MANUFACTURING SYSTEMS ENGINEERING

STANLEY B. GERSHWIN

Massachusetts Institute of Technology

PTR Prentice Hall
Englewood Cliffs, New Jersey 07632

Library of Congress Cataloging-in-Publication Data

GERSHWIN, S. B.
   Manufacturing systems engineering / Stanley B. Gershwin
      p.   cm.
   Includes bibliographical references and index.
   ISBN 0-13-560608-X
   1. Production engineering.   I. Title.
   TS176.G48   1994
   658.5–dc20   93-25841
                                                                 CIP

Acquisitions Editor: Michael Hays
Buyer: Mary McCartney
Cover Design: Ben Santora
Editorial Assistant: Kim Intindola
Editorial/production Supervision: Lisa Iarkowski

 © 1994 PTR Prentice Hall
Prentice-Hall, Inc.
A Paramount Communications Company
Englewood Cliffs, NJ 07632

The publisher offers discounts on this book when ordered in bulk quantities.
For more information, contact:

         Corporate Sales Department
         PTR Prentice Hall
         113 Sylvan Avenue
         Englewood Cliffs, NJ 07632
         Phone: 201-592-2863
         FAX: 201-592-2249

Printed in the United States of America
10 9 8 7 6 5 4 3 2 1

ISBN 0-13-560608-X

Prentice-Hall International (UK) Limited, *London*
Prentice-Hall of Australia Pty. Limited, *Sydney*
Prentice-Hall of Canada, Inc., *Toronto*
Prentice-Hall Hispanoamericana S.A., *Mexico*
Prentice-Hall of India Private Limited, *New Delhi*
Prentice-Hall of Japan, Inc., *Tokyo*
Simon & Schuster Asia Pte. Ltd., *Singapore*
Editora Prentice-Hall do Brasil, Ltda., *Rio de Janeiro*

To Fran and Julz

Contents

List of Figures

List of Tables

Preface

The purpose of this book is to provide a fundamental description and analysis of some of the most important phenomena in material flow in manufacturing systems. It has a point of view; that disruptions, while undesirable, are a fact of life in a factory. While effort should be expended to reduce them, or even to eliminate some of them, some disruption is inevitable, and we should develop ways of limiting their effects. The book describes some potentially disruptive events that affect production, the control actions that managers can take in anticipation of or in response to the disruptions, and the consequences of the control actions. The goal is to contribute to the development of a rigorous, and useful, manufacturing systems science.

Chapter 1 is an introduction to the field. In non-technical language, it describes issues and phenomena that arise when manufacturing resources are combined into systems. Chapter 2, on Markov chains and processes, supplies some mathematical tools that are needed for the next several chapters. Chapters 3 and 4 describe transfer lines and Chapter 5 generalizes these models to include assembly. Queuing network models, and their application to manufacturing systems, are described in Chapter 6. Chapters 7 and 8, on linear and dynamic programming, supply the additional mathematical background required for the remaining chapters on flexible, and other, manufacturing systems. Chapter 9 treats the real-time scheduling of flexible manufacturing systems in which failures can disrupt production; Chapter 10 presents a framework for dealing with more events, and for simplifying the real-time scheduling computations for more complex systems. Chapter 11 describes the issues that arise when systems are less than ideally flexible, and provides some solutions. Chapter 12 combines the buffer issues in Chapters 3, 4, and 5 with the real-time scheduling problems of Chapter 9. Finally, Chapter 13 synthesizes some of the issues of the first half of the book with the solutions of the second half. A precedence diagram, for reading the chapters, appears in Figure 0.1. The dashed arrow between Chapter 4 and Chapter 12 is meant to indicate that while the latter can be studied without a deep understanding of Chapter 4, it has been influenced by the earlier chapter's contents.

This book is aimed at graduate students and professionals in industrial engineering, manufacturing engineering, and operations research. A reader who fully assimilates this

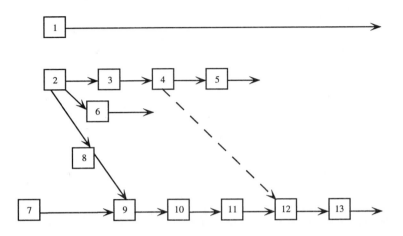

Figure 0.1: Chapter Precedence

book will gain some knowledge of Markov processes, linear programming, and dynamic programming. These topics are covered enough to make the rest of the text comprehensible, and to form an introduction to a more thorough and rigorous treatment of them. More importantly, that reader will learn some issues that arise in the design and operation of manufacturing systems, and methods for dealing with these issues.

Many people seem to confuse *simulation* and *analytical computation*. It is important for readers to know what they are and how they differ, and to know that this book has very little of the former, and plenty of the. latter. The best way to explain the difference is to imagine two computer programs that evaluate the area of a room. A simulation program would conceptually lay out tiles on the floor. If the room were an 8 foot by 10 foot rectangle, it would put the first tile in a corner, put another one next to it, another one next to that one, and so forth. It would keep track of how many tiles it had put down, and where on the floor it was. When it reaches a wall, it would start another row. It would continue until it completed the floor, and then it would report that it had put down 80 tiles, so the floor space is 80 square feet.

An analytical program would multiply 8 by 10 and get 80.

This highly unfair example reveals some of the advantages of analytical methods over simulation, but it conceals their disadvantages. The advantage of analytical methods is that they are fast, and analytic computer programs can be relatively simple. The disadvantage is that analytic methods are not always available. That is, not all problems have nice compact formulas for solutions. In this case, imagine if the room were irregularly shaped: simulation (with tiles of various sizes, depending on the accuracy needed) would be the only way to get a useful result.

One of the goals of this book is to find as many rectangular or almost rectangular rooms as possible in the factory. There are limits to what can be done this way, but there are many powerful and useful results that are available and that are not widely known.

The main prerequisite for readers of this book is a general mathematical and engineering background and an ability to face down a page of equations without debilitating fear. They should also know something about difference and differential equations; an elementary course in probability is required for Chapter 2; and some familiarity with optimization would be helpful for later chapters.

Acknowledgments I am indebted to many former and present students who collaborated on the technical ideas described here, including Irvin Schick, Joseph Kimemia, Mostafa Ammar, Garrett Van Ryzin, Sherman Xiewei Bai, James Violette, Mitchell Burman, Stephanie Connolly, Cathy Strosser, Yong Choong, N. Srivatsan, Elena Otero, and Sungsu Ahn; and to other collaborators, who include Michael Caramanis, Ali Sharifnia, Yves Dallery, Oded Maimon, Jean Lasserre, Stephane Dauzere-Peres, Oded Berman, Ramakrishna Akella, and Sheldon Lou.

I am also grateful for the many students, more senior colleagues, and others who took the time to criticize the manuscript. They include N. Srivatsan, Ali Sharifnia, Walt Tribula, El-Kebir Boukas, Taketoshi Yoshida, Rajan Suri, Y. Narahari, Kenneth McKay, Katherine F. Allou, and Frances Allou Gershwin. They made many valuable suggestions, and caught many potentially embarrassing errors. I am responsible for those that remain, of course.

John Buzacott, Y. C. Ho, P. R. Kumar, Suresh Sethi, and Rajan Suri have been great friends and important influences for many years. I am grateful for their advice and guidance.

I also must thank my many 2.852 students at MIT who found numerous typos in the various versions of the manuscript over the years, and who served as involuntary human experimental subjects for the homework exercises. They have been generous with advice.

I am also grateful for the secretarial assistance provided by Diane de Alderete and Susan Imrie. Many figures were drawn by Diane de Alderete and Arthur Giordani.

Diane de Alderete gave more of her time and energy than anyone could expect. Sungsu Ahn and N. Srivatsan provided last minute emergency rescues. Fran Gershwin was always there to bail me out of a crisis, and to keep me more or less rational.

I have been fortunate to have research support from many sources, including NSF, IBM, ARPA, the US Army, and the MIT Leaders for Manufacturing Program.

Chapter 1

Introduction

1.1 Overview

Manufacturing is one of the few ways that wealth is created. It is one of the oldest economic activities of humanity and is full of tradition and craft. Like all important human enterprises, it is subject to constant scrutiny and to constant technological change. However, in some important areas in manufacturing, *ad hoc* techniques and intuition are more prevalent than systematic methods. Sometimes, modern tools (like computers) are used only to make existing practices permanent. Unfortunately, existing practices are often not adequate.

The purpose of this book is to explore some important *systems* problems in manufacturing. These are problems that arise when several resources are used together to manufacture something — virtually the only way anything is made. When manufacturing systems are created, a danger arises that these resources may interfere with one another. For example, if a part must pass through two machines before it is complete, and one of those machines is out of order (*down*, *failed*, or other terms) then the other cannot be used. As a result, some capacity is lost because a perfectly good machine is forced to wait. This can be prevented (up to a point) if some parts have been stored for the operational machine to work on, and there is space to put the pieces it completes while the other is down. In designing such a system, one must ask, *How much space should be allocated for this purpose?* and *How much material storage (in-process inventory) should be allowed for this purpose?*

In a more complicated factory, where there are many part types and alternate production paths, a failure can be mitigated by using the remaining capacity for the production of parts that do not require the machine that is down. In designing the control policy for such a system, one must ask, *When a failure occurs, how should production be shifted so that the operational machines are well utilized without making unnecessary inventory?*

Other issues are also likely to arise in most factories. Usually, some time or cost must be expended to change a machine over from producing one part type to producing another. This is called *changing a setup* or *setting up* or *changing tooling*. (When such changes can be made at no cost, we call such a machine, or system, *flexible*.) Such setup changes must

1

be scheduled; we must choose when we will do them. If they occur too often, production time is lost and costs are incurred. The consequence is that costs go up and the factory may not be able to meet demand. On the other hand, if they occur too infrequently, inventory and delays increase; the consequence is that other costs go up. The only way to deal with this is to plan a setup change frequency on a system-wide basis, taking costs and capacity into account, and not to react to an immediate demand without this perspective. Of course, setup changes must be scheduled in a way that anticipates and reacts to machine failures. In addition, maintenance must be scheduled; engineering changes must be anticipated and reacted to, and so forth.

Manufacturing, like other fields of engineering, is a constant fight with uncertainty and deviation. Whether many, few, or only one copy of an item must be made, their physical properties (size, material, weight, etc.) must be close to a plan, or product specification. Any deviation from that plan is bad. This is the requirement of *product quality*.

Just as importantly, these items must be delivered to a customer according to a plan (or delivery schedule), and any deviation from that plan is also bad. We have already mentioned some causes of delivery deviation: machine failures, setup changes, engineering changes. There are many others. There are a variety of ways of reducing this deviation. They include *final inventory*, in which the product is made earlier than it is needed; *in-process inventory*, in which some operations on the product are performed earlier than they are needed; and *redundancy*, in which some production resources are backed up, so that, for example, there is an alternate machine to do an operation when a machine fails. The first two are ant-*vs.*-grasshopper strategies: the ant keeps working even in the absence of demand. Later, when it is impossible to produce, he can satisfy his demand from his inventory. The grasshopper, with nothing stored, starves.

Unfortunately, these strategies, which are chosen to reduce risks, are themselves costly and risky. Demand may change so that the stored product, or the extra machine, is not needed. The money that was invested in buying the extra machine or producing the inventory is lost.

To help answer these questions, we use modern techniques of Markov process modeling and dynamic programming. The premise underlying this book is that the answers are not always obvious, even when all possible data is available. These problems can be extraordinarily complex, even for simple systems, because of the large number of different states the manufacturing system may be in, and because of the large number of design alternatives available. Systematic means must be found for dividing one enormous problem into many small conquerable problems, and then reconstituting the solution.

There is another set of solutions, which is not treated here. To reduce the effects of failures, reduce the frequency and duration of failures. That is, make machines more reliable and easier to service. If it is costly to change setups, change the machines or the procedures so that it is less costly. These are often, but not always, better than adding storage or redundancy. The methods of this book can sometimes help the decision of which approach to take.

Even though manufacturing is very old, it is an essential component of all modern economies. The magnitudes of trade surpluses and deficits are thought to play a major role in determining the well-being of nations, and of the world economic system, and the relative health of a nation's manufacturing sector is a principal influence on its trade surplus or deficit. In fact, since the sizes of inventories are thought to affect the severity of economic recessions, reducing inventories can have positive consequences for the global economy, and not only individual companies. The main goal of this book is to contribute to the development of a rigorous science of manufacturing systems, and thus to the capacity to utilize resources efficiently for production.

As technology continues to develop, we can expect a greater use of computers in factories. They will be used — in *Computer-Integrated Manufacturing* — to consolidate important information and to distribute it among production, design, marketing, and financial organizations within a firm. Within production, they will be used for both long term planning and short term control. A variety of algorithms for such computer applications is provided in this book.

1.2 Definitions

Manufacturing Manufacturing is the transformation of material into something useful and portable. This definition excludes the construction of buildings and bridges, since they are built where they are to be used. If we take a broad view of "portable," it includes battleships and 747s. For the purposes of this book, however, we restrict our attention to the manufacture of larger numbers of smaller items. Alternate terms are *production, fabrication*, and others.

Essential to manufacturing is predictability and repeatability. A manufacturing firm wants to know in advance exactly how a given product will come out, and, most often, it wants to repeat an operation many times in exactly the same way. That is, the firm makes a promise to its customers to deliver a product — most often, many copies of that product — with certain characteristics. If it disappoints its customers, it will suffer economic consequences. That promise extends to the delivery schedule. The firm must deliver a specified number of copies of its products at specified times, and it will suffer if its customers are not satisfied. To state it another way: the accuracy of the delivery schedule of a product is just as important as the accuracy of its physical characteristics.

Discrete and Continuous Manufacturing Discrete manufacturing produces distinct items (for example, automobiles, integrated circuits). Continuous manufacturing produces quantities of material (such as oil refining). We emphasize discrete manufacturing although many results apply to continuous manufacturing as well.

Manufacturing System A manufacturing system is a set of machines, transportation elements, computers, storage buffers, and other items that are used together for manufacturing. People are also part of the system. Alternate terms are *factory, production system*, and *fabrication facility*. Subsets of manufacturing systems, which are themselves systems, are sometimes called *cells, work centers* or *work stations*.

System Design   Manufacturing system design is the choice of machines, buffers, transport system, computer and communication system, operators, repair personnel, and so forth.

Scheduling and Real-Time Decision-Making   Scheduling is the choice of times for future controllable events. (Controllable events are those whose times can be chosen. Part loading is a controllable event; machine failures are not. See Chapters 9 and 10.) Because the best times for some controllable future events depend on intervening uncontrollable events, schedules must be changed as events occur. Consequently, decisions must be made in real time.

1.3   Issues and Performance Measures

Production Rate   A manufacturing system's *production rate* is the number of parts that it produces per time unit. This may be a vector, if the system can make more than one part type. It is also called *throughput*, especially in the single part type case.

Capacity   The *capacity* of a manufacturing system is its maximum production rate, if the system produces only one part type. In this case, it is a number, and we want it to be as large as possible. If the system can make more than one part type, capacity is a more complex concept, which cannot be measured by a single number.[1] This is because (a) different part types make different demands on a factory's resources; (b) the more a system makes of one type, the less it makes of another; (c) the capacity varies over time as resources become available or unavailable due to failure, maintenance, changes of tooling, coffee breaks, etc.; and (d) how you view the capacity of a system depends on the time period over which you are considering it — the short term view of capacity considers the current repair state, set up, and so forth, whereas the long term capacity takes the *average* reliability and average set up state into account. The calculation of capacity, and its efficient utilization, is the major theme of this book. We provide precise definitions of capacity in Chapters 9 and 10. Essentially, we define the capacity of a manufacturing system to be the set of possible production rate *vectors*, where each component of the vector is the production rate of one of the part types. This is a somewhat abstract definition, but it captures the nature of capacity.

In-Process Inventory   In-process inventory is material found in a manufacturing system — in machines, in storage areas, in the transportation subsystem, in inspection stations — at any time. We want this to be as small as possible for a variety of reasons:

- inventory costs money to create, but generates no revenue while it is in the factory or the warehouse;

---

[1]It cannot, and therefore should not, but it often is. We cannot use scientific techniques to provide a better estimate of such a number than already exists, since such a number is not meaningful (except for the single-part type systems of Chapters 3–5). All we can do is make the picture look complicated. But that is not our fault; the capacity picture *is* complicated.

- the more the inventory, the longer it takes to produce a product, on the average, and therefore the longer the factory makes the customer wait;

- the more time items spend in the factory, the more they are vulnerable to damage;

- the more time items spend in the factory, the more time elapses between production and use, so that if there is a problem in production it does not show up for a long time, during which many faulty parts are made; and,

- the space, and material-handling equipment needed for inventory costs money.

Inventory is also called *work-in-process,* or *WIP.*

Cycle Time Cycle time is the average amount of time that a part (of a given type) spends in a manufacturing system. We want this to be as small as possible for some of the same reasons that we want inventory to be small. It is also called *throughput time* or *lead time.*

There is some ambiguity in these terms, because they are also sometimes defined as the average amount of time between the order and the delivery of a part. We use the former definition. A related concept is called *working time,* or *touch time.* It is the actual time a part is worked on while it is in a factory. This can be as little as 1.5% of the cycle time (Merchant, 1983).

The relationship between production, or arrival, rate (λ), in-process inventory (L), and cycle time (W) is given by *Little's law* (Little, 1961):

$$L = \lambda W.$$

(This is the notation that Little's law usually appears in. We use different notation throughout the text.)

One problem that manufacturing suffers from is the non-universality of terminology. Different people have different words for the same concept, and even use the same words for different concepts. *Cycle time* is sometimes used to mean the length of time a machine requires for an operation.

Responsiveness to Customers Responsiveness to customers is one of the things that determines whether a manufacturing firm survives. However, it is a complex issue. We want to promise delivery of a potential order as early as possible. We also want to deliver the order as close as possible to the specified date. We want to be able to deliver orders of all sizes, including prototypes or samples. These objectives conflict with one another.

Flexibility Flexibility is the ability of a system to do more than one thing. It is the existence of choices or options in the system. We distinguish two kinds of flexibility:

Product Flexibility Product flexibility is the ability of a manufacturing system to produce different part types. We can quantify it as the number of different part types that a system can produce during a specified time period. A *flexible manufacturing* *system* or *FMS* is a manufacturing system that can produce more than one part type with little time lost or expense for changeover.

Product flexibility contributes to improved customer responsiveness. It also allows the same capital investment to be used over a long period of time, as the market changes.

Process Flexibility Process flexibility is the ability of a manufacturing system to produce the same part type in different ways. A system that is process-flexible is also said to have *multiple routes*.

Other Measures In our quest to understand the events that influence the flow of material in a factory, we are neglecting issues that are of equal significance. The reader should not be misled by the analytic fireworks in later chapters to forget these concerns:

Quality of product is of paramount importance in manufacturing. It is not studied here only because we concentrate on issues closely related to material movement.[2] *Yield* is the fraction of parts — at either final or intermediate stages — that pass inspection, that is, that are measured to satisfy quality standards. *Costs* include expenses for raw material, labor, and capital.

Goldratt and his co-authors (Goldratt and Cox, 1986; Goldratt and Fox, 1986) say that the goal of a factory is to make money, and that there are three important measures (which are defined in monetary rather than physical units): *throughput, inventory,* and *operating expenses.* The first should be maximized and the last two should be minimized. The prediction and improvement of throughput and inventory are the main topics of this book.

Objectives of a Manufacturing Firm A manufacturer has a variety of objectives. They are all important, and their relative importance changes with time due to changes in market conditions and technology. They include:

- to make the most money

- to maintain the market share, or to meet a specified market share

- to stay in business as long as possible

- to make only high quality products, and to sell just enough to stay in business

- to be known as the technological leader

There are tradeoffs among these objectives and the measures described above.

---

[2]Actually, one could probably make the argument that a delivery schedule is part of the product, and that meeting the schedule is as much a quality issue as meeting other product specifications.

1.4 Manufacturing System Challenges

Complexity A manufacturing system may make thousands of part types (not just parts) during a year. There may be hundreds of machines. At each moment, the managers are faced with hundreds of decisions, such as: which part should be loaded onto each machine next? The consequences of each decision are hard to predict.

Information Because of the complexity of many manufacturing systems, the amount of information required to make good decisions is immense. (Database design for manufacturing systems has received much recent attention.) In fact, obtaining good information has been so difficult that practitioners and software designers have tended to assume that actual decision-making is trivial once the information is available. We do not make that assumption.

On the other hand, we assume that information is available. At present, this assumption is not universally true, and this may make some of the techniques described below difficult to implement. However, a great deal of effort is being expended to develop an information infrastructure that will provide the data that is required, and manufacturing firms can be expected to be ready for these methods in the near future.

Randomness Many important events are random, including the failures of machines, the arrival of demands, the arrival of raw materials, the change of a design (and therefore of one or more manufacturing steps), the arrival or departure of workers, etc. Such randomness affects the performance of the system, and does not make decision-making any easier.

Heterogeneity This characteristic may be the least tractable of all, and, perhaps for that reason, it receives the least attention in the research literature. Many different *kinds* of events occur. Operations, failures, tool changes, maintenance, demand changes, etc. all have different characteristics. This makes modeling difficult, and it requires the modeler to have good judgment about what is most important. It means that an accurate prediction of system performance requires a model that is demanding to describe, much less to analyze.

Limitations, constraints, and tradeoffs Generally, only one part may be processed at one machine at a time. When more than one part can be processed (*e.g.*, in semiconductor fabrication), the number of parts is still limited. Since some time is required to do any operation, the production capacity is limited. In addition, there are precedence constraints. Some operations must be done before others. Consequently, a machine may be idle while another has a long queue (waiting line) because operations cannot be done at the former before other operations are done at the latter. (Example: to build printed circuit cards, insertion is done before soldering, which is done before testing.) Storage space is expensive and sometimes limited. In Chapters 3-5, we study systems in which a full buffer (storage area) prevents a machine from doing operations. This also limits system capacity.

For most systems (if everything else is equal), increasing storage space (a penalty) increases in-process inventory (a penalty) and increases capacity (a benefit). We want to quantify these relationships, alter a system to increase the net benefit, and find the best operating point for a given system.

Other impediments   There are problems that lie outside the scope of this book, but which limit the possibility of applying these methods. For example, if company policies are to ship finished goods once per week, it is impossible to reduce inventory to less than a week's worth just before shipment. There is nothing to be gained by changing setups more than once per week per part type, even if that could reduce inventory. There may be very good reasons to ship only once per week: for example because the factory is at a remote location and the cheapest means of transportation is by boat, if the boat is filled up. Or, the reasons may have been valid long ago but nobody wants to change. Also, maybe manufacturing in a remote location is not as cheap as it appears.

Another difficulty which is out of the hands of the manufacturing or industrial engineer is the incentive structure of the firm. If a worker (in a blue collar or a suit) is rewarded for high production volume, that is what the worker is going to try to deliver. There may be editorials in the company newsletter about meeting the needs of customers, and sermons about quality, but if people are paid for how much they make, that is what they will focus their attention on. Consequently, it will do little good to develop a sophisticated scheduling system that carefully allocates available capacity to the part types that are most needed; it will simply be ignored if the company communicates, by means of its incentive system, that it is really interested in total volume.

To "think globally and act locally" looks good on a bumper sticker, but sometimes global acting is required as well.

1.5   Current Practices

Current scheduling practices are often *ad hoc* and chaotic. Sometimes, scheduling software or simple back-of-the-envelope calculations determine some decisions, but the decisions are revised — not always systematically — when one of the random events occurs. The behavior of the system is often unpredictable, so parts that are especially far behind are often expedited (moved to the front of the queue). This adds to the unpredictability of the system.

There are some systematic methods such as MRP (Materials Requirements Planning) for high level planning (in which fixed, but often somewhat arbitrary times are assigned to each production stage), and Kanban (in which a fixed number of parts are allowed into a production stage), but these common-sense rules are difficult to analyze in a systematic way.

Simulation is widely used in the design of manufacturing systems, but this tool is easy to misuse. As we argue in Chapter 9, the policy by which a manufacturing system is operated is important, in that it can have a major effect on how the system performs. Unfortunately, this aspect — as well as many others — is usually neglected in the simulation of a system. Most often, the operating policy is buried deep in the simulation code, is simplistic, and is very different from the way that the system will actually be operated. Consequently, predictions of system behavior based on simulation are often misleading.

In addition, simulation code can often get so complicated that it is hard to know what is really in it. When complex computer programs crash, or produce results that deviate from the author's or user's expectations, they are debugged and often modified until they conform. What remains are the more subtle bugs as well as the implicit assumptions. This can lead to programs that reproduce their creator's prejudices more than they inform about reality.

Finally, simulations are usually time-consuming. This can make them expensive and clumsy tools for the design of a complex system, or for the design of an operating policy.

Literature There is a vast research literature on manufacturing systems. A small fraction of it is listed in the bibliographies of this and the later chapters. There is also a non-research literature which deals with material flow, factory design, and other problems. Some of this material is also listed at the end of this chapter. The literature reflects the wide disparity of the field: some of it is based on common sense and some is based on elaborate mathematics.

1.6 Objective and Method of this Book

Objective Excess inventories, long lead times, and uncertain delivery dates are caused by randomness and lack of synchronization. There are only two possible solutions: reduce the randomness (due to machine failures, engineering changes, customer orders, and so forth) and reasons for the lack of synchronization (costly setup changes, large batch machines, and others); or respond to them in a way that limits their disruptive effects. Both strategies should be pursued; this book is devoted to the second. The objective is to present tools for that strategy, as well as tools for assessing the effects of randomness and lack of synchronization, and to educate the reader so that he or she can further develop these tools. These tools are designed to help the architect or operator of a manufacturing system to meet the firm's objectives by evaluating or optimizing a system.

The longer term goal is to contribute to the development of manufacturing science. There are many authors who propose insightful ideas for reducing waste and focusing energies, but their recommendations invariably lack the quantitative precision that engineers need. The reason is that such precise tools are not widely known, or in many cases do not exist. Some tools are provided here; just as important, foundations are developed for others to build more tools on in the future.

Methods We emphasize mathematical modeling and use mathematical methods to attempt to understand the behavior of systems. This is not the only way to proceed; there are other methodologies (simulation, artificial intelligence) that do not use mathematical models. The advantage of mathematical modeling is that, in the long run, it can lead to the deepest understanding of the system, and provide the most practical results. For example, an analytic model of a transfer line can be solved quickly by a computer, and can be embedded in an optimization algorithm. This way, it can be used to design lines. Simulations can be used in that way also, but such an optimization would be awkward and time-consuming. (This difference is demonstrated in the exercises in Chapters 3 and 4.) Probably the best way to proceed would be to use both kinds of models: analytic/optimization to quickly bring the design into the ballpark; and simulation to verify and fine-tune. The primary tools are Markov chains and dynamic programming.

Overview   Most often, science works most efficiently by studying the simplest possible system that exhibits a phenomenon. When that system is well-understood, a new phenomenon is added in a way such that the next system becomes the simplest system that exhibits that phenomenon. The initial systems to be studied appear to be simplistic and academic but, if the process is successful, the later systems are quite realistic. Following that process, Chapters 3-5 describe the behavior of manufacturing systems that are completely inflexible in that they produce only a single part type, and have no alternate routes. The operating rule is very simple: whenever a machine can do an operation, it does it. Chapter 3 describes the simplest models: long lines without buffers or with infinite buffers, or two-machine lines that can be solved analytically. Solution, in this case, means finding long-time average values of important performance measures, including production rate and amounts of WIP. Chapter 4 adds complexity by treating long lines with finite buffers. The analysis of these systems is more difficult because they cannot be solved analytically. Chapter 5 adds more features: assembly and disassembly. Chapter 6 studies systems with multiple part types, but with infinite buffers (and without assembly and disassembly). In these systems, the next part type to be processed by a machine, or the next machine a part visits, is not fixed. However, the queuing network models of this chapter do not describe how to make such choices; they only describe the long-term average consequences of dealing with more than one part type simultaneously. The mathematical background for Chapters 3-6 is supplied in Chapter 2.

The later chapters deal with manufacturing systems with choice. Methods are described for making scheduling decisions in real time. This is because some decisions — for example, which part to load on a machine next; whether or not to let a machine be idle for a short time — can only be made after random events occur. If there is a surplus of one part type, and a backlog of another, the system's capacity should be directed to the backlogged part. This can only be determined after the surplus and backlog exist. We use the term *scheduling* for this, even though scheduling is usually to mean short term advanced planning. Chapter 9 supplies the real-time decision algorithms for the simplest model of a flexible manufacturing system, in which only two kinds of events take place: operations and machine failures. In Chapter 10, a framework is created for dealing with many other kinds of events, such as setup changes, so that the resulting decision algorithms are less restrictive and applicable to realistic systems.

The scheduling of setup changes is studied in more depth in Chapter 11. In Chapters 9-11, buffers are not considered. Decisions about any portion of the system are immediately influenced by events in every other portion of the system. This is not appropriate in large systems. Consequently, the model of Chapter 9 is generalized in Chapter 12 by using the decomposition ideas of Chapter 4. Finally, the methods of Chapters 9-12 are synthesized in Chapter 13. This chapter deals with the scheduling of general manufacturing systems: systems with many different kinds of events, and with buffers that break the system into sub-systems. The framework of Chapter 10 is generalized. The mathematical background of the later chapters is supplied in Chapters 7 and 8.

Engineering Discipline The point of view of this book is that manufacturing is an engineering discipline, just as intellectually demanding and worthy of respect as mechanical, electrical, chemical, and other established fields of engineering. If the last statement sounds a little defensive or even insecure, it is because manufacturing engineering has not always been treated that way, by its colleagues or by its own practitioners.

Here, we propose to identify the components of an engineering discipline:

- *Science* is the activity of collecting and organizing information about the real world. Often, this information is put in the form of mathematical models. The activity of creating new mathematical models is science. The method of science is to simplify: the scientist tries to find the simplest system that exhibits the phenomenon under study. This is done in physical and biological experimentation, and in mathematical modeling. Once a phenomenon is understood in its purest form, mathematicians and engineers can deal with its interactions with other phenomena. Science, defined this way, is not the solving of problems, but only the gathering of information for the purpose of gaining understanding.

  It is difficult to do science, in this pure sense, in manufacturing because

  - Science is generally the study of the *natural* world, whereas manufacturing is artificial. However, much of the phenomena that must be studied are almost natural, in that they are *uncontrollable*, as defined in Chapter 10.

  - Many of the phenomena that we need to understand are *bad*, such as machine failures, time lost for setup changes, etc. Phenomena of other branches of science or engineering often are neutral — neither good nor bad, but simply interesting facts — and often can be exploited for some future purpose later. Bad events in factories are just bad. Machine failures, material absences, and long setup times have no redeeming social value, and can never be exploited for any purpose later.

  - Everything about a factory is urgent and practical. A dollar spent on reducing the frequencies or durations of bad phenomena would appear to be better spent than a dollar spent on understanding them. It is hard to justify allowing an employee to act like a disinterested scientist while there are expensive problems to solve.

- *Mathematics* is the activity of analyzing statements — including the mathematical models created by scientists — to create new statements. Its source of information (axioms or assumptions) may be science, and its methods are logical and computational. Mathematics is not an end in itself. Its goal is to produce interesting — useful — new statements. Some of these statements, which include models, design methods, algorithms, and qualitative results, form a branch of engineering.

- *Application* is the goal of engineering. It is the activity of affecting the real world in useful ways, using the results of science and mathematics.

There is considerable research literature on manufacturing systems and related topics. Little of it is applied, however. This is only one of many fields in which there is a *gap* between theory and practice. Many theoreticians and some practitioners blame this on the ignorance and lack of sophistication of the practitioners, but (in my opinion) this is unfair. Some of the reason for the gap is due to the absence of science in the theoreticians' work.

This book contains some science and a lot of mathematics. The science consists of a discussion and mathematical representation of realistic factory problems and phenomena. The mathematics is used to make predictions about behavior and to design operating policies. The goal is to provide tools that will be useful to an engineer.

One source of confusion is the purpose of mathematical and other models, and the relationship between the mathematics and the real world. Clarifying this point is important in a book about manufacturing systems, since this is a practical area in which the gap between theoreticians and practitioners is very wide.

All models — from vague intuition to very elaborate mathematical/computational systems with thousands of statements used in economic forecasting — have some specific purpose. Good models have well-defined purposes, and their performances can be judged according to their purposes. Poor models are often constructed without a clear purpose in mind. All models are simplifications of reality. The modeler must consciously decide what the tradeoff will be between tractability and accuracy. It is tempting to be conservative and include all possible details, but a model with too much detail cannot be analyzed. One way of viewing this is to say that mathematics is too weak and narrow a discipline to apply to real problems without a great deal of help from the user. In any case, one should consider results from such models as starting points. Before any irrevocable decisions are made, other forms of analysis, such as simulation or small scale experimentation, should also be used.

The most obvious simplification in this book is the representation of discrete material by means of continuous variables. Since parts are discrete, this could not possibly be accurate — could it? Answer: It could be *sufficiently* accurate for some purposes. We must be sure we know the purpose of the model before we create it or try to answer that question or apply the results.

Another usual assumption that sometimes looks disturbing is that storage areas can hold an infinite amount of material. Of course they cannot. *Sometimes*, however, it is helpful not to have to bother with the upper bound, and it is rare that more than a few parts appear in a buffer. But this can be a trap. Sometimes, as we will see, the finiteness of a buffer is its most important characteristic.

Not only are quantities approximate, but concepts can also be approximate. For example, we define a *controllable event* in Chapter 10 as one whose time of occurrence can be chosen, and an *uncontrollable event* as one whose time cannot. In reality, some events can sometimes be chosen, or can be influenced but not chosen precisely, or can be chosen by some people and not by others. It is not fruitful — or accurate — to classify all events as one or the other, under all conditions. Rather, the methods of Chapter 10 should be used with care, and events should be classified as one or the other under limited circumstances.

A successful mathematical model is one that takes into account all important influences on a system. (*Important* is the key word here, and it is why a great deal of mature judgment is required of a model builder.) It is not sensitive to phenomena that are not included. Therefore, the modeler must include all phenomena that affect the system in a significant way. Some mathematical models are difficult to extend. That is, it is not easy to modify the model to include more phenomena. This is not desirable, but is often unavoidable. The models in Chapters 3-5 are like this. The models in Chapter 10 and following are less limited in this way.

Unfortunately the term "application" can be misleading. It suggests that there are a set of mathematical tools available and waiting to be used. The user need only put in a set of data into a computer program, and the result will pop out. In fact, there are some useful tools like that, such as linear programming. Most often, however, new mathematics must be developed from broad concepts. In this book, for example, we describe Markov processes in Chapter 2 and we use those concepts to develop transfer line models in Chapter 3. But the application is not a simple matter of plugging numbers or symbols into a set of equations. Much effort is required to develop a reasonably accurate, reasonably tractable set of equations and methods.

To reiterate: a mathematical model must be designed with a purpose in mind. It is a simplification of reality. A model, and all the approximations that enter into its analysis, are only accurate over a limited range of parameters and phenomena. It must be based on empirical observation.

Sophistication Much of the academic literature, perhaps including material that appears in these pages, has been criticized as too sophisticated for most manufacturers. Such a statement can have at least two possible meanings.

- *Most manufacturing people are not educated enough for it.* This is unfortunate and it need not be the case. Most manufacturing people are certainly intelligent enough for it, in the author's experience. (Most people who have not been dazzled by education know the difference between *education* and *intelligence*.) However, manufacturing systems engineering has not been taught in a way that is both useful and intellectually demanding.

- *Real problems are much simpler and more basic than are described in the literature. The solutions needed are also much simpler and more basic.* This is true sometimes, but not always. A useful goal of abstraction is to find the common attributes of a wide variety of systems, and to teach the systems in a unified way. Thus, a little bit of sophistication can be an efficient way to study a wide variety of systems. In addition, manufacturing systems can be expected to grow, not diminish in complexity, and sophisticated tools — and sophisticated people — will always be needed.

State of the Art Both as a practice and as a theoretical research area, manufacturing systems engineering is still in an early stage of development. Practitioners are often successful in operating a factory satisfactorily without having communicated the reasons for their success in a generalizable way. Theoreticians have not settled on an agreed-upon set of models in the same way that physicists, mechanical engineers, and biological scientists have.

Practitioners have not settled on an agreed-upon terminology; see the comments above on "cycle time." Research and debate are active, and this book is intended to be part of that debate.

As a consequence, the contents of books like this are very much determined by the opinions and tastes of the authors. That which seems important today may not remain important. A successful practitioner or researcher will not blindly apply the methods described here, but will use them as a starting point in an investigation of real phenomena in real systems.

In some ways, manufacturing systems engineering is like an 18th century science that is practiced with 20th century technology. There is a great deal of knowledge, wisdom and experience, and the computer is used to collect information and support the practices that have been developed based on that experience. However, modern sciences and engineering fields have passed through the systematic data collection and model-building of the 19th century, and manufacturing must also pass through that phase.

1.7   Other issues

Our focus is narrow. We do not deal with issues closely related to labor relations, quality, process planning, learning, and others. The reader should keep them in mind, and be aware that they are related to the material flow issues described here. Extending the models described here to include them would be important research contributions.

If production rates are increased without any other changes, *labor relations* may suffer. Conversely, poor labor relations can lead to long operation times or disruptions which adversely affect factory performance. This is an enormous and complicated area which is heavily laden with emotion and politics.

Quality is of major importance. If quality is assured more by inspection than by careful fabrication, material flow is complicated because there is either a large rejection rate or a large rework rate. (In any case, this is generally viewed as a poor route to quality.) *Process planning* is the activity of designing the production steps in the manufacture of an item. The primary concerns are the physical transformations involved, and the assurance of quality, but there are often alternative processes or alternative ways of performing a given process. These alternatives can affect the flow of material in the system. They can influence the duration of operations, the existence of alternate routes, the cost of changing setups, and other effects. The choice among alternate routes is discussed briefly at the end of Chapter 9.

When things go wrong in a production system, there are two responses possible: (1) take some action to respond to the disruption and prevent it from doing too much damage, and (2) study the source of the disruption to prevent it from happening again. The latter is *learning*. Both responses are valid, but they can be, in practice, polar opposites. For example, if machine failure is important in a factory, its effects can be mitigated by building buffers, so that if one machine goes down, its neighbors can keep working. However, besides costing money, such buffers hide the failures, so that there is little incentive to improve the machines and little information to guide their improvement. (Learning is an important part of the Just In Time philosophy.[3])

In this book, we assume that machine capabilities are fixed, and we ignore learning. We do not do this to suggest that this is a bad or unimportant strategy. Rather, we feel that we must thoroughly understand the performance of fixed systems before we can hope to quantify the effects of learning.

Other important systems issues are related to systems design. We touch on design in the exercises in Chapters 3 and 4 but do not make it a focus of the book. In those chapters, we ask the reader to select optimal buffer sizes and the best machines (among competing vendors) for the operations in transfer lines. There are many more design issues in more complex systems. For example, if a firm must make many different parts, how should it design production systems to take advantage of any commonalities among the parts so that machines may be used for more than one of them? This is related to setup changes (Chapter 11) and is called *group technology*.

Another important set of issues which are not discussed here are related to the computer systems that support advanced manufacturing systems. (For some people, these are the *only* issues that are important.) They include the organization of computer hardware and software, the design of databases, network protocols, etc.

Simplicity *Simplicity* is not likely to be among the attributes that most people would use in describing this book. However, a certain kind of simplicity is a goal, particularly of the chapters that deal with system scheduling.

Complex systems that are poorly understood become increasingly complex over time. We experience such systems constantly in our daily lives, and such experiences are frustrating and wearing. Examples are unfortunately abundant: they include the tax code, the medical insurance system, many aspects of the legal system, price, wage, and rent control schemes, and many government social service agencies.

I would propose the following mechanism to explain this phenomenon: when a system is poorly understood, simple rules are created to achieve some goal. They fail to move the system toward the goal. Instead, problems appear. More well-intentioned but misguided rules are added to solve the problems, but they only lead to new problems. This continues until nobody really understands what the rules are, what the goals of the organization are, or what the consequence of new rules would be. It also becomes increasingly difficult to change the system because of its dispiriting complexity, and because of the efforts of a minority of people who are well served by it.

For example, in a manufacturing system, which has a goal of satisfying customers, an apparently reasonable rule would be to *establish priorities for jobs, and to do the jobs with the highest priorities first.* Priorities can be assigned in various ways, but most often, the degree of lateness has a great deal to do with it. After some time, difficulties are observed. More and more jobs are later and later, and soon they are all in the same priority class: the highest. In this example, the problem arises because setup changes are performed too often. Orders arrive, after all, according to customers' needs, not the manufacturer's convenience.

---

[3]However, as one of my students (James Violette) once said, reducing inventory in order to find trouble spots is a little like walking barefoot to find broken glass.

A new rule is then added to solve the problems created by the old rule. *Among all the highest priority jobs, first do the jobs that go to the most valuable customers.* This, however, does not solve the problem; it only shifts the burden. The less important customers will eventually go elsewhere for better service, and only the most important customers may be left. Which job, now, do we serve first? This calls for another rule.

Nobody wants to jettison the lateness priority rule: it seems to make sense. Certainly nobody wants to drop the valuable customer rule. Perhaps the problem is simply that the factory is operating at its capacity, and the only way to satisfy more customers would be to buy more capital equipment. However, a glance at the shop shows a great deal of unproductive activity, particularly setup changes. It also shows idleness, since some machines are starved or blocked by others. There would seem to be some other solution.

A related example from classical science is the Ptolemaic system of astronomy. Timothy Ferris, in *Coming of Age in the Milky Way* (Ferris, 1988) describes the development of what we know as the Ptolemaic model of the universe. First, the earth was considered to be at the center of the universe, and the sun, moon, planets, stars, and other heavenly bodies revolved around it in large concentric spheres. But this did not survive careful observation, so more spheres were added. The new spheres were not concentric; they rotated about points on the earlier spheres. The more precise the observation, the more spheres were needed. Eventually, Ptolemy's system became hopelessly complex. Putting the sun at the center of the solar system simplified things and made them comprehensible.

When rules proliferate, the system is poorly understood. Additional rules are worse than band-aids to cure cancer: they are the cancer. The only solution is to develop an understanding of the system. This understanding may be difficult to achieve, but the operating policies that result from such an understanding will be surprisingly simple, and the system will work.

Bibliography

[1] R. N. Anthony (1965), *Planning and Control Systems: A Framework for Analysis,* Harvard University, 1965.

[2] R. G. Askin and C. R. Standridge (1993), *Modeling and Analysis of Manufacturing Systems*, Wiley, 1993.

[3] M. Baudin (1990), *Manufacturing Systems Analysis With Application to Production Scheduling*, Yourdon Press Computing Series, Prentice Hall, 1990.

[4] J. A. Buzacott and J. G. Shanthikumar (1992), editors, *Queueing Systems Theory and Applications, Special Issue on Queueing Models of Manufacturing Systems*, Volume 12, No. 1-2, December, 1992.

[5] J. A. Buzacott and J. G. Shanthikumar (1993), *Stochastic Models of Manufacturing Systems*, Prentice Hall, 1993.

[6] A. Dear (1988), *Working Towards Just-In-Time*, Van Nostrand Reinhold.

[7] A. A. Desrochers (1990), *Modeling and Control of Automated Manufacturing Systems*, IEEE Computer Society Press, Washington.

[8] Timothy Ferris (1988), *Coming of Age in the Milky Way*, Doubleday, 1988.

[9] E. M. Goldratt and J. Cox (1986) *The Goal*, North River Press, 1986.

[10] E. M. Goldratt and R. E. Fox (1986) *The Race*, North River Press, 1986.

[11] R. H. Hayes, S. C. Wheelwright, and K. Clark (1988), *Dynamic Manufacturing — Creating the Learning Organization*, The Free Press, Macmillan, 1988.

[12] A. Kusiak (1990), *Intelligent Manufacturing Systems,* Prentice Hall, 1990.

[13] J. D. C. Little (1961) "A Proof for the Queuing Formula: $L = \lambda W$," *Operations Research*, Vol. 9, No. 3, pp. 383-387.

[14] E. Merchant (1983), "Production: A Dynamic Challenge," *IEEE Spectrum*, Vol. 25, No. 5, pp. 36-39, May, 1983.

[15] K. N. McKay (1992), "Production Planning and Scheduling: A Model for Manufacturing Decisions Requiring Judgment," Ph. D. Thesis, University of Waterloo, Waterloo, Ontario, Canada.

[16] Y. Monden (1983), "Toyota Production System — Practical Approach to Production Management," Industrial Engineering and Management Press, Institute of Industrial Engineers.

[17] F. A. Rodammer and K. P. White (1988), "A Recent Survey of Production Scheduling," *IEEE Transactions on Systems, Man, and Cybernetics*, Vol. 18, No. 6, pp. 841-851, November/December, 1988.

[18] R. I. Schonberger (1986), *World Class Manufacturing — The Lessons of Simplicity Applied*, The Free Press, Macmillan.

[19] E. A. Silver and R. Peterson (1985), *Decision Systems for Inventory Management and Production Planning*, Second Edition, Wiley, 1985.

[20] S. B. Smith (1989), *Computer-Based Production and Inventory Control*, Prentice Hall, 1989.

[21] N. Viswanadham and Y. Narahari (1992), *Performance Modeling of Automated Manufacturing Systems*, Prentice Hall, 1992.

[22] J. P. Womack, D. T. Jones, and D. Roos (1990), *The Machine That Changed the World*, Rawson Associates, Macmillan, 1990.

Chapter 2

Markov Chains and Processes

2.1 Types

The focus of this book is the study of dynamic systems that are useful for the analysis, design, and operation of manufacturing systems. Dynamic systems are mathematical models that represent the change of important quantities over time. Dynamic systems may be classified according to many attributes:

- The time index may be discrete or continuous.

- The state may be discrete or continuous or mixed.

- The system may be stochastic (random) or deterministic.

- The system may describe the evolution of a process, or it may involve optimization to determine values of important decision variables as functions of time or the state.

For our purposes, *discrete* means that there are a set of items or quantities that may be counted using integers. *Continuous* means that the item in question must be measured by real numbers, or sets of real numbers, not restricted to the integers.[1]

In this chapter, we study systems that are stochastic and in which there are no decision variables. We use the results calculated here in Chapters 3-5 to describe simple manufacturing systems. These systems operate on only one part type and there are no real-time production decisions to be made. (Some features are generalized, but others are less general, in Chapter 6.) In Chapter 8, we introduce decision variables, and use the results in determining real-time operating policies for manufacturing systems in subsequent chapters.

---

[1]Strictly speaking, *continuous* applies to functions, not numbers, and is opposed to *discontinuous*. *Real* is the more correct term when applied to numbers. However, *real* makes most sense in opposition to *imaginary* or *complex*. We prefer *continuous* (as opposed to *discrete*) for numbers.

2.1.1 The index

A *Markov process* or *chain* is a kind of probabilistic dynamic system (that is, a kind of *stochastic process*) in which the future behavior depends only on the present, not the past. Stochastic processes have an *index* (sometimes called the *parameter*, although this term has other meanings) which is a one-dimensional time (or time-like) variable (usually represented t), and a *state*.

The index may be discrete or continuous. When it is discrete, it usually is allowed to take on all integer values, or all positive integer values. Such Markov processes are often characterized by difference equations. When the index is continuous, it is real and takes on all real values or all positive real values. The Markov process is often described by a set of differential equations.

2.1.2 The state

The state of a Markov process may be discrete, it may be continuous, or it may have both discrete and continuous parts. At any time t there is a probability distribution $f(x, t)$ for the state x. In general, x is multidimensional and may reside in any kind of space, bounded or unbounded. We will frequently use X to represent a *random variable*, a mapping from *sample space* (where the random events, like the throws of the dice, are taking place) to the space of x, the variable of interest.

2.1.3 Probability distributions

Let $\mathbf{R}$ be the real number line, and $\mathbf{R}^n$ be n-dimension vector space. Let x and $X \in \mathbf{R}^n$. Then a *probability density* $f(x)$ is defined by

$$f(x)\delta x_1 \ldots \delta x_n = \quad \text{prob}\ [x_1 \leq X_1 \leq x_1 + \delta x_1, \ldots, x_n \leq X_n \leq x_n + \delta x_n]$$
$$+o(\delta x_1 \ldots \delta x_n) \tag{2.1}$$

wherever this statement makes sense. (The notation $o(\delta x)$ represents quantities that are not treated in detail because they approach 0 faster than δx, as δx approaches 0.) However, it does not always make sense, since there are important cases in which it is possible for $f(x)$, defined this way, to be infinite for some values of x. Therefore, a richer structure is required. This kind of thing is discussed in great mathematical detail and rigor in an area called *measure theory*.

In (2.1), no value of x can have nonzero probability. That is, the probability of finding the state at any particular point is 0. The probability of finding it in an n-dimensional region S, however, may be nonzero, and can be calculated by integrating $f(x)$ over the region:

$$\text{prob}\ [X \in S] = \int_S f(x)dx_1 \ldots dx_n.$$

This integral is 1 if S is the whole space. That is,

$$\text{prob } [X \in \mathbf{R}^n] = \int_{\mathbf{R}^n} f(x)dx_1 \ldots dx_n = 1.$$

This is called *normalization*.

Imagine a stochastic process in which a particle can move to the left or right on an interval, but when it reaches either end point, it tends to stay there for a while. In that case, the end points have nonzero probability while the interior points have zero probability (although nonzero density). We say that the end points have *probability mass*. More generally, imagine a particle moving over a two-dimensional region. The boundaries can be sticky as in the interval above. There could even be a line in the interior which has this sticky behavior. Most of the interior has a usual two-dimensional density. However, the sticky lines have one-dimensional densities along them. This is because the particle could hit the boundaries or internal lines at any point. There is a one-dimensional density along each of these lines, which, when integrated along the lines, gives the probability of finding the point on the line. There could even be especially sticky points — *mass points* — which themselves have nonzero probabilities.

An example appears in Section 2.6.2. An unreliable machine falls behind production requirements when it fails, and can catch up when it is operational. It is operated so that the surplus, the difference between actual production and demand, never gets too large. That is, when the machine is up, the surplus is allowed to grow only up to a certain value, Z. When it reaches that value, production is slowed so that the surplus stays constant. On the other hand, when the machine is down, the surplus can decrease indefinitely. When the surplus is negative, it becomes a backlog. In this example, the surplus has a probability distribution which has two parts: a mass at Z, and a density function on $(-\infty, Z)$.

In general, if the continuous component of the state is defined in a subset R of $\mathbf{R}^n$, there could be n-dimensional subsets of R in which the density is n-dimensional; there could be $n - 1$-dimensional subsets in which the density is $n - 1$-dimensional, $\ldots$, 2-dimensional subsets of R in which the density is 2-dimensional, 1-dimensional subsets of R in which the density is 1-dimensional, and *mass* points which have a nonzero probability. (There also may be a discrete component of the state.)

Let g be a function defined on $\mathbf{R}^n$. Then we define the *mean* or *average expected value* of g to be

$$\bar{g} = \int_{\mathbf{R}^n} g(x)f(x)dx_1 \ldots dx_n.$$

In particular, the mean value of x is

$$\bar{x} = \int_{\mathbf{R}^n} xf(x)dx_1 \ldots dx_n.$$

Here x and $\bar{x}$ are members of $\mathbf{R}^n$, that is, vectors.

2.2   Discrete Time, Discrete State

2.2.1   Conditional probability

The basic concepts of Markov processes can be developed from the discrete time, discrete state case, and that case can be developed from the notion of conditional probability.

Intuitively, an *event* is an occurrence, as we usually think of it. Technically, it is a subset of the sample space. For example, getting an odd number on a pair of dice is simply the event of throwing a 3, 5, 7, 9, or 11. Since an event is a set of samples, we can say that an event is *true* if a sample is a member of the event. This is the same as saying that the event has happened.

Let A and B be events. Then (A and B) is an event. ((A and B) is true if A is true and B is true.) The probabilities of all these events are prob(A), prob(B), and prob(A and B). The *conditional probability* of A given B is the probability that A occurs given that we know that B has occurred. It is

$$\text{prob}\,(A \mid B) = \frac{\text{prob}\,(A \text{ and } B)}{\text{prob}\,(B)}.$$

For example, let A be the event of throwing an odd number with a single die. Then $A = \{1, 3, 5\}$. Let B be the event of throwing a number less than or equal to 3 with the single die. Then, $B = \{1, 2, 3\}$ and prob $(B) = 1/2$. The event (A and B) is $\{1, 3\}$ and its probability is prob $(A \text{ and } B) = 1/3$. The probability of throwing an odd number, given that we know that it is less than or equal to 3, is prob $(A \mid B) = 2/3$.

Let $B = (C \text{ or } D)$. (B is true if C is true *or* D is true.) Assume that (C and D) $= \emptyset$, the empty set. (That is, C and D are *mutually exclusive*. If C is true, then D must be false, and *vice versa*.) Then,

$$\text{prob}\,(A \mid C) = \frac{\text{prob}\,(A \text{ and } C)}{\text{prob}(C)},$$

$$\text{prob}\,(A \mid D) = \frac{\text{prob}\,(A \text{ and } D)}{\text{prob}(D)}.$$

Then, since (C and D) $= \emptyset$,

$$\text{prob}\,(A \text{ and } B) = \text{prob}\,(A \text{ and } C) + \text{prob}\,(A \text{ and } D)$$

or,

$$\text{prob}\,(A \mid B)\,\text{prob}\,(B) = \text{prob}\,(A \mid C)\text{prob}\,(C) + \text{prob}\,(A \mid D)\text{prob}\,(D)$$

so

$$\text{prob}\,(A \mid B) = \text{prob}\,(A \mid C)\text{prob}\,(C \mid B) + \text{prob}\,(A \mid D)\text{prob}\,(D \mid B).$$

An important case is when $(C \text{ or } D) = B$ is the universal set, so that $(A \text{ and } B) = A$. Then

$$\text{prob } (A) = \text{prob } (A \mid C)\text{prob } (C) + \text{prob } (A \mid D)\text{prob } (D).$$

More generally, if A and $\mathcal{E}_1, \ldots \mathcal{E}_k$ are events and

$$\mathcal{E}_i \text{ and } \mathcal{E}_j = \emptyset, \text{ for all } i \neq j$$

and

$$\bigcup_j \mathcal{E}_j = \text{ the universal set}$$

(that is, the set of $\mathcal{E}_j$ sets is *collectively exhaustive*) then

$$\sum_j \text{prob } (\mathcal{E}_j) = 1$$

and

$$\text{prob } (A) = \sum_j \text{prob } (A|\mathcal{E}_j) \text{ prob } (\mathcal{E}_j). \tag{2.2}$$

Equation (2.2) is central to the derivation of transition equations of Markov chains and Markov processes. It is sometimes called the *total probability theorem*. Some useful generalizations of (2.2) are

$$\text{prob } (A|B) = \sum_j \text{prob } (A|B \text{ and } \mathcal{E}_j) \text{ prob } (\mathcal{E}_j|B),$$

$$\text{prob } (A \text{ and } B) = \sum_j \text{prob } (A|B \text{ and } \mathcal{E}_j) \text{ prob } (\mathcal{E}_j \text{ and } B).$$

2.2.2 The geometric distribution

Consider a probabilistic system consisting of two states: 0 and 1. Let $\mathbf{p}(\alpha, t)$ be the probability of being in state α at time t, where $\alpha = 0$ or 1. Assume that

$$\mathbf{p}(1, 0) = 1. \tag{2.3}$$

Assume that the system can go from state 1 to state 0, but not from 0 to 1. Let p be the conditional probability that the system is in state 0 at time $t + 1$, given that it is in state 1 at time t. Symbolically,

$$p = \text{ prob } \left[\alpha(t+1) = 0 \middle| \alpha(t) = 1 \right].$$

Then, since

$$\mathbf{p}(0, t+1) \quad = \text{prob} \left[\alpha(t+1) = 0 \middle| \alpha(t) = 1 \right] \text{prob} \left[\alpha(t) = 1 \right]$$

$$+ \text{prob} \left[\alpha(t+1) = 0 \middle| \alpha(t) = 0 \right] \text{prob} \left[\alpha(t) = 0 \right],$$

we have[2]

$$\mathbf{p}(0, t+1) = p\mathbf{p}(1, t) + \mathbf{p}(0, t), \tag{2.4}$$

$$\mathbf{p}(1, t+1) = (1-p)\mathbf{p}(1, t),$$

and, the normalization equation,

$$\mathbf{p}(1, t) + \mathbf{p}(0, t) = 1. \tag{2.5}$$

The solution to (2.3), (2.4), (2.5) is

$$\mathbf{p}(0, t) \quad = \quad 1 - (1-p)^t, \tag{2.6}$$
$$\mathbf{p}(1, t) \quad = \quad (1-p)^t. \tag{2.7}$$

[Note that the equation for $\mathbf{p}(1, t+1)$ is not needed in determining (2.6) and (2.7).] The graphs of (2.6) and (2.7), with $p = 0.1$, appear in Figure 2.1.

Recall that once the system makes the transition from 1 to 0 it can never go back. The probability that the transition takes place at t is

$$\text{prob} \left[\alpha(t) = 0 \text{ and } \alpha(t-1) = 1 \right] = (1-p)^{t-1}p.$$

The time of the transition from 1 to 0 is said to be *geometrically distributed with parameter* p. The expected transition time is $1/p$. The geometric distribution is widely used because of its analytic tractability. In later sections, we typically assume that an operational machine's time to failure is geometrically distributed with parameter p, and that a failed machine's time to repair is geometrically distributed with parameter r.

Note that in this example, the probability of a transition from 1 to 0 at time $t + 1$ depends only on the value of the state at time t, and not on its earlier values. In this case, this observation is trivial, since if the state is 1 at time t, it must have been 1 at all earlier times. Nevertheless, this is a simple Markov chain.

---

[2]Equations (2.3), (2.4), and (2.5) form a set of *difference equations*. Difference equations are similar to differential equations, and the solution techniques are closely related. See Goldberg (1958) and Luenberger (1979).

Geometric Distribution

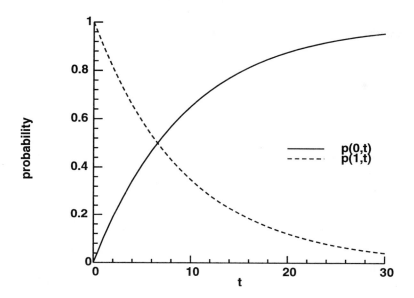

Figure 2.1: Probabilities as a Function of Time — Geometric Distribution

2.2.3 Markov chains

The basic assumption is

$$\text{prob } [X(t+1) = x(t+1) \mid X(t) = x(t),$$
$$X(t-1) = x(t-1), X(t-2) = x(t-2), \ldots]$$

$$= \text{ prob } [X(t+1) = x(t+1) \mid X(t) = x(t)].$$

This means that the probability that we would estimate for the system being in some state at time $t+1$ given the information on where the state was at time t, $t-1$, $t-2$, and so forth, is exactly the same as the probability that we would estimate given only the information on where the state was at time t. Once we know where the state was at time t, the prior history is irrelevant.

Let

$$\text{prob } [X(t+1) = i \mid X(t) = j] = P_{ij} \qquad (2.8)$$

and let

$$\mathbf{p}_i(t) = \text{ prob } (X(t) = i).$$

This is the probability distribution of the state of the system at time t. P_{ij} is called the *transition probability*. Consider Equation (2.2) in which A is the event $\{X(t+1) = i\}$, and $\{\mathcal{E}_j\}$ is the event $\{X(t) = j\}$. Then (2.2) becomes

$$\mathbf{p}_i(t+1) = \sum_j P_{ij}\mathbf{p}_j(t). \qquad (2.9)$$

This is the statement of the dynamics of the system. The normalization equation is

$$\sum_i \mathbf{p}_i(t) = 1, \text{ for all } t. \qquad (2.10)$$

It is useful to define the matrix $P^{(n)}$, the nth power of P. Then

$$\mathbf{p}_i(t) = \sum_j P_{ij}^{(t)}\mathbf{p}_j(0).$$

Reminder   Before we go any further, it is worthwhile to remind the reader of what $\mathbf{p}_i(t)$ means. It is the probability of finding the state equal to i at time t. Since we are discussing probability, we don't know if the state is actually at i at that time, if the probability is less than 1. On the other hand, if we actually look at the system, then we either observe that the state is i or it is not. Consequently, if we observe at time t, $\mathbf{p}_i(t)$ is either 1 or 0.

Suppose we observe the system at time t and find that the state is, in fact, i, so $\mathbf{p}_i(t) = 1; \mathbf{p}_j(t) = 0, j \neq i$. Assume that the transition probabilities P_{ij} are small, for $i \neq j$. Then, if we do not observe the system again, $\mathbf{p}_i(t+1)$ will be close to 1, and all other probabilities $\mathbf{p}_j(t+1)$ will be small or 0. If we continue not observing the system, $\mathbf{p}_i(s)$ will generally continue to decrease, for $s > t$ and other $\mathbf{p}_j(s)$ will generally continue to increase or remain constant. (This is actually a bit of a simplification. The behavior of probabilities as a function of time is a very complicated subject, and the probabilities are hard to compute.) In the long run, for many systems $\mathbf{p}_j(s)$ will approach a limit called the *steady state probability distribution*. (See Section 2.2.5.) It is important to remember that no observations were performed after t. If an observation were performed, the probability distribution would collapse back to being either 0 or 1.

Graph of a Markov Chain   It is convenient to represent a Markov chain with a directed graph. The nodes of the graph are the states i. An arc exists from node j to node i if $P_{ij} > 0$. The arcs are usually labeled with P_{ij}. The graph of the geometric distribution is shown in Figure 2.2.

2.2.4   Example: machine reliability

Problem   A machine can be in two states: *operational* (also called *up* or *working*) and *under repair (down* or *failed)*. It does an operation in a fixed time period, which is the time unit. Thus, while it is working, its production rate is one part per time unit. The

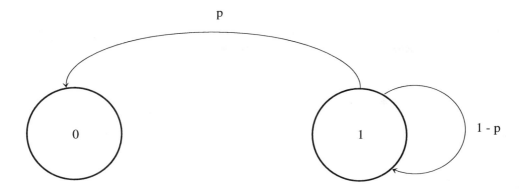

Figure 2.2: Graph of Markov Chain for Geometric Distribution

probability that a failure occurs during an operation (while the machine is up) is p. The probability that a repair is completed during a time unit while the machine is down is r. The graph of this Markov chain is shown in Figure 2.3.

What is the long run average production rate of the machine?

Solution   We often use 1 for up and 0 for down. The probability distribution satisfies

$$\mathbf{p}(0, t+1) = \mathbf{p}(0, t)(1 - r) + \mathbf{p}(1, t)p, \tag{2.11}$$
$$\mathbf{p}(1, t+1) = \mathbf{p}(0, t)r + \mathbf{p}(1, t)(1 - p). \tag{2.12}$$

To solve (2.11) and (2.12), we observe that this is a set of linear difference equations with constant coefficients. Consequently, the solution will be a sum of vectors of the form

$$\mathbf{p}(t) = aX^t$$

where X is a scalar and

$$\mathbf{p}(t) = \begin{pmatrix} \mathbf{p}(0, t) \\ \mathbf{p}(1, t) \end{pmatrix}; \qquad a = \begin{pmatrix} a(0) \\ a(1) \end{pmatrix}.$$

For each of these vectors,

$$a(0)X^{t+1} = a(0)X^t(1 - r) + a(1)X^t p,$$
$$a(1)X^{t+1} = a(0)X^t r + a(1)X^t(1 - p),$$

and, since we may assume $X \neq 0$,

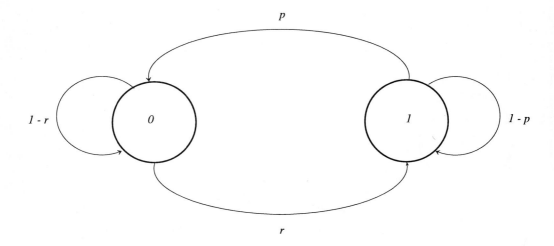

Figure 2.3: Graph of Markov Chain for Discrete Time Unreliable Machine Model

$$
\begin{aligned}
a(0)X &= a(0)(1-r) + a(1)p, \\
a(1)X &= a(0)r + a(1)(1-p),
\end{aligned}
$$

or,

$$
\begin{aligned}
X &= 1 - r + \frac{a(1)}{a(0)}p, \\
X &= \frac{a(0)}{a(1)}r + 1 - p.
\end{aligned}
$$

Then, if we eliminate $a(1)/a(0)$ from these equations, we find

$$
X = 1 - r + \frac{rp}{X - 1 + p}
$$

or,

$$
(X - 1 + r)(X - 1 + p) = rp.
$$

This is a quadratic equation with two solutions:

$$
X = 1 \text{ and } X = 1 - r - p.
$$

Since there are two Xs, there are two a vectors and two terms in the sums for $\mathbf{p}(0, t)$ and $\mathbf{p}(1, t)$. There is not enough information here to completely determine the vectors, but we can establish the ratio $a(1)/a(0)$. If $X = 1$ then

$$\frac{a(1)}{a(0)} = \frac{r}{p}.$$

If $X = 1 - r - p$, then

$$\frac{a(1)}{a(0)} = -1.$$

The solution of (2.11) and (2.12) is therefore (after some simplification),

$$\mathbf{p}(0, t) = \mathbf{p}(0, 0)(1 - p - r)^t + \frac{p}{r + p} \left[1 - (1 - p - r)^t \right], \tag{2.13}$$

$$\mathbf{p}(1, t) = \mathbf{p}(1, 0)(1 - p - r)^t + \frac{r}{r + p} \left[1 - (1 - p - r)^t \right]. \tag{2.14}$$

A graph of $\mathbf{p}(1, t)$ appears in Figure 2.4. In that graph, $p = 0.01$, $r = 0.09$, and $\mathbf{p}(1, 0)$ = 0.1.

2.2.5 Steady state

The limit of (2.13)-(2.14) as $t \to \infty$ is

$$\mathbf{p}(0) = \frac{p}{r + p}, \tag{2.15}$$

$$\mathbf{p}(1) = \frac{r}{r + p} \tag{2.16}$$

which is the solution of

$$\mathbf{p}(0) = \mathbf{p}(0)(1 - r) + \mathbf{p}(1)p, \tag{2.17}$$

$$\mathbf{p}(1) = \mathbf{p}(0)r + \mathbf{p}(1)(1 - p). \tag{2.18}$$

These equations are what (2.11)-(2.12) become if we assume

$$\mathbf{p}(0, t + 1) = \mathbf{p}(0, t),$$
$$\mathbf{p}(1, t + 1) = \mathbf{p}(1, t).$$

A *steady state* probability distribution $\mathbf{p}$ is one that satisfies Equation (2.9) with

$$\mathbf{p}_j = \mathbf{p}_j(t + 1) = \mathbf{p}_j(t)$$

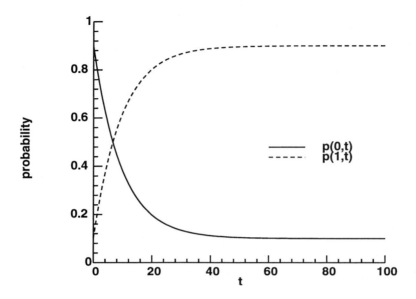

Figure 2.4: Probabilities as a Function of Time — Discrete Time Unreliable Machine

If a steady state distribution exists and is unique, it is *ergodic* and satisfies

$$\mathbf{p}_j = \lim_{t \to \infty} \mathbf{p}_j(t).$$

Uniqueness means that the limiting distribution is independent of the initial distribution $\mathbf{p}_j(0)$. Precise conditions are known that guarantee that a steady state exists, that it satisfies this limit, and that it is unique. Most examples in this book have a unique steady state distribution; counter-examples include the gambler's ruin problem, which has a non-unique steady state distribution; and the $M/M/1$ queue when the arrival rate exceeds the service rate, which does not have a steady state distribution. Intuitively, a steady state exists if the system has only a finite set of states, or, if it has an infinite number of states, it spends almost all its time among a finite set of states.

Meaning of steady state   This is often a confusing concept. It does *not* mean that the system is settling down in any sense. Knowing the steady state distribution tells us nothing about the dynamics of the system, or what state it will be in at any given time. The existence of a steady state distribution says nothing about the state of the system at any time in the future.

The steady state distribution tells something about the state of our *knowledge* of the system and of its future. If we know the state at time 0, we might have a good idea of the state at time 1. In the example above, if $r = p = 0.01$, and the machine is up at time 0, it is very likely to be up at time 1. However, our estimate of the state of the system depends less on our knowledge of the present as we contemplate the further future. The effect of $p(0,0)$ and $p(1,0)$ fades away as t grows. In particular, $p(0,1000)$ and $p(1,1000)$ are almost indistinguishable from $p(0,10000)$ and $p(1,10000)$. Thus, we (loosely) say "the system has reached steady state at time 1000." It would be more correct to say "our state of knowledge at time 0 of the system at time t has reached steady state at time $t = 1000$."

Another, more intuitive, meaning of steady state is that the performance measures appear to be close to constant over time. In this example, $\mathbf{p}(1,t)$ represents the availability of the machine; if it produces one part per time unit, the probability that it will produce a part at time t is $\mathbf{p}(1,t)$. Thus, $\mathbf{p}(1,t)$ is essentially the production rate. Here, the system reaches steady state when this performance measure approaches a limit. Unfortunately, the two meanings can sometimes conflict and cause confusion. Imagine that we observe the machine for a long period of time, and that we measure its production rate at intervals. If the rates we measure stay reasonably close to constant over all the intervals, we would like to say that the system is in steady state. However, this meaning is clearly different from the first, since we are observing the system, therefore resetting the probability distribution to 0 or 1. We use the first meaning of steady state throughout this book.

2.2.6   Example: gambler's ruin

Assume that you have i dollars and the house has $N - i$ dollars. At each turn, a coin is flipped. If it is heads, you gain a dollar and the house loses a dollar. If it is tails, *vice versa*. The game is over if either you or the house runs out of money. Let the bias of the coin, the probability of heads, be p. What is the probability that you win, in other words, that the house runs out of money first?

Solution   Let $w(i)$ be the probability that you win, given that you now have i dollars. ($w(i)$ is not the steady state probability distribution). Then

$$
\begin{aligned}
w(0) &= 0 \\
w(N) &= 1
\end{aligned}
$$

The first equation says that if you have 0 the game is already over and you have lost. The second equation says that if you have N the game is over and you have won. To complete the model, we must slightly extend Equation (2.2). Let B be an event. Then

$$
\text{prob}\,(A|B) = \sum_j \text{prob}\,(A|\mathcal{E}_j \text{ and } B)\,\text{prob}\,(\mathcal{E}_j|B).
$$

We can use this equation to determine the probability of winning, given that you have i, for each outcome: getting heads or tails. Let A be the event that you win, $\mathcal{E}_1$ be the event

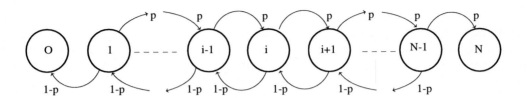

Figure 2.5: Graph of Markov Chain for Gambler's Ruin Problem

that the coin comes up heads, and $\mathcal{E}_2$ be the event that the coin comes up tails, and B be the event that you now have i dollars. Then this equation becomes

$$\text{prob (win } | i) = \quad \text{prob (win } | i \text{ and heads) prob (heads } | i)$$

$$+ \text{ prob (win } | i \text{ and tails) prob (tails } | i).$$

If you have i and get heads, you now have $i + 1$. If you have i and get tails, you now have $i - 1$. Therefore,

$$w(i) = w(i + 1)p + w(i - 1)(1 - p).$$

The graph of the Markov chain is shown in Figure 2.5. The solution of this equation, if $p \neq \frac{1}{2}$, is

$$w(i) = \frac{\left[\frac{1-p}{p}\right]^i - 1}{\left[\frac{1-p}{p}\right]^N - 1}. \tag{2.19}$$

The evils of gambling   If you start with \$10 and the house has \$90, and $p = .51$ (a coin biased in *your* favor), the probability of winning is only about .336. If the coin is not biased in your favor, your odds of breaking the bank are not better.

Steady State   In this case, an ergodic steady state probability distribution does not exist. There are an infinite set of steady state distributions. They are all convex combinations of

$$\mathbf{p}(0) = 1; \mathbf{p}(n) = 0, n > 0,$$

and

$$\mathbf{p}(N) = 1; \mathbf{p}(n) = 0, n < N.$$

That is, any distribution such that $\mathbf{p}(0) + \mathbf{p}(N) = 1$, $\mathbf{p}(j) = 0, 1 \leq j \leq N - 1$ is a steady state distribution.

2.2.7 Classification of states

A chain is *irreducible* if and only if each state can be reached from each other state after one or more transition. State i is *periodic* with period $m > 1$ if $P_{ii}^{(n)} = 0$ unless $n = km$ and m is the largest such integer.

Let f_{ij} be the probability that, if the system is in state j, it will at some later time be in state i. State i is *transient* if $f_{ij} < 1$. If a steady state distribution exists, and i is a transient state, its steady state probability is 0. The states can be uniquely divided into sets $T, C_1, \ldots C_n$ such that T is the set of all transient states and $f_{ij} = 1$ for i and j in the same set C_m and $f_{ij} = 0$ for i in some set C_m and j not in that set. If there is only one set C, the chain is irreducible. The sets C_m are called *final classes* or *absorbing classes* and T is the *transient class*. In the gambler's ruin problem, the final classes are $\{0\}$ and $\{N\}$ and $T = \{1, 2, \ldots, N - 1\}$.

Transient states cannot be reached from any other states except possibly other transient states. If state i is in T, there is no state j in any set C_m such that there is a sequence of possible transitions (transitions with nonzero probability) from j to i.

2.2.8 Classification of Markov processes

It is possible to define a variety of Markov processes that generalize the Markov chain defined in Section 2.2.3. The basic idea of a Markov process is that all information about the future evolution of its state exists in the present. One need not remember anything about the past as long as the current state is completely known. Systems that have this characteristic can have discrete or continuous times; and discrete, continuous, or mixed state spaces. Markov process with continuous time and discrete state are described in Section 2.3. Section 2.4 discusses systems with discrete time and continuous state. Continuous time Markov processes with continuous state are mentioned briefly in Section 2.5. Section 2.6 presents an important class of Markov processes with continuous time and mixed state. This material is important background for the manufacturing systems scheduling in Chapter 9 and following.

2.3 Continuous Time, Discrete State

2.3.1 Transition equations

Here, we have

$$\text{prob } [X(t) \in E \mid X(s) = x(s), \text{ all } s < \tau] = \text{prob } [X(t) \in E \mid X(\tau) = x(\tau)]$$

where E is any set of discrete points and t is any continuous time $> \tau$. The quantity on the left is the conditional probability that the random variable X is in set E at time t, given its entire history in the time before τ, which is earlier than t. The quantity on the right is the probability that the random variable X at time t is in set E, given *only* its value at time

τ. The fact that the conditional probability is not affected by the additional information in the earlier history is what makes $X(t)$ a Markov process.

Let $\mathcal{E}_j$ be the event $\{X(\tau) = j\}$ and A be the event $\{X(t) = i\}$. Then (2.2) becomes

$$\text{prob } (X(t) = i) = \sum_j \text{ prob } (X(t) = i \mid X(\tau) = j) \text{ prob } (X(\tau) = j).$$

In this equation, replace t by $t + \delta t$ and τ by t. It becomes

$$\text{prob } (X(t + \delta t) = i) = \sum_j \text{ prob } [X(t + \delta t) = i \mid X(t) = j] \text{ prob } (X(t) = j).$$

Assume δt is small, and assume that λ_{ij} exists for all $i \neq j$ such that

$$\text{prob } [X(t + \delta t) = i \mid X(t) = j] = \lambda_{ij}\delta t + o(\delta t). \tag{2.20}$$

(Note that some authors define λ this way and some reverse the subscripts.) Then

$$\text{prob } (X(t + \delta t) = i) \quad = \quad \sum_{j \neq i} \lambda_{ij}\delta t \text{ prob } (X(t) = j)$$

$$+ \text{ prob } (X(t + \delta t) = i | X(t) = i) \text{ prob } (X(t) = i) + o(\delta t).$$

Define

$$\mathbf{p}_i(t) = \text{ prob } (X(t) = i).$$

Then

$$\mathbf{p}_i(t + \delta t) = \sum_{j \neq i} \lambda_{ij}\mathbf{p}_j(t)\delta t + \text{ prob } (X(t + \delta t) = i \mid X(t) = i)\mathbf{p}_i(t) + o(\delta t).$$

The conditional probabilities satisfy

$$1 = \sum_j \text{ prob } (X(t + \delta t) = j \mid X(t) = i)$$

so

$$\text{prob } (X(t + \delta t) \quad = \quad i \mid X(t) = i) = 1 - \sum_{j \neq i} \text{ prob } (X(t + \delta t) = j \mid X(t) = i)$$

$$= \quad 1 - \sum_{j \neq i} \lambda_{ji}\delta t + o(\delta t).$$

Thus,

$$\mathbf{p}_i(t + \delta t) = \sum_{j \neq i} \lambda_{ij} \mathbf{p}_j(t)) \delta t + \left[1 - \sum_{j \neq i} \lambda_{ji} \delta t \right] \mathbf{p}_i(t) + o(\delta t).$$

It is convenient to define

$$\lambda_{ii} = - \sum_{j \neq i} \lambda_{ji} \tag{2.21}$$

so that

$$\mathbf{p}_i(t + \delta t) = \sum_{j \neq i} \lambda_{ij} \mathbf{p}_j(t)) \delta t + [1 + \lambda_{ii} \delta t] \, \mathbf{p}_i(t) + o(\delta t) \tag{2.22}$$

or

$$\mathbf{p}_i(t + \delta t) = \sum_{j} \lambda_{ij} \mathbf{p}_j(t) \delta t + \mathbf{p}_i(t) + o(\delta t). \tag{2.23}$$

Note that λ_{ii} is nothing other than a convenient definition. It does not have meaning the way λ_{ij} does, for $i \neq j$, in (2.20). It is certainly not a probability rate; it is negative. Many people, when they first encounter λ_{ii}, confuse themselves by finding a meaning which does not exist. The matrix of λ_{ij} is often called the *infinitesimal generator* of process X.

We can write a first order Taylor expansion of the left side of Equation (2.23):

$$\mathbf{p}_i(t) + \frac{d\mathbf{p}_i}{dt} \delta t = \sum_{j} \lambda_{ij} \mathbf{p}_j(t) \delta t + \mathbf{p}_i(t) + o(\delta t)$$

or,

$$\frac{d\mathbf{p}_i}{dt} = \sum_{j} \lambda_{ij} \mathbf{p}_j(t), \text{ all } i. \tag{2.24}$$

A *steady state* probability distribution $\mathbf{p}_i(t)$ is one that satisfies this equation with

$$\frac{d\mathbf{p}_i(t)}{dt} = 0, \text{ all } i.$$

That is,

$$0 = \sum_{j} \lambda_{ij} \mathbf{p}_j, \text{ all } i. \tag{2.25}$$

The *ergodic* distribution is the unique steady state distribution, if it exists.

Graphs   Continuous time, discrete state Markov processes can also be represented by graphs. The nodes are the states; the arcs from j to i are labeled with λ_{ij}.

Comparison with discrete time, discrete state systems   In Equation (2.8), P_{ij} is a *probability*, a pure number. By contrast, λ_{ij} is a *rate* with units of 1/time. In the examples in Section 2.3, p and r are probabilities, whereas in this section, the same symbols represent rates. This is a frequent source of confusion for people new to this subject.

2.3.2   Balance equations

Equation (2.25) can be written in another form. First, separate out the term in which $j = i$:

$$0 = \sum_{j \neq i} \lambda_{ij}\mathbf{p}_j + \lambda_{ii}\mathbf{p}_i.$$

From (2.21), the definition of λ_{ii},

$$0 = \sum_{j \neq i} \lambda_{ij}\mathbf{p}_j - \sum_{j \neq i} \lambda_{ji}\mathbf{p}_i.$$

This can be written

$$\mathbf{p}_i \sum_{j \neq i} \lambda_{ji} = \sum_{j \neq i} \lambda_{ij}\mathbf{p}_j. \tag{2.26}$$

The left side of (2.26) is the rate at which the system leaves state i. The right side is the rate at which the system enters state i. In steady state, these rates must be equal. These equations are often called *balance equations* (or sometimes *global balance*, or *full balance*, or other variation).

2.3.3   The exponential distribution

The exponential distribution is the continuous time counterpart of the geometric distribution. Again, let the probabilistic system consist of two states: 0 and 1. Let $\mathbf{p}(\alpha, t)$ be the probability of being in state α at time t, $\alpha = 0$ or 1. Assume that

$$\mathbf{p}(1,0) = 1. \tag{2.27}$$

Assume that the system can go from state 1 to state 0, but not from 0 to 1. Let $p\delta t$ be approximately the conditional probability that the system is in state 0 at time $t + \delta t$, given that it is in state 1 at time t. More precisely,

$$p\delta t = \text{ prob } \left[\alpha(t + \delta t) = 0 \Big| \alpha(t) = 1\right] + o(\delta t).$$

This equation expresses the *memoryless* property of the exponential distribution. The probability of a transition during an interval of length δt, given that the transition has not yet occurred, is independent of when you are considering it. For example, if a machine's time to fail is exponentially distributed with mean 100 hours, and its most recent repair was completed at 9:00, the probability of it failing between 9:00 and 10:00 is about .01. If it has not failed by 5:00, its probability of failing between 5:00 and 6:00 is about .01. If it has not failed during 100 hours of operation, its probability of failing in its 101st hour is about .01. If it has not failed during 1000 hours of operation, its probability of failing in its 1001st hour is still about .01. Thus, if you know that a random variable is exponentially distributed, and you know its mean, it will not help you to know how long it has been in its current state if you want to estimate the probability of a transition. The graph of the exponential distribution is shown in Figure 2.6.

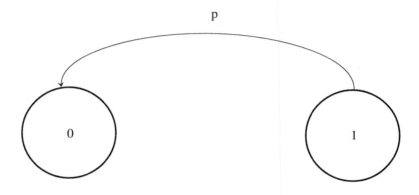

Figure 2.6: Graph of Markov Process for Exponential Distribution

Consider Equation (2.2) in which A is the event $\{X(t+\delta t) = 0\}$, $\mathcal{E}_1$ is the event $\{X(t) = 1\}$, and $\mathcal{E}_2$ is the event $\{X(t) = 0\}$. Then (2.2) becomes

$$\mathbf{p}(0, t+\delta t) \quad = \quad \text{prob}\left[\alpha(t+\delta t) = 0 \Big| \alpha(t) = 1\right] \text{ prob }[\alpha(t) = 1]$$

$$+ \text{ prob}\left[\alpha(t+\delta t) = 0 \Big| \alpha(t) = 0\right] \text{ prob}[\alpha(t) = 0].$$

Then

$$\mathbf{p}(0, t+\delta t) = p\delta t\mathbf{p}(1, t) + \mathbf{p}(0, t) + o(\delta t) \tag{2.28}$$

or,

$$\frac{d\mathbf{p}(0, t)}{dt} = p\mathbf{p}(1, t). \tag{2.29}$$

Similarly,

$$\mathbf{p}(1, t + \delta t) = \quad \text{prob} \left[\alpha(t + \delta t) = 1 \middle| \alpha(t) = 1 \right] \text{prob} \left[\alpha(t) = 1 \right]$$

$$+ \text{prob} \left[\alpha(t + \delta t) = 1 \middle| \alpha(t) = 0 \right] \text{prob} \left[\alpha(t) = 0 \right],$$

so

$$\mathbf{p}(1, t + \delta t) = (1 - p\delta t)\mathbf{p}(1, t) + (0)\mathbf{p}(0, t) + o(\delta t). \tag{2.30}$$

The coefficient of $\mathbf{p}(0, t)$ is 0 because, in this system, there is no way of going from 0 to 1. Then,

$$\frac{d\mathbf{p}(1, t)}{dt} = -p\mathbf{p}(1, t). \tag{2.31}$$

The solution to (2.27), (2.31) is

$$\mathbf{p}(0, t) = 1 - e^{-pt}, \tag{2.32}$$
$$\mathbf{p}(1, t) = e^{-pt}. \tag{2.33}$$

Recall that once the system makes the transition from 1 to 0 it can never go back, in this model. The probability that the transition takes place in $[t, t + \delta t]$ is

$$\text{prob} \left[\alpha(t + \delta t) = 0 \text{ and } \alpha(t) = 1 \right] = e^{-pt} p \delta t.$$

The time of the transition from 1 to 0 is said to be *exponentially distributed* with rate p. The expected transition time is $1/p$. The exponential distribution is widely used because of its analytic tractability. In later sections, we typically assume that an operational machine's time to failure is exponentially distributed with parameter p, and that a failed machine's time to repair is exponentially distributed with parameter r.

2.3.4   The meaning of it all

Before we go further, now is a good time to reflect on the meaning of the models and assumptions that we have introduced, and to establish the connection with the real world. Many people find such models to be overly simplistic, not representative of the real complexities that are found in factories and elsewhere. How useful will all these mathematical calisthenics prove to be?

Figure 2.7 is a graph of $e^{-pt} p$, and, superimposed on it, is a set of samples of failure times of a machine. They are organized as a set of bars, so that the height of each bar represents the number of times the failure time fell within the width of that bar. Note that the bars generally follow the exponential curve, but some are above and some are below. Had we taken more samples, and performed sophisticated statistical tests, we could say that, with some confidence, the machine fails according to an exponential distribution, or that it does not.

Note that the exponential density function decreases but does not go to zero as t goes to ∞. That is, prob$[t > T] > 0$ for all $t > 0$. There is a very small probability of a very large outcome.

For most purposes, the details of the shape of the curve are not as important as its gross features. The most important features of a probability distribution are its mean, its variance[3], and its general shape: whether the density has one, two, or more local maximums. If we made a small change to the curve in Figure 2.7 without changing its mean, variance, and general shape, the samples would fit about equally well. Consequently, the effect of the failures of this machine on other machines, material flow, and the overall performance of the system would not be greatly affected.

It is important to remember that we have not postulated any reason why a distribution should be exponential. Certainly it is desirable that it is, because it greatly simplifies the mathematics. Certainly, however, not everything is exponentially distributed. The practitioner must observe the system, and see whether this or any other distribution is at least a plausible representation of the observations. In many cases, the memoryless property of the exponential distribution is a statement of ignorance: the fact that the system has gone so long without a transition gives us no information about whether a transition is any more likely. In many cases, there may be many independent reasons for a transition to occur. Each may be distributed according to some non-exponential distribution, but it may be uncertain whether each will actually occur, or, among those that do, which will occur first. The effect of all this uncertainty may be to produce a distribution close to exponential.

2.3.5 Example: unreliable machine

This is similar to the discrete time, discrete state unreliable machine. A machine can be in two states: up or down. The probability that an operation is completed during an interval $[t, t + \delta t]$ while the machine is up is $\mu \delta t$. The probability that a failure occurs during an interval $[t, t + \delta t]$ while the machine is up is $p \delta t$. The probability that a repair is completed during an interval $[t, t + \delta t]$ while the machine is down is $r \delta t$. What is the long run average production rate of the machine?

The graph of this Markov process is shown in Figure 2.8. Note that the directed links are labeled with probability rates, not probabilities, and that the so-called self-loops, the links leading from a state back to itself, are not drawn. The probability distribution satisfies

$$\mathbf{p}(0, t + \delta t) = \mathbf{p}(0, t)(1 - r\delta t) + \mathbf{p}(1, t)p\delta t + o(\delta t)$$

---

[3]The *variance* of a scalar random variable x is $E(x - E(x))^2$, where E is the expectation operation. The *standard deviation* is the square root of the variance. In a graph like Figure 2.7, the variance and standard deviation are indicators of how widely spread the density function is. Variance and standard deviation are very important concepts, but they are defined in a footnote because they are not used very much in this book. This is unfortunate because variation and deviation (and their reduction) are very important to manufacturers. They play a small role here because, frankly, the variances of the processes described in this book have been little studied. This neglect should be remedied. See Section 3.2.

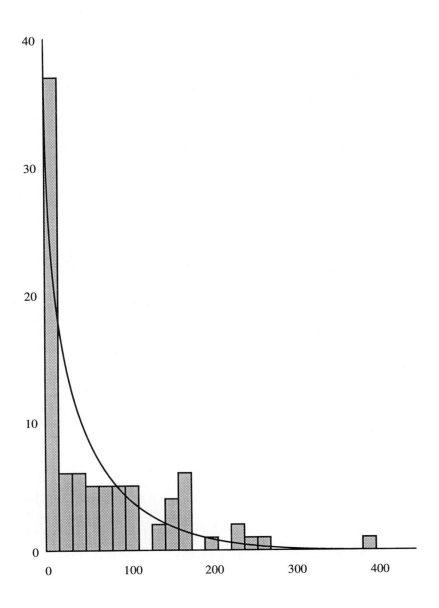

Figure 2.7: Exponential Density Function and Samples

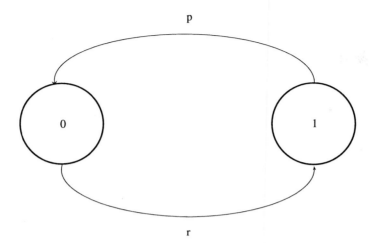

Figure 2.8: Graph of Markov Chain for Continuous Time Unreliable Machine Model

$$\mathbf{p}(1, t + \delta t) = \mathbf{p}(0, t) r \delta t + \mathbf{p}(1, t)(1 - p \delta t) + o(\delta t)$$

or

$$\frac{d\mathbf{p}(0, t)}{dt} = -\mathbf{p}(0, t) r + \mathbf{p}(1, t) p$$

$$\frac{d\mathbf{p}(1, t)}{dt} = \mathbf{p}(0, t) r - \mathbf{p}(1, t) p.$$

The solution is

$$\mathbf{p}(0, t) \quad = \quad \frac{p}{r + p} + \left[\mathbf{p}(0, 0) - \frac{p}{r + p} \right] e^{-(r+p)t} \tag{2.34}$$

$$\mathbf{p}(1, t) \quad = \quad 1 - \mathbf{p}(0, t). \tag{2.35}$$

As $t \rightarrow \infty$, we have

$$\mathbf{p}(0) = \frac{p}{r + p}; \mathbf{p}(1) = \frac{r}{r + p}.$$

The average production rate is $\mathbf{p}(1)\mu$ or $\dfrac{r\mu}{r + p}$.

2.3.6   The $M/M/1$ queue

This is the simplest queuing theory model. It has very few assumptions, and they are rarely satisfied in reality. It is a good way to get into the subject, however, because anything more realistic is much more complicated. In spite of its unreality, we can learn something from it.

Consider a queuing system with an infinite amount of storage space. Parts arrive according to a *Poisson process*. That is, the interarrival times are exponentially distributed, which means that if a part arrives at time s, the probability that the next part arrives during the interval $[s + t, s + t + \delta t]$ is $e^{-\lambda t}\lambda\delta t + o(\delta t)$. λ is the *arrival rate*. Similarly, the service times are exponentially distributed, which means that if an operation is completed at time s and the buffer is not empty, the probability that the next operation is completed during the interval $[s + t, s + t + \delta t]$ is $e^{-\mu t}\mu\delta t + o(\delta t)$. μ is the *service rate*.

Let $\mathbf{p}(n, t)$ be the probability that there are n parts in the system at time t. Then,

$$\mathbf{p}(n, t + \delta t) = \mathbf{p}(n - 1, t)\lambda\delta t + \mathbf{p}(n + 1, t)\mu\delta t + \mathbf{p}(n, t)(1 - (\lambda\delta t + \mu\delta t)) + o(\delta t),$$
$$n > 0 \quad (2.36)$$

and

$$\mathbf{p}(0, t + \delta t) = \mathbf{p}(1, t)\mu\delta t + \mathbf{p}(0, t)(1 - \lambda\delta t) + o(\delta t). \tag{2.37}$$

These equations are application of Equation (2.2). In (2.36), A is the event {there are n parts in the system at time $t + \delta t$}, $\mathcal{E}_1$ is the event {there are $n - 1$ parts in the system at time t}, $\mathcal{E}_2$ is the event {there are $n + 1$ parts in the system at time t}, and $\mathcal{E}_3$ is the event {there are n parts in the system at time t}. In (2.37), A is the event {there is 1 part in the system at time $t + \delta t$}, $\mathcal{E}_1$ is the event {there are no parts in the system at time t}, and $\mathcal{E}_2$ is the event {there is 1 part in the system at time t}. Equations (2.36) and (2.37) become

$$\frac{\partial \mathbf{p}(n, t)}{\partial t} = \mathbf{p}(n - 1, t)\lambda + \mathbf{p}(n + 1, t)\mu - \mathbf{p}(n, t)(\lambda + \mu), n > 0$$

and

$$\frac{\partial \mathbf{p}(0, t)}{\partial t} = \mathbf{p}(1, t)\mu - \mathbf{p}(0, t)\lambda.$$

If a steady state distribution exists, it satisfies

$$0 = \mathbf{p}(n - 1)\lambda + \mathbf{p}(n + 1)\mu - \mathbf{p}(n)(\lambda + \mu), n > 0$$

and

$$0 = \mathbf{p}(1)\mu - \mathbf{p}(0)\lambda.$$

Let $\rho = \lambda/\mu$. These equations are satisfied by

$$\mathbf{p}(n) = (1 - \rho)\rho^n, n \geq 0 \tag{2.38}$$

if $\rho < 1$. The average number of parts in the system is

$$\bar{n} = \sum_n n\mathbf{p}(n) = \frac{\rho}{1-\rho} = \frac{\lambda}{\mu - \lambda}. \tag{2.39}$$

From Little's law, the average delay experienced by a part is

$$W = \frac{1}{\mu - \lambda}.$$

Figure 2.9 is a graph of W as a function of λ, with $\mu = 1$.

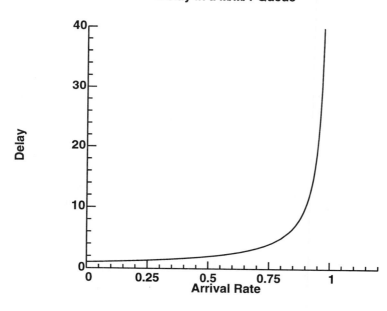

Figure 2.9: Delay *versus* Arrival Rate

2.3.7 Interpretation

The most important characteristic of this system is that the arrival process is not affected by the number of parts in the system, but the departure process is turned off when the buffer is empty.

The condition $\rho < 1$ or $\lambda < \mu$ means that the rate at which parts arrive is less than the rate at which parts can be processed. This means that if, at some time, there happen to be many parts in the system, that number will probably decrease over time. On the other hand, if the system is empty, a part will arrive sooner or later. If, by chance, more parts than average arrive during a period, the system may accumulate a few parts. Thus the number of parts in the system will increase and decrease, but not get very far from 0 very often.

On the other hand, if $\lambda > \mu$, parts will tend to accumulate in the system. Parts arrive faster than they can be processed, and the arrival mechanism is never turned off. In fact, if the system is started empty at time 0, the number of parts in the system at time t is close to $(\lambda - \mu)t$. The probability of finding the system empty approaches 0. In this case, there is no steady state probability distribution.

The *capacity* of this system is μ. This is the greatest rate at which parts can enter and leave the system. The delay and the average number of parts in the system increase dramatically as the arrival rate approaches the capacity. These quantities are much harder to calculate in other systems, but this behavior is characteristic of all systems with waiting.

There are only two ways of reducing delay: increase the capacity, or change the relationship between throughput and delay. The first approach involves changing the manufacturing process; the second involves scheduling.

2.4   Discrete Time, Continuous State

Here, we have

$$\text{prob } [X(t) \in E \mid X(s), s < \tau] = \text{ prob } [X(t) \in E \mid X(\tau)]$$

where E is any set in $\mathbf{R}^n$ and t is any member of the discrete set it belongs to (such as the set of integers). To characterize the process, we need a function $f(x, t)$ which is a density function of x that varies over a discrete set of t values.

2.5   Continuous Time, Continuous State

We have

$$\text{prob } [X(t) \in E \mid X(s), s < \tau] = \text{ prob } [X(t) \in E \mid X(\tau)]$$

where E is any set in $\mathbf{R}^n$ and t is any continuous value.

To characterize the process, we need a function $f(x, t)$ which is a density function of x that varies over a continuous set of t values. Most often, it satisfies a partial differential equation over x and t:

$$\frac{\partial f}{\partial t} = G\left(f, \frac{\partial f}{\partial x} \right).$$

The most usual example of this process is a *diffusion*, or *Brownian motion* process, where the state changes direction at essentially every time instant.

2.6 Continuous Time, Continuous and Discrete State

2.6.1 General formulation

This sounds more complicated than the last case, but actually, its behavior can be simpler. An example is where all the randomness originates in the discrete portion of the state. Now the continuous portion evolves in a smooth manner. It is much easier to solve the resulting differential equations than in the diffusion case.

To deal with this case, let $x(t)$ be the continuous portion of the state and $\alpha(t)$ be the discrete portion. As an even more special case, assume that α evolves according to an independent Markov process, and that the dynamics of x are driven by α. In fact, assume the following class of systems:

$$\text{prob } [\alpha(t + \delta t) = i \mid \alpha(t) = j] = \lambda_{ij}\delta t + o(\delta t) \text{ if } j \neq i, \tag{2.40}$$

$$\frac{dx}{dt} = G(x(t), \alpha(t)).$$

The behavior of α is exactly the same as that of X in Section 2.3. Equation (2.40) is the same as Equation (2.20). Note that this is not a completely general continuous time, mixed state system. In particular, once α takes a value, x behaves deterministically. All the randomness comes from α, and x does not influence α.

We are seeking a function which is a probability density for x and a probability mass for α. That is,

$$f(x, \beta, t)\delta x_1 \delta x_2 \ldots \delta x_n = \quad \text{prob } [x_1 \leq X_1(t) \leq x_1 + \delta x_1, x_2 \leq X_2(t) \leq x_2 + \delta x_2,$$

$$\ldots, x_n \leq X_n(t) \leq x_n + \delta x_n, \alpha(t) = \beta]$$

$$+o(\delta x_1 \ldots \delta x_n).$$

Assume that the initial value of this function, $f(x, \alpha, 0)$ has been specified. Then the evolution of $f(x, \alpha, t)$ is determined as follows:

$$f(x, i, t + \delta t) = \sum_{j \neq i} f(x^j, j, t)\lambda_{ij}\delta t + f(x^i, i, t) \left[1 - \sum_{j \neq i} \lambda_{ji}\delta t\right] + o(\delta t) \tag{2.41}$$

where

$$x^j = x - G(x, j)\delta t + o(\delta t) \text{ for all } j, \text{ including } j = i$$

is the approximate value of $x(t)$ in order for $x(t + \delta t)$ to be x, if α is j during $(t, t + \delta t)$. Equation (2.41) (if it were multiplied by $\delta x_1 \delta x_2 \ldots \delta x_n$) is again an application of (2.2) in which

- A is the event $\{x_1 \leq X_1(t + \delta t) \leq x_1 + \delta x_1,\ x_2 \leq X_2(t + \delta t) \leq x_2 + \delta x_2,\ \ldots,$ $x_n \leq X_n(t + \delta t) \leq x_n + \delta x_n,\ \alpha(t + \delta t) = i\}$, and

- $\mathcal{E}_j$ is the event $\{x_1 - G_1(X, j)\delta t \leq X_1(t) \leq x_1 + \delta x_1 + G_1(X, j)\delta t,\ x_2 - G_2(X, j)\delta t \leq X_2(t) \leq x_2 + \delta x_2 + G_2(X, j)\delta t, \ldots, x_n - G_n(X, j)\delta t \leq X_n(t) \leq x_n + \delta x_n + G_n(X, j)\delta t,$ $\alpha(t) = j\}$.

As usual, we define

$$\lambda_{ii} = -\sum_{j \neq i} \lambda_{ji}.$$

The first term of (2.41) represents all the ways the state could have gotten to (x, i) at time $t + \delta t$ in which $\alpha(t) \neq i$, and the second represents the only way the state could get there when $\alpha(t) = i$. From this,

$$f(x, i, t + \delta t) = \sum_{j \neq i} f(x - G(x, j)\delta t, j, t)\lambda_{ij}\delta t + f(x - G(x, i)\delta t, i, t)\left[1 + \lambda_{ii}\delta t\right] + o(\delta t).$$

This equation is analogous to (2.22). Expanding to first order in δt,

$$f(x, i) + \frac{\partial f(x, i)}{\partial t}\delta t = \sum_{j \neq i} f(x, j)\lambda_{ij}\delta t + \left[f(x, i) - \frac{\partial f(x, i)}{\partial x}G(x, i)\delta t\right]\left[1 + \lambda_{ii}\delta t\right]$$
$$+ o(\delta t)$$
$$= \sum_{j \neq i} f(x, j)\lambda_{ij}\delta t + f(x, i) - \frac{\partial f(x, i)}{\partial x}G(x, i)\delta t + f(x, i)\lambda_{ii}\delta t$$
$$+ o(\delta t)$$

in which we have dropped the t argument to simplify notation. If we subtract $f(x, i)$ from both sides, divide through by δt, and let δt approach 0,

$$\frac{\partial f(x, i)}{\partial t} = \sum_j f(x, j)\lambda_{ij} - \frac{\partial f(x, i)}{\partial x}G(x, i) \text{ for all } i.$$

This is a set of partial differential equations which are analogous to (2.24). In steady state,

$$0 = \sum_j f(x, j)\lambda_{ij} - \frac{\partial f(x, i)}{\partial x}G(x, i) \text{ for all } i.$$

In addition, boundary conditions must be specified.

2.6.2 Production surplus from an unreliable machine

Consider the unreliable machine described in Section 2.3.3 that can change repair state in continuous time, but now with a continuous production process. Think of it as a random valve controlling the flow of a fluid. When the valve is open, it produces material at rate μ per unit time; when it is closed, it produces at rate 0. In later chapters, we discuss situations in which such a continuous production model makes sense.

We can regulate this process. If it produces more than a desired amount, we can slow it down. (If it produces too little, however, there is nothing we can do.) **Question:** how close to a desired average rate — d per unit time — will it produce? Let us design a simple regulation strategy.

Before introducing a mathematical model, we make an observation. We only have an interesting problem if $d < \mu$. In fact, it really only makes sense if

$$d < \frac{\mu r}{r + p}. \tag{2.42}$$

Model Let α represent the machine state: $\alpha = 1$ means the machine is up; $\alpha = 0$ means the machine is down. Let $u(t)$ be the production rate at time t. It can be controlled: if the machine is up, we can choose any u in

$$0 \leq u \leq \mu.$$

If the machine is down, we must have $u = 0$. These two statements can be combined as

$$0 \leq u \leq \mu\alpha.$$

In later chapters, we call this the *capacity set*. It is a random set that changes over time as the machine state changes. Let x represent the *surplus*, the difference between production and requirements. It satisfies

$$\frac{dx}{dt} = u - d. \tag{2.43}$$

If x is positive, we have produced too much. If x is negative, we have produced too little. We would like to regulate the production process, so that x is never too far from 0. Here we analyze a control law $u(x, \alpha)$. We synthesize such laws in Chapter 9.

Control law Define $Z \geq 0$ to be an important value of x. Z is called the *hedging point*.

- if $x < Z, u = \mu\alpha$.

- if $x = Z, u = d\alpha$.

- if $x > Z, u = 0$.

The first condition says that when x is not at its maximum desirable value, the system is run at its maximum rate (μ when the machine is up; 0 when it is down). When the machine is up, (2.43) implies that x is increasing. The second condition says that if x is at the boundary and the machine is working, we only run it at rate d. Consequently, x remains at Z, according to (2.43). This is important: it implies that x cannot ever exceed Z (unless, of course, the system is initialized with $x > Z$). If the machine is down, u is 0 and x decreases, so that x leaves Z as soon as the failure occurs.

Probability Distribution and Transition Equations   For $x < Z$, define $f(x, \alpha, t)$ as

$$f(x, \alpha, t)\delta x = \text{ prob } (x \leq X(t) \leq x + \delta x \text{ and the machine state is } \alpha \text{ at time } t).$$

$P(Z, \alpha, t)$ is a probability mass. For $x < Z$,

$$f(x, 0, t + \delta t) = f(x + d\delta t, 0, t)(1 - r\delta t) + f(x, 1, t)p\delta t + o(\delta t)$$

or, in steady state, where we drop the t arguments of $f(x, \alpha, t)$ and $P(Z, \alpha, t)$,

$$f(x, 0) = f(x + d\delta t, 0)(1 - r\delta t) + f(x, 1)p\delta t + o(\delta t). \tag{2.44}$$

This is because the state could get to $(x, 0)$ from $(x + d\delta t, 0)$ if no repair occurs, or from $(x, 1)$ if the machine is up and a failure occurs. All this is an approximation, and is only accurate to within $o(\delta t)$; a more accurate argument of $f(x, 1)$ would be some $x' \in [x - (\mu - d)\delta t, x + d\delta t]$. If the failure occurs early in the interval, then x' must have been $x + d\delta t$; if it occurs late, then x' must have been $x - (\mu - d)\delta t$. However, the difference between either end of the interval and x is on the order of δt, and if we expanded f, the δt term would be multiplied by the $p\delta t$ coefficient, so it would be dropped. Therefore, we may as well consider $f(x, 1)$ to be evaluated at x, rather than x'.

To analyze (2.44), we must expand $f(x + d\delta t, 0)$. It is given by

$$f(x + d\delta t, 0) = f(x, 0) + \frac{\partial f}{\partial x}(x, 0)d\delta t + o(\delta t).$$

Consequently, (2.44) is

$$f(x, 0) = f(x, 0) - f(x, 0)r\delta t + \frac{\partial f}{\partial x}(x, 0)d\delta t + f(x, 1)p\delta t + o(\delta t),$$

or,

$$0 = -f(x, 0)r + \frac{\partial f}{\partial x}(x, 0)d + f(x, 1)p.$$

Similarly, for $x < Z$,

$$f(x, 1) = f(x, 0)r\delta t + f(x - (\mu - d)\delta t, 1)(1 - p\delta t) + o(\delta t). \tag{2.45}$$

This is because if the system is at $(x, 1)$ at time $t + \delta t$, we must have

$$x(t + \delta t) = x(t) + (\mu - d)\delta t.$$

Expanding leads to

$$f(x, 1) = f(x, 0)r\delta t + f(x, 1) - f(x, 1)p\delta t - \frac{\partial f(x, 1)}{\partial x}(\mu - d)\delta t + o(\delta t)$$

or,

$$0 = f(x, 0)r - f(x, 1)p - \frac{\partial f(x, 1)}{\partial x}(\mu - d).$$

Boundary conditions must be satisfied at $x = Z$. To get to $(Z, 1)$ from $(x, 1)$, where $x \leq Z$,

$$
\begin{aligned}
P(Z, 1) \quad = \quad & P(Z, 1)(1 - p\delta t) + \text{ prob } (Z - (\mu - d)\delta t < X < Z, \alpha = 1)(1 - p\delta t) \\
& + o(\delta t). \quad\quad\quad (2.46)
\end{aligned}
$$

That is, the state can be at $(Z, 1)$ at time $t + \delta t$ if it were at the same state at time t and no failure occurred in $[t, t + \delta t]$ (because when the state is at $(Z, 1)$, x does not change); or the surplus could have been just below Z at time t and the machine did not go down in $[t, t + \delta t]$. We need not consider transitions from states of the form $(x, 0)$, in which

$$Z - (\mu - d)\delta t \leq x \leq Z$$

because the corresponding terms would be on the order of $(\delta t)^2$.

Note that

$$\text{prob } (Z - (\mu - d)\delta t < X < Z, \alpha = 1) = f(Z, 1)(\mu - d)\delta t \quad\quad\quad (2.47)$$

so that, to first order,

$$P(Z, 1) = P(Z, 1) - p\delta t P(Z, 1) + f(Z, 1)(\mu - d)\delta t + o(\delta t),$$

or,

$$0 = -pP(Z, 1) + f(Z, 1)(\mu - d).$$

To get to the interior from $x = Z$, observe that

$$
\begin{aligned}
\text{prob } (Z - \delta x < X < Z, 0) \quad & = f(Z, 0)\delta x + o(\delta t) \\
& = P(Z, 1)p\delta t + o(\delta t)
\end{aligned}
\quad\quad\quad (2.48)
$$

where $\delta x = d\delta t$. The first equation is true by definition; the second due to the failure of the machine when $x = Z$. There are no other transitions whose probability is first order in δt. Thus,

$$f(Z,0)d = P(Z,1)p$$

or

$$f(Z,1)(\mu - d) = f(Z,0)d.$$

To summarize, we must solve the following boundary value problem:

$$0 = -f(x,0)r + \frac{\partial f}{\partial x}(x,0)d + f(x,1)p \tag{2.49}$$

$$0 = f(x,0)r - f(x,1)p - \frac{\partial f(x,1)}{\partial x}(\mu - d) \tag{2.50}$$

$$0 = -pP(Z,1) + f(Z,1)(\mu - d) \tag{2.51}$$

$$f(Z,1)(\mu - d) = f(Z,0)d. \tag{2.52}$$

Solution of Transition Equations   To solve (2.49)-(2.52), we try the following reasonable guess:

$$f(x,\alpha) = A(\alpha)e^{bx}$$

where $A(1), A(0)$, and b must be determined. Plugging into (2.49), and dividing by e^{bx}

$$0 = -A(0)r + bA(0)d + A(1)p. \tag{2.53}$$

From (2.50),

$$0 = A(0)r - A(1)p - bA(1)(\mu - d). \tag{2.54}$$

From (2.52),

$$A(1)(\mu - d) = A(0)d. \tag{2.55}$$

From (2.53)-(2.55) we find that

$$b = \frac{r}{d} - \frac{p}{\mu - d}.$$

Renaming $A(0)$ as A, we can now complete the solution:

$$f(x,0) = Ae^{bx} \tag{2.56}$$

$$f(x,1) = A\frac{d}{\mu - d}e^{bx}$$

(2.57)

$$P(Z,1) = A\frac{d}{p}e^{bZ}$$

(2.58)

$$P(Z,0) = 0$$

(2.59)

Now A is a normalizing constant, chosen so that

$$1 = P(Z,1) + \int_{-\infty}^{Z} [f(x,0) + f(x,1)]\,dx.$$

(2.60)

Comments and Interpretation

1. We have assumed that a steady state solution exists, and that A can be determined from the normalization Equation (2.60). However, for the integral in (2.60) to be finite, it is necessary that b be positive. Physically, it means that on the average, more surplus is produced during periods while the machine is working at full speed than is lost while the machine is down. Because the average length of an up period is $1/p$, the average amount of surplus gained during an up period while the machine is working at its maximum (that is, while $x < Z$) is

$$\frac{\mu - d}{p}.$$

Similarly, the average length of a down period is $1/r$, and the average amount of surplus lost during a down period is

$$\frac{d}{r}.$$

For x not to drift to $-\infty$ (and thus for a steady state solution to exist), we must have

$$\frac{\mu - d}{p} > \frac{d}{r}$$

or

$$\frac{p}{\mu - d} < \frac{r}{d}$$

which implies that b is positive. Note that this is equivalent to (2.42).

2. Let

$$C = Ae^{bZ}.$$

Then

$$f(x, 0) = Ce^{-b(Z-x)}$$

$$f(x, 1) = C\frac{d}{\mu - d}e^{-b(Z-x)}$$

$$P(Z, 1) = C\frac{d}{p}$$

$$P(Z, 0) = 0$$

This manipulation makes clear that the probability distribution really depends on $Z - x$. If Z is changed, the whole distribution shifts without changing its shape.

Figure 2.10 is a graph of the probability density $f(x, 0)$. The heavy vertical line indicates the location of the probability mass. The height is *not* drawn to scale.

2.7   Preview

Now that we have established a vocabulary for random dynamic processes, we can describe — in more precise terms than before — what appears in later chapters.

Chapters 3 to 6 extend the material in this chapter to the movement of parts in manufacturing systems. In particular, they build on the unreliable machine and $M/M/1$ models. Chapter 3 describes two-machine, one-finite-buffer transfer lines as Markov processes with discrete or continuous time, and with discrete or mixed state. The steady state distributions are calculated, and they are used to determine the average production rates and in-process inventories. In Chapter 4, it is pointed out that the steady state distribution cannot practically be calculated (or even written) for a line with more than two machines and more than one finite buffer, so approximate decomposition methods are developed to determine average production rates and in-process inventories. Chapter 5 generalizes these models to include assembly. The models of Chapters 3 to 5 are limited in that there is only one route through the system, which all parts take. There is also no opportunity for control, that is, human or machine decision-making about material movement.

Chapter 6 describes a different kind of extension. Machines are reliable, although operation times may vary from part to part. Different parts may take different routes through the system, and the route choice may be random. There may be different classes of parts, with different routing probabilities. For this class of models (*Jackson networks*), analytic or

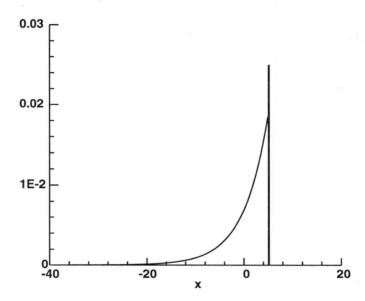

Figure 2.10: Probability Distribution of Controlled Machine

practical solutions exist when buffers are infinite. There is still no opportunity for human or machine decision-making.

The remainder of the book deals with choice in material flow systems. It builds on the material in Section 2.6.2. Some mathematical preliminaries are required first: Chapter 7 is a *very* brief introduction to linear programming which introduces some concepts needed later. Chapter 8 is a slightly longer introduction to dynamic programming. Dynamic programming can be thought of as (1) the mathematics of decision-making over time, or (2) an extension of Markov processes in which a decision-maker has an influence over the outcome of events.

Chapter 9 is an extension of Section 2.6.2 in which the goal is to determine Z for single part type systems, or to generalize the control law when there are more than one part type. In Chapter 9, there are still only two kinds of events (operations and failures), and buffers do not play a role. Later chapters allow more kinds of events and buffers.

Exercises

1. Prove (2.6)-(2.7).

2. Prove that the expected transition time of a geometrically distributed random variable with parameter p is $1/p$.

3. Prove (2.13)-(2.14).

4. **Machine reliability, part 2**   A machine has two failure modes: when it is up, it can go to failure mode 1 with probability p_1, it can go to failure mode 2 with probability p_2, or it can stay up (and make a part) with probability $1 - p_1 - p_2$. If it is down in mode i, it can go up with probability r_i. Draw the graph of this Markov chain. Assume that the production rate is 1 in the up state and 0 in the two down states. What is the long term average production rate?

5. **Machine reliability, part 3**   A machine has two working modes: recently repaired (1) and wearing out (2). When it is down (0), it has probability r of going to state 1 and $1 - r$ of not changing. When it is in state 1, it has probability p_1 of going to 0, s of going to 2, and $1 - p_1 - s$ of staying where it is and producing a part. In state 2, it has probability p_2 of going to 0 and $1 - p_2$ of staying at 2 and producing a part. When the system is in state 1 or state 2, it produces exactly one part each time unit if it does not fail. When it is in state 0, it produces no parts. Draw the graph of this Markov chain. What is the long term average production rate?

6. Prove (2.19).

7. In the gambler's ruin problem, what is $w(i)$ if $p = \frac{1}{2}$?

8. For the gambler's ruin problem, let $\mathbf{p}(n, t)$ be the probability of your having n dollars at time t. Write the transition equations for $\mathbf{p}(n, t)$. Prove the statement about the steady state distribution. *Hint:* be sure to include in the equations the fact that if $n(t) = 0$ or N then $n(t + 1) = n(t)$ with certainty.

9. Prove that (2.32)-(2.33) satisfies (2.27), (2.31).

10. Prove that the expected transition time of an exponentially distributed random variable with parameter p is $1/p$.

11. Prove (2.34)-(2.35).

12. Derive the balance equations for the $M/M/1$ queue.

13. Prove (2.38).

14. Prove (2.39).

15. Show that in an $M/M/1$ queue, the long term average throughput, the rate that parts leave the system, is $\min(\lambda, \mu)$. *Hint:* assume that if $\lambda > \mu$,

$$\lim_{t \to \infty} \mathbf{p}(0, t) = 0$$

as described in Section 2.3.7.

16. Explain why b must be positive on physical grounds. Produce a different answer than the one in "Comments and Interpretation." *Hint:* what does $\frac{r}{r+p}$ mean?

17. Explain Equations (2.44), (2.45), (2.46), (2.47), (2.48), (2.59) as an example of (2.2). Identify A and $\mathcal{E}_i$ in each equation.

18. What is the relationship between C and Z? Why does this make intuitive sense? The purpose of the control policy of Section 2.6.2 was to keep x not too far from 0. Complete the analysis (in one possible way) by finding the normalizing constant A (or C), and choosing Z so that

$$Ex = \int_{-\infty}^{Z} x(f(x,0) + f(x,1))dx + Z(P(Z,0) + P(Z,1)) = 0.$$

(A different way of completing the analysis is described in Chapter 9.)

Bibliography

[1] A. T. Bharucha-Reid, *Elements of the Theory of Markov Processes and their Applications*, McGraw-Hill, 1960.

[2] L. Breiman, *Probability*, Addison-Wesley, 1968.

[3] K. L. Chung, *Markov Chains with Stationary Transition Probabilities*, Springer-Verlag, 1960.

[4] R. B. Cooper, *Introduction to Queueing Theory*, Macmillan, 1972.

[5] D. R. Cox and W. L. Smith, *Queues*, Methuen, 1967.

[6] A. W. Drake, *Fundamentals of Applied Probability Theory*, McGraw-Hill, 1967.

[7] W. Feller, *An Introduction to Probability Theory and its Applications*, Volumes I and II, Wiley, 1966.

[8] S. Goldberg, *Introduction to Difference Equations, with Illustrative Examples from Economics, Psychology, and Sociology*, Wiley, 1958.

[9] R. A. Howard, *Dynamic Probabilistic Systems; Volume I: Markov Models*, Wiley, 1971.

[10] L. Kleinrock, *Queuing Systems; Volume I: Theory*, Wiley, 1975.

[11] D. G. Luenberger, *Introduction to Dynamic Systems — Theory, Models, and Applications*, Wiley, 1979.

[12] P. A. P. Moran, *The Theory of Storage*, Methuen, 1959.

[13] E. Parzen, *Stochastic Processes*, Holden-Day, 1962.

[14] S. M. Ross, *Stochastic Processes*, Wiley, 1983.

[15] S. M. Ross, *Introduction to Probability Models*, Wiley, 1985.

[16] S. M. Ross, *Introduction to Probability and Statistics for Engineers and Scientists*, Wiley, 1987.

Chapter 3

Transfer Lines

3.1 Introduction

Transfer Lines A *transfer line* is a manufacturing system with a very special structure. It is a linear network of service stations or machines $(M_1, M_2, \ldots, M_k)$ separated by buffer storages $(B_1, B_2, \ldots, B_{k-1})$. Material flows from outside the system to M_1, then to B_1, then to M_2, and so forth until it reaches M_k after which it leaves. Figure 3.1 depicts a transfer line. The squares represent machines and the circles represent buffers. Other terms include *tandem queuing system*, *flow line*, and *production line*.

If machine behavior were perfectly predictable and regular, there would be no need for buffers. However, all machines eventually fail, and some stations require an unpredictable, or predictable but not constant, amount of time to complete their operations. This unpredictability or irregularity has the potential for disrupting the operations of adjacent machines, or even machines further away, and buffers are used to reduce this potential. The purpose of this chapter, and Chapters 4 and 5, is to assess the effects of this uncertainty on the performance of the system. The system performance is measured in production rate and amount of average in-process inventory.

Here and elsewhere we assume that machines are either up or down. There is no middle ground in our models. In reality, machines can sometimes be partially operational. For

Figure 3.1: Five-Machine Transfer Line

example, a flexible machine is one that can operate on several different part types. If one tool wears out, the set of parts that the machine can work on may be restricted. Another example of a more general system is where a box in Figure 3.1 represents two or more machines in parallel. This is frequently done when a given speed can be achieved for less money with two cheap machines than with one expensive machine. In that case, the number of repair states for that stage is one more than the number of machines in parallel. In this chapter, however, we deal with systems with only one part type, and machine repair states are binary.

When a failure occurs, or when a machine takes an exceptionally long time to complete an operation, the level in the adjacent upstream storage may rise. If the disruption persists long enough, that storage fills up and forces the machine upstream of it to stop processing parts. Such a forced down machine is *blocked*. Similarly, the level of the adjacent downstream storage may fall during a failure, as the downstream machines drain its contents. If the failure persists long enough, the adjacent downstream storage empties and the machine downstream of it stops processing parts. Such a forced down machine is *starved*. These effects propagate up and down the line if the repair is not done promptly.

By supplying both workpieces and room for workpieces, interstage buffer storages partially decouple adjacent machines. While machine failures are inevitable, the effects of a failure of one of the machines on the operation of others is mitigated by the buffer storages. When storages are empty or full, however, this decoupling effect cannot take place. Thus, as storage sizes increase, the probability of storages being empty or full decreases and the effects of failures on the production rate of the system are reduced. However, an undesirable consequence of buffers is in-process inventory. As buffer sizes increase, more partially completed material is present between processing stages.

Inventory — *work-in-process*, or *WIP* — is undesirable. This is because:

1. it costs money to create, but as long as it sits in buffers, it generates no revenue.

2. the average *lead time* — the average amount of time between when an item is ordered and when it is delivered — is proportional to the average amount of inventory (because of *Little's law* (Little, 1961)). This time is undesirable because

   (a) customers do not want to wait; and

   (b) if there is a problem in production, this much time elapses before the problem is found. During that time, many faulty parts are made.

3. inventory in a factory or a warehouse are vulnerable to damage (due to material handling or leaky roofs) or "shrinkage" (theft). The more items, the more time they spend, the more vulnerable they are.

4. the space and the material-handling equipment needed for inventory costs money.

Failures occur in ways that are difficult or impossible to predict. The literature is full of random models of machine failure, but other situations can arise. For example, some machines fail — or require maintenance — after a known number of operations. Machine tools in which cutting edges wear in predictable ways, and chemical vapor deposition machines in semiconductor fabrication, behave this way. (In CVD, just as much material is deposited on the inside of the machine as is deposited on the wafers, and it must be removed before too much accumulates.)

More generally, we can distinguish between *time dependent* and *operation dependent* failures (Buzacott and Hanifin, 1978). Both can be random or deterministic; the former depend only on the amount of time since the last repair, and the latter depend only on the number of operations that have been performed since the last repair. Examples of time dependent failures include power failures; tool breaks are operation dependent. In Chapters 3-5, we generally deal with operation dependent failures; in Chapter 9 and later, we assume time dependent failures.[1]

Why study transfer lines?   We study transfer lines for two major reasons.

1. They are of economic importance. They are used in high volume manufacturing, particularly automobile production. They make engine blocks, transmission cables, cylinders, connecting rods, etc. Their capital costs range from $100,000 to $30,000,000.

2. They represent the simplest form of an important phenomenon: the interactions of manufacturing stages, and their decoupling by means of buffers. By studying coupling and decoupling in this context, we may learn something useful that we can apply to more complex systems.

By focusing on failures, we study the simplest kind of disruption that affects these and other systems. Interruptions of raw material supplies, absences of workers, and absences of tooling can be very similar to failures; and maintenance and setup changes have important characteristics in common. There are important differences: some disruptions, like setup changes, are under the control of the management or operators, and others, such as failures, are not. We discuss characteristics of disruptions in Chapter 10.

Transfer line behavior   There are two factors that limit the production rate of a production line: (1) it cannot work at a greater rate than its slowest machine; and (2) it is limited by the variability and lack of synchronization of events. The only ways of increasing the production rate of such a system are to (1) increase the production rate of the machines, starting with the slowest; and (2) either reduce the frequency and duration of unsynchronized, disruptive events, or install in-process buffers.

If a manufacturing firm is fortunate enough to have a transfer or production line in which failures or other disruptions do not play a role, it is doubly fortunate: it avoids the expense — in the form of reduced production rate, increased inventory, and highly variable production, from week to week — that such disruptions cause; and it is spared the strenuous

---

[1]I may as well be honest about it: We make that assumption because it makes the models easier to analyze. In my opinion, this compromise does not cause much of an error, but operation dependent failures would definitely be better. There is still plenty of work to do.

mathematics to follow. Otherwise, it must deal with the disruptions, either by eliminating them, or by eliminating their consequences.

The essence of transfer lines is their variability. Unfortunately, the emphasis in the literature has been the calculation of steady state performance measures, and this is the material that we present. Very few papers have attempted to calculate the variance of these measures — to estimate the variability of production and buffer levels from one week to the next.

The study of transfer lines tells us that space for in-process inventory can affect production rate, but only at a price: in-process inventory, and associated delays. It tells us that for storage to make a difference,

1. the line should be close to balanced (that is, the machines should be close to equally productive). If it is not balanced, some buffers will be chronically empty and some will be chronically full. Increasing buffer sizes will have almost no effect on production rate, but will tend to keep more material in the nearly full buffers.

2. the size of the buffer should be comparable to the magnitude of the disruptions, when measured in comparable units. That is, the number of parts a buffer can hold should be roughly the same as the number of parts one nearby machine could make while another nearby machine is down.

3. the difference in production rate between the line with no buffers and with infinite buffers should be large. These bounds are calculated in Section 3.3.

Difficulties   Markov chain models of such systems are difficult to treat because of their large state spaces and their indecomposability:

Large state space: When the system is modeled as a discrete-space Markov chain or process, the number of distinct states is the product of the number of different machine states and the number of distinct buffer levels. For example, consider a system in which each machine can be in two states: operational or under repair. Buffer B_i can be in $N_i + 1$ states: $n_i = 0, 1, ..., N_i$, where n_i is the amount of material in B_i and N_i is its size. As a result, the Markov chain representation of a k-machine line with $k - 1$ buffers has M distinct states, where

$$M = 2^k \prod_{i=0}^{k-1} (N_i + 1).$$

A 20-machine line with 19 buffers each of size 10, for example, has over 6.41×10^{25} states. This is not only too large for the steady-state probability distribution to be calculated in a brute force way by computer today; it is a good bet that it can *never* be computed in that way.[2]

---

[2]I hate to be pessimistic about the future of technology, but this number is about the same as the number of molecules in 2,300 liters of gas at sea level.

Indecomposability: Many models of queuing networks are decomposable; that is, portions of the system can be treated as though they are isolated from other portions. In practice, systems are decomposed so that each portion has exactly one storage area. The mathematical models break up exactly into smaller models, with simple relationships among the small models. The Markov chain models of transfer lines do not have this property. We derive an *approximate* decomposition in Chapter 4, but no exact decomposition exists.

Because of these difficulties, most practical work on estimating transfer line behavior is done by rules of thumb or by simulation.

Modeling The material in this chapter and in Chapters 4 and 5 is intended to provide analytic models of transfer lines and assembly/disassembly systems, and efficient methods to assess performance measures based on these models. Because of the difficulties described above, approximations for large systems are described Chapters 4 and 5.

Three different kinds of models are described in these chapters which are based on the different kinds of Markov processes in Chapter 2: discrete state, discrete time; discrete state, continuous time; and mixed state, continuous time. In some cases, the choice of model is dictated by the system being studied, but there are also important situations where the choice of model is up to the analyst. This is because no model is *exactly* right, and judgment is required in fitting mathematics to reality. Often, in those cases, the choice of model is not very important because all give similar results. This is illustrated in the graphs of the exponential (discrete state, continuous time) and continuous (mixed state, continuous time) two-machine lines, and in some of the exercises.

3.2 Variability

The methods of this and the next two chapters are designed to calculate *steady-state, mean* values of production rate and buffer levels (inventory). However, variability is important. Even though these methods provide very accurate predictions of average behavior, week to week variations can be surprisingly large.

To illustrate this point, we construct and analyze a representative system. (This is not a real line, but a simplified example of a class of realistic systems.) Consider a deterministic processing time transfer line consisting of 20 machines and 19 buffers. Deterministic processing time lines are described in detail in Section 3.5, and long lines are analyzed in Section 4.2. To simplify the discussion, we assume that all the machines and all the buffers are identical. (This is not necessary for the analysis technique, but it saves the trouble of describing each individual machine and buffer.) The system does operations with a one-minute cycle. It is run for two shifts (16 hours) a day, five days a week, or 4800 minutes per week. If it never failed, it could produce 4800 parts per week. Each machine has a mean time to fail (MTTF) of 3880 minutes, or just under 65 hours. It has a mean time to repair (MTTR) of 120 minutes. Each machine, if it were operating without interference from other machines, would thus be available 97% of the time, and could produce 4656 parts per week. (In terms of quantities that are defined in Section 3.5, each machine has $r = .00833$ and $p = .000258$.) The buffers are all assumed to have a capacity of 10 parts.

Using the decomposition technique of Section 4.2, we find that the average production rate of the line is .6764 parts per minute, or 3247 parts per week.

A simulation model of this line was run for 100 weeks. Its average production rate during the whole interval was .6769 parts per minute, about 2 parts per week greater than the analytic technique.[3] However, there was tremendous variability from week to week. For example, Figure 3.2[4] is a graph of weekly production.

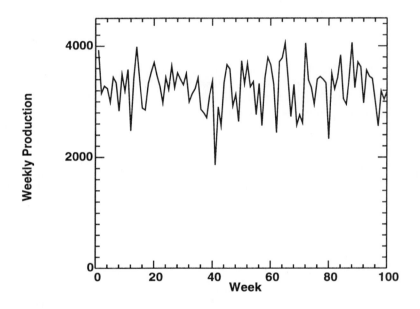

Figure 3.2: Production Variability

It is apparent that there are wide variations in weekly performance. In fact, the production of the worst week during this 100-week period was 1863 parts, or 57% of average, and the best week's production was 4061 parts, or 125% of average. The standard deviation was 403 parts, or 12.4% of the weekly average.

Conclusions We can draw the following conclusions from this example.

1. First, randomness can be extremely important on a day-to-day and week-to-week basis in a manufacturing system, and not just on a minute-to-minute basis. That is, there

---

[3]Incidentally, the analytic approximation took seconds on a personal computer (a 20 megahertz 80386 machine) while the simulation took hours — a ratio on the order of thousands. Consequently, the approximation is a much better tool for line design, as you will see when you do some of the exercises of this chapter and the next.

[4]reprinted from Gershwin (1993) with permission from Elsevier Scienc Publishers

can be large, nerve-wracking variations in performance which can affect customer satisfaction. Life with this system consists of periods when the line easily exceeds requirements alternating with periods of high pressure, anxiety, and complaints. Furthermore, although the predicted average performance will be observed in the long run, we have to live in the short run. One hundred weeks may be too long to wait to get the required production rate; very few manufacturing processes or products last that long without a major change. The only ways of reducing these variations are either to increase the reliability of the machines (decrease time to repair or increase time to fail), or to increase inventory space (the in-process buffers downstream storage).

2. Second, in spite of the randomness, the models are accurate. Engineers, who live with the enormous variability that these systems exhibit, reasonably conclude that simple mathematical or simulation models cannot capture the diversity of the disruptions that occur on these systems, and therefore that such models cannot predict performance. They point out that there are many reasons for machines to go down, and many reasons why repairs can take the lengths of time they do. A line can look completely different from one week to the next.

   The models work because the uptime and downtime probability distributions *summarize* all the different causes for these disruptions. As long as the distributions in the analytic and simulation models correspond reasonably closely with observed uptime and downtime distributions, the reasons for any given event do not matter. Analytic and simulation models of these systems are designed specifically to reflect the effects of random disruptions.

3. Third, there is an important gap in the research literature. There are almost no published papers on the variability of performance of transfer lines. Although the analytic decomposition is extremely accurate in predicting mean performance, it has nothing to say about the variance of the number of parts produced in a week, or the variance of buffer levels.

3.3 Zero Buffers and Infinite Buffers

These extreme cases are important because they define the limits of buffer effectiveness and they are easy to evaluate. They determine upper and lower bounds of production rates. If the lower bound is greater than the required production rate, there is no need for a buffer in the line; if the upper bound is less than the required production rate, no amount of buffering will allow the line to achieve it.

Most of the material in this section is taken from Buzacott (1967). Assume the line has k machines. Machines are assumed to have equal, constant operation times. The operation time is chosen to be the time unit. Machines can only fail while they are working. Both down times and up times are distributed geometrically. The probability of Machine M_i failing during a time unit when it is operating is p_i, and the probability of Machine M_i being repaired during a time unit when it is down is r_i. We also make one of the most

common assumptions in this literature: the first machine is never starved and the last is
never blocked.

As earlier, we use

$$e_i = \frac{r_i}{r_i + p_i} \tag{3.1}$$

for the isolated efficiency of Machine M_i.

3.3.1   Zero buffers

Operation dependent failures   Lines with buffers of size zero have no decoupling between stages. Consequently, as soon as any machine fails, the whole line is forced to wait.
We ignore the possibility that two machines may fail simultaneously, so only one machine
may be down at any time. We also assume *operation dependent failures*, which means that
a machine may only fail when it is operating. This is the most important kind of failure in
a transfer line (Buzacott and Hanifin, 1978).

Consider a long time interval of length T during which Machine M_i fails m_i times,
$i = 1, \ldots k$. If no machine ever failed, the line would produce T parts. If we assume that
the average time to repair of M_i is $1/r_i$ time units each time it fails, the total system down
time is close to

$$D = \sum_{i=1}^{k} \frac{m_i}{r_i}$$

so the total up time is approximately

$$U = T - \sum_{i=1}^{k} \frac{m_i}{r_i}.$$

Since the system produces one part per time unit while it is working, it produces U parts
during the interval of length T. Note that, approximately,

$$m_i = p_i U.$$

This is because M_i can only fail while it is operational. Thus,

$$U = T - U \sum_{i=1}^{k} \frac{p_i}{r_i},$$

or,

$$\frac{U}{T} = E_{ODF} = \frac{1}{1 + \sum_{i=1}^{k} \frac{p_i}{r_i}}. \tag{3.2}$$

E_{ODF} is the *efficiency* of the line. It is the ratio of the number of parts produced to the number that would have been produced if there were no failures. In this context, it is the same as the *production rate* since it measures the average number of parts produced per time unit. We use the subscript to emphasize that we are considering operation dependent failures here and time dependent failures in the next paragraph. In the rest of this chapter, however, we deal with operation dependent failures and we drop the subscript. Note that E_{ODF} is a function of the ratio p_i/r_i and not p_i or r_i separately. In the special case of $k = 1$, (3.2) reduces to the isolated efficiency formula for a single machine (3.1). In the limit, as a line without buffers gets very long, its production rate goes to 0.

There is no point in having machines that can operate at different speeds in a transfer line without buffers; while all machines are operational, they must all work at the speed of the slowest machine. In Sections 3.7-3.10 and Chapter 4, we show the effects of buffers on systems with machines whose speeds differ.

Time dependent failures Time dependent failures can occur whether or not a machine is operating. For example, a fuse in a machine's electrical system could burn out independently of how many operations the machine has performed. It is only influenced by how long the machine has been powered, and how many times it has been turned on and off. A common error in estimating efficiency of a transfer line without buffers is to treat operation dependent failures as though they are time dependent.

In the time dependent case, the machines' failure and repair behavior are independent of one another. Each machine may fail without regard to whether others are working or not, because it fails independently of whether it is performing operations or not. Therefore,

$$E_{TDF} = \prod_{i=1}^{k} e_i. \tag{3.3}$$

This can make a difference: if $e_i = .98$ for all machines in the line and $k = 20$, then $E_{ODF} = .71$ and $E_{TDF} = .67$. If the e_is are smaller, the difference is greater.

3.3.2 Infinite buffers

Consider a two-machine line with an infinite buffer. Suppose that the machines are such that, if they were operated in isolation (that is, with an unlimited, uninterrupted source of parts and an unlimited sink), the first machine could produce $u_1 T$ parts, on the average, during a long interval of length T, and the second could produce $u_2 T$. Thus, the isolated production rates of the machines are u_1 and u_2. There are three cases to consider: $u_1 < u_2, u_1 = u_2, u_1 > u_2$.

If $u_1 < u_2$, then the amount of material that enters the buffer is less than the second machine is capable of removing. The buffer is frequently empty, and the second machine is frequently idle. Thus, we can expect that the buffer never accumulates much material. It can accumulate some because of the lack of synchronization between the machines: sometimes, the second machine is down while the first is up. Consequently, about $u_1 T$ parts leave the second machine, and the production rate of the system is u_1, the same as that of the first, the slowest machine. In important probabilistic models of such systems (like the $M/M/1$ queue, or the two-machine deterministic processing time line with an infinite buffer, described below), a steady state buffer level probability distribution exists and satisfies

$$\lim_{L \to \infty} \quad \lim_{t \to \infty} \quad \mathrm{prob}(n(t) > L) = 0$$

and a mean buffer level $\bar{n}$ exists and is independent of the initial condition $n(0)$.

If $u_1 > u_2$, then the amount of material that enters the buffer is more than the second machine is capable of removing. During the interval of length T, the net increase in buffer level is close to $(u_1 - u_2)T$. Since the buffer is rarely empty, the second machine is rarely forced to be idle, so the amount of material leaving the system is $u_2 T$, and the production rate is that of the second, the slowest machine. In general, no steady-state probability distribution exists. There may be a time-varying distribution whose mean satisfies

$$\lim_{t \to \infty} \quad \mathrm{prob}(n(t) > L) = 1 \quad \forall L.$$

The most complex case is where $u_1 = u_2$. Now, while the buffer is not empty, the amount of material that the first machine puts into the buffer is exactly the amount that the second machine can remove, on the average. When the buffer does not become empty, the probability of its level going up a given amount is equal to the probability of its level going down the same amount. The buffer level has no upper bound, but it does have a lower bound: zero. Describing how this case behaves requires a more precise analysis than the other two cases, but it is reasonable to assume that the expected amount of material in the buffer does not level off, as in the first case, or increase as in the second case. Instead, it can fluctuate wildly. It is also reasonable to assume that the system production rate is the same as that of both machines.

To conclude: the production rate is the same as that of the slower machine in the two-machine line. The average level is finite if the first machine is slower than the second, and infinite if the second machine is slower.

We can use this conclusion to analyze longer lines with infinite buffers. Recall that in the argument that led to the last conclusion, we did not consider the statistical details of the behavior of the machines; we only cared which machine was faster on the average, in the long run.

For each buffer i, $i = 1, \ldots, k - 1$, treat the whole upstream part of the line as a single machine whose speed is u_1^i, and the whole downstream part of the line as a single machine whose speed is u_2^i. Since we know that the throughput of the line will be equal to that of the slowest of those two parts, we can analyze the slowest part in the same way. We keep breaking the line up and discarding the faster part until we are left with the slowest machine, and that determines the speed of the line. As an alternative approach, consider the slowest machine in the line. (If there are more than one machine that operates at the same slow speed, consider the one furthest upstream.) If it is the first machine in the line, its downstream buffer behaves like the first two-machine case ($u_1 < u_2$), and the line speed is the same as its speed. If it is not the first machine, its upstream buffer will accumulate material in the same way as the second two-machine case, and its downstream buffer will behave just as in the first two-machine case. Again, its speed is that of the whole line.

If all machines operate at the same speed, that speed will be the speed of the line, and the buffer levels will all fluctuate. Therefore, the production rate of a line composed of identical machines and infinite buffers is that of each of the machines, independent of the length of the line.

Question: We have seen that as lines with buffers of size 0 and identical machines increase in length, their production rates go to 0, and that as lines with buffers of size infinity and identical machines increase in length, their production rates stay constant. How do lines with finite buffers and identical machines behave as they increase in length? It is reasonable to assume that their production rates decrease, but to what? To 0, or to a nonzero value? We furnish a conjecture in Sections 4.2.3 and 4.3.4.

3.4 Discussion of Some General Assumptions

1. *Zero buffers and line balancing.* If there are no buffers in a line, and the operation times of all the machines are different, then there is inefficiency even while no machine is down. This is because all machines that are faster than the slowest must wait for the slowest to complete its (or their) operations. This is undesirable, and lines without buffers should be designed so that all machines work at the same speed. This is called the *line balancing* problem.

   In metal cutting systems, each station of a line may perform several cuts. That is, there are several cutting tools, and they make their holes either simultaneously or sequentially, depending on mechanical considerations. As the line is designed, the designer may have some choice as to where — at which station — a given operation may be placed. There are always constraints: some operations must be performed strictly before others; finishing operations may not be put on the same "head" as roughing operations; the total amount of power at a station may be limited. The line balancing design problem is to assign operations to stations in a way that satisfies all the constraints and maximizes the speed of the slowest machine.

2. *Unlimited repair personnel.* In general, we assign a repair rate or probability to each machine, which is independent of the state of the rest of the system. This is of no consequence in the zero-buffer case, since only one machine may be down at a time. However, it is important for the infinite buffer case, as well as all the finite buffer cases to follow. Essentially, this means that the repair process at each machine depends only on the characteristics of the machine, and not on any system-wide properties.

   A counter-example would be a system in which there are a limited number (R) of repair personnel. If the number of machines that are down is less than or equal to R, the repair process is like the one we describe here. If it is greater than R, a repair queue is formed, and machines that fail are forced to be wait until a repair person is available.

3. *Uncorrelated failures.* This assumption is analogous to the assumption of unlimited repair personnel. Each machine's failure process is assumed to be independent of the state of the rest of the system. This excludes such events as a power failure or loss of coolant that affects the whole line, a shipment of poor quality raw parts, which causes failures of machines, or a tool that is so worn that it degrades workpiece quality badly enough to cause excess wear on the next tool. In that case, both tools are likely to wear out together, and thus precipitate machine failures.

4. *Perfect yield.* Quality is not treated in the models presented here. All parts are assumed perfect. There is no inspection procedure, no rework, and no rejects. These phenomena are certainly important, but there is only a limited literature that deals with them in the present context.

5. *The first machine is never starved and the last is never blocked.* This is a widespread assumption in the transfer line literature. In reality, vendors sometimes fail to deliver, and sales are sometimes less than expected. This could be remedied by describing a model with a random arrival process to the first machine and a random departure process from the last machine. An easier approach would be to use the first machine in the model to represent the arrivals of material. In that case, the first buffer in the model represents the raw material inventory of the factory, and the second machine of the model represents the first machine of the line. Similarly, the last machine of the model could represent the demand or sales process, and the last buffer is the finished goods inventory. The next-to-last machine of the model is the last machine of the line.

On the other hand, sometimes the line is turned off when there are no raw parts to process (Strosser, 1991). In that case, starvation has no effect on the dynamics of the line; instead, it reduces the time during which the line operates. This makes it possible to predict performance for a line operated in this manner using the tools described in this chapter and the next.

6. *Blocking.* There are a variety of models of blocking (Dallery and Gershwin, 1992). Some models prevent a machine from doing an operation if the downstream buffer is full; others allow the operation, but require the part to wait in the machine's working area until the buffer is no longer full. Since the effect of the difference between blocking models is no greater than the effect of changing all buffer sizes by 1, the blocking models in this book were chosen for their simplicity and symmetry with the starvation models rather than a precise representation of events.[5]

---

[5] However, not everyone agrees with this approach. See Altiok and Stidham (1982).

3.5 Deterministic Processing Time Model

The purpose of developing Markov process models of transfer lines is to predict the performance of a line. Such predictions are vital to line design and to the creation of delivery schedules. To do this, we first describe the model assumptions very precisely (Section 3.5.1); then we describe the performance measures in terms of the parameters and states of the model (Section 3.5.2); we specialize this to a two-machine line in Section 3.6 and we study longer lines of this kind in Section 4.2.

In this model, the lengths of time that parts spend in machines are

- *fixed;*

- *known in advance;* and

- *the same for all machines*

when the machines do not fail during an operation. All operational machines start their operations at the same instant. Consequently, the time may be considered discrete. In addition, the state is discrete, since machines may be either up or down, and since the parts are discrete. The times that failures occur, and the lengths of time that machines are down, are random. Therefore (since we assume that the random processes are all memoryless) this is a discrete time, discrete state Markov chain. This class of systems is described in Section 2.2.

While a machine is working (operational and neither starved nor blocked), a fixed amount of time is required to process a part. This time is the same for all machines and is taken as the time unit. During a time unit when Machine M_i is working, it has probability p_i of failing. Its mean time to fail (MTTF) in *working* time (not simply clock time) is thus $1/p_i$. When a machine is not working, due to starvation or blockage, it cannot fail. Such *idle* time is not counted in $1/p_i$. After a machine has failed, it is under repair and it has probability r_i of being repaired during a time unit. Its mean time to repair (MTTR) is therefore $1/r_i$. This is measured in clock time, not in working time. The buffer is a storage element. Parts pass through a buffer with a transportation delay that is negligible compared to service times in the machines, except for the delay caused by other parts in the queue. This is the simplest model for studying failures and storage constraints. Its major important limitation is that all machines are required to have the same processing time.

3.5.1 Model assumptions, notation, terminology, and conventions

1. Material flows from outside the system to Machine M_1, to Buffer $B_1, \ldots$ to Buffer B_{i-1}, to Machine M_i, to Buffer $B_i, \ldots$, to Machine M_k, and then out of the system.

2. Let α_i indicate the repair state of Machine M_i. If $\alpha_i = 1$, the machine is *operational* (sometimes called *up*); if $\alpha_i = 0$, it is *under repair* (also called *failed* or *down*).

3. A machine is *starved* if its upstream buffer is empty. It is *blocked* if its downstream buffer is full.

4. An inexhaustible supply of workpieces is available upstream of the first machine in the line, and an unlimited storage area is present downstream of the last machine. Thus, the first machine is never starved, and the last machine is never blocked.

5. All machines have equal and constant service times. Time is scaled so that this machine cycle takes one time unit. Transportation takes negligible time compared to machining times. All operating machines start their operations at the same instant.

6. The amount of material in Buffer i at time t is $n_i(t)$, $0 \le n_i(t) \le N_i$. A buffer gains or loses at most one piece during a time unit. One piece is inserted into the buffer if the upstream machine is working (operational and neither starved nor blocked). One piece is removed if the downstream machine is working.

7. The state of the system is

$$s = (n_1, \ldots, n_{k-1}, \alpha_1, \ldots, \alpha_k).$$

8. Machines are assumed to have geometrically distributed times between failures and times to repair. If Machine M_i begins processing a workpiece, there is a constant probability p_i that it fails during that cycle. Thus, the mean operating time (in cycles) between failures is $1/p_i$.

9. *Operation dependent failures:* Machines fail only while processing workpieces. Thus, if Machine M_i is operational but starved or blocked, it cannot fail. That is,

$$\text{prob } [\alpha_i(t+1) = 0 \mid n_{i-1}(t) = 0, \alpha_i(t) = 1, n_i(t) < N_i] = 0,$$

$$\text{prob } [\alpha_i(t+1) = 1 \mid n_{i-1}(t) = 0, \alpha_i(t) = 1, n_i(t) < N_i] = 1,$$

$$\text{prob } [\alpha_i(t+1) = 0 \mid n_{i-1}(t) > 0, \alpha_i(t) = 1, n_i(t) = N_i] = 0,$$

$$\text{prob } [\alpha_i(t+1) = 1 \mid n_{i-1}(t) > 0, \alpha_i(t) = 1, n_i(t) = N_i] = 1.$$

When Machine M_i is working, it has probability p_i of failing. That is,

$$\text{prob } [\alpha_i(t+1) = 0 \mid n_{i-1}(t) > 0, \alpha_i(t) = 1, n_i(t) < N_i] = p_i, \qquad (3.4)$$

$$\text{prob } [\alpha_i(t+1) = 1 \mid n_{i-1}(t) > 0, \alpha_i(t) = 1, n_i(t) < N_i] = 1 - p_i. \qquad (3.5)$$

10. Similarly, if Machine M_i is failed at the beginning of a cycle, there is a constant probability r_i that it is repaired during that cycle. Thus, the mean time (in cycles) to repair is $1/r_i$. When Machine M_i is under repair, it has probability r_i of becoming operational during each time unit. That is,

$$\text{prob } [\alpha_i(t+1) = 1 \mid \alpha_i(t) = 0] = r_i, \qquad (3.6)$$

$$\text{prob } [\alpha_i(t+1) = 0 \mid \alpha_i(t) = 0] = 1 - r_i. \qquad (3.7)$$

11. Workpieces are not destroyed or rejected at any stage in the line. Partly processed workpieces are not added into the line. When a machine breaks down, the workpiece it was operating on is returned to the upstream storage to wait for the machine to be repaired so that processing can resume.

12. *Convention*: Repairs and failures occur at the beginnings of time units, and changes in buffer levels take place at the end of the time units. Thus, during periods while starvation and blockage do not influence Buffer i,

$$n_i(t+1) = n_i(t) + \alpha_i(t+1) - \alpha_{i+1}(t+1). \tag{3.8}$$

More generally,

$$n_i(t+1) = n_i(t) + \mathcal{I}_{ui}(t+1) - \mathcal{I}_{di}(t+1), \tag{3.9}$$

where $\mathcal{I}_{ui}(t+1)$ is the indicator of whether flow arrives at Buffer i from upstream. That is,

$$\mathcal{I}_{ui}(t+1) = \begin{cases} 1 \text{ if } \alpha_i(t+1) = 1 \text{ and } n_{i-1}(t) > 0 \text{ and } n_i(t) < N_i, \\ 0 \text{ otherwise.} \end{cases}$$

The indicator $\mathcal{I}_{di}(t+1)$ of flow leaving Buffer i is defined similarly:

$$\mathcal{I}_{di}(t+1) = \begin{cases} 1 \text{ if } \alpha_{i+1}(t+1) = 1 \text{ and } n_i(t) > 0 \text{ and } n_{i+1}(t) < N_{i+1} \\ 0 \text{ otherwise.} \end{cases}$$

13. In the Markov chain model, there is a set of transient states, and a single final class. Thus, a unique steady state distribution exists. The model is studied in steady state. That is, we calculate the stationary probability distribution.

By Assumption 9, a machine that is processing a part has a probability of failure p_i. When the machine is operational but forced down (either starved or blocked), it cannot fail. The probability that an operating machine remains operational is $1 - p_i$. The probability that a failed machine is repaired by the end of any cycle is r_i, independent of storage levels. A failed machine remains down at the end of a cycle with probability $1 - r_i$.

Once machine transitions take place, the new storage level is determined (Assumption 12). This value is dependent on the new states of the adjacent machines. If the upstream machine is processing a part, the part is added to the storage; if the downstream machine is processing a part, it is removed from the storage. The new storage level also depends on the storage levels immediately upstream and downstream at the end of the previous cycle. For example, if Machine M_i is operational and the upstream storage was not empty, a new piece enters storage i.

The failure and repair probabilities are used in obtaining the state transition probabilities, defined by

$$T(s, s') = \text{prob} \ (s(t+1) = s \mid s(t) = s').$$ (3.10)

Here, $T(s, s')$ is P_{ij} of Equation (2.8). To make the notation compact, we write

$$s' = (n_1(t), \ldots, n_{k-1}(t), \beta_1, \ldots, \beta_k).$$

That is, s is the state at time $t + 1$ and s' is the state at time t. In particular, α is the machine repair state at time $t + 1$ and β is the machine repair state at time t.

For much of what follows, it is important to note that (3.10) is the product of (3.6) or (3.7) or (3.4) or (3.5) for all i, whenever the buffer levels satisfy (3.9), and 0 otherwise. The steady state probability distribution satisfies

$$\mathbf{p}(s) = \sum_{s'} T(s, s') \mathbf{p}(s').$$ (3.11)

Then, if $n(t)$ and $n(t + 1)$ satisfy (3.8) (that is, if all the buffer states are interior — between 2 and $N - 2$ — at both times t and $t + 1$),

$$T(s, s') = \prod_{i=1}^{k} \left(p_i^{1-\alpha_i} (1 - p_i)^{\alpha_i} \right)^{\beta_i} \left((1 - r_i)^{1-\alpha_i} r_i^{\alpha_i} \right)^{1-\beta_i}.$$ (3.12)

This is the product of (3.4), (3.5), (3.6), and (3.7). In (3.12), α_i is the machine state at time $t + 1$, which is part of s; β_i is the machine state at time t, which is part of s'. A less compact form for $T(s, s')$ can be developed using (3.9) when s or s' is on the boundary — when some $n_i(t)$ or $n_i(t + 1)$ is 0 or 1 or N_{i-1} or N_i.

3.5.2   Performance measures

The steady state *production rate* (*throughput, flow rate*, or *efficiency*) of Machine M_i is the probability that Machine M_i produces a part in a time step. It is the probability that Machine M_i is operational and neither starved nor blocked in time step t. It is equivalent, and more convenient, to express it as the probability that Machine M_i is operational and neither starved nor blocked in time step $t + 1$, or

$$E_i = \text{prob} \ (\alpha_i(t+1) = 1, n_{i-1}(t) > 0, n_i(t) < N_i) = \text{prob} \ (\mathcal{I}_{ui}(t+1) = 1).$$

This is an awkward expression because it involves states at two different time steps. We therefore transform it into a statement about the state of the system at a single time step:

$$\begin{aligned} E_i \ = \ & \text{prob} \ (\alpha_i(t+1) = 1, n_{i-1}(t) > 0, n_i(t) < N_i) \\[6pt] = \ & \text{prob} \ (\alpha_i(t+1) = 1 \mid n_{i-1}(t) > 0, \alpha_i(t) = 1, n_i(t) < N_i) \\ & \quad \text{prob} \ (n_{i-1}(t) > 0, \alpha_i(t) = 1, n_i(t) < N_i) \\ & + \text{prob} \ (\alpha_i(t+1) = 1 \mid n_{i-1}(t) > 0, \alpha_i(t) = 0, n_i(t) < N_i) \\ & \quad \text{prob} \ (n_{i-1}(t) > 0, \alpha_i(t) = 0, n_i(t) < N_i). \end{aligned}$$

From (3.5) and (3.6), this can be written

$$E_i = (1 - p_i) \text{ prob } (n_{i-1}(t) > 0, \alpha_i(t) = 1, n_i(t) < N_i)$$
$$+ r_i \text{ prob } (n_{i-1}(t) > 0, \alpha_i(t) = 0, n_i(t) < N_i).$$

It is possible to show that (Dallery and Gershwin, 1992)[6]

$$r_i \text{ prob } (n_{i-1}(t) > 0, \alpha_i(t) = 0, n_i(t) < N_i) =$$
$$p_i \text{ prob } (n_{i-1}(t) > 0, \alpha_i(t) = 1, n_i(t) < N_i)$$

and we do so for two-machine lines below. This equation is useful for establishing (3.17) and, from the previous equation (after dropping the t arguments), that

$$E_i = \text{ prob } (\alpha_i = 1, n_{i-1} > 0, n_i < N_i). \tag{3.13}$$

The steady state average level of Buffer i is

$$\bar{n}_i = \sum_s n_i \text{ prob } (s). \tag{3.14}$$

Formulas for these and related quantities for two-machine lines are presented below.

Conservation of Flow Because there is no mechanism for the creation or destruction of material, flow is conserved, or

$$E = E_1 = E_2 = \ldots = E_k. \tag{3.15}$$

This statement should be proved, and not simply asserted. However, it has turned out to be surprisingly tricky to prove using the transition equations. In the two-machine case, it can be proved from the analytic solution developed below.

The Flow Rate-Idle Time Relationship Define e_i to be the *isolated production rate* of Machine M_i. It is what the production rate of M_i would be if it were never impeded by other machines or buffers. It is given by

$$e_i = \frac{r_i}{r_i + p_i} \tag{3.16}$$

and it represents the fraction of time that M_i is operational. The actual production rate E_i of M_i is less because of blocking or starvation. It satisfies

$$E_i = e_i \text{ prob } [n_{i-1} > 0 \text{ and } n_i < N_i]. \tag{3.17}$$

This may look surprising. It seems to suggest that the events of a machine being down and its adjacent buffers being empty or full are independent. However, failures may occur

---

[6]This equation says that, in steady state, there is a repair for every failure of Machine i.

only while machines are not idle due to starvation or blockage. Furthermore, B_{i-1} can become empty and B_i can become full only when M_i is operational. Therefore, an idle period can be thought of as a hiatus in which a clock, measuring working time until the next machine state change event, is not running. The fraction of non-idle time that M_i is operational is thus the same as the fraction of time it would be operational if it were not in a system with other machines and buffers.

This is proved below for the two-machine case.

The Approximate Flow Rate-Idle Time Relationship   It is useful to observe that

$$\text{prob}\ (n_{i-1} = 0 \text{ and } n_i = N_i) \approx 0. \tag{3.18}$$

The probability of this event is small because such states can only be reached from states in which $n_{i-1} = 1$ and $n_i = N_i - 1$ by means of a transition in which

1. Machine M_{i-1} is either under repair or starved, and

2. $\alpha_i = 1$, and

3. Machine M_{i+1} is either under repair or blocked.

The production rate may therefore be approximated by

$$E_i \approx e_i \left(1 - \text{prob}\ (n_{i-1} = 0) - \text{prob}\ (n_i = N_i)\right). \tag{3.19}$$

This result is needed in the decomposition method described in Chapter 4.

3.6   Deterministic Two-Machine Line

The two-machine line is the simplest non-trivial case of a transfer line. Since there is only one buffer, there is no issue of decomposability. In general, any model of a two-machine, one-buffer line can be solved numerically for any reasonably-sized buffer, but an analytic solution is possible for this and some other models. An analytic solution is desirable because such solutions are often — although not always — better behaved numerically and often require less computer time than matrix methods.

We use the analytic solution developed here in the long-line decomposition method described in Chapter 4. Speed, accuracy, and ease of programming are important, since it is used as a subroutine that is called many times by the main algorithm.

This two-machine method was extended, somewhat clumsily, to three-machine, two-buffer lines (Gershwin and Schick, 1983). The resulting technique was slow and was practical only for small buffers. It could not be usefully extended to longer lines.

3.6.1   Transition equations

In the two-machine case, the state of the system is $s = (n, \alpha_1, \alpha_2)$ where n is the buffer level $(0 \leq n \leq N)$ and α_i is the repair state of Machine i $(i = 1, 2, \alpha_i = 0, 1)$.

Transient States The assumptions of the model imply that certain states are transient, that is, they have zero steady state probability. Transient states cannot be reached from any state except possibly other transient states. (See Section 2.2.7.) These states are all on the boundaries: for all such states, $n = 0, 1, N - 1$, or N. Equation (3.9) is the key for understanding the following explanations.

(0,1,0) is transient because it cannot be reached from any state. If $\alpha_1(t+1) = 1$ and $\alpha_2(t+1) = 0$, then $n(t+1) = n(t) + 1$.

(0,1,1) is transient because it cannot be reached from any state. If $n(t) = 0$ and $\alpha_1(t+1) = 1$ and $\alpha_2(t+1) = 1$, then $n(t+1) = 1$ since M_2 is starved and thus not able to operate. If $n(t) > 0$ and $\alpha_1(t+1) = 1$ and $\alpha_2(t+1) = 1$, then $n(t+1) = n(t)$.

(0,0,0) is transient because it can be reached only from itself or (0,1,0). It can be reached from itself if neither machine is repaired; it can be reached from (0,1,0) if the first machine fails while attempting to make a part. It cannot be reached from (0,0,1) or (0,1,1) since the second machine cannot fail. Otherwise, if $\alpha_1(t+1) = 0$ and $\alpha_2(t+1) = 0$, then $n(t+1) = n(t)$.

(1,1,0) is transient because it can be reached only from (0,0,0) or (0,1,0). If $\alpha_1(t+1) = 1$ and $\alpha_2(t+1) = 0$, then $n(t+1) = n(t)+1$. Therefore, $n(t) = 0$. However, (1,1,0) cannot be reached from (0,0,1) since Machine 2 cannot fail. (For the same reason, it cannot be reached from (0,1,1), but since the latter is transient, that is irrelevant.)

Similarly, $(N,0,0)$, $(N,0,1)$, $(N,1,1)$, and $(N-1,0,1)$ are transient.

The set of states that are transient depends crucially upon the assumptions and conventions. If machines could fail while they are starved, or if buffer levels changed first and then machine states, the list of transient states would be different. The non-transient states are divided into three groups: the internal states $(2 \le n \le N - 2)$, the lower boundary states $(n \le 1)$, and the upper boundary states $(n \ge N - 1)$.

Lower boundary equations $n \le 1$

The system can get from (0,0,1) to (0,0,1) if the first machine is not repaired. Since the second machine is starved, it cannot fail, and the probability of the transition is $1 - r_1$. It can move from (1,0,0) to (0,0,1) if the first machine stays down and the second is repaired. The probability of this is $(1 - r_1)r_2$. The probability of the transition from (1,0,1) to (0,0,1) is $(1 - r_1)(1 - p_2)$ since the first machine stays down and the second stays up. The probability of the transition from (1,1,1) to (0,0,1) is $p_1(1 - p_2)$ since the first machine goes down and the second stays up. No other transitions from non-transient states are possible. Consequently, the first equation is:

$$\mathbf{p}(0,0,1) = \quad (1 - r_1)\mathbf{p}(0,0,1) + (1 - r_1)r_2\mathbf{p}(1,0,0)$$
$$+(1 - r_1)(1 - p_2)\mathbf{p}(1,0,1) + p_1(1 - p_2)\mathbf{p}(1,1,1). \tag{3.20}$$

The other equations are similar:

$$\mathbf{p}(1,0,0) = (1-r_1)(1-r_2)\mathbf{p}(1,0,0) + (1-r_1)p_2\mathbf{p}(1,0,1) + p_1 p_2 \mathbf{p}(1,1,1) \tag{3.21}$$

$$\begin{aligned}\mathbf{p}(1,0,1) =\ & (1-r_1)r_2\mathbf{p}(2,0,0) + (1-r_1)(1-p_2)\mathbf{p}(2,0,1) + p_1 r_2 \mathbf{p}(2,1,0) \\ & + p_1(1-p_2)\mathbf{p}(2,1,1)\end{aligned} \tag{3.22}$$

$$\begin{aligned}\mathbf{p}(1,1,1) =\ & r_1 \mathbf{p}(0,0,1) + r_1 r_2 \mathbf{p}(1,0,0) + r_1(1-p_2)\mathbf{p}(1,0,1) \\ & + (1-p_1)(1-p_2)\mathbf{p}(1,1,1)\end{aligned} \tag{3.23}$$

$$\mathbf{p}(2,1,0) = r_1(1-r_2)\mathbf{p}(1,0,0) + r_1 p_2 \mathbf{p}(1,0,1) + (1-p_1)p_2 \mathbf{p}(1,1,1) \tag{3.24}$$

Internal equations $2 \le n \le N-2$

Internal states are those in which $2 \le n \le N-2$. (In order that any n satisfy this, it is necessary that $N \ge 4$. Consequently, this analysis does not apply to systems in which $N = 0, 1, 2,$ or 3.) *Internal transition equations* ((3.25)-(3.28)) are those that involve only internal states. They are the equations in which the final state s is internal, and all the initial states s' such that the transition probability ($T(s,s')$ in (3.10)) is nonzero are internal.

$$\begin{aligned}\mathbf{p}(n,0,0) =\ & (1-r_1)(1-r_2)\mathbf{p}(n,0,0) + (1-r_1)p_2\mathbf{p}(n,0,1) \\ & + p_1(1-r_2)\mathbf{p}(n,1,0) + p_1 p_2 \mathbf{p}(n,1,1)\end{aligned} \tag{3.25}$$

$$\begin{aligned}\mathbf{p}(n,0,1) =\ & (1-r_1)r_2\mathbf{p}(n+1,0,0) + (1-r_1)(1-p_2)\mathbf{p}(n+1,0,1) \\ & + p_1 r_2 \mathbf{p}(n+1,1,0) + p_1(1-p_2)\mathbf{p}(n+1,1,1)\end{aligned} \tag{3.26}$$

$$\begin{aligned}\mathbf{p}(n,1,0) =\ & r_1(1-r_2)\mathbf{p}(n-1,0,0) + r_1 p_2 \mathbf{p}(n-1,0,1) \\ & + (1-p_1)(1-r_2)\mathbf{p}(n-1,1,0) + (1-p_1)p_2 \mathbf{p}(n-1,1,1)\end{aligned} \tag{3.27}$$

$$\begin{aligned}\mathbf{p}(n,1,1) =\ & r_1 r_2 \mathbf{p}(n,0,0) + r_1(1-p_2)\mathbf{p}(n,0,1) + (1-p_1)r_2 \mathbf{p}(n,1,0) \\ & + (1-p_1)(1-p_2)\mathbf{p}(n,1,1)\end{aligned} \tag{3.28}$$

Upper boundary equations $n \ge N-1$

$$\begin{aligned}\mathbf{p}(N-2,0,1) =\ & (1-r_1)r_2\mathbf{p}(N-1,0,0) + p_1 r_2 \mathbf{p}(N-1,1,0) \\ & + p_1(1-p_2)\mathbf{p}(N-1,1,1)\end{aligned} \tag{3.29}$$

$$\begin{aligned}\mathbf{p}(N-1,0,0) =\ & (1-r_1)(1-r_2)\mathbf{p}(N-1,0,0) + p_1(1-r_2)\mathbf{p}(N-1,1,0) \\ & + p_1 p_2 \mathbf{p}(N-1,1,1)\end{aligned} \tag{3.30}$$

$$\begin{aligned}\mathbf{p}(N-1,1,0) =\ & r_1(1-r_2)\mathbf{p}(N-2,0,0) + r_1 p_2 \mathbf{p}(N-2,0,1) \\ & + (1-p_1)(1-r_2)\mathbf{p}(N-2,1,0) + (1-p_1)p_2 \mathbf{p}(N-2,1,1)\end{aligned} \tag{3.31}$$

$$\begin{aligned}\mathbf{p}(N-1,1,1) =\ & r_1 r_2 \mathbf{p}(N-1,0,0) + (1-p_1)r_2 \mathbf{p}(N-1,1,0) \\ & + (1-p_1)(1-p_2)\mathbf{p}(N-1,1,1) + r_2 \mathbf{p}(N,1,0)\end{aligned} \tag{3.32}$$

$$\begin{aligned}\mathbf{p}(N,1,0) =\ & r_1(1-r_2)\mathbf{p}(N-1,0,0) + (1-p_1)(1-r_2)\mathbf{p}(N-1,1,0) \\ & + (1-p_1)p_2 \mathbf{p}(N-1,1,1) + (1-r_2)\mathbf{p}(N,1,0)\end{aligned} \tag{3.33}$$

Note that these equations are appropriate only for lines in which $N \geq 4$.

Normalization Equation (2.10)

$$1 = \sum_{n=0}^{N} \sum_{\alpha_1=0}^{1} \sum_{\alpha_2=0}^{1} \mathbf{p}(n, \alpha_1, \alpha_2). \tag{3.34}$$

3.6.2 Performance measures

The most important performance measures are *efficiencies, probabilities of starvation and blockage*, and *average buffer level*. The average buffer level is also the *average work-in-process (WIP) inventory*.

The efficiency E_i of Machine i is the probability that it can do an operation at any time. E_1 is the probability that M_1 is operational and not blocked:

$$E_1 = \sum_{\substack{n < N \\ \alpha_1 = 1}} \mathbf{p}(n, \alpha_1, \alpha_2). \tag{3.35}$$

E_2 is the probability that M_2 is operational and not starved:

$$E_2 = \sum_{\substack{n > 0 \\ \alpha_2 = 1}} \mathbf{p}(n, \alpha_1, \alpha_2). \tag{3.36}$$

The probabilities of starvation and blockage are:

$p_s = \mathbf{p}(0, 0, 1)$, the probability of starvation,

$p_b = \mathbf{p}(N, 1, 0)$, the probability of blockage.

The average buffer level is:

$$\bar{n} = \sum_{\text{all } s} n\mathbf{p}(n, \alpha_1, \alpha_2).$$

3.6.3 Identities

Repair frequency equals failure frequency For every repair, there is a failure (in steady state). This seems self-evident, so it is reassuring that the transition equations satisfy this condition. This equation is used in the decomposition described in Chapter 4. When the system is in steady state,

$$r_1 \text{ prob } [\{\alpha_1 = 0\} \text{ and } \{n < N\}] = p_1 \text{ prob } [\{\alpha_1 = 1\} \text{ and } \{n < N\}]. \tag{3.37}$$

If we define

$$D_1 = \text{prob}\ [\{\alpha_1 = 0\}\ \text{and}\ \{n < N\}], \tag{3.38}$$

then (3.37) becomes

$$r_1 D_1 = p_1 E_1. \tag{3.39}$$

Proof: The left side is the probability that the state leaves the set of states

$$\mathcal{S}_0 = \{\{\alpha_1 = 0\}\ \text{and}\ \{n < N\}\}.$$

This is because the only way the system can leave $\mathcal{S}_0$ is for M_1 to get repaired. (Since M_1 is down, the buffer cannot become full.) The probability that the state leaves $\mathcal{S}_0$ is the probability that the state is in $\mathcal{S}_0$ (D_1) times the probability of a repair of M_1 (r_1).

The right side is the probability that the state enters $\mathcal{S}_0$. When the system is in steady state, the only way for the state to enter $\mathcal{S}_0$ is for it to be in set

$$\mathcal{S}_1 = \{\{\alpha_1 = 1\}\ \text{and}\ \{n < N\}\}$$

in the previous time unit. This is because the set

$$\{\{\alpha_1 = 0\}\ \text{and}\ \{n = N\}\}$$

is transient. The probability that the state enters $\mathcal{S}_0$ is the probability that the state is in $\mathcal{S}_1(E)$ times the probability of a failure of $M_1(p_1)$.

An alternate proof appears in Exercise 5. It is equivalent, but less intuitive because it only involves the manipulation of equations.

Conservation of Flow E_1 is the probability that a part passes through M_1 in a time unit and E_2 is the probability that a part passes through M_2 in a time unit. For the system to be in steady state, these quantities must be equal. We prove that equality here.

It is important to note that, by proving conservation of flow, we are not proving anything about transfer lines. Instead, we are verifying that we have done a good job in constructing the model. We did not include any mechanism for creation or destruction of material, and the system is analyzed in steady state. If material were not conserved, there would be something seriously wrong with the model.

From (3.36), (3.35),

$$E_1 = \sum_{n=0}^{N-1} \mathbf{p}(n,1,0) + \sum_{n=0}^{N-1} \mathbf{p}(n,1,1),$$

$$E_2 = \sum_{n=1}^{N} \mathbf{p}(n,0,1) + \sum_{n=1}^{N} \mathbf{p}(n,1,1).$$

Then

$$E_1 - E_2 = \sum_{n=0}^{N-1} \mathbf{p}(n,1,0) - \sum_{n=1}^{N} \mathbf{p}(n,0,1)$$

because the appropriate boundary states are transient. It is convenient to write this as

$$E_1 - E_2 = \sum_{n=1}^{N-2} \mathbf{p}(n+1,1,0) - \sum_{n=1}^{N-2} \mathbf{p}(n,0,1)$$

and it is true, again, because of transient boundary states.

If we add Equations (3.20), (3.21), (3.23), (3.24), and cancel everything that can be canceled, we find the following remarkable fact:

$$\mathbf{p}(2,1,0) = \mathbf{p}(1,0,1). \tag{3.40}$$

Then add (3.25), (3.26), (3.27), (3.28), with (3.26) evaluated at $n-1$ and (3.27) evaluated at $n+1$. The sum simplifies to:

$$\mathbf{p}(n,0,0) \quad + \quad \mathbf{p}(n-1,0,1) \quad + \quad \mathbf{p}(n+1,1,0) \quad + \quad \mathbf{p}(n,1,1) =$$

$$\mathbf{p}(n,0,0) \quad + \quad \mathbf{p}(n,0,1) \quad + \quad \mathbf{p}(n,1,0) \quad + \quad \mathbf{p}(n,1,1),$$

or,

$$\mathbf{p}(n+1,1,0) - \mathbf{p}(n,0,1) = \mathbf{p}(n,1,0) - \mathbf{p}(n-1,0,1), n = 2,\dots,N-2. \tag{3.41}$$

If $\delta(n) = \mathbf{p}(n+1,1,0) - \mathbf{p}(n,0,1)$, then $\delta(1) = 0$ by (3.40) and $\delta(n+1) = \delta(n)$, for $n = 2,\dots,N-2$ by (3.41). Thus $\delta(n) = 0$ for $n = 1,\dots,N-2$ by induction.[7] Since

$$E_1 - E_2 = \sum_{n=1}^{N-2} \delta(n),$$

then

$$E_1 = E_2 = E.$$

Flow Rate-Idle Time

$$E = e_1(1 - p_b). \tag{3.42}$$

---

[7]An alternative proof that $\delta(n) = 0$ is to observe that the only way for the buffer level to go above n is for the state to go through $(n+1,1,0)$, and the only way for the buffer level to go below n is for the state to go through $(n,0,1)$. In steady state, the buffer level goes above n just as often as it goes below n. Consequently, $\mathbf{p}(n+1,1,0) = \mathbf{p}(n,0,1)$. This observation was due to Kate Gasser.

Proof: From the definitions of E_1 and D_1, we have

$$\text{prob}\,[n < N] = E + D_1,$$

or

$$1 - p_b = E + \frac{p_1}{r_1}E = \frac{E}{e_1}.$$

Similarly,

$$E = e_2(1 - p_s) \tag{3.43}$$

See Exercise 12.

Suggested Reading: Read Buzacott (1967). Compare the two-machine models with the one described here.

3.6.4   Solution technique

Overview   In this section, we describe a technique for obtaining an analytic solution for the two-machine deterministic processing time line. In later sections, we extend the method for other models.

To find the steady-state probability distribution of an M-state Markov chain, it is necessary to solve a set of M linear transition equations in M unknowns. In the problem discussed here, $M = 4(N + 1)$. The three Markov process models of the two-machine transfer lines that we discuss in this chapter have a structure that can be exploited.

The probability distribution $\mathbf{p}$ can be thought of as a vector whose index is the state s. This vector can be partitioned as follows:

$$\mathbf{p} = \begin{pmatrix} \mathbf{p}^l \\ \mathbf{p}^i \\ \mathbf{p}^u \end{pmatrix}$$

where l refers to lower boundary states, i refers to internal states, and u refers to upper boundary states. Recall that there are generally far more internal states that others, so if we can find the internal probabilities easily, we have solved most of the problem. The transition matrix T can be partitioned correspondingly:

$$T = \begin{pmatrix} T^{ll} & T^{li} & 0 \\ T^{il} & T^{ii} & T^{iu} \\ 0 & T^{ui} & T^{uu} \end{pmatrix}$$

in which the off-diagonal partitions have zeros in most positions. Then we seek $\mathbf{p}$ to satisfy

$$\begin{aligned} \mathbf{p}^l &= T^{ll}\mathbf{p}^l + T^{li}\mathbf{p}^i \\ \mathbf{p}^i &= T^{il}\mathbf{p}^l + T^{ii}\mathbf{p}^i + T^{iu}\mathbf{p}^u \\ \mathbf{p}^u &= \phantom{T^{il}\mathbf{p}^l +} T^{ui}\mathbf{p}^i + T^{uu}\mathbf{p}^u \end{aligned} \tag{3.44}$$

as well as normalization (3.34) which can be written

$$1 = \nu^{l^T}\mathbf{p}^l + \nu^{i^T}\mathbf{p}^i + \nu^{u^T}\mathbf{p}^u$$

where ν^l, ν^i, and ν^u are vectors of 1s of appropriate dimensions.

We can easily find a set of ℓ vectors $\xi_1, \ldots, \xi_\ell$ which have the same dimensionality as $\mathbf{p}$, which are partitioned the same way, and which satisfy the internal equations:

$$\xi_j^i = T^{il}\xi_j^l + T^{ii}\xi_j^i + T^{iu}\xi_j^u, j = 1, \ldots, \ell.$$

Consequently, if the probability distribution vector $\mathbf{p}$ is expressed as a linear combination of these vectors,

$$\mathbf{p} = \sum_{j=1}^{\ell} C_j \xi_j \tag{3.45}$$

then $\mathbf{p}$ also satisfies the internal equations,

$$\mathbf{p}^i = T^{il}\mathbf{p}^l + T^{ii}\mathbf{p}^i + T^{iu}\mathbf{p}^u.$$

In order to satisfy the remaining ℓ equations, the ℓ coefficients C_j must be appropriately chosen. Substituting (3.45) into (3.44),

$$\sum_{j=1}^{\ell} C_j \xi_j^l = T^{ll} \sum_{j=1}^{\ell} C_j \xi_j^l + T^{li} \sum_{j=1}^{\ell} C_j \xi_j^i$$

$$\sum_{j=1}^{\ell} C_j \xi_j^i = T^{il} \sum_{j=1}^{\ell} C_j \xi_j^l + T^{ii} \sum_{j=1}^{\ell} C_j \xi_j^i + T^{iu} \sum_{j=1}^{\ell} C_j \xi_j^u$$

$$\sum_{j=1}^{\ell} C_j \xi_j^u = T^{ui} \sum_{j=1}^{\ell} C_j \xi_j^i + T^{uu} \sum_{j=1}^{\ell} C_j \xi_j^u$$

which can be simplified to

$$0 = \sum_{j=1}^{\ell} C_j \left(\xi_j^l - T^{ll}\xi_j^l - T^{li}\xi_j^i \right)$$

$$0 = \sum_{j=1}^{\ell} C_j \left(\xi_j^u - T^{ui}\xi_j^i - T^{uu}\xi_j^u \right).$$

If the ξ_js are chosen well, some of these are satisfied automatically the same way that the internal equations are satisfied. The normalization equation (3.34) becomes

$$1 = \sum_{j=1}^{\ell} C_j \left(\nu^{l^T}\xi_j^l + \nu^{i^T}\xi_j^i + \nu^{u^T}\xi_j^u \right).$$

This requires solving ℓ linear equations in ℓ unknowns (where ℓ is the number of these equations not solved automatically by the choice of ξ_j). Since ℓ is much smaller than M, it is relatively easy to do. For example, for the two-machine transfer line $M = 4(N + 1)$ and $\ell = 2$. (Actually, M is a little less than that, since we have identified the transient states, and we know what their steady state probabilities are.) In the following, we follow this plan for the two-machine deterministic processing time line. In later sections, we do it for the exponential and continuous lines.

Internal Equations   When a state is internal, all the operational machines can transfer parts from their upstream to their downstream storages. In other words, no machine is starved or blocked. The final level of the buffer storage is given in terms of its initial level and the final operating conditions of adjacent machines by

$$n(t + 1) = n(t) + \alpha_1(t + 1) - \alpha_2(t + 1). \tag{3.46}$$

This is in keeping with the convention (Assumption 12) that in each cycle, machine states change before storage levels. In the following, we use α_i for $\alpha_i(t+1)$ and β_i for $\alpha_i(t)$.

A close look at (3.25)-(3.28) reveals that n appears on the left side, and that $n, n-1$, and $n+1$, and no other storage levels appear on the right. This suggests that a reasonable guess for ξ might be

$$\xi(n, \alpha_1, \alpha_2) = X^n \phi(\alpha_1, \alpha_2).$$

To determine if it is a good guess, plug it into (3.25)-(3.28). When we do, we find that X^n appears on both sides (more or less). After canceling that factor, these equations become

$$\phi(0,0) = (1-r_1)(1-r_2)\phi(0,0) + (1-r_1)p_2\phi(0,1) + p_1(1-r_2)\phi(1,0) + p_1p_2\phi(1,1) \tag{3.47}$$

$$\begin{aligned} X^{-1}\phi(0,1) = \quad & (1-r_1)r_2\phi(0,0) + (1-r_1)(1-p_2)\phi(0,1) + p_1r_2\phi(1,0) \\ & + p_1(1-p_2)\phi(1,1) \end{aligned} \tag{3.48}$$

$$X\phi(1,0) = r_1(1-r_2)\phi(0,0) + r_1p_2\phi(0,1) + (1-p_1)(1-r_2)\phi(1,0) + (1-p_1)p_2\phi(1,1) \tag{3.49}$$

$$\phi(1,1) = r_1r_2\phi(0,0) + r_1(1-p_2)\phi(0,1) + (1-p_1)r_2\phi(1,0) + (1-p_1)(1-p_2)\phi(1,1) \tag{3.50}$$

Now we notice that wherever the first argument of ϕ is 0, its coefficient has $(1 - r_1)$ as a factor, and that wherever the first argument of ϕ is 1, its coefficient has p_1 as a factor. Similarly, wherever the second argument of ϕ is 0, its coefficient has $(1 - r_2)$ as a factor, and that wherever the second argument of ϕ is 1, its coefficient has p_2 as a factor. This suggests that another possible guess is $\phi(\alpha_1, \alpha_2) = Y_1^{\alpha_1} Y_2^{\alpha_2}$. If we try this expression, Equations (3.47)-(3.50) become, after factoring,

$$1 = (1 - r_1 + Y_1p_1)(1 - r_2 + Y_2p_2) \tag{3.51}$$

$$X^{-1}Y_2 = (1 - r_1 + Y_1p_1)(r_2 + Y_2(1 - p_2)) \tag{3.52}$$

$$XY_1 = (r_1 + Y_1(1 - p_1))(1 - r_2 + Y_2 p_2) \tag{3.53}$$

$$Y_1 Y_2 = (r_1 + Y_1(1 - p_1))(r_2 + Y_2(1 - p_2)) \tag{3.54}$$

Since the last equation is a product of the other three, there are only three independent equations in three unknowns here. They may be simplified further:

$$1 = (1 - r_1 + Y_1 p_1)(1 - r_2 + Y_2 p_2) \tag{3.55}$$

$$XY_1 = \frac{r_1 + Y_1(1 - p_1)}{1 - r_1 + Y_1 p_1} \tag{3.56}$$

$$X^{-1} Y_2 = \frac{r_2 + Y_2(1 - p_2)}{1 - r_2 + Y_2 p_2} \tag{3.57}$$

Equations (3.55)-(3.57) are called the *parametric equations*. To solve them, we begin by multiplying (3.56) and (3.57) to eliminate X, and we simplify with (3.55):

$$Y_1 Y_2 = (r_1 + Y_1(1 - p_1))(r_2 + Y_2(1 - p_2)). \tag{3.58}$$

Solving (3.55) for Y_2:

$$Y_2 = \frac{1}{p_2}\left[\frac{1}{1 - r_1 + Y_1 p_1} - (1 - r_2)\right]. \tag{3.59}$$

Plugging (3.59) into (3.58):

$$Y_1 \frac{1}{p_2}\left[\frac{1}{1 - r_1 + Y_1 p_1} - (1 - r_2)\right] =$$

$$(r_1 + Y_1(1 - p_1))\left(r_2 + \frac{1 - p_2}{p_2}\left[\frac{1}{1 - r_1 + Y_1 p_1} - (1 - r_2)\right]\right). \tag{3.60}$$

Multiplying both sides by $p_2(1 - r_1 + Y_1 p_1)$:

$$Y_1\left[1 - (1 - r_2)(1 - r_1 + Y_1 p_1)\right] =$$

$$(r_1 + Y_1(1 - p_1))\left[r_2 p_2(1 - r_1 + Y_1 p_1) + [1 - (1 - r_2)(1 - r_1 + Y_1 p_1)(1 - p_2)]\right]. \tag{3.61}$$

This is a quadratic equation in Y_1. After a heroic effort, it can be written

$$
\begin{aligned}
0 = {}& Y_1^2 (p_1 + p_2 - p_1 p_2 - p_1 r_2) \\
& - Y_1 (r_1 (p_1 + p_2 - p_1 p_2 - p_1 r_2) + p_1 (r_1 + r_2 - r_1 r_2 - r_1 p_2)) \\
& + r_1 (r_1 + r_2 - r_1 r_2 - r_1 p_2).
\end{aligned} \tag{3.62}
$$

Equation (3.62) has two solutions:

$$Y_{11} = \frac{r_1}{p_1},$$
$$Y_{12} = \frac{r_1 + r_2 - r_1 r_2 - r_1 p_2}{p_1 + p_2 - p_1 p_2 - p_1 r_2}.$$

By using (3.55) and (3.57), we can determine the corresponding X_j and Y_{2j}. The complete solutions are:

$$\left. \begin{array}{l} Y_{11} = \dfrac{r_1}{p_1} \\[2em] Y_{21} = \dfrac{r_2}{p_2} \\[2em] X_1 = 1 \end{array} \right\} \tag{3.63}$$

$$\left. \begin{array}{l} Y_{12} = \dfrac{r_1 + r_2 - r_1 r_2 - r_1 p_2}{p_1 + p_2 - p_1 p_2 - p_1 r_2} \\[2em] Y_{22} = \dfrac{r_1 + r_2 - r_1 r_2 - p_1 r_2}{p_1 + p_2 - p_1 p_2 - p_2 r_1} \\[2em] X_2 = \dfrac{Y_{22}}{Y_{12}} \end{array} \right\} \tag{3.64}$$

We now have the complete internal solution:

$$\mathbf{p}(n, \alpha_1, \alpha_2) = C_1 X_1^n Y_{11}^{\alpha_1} Y_{21}^{\alpha_2} + C_2 X_2^n Y_{12}^{\alpha_1} Y_{22}^{\alpha_2}. \tag{3.65}$$

To complete the solution, we have to (1) complete the ξ_j vectors (in other words, develop expressions for $\mathbf{p}(n, \alpha_1, \alpha_2)$ when $n = 0, 1, N-1$, or N), and (2) find equations for C_j.

Boundary Equations   Every term on the right side of (3.22) is of internal form. Therefore it is easy to show that

$$\xi(1, 0, 1) = XY_2,$$

or, equivalently,

$$\mathbf{p}(1, 0, 1) = C_1 X_1 Y_{21} + C_2 X_2 Y_{22}.$$

Recall that

$$\mathbf{p}(2, 1, 0) = \mathbf{p}(1, 0, 1).$$

Then

$$\sum_{j=1,2} C_j X_j^2 Y_{1j} = \sum_{j=1,2} C_j X_j Y_{2j},$$

or,

$$\sum_{j=1,2} C_j X_j \left[X_j Y_{1j} - Y_{2j} \right] = 0.$$

Note that if $j = 2, X_j Y_{1j} - Y_{2j} = 0$. If $e_1 \neq e_2$ and $j = 1$, then $X_j Y_{1j} - Y_{2j} \neq 0$. Therefore, if $e_1 \neq e_2$, $C_1 = 0$. That is, there is only one vector ξ, and the coefficient C_2 is simply a normalization coefficient. We therefore drop the j subscript in the following.

At the lower boundary, $\mathbf{p}(0,0,1), \mathbf{p}(1,0,0)$, and $\mathbf{p}(1,1,1)$ remain unknown, and they must satisfy (3.20), (3.21), (3.23), and (3.24). The fact that there are four equations in three unknowns is not a problem; we have already taken care of the extra equation when we added them all up and required that $C_1 = 0$.

To determine the remaining lower boundary probabilities, note that (3.20) can be written

$$r_1 \mathbf{p}(0,0,1) = (1 - r_1) r_2 \mathbf{p}(1,0,0) + (1 - r_1)(1 - p_2) \mathbf{p}(1,0,1)$$
$$+ p_1 (1 - p_2) \mathbf{p}(1,1,1). \tag{3.66}$$

If we plug this into (3.23), we get

$$\mathbf{p}(1,1,1) = r_2 \mathbf{p}(1,0,0) + (1 - p_2) C X Y_2 + (1 - p_2) \mathbf{p}(1,1,1)$$

or,

$$p_2 \mathbf{p}(1,1,1) = r_2 \mathbf{p}(1,0,0) + (1 - p_2) C X Y_2. \tag{3.67}$$

Equation (3.21) can be written

$$(r_1 + r_2 - r_1 r_2) \mathbf{p}(1,0,0) = (1 - r_1) p_2 C X Y_2 + p_1 p_2 \mathbf{p}(1,1,1). \tag{3.68}$$

The last two equations involve two unknowns. If we eliminate $\mathbf{p}(1,1,1)$ and simplify, we get

$$(r_1 + r_2 - r_1 r_2 - p_1 r_2) \mathbf{p}(1,0,0) = (p_1 + p_2 - p_1 p_2 - p_2 r_1) C X Y_2.$$

But the definition of Y_2 (3.64) implies that

$$\mathbf{p}(1,0,0) = C X.$$

Equation (3.67) then becomes

$$p_2 \mathbf{p}(1,1,1) = C X (r_2 + (1 - p_2) Y_2)$$

which is

$$\mathbf{p}(1,1,1) = \frac{CX}{p_2} \frac{r_1 + r_2 - r_1 r_2 - r_1 p_2}{p_1 + p_2 - p_1 p_2 - r_1 p_2}.$$

Finally, $\mathbf{p}(0,0,1)$ is obtained from (3.66):

$$\mathbf{p}(0,0,1) = CX \frac{r_1 + r_2 - r_1 r_2 - r_1 p_2}{r_1 p_2}.$$

The upper boundary equations and states are treated in exactly the same way.

Summary of Steady-State Probabilities   We summarize all the two-machine probabilities here.

$$
\begin{aligned}
\mathbf{p}(0,0,0) &= 0 & (3.69)\\
\mathbf{p}(0,0,1) &= CX\frac{r_1 + r_2 - r_1 r_2 - r_1 p_2}{r_1 p_2} & (3.70)\\
\mathbf{p}(0,1,0) &= 0 & (3.71)\\
\mathbf{p}(0,1,1) &= 0 & (3.72)\\
\mathbf{p}(1,0,0) &= CX & (3.73)\\
\mathbf{p}(1,0,1) &= CXY_2 & (3.74)\\
\mathbf{p}(1,1,0) &= 0 & (3.75)\\
\mathbf{p}(1,1,1) &= \frac{CX}{p_2}\frac{r_1 + r_2 - r_1 r_2 - r_1 p_2}{p_1 + p_2 - p_1 p_2 - r_1 p_2} & (3.76)\\
\mathbf{p}(N-1,0,0) &= CX^{N-1} & (3.77)\\
\mathbf{p}(N-1,0,1) &= 0 & (3.78)\\
\mathbf{p}(N-1,1,0) &= CX^{N-1}Y_1 & (3.79)\\
\mathbf{p}(N-1,1,1) &= \frac{CX^{N-1}}{p_1}\frac{r_1 + r_2 - r_1 r_2 - p_1 r_2}{p_1 + p_2 - p_1 p_2 - p_1 r_2} & (3.80)\\
\mathbf{p}(N,0,0) &= 0 & (3.81)\\
\mathbf{p}(N,0,1) &= 0 & (3.82)\\
\mathbf{p}(N,1,0) &= CX^{N-1}\frac{r_1 + r_2 - r_1 r_2 - p_1 r_2}{p_1 r_2} & (3.83)\\
\mathbf{p}(N,1,1) &= 0 & (3.84)\\
\mathbf{p}(n,\alpha_1,\alpha_2) &= CX^n Y_1^{\alpha_1} Y_2^{\alpha_2}, 2 \le n \le N-2; \alpha_1 = 0,1; \alpha_2 = 0,1 & (3.85)
\end{aligned}
$$

where

$$Y_1 = \frac{r_1 + r_2 - r_1 r_2 - r_1 p_2}{p_1 + p_2 - p_1 p_2 - p_1 r_2} \qquad (3.86)$$

$$Y_2 = \frac{r_1 + r_2 - r_1 r_2 - p_1 r_2}{p_1 + p_2 - p_1 p_2 - r_1 p_2} \tag{3.87}$$

$$X = \frac{Y_2}{Y_1} \tag{3.88}$$

and C is a normalizing constant.

Observation: Some of the expressions for boundary state probabilities are of internal form, and some are not. For reasonable values of the r_i and p_i parameters, the nonzero boundary probabilities that are not of internal form are much larger than internal probabilities. This is because the system tends to spend much more time at those states than at internal states.

There is nothing special about any particular internal state. When the system is in an internal state, it remains there if the machine states are the same, or it leaves if they are different. However, if Machine M_1 fails, the buffer may empty. (If M_1 is repaired before the buffer empties, the system is left at some other internal state, which is no more special than the one it was at before.) Whenever the buffer empties, regardless of what state the system was at before the failure, the system is in state (0,0,1). Furthermore, it stays there for a long time: until the repair occurs. This is because M_2 cannot fail, and the buffer level cannot change. Consequently, the state has high probability. When the repair occurs, the state changes to (1,1,1). This is because one piece enters the buffer and none leaves during that time unit. The state remains there for a long time: until M_1 or M_2 fails.

Limits If a failure or repair probability goes to zero, or if a buffer becomes very large, we can guess what will happen to the steady state production rate and in-process inventory.[8] In the following, we prove that the mathematical model agrees with our intuition, and perhaps tells us something that we might not have guessed.

$$
\begin{array}{lll}
\text{If } r_1 \to 0, & \text{then} & E \to 0, p_s \to 1, p_b \to 0, \text{ and } \bar{n} \to 0. \\
\text{If } r_2 \to 0, & \text{then} & E \to 0, p_b \to 1, p_s \to 0, \text{ and } \bar{n} \to N. \\
\text{If } p_1 \to 0, & \text{then} & p_s \to 0, E \to 1 - p_b \to e_2, \text{ and } \bar{n} \to N - e_2. \\
\text{If } p_2 \to 0, & \text{then} & p_b \to 0, E \to 1 - p_s \to e_1, \text{ and } \bar{n} \to e_1. \\
\text{If } N \to \infty \text{ and } e_1 < e_2, & \text{then} & E \to e_1, p_b \to 0, \text{ and } p_s \to 1 - \frac{e_1}{e_2}.
\end{array}
$$

Proof: combining conservation of flow and the flow rate-idle time relationship, we can write

$$E = \frac{r_1}{r_1 + p_1}(1 - p_b) = \frac{r_2}{r_2 + p_2}(1 - p_s). \tag{3.89}$$

Let $r_1 \to 0$. Then to maintain equality (3.89), $E \to 0$ and $p_s \to 1$. $p_s \to 1$ means that $\mathbf{p}(n, \alpha_1, \alpha_2) \to 0$ for all $n \neq 0$. Consequently, $p_b \to 0$ and $\bar{n} \to 0$. Similarly for $r_2 \to 0$.

Let $p_1 \to 0$. Then there are only two nonzero steady-state probabilities: $\mathbf{p}(N, 1, 0)$ and $\mathbf{p}(N - 1, 1, 1)$. All other states s have $\mathbf{p}(s) = 0$. This is true because, before normalization, those probabilities are much larger than any other when p_1 is small. The normalization constant C is very small and dominated by those terms. As $p_1 \to 0, C \to 0$, and all probabilities

---

[8]Suggestion: guess what will happen before you read further.

except those whose expressions have p_1 in the denominator go to 0. Consequently, $p_s \to 0$ and $E \to e_2$. Because they are the only two nonzero probabilities in the limit, $\mathbf{p}(N, 1, 0)$ and $\mathbf{p}(N-1, 1, 1)$ satisfy

$$\mathbf{p}(N, 1, 0) + \mathbf{p}(N-1, 1, 1) \to 1.$$

From (3.76) and (3.83),

$$\frac{\mathbf{p}(N, 1, 0)}{\mathbf{p}(N-1, 1, 1)} \to \frac{r_2}{p_2}$$

so

$$\mathbf{p}(N-1, 1, 1) \to e_2$$
$$\mathbf{p}(N, 1, 0) \to 1 - e_2$$

and

$$\bar{n} \to (N-1)\mathbf{p}(N-1, 1, 1) + N\mathbf{p}(N, 1, 0) \to N - e_2.$$

To interpret this behavior, note that Machine 1 almost never fails. Consequently, the buffer is almost always full or it is holding one part less than full. It is full if Machine 2 is down (which it is $1 - e_2$ of the time). When Machine 2 is up, the buffer level drops to $N - 1$.

The limits for $p_2 \to 0$ follow similarly.

To study the effects of $N \to \infty$, we make use of the solution form:

$$\mathbf{p}(n, \alpha_1, \alpha_2) = C X^n Y_1^{\alpha_1} Y_2^{\alpha_2}$$

for $n = 2, \ldots, N-2$. We have already demonstrated that if $e_1 = e_2$, then $X = 1$. It can be shown (Exercise 13) that if $e_1 > e_2$, $X > 1$, and if $e_1 < e_2$, $X < 1$.

Consequently, if $e_1 > e_2$, no limiting steady-state probability distribution exists as $N \to \infty$. On the other hand, if $e_1 < e_2$, a limiting distribution does exist because the probabilities approach 0 exponentially. In that case, the probability p_b of filling the buffer approaches 0 and, from (3.89),

$$E = e_1,$$

$$p_s = 1 - \frac{e_1}{e_2}.$$

Note that the production rate is that of the slower machine, which is exactly what we said earlier for lines with infinite buffers.

3.6.5 Numerical results and qualitative observations

Figure 3.3 demonstrates the effects of buffer size N and Machine 1 repair rate r_1 on the production rate (E) of the system. The system parameters are $p_1 = 0.1, r_2 = 0.1$, and $p_2 = 0.1$. On the lowest graph, $r_1 = 0.06$; and for the others, $r_1 = 0.08, 0.10, 0.12$, and 0.14. The production rate increases monotonically with N and r_1. Note that the line is balanced when $r_1 = 0.1$; when $r_1 < 0.1$, the first machine is less efficient than the second; and when $r_1 > 0.1$, the first machine is more efficient than the second. All lines approach limits, but the top two lines clearly approach the *same* limit. This is because, for $r_1 < 0.1$, the limiting production rate, as $N \to \infty$, is the efficiency of the first machine ($r_1/(r_1 + p_1)$), and this is a function of r_1, which differs in the bottom two lines. For $r_1 > 0.1$, the limiting production rate is the efficiency of the second machine ($r_2/(r_2 + p_2)$), which is not a function of r_1. Since the limiting production rate, when $r_1 = 0.1$, is the same as when $r_1 > 0.1$, the middle line approaches the same limit as the top lines.

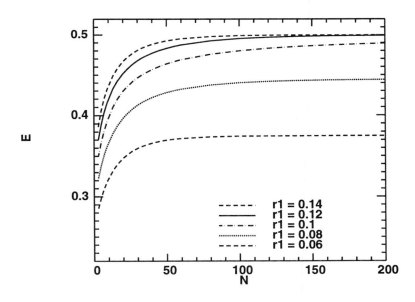

Figure 3.3: Effect of Repair Rate and Buffer Size on Production Rate

Figure 3.4 demonstrates the effects of buffer size N and Machine 1 repair rate on the average amount of material $\bar{n}$ in the buffer for the same set of systems. In the two graphs with $r_1 < 0.1$, $(\bar{n})$ approaches finite limits. In the two graphs with $r_1 > 0.1$, $\bar{n}$ seems to increase without limit; in fact, $N - \bar{n}$ approach finite limits. In the middle graph, where $r_1 = 0.1$, $\bar{n}$ is exactly $N/2$ for all N.

This behavior can be explained as follows: as the buffer size N increases, the amount of

Deterministic Two-Machine Line

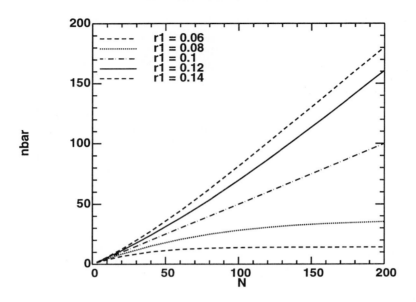

Figure 3.4: Effect of Repair Rate and Buffer Size on Average Buffer Level

material in the buffer increases. When r_1 is small and N is large enough, the first machine is the bottleneck and the buffer is not full very often. Therefore, since the only way that the buffer can affect things is by its filling or emptying, increasing the buffer size is not likely to have much of an effect on production rate or average buffer level. (This is a little like the $M/M/1$ queue of Section 2.3. The details are entirely different, but for both, there is a large storage area with parts arriving and departing at random.)

When r_1 is large and N is large enough, the second machine is the bottleneck and the buffer is likely to be full quite a lot. Again, increasing the buffer size is not likely to have much of an effect on production rate. However, it will affect average buffer level. This is because, since the first machine adds pieces faster than the second can take them away, the amount of free space in the buffer is rarely very large, no matter how large the buffer is. In fact, if we think of the movement of spaces or holes in the system as exactly complementary to the movement of parts, then we are simply reversing the line, and considering the effect of the repair rate of the first machine of the reversed line being small. The middle case is where $r_1 = r_2$. In this case, it is not hard to show that $\bar{n} = N/2$.

An important conclusion is that the optimal choice of some system parameters (for example, N) is a function of others (r_1, p_1, r_2, p_2). In particular, if the first machine were slower than the second, we might be willing to allow N to be larger than if the first machine were faster.

Figures 3.5, 3.6, and 3.7 show the effects of buffer size on production rate, average buffer level, and probabilities of blockage and starvation. The machine parameters are $r_1 = 0.09, p_1 = 0.01, r_2 = 0.08$, and $p_2 = 0.009$. Figures 3.8, 3.9, and 3.10 show the effects of Machine 1 repair rate on production rate, average buffer level, and probabilities of blockage and starvation. The system parameters are $N = 20, p_1 = 0.01, r_2 = 0.08$, and $p_2 = 0.009$.

Figure 3.11 shows production rate as a function of Machine 1 repair probability, while Machine 1 failure probability is allowed to vary in such a way as to keep Machine 1 isolated efficiency constant. In this example, $N = 10, r_2 = 0.8, p_2 = 0.09$, and r_1 and p_1 are chosen so that

$$\frac{r_1}{r_1 + p_1} = e_1 = 0.9.$$

The point of this example is to emphasize that both r_1 and p_1 — both MTTR and MTTF — are important in determining production rate in a system with storage, and not just isolated efficiency. The maximum production rate is 0.89, and the minimum is 0.82 — a substantial difference.

In general, production rate E increases monotonically and saturates as a function of parameters N, r_1, and r_2; and it decreases monotonically to 0 as a function of p_1 and p_2. On the other hand, the average buffer level $\bar{n}$ increases with N, r_1, and p_2 and it decreases with p_1 and r_2. How $\bar{n}$ increases with N depends on which machine is faster, or whether they are equal.

3.7 Exponential Model

In this and Section 3.8, we model a transfer line as a discrete state, continuous time Markov process (Section 2.3). The behavior of Machine M_i is characterized by three exponentially distributed random variables: the service time (with mean $1/\mu_i$), the time to fail (with mean $1/p_i$ — abbreviated MTTF) and the time to repair (with mean $1/r_i$ — abbreviated MTTR). Failures are still operation dependent. The buffers are each of finite storage size $(C_1, C_2, ..., C_{k-1})$. It is convenient to define $N_i = C_i + 2$ as an extended storage size between M_i and M_{i+1}. N_i includes the parts that are in the work areas of M_i and M_{i+1}.

This model is more flexible than the previous because the machines have three parameters. The machines are not all required to operate at the same speed. This flexibility comes at the price of a somewhat more complex calculation to find the steady state probability distribution.

3.7.1 Model assumptions, notation, terminology, and conventions

All assumptions, notation, terminology, and conventions are exactly the same as those of the deterministic processing time line, except the following:

1. Service, failure and repair times for M_i are assumed to be exponential random variables with parameters μ_i, p_i and r_i; $i = 1, \ldots k$. These quantities are the *service rate, failure rate* and *repair rate*, respectively.

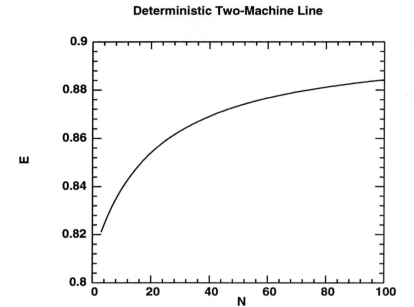

Figure 3.5: Effect of Buffer Size on Production Rate — Deterministic Processing Time Line

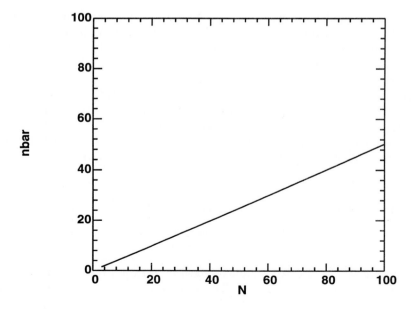

Figure 3.6: Effect of Buffer Size on Average Buffer Level — Deterministic Processing Time Line

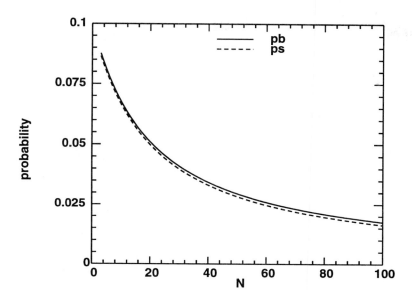

Figure 3.7: Effect of Buffer Size on Probability of Blockage and Starvation — Deterministic Processing Time Line

When a machine is under repair, it remains in that state for a period of time which is exponentially distributed with mean $1/r_i$. This period is unaffected by the states of the other machines or of the storages.

When a machine is operational, it operates on a piece if it is not starved or blocked. It continues operating until either it completes the piece or a failure occurs, whichever happens first. Either event can happen during the time interval $(t, t + \delta t)$ with probability approximately $\mu_i \delta t$ or $p_i \delta t$ respectively, for small δt.

2. The state of Buffer B_i is denoted by the integer n_i. This is the number of pieces in Buffer B_i plus the piece in Machine M_{i+1}. When M_i is blocked, n_i also includes the finished piece in M_i. The storage size between M_i and M_{i+1} is denoted by $C_i + 1$ which includes one space in M_{i+1}.

Machine M_i is blocked at the instant when it has completed a piece and there is no storage space in B_i. The convention for blockage is $n_i = N_i = C_i + 2$. Machine M_i is starved at the instant when it has completed a piece and there is no piece in B_{i-1}.

Since time is continuous, and all times between events are exponentially distributed, no two events can happen at the same instant. There is no longer any need for the convention that buffers change state only after machines. In fact, buffers change state only after

Deterministic Two-Machine Line

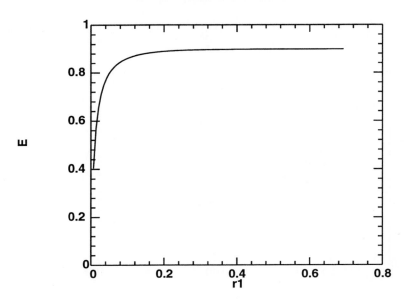

Figure 3.8: Effect of Machine 1 Repair Rate on Production Rate — Deterministic Processing Time Line

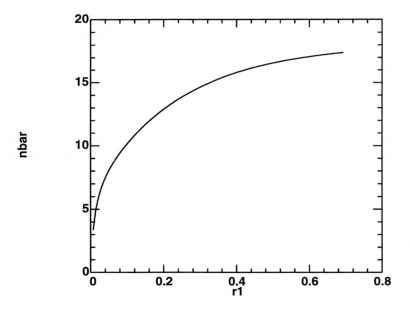

Figure 3.9: Effect of Machine 1 Repair Rate on Average Buffer Level — Deterministic Processing Time Line

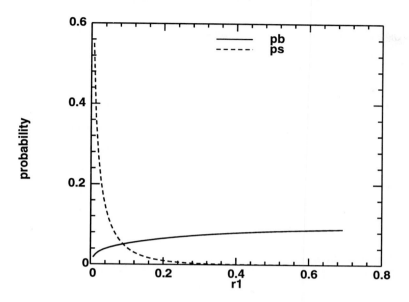

Figure 3.10: Effect of Machine 1 Repair Rate on Probability of Blockage and Starvation — Deterministic Processing Time Line

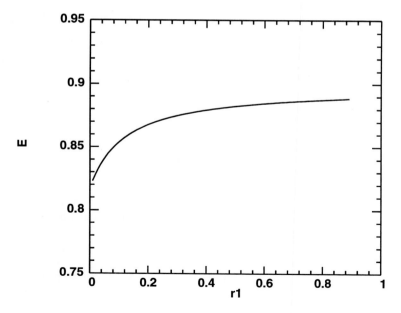

Figure 3.11: Effect of Machine 1 Variability with Constant Isolated Efficiency on Production Rate — Deterministic Processing Time Line

machines complete operations.

3.7.2   Performance measures

The probability that Machine M_i is processing a workpiece is termed the *efficiency*, E_i, and is given by

$$E_i = \text{prob } [\alpha_i = 1, n_{i-1} > 0, n_i < N_i]. \tag{3.90}$$

The *production rate* (throughput rate) of Machine M_i, in parts per time unit, is

$$P_i = \mu_i E_i. \tag{3.91}$$

Conservation of Flow
    Since there is no creation or destruction of workpieces, flow is conserved. That is

$$P = P_1 = P_2 = \ldots = P_k. \tag{3.92}$$

Flow Rate-Idle Time Relationship
    The *isolated efficiency* e_i of Machine M_i is, as usual,

$$e_i = \frac{r_i}{r_i + p_i} \tag{3.93}$$

and it represents the fraction of time that M_i is operational. The *isolated production rate*, ρ_i is then given by

$$\rho_i = \mu_i e_i. \tag{3.94}$$

and it represents what the production rate of M_i would be if it were never impeded by other machines or buffers. The actual production rate P is less because of blocking and starvation.

    The flow rate-idle time relation can be stated as

$$E_i = e_i \text{ prob } [n_{i-1} > 0 \text{ and } n_i < N_i]. \tag{3.95}$$

or

$$P = \rho_i \text{ prob } [n_{i-1} > 0 \text{ and } n_i < N_i]. \tag{3.96}$$

    While it is possible for $n_{i-1} = 0$ and $n_i = N_i$ simultaneously, it is not likely. This corresponds to an event in which M_i finishes a piece and finds that it is both blocked and starved. The probability of this event is small because such states can only be reached from states in which $n_{i-1} = 1$ and $n_i = N_i - 1$ by means of a transition in which

1. Machine M_{i-1} is either under repair, starved, or taking a long time to process a piece, and

2. $\alpha_i = 1$, and

3. Machine M_{i+1} is either under repair, blocked, or taking a long time to process a piece.

The production rate may therefore be approximated by

$$P_i \approx \rho_i \left(1 - \text{prob} \left[n_{i-1} = 0 \right] - \text{prob} \left[n_i = N_i \right] \right). \tag{3.97}$$

However, if there is a great variation in efficiencies and service rates among the machines, this assumption may not hold and this may break down. In particular, if μ_i is much larger than μ_{i-1} and μ_{i+1}, then the probability that $n_{i-1} = 0$ and $n_i = N_i$ simultaneously can be large.

This discussion is, of course, similar to the corresponding observation for the deterministic processing time line. It will be useful in the decomposition of a long line with exponential machines and finite buffers.

3.8 Exponential Two-Machine Line

In this section, we study the exponential two-machine transfer line. The state of the system is represented by

$$s = (n, \alpha_1, \alpha_2)$$

with $n = 0, 1, \ldots, N; \alpha_i = 0, 1; i = 1, 2$.

3.8.1 Balance equations

Instead of studying the system by means of the transition equations, we use the balance equations, which equate the rate of leaving a state with the rate of entering it, to obtain the steady state distribution. Recall that for a continuous time, discrete space Markov process (Section 2.3),

$$\frac{d\mathbf{p}_i(t)}{dt} = \sum_j \lambda_{ij} \mathbf{p}_j(t) \tag{3.98}$$

where $\lambda_{ij} > 0, j \neq i$, and

$$\lambda_{ii} = - \sum_{j \neq i} \lambda_{ji}.$$

In steady state $d\mathbf{p}_i/dt = 0$, and the negative term of (3.98) can be moved to the left side, so (3.98) becomes

$$\mathbf{p}_i \sum_{j \neq i} \lambda_{ji} = \sum_{j \neq i} \lambda_{ij} \mathbf{p}_j. \tag{3.99}$$

The left side is the rate of the system leaving state i, and the right side is the rate of entering it.

We distinguish four sets of equations, corresponding to the values of α_1 and α_2.

$\alpha_1 = a_2 = 0$:

$$\mathbf{p}(n,0,0)(r_1 + r_2) = \mathbf{p}(n,1,0)p_1 + \mathbf{p}(n,0,1)p_2, 1 \le n \le N-1, \tag{3.100}$$

$$\mathbf{p}(0,0,0)(r_1 + r_2) = \mathbf{p}(0,1,0)p_1, \tag{3.101}$$

$$\mathbf{p}(N,0,0)(r_1 + r_2) = \mathbf{p}(N,0,1)p_2. \tag{3.102}$$

The left sides of these equations represent the rate at which the state leaves $(n,0,0)$. They reflect the fact that the system leaves state $(n,0,0)$ only when the repair of a machine is complete. The right sides represent the rates at which the system enters state $(n,0,0)$. The system can reach state $(n,0,0)$ either from state $(n,1,0)$ (if $n < N$) if Machine M_1 fails or from $(n,0,1)$ (if $n > 0$) if Machine M_2 fails. Note that the definition of internal states is different here from in the deterministic processing time case: here (n,α_1,α_2) is an internal state if $1 \le n \le N-1$.

The other three sets of equations can be derived similarly.

$\alpha_1 = 0, \alpha_2 = 1$:

$$\begin{aligned}
\mathbf{p}(n,0,1)(r_1 + \mu_2 + p_2) &= \mathbf{p}(n,0,0)r_2 + \mathbf{p}(n,1,1)p_1 \\
&\quad + \mathbf{p}(n+1,0,1)\mu_2, 1 \le n \le N-1
\end{aligned} \tag{3.103}$$

$$\mathbf{p}(0,0,1)r_1 = \mathbf{p}(0,0,0)r_2 + \mathbf{p}(0,1,1)p_1 + \mathbf{p}(1,0,1)\mu_2 \tag{3.104}$$

$$\mathbf{p}(N,0,1)(r_1 + \mu_2 + p_2) = \mathbf{p}(N,0,0)r_2 \tag{3.105}$$

$\alpha_1 = 1, \alpha_2 = 0$:

$$\begin{aligned}
\mathbf{p}(n,1,0)(p_1 + \mu_1 + r_2) &= \mathbf{p}(n-1,1,0)\mu_1 + \mathbf{p}(n,0,0)r_1 \\
&\quad + \mathbf{p}(n,1,1)p_2, 1 \le n \le N-1
\end{aligned} \tag{3.106}$$

$$\mathbf{p}(0,1,0)(p_1 + \mu_1 + r_2) = \mathbf{p}(0,0,0)r_1 \tag{3.107}$$

$$\mathbf{p}(N,1,0)r_2 = \mathbf{p}(N-1,1,0\mu_1 + \mathbf{p}(N,0,0)r_1 + \mathbf{p}(N,1,1)p_2 \tag{3.108}$$

$\alpha_1 = 1, \alpha_2 = 1$:

$$\begin{aligned}
\mathbf{p}(n,1,1)(p_1 + p_2 + \mu_1 + \mu_2) &= \mathbf{p}(n-1,1,1)\mu_1 + \mathbf{p}(n+1,1,1)\mu_2 \\
&\quad + \mathbf{p}(n,1,0)r_2 + \mathbf{p}(n,0,1)r_1, 1 \le n \le N-1
\end{aligned} \tag{3.109}$$

$$\mathbf{p}(0,1,1)(p_1 + \mu_1) = \mathbf{p}(1,1,1)\mu_2 + \mathbf{p}(0,1,0)r_2 + \mathbf{p}(0,0,1)r_1 \tag{3.110}$$

$$\mathbf{p}(N,1,1)(p_2 + \mu_2) = \mathbf{p}(N-1,1,1)\mu_1 + \mathbf{p}(N,1,0)r_2 + \mathbf{p}(N,0,1)r_1 \tag{3.111}$$

3.8.2 Performance measures

Efficiency E_i is defined as the probability that the ith machine is operating on a piece, or the fraction of time in which the ith machine produces pieces. Efficiency is no longer the same as production rate, as it was in the deterministic processing time model. We can express the efficiencies in terms of the steady state probabilities as:

$$E_1 = \sum_{n=0}^{N-1} \sum_{\alpha_2=0}^{1} \mathbf{p}(n, 1, \alpha_2), \tag{3.112}$$

$$E_2 = \sum_{n=1}^{N} \sum_{\alpha_1=0}^{1} \mathbf{p}(n, \alpha_1, 1). \tag{3.113}$$

In Section 3.8.3 we show that

$$\mu_1 E_1 = \mu_2 E_2. \tag{3.114}$$

The quantity $\mu_i E_i$ can be interpreted as the rate at which pieces emerge from Machine i. Equation (3.114) is then a conservation of flow law, and we can define

$$P = \mu_i E_i \tag{3.115}$$

as the *production rate* of the system.

Another important measure of system performance is the *expected in-process inventory*. This can be written

$$\bar{n} = \sum_{n=0}^{N} \sum_{\alpha_1=0}^{1} \sum_{\alpha_2=0}^{1} n\mathbf{p}(n, \alpha_1, \alpha_2). \tag{3.116}$$

3.8.3 Identities

First, we show that some of the steady state probabilities are zero.
Transient States

$$\mathbf{p}(0, 0, 0) = \mathbf{p}(0, 1, 0) = \mathbf{p}(N, 0, 0) = \mathbf{p}(N, 0, 1) = 0. \tag{3.117}$$

Proof: Combining Equations (3.101) and (3.107) yields:

$$\mathbf{p}(0, 0, 0)r_2 + \mathbf{p}(0, 1, 0)(\mu_1 + r_2) = 0.$$

Since probabilities are non-negative, $\mathbf{p}(0, 0, 0) = \mathbf{p}(0, 1, 0) = 0$. Combining Equations (3.102) and (3.105) yields:

$$\mathbf{p}(N, 0, 0)r_1 = \mathbf{p}(N, 0, 1)(r_1 + \mu_2) = 0. \tag{3.118}$$

This implies that $\mathbf{p}(N, 0, 0) = \mathbf{p}(N, 0, 1) = 0$.

Repair frequency equals failure frequency   Equation (3.119) asserts that the rate of transitions from the set of states in which Machine 1 is under repair to the set of states in which Machine 1 is operational is equal to the rate of transitions in the opposite direction. This is essentially the same as (3.39), and is similarly reassuring.

$$r_1 \sum_{n=0}^{N} \sum_{\alpha_2=0}^{1} \mathbf{p}(n,0,\alpha_2) = p_1 \sum_{n=0}^{N-1} \sum_{\alpha_2=0}^{1} \mathbf{p}(n,1,\alpha_2). \tag{3.119}$$

Proof: Add Equations (3.100)-(3.105):

$$\sum_{n=0}^{N} \mathbf{p}(n,0,0)(r_1+r_2) + \sum_{n=1}^{N} \mathbf{p}(n,0,1)(r_1+\mu_2+p_2) + \mathbf{p}(0,0,1)r_1$$

$$= p_1 \sum_{n=0}^{N-1} \mathbf{p}(n,1,0) + p_2 \sum_{n=1}^{N} \mathbf{p}(n,0,1) + r_2 \sum_{n=0}^{N} \mathbf{p}(n,0,0) \tag{3.120}$$

$$+ p_1 \sum_{n=0}^{N-1} \mathbf{p}(n,1,1) + \mu_2 \sum_{n=0}^{N-1} \mathbf{p}(n+1,0,1).$$

This can be reduced to

$$r_1 \sum_{n=0}^{N} \mathbf{p}(n,0,0) + r_1 \sum_{n=0}^{N} \mathbf{p}(n,0,1) = p_1 \sum_{n=0}^{N-1} \mathbf{p}(n,1,0) + p_1 \sum_{n=0}^{N-1} \mathbf{p}(n,1,1) \tag{3.121}$$

which is equivalent to (3.119).

Helpful equation   Equation (3.122) is analogous to (3.41), and is also helpful in establishing conservation of flow.

$$\mu_1 \sum_{\alpha_2=0}^{1} \mathbf{p}(n,1,\alpha_2) = \mu_2 \sum_{\alpha_1=0}^{1} \mathbf{p}(n+1,\alpha_1,1), 0 \leq n \leq N-1. \tag{3.122}$$

Proof: by induction. For $n=0$, add Equations (3.101), (3.104), (3.107) and (3.110). From 3.117,

$$\mathbf{p}(0,0,1)r_1 + \mathbf{p}(0,1,1)(p_1+\mu_1) =$$
$$\mathbf{p}(0,1,1)p_1 + \mathbf{p}(1,0,1)\mu_2 + \mathbf{p}(1,1,1)\mu_2 + \mathbf{p}(0,0,1)r_1, \tag{3.123}$$

or,

$$\mathbf{p}(0,1,1)\mu_1 = \mathbf{p}(1,0,1)\mu_2 + \mathbf{p}(1,1,1)\mu_2. \tag{3.124}$$

Since $\mathbf{p}(0,1,0)=0$ this is equivalent to

$$\mu_1 \sum_{\alpha_2=0}^{1} \mathbf{p}(0,1,\alpha_2) = \mu_2 \sum_{\alpha_1=0}^{1} \mathbf{p}(1,\alpha_1,1) \tag{3.125}$$

which is Equation (3.122) with $n = 0$.

Assume that Equation (3.122) holds for $n = m \leq N - 2$. We show that this implies (3.122) for $n = m + 1$. Add Equations (3.100), (3.103), (3.106), and (3.109) with $n = m + 1$ for $(1 \leq m + 1 \leq N - 1)$. This yields

$$\mathbf{p}(m + 1, 0, 0)(r_1 + r_2) + \mathbf{p}(m + 1, 1, 0)(p_1 + \mu_1 + r_2)$$
$$+ \mathbf{p}(m + 1, 0, 1)(r_1 + \mu_2 + p_2) + \mathbf{p}(m + 1, 1, 1)(p_1 + p_2 + \mu_1 + \mu_2)$$

$$\begin{aligned}
= \quad & \mathbf{p}(m + 1, 1, 0)p_1 + \mathbf{p}(m + 1, 0, 1)p_2 + \mathbf{p}(m + 1, 0, 0)r_2 + \mathbf{p}(m + 1, 1, 1)p_1 \quad (3.126)\\
& + \mathbf{p}(m + 2, 0, 1)\mu_2 + \mathbf{p}(m, 1, 0)\mu_1 + \mathbf{p}(m + 1, 0, 0)r_1 \\
& + \mathbf{p}(m + 1, 1, 1)p_2 + \mathbf{p}(m, 1, 1)\mu_1 + \mathbf{p}(m + 2, 1, 1)\mu_2 \\
& + \mathbf{p}(m + 1, 1, 0)r_2 + \mathbf{p}(m + 1, 0, 1)r_1.
\end{aligned}$$

This can be reduced to

$$\mathbf{p}(m + 1, 1, 0)\mu_1 + \mathbf{p}(m + 1, 0, 1)\mu_2 + \mathbf{p}(m + 1, 1, 1)(\mu_1 + \mu_2)$$
$$= \mathbf{p}(m, 1, 0)\mu_1 + \mathbf{p}(m, 1, 1)\mu_1 + \mathbf{p}(m + 2, 0, 1)\mu_2 + \mathbf{p}(m + 2, 1, 1)\mu_2. \tag{3.127}$$

But by induction

$$\mathbf{p}(m, 1, 0)\mu_1 + \mathbf{p}(m, 1, 1)\mu_1 = \mathbf{p}(m + 1, 0, 1)\mu_2 + \mathbf{p}(m + 1, 1, 1)\mu_2 \tag{3.128}$$

and therefore (3.127) becomes

$$\mu_1 \sum_{\alpha_2 = 0}^{1} \mathbf{p}(m + 1, 1, \alpha_2) = \mu_2 \sum_{\alpha_1 = 0}^{1} \mathbf{p}(m + 2, \alpha_1, 1). \tag{3.129}$$

Therefore, Equation (3.122) holds for $0 \leq n \leq N - 2$. To prove (3.126) for $n = N - 1$ add, Equations (3.102), (3.105), (3.108), and (3.111) to yield, after taking the transient states into account,

$$\mathbf{p}(N, 1, 0)r_2 + \mathbf{p}(N, 1, 1)(p_2 + \mu_2) =$$
$$\mathbf{p}(N - 1, 1, 0)\mu_1 + \mathbf{p}(N, 1, 1)p_2 + \mathbf{p}(N - 1, 1, 1)\mu_1 + \mathbf{p}(N, 1, 0)r_2 \tag{3.130}$$

or

$$\mathbf{p}(N, 1, 1)\mu_2 = \mathbf{p}(N - 1, 1, 0)\mu_1 + \mathbf{p}(N - 1, 1, 1)\mu_1 \tag{3.131}$$

or

$$\mu_1 \sum_{\alpha_2 = 0}^{1} \mathbf{p}(N - 1, 1, \alpha_2) = \mu_2 \sum_{\alpha_1 = 0}^{1} \mathbf{p}(N, \alpha_1, 1) \tag{3.132}$$

since $\mathbf{p}(N, 0, 1) = 0$. This is Equation (3.122) for $n = N - 1$, so (3.126) is proven.

Conservation of Flow   The rates of transitions between the set of states in which Machine 1 can produce a piece and the set of states in which Machine 2 can produce a piece are equal.

$$\mu_1 \sum_{n=0}^{N-1} \sum_{\alpha_2=0}^{1} \mathbf{p}(n,1,\alpha_2) = \mu_2 \sum_{n=1}^{N} \sum_{\alpha_1=0}^{1} \mathbf{p}(n,\alpha_1,1). \tag{3.133}$$

Proof: Equation (3.133) is Equation (3.122) summed for $n = 0, ..., N-1$.

Flow Rate-Idle Time Relationship   Just as in the deterministic processing time case,

$$E_1 = e_1 \text{ prob } (n < N), \tag{3.134}$$

$$E_2 = e_2 \text{ prob } (n > 0). \tag{3.135}$$

The proofs are identical.

Limits   These limits should be compared with those of Section 3.6.4:

$$\text{If } \rho_i \to 0, \text{ then } P \to 0, E_i \to e_i, \text{ and } E_j \to 0, \text{for } j \neq i. \tag{3.136}$$

$$\text{If } \rho_i \to \infty, \text{ then } P \to \rho_j, E_i \to 0, \text{ and } E_j \to e_j, \text{for } j \neq i. \tag{3.137}$$

These results are quite general, since $\rho_i \to 0$ if $\mu_i \to 0$, $r_i \to 0$, or $p_i \to \infty$; and $\rho_i \to \infty$ if $\mu_i \to \infty$.

Proof: We can combine several results and write

$$P = \rho_1 \text{ prob } (n < N) = \rho_2 \text{ prob } (n > 0).$$

If $\rho_1 \to 0$, then $P \to 0$ and prob$(n > 0) \to 0$. Consequently, from (3.135), $E_2 \to 0$. Since prob$(n = 0) \to 1$, then prob$(n < N) \to 1$. Then, from (3.134), $E_1 \to e_1$. The rest of the statements can be proved similarly.

By the same techniques, it is possible to establish that

- If $\rho_1 \to 0$, then $\bar{n} \to 0$.

- If $\rho_1 \to \infty$, then $\bar{n} \to N$.

- If $\rho_2 \to 0$, then $\bar{n} \to N$.

- If $\rho_2 \to \infty$, then $\bar{n} \to 0$.

3.8.4 Solution of balance equations

In this section, we develop a solution technique for the balance equations. As in the deterministic processing time case, it is based on separating the internal and boundary states equations. A solution is obtained for the internal equations which has some unknown parameters, or degrees of freedom. The solution is completed using some of the boundary equations, and the parameters are determined by using the rest of the boundary equations.

Analysis of the Internal Equations We define internal states as states (n, α_1, α_2) where $1 \leq n \leq N-1$. Note that this differs from the deterministic processing time system. Internal equations are the balance equations that do not include any boundary states. The rest are called boundary equations. Following the analysis of the deterministic processing time line, we guess a solution for the internal equations of the form

$$\mathbf{p}(n, \alpha_1, \alpha_2) = CX^n Y_1^{\alpha_1} Y_2^{\alpha_2}, 1 \leq n \leq N - 1 \tag{3.138}$$

where C, X, Y_1, Y_2 are parameters to be determined.

By substituting (3.138) into the internal equations we find that those equations are satisfied if X, Y_1, Y_2 satisfy the following three non-linear *parametric* equations:

$$p_1 Y_1 + p_2 Y_2 - r_1 - r_2 = 0 \tag{3.139}$$

$$\mu_1 \left(\frac{1}{X} - 1 \right) - p_1 Y_1 + r_1 + \frac{r_1}{Y_1} - p_1 = 0 \tag{3.140}$$

$$\mu_2(X - 1) - p_2 Y_2 + \frac{r_2}{Y_2} + r_2 - p_2 = 0 \tag{3.141}$$

This is because the internal equations [Equations (3.100), (3.103), (3.106), and (3.109)] can be written

$$\mathbf{p}(n, \alpha_1, \alpha_2)(r_1^{1-\alpha_1} p_1^{\alpha_1})$$

$$\begin{aligned} = \quad & (\mathbf{p}(n - 1, \alpha_1, \alpha_2) - \mathbf{p}(n, \alpha_1, \alpha_2))\mu_1 \alpha_1 \\ + \quad & (\mathbf{p}(n + 1, \alpha_1, \alpha_2) - \mathbf{p}(n, \alpha_1, \alpha_2))\mu_2 \alpha_2 \\ + \quad & \mathbf{p}(n, 1 - \alpha_1, \alpha_2)r_1^{\alpha_1} p_1^{1-\alpha_1} + \mathbf{p}(n, \alpha_1, 1 - \alpha_2)r_2^{\alpha_2} p_2^{1-\alpha_2}. \end{aligned} \tag{3.142}$$

If $\mathbf{p}(n, \alpha_1, \alpha_2)$ is given by (3.138), Equation (3.142) becomes

$$X^n Y_1^{\alpha_1} Y_2^{\alpha_2} \left(r_1^{1-\alpha_1} p_1^{\alpha_1} + r_2^{1-\alpha_2} p_2^{\alpha_2} \right)$$

$$= X^n Y_1^{\alpha_1} Y_2^{\alpha_2} \mu_1 \alpha_1 \left(\tfrac{1}{X} - 1 \right)$$

$$+ X^n Y_1^{\alpha_1} Y_2^{\alpha_2} \mu_2 \alpha_2 (X - 1) + X^n Y_1^{1-\alpha_1} Y_2^{\alpha_2} r_1^{\alpha_1} p_1^{1-\alpha_1}$$

$$- X^n Y_1^{\alpha_1} Y_2^{1-\alpha_2} r_2^{\alpha_2} p_2^{1-\alpha_2}. \tag{3.143}$$

or

$$r_1^{1-\alpha_1} p_1^{\alpha_1} + r_2^{1-\alpha_2} p_2^{\alpha_2}$$

$$= \mu_1 \alpha_1 \left(\tfrac{1}{X} - 1 \right) + \mu_2 \alpha_2 (X - 1) \tag{3.144}$$

$$+ Y_1^{1-2\alpha_1} r_1^{\alpha_1} p_1^{1-\alpha_1} + Y_2^{1-2\alpha_2} r_2^{\alpha_2} p_2^{1-\alpha_2}$$

or, finally,

$$0 = \left\{ \mu_1 \alpha_1 \left(\frac{1}{X} - 1 \right) + Y_1^{1-2\alpha_1} r_1^{\alpha_1} p_1^{1-\alpha_1} - r_1^{1-\alpha_1} p_1^{\alpha_1} \right\}$$
$$+ \left\{ \mu_2 \alpha_2 (X - 1) + Y_2^{1-2\alpha_2} r_2^{\alpha_2} p_2^{1-\alpha_2} - r_2^{1-\alpha_2} p_2^{\alpha_2} \right\}. \tag{3.145}$$

Equation (3.139) follows when $\alpha_1 = \alpha_2 = 0$. Equations (3.140) and (3.141) result from $\alpha_1 = 1, \alpha_2 = 0$ and $\alpha_2 = 1$, respectively. When $\alpha_1 = \alpha_2 = 1$, the result is the sum of Equations (3.140) and (3.141).

Equations (3.139)-(3.141) can be reduced to the following fourth degree polynomial in Y_1:

$$p_1^3 Y_1^4$$

$$+ \quad \left[-\mu_2 p_1^2 - 3p_1^2 r_1 - p_1^2 r_2 - p_2 p_1^2 + \mu_1 p_1^2 + p_1^3 \right] Y_1^3$$

$$+ \quad \left[2\mu_2 p_1 r_1 - r_2 p_1 \mu_1 - 2r_1 p_1 \mu_1 - p_2 p_1 \mu_1 - \mu_2 p_1^2 - 3p_1^2 r_1 \right.$$
$$\left. -p_1^2 r_2 - p_2 p_1^2 + \mu_2 r_2 p_1 + 3r_1^2 p_1 + 2p_1 r_1 r_2 + 2p_1 p_2 r_1 \right] Y_1^2$$

$$+ \quad \left[2p_1 p_2 r_1 + \mu_1 r_1^2 + \mu_1 r_1 r_2 + r_1 \mu_1 p_2 + p_1 r_2 \mu_2 + 2p_1 r_1 \mu_2 \right.$$
$$\left. +3p_1 r_1^2 + 2r_1 r_2 p_1 - \mu_2 r_1^2 - r_1 r_2 \mu_2 - r_1^2 p_2 - r_1^3 - r_1^2 r_2 \right] Y_1$$

$$+ \quad \left[-r_1 \mu_2 (r_1 + r_2) - r_1^2 r_2 - r_1^3 - r_1^2 p_2 \right] = 0. \tag{3.146}$$

It is easy to verify that one solution is

$$Y_{11} = \frac{r_1}{p_1} \tag{3.147}$$

and by substituting (3.147) in (3.139) and (3.140) we obtain:

$$Y_{21} = \frac{r_2}{p_2} \tag{3.148}$$

and

$$X_1 = 1. \tag{3.149}$$

The other three solutions to (3.146) can be obtained by solving a cubic equation. We can write (3.146) as

$$p_1^2(p_1 Y_1 - r_1)(Y_1^3 + sY_1^2 + tY_1 + u) = 0 \tag{3.150}$$

where s, t and u are given by

$$
\begin{aligned}
s &= \frac{1}{p_1}(-\mu_2 - 2r_1 - r_2 - p_2 + \mu_1 + p_1) \\
t &= \frac{1}{p_1^2}(\mu_2 r_1 - r_2 \mu_1 - r_1 \mu_1 - p_2 \mu_1 - \mu_2 p_1 \\
&\quad -2p_1 r_1 - p_1 r_2 - p_1 p_2 + \mu_2 r_2 + r_1^2 + r_1 r_2 + r_1 p_2) \\
u &= \frac{1}{p_1^2}(\mu_2(r_1 + r_2) + r_1 r_2 + r_1^2 + r_1 p_2).
\end{aligned}
\tag{3.151}
$$

The three values of Y_1 — other than (3.147) — that satisfy (3.150) are[9]

$$Y_{12} = 2\sqrt{-\frac{a}{3}}\cos\left(\frac{\phi}{3}\right) - \frac{s}{3} \tag{3.152}$$

$$Y_{13} = 2\sqrt{-\frac{a}{3}}\cos\left(\frac{\phi}{3} + \frac{2\pi}{3}\right) - \frac{s}{3} \tag{3.153}$$

$$Y_{14} = 2\sqrt{-\frac{a}{3}}\cos\left(\frac{\phi}{3} + \frac{4\pi}{3}\right) - \frac{s}{3} \tag{3.154}$$

where

$$a = \frac{1}{3}(3t - s^2) \tag{3.155}$$

$$b = \frac{1}{27}(2s^3 - 9st + 27u) \tag{3.156}$$

and

$$\phi = \arccos\left[\frac{-b}{2\sqrt{\frac{-a^3}{27}}}\right]. \tag{3.157}$$

---

[9] *Handbook of Chemistry and Physics*, Chemical Rubber Publishing Company

To summarize,

$$\mathbf{p}(n, \alpha_1, \alpha_2) = \sum_{j=1}^{4} c_j X_j^n Y_{1j}^{\alpha_1} Y_{2j}^{\alpha_2} \text{ for } n = 1, \dots, N-1. \tag{3.158}$$

where Y_{1i} is given by (3.152)-(3.154); Y_{2j} and X_j, for $j = 2, 3, 4$, are obtained from (3.139) and (3.140); and $c_j, j = 1, 2, 3, 4$ are parameters to be determined.

Analysis of the Boundary Equations   There are a total of eight boundary states. Four of them are transient; their steady state probabilities are 0. The other four are:

$$\mathbf{p}(0, 0, 1) = \frac{1}{r_1} \sum_{j=1}^{4} c_j (p_1 Y_{1j} Y_{2j} + \mu_2 X_j Y_{2j}) \tag{3.159}$$

$$\mathbf{p}(0, 1, 1) = \sum_{j=1}^{4} c_j Y_{1j} Y_{2j} \tag{3.160}$$

$$\mathbf{p}(N, 1, 0) = \frac{1}{r_2} \sum_{j=1}^{4} c_j X_j^{N-1} (\mu_1 Y_{1j} + p_2 X_j Y_{1j} Y_{2j}) \tag{3.161}$$

$$\mathbf{p}(N, 1, 1) = \sum_{j=1}^{4} c_j X_j^N Y_{1j} Y_{2j} \tag{3.162}$$

(Note that (3.160) and (3.162) are in internal (3.158) form.) Furthermore, the coefficients c_j satisfy

$$c_1 = 0 \tag{3.163}$$

$$\sum_{j=2}^{4} c_j Y_{1j} = 0 \tag{3.164}$$

$$\sum_{j=2}^{4} c_j X_j^N Y_{2j} = 0 \tag{3.165}$$

and the normalization equation,

$$\sum_{n=0}^{N} \sum_{\alpha_1=0}^{1} \sum_{\alpha_2=0}^{1} \mathbf{p}(n, \alpha_1, \alpha_2) = 1. \tag{3.166}$$

Proof: The expressions (3.158)-(3.162) and (3.117) satisfy all the balance equations (3.100)-(3.111) identically except for (3.110) and (3.106) for $n = 1$, and (3.111) and (3.103) for $n = N - 1$. Equation (3.110) becomes

$$0 = \sum_{j=1}^{4} c_j Y_{2j} (\mu_1 Y_{1j} - \mu_2 X_j Y_{1j} - \mu_2 X_j). \tag{3.167}$$

Equation (3.106) for $n = 1$, becomes

$$0 = \sum_{j=1}^{4} c_j X_j \left[(p_1 + \mu_1 + r_2) Y_{1j} - r_1 - p_2 Y_{1j} Y_{2j} \right]. \tag{3.168}$$

Equation (3.111) becomes

$$0 = \sum_{j=1}^{4} c_j X_j^{N-1} Y_{1j} (\mu_2 X_j Y_{2j} - \mu_1 Y_{2j} - \mu_1) \tag{3.169}$$

and Equation (3.103), for $n = N - 1$, is

$$0 = \sum_{j=1}^{4} c_j X_j^{N-1} [(r_1 + \mu_2 + p_2) Y_{2j} - r_2 - p_1 Y_{1j} Y_{2j}]. \tag{3.170}$$

Equation (3.168) can be transformed by observing that

$$(p_1 + \mu_1 + r_2) Y_{1j} - r_1 - p_2 Y_{1j} Y_{2j}$$

$$= (p_1 Y_{1j} - r_1) + \mu_1 Y_{1j} + Y_{1j} (r_2 - p_2 Y_{2j}) \tag{3.171}$$

$$= (p_1 Y_{1j} - r_1) + \mu_1 Y_{1j} - Y_{1j} (r_1 - p_1 Y_{1j}) \tag{3.172}$$

(because of Equation (3.139)), and,

$$= (p_1 Y_{1j} - r_1)(1 + Y_{1j}) + \mu_1 Y_{1j}. \tag{3.173}$$

Note that Equation (3.140) can be written

$$\mu_1 \left(\frac{1}{X_j} - 1 \right) = (p_1 Y_{1j} - r_1) \frac{1 + Y_{1j}}{Y_{1j}} \tag{3.174}$$

so that expression (3.173) is

$$\mu_1 \left(\frac{1}{X_j} - 1 \right) Y_{1j} + \mu_1 Y_{1j} = \mu_1 \frac{Y_{1j}}{X_j}. \tag{3.175}$$

Thus, Equation (3.168) is now

$$0 = \sum_{j=1}^{4} c_j Y_{1j}. \tag{3.176}$$

The same sequence of steps can be applied to Equation (3.170) to yield

$$0 = \sum_{j=1}^{4} c_j X_j^N Y_{2j}. \tag{3.177}$$

To analyze (3.167), first observe that Equation (3.174) implies

$$\mu_1 Y_{1j} - \mu_2 X_j (Y_{1j} + 1) = \mu_1 Y_{1j} - \frac{\mu_2 X_j \mu_1 \left(\frac{1}{X_j} - 1\right) Y_{1j}}{p_1 Y_{1j} - r_1} \tag{3.178}$$

if $p_1 Y_{1j} - r_1 \neq 0$. Recall that $p_1 Y_{11} - r_1 = 0$ so (3.178) is true only for $j \neq 1$. Equation (3.141) can be written

$$\mu_2 (X_j - 1) = (p_2 Y_{2j} - r_2) \left(\frac{1 + Y_{2j}}{Y_{2j}}\right) \tag{3.179}$$

so that (3.178) can be transformed to

$$-\mu_1 Y_{1j} / Y_{2j}, \tag{3.180}$$

with the use of (3.140), still assuming

$$p_1 Y_{1j} - r_1 \neq 0.$$

Equation (3.167) can now be written

$$0 = c_1 Y_{21} (\mu_1 Y_{11} - \mu_2 X_1 Y_{11} - \mu_2 X_1) - \mu_1 \sum_{j=2}^{4} c_j Y_{1j} \tag{3.181}$$

or, using (3.147)-(3.149),

$$0 = c_1 \frac{r_2}{p_2} (\mu_1 \frac{r_1}{p_1} - \mu_2 \frac{r_1}{p_1} - \mu_2) - \mu_1 \sum_{j=2}^{4} c_j Y_{1j}. \tag{3.182}$$

Finally, we observe that (3.176) implies that

$$\sum_{j=2}^{4} c_j Y_{1j} = -c_1 \frac{r_1}{p_1} \tag{3.183}$$

so that (3.182) can be written, after some transformation, as

$$0 = c_1 \left[\frac{\mu_1 r_1}{r_1 + p_1} - \frac{\mu_2 r_2}{r_2 + p_2} \right]. \tag{3.184}$$

By the same sort of manipulations, Equation (3.169) can also be transformed into Equation (3.184).

To complete the proof, two cases must be considered. If

$$\frac{\mu_1 r_1}{r_1 + p_1} \neq \frac{\mu_2 r_2}{r_2 + p_2} \tag{3.185}$$

then (3.163) follows from (3.184); and (3.164) and (3.165) follow from (3.163), (3.176), and (3.177).

If

$$\frac{\mu_1 r_1}{r_1 + p_1} = \frac{\mu_2 r_2}{r_2 + p_2} \tag{3.186}$$

then c_1 is not determined by (3.184). However, in this case $Y_1 r_1 / p_1$ is a double root of (3.146). That is, one of the values of Y_{1j} given by (3.152)-(3.154) ($j = 2, 3, 4$) is r_1/p_1. Then there are only three independent sets of parameters (X_j, Y_{1j}, Y_{2j}) and the coefficients c_j are given by (3.164)-(3.166).

The coefficients c_2, c_3, and c_4 can be found by solving (3.164) and (3.165) and the normalization equation (3.166).

The quantities

$$\rho_i = \frac{\mu_i r_i}{r_i + p_i} \tag{3.187}$$

that appear in Equation (3.184) have physical significance. Recall that the ratio

$$e_i = \frac{r_i}{r_i + p_i}$$

is the isolated efficiency, the fraction of time Machine i would be available (not under repair) if it were in isolation. Since μ_i is the production rate while it is operational, $\rho_i = \mu_i e_i$ is the production rate in isolation, the production rate it would have if it were not part of a system with other machines and storages.

The Algorithm   To summarize, the steady state probabilities are evaluated by means of the following:

- Step 1: Find $Y_{1j}, Y_{2j}, X_j; j = 2, 3, 4$ using (3.152)-(3.154) and (3.139)-(3.140).

- Step 2: Solve Equations (3.164)-(3.166) to obtain $c_j; j = 2, 3, 4$.

- Step 3: Use (3.117) and Equations (3.158)-(3.162) to evaluate all probabilities. These probabilities can be used to evaluate the measures of performance.

3.8.5   Numerical results and qualitative observations

Figures 3.12-3.16 are graphs of performance of both exponential processing time lines (solid) and continuous material lines (dashed) with the same parameters. Their behaviors are similar in most respects, but not the same; and in one case, they are quite different.

Figures 3.12 and 3.13 show the effects of buffer size on production rate P and average buffer level $\bar{n}$. The machine parameters are $r_1 = 0.09, p_1 = 0.01, \mu_1 = 1.1, r_2 = 0.08, p_2 = 0.009$ and $\mu_2 = 1.0$.

Figures 3.14 and 3.15 show the effects of Machine 2 service rate on system production rate and average buffer level. The parameters are the same as in the previous graphs. The buffer size N is 20. Their shapes are due to the fact that when μ_2 is small, Machine 2 is the bottleneck in the system. The buffer is nearly always full, and the production rate is extremely low. In fact, increases in μ_2 translate directly into increases in P, since Machine 1 is so far from being the bottleneck. When μ_2 is large, Machine 1 is the bottleneck. The buffer is nearly always empty, and the production rate is the maximum production rate of Machine 1 in isolation.

Figure 3.16 shows the effects of Machine 1 repair rate on average buffer level. The parameters are the same as in the previous cases.

The exponential and continuous graphs in Figures 3.12-3.15 are very close to one another. By contrast, the exponential and continuous graphs in Figure 3.16 differ substantially.

3.9   Continuous Model

In this section and the next, we model a transfer line as a continuous time, mixed state Markov process (Section 2.6). Physically, the material that is processed is treated as though it is a continuous fluid. The assumptions on which this model is based are more general than those of the deterministic model in that the machines can operate at different speeds. In addition, the rate of machine failure is affected by the buffer level: whether it is empty, full, or in between.

The quantity μ_i is the speed at which Machine i processes material while it is operating and not constrained by the other machine or the buffer. It is a constant, in that μ_i does not depend on the repair state of the other machine or the buffer level.

In the following, we list a set of assumptions on machine and buffer behavior. These assumptions imply that the storage gains material from Machine 1 at a rate of μ_1 when that machine is operational and not blocked. It gains no material otherwise. It loses material to Machine 2, when it is operational and not starved, at rate μ_2. The probability of repair of a machine is unaffected by storage levels or by the states of other machines.

The probability of failure is affected by storage level because of the different machine speeds. When the storage is neither empty nor full and both machines are operational, Machine 1 processes $\mu_1 \delta t$ material during an interval of length δt, and Machine 2 processes $\mu_2 \delta t$.

However, when the storage is empty and both machines are operational, consider the case in which $\mu_1 < \mu_2$. Both machines process $\mu_1 \delta t$ during an interval of length δt. Consequently,

Exponential and Continuous Two-Machine Lines

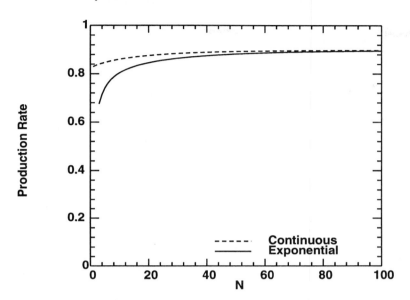

Figure 3.12: Effect of Buffer Size on Production Rate — Exponential Processing Time and Continuous Material Lines

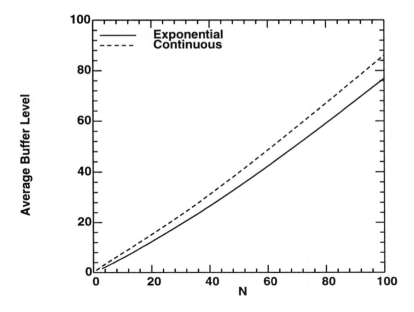

Figure 3.13: Effect of Buffer Size on Average Buffer Level — Exponential Processing Time and Continuous Material Lines

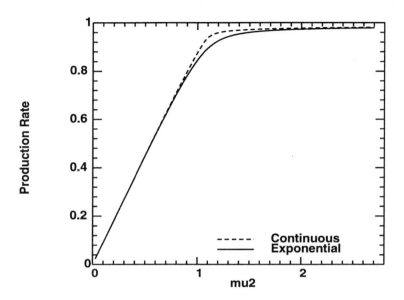

Figure 3.14: Effect of Machine 2 Service Rate on Production Rate — Exponential Processing Time and Continuous Material Lines

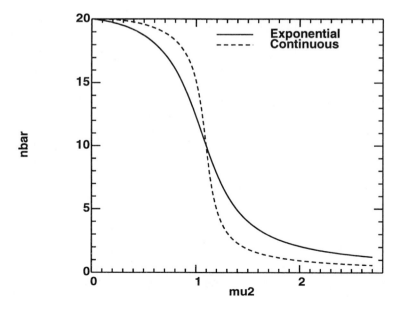

Figure 3.15: Effect of Machine 2 Service Rate on Average Buffer Level — Exponential Processing Time and Continuous Material Lines

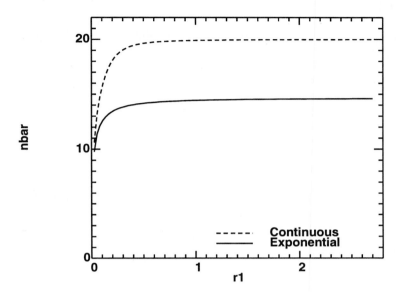

Figure 3.16: Effect of Machine 1 Repair Rate on Average Buffer Level — Exponential Processing Time and Continuous Material Lines

Machine 1 is operating at full speed but Machine 2 is operating at less than full speed. Or, Machine 2 may be viewed as working only $(\mu_1/\mu_2)\,\delta t$ during that interval and as idle the rest of the time. It is then natural to assume that the failure probability of Machine 1 is its usual value, $p_1\delta t$, whereas that of Machine 2 is $(\mu_1/\mu_2)p_2\delta t$. Similar reasoning applies when $\mu_1 > \mu_2$ on the $x = N$ boundary.

If $x = 0$ and the first machine is under repair, the second machine cannot fail. This is because it has no material to process. Similarly, the first machine processes no material when the storage is full and the second machine is not operational. Consequently, it cannot fail.

3.9.1 Model assumptions, notation, terminology, and conventions

During time interval $(t, t + \delta t)$:

When $0 < x < N$

  1. the change in x is $(\alpha_1\mu_1 - \alpha_2\mu_2)\delta t$

2. the probability of repair of Machine i, that is, the probability that $\alpha_i(t+\delta t) = 1$ given that $\alpha_i(t) = 0$, is $r_i \delta t$

3. the probability of failure of Machine i, that is, the probability that $\alpha_i(t+\delta t) = 0$ given that $\alpha_i(t) = 1$, is $p_i \delta t$.

When $x = 0$

1. the change in x is $(\alpha_1 \mu_1 - \alpha_2 \mu_2)^+ \delta t$

   (That is, when $x = 0$, it can only increase.)

2. the probability of repair is $r_i \delta t$

3. if Machine 1 is down, Machine 2 cannot fail. If Machine 1 is up, the probability of failure of Machine 2 is $p_2^b \delta t$, where

$$p_2^b = \frac{p_2 \mu}{\mu_2} \tag{3.188}$$

$$\mu = \min(\mu_1, \mu_2). \tag{3.189}$$

This is because, when the buffer is empty, the second machine can operate no faster than the first. If the first is faster than the second, the second operates as it does normally, and the buffer is immediately not empty. If the first is slower than the second, it limits the speed of the second when the buffer is empty. We assume here that the failure rate of a machine is proportional to its operating speed (with a proportionality constant that varies from machine to machine).

The probability of failure of Machine 1 is $p_1 \delta t$.

When $x = N$

1. the change in x is $(\alpha_1 \mu_1 - \alpha_2 \mu_2)^- \delta t$

2. the probability of repair is $r_i \delta t$

3. if Machine 2 is down, Machine 1 cannot fail. If Machine 2 is up, the probability of failure of Machine 1 is $p_1^b \delta t$, where

$$p_1^b = \frac{p_1 \mu}{\mu_1}.$$

The first machine can fail only if the second is operational. The probability of failure of Machine 2 is $p_2 \delta t$.

3.9.2 Performance measures

Performance measures for continuous material lines are similar to those for exponential processing time lines. The probability that Machine M_i is processing a workpiece is termed the *efficiency*, E_i, and is given by

$$E_i = \text{prob} \left[\alpha_i = 1, x_{i-1} > 0, x_i < N_i \right]. \tag{3.190}$$

The *production rate* (throughput rate) of Machine M_i, in parts per time unit, is

$$P_i = \mu_i E_i. \tag{3.191}$$

Conservation of Flow

Since there is no creation or destruction of material, flow is conserved. That is,

$$P = P_1 = P_2 = \ldots = P_k. \tag{3.192}$$

Flow Rate-Idle Time Relationship

The *isolated efficiency* e_i of Machine M_i is, as usual,

$$e_i = \frac{r_i}{r_i + p_i} \tag{3.193}$$

and it represents the fraction of time that M_i is operational. The *isolated production rate*, ρ_i is then given by

$$\rho_i = \mu_i e_i \tag{3.194}$$

and it represents what the production rate of M_i would be if it were never impeded by other machines or buffers. The actual production rate P_i is less because of blocking and starvation.

The flow rate-idle time relation is

$$P_i = \rho_i \, \text{prob} \left[x_{i-1} > 0 \text{ and } x_i < N_i \right]. \tag{3.195}$$

In the continuous case, it is impossible for a machine to become starved and blocked simultaneously. Consequently,

$$P_i = \rho_i \left(1 - \text{prob} \left[x_{i-1} = 0 \right] - \text{prob} \left[x_i = N_i \right] \right). \tag{3.196}$$

Note that this is *not* an approximation.

3.10 Continuous Two-Machine Line

3.10.1 Transition equations

Intermediate Storage Levels When the storage is neither empty nor full, its level can rise or fall depending on the states of adjacent machines. Since it can change only a small amount during a short time interval, it is natural to use differential equations to describe its behavior.

For example, the probability of finding both machines operational with a storage level between x and $x + \delta x$ at time $t + \delta t$ is given by $f(x, 1, 1, t + \delta t)\delta x$, where

$$
\begin{aligned}
f(x, 1, 1, t + \delta t) \;=\; & (1 - (p_1 + p_2)\delta t)f(x - \mu_1\delta t + \mu_2\delta t, 1, 1, t) \\
& + r_1\delta t f(x + \mu_2\delta t, 0, 1, t) + r_2\delta t f(x - \mu_1\delta t, 1, 0, t) + o(\delta t).
\end{aligned}
$$

This is because

1. If both machines are operational at time t and the storage level is between

   $$x - \mu_1\delta t + \mu_2\delta t$$

   and

   $$x - \mu_2\delta t + \mu_2\delta t + \delta x,$$

   then there will be no failures before $t + \delta t$ with probability

   $$(1 - p_1\delta t)(1 - p_2\delta t)$$

   and, at time $t + \delta t$, the storage level will be between x and $x + \delta x$.

2. If, at time t, the first machine is under repair and the second is operational, the probability that both machines will be operational at time $t + \delta t$ is, to first order, $r_1\delta t$. During that time interval, the storage loses $\mu_2\delta t$.

3. Similarly for the third term.

Letting $\delta t \to 0$, this equation becomes

$$
\begin{aligned}
\frac{\partial f}{\partial t}(x, 1, 1) \;=\; & -(p_1 + p_2)f(x, 1, 1) + (\mu_2 - \mu_1)\frac{\partial f}{\partial x}(x, 1, 1) \\
& + r_1 f(x, 0, 1) + r_2 f(x, 1, 0)
\end{aligned}
\tag{3.197}
$$

(where the t argument is suppressed).

The other three equations that describe the internal storage behavior are

$$\frac{\partial f}{\partial t}(x,0,0) = -(r_1 + r_2)f(x,0,0) + p_1 f(x,1,0) + p_2 f(x,0,1) \tag{3.198}$$

$$\frac{\partial f}{\partial t}(x,0,1) = \mu_2 \frac{\partial f}{\partial x}(x,0,1) - (r_1 + p_2)f(x,0,1) + p_1 f(x,1,1) + r_2 f(x,0,0) \tag{3.199}$$

$$\frac{\partial f}{\partial t}(x,1,0) = -\mu_1 \frac{\partial f}{\partial x}(x,1,0) - (p_1 + r_2)f(x,1,0) + p_2 f(x,1,1) + r_1 f(x,0,0) \tag{3.200}$$

Boundary Behavior While the internal behavior of the system can be described by probability density functions, there may be a nonzero probability of finding the system in a given boundary state. For example, if $\mu_1 < \mu_2$ and both machines are operational, the level of storage tends to decrease. If both machines remain operational for enough time, the storage will be empty ($x = 0$). Once at state (0,1,1) the system will remain there until a machine fails. This behavior differs from that of an internal state (such as $(x,1,1)$, for some $x, 0 < x < N$) because there are no internal states that are very much more likely to be reached than other states, or at which the system is likely to remain for a particularly long time.

There are eight boundary states ((x,α_1,α_2) where $x = 0$ or N, $\alpha_1 = 0$ or $1, \alpha_2 = 0$ or 1) and that many equations. There are different versions of some of these equations for $\mu_1 < \mu_2, \mu_1 = \mu_2$, and $\mu_1 > \mu_2$.

Lower Boundary: $x = 0$

- *Boundary-to-Boundary Equations*

  If the system is in state (0,0,0) at time $t+\delta t$, it could have been in state (0,0,0) or state (0,1,0) at time t, if δt is sufficiently small. The (0,0,0)-(0,0,0) transition probability is $(1 - (r_1 + r_2)\delta t)$ and the (0,1,0)-(0,0,0) transition probability is $p_1 \delta t$. Thus

  $$\mathbf{p}(0,0,0,t + \delta t) = (1 - (r_1 + r_2)\delta t)\mathbf{p}(0,0,0,t) + p_1 \delta t \mathbf{p}(0,1,0,t) + o(\delta t). \tag{3.201}$$

  It is not necessary to consider transitions directly from the interior, that is, from states like $(\delta x, 0, 1)$. This is because, from such a state, either the amount of material in the buffer goes to 0 first, or the machine states go to (0,0) first. If the amount of material goes to 0, the second machine cannot fail. If the machine states go to (0,0), the buffer cannot empty. In either case, the state cannot go to (0,0,0).

  As $\delta t \to 0$, (3.201) becomes

  $$\frac{d}{dt}\mathbf{p}(0,0,0) = -(r_1 + r_2)\mathbf{p}(0,0,0) + p_1 \mathbf{p}(0,1,0). \tag{3.202}$$

  We can also conclude that

  $$\mathbf{p}(0,1,0) = 0 \tag{3.203}$$

since, if the system ever reaches that state, it leaves instantly. The buffer immediately accumulates material and the state changes. Thus, (3.202) can be further simplified, which is done below.

- *Interior-to-Boundary Equations*

To arrive at state (0,0,1) at time $t + \delta t$, the system may have been in one of four sets of states at time t. It could have been in state (0,0,0) with a repair of the second machine. It could have been in state (0,0,1) with no repair of the first machine. (The second could not have failed since it was starved.) It could have been in state (0,1,1) with the first machine failing and the second not failing. It could have been in any state $(x, 0, 1)$ where $0 < x \leq \mu_2 \delta t$ if no repair of the first machine or failure of the second occurred. If the second order terms are ignored,

$$
\begin{aligned}
\mathbf{p}(0, 0, 1, t + \delta t) \;=\;& r_2 \delta t \mathbf{p}(0, 0, 0, t) + (1 - r_1 \delta t) \mathbf{p}(0, 0, 1, t) + p_1 \delta t \mathbf{p}(0, 1, 1, t) \\
& + \int_0^{\mu_2 \delta t} f(x, 0, 1, t) dx
\end{aligned}
\tag{3.204}
$$

or,

$$
\frac{d}{dt} \mathbf{p}(0, 0, 1) = r_2 \mathbf{p}(0, 0, 0) - r_1 \mathbf{p}(0, 0, 1) + p_1 \mathbf{p}(0, 1, 1) + \mu_2 f(0, 0, 1).
\tag{3.205}
$$

The character of this and the remaining interior-to-lower boundary equation depends on whether $\mu_1 \leq \mu_2$ or $\mu_1 > \mu_2$. If $\mu_1 \leq \mu_2$, it is possible to get to (0,1,1) from (0,1,1) if no failures occur; from (0,0,1) if the first machine is repaired; and from $(x, 1, 1)$ (where $0 < x \leq (\mu_2 - \mu_1)\delta t$) if no failures occur.

Symbolically (to first order)

$$
\begin{aligned}
\mathbf{p}(0, 1, 1, t + \delta t) \;=\;& (1 - (p_1 + p_2^b)\delta t)\mathbf{p}(0, 1, 1, t) + r_1 \delta t \mathbf{p}(0, 0, 1, t) \\
& + \int_0^{(\mu_2 - \mu_1)\delta t} f(x, 1, 1, t) dx,
\end{aligned}
\tag{3.206}
$$

or,

$$
\begin{aligned}
\frac{d}{dt} \mathbf{p}(0, 1, 1) \;=\;& -(p_1 + p_2^b)\mathbf{p}(0, 1, 1) + r_1 \mathbf{p}(0, 0, 1) \\
& + (\mu_2 - \mu_1)f(0, 1, 1), \text{ if } \mu_1 \leq \mu_2.
\end{aligned}
\tag{3.207}
$$

If $\mu_1 > \mu_2$, it is not possible to get from (0,1,1) at t to (0,1,1) at $t + \delta t$, if δt is small. This is because when both machines are working, material accumulates in the buffer.

For the same reason, if the system is in state $(0,0,1)$ at time t and the first machine is repaired during $(t, t + \delta t)$, there will be some material in the buffer at time $t + \delta t$. Finally, if at t the state is $(x, 1, 1)$ and no failure occurs in $(t, t + \delta t)$, the state at $t + \delta t$ is $(x', 1, 1)$ where $x' > x$. Thus, there is no way of getting to state $(0, 1, 1)$, so

$$\mathbf{p}(0, 1, 1) = 0 \text{ if } \mu_1 > \mu_2. \tag{3.208}$$

- *Boundary-to-Interior Equations*

To be in state $(x, 1, 0)$ at time $t + \delta t$, where $0 < x < \mu_1 \delta t$, the system can either have been in an internal state at time t or at a boundary state some time during the time interval $(t, t + \delta t)$. The only possible internal states are $(x, 1, 1)$ or $(x, 0, 0)$, but their probabilities would contribute second order terms in the following equation. Accounting only for terms that are of zero'th and first order in δt:

$$\int_0^{\mu_1 \delta t} f(x, 1, 0, t + \delta t) dx = \int_t^{t+\delta t} \left(r_1 \mathbf{p}(0, 0, 0, s) + p_2^b \mathbf{p}(0, 1, 1, s) \right) ds$$
$$+ (1 - (p_1 + r_2)\delta t)\mathbf{p}(0, 1, 0, t). \tag{3.209}$$

The zero'th order term in this equation is

$$0 = \mathbf{p}(0, 1, 0, t) \tag{3.210}$$

which means that the system cannot persist in state $(0,1,0)$. If the first machine is operational and the second is not, material will instantly accumulate in the buffer. Note that (3.210) is consistent with (3.203) and that (3.202) is now

$$\frac{d}{dt}\mathbf{p}(0, 0, 0) = -(r_1 + r_2)\mathbf{p}(0, 0, 0). \tag{3.211}$$

The first order terms in (3.209) are

$$\mu_1 f(0, 1, 0) = r_1 \mathbf{p}(0, 0, 0) + p_2^b \mathbf{p}(0, 1, 1). \tag{3.212}$$

If $\mu_1 > \mu_2$, it is possible to reach state $(x, 1, 1)$ (where $0 < x \leq (\mu_1 - \mu_2)\delta t$) from the boundary. Due to (3.208) and (3.210), the balance equation is, to first order,

$$\int_0^{(\mu_1 - \mu_2)\delta t} f(x, 1, 1, t + \delta t) dx = r_1 \int_t^{t+\delta t} \mathbf{p}(0, 0, 1, s) ds \tag{3.213}$$

or,

$$(\mu_1 - \mu_2)f(0, 1, 1) = r_1 \mathbf{p}(0, 0, 1) \text{ if } \mu_1 > \mu_2. \tag{3.214}$$

If $\mu_1 \leq \mu_2$, $(x, 1, 1)$ can only be reached from states (x', α_1, α_2) where $x' \geq x$. Consequently, there is no counterpart to (3.214) if $\mu_1 \leq \mu_2$.

Upper Boundary: $x = N$

Analogous phenomena occur on the upper boundary. Therefore the transition equations are only stated and not derived here.

- *Boundary-to-Boundary Equation*

$$\frac{d}{dt}\mathbf{p}(N,0,0) = -(r_1 + r_2)\mathbf{p}(N,0,0) \tag{3.215}$$

- *Interior-to-Boundary Equations*

$$\frac{d}{dt}\mathbf{p}(N,1,0) = r_1\mathbf{p}(N,0,0) - r_2\mathbf{p}(N,1,0) + p_2\mathbf{p}(N,1,1) + \mu_1 f(N,1,0) \tag{3.216}$$

$$\frac{d}{dt}\mathbf{p}(N,1,1) = -(p_1^b + p_2)\mathbf{p}(N,1,1) + (\mu_1 - \mu_2)f(N,1,1)$$
$$+ r_2\mathbf{p}(n,1,0) \text{ if } \mu_1 \geq \mu_2 \tag{3.217}$$

$$\mathbf{p}(N,1,1) = 0 \text{ if } \mu_1 < \mu_2 \tag{3.218}$$

- *Boundary-to-Interior Equations*

$$\mathbf{p}(N,0,1) = 0 \tag{3.219}$$

$$\mu_2 f(N,0,1) = r_2\mathbf{p}(N,0,0) + p_1^b\mathbf{p}(N,1,1) \tag{3.220}$$

$$(\mu_2 - \mu_1)f(N,1,1) = r_2\mathbf{p}(N,1,0) \text{ if } \mu_1 < \mu_2 \tag{3.221}$$

Normalization   The sum of all probabilities is always 1. Thus,

$$\sum_{\alpha_1=0}^{1}\sum_{\alpha_2=0}^{1}\left[\int_0^N f(x,\alpha_1,\alpha_2)dx + \mathbf{p}(0,\alpha_1,\alpha_2) + \mathbf{p}(N,\alpha_1,\alpha_2)\right] = 1. \tag{3.222}$$

Informal Discussion of Transient Behavior   In the analysis to follow, the steady state solution of these equations is sought so that all time derivatives vanish. However, some additional explanation is required to clarify the transient behavior of this system. In a transient analysis, it should be possible to choose any positive functions $f(x,\alpha_1,\alpha_2,t)$ and positive values $\mathbf{p}(0,\alpha_1,\alpha_2,t), \mathbf{p}(N,\alpha_1,\alpha_2,t)$ at time $t = 0$ which satisfy (3.222), and to use the equations above to propagate these densities and probabilities for all $t > 0$.

This would seem to be precluded by equations such as (3.208), (3.210), and (3.212). That is, these equations seem to impose conditions that the probabilities and densities must satisfy at all times, including $t = 0$. To see that this is not the case, consider (3.209). If at $t = 0$ (3.210) is not satisfied, (3.209) says that all the probability in $\mathbf{p}(0, 1, 0)$ is transferred into $f(x, 1, 0)$ for x in the interval $(0, \mu_1 \delta t)$, where δt is small. Informally, this means that the value assigned to $\mathbf{p}(0, 1, 0)$ appears as the magnitude of an impulse in $f(x, 1, 0)$ at $x = 0$. Immediately, according to (3.210), $\mathbf{p}(0, 1, 0)$ goes to zero.

The general rule is: if a mass should be zero and is not zero initially, treat the adjacent internal density as initialized with that mass as an impulse, and replace that mass with 0 at $t = 0+$.

3.10.2   Performance measures

Production Rate   The production rate P_2 is the rate at which material leaves the second machine. When the storage is not empty and the second machine is operational, the rate is μ_2. When the storage is empty but both machines are operational, the rate is $\mu = \mu_1$. Otherwise, no material emerges from the system. Consequently,

$$P_2 = \mu_2 \left[\int_0^N (f(x, 0, 1) + f(x, 1, 1))dx + p(N, 1, 1) \right] + \mu_1 \mathbf{p}(0, 1, 1). \tag{3.223}$$

By similar reasoning, the rate that material enters the first machine is

$$P_1 = \mu_1 \left[\int_0^N (f(x, 1, 0) + f(x, 1, 1))dx + \mathbf{p}(0, 1, 1) \right] + \mu_2 \mathbf{p}(N, 1, 1). \tag{3.224}$$

In the following section, we show that these two quantities are equal, and therefore we drop the subscripts.

In-Process Inventory   The average in-process inventory is given by

$$\bar{x} = \sum_{\alpha_1=0}^1 \sum_{\alpha_2=0}^1 \left[\int_0^N x f(x, \alpha_1, \alpha_2)dx + N\mathbf{p}(N, \alpha_1, \alpha_2) \right]. \tag{3.225}$$

3.10.3   Identities

The transition equations have a steady state solution in which all time derivatives vanish. From some of the boundary equations,

$$\mathbf{p}(0, 0, 0) = \mathbf{p}(0, 1, 0) = \mathbf{p}(N, 0, 0) = \mathbf{p}(N, 0, 1) = 0 \tag{3.226}$$

and

$$\mathbf{p}(0, 1, 1) = 0 \text{ if } \mu_1 > \mu_2, \tag{3.227}$$

$$\mathbf{p}(N, 1, 1) = 0 \text{ if } \mu_1 < \mu_2. \tag{3.228}$$

The following is reminiscent of (3.41) and (3.122). Like those equations, it is used in establishing conservation of flow.

$$(\mu_2 - \mu_1)f(x, 1, 1) + \mu_2 f(x, 0, 1) - \mu_1 f(x, 1, 0) = 0, 0 \le x \le N. \tag{3.229}$$

Proof: If the steady state versions of the internal differential Equations (3.197)-(3.200) are added,

$$0 = \frac{d}{dx}\left[(\mu_2 - \mu_1)f(x,1,1) + \mu_2 f(x,0,1) - \mu_1 f(x,1,0)\right] \tag{3.230}$$

results. (The full, rather than partial, derivative symbol is used since time dependence is ignored and so x is the only continuous variable.) Therefore,

$$(\mu_2 - \mu_1)f(x,1,1) + \mu_2 f(x,0,1) - \mu_1 f(x,1,0) = K \tag{3.231}$$

where K is some constant to be determined. The proof is complete when we establish that K is 0. We can find K by evaluating (3.231) for some particular value of x, for example, $x = 0$.

If $\mu_2 > \mu_2$, Equation (3.205) is

$$r_1 \mathbf{p}(0,0,1) = \mu_2 f(0,0,1). \tag{3.232}$$

Comparing this with (3.214),

$$0 = (\mu_2 - \mu_1)f(0,1,1) + \mu_2 f(0,0,1). \tag{3.233}$$

In addition, when $\mu_1 > \mu_2$, (3.212) implies

$$\mu_1 f(0,l,0) = 0. \tag{3.234}$$

Combining this with (3.233) results in

$$(\mu_2 - \mu_1)f(x,1,1) + \mu_2 f(x,0,1) - \mu_1 f(x,1,0) = 0 \tag{3.235}$$

when $x = 0$, if $\mu_1 > \mu_2$.

If $\mu_1 \leq \mu_2$, Equation (3.235) results from combining (3.205), (3.207) and (3.212). (The corresponding result can be obtained at $x = N$ in a similar manner.) Consequently the proof is complete. A similar result was proved (3.122) for the discrete material, exponential processing time model.

Conservation of Flow

$$P_1 = P_2 \tag{3.236}$$

Proof: Subtracting (3.224) from (3.223) yields

$$P_2 - P_1 = \int_0^N \left[(\mu_2 - \mu_1)f(x,1,1) + \mu_2 f(x,0,1) - \mu_1 f(x,1,0)\right] dx. \tag{3.237}$$

Equation (3.229) implies that the integral vanishes and therefore Equation (3.236) is proved.

Blocking, Starvation, and Production Rate The probability of blocking p_b is the probability that a machine is unable to operate because its downstream buffer is full. In the two-machine case, only Machine 1 can be blocked. This probability is not simply that of the buffer being full, since production can continue (at a reduced rate if $\mu_2 < \mu_1$) if both machines are operational. Instead, it is

$$p_b = \mathbf{p}(N, 1, 0) + (1 - \frac{\mu_2}{\mu_1})\mathbf{p}(N, 1, 1). \tag{3.238}$$

Recall that if $\mu_2 > \mu_1$, $\mathbf{p}(N, 1, 1) = 0$.

Similarly, the probability of starvation is given by

$$p_s = \mathbf{p}(0, 0, 1) + (1 - \frac{\mu_1}{\mu_2})\mathbf{p}(0, 1, 1). \tag{3.239}$$

In this context, we can define *efficiency* E_i by the following:

$$E_i = \frac{P}{\mu_i}, i = 1, 2. \tag{3.240}$$

Repair frequency equals failure frequency The continuous analog of (3.39) is established here. We define

$$D_1 = \mathbf{p}(0, 0, 1) + \int_0^N (f(x, 0, 0) + f(x, 0, 1))dx, \tag{3.241}$$

$$D_2 = \mathbf{p}(N, 1, 0) + \int_0^N (f(x, 0, 0) + f(x, 1, 0))dx. \tag{3.242}$$

Then

$$p_i E_i = r_i D_i, i = 1, 2. \tag{3.243}$$

Note that D_i is the probability that Machine i is under repair.

Proof: The proof is presented for $i = 1$ only. A similar proof holds for $i = 2$. Equations (3.224), (3.223), and (3.241) imply

$$\begin{aligned}
p_1 E_1 - r_1 D_1 &= p_1 \mathbf{p}(0, 1, 1) - r_1 \mathbf{p}(0, 0, 1) \\
&+ \int_0^N [p_1(f(x, 1, 0) + f(x, 1, 1)) - r_1(f(x, 0, 0) + f(x, 0, 1))]\, dx \\
&+ p_1 \frac{\mu_2}{\mu_1}\mathbf{p}(N, 1, 1).
\end{aligned} \tag{3.244}$$

By means of (3.198) and (3.199), the integrand in (3.244) can be transformed to

$$-\mu_2 \frac{d}{dx}f(x, 0, 1).$$

Consequently, (3.244) can be written

$$p_1 E_1 - r_1 D_1 =$$

$$p_1 \mathbf{p}(0,1,1) - r_1 \mathbf{p}(0,0,1) - \mu_2(f(N,0,1) - f(0,0,1)) + p_1 \frac{\mu_2}{\mu_1} \mathbf{p}(N,1,1). \qquad (3.245)$$

This can be further transformed, by means of the steady state version of (3.205), into

$$p_1 E_1 - r_1 D_1 = -\mu_2 f(N,0,1) + p_1 \frac{\mu_2}{\mu_1} \mathbf{p}(N,1,1). \qquad (3.246)$$

In the steady state version of (3.220), $P(N,0,0)$ is 0. Therefore, (3.246) becomes

$$p_1 E_1 - r_1 D_1 = 0$$

and the proof is complete.

Flow Rate-Idle Time

$$P = \mu_1 e_1 (1 - p_b) \qquad (3.247)$$

$$P = \mu_2 e_2 (1 - p_s) \qquad (3.248)$$

where, as usual,

$$e_i = \frac{r_i}{r_i + p_i}, i = 1,2 \qquad (3.249)$$

is the isolated efficiency. This is significant for two reasons. First, it helps to justify the model. This is because

$$\rho_i = \mu_i e_i \qquad (3.250)$$

is the isolated production rate of Machine i, the rate at which material would be processed by Machine i if it were not limited by interaction with other machines and buffers (that is, by starvation or blockage). Equation (3.247) says that the production rate is the isolated production rate of the first machine times the probability it is not blocked and (3.248) has a similar interpretation.

The second reason is that (3.247) and (3.248) may prove useful in evaluating the production rate, or in decomposing larger systems.

To prove (3.247), we note that

$$E_1 + D_1 = 1 - \mathbf{p}(N,0,1) - (1 - \frac{\mu_2}{\mu_1})\mathbf{p}(N,1,1), \qquad (3.251)$$

or, from (3.238) and (3.243),

$$E_1(1 + \frac{p_1}{r_1}) = 1 - p_b \qquad (3.252)$$

from which (3.247) follows. The proof of (3.248) is similar.

Limits By letting machine parameters become very small or very large, limiting results can be obtained from (3.247) and (3.248).

If $\rho_i \to 0$, then $P \to 0, E_i \to e_i$, and $E_j \to 0, j \neq i$. (3.253)

If $\rho_i \to \infty$, then $P \to \rho_j, E_i \to 0$, and $E_j \to e_j, j \neq i$. (3.254)

- If $\rho_1 \to 0$, then $\bar{n} \to 0$.

- If $\rho_1 \to \infty$, then $\bar{n} \to N$.

- If $\rho_2 \to 0$, then $\bar{n} \to N$.

- If $\rho_2 \to \infty$, then $\bar{n} \to 0$.

The results and interpretation are identical with the exponential case (3.136) and (3.137).

3.10.4 Solution technique

It is natural to assume an exponential form for the solution to the steady state density equations, since (3.197)-(3.200) are coupled ordinary linear differential equations. A solution of the form

$$f(x, \alpha_1, \alpha_2) = C e^{\lambda x} Y_1^{\alpha_1} Y_2^{\alpha_2} \qquad (3.255)$$

(where C, λ, Y_1, Y_2 are parameters to be determined) is assumed. Expression (3.255) satisfies the steady state version of (3.197)-(3.200) if

$$\sum_{i=1}^{2} (p_i Y_i - r_i) = 0, \qquad (3.256)$$

$$-\mu_1 \lambda = (p_1 Y_1 - r_1) \frac{1 + Y_1}{Y_1} \qquad (3.257)$$

$$\mu_2 \lambda = (p_2 Y_2 - r_2) \frac{1 + Y_2}{Y_2} \qquad (3.258)$$

These are three equations in three unknowns, which are called the *parametric equations*. Different parametric equations have already been described for the deterministic and exponential cases. One solution is

$$Y_1 = \frac{r_1}{p_1}$$
$$Y_2 = \frac{r_2}{p_2}$$
$$\lambda = 0$$

By eliminating λ and Y_2 from (3.256)-(3.258), and removing a $(p_1 Y_1 - r_1)$ factor, they reduce to a single quadratic equation in Y_1:

$$-(\mu_2 - \mu_1) p_1 Y_1^2 + [(\mu_2 - \mu_1)(r_1 + r_2) - (\mu_2 p_1 + \mu_1 p_2)] Y_1 + \mu_2(r_1 + r_2) = 0. \quad (3.259)$$

Special Case: $\mu_1 = \mu_2 = \mu$ Equation (3.259) suggests that $\mu_1 = \mu_2$ is a special case since it reduces to a linear equation. In that case

$$Y_1 = \frac{r_1 + r_2}{p_1 + p_2}, \tag{3.260}$$

Equation (3.256) implies

$$Y_2 = \frac{r_1 + r_2}{p_1 + p_2}, \tag{3.261}$$

and (3.257) or (3.258) yields

$$\lambda = \frac{1}{\mu}(r_1 p_2 - r_2 p_1)(\frac{1}{p_1 + p_2} + \frac{1}{r_1 + r_2}). \tag{3.262}$$

To complete the solution, the boundary conditions yield

$$\mathbf{p}(0,0,1) = C\frac{\mu}{r_1 p_2}(r_1 + r_2) \tag{3.263}$$

$$\mathbf{p}(0,1,1) = C\frac{\mu}{p_2}\frac{r_1 + r_2}{p_1 + p_2} \tag{3.264}$$

$$\mathbf{p}(N,1,0) = C\frac{\mu}{p_1 r_2}e^{\lambda N}(r_1 + r_2) \tag{3.265}$$

$$\mathbf{p}(N,1,1) = C\frac{\mu}{p_1}e^{\lambda N}\frac{r_1 + r_2}{p_1 + p_2} \tag{3.266}$$

and C is obtained from the normalization equation (3.222).

General Case: $\mu_1 \neq \mu_2$ Here (3.255) is replaced by a sum of two terms corresponding to the two solutions Y_{1j} of (3.259):

$$f(x,\alpha_1,\alpha_2) = \sum_{j=1}^{2} C_j e^{\lambda_j x}Y_{1j}^{\alpha_1}Y_{2j}^{\alpha_2}. \tag{3.267}$$

This is the usual approach to solving ordinary differential equation problems. The Y_{ij} and λ_j parameters are obtained from (3.256) and (3.257) or (3.258).

Because of the nature of the boundary conditions, two cases must be considered.

$\mu_1 > \mu_2$ From (3.208),

$$\mathbf{p}(0,1,1) = 0. \tag{3.268}$$

Equation (3.214) implies

$$\mathbf{p}(0,0,1) = \frac{\mu_1 - \mu_2}{r_1}\sum_{j=1}^{2} C_j Y_{1j}Y_{2j}. \tag{3.269}$$

Equation (3.212) requires that $f(0, 1, 0) = 0$ or

$$\sum_{j=1}^{2} C_j Y_{1j} = 0. \tag{3.270}$$

Since $\mu_2 < \mu_1$, Equation (3.220) is

$$\mathbf{p}(N, 1, 1) = \frac{\mu_1}{p_1} f(N, 0, 1) \tag{3.271}$$

or

$$\mathbf{p}(N, 1, 1) = \frac{\mu_1}{p_1} \sum_{j=1}^{2} C_j e^{\lambda_j N} Y_{2j}. \tag{3.272}$$

From (3.216) we find

$$\mathbf{p}(N, 1, 0) = \frac{\mu_1}{r_2 p_1}(r_1 + r_2) \sum_{j=1}^{2} C_j e^{\lambda_j N}. \tag{3.273}$$

Not all of the boundary equations have been used in deriving these expressions. These expressions do, however, satisfy all of them.

To obtain the constants C_1 and C_2, two linear equations are needed. One is (3.270). The other is the normalization equation. If all the indicated integrals and sums in (3.222) are performed, it reduces to an equation of the form

$$A_1 C_1 + A_2 C_2 = 1 \tag{3.274}$$

where A_j depends on the problem data, $j = 1, 2$. Equations (3.270) and (3.274) determine C_1 and C_2 and thus the solution is complete. A special situation arises if $\lambda_1 = \lambda_2$. A solution to (3.259) is

$$Y_{1j} = \frac{r_1}{p_1}$$

which implies that

$$Y_{2j} = \frac{r_2}{p_2}$$

and $\lambda_j = 0$. This solution always has coefficient $C_j = 0$.

$\mu_1 < \mu_2$ The analysis for this case is similar. The densities are given by (3.267). The boundary probabilities are

$$\mathbf{p}(0, 0, 1) = \frac{\mu_2}{r_1 p_2}(r_1 + r_2) \sum_{j=1}^{2} C_j \tag{3.275}$$

$$\mathbf{p}(0,1,1) = \frac{\mu_2}{p_2} \sum_{j=1}^{2} C_j Y_{1j} \tag{3.276}$$

$$\mathbf{p}(N,1,0) = \frac{\mu_2 - \mu_1}{r_2} \sum_{j=1}^{2} C_j e^{\lambda_j N} Y_{1j} Y_{2j} \tag{3.277}$$

$$\mathbf{p}(N,1,1) = 0 \tag{3.278}$$

Here, C_1 and C_2 are determined from (3.274) and (3.277), where $A_j, j = 1, 2$, are determined from (3.222), (3.267), and (3.275)-(3.277). Similar comments to those after (3.274) apply here when $\lambda_1 = \lambda_2$.

Production rate   The production rate can be evaluated from (3.223) or (3.224). However, it is easier to use (3.247) or (3.248) where p_b and p_s are given by (3.238) and (3.239).

In-process inventory   If $\mu_1 = \mu_2$ and $\lambda \neq 0$, (3.225) becomes

$$\bar{x} = C \left(\frac{1+Y}{\lambda}\right)^2 \left[e^{\lambda N}(\lambda N - 1) + 1\right] + N(\mathbf{p}(N,1,0) + \mathbf{p}(N,1,1)). \tag{3.279}$$

If $\mu_1 = \mu_2$ and $\lambda = 0$, this must be replaced by

$$\bar{x} = \frac{C}{2} \left(N(1+Y)\right)^2 + N(\mathbf{p}(N,1,0) + \mathbf{p}(N,1,1)). \tag{3.280}$$

If $\mu_1 \neq \mu_2$, the average in-process inventory is

$$\bar{x} = \sum_{j=1}^{2} C_j \left(\frac{1+Y_{1j}}{\lambda_j}\right) \left(\frac{1+Y_{2j}}{\lambda_j}\right) \left[e^{\lambda_j N}(\lambda_j N - 1) + 1\right] \tag{3.281}$$

$$+ N(\mathbf{p}(N,1,0) + \mathbf{p}(N,1,1)) \tag{3.282}$$

as long as both $\lambda_j \neq 0$. If λ_1 or λ_2 is zero, the corresponding term in the summation must be replaced by

$$\frac{C_j}{2} N^2 (1 + Y_{1j})(1 + Y_{2j}). \tag{3.283}$$

3.10.5 Numerical results and qualitative observations

Graphs of performance of the continuous material, two-machine line appear in Figures 3.12, 3.13, 3.14, 3.15, and 3.16. The system parameters are exactly the same as in the exponential processing time lines whose performance appears in the same graphs.

Figures 3.12 and 3.13 show the effects of buffer size on production rate P and average buffer level $\bar{x}$. Figures 3.14 and 3.15 show the effects of Machine 2 service rate on system production rate and average buffer level. Figure 3.16 shows the effects of Machine 1 repair rate on average buffer level.

In comparing the exponential and continuous graphs, we observe that they are very similar, except that the continuous graphs seem to change more abruptly. Corresponding exponential graphs seem to be smoother. Numerically, they are fairly close except for Figure 3.16. When r_1 is large, the limiting average buffer level in the exponential case is less than 15, whereas in the continuous case it is very close to 20. *Can you think of an intuitive explanation for the difference?*

Relationship between Deterministic and Continuous Models Figure 3.17 is a graph of deterministic processing time results. Each point is the production rate of a two-machine line in which

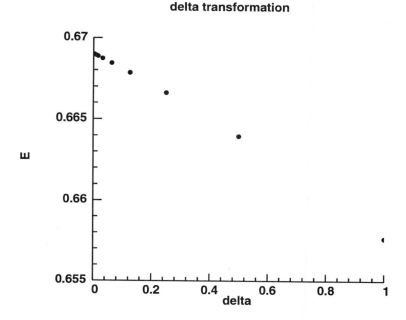

Figure 3.17: Relationship between Deterministic and Continuous Models

$$r_1' = r_1\Delta$$
$$p_1' = p_1\Delta$$
$$r_2' = r_2\Delta$$
$$p_2' = p_2\Delta$$
$$N' = \frac{N}{\Delta}$$

and

$$r_1 = 0.2$$
$$p_1 = 0.05$$
$$r_2 = 0.15$$
$$p_2 = 0.05$$
$$N = 4$$

and Δ takes a different value for each point. In each case, $1/\Delta$ is an integer. This set of points evidently approaches a limit as $\Delta \to 0$. In fact, it can be shown (Gershwin and Schick, 1980) that the limit is given by the production rate of a continuous time line whose parameters are r_1, p_1, r_2, p_2, and N as above, and $\mu_1 = \mu_2 = 1$.

The reason for this is that the pieces in a $r_1', p_1', r_2', p_2', N'$ system are like the pieces in a r_1, p_1, r_2, p_2, N system broken into $1/\Delta$ smaller pieces. The number of pieces that can fit in the buffer ($N' = N/\Delta$) is larger, but the processing time is smaller. Therefore, the probability of an event during the smaller processing time (r_i' and p_i') is smaller. In the limit, the material is much like a fluid.

Reading Assignment: Read Wijngaard (1979). Compare the two-machine model with the one described here.

3.11   Research Problems

While there has been a great deal of research on transfer lines, there is still plenty of work to do. For example,

1. Study *mixed lines*: lines in which the machines are described by different models. Also consider line with machines that have multiple failure modes.

2. For Markov process models of transfer lines with more than two machines, demonstrate conservation of flow and the flow rate-idle time relationship by using the transition or balance equations. Devise proof techniques that will be useful for new models of lines, such as those developed for the first research problem.

3. Note how the points in Figure 3.17 appear to form a straight line. Find the slope of this line. This would allow a much better approximation than simply using the continuous model instead of the deterministic processing time model. (The intercept is determined by the continuous limit, when $\Delta \to 0$.) Extend the analysis to a similar limit for the exponential processing time line.

4. Jacobs and Meerkov (1993) study *due time performance*, the frequency with which a production system meets production commitments. This is an important performance measure, which is closely related to production variance, and which has been inexplicably neglected. It should be studied extensively.

Other research problems are suggested in Dallery and Gershwin (1992).

Exercises

1. Generalize (3.2) and (3.3) by deriving E for a manufacturing system in which some machines have operation dependent failures and others have time dependent failures.

2. Demonstrate (3.12).

3. Show that $(N, 0, 0)$, $(N, 0, 1)$, $(N, 1, 1)$, and $(N - 1, 0, 1)$ are transient in the deterministic processing time two-machine line.

4. Write the transition equations for two-machine deterministic processing time lines in which $N = 1, 2$, and 3. Draw the state transition graphs.

5. Prove (3.37) in a different way. Add Equations (3.25) and (3.26) to get an expression for $\mathbf{p}(n, 0, 0) + \mathbf{p}(n - 1, 0, 1), n = 2, \ldots, N - 2$. *(Be careful!)* Add another pair of equations to get an expression for $\mathbf{p}(1, 0, 0) + \mathbf{p}(0, 0, 1)$. Similarly find an expression for $\mathbf{p}(N - 1, 0, 0) + \mathbf{p}(N - 2, 0, 1)$. Now add them all up, and the result follows.

6. Prove the equation analogous to (3.39) for Machine 2.

7. Verify (3.63) and (3.64) by plugging (3.63) and (3.64) into (3.65) and the result into (3.25)-(3.28).

8. Verify that if $e_1 = e_2$, the two sets of solutions, (3.63) and (3.64), are the same. What does this imply about the solution (3.65)?

9. In the analytic solution of the two-machine deterministic processing time line, how are C_1 and C_2 determined if $e_1 = e_2$?

10. Demonstrate that (3.24) is satisfied by (3.69)-(3.88).

11. Derive the upper boundary probabilities of the two-machine deterministic processing time line.

12. For the two-machine deterministic processing time line, prove

$$E = e_2(1 - p_s).$$

13. For the two-machine deterministic processing time line, prove that if $e_1 > e_2$, then $X > 1$. Also, prove that if $e_1 < e_2$, then $X < 1$. Prove that if $X = 1$, $r_1/p_1 = r_2/p_2$.

14. Write a computer program (in any language you choose) to evaluate the two-machine deterministic processing time line. Using X, Y_1, and Y_2 from (3.86)-(3.88), find the *unnormalized* probabilities by ignoring C in (3.69)-(3.85). Finally, calculate C by satisfying the normalization condition. Evaluate E and $\bar{n}$. Debug your program by comparing results with the graphs.

15. Write a computer program to *simulate* the deterministic processing time line. Do not restrict it to two-machine lines. Evaluate E and $\bar{n}_i$. Compare results with the program written for Exercise 14. Compare the speeds of the two programs, when you run the simulation long enough to reduce the error to acceptable results. Try the following line design problem using the simulation rather than the analytic program, and decide if simulation is practical for this.

16. Generalize the simulation program of Exercise 15 to include a nonzero minimum buffer level (n_i^{min}). That is, buffer levels are not allowed to be less than some minimum value. If Buffer $i - 1$ reaches that value (if $n_i = n_i^{min}$), Machine i is not allowed to work until n_i increases. By means of simulation experiments, show that the production rate depends only on the difference between the minimum and the maximum buffer level (n_i^{max}), and therefore that the production rate is the same as if the minimum buffer level were 0 and the maximum level were $N_i = n_i^{max} - n_i^{min}$. What can you say about the average buffer level? Show experimentally that if the minimum and maximum buffer levels are the same, the production rate is the same as for lines with buffers of size 0, and that Equation (3.2) predicts the production rate. This demonstrates that buffers are useful only when their levels are allowed to vary. Can you state and solve the transition equations for a two- machine line with a nonzero buffer level?

17. Using the program written for Exercise 14, recommend the cheapest configuration of a two-machine deterministic processing time line. We can run the line at a speed (that is, operational machine speed) of 1 part per minute or 2 parts per minute. The demand on the system requires a long run production rate of .58 parts per minute.

If we run it at 1 part per minute, we have a choice of two models for the first machine: one with $(r, p) = (.01, .008)$ and a cost of \$10,000; and one with $(r, p) = (.01, .006)$ and a cost of \$20,000. There is only one model available for the second machine, and its parameters are $(r, p) = (.01, .006)$ and its cost is \$20,000.

If we run it at 2 parts per minute, we have a choice of two models for the first machine: one with $(r, p) = (.005, .009)$ and a cost of \$20,000; and one with $(r, p) = (.005, .007)$ and a cost of \$30,000. There is only one model available for the second machine, and its parameters are $(r, p) = (.005, .007)$ and its cost is \$30,000. Assuming that both machines must operate at the same speed, what is the optimal combination of machines and buffer sizes if parts cost \$50 each? What is it if parts cost \$70 each? \$400? Here, we interpret optimal as meaning that the system is able to meet the specified demand rate, and the sum of capital cost and inventory holding cost is minimized.

18. Prove the equation analogous to (3.119) for Machine 2.

19. Using the program of Exercise 14 see if you can observe a relationship between $\bar{n}$ and $\bar{n}'$ in the relationship between the deterministic and continuous models of Section 3.10.5.

20. Derive equations for the deterministic processing time two-machine line with the *opposite convention* from Assumption 12.

21. Write a computer program to evaluate the two-machine exponential processing time line. Calculate X_j, Y_{1j}, and Y_{2j} from (3.152)-(3.157) and (3.139) and (3.140). Calculate c_j from (3.164)-(3.166). Evaluate E and $\bar{n}$. Debug your program by comparing results with the graphs.

22. Prove (3.243) for Machine 2.

23. Write a computer program to evaluate the two-machine continuous material line using the method of Section 3.10.4. Be careful to consider all cases. Evaluate E and $\bar{n}$. Debug your program by comparing results with the graphs.

24. Let $\mu_1 = \mu_2 = 1$. For what values of r_i and p_i and N are the results (E and $\bar{n}$) of the exponential model close to those of the deterministic processing time model? (That is, use the same r_i and p_i in both models, even though they are probabilities in the deterministic processing time model and rates in the exponential model.) Find some values by numerical experimentation, and interpret them.

25. Repeat Exercise 24 for the deterministic processing time and continuous material models.

26. For what values of μ_i, r_i, and p_i and N are the results of the continuous model close to those of the exponential model? Find some values by numerical experimentation, and interpret them.

27. Consider a continuous material, exponential repair and failure, two-machine transfer line model. Let $\mu_1 = 2400/\text{day}$ and $\mu_2 = 2100/\text{day}$. Assume that the second machine never fails. (For computation purposes, let $p_2 = 1.0 \times 10^{-5}$ and $r_2 = 1.0$.)

Graph P *vs.* r_1, in which p_1 varies with r_1 such that

$$e_1 = \frac{r_1}{r_1 + p_1} = 0.9$$

Let the range be $0.9 \times 10^{-3} \leq r_1 \leq 0.9 \times 10^{-1}$. Draw one graph with $N = 3500$, a second with $N=35,000$, and the third with $N=175,000$.

Graph N *vs.* r_1, in which N is chosen to maintain $P =2000$/day. Use the same range for r_1, and calculate p_1 the same way.

What does this say about the effect of variability on production rate, even when e is kept constant?

What does this say about the amount of storage space necessary to maintain a production rate, for differing levels of variability?

Suppose the units are not parts but *calories*. Suppose we are not contemplating a set of manufacturing systems, but rather a set of *people*. Suppose the first machine represents the variability of supply of *food*, and the second represents *human energy consumption*. Suppose that the buffer represents *body fat*, at 3500 calories per pound. Finally, suppose humans need 2000 calories/day on average to survive.

What does this problem say about the body fat of people who survive in various environments? That is, how much body fat does a person need to carry in order to survive droughts that occur once every 2.7 years (1000 days), on the average, and last about 3.7 months (100 days), on the average? On the other hand, how much fat is needed to survive one-day interruptions of food supply that occur about once every 10 days?

28. Transfer line design. The Tech Manufacturing Company is contemplating the acquisition of a transfer line to make its highly successful Tech-o-Tronic brand of desktop widgets.

    The making of widgets is a two-step process. It requires rough drilling, and finished reaming. Several different vendors have been invited to submit bids for the machines and buffer that will make up the line.

    It is your job to pick the least expensive combination of machines and buffers that produces the required production rate of 5.5 parts per hour. Which of the following machines should the company purchase, and what size buffer should it have to minimize cost? Use one of the computer programs written for the earlier exercises. Justify your answer. An answer within 1% of the optimum will be judged correct.

    The following is a summary of the information supplied by the vendors.

    The ALPHA Machine Tool Company has a rough drilling machine that costs $25,000 that can do 0.11 operations per minute on the average and has a mean time to fail of 40 working hours and a mean time to repair of 2 hours.

    The ALPHA Machine Tool Company has a final reaming machine that costs $50,000 that can do 6.3 operations per hour on the average and has a mean time to fail of 50 working hours and a mean time to repair of 2 hours.

    The BETA Machine Tool Company has a rough drilling machine that costs $20,000 that can do an average of 1 operation per 10 minutes and has a mean time to fail of

15 hours of operation and a mean time to repair of 180 minutes.

The BETA Machine Tool Company has a final reaming machine that costs $45,000 that can do an average of 6 operations per hour and has a mean time to fail of 200 operations and a mean time to repair of 2 hours.

The GAMMA Machine Tool Company has a machine that can do both rough drilling and final reaming. It costs $80,000 and can process (perform both operations on) an average of 1 part per 10 minutes and has a mean time to fail of 40 hours and a mean time to repair of 2 hours.

Assume that the buffer space is free but the value of parts in storage between the drilling and reaming stages is $1,000 per part.

In the optimal line, what is the average lead (cycle) time? *Hint:* See Chapter 1.

29. Consider deterministic processing time Transfer Line L in which $r_1 = .09$, $p_1 = .01$, $N = 10$, $r_2 = .1$, and $p_2 = .1$; and Transfer Line L' which is the same as Transfer Line L except that $r_1' = .001$, $p_1' = .0001$. Note that the isolated efficiencies of the first machines satisfy $e_1 < e_1'$. If we evaluate the line efficiencies, we find that $E = .4909$ and $E' = .4776$, so $E > E'$. (Verify your computer program, if you wrote one, with these numbers.) Explain this apparent paradox: how can line efficiency go down when the efficiency of one machine goes up and the other machine and the buffer stay the same?

Bibliography

[1] T. Altiok and S. Stidham Jr. (1982), "A Note on Transfer Lines with Unreliable Machines, Random Processing Times, and Finite Buffers," *IIE Transactions*, Vol. 14, No. 2, pp. 125-127.

[2] J. A. Buzacott (1967), "Automatic Transfer Lines with Buffer Stocks," *International Journal of Production Research*, Vol. 5, No. 3, pp. 183-200.

[3] J. A. Buzacott (1972), "The Effect of Station Breakdown and Random Processing Times on the Capacity of Flow Lines with In-Process Storage," *AIIE Transactions*, Vol. 4, No. 4, 308-312.

[4] J. A. Buzacott and L. E. Hanifin (1978), "Models of Automatic Transfer Lines with Inventory Banks — A Review and Comparison," *AIIE Transactions*, Vol. 10, No. 2, 197-207.

[5] J. A. Buzacott and J. G. Shanthikumar (1993), *Stochastic Models of Manufacturing Systems*, Prentice Hall, 1993.

[6] Y. Dallery and S. B. Gershwin (1992), "Manufacturing Flow Line Systems: A Review of Models and Analytical Results," *Queueing Systems Theory and Applications, Special Issue on Queueing Models of Manufacturing Systems*, Volume 12, No. 1-2, December, 1992, pp. 3-94.

[7] S. B. Gershwin (1993), "Variance of Output of a Tandem Production System," *Queuing Networks with Finite Capacity*, Proceedings of the Second International Workshop held in Research Triangle Park, North Carolina, May 28-29, 1992, Edited by R. Onvural and I Akyldiz, Elsevier, to appear.

[8] S. B. Gershwin and O. Berman (1978), "Analysis of Transfer Lines Consisting of Two Unreliable Machines with Random Processing Times and a Finite Storage Buffer," Massachusetts Institute of Technology Laboratory for Information and Decision Systems Report ESL-R-834-7, 1978.

[9] S. B. Gershwin and O. Berman (1981), "Analysis of Transfer Lines Consisting of Two Unreliable Machines with Random Processing Times and Finite Storage Buffers," *AIIE Transactions*, Vol. 13, No. 1, March, 1981, pp. 2-11.

[10] S. B. Gershwin and I. C. Schick (1983), "Modeling and Analysis of Three-Stage Transfer Lines with Unreliable Machines and Finite Buffers," *Operations Research,* Vol. 31, No. 2, March-April, 1983, pp. 354-380.

[11] S. B. Gershwin and I. C. Schick (1980), "Continuous Model of an Unreliable Two-Stage Material Flow System with a Finite Interstage Buffer," Massachusetts Institute of Technology Laboratory for Information and Decision Systems Report LIDS-R-1039, September, 1980.

[12] D. Jacobs and S. M. Meerkov (1993), "Due Time Performance in Lean and Mass Manufacturing Environments," University of Michigan Department of Electrical Engineering and Computer Science Report No. CGR-93-5, February, 1993.

[13] J. D. C. Little (1961) "A Proof for the Queuing Formula: $L = \lambda W$," *Operations Research,* Volume 9, Number 3, pp. 383-387.

[14] C. M. Strosser, "Diagnosis of Production Shortfall in a Transfer Line by Means of Analytic and Simulation Methods," MIT Master's Thesis, May, 1991.

[15] J. Wijngaard (1979), "The Effect of Interstage Buffer Storage the Output of Two Unreliable Production Units in Series, with Different Production Rates," *AIIE Transactions* Vol. 11, No. 1, 42-47.

Chapter 4

Decomposition of Long Transfer Lines

4.1 Introduction

The two-machine lines of Chapter 3 can be solved analytically, and this means that fast computer programs can be written to determine production rates, average in-process inventories, and other measures. However, no such exact analytical solution exists for longer lines (Figure 4.1[1]), and brute force numerical techniques are unsatisfactory because of the sizes of the state spaces.

In this chapter, we describe approximate decomposition methods for long deterministic processing time lines and long exponentially distributed repair-failure-processing time lines. These methods are based on a representation of a $(k-1)$-buffer system by $k-1$ single-buffer

---

[1]Reprinted with permission from *Operations Research*, Vol. 35, No. 2, 1987, copyright 1987, Operations Research Society of America. No further reproduction permitted without the consent of the copyright owner.

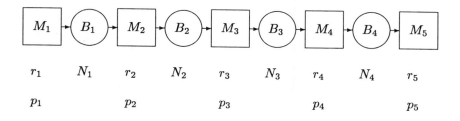

Figure 4.1: Five-Machine Deterministic Processing Time Flow Line

systems. The parameters of the single-buffer systems are determined by relationships among the flows through the buffers of the original system. A simple algorithm is developed to calculate the parameters. Numerical and simulation experience indicate that the method determines throughput and average buffer levels accurately, although analytic proofs and bounds are not available. In Sections 4.2 and 4.3, we discuss the decomposition equations for the two transfer line models. In Section 4.2.2, we present solution techniques for the equations. For an analysis of a continuous model of a long transfer line, see Dallery, David, and Xie (1989).

Consider Figure 4.2[2], a set of two-machine lines $L(i), i = 1, \ldots, k-1$. Their buffers have the same sizes as those of L in Figure 4.1. Pseudo-machine $M_u(i)$ models the part of the line upstream of B_i and $M_d(i)$ models the part of line downstream from B_i. We seek the parameters of the pseudo-machines so that the behavior of the material flow in the buffers of the two-machine lines closely matches that of the flow in the buffers of the long line. That is, parameters are chosen so that:

1. The rate of flow into and out of Buffer B_i in line $L(i)$ approximates that of Buffer B_i in line L.

2. The probability of the buffer of line $L(i)$ being empty or full is close to that of B_i in L being empty or full.

3. The probability of resumption of flow into (and out of) the buffer in line L(i) in a time interval after a period during which it was interrupted is close to the probability of the corresponding event in L.

4. Finally, the average amount of material in the buffer of line $L(i)$ approximates the material level in Buffer B_i in L.

In order to find such parameter values, we use relationships among parameters and measures of a transfer line. In analyzing the deterministic processing time model, we find repair and failure probabilities $r_u(1)$, $p_u(1)$, $r_d(1)$, $p_d(1)$, $r_u(2)$, $p_u(2)$, etc. For the exponential model, we must find repair, failure, and processing time rates $r_u(1)$, $p_u(1)$, $\mu_u(1)$, $r_d(1)$, $p_d(1)$, $\mu_d(1)$, $r_u(2)$, $p_u(2)$, $\mu_u(2)$, etc.

Justification   Figures 4.3[3], 4.4[4], 4.5[5], and 4.6[6] contain data from a set of simulations of two-machine deterministic processing time transfer lines (Schick, 1978; Schick and Gershwin, 1978). The machine parameters are $r_1 = r_2 = .2$, $p_1 = .1$, and $p_2 = .05$. Different simulations were performed with different buffer sizes: 4, 8, and 16. The horizontal axes of Figures 4.3-4.5 represent durations of intervals in which parts emerged from the second

---

[2]Reprinted with permission from *Operations Research*, Vol. 35, No. 2, 1987, copyright 1987, Operations Research Society of America. No further reproduction permitted without the consent of the copyright owner.

[3]with permission of the Massachusetts Institute of Technology

[4]with permission of the Massachusetts Institute of Technology

[5]with permission of the Massachusetts Institute of Technology

[6]with permission of the Massachusetts Institute of Technology

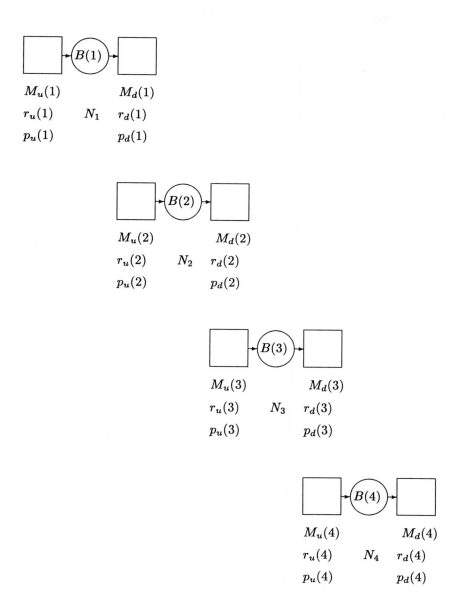

Figure 4.2: Deterministic Processing Time Transfer Line Decomposition

machine without a break. That is, 30 depicts an interval of length 30 in which exactly 30 parts were made. A part was not made on the last time step before the interval or on the first time step after it. The horizontal axis of Figure 4.6 represents the durations of interruptions, intervals in which parts were not produced. The vertical axes show the frequencies that intervals of these lengths appeared in the simulations.

The fact that the points line up very close to straight lines suggest that the output production intervals and interruption intervals have distributions which are very close to geometric. As a consequence, an observer who could only see the graphs (but not the system that produced them) would have no way of telling whether the graphs were generated by a two-machine line, or by a single machine in isolation.

This suggests that if another buffer and machine were added to the two-machine line, that buffer would experience the same behavior as if it were connected to a single machine. In that case, analyzing a three-machine, two-buffer line reduces to (1) analyzing the first two-machine, one-buffer subsystem, (2) determining the parameters of an equivalent machine, and (3) analyzing the two-machine system that consists of the equivalent machine, the second buffer, and the third machine. That is, only two-machine systems would have to be studied. Analyzing a longer line would involve more of the same steps, and also only two-machine systems.

In fact, the methods described in this chapter are a little more complicated (and probably more accurate) than that because they consider the corresponding intervals at the first machine, and their effects on the upstream buffers. However, they only involve the analysis of two-machine lines. Note that we were not able to distinguish among the distributions of interruption durations corresponding to different buffer sizes. This was attributed to the fact that the repair probabilities of the two machines were the same.

Notation   In the following, integer subscripts refer to machines and buffers in the original, or real, line. When an integer appears in parentheses, it refers to the indicated two-machine line. For example, $p_s(i-1)$ is the probability of starvation in $L(i-1)$. It is the fraction of time that $B(i-1)$ is empty and $M_d(i-1)$ is unable to work because of it. It is approximately the probability that B_{i-1} is empty. In many cases, we use B_i and $B(i)$ interchangeably. Other subscripts include u and d for upstream and downstream; and s and b for starvation and blocking.

4.2   Deterministic Processing Time Model

4.2.1   Equations

We assume that the random behaviors governing flow into and out of B_i can be characterized by four geometrically distributed random variables with parameters $p_u(i), r_u(i), p_d(i)$, and $r_d(i)$. The key to the decomposition method is to find these parameters so that the material flow into and out of the buffers of the two-machine lines closely matches the flow into and out of the corresponding buffers of the long line L. Because there are four parameters

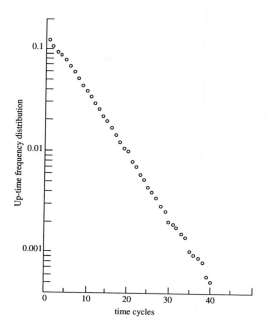

Figure 4.3: Up-Time Frequency Distribution for a Two-Machine Line with $N = 4$

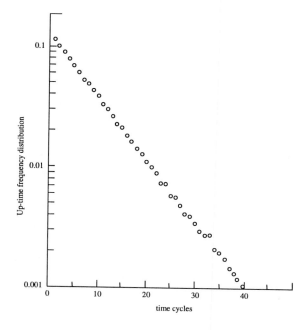

Figure 4.4: Up-Time Frequency Distribution for a Two-Machine Line with $N = 8$

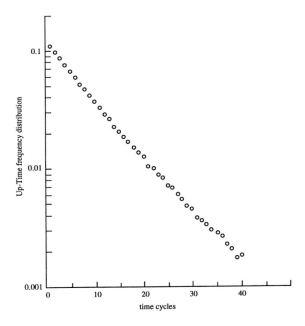

Figure 4.5: Up-Time Frequency Distribution for a Two-Machine Line with $N = 16$

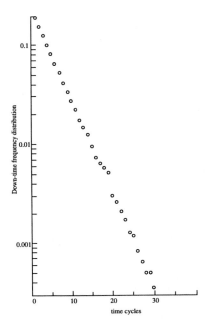

Figure 4.6: Down-Time Frequency Distribution for a Two-Machine Line

per two-machine line (per buffer in the long line), four equations per buffer, or $4(k-1)$ conditions, are required to determine them.

The decomposition method is based on the equation of conservation of flow, the flow rate-idle time relationship, and the resumption of flow equations developed below. The approach is to characterize the most important features of the transfer line in a simple approximate way, and to find a solution to the resulting set of equations.

Let $E(i)$ be the efficiency or production rate of two-machine line $L(i)$. Let $p_s(i)$ be the probability of starving $M_d(i)$ and let $p_b(i)$ be the probability of blocking $M_u(i)$. $E(i), p_s(i)$, and $p_b(i)$ are functions of the four unknowns $r_u(i), p_u(i), r_d(i), p_d(i)$ through the two-machine line formulas.

Conservation of Flow   One set of conditions is related to conservation of flow:

$$E(i) = E(1), i = 2, \ldots, k-1. \tag{4.1}$$

Flow Rate-Idle Time   The second set of conditions follows from the approximate flow rate-idle time relationship (3.19),

$$E(i) = e_i \left(1 - p_s(i-1) - p_b(i)\right), i = 2, \ldots, k-1. \tag{4.2}$$

In two-machine lines $L(i-1)$ and $L(i)$, the two-machine flow rate-idle time relationships (3.42), (3.43) are

$$E(i) = e_u(i) \left[1 - p_b(i)\right]$$

and

$$E(i-1) = e_d(i-1) \left[1 - p_s(i-1)\right].$$

These can be written

$$p_s(i-1) = 1 - \frac{E(i-1)}{e_d(i-1)}$$

$$p_b(i) = 1 - \frac{E(i)}{e_u(i)}$$

Then (4.2) becomes

$$E(i) = e_i \left(\frac{E(i-1)}{e_d(i-1)} + \frac{E(i)}{e_u(i)} - 1 \right), i = 2, \ldots, k-1, \tag{4.3}$$

or, since $E(i-1) = E(i)$,

$$1 = e_i \left(\frac{1}{e_d(i-1)} + \frac{1}{e_u(i)} - \frac{1}{E(i)} \right), i = 2, \ldots, k-1. \tag{4.4}$$

Finally, we observe that

$$\frac{1}{e_d(i-1)} = \frac{p_d(i-1) + r_d(i-1)}{r_d(i-1)}$$

$$\frac{1}{e_u(i)} = \frac{p_u(i) + r_u(i)}{r_u(i)}$$

which implies that (4.4) can be written

$$\frac{p_d(i-1)}{r_d(i-1)} + \frac{p_u(i)}{r_u(i)} = \frac{1}{E(i)} + \frac{1}{e_i} - 2, i = 2, \ldots, k-1. \tag{4.5}$$

Resumption of Flow   In the following, we derive a set of equations of the form

$$r_u(i) = r_u(i-1)X(i) + r_i(1 - X(i)), i = 2, \ldots, k-1 \tag{4.6}$$

$$r_d(i-1) = r_d(i)Y(i) + r_i(1 - Y(i)), i = 2, \ldots, k-1 \tag{4.7}$$

which show the relationship between repair probabilities in neighboring two-machine lines and in the original line. To characterize the repair probabilities in the two-machine lines, we consider the meaning of failure and repair in those systems.

Pseudo-machine $M_u(i)$ in line $L(i)$ represents, to Buffer B_i, everything upstream of B_i in line L. Thus, at time t,

$$\left.\begin{array}{l} \{\alpha_u(i) = 1\} \text{ iff } \{\alpha_i(t) = 1\} \text{ and } \{n_{i-1}(t-1) > 0\} \\[2mm] \{\alpha_u(i) = 0\} \text{ iff } \{\alpha_i(t) = 0\} \text{ or } \{n_{i-1}(t-1) = 0\} \end{array}\right\} \tag{4.8}$$

Note that $\{\alpha_u(i)$ and $\{n_i(t-1) < N_i\}\}$ is very much like $\mathcal{I}_{ui}$ of Section 3.5.1.

A failure of $M_u(i)$ represents either a failure of machine M_i or the emptying of Buffer B_{i-1}. The emptying of B_{i-1}, in turn, is due to a failure of M_{i-1} or the emptying of B_{i-2}. That is, the emptying of B_{i-1} is due to a failure of $M_u(i-1)$. A failure of $M_u(i)$ therefore results from either a failure of machine M_i or a failure of $M_u(i-1)$. The repair of $M_u(i)$ is the termination of whichever condition was in effect. Consequently, the probability of repair of $M_u(i)$ is r_i if the cause of failure is the failure of M_i and it is $r_u(i-1)$ otherwise. This leads to Equation (4.6), in which $X(i)$ is the conditional probability that $M_u(i-1)$ is down given that $M_u(i)$ is down.

We now make this more precise. The probability that M_i produces a part at time $t+1$ given that it did not produce and was not blocked at time t is

$$r_u(i) = \text{prob } [n_{i-1}(t) > 0 \text{ and } \alpha_i(t+1) = 1 \,|$$

$$\{n_{i-1}(t-1) = 0 \text{ or } \alpha_i(t) = 0\} \text{ and } n_i(t-1) < N_i]. \tag{4.9}$$

We have made an important assumption here: that $r_u(i)$ is independent of t. This is the assumption that the lengths of time intervals in which no material appears at B_i is distributed geometrically.

To analyze this expression, we analyze

$$\text{prob }(U|V \text{ or } W) = \frac{\text{prob }(U \text{ and } (V \text{ or } W))}{\text{prob }(V \text{ or } W)} = \frac{\text{prob }((U \text{ and } V) \text{ or } (U \text{ and } W))}{\text{prob }(V \text{ or } W)}$$

where U, V, and W are events. If we assume that V and W are disjoint, then $(U \text{ or } V)$ and $(U \text{ or } W)$ are disjoint. As a consequence,

$$\text{prob }(U|V \text{ or } W) = \frac{\text{prob }(U \text{ and } V)}{\text{prob }(V \text{ or } W)} + \frac{\text{prob }(U \text{ and } W)}{\text{prob }(V \text{ or } W)}.$$

To analyze the first term, note that

$$\text{prob }(U \text{ and } V) = \text{prob }(U|V)\text{prob }(V)$$

and

$$\text{prob }(V|V \text{ or } W) = \frac{\text{prob }(V \text{ and } (V \text{ or } W))}{\text{prob }(V \text{ or } W)} = \frac{\text{prob }(V)}{\text{prob }(V \text{ or } W)}$$

and the second term is similar. Consequently,

$$\text{prob }(U|V \text{ or } W) = \quad \text{prob }(U|V)\text{prob }(V|V \text{ or } W)$$

$$+\text{prob }(U|W)\text{prob }(W|V \text{ or } W). \tag{4.10}$$

Let

$$
\begin{aligned}
U &= \{n_{i-1}(t) > 0 \text{ and } \alpha_i(t+1) = 1\}, \\
V &= \{n_{i-1}(t-1) = 0 \text{ and } n_i(t-1) < N_i\}, \\
W &= \{\alpha_i(t) = 0 \text{ and } n_i(t-1) < N_i\}.
\end{aligned}
$$

Note that $\{n_{i-1}(t-1) = 0\}$ and $\{\alpha_i(t) = 0\}$ are disjoint events. They are disjoint because if $n_{i-1}(t-1) = 0$, then M_i could not fail at time t; and if M_i were down earlier than t, $n_{i-1}(t-1)$ could not be 0. Consequently V and W are disjoint.

Breaking down (4.9) according to (4.10) gives

$$r_u(i) = A(i-1)X(i) + B(i)X'(i), \tag{4.11}$$

where

$$A(i-1) = \quad \text{prob }\left[n_{i-1}(t) > 0 \text{ and } \alpha_i(t+1) = 1\right|$$

$$\left. n_{i-1}(t-1) = 0 \text{ and } n_i(t-1) < N_i\right], \tag{4.12}$$

$$X(i) = \text{prob} \left[n_{i-1}(t-1) = 0 \text{ and } n_i(t-1) < N_i \right|$$

$$\{n_{i-1}(t-1) = 0 \text{ or } \alpha_i(t) = 0\} \text{ and } \{n_i(t-1) < N_i\} \right], \quad (4.13)$$

$$B(i) = \text{prob} \left[n_{i-1}(t) > 0 \text{ and } \alpha_i(t+1) = 1 \mid \alpha_i(t) = 0 \text{ and } n_i(t-1) < N_i \right], \quad (4.14)$$

$$X'(i) = \text{prob} \left[\alpha_i(t) = 0 \text{ and } n_i(t-1) < N_i \mid \{n_{i-1}(t-1) = 0 \text{ or } \alpha_i(t) = 0\} \right. \quad (4.15)$$

$$\text{and } n_i(t-1) < N_i \big].$$

We now evaluate all four conditional probabilities.

To analyze (4.14), recall that $\alpha_i(t) = 0$ implies that $n_i(t-1) < N_i$ since if Buffer $i-1$ were full, Machine i could not fail, and if Machine i fails, Buffer $i-1$ could not become full. Also, $\alpha_i(t) = 0$ implies that $n_{i-1}(t-1) > 0$ for similar reasons. Equation (3.8) then implies that $n_{i-1}(t) > n_{i-1}(t-1)$, so $n_{i-1}(t) > 0$. Consequently, (4.14) is equivalent to

$$B(i) = \text{prob} \left[\alpha_i(t+1) = 1 \mid \alpha_i(t) = 0 \right],$$

or,

$$B(i) = r_i.$$

The first quantity, $A(i-1)$, is the probability of Buffer B_{i-1} making the transition from empty to non-empty. Buffer B_{i-1} being empty implies that machine M_{i-1} is either down or starved. This is equivalent to saying that $M_u(i-1)$ is down. The only way that B_{i-1} can become non-empty immediately after being empty is for $M_u(i-1)$ to recover. The probability of this event is, by definition, $r_u(i-1)$. Therefore,

$$A(i-1) = r_u(i-1).$$

We now show that

$$X(i) = \frac{p_s(i-1)r_u(i)}{p_u(i)E(i)}. \quad (4.16)$$

Equation (4.13) can be written

$$X(i) = \frac{\text{prob } [n_{i-1}(t-1) = 0 \text{ and } n_i(t-1) < N_i]}{\text{prob } [\{n_{i-1}(t-1) = 0 \text{ or } \alpha_i(t) = 0\} \text{ and } n_i(t-1) < N_i]}. \quad (4.17)$$

We have observed that the probability of B_{i-1} being empty and B_i being full at the same time is small (Section 3.5.2). Therefore, the numerator of (4.17) is approximately the probability of B_{i-1} being empty. We assume B_{i-1} in $L(i)$ has the same probability of being empty as B_{i-1} in L, so the numerator is $p_s(i-1)$.

The denominator of (4.17) is, according to (4.8), the probability of the following event (the time arguments are suppressed):

$$\{\alpha_u(i) = 0\} \text{ and } \{n_i < N_i\}. \tag{4.18}$$

The probability of this event can be calculated by making use of Equation (3.39) of Section 3.6.3:

$$r_u(i)\text{prob } [\{\alpha_u(i) = 0\} \text{ and } \{n_i < N_i\}]$$

$$= p_u(i)\text{prob } [\{\alpha_u(i) = 1\} \text{ and } \{n_i < N_i\}] = p_u(i)E(i). \tag{4.19}$$

Thus, the denominator of (4.17) is

$$\text{prob } [\{\alpha_u(i) = 0\} \text{ and } \{n_i < N_i\}] = \frac{p_u(i)E(i)}{r_u(i)} \tag{4.20}$$

and (4.16) is established.

A comparison of (4.13) and (4.15) shows that the events are complementary. Therefore

$$X'(i) = 1 - X(i). \tag{4.21}$$

All quantities in (4.11) have now been evaluated, and the result is (4.6), in which $X(i)$ is given by (4.16). A similar analysis yields Equation (4.7) for the second pseudo-machine in the i-1st line, where

$$Y(i) = \frac{p_b(i)r_d(i-1)}{p_d(i-1)E(i-1)}. \tag{4.22}$$

Finally, there are boundary conditions:

$$\left.\begin{array}{l} r_u(1) = r_1 \\[2ex] p_u(1) = p_1 \\[2ex] r_d(k-1) = r_k \\[2ex] p_d(k-1) = p_k \end{array}\right\} \tag{4.23}$$

There are a total of $4(k-1)$ equations among (4.1), (4.5), (4.6), (4.7), and (4.23) in $4(k-1)$ unknowns: $r_u(i), p_u(i), r_d(i), p_d(i), i = 1, \ldots, k-1$.

An algorithm to solve these equations is presented in Section 4.2.2. It is important to emphasize that we have no proof that these equations are good approximations, and no bounds on the errors. There is, however, considerable evidence — comparisons of solutions of these equations with simulation — that the results are close enough for any practical purposes.

4.2.2   Dallery-David-Xie algorithm

An algorithm was formulated by Dallery, David, and Xie (1988) to solve the decomposition equations of Section 4.2.1. Dallery, David, and Xie observed that since one of the equations that must be satisfied is the conservation-of-flow equation (4.1), then wherever $E(i)$ appears in an equation, it can be replaced with $E(i-1)$ or $E(i+1)$ if that is more convenient.

Two quantities are introduced:

$$I_u(i) = \frac{p_u(i)}{r_u(i)}$$

$$I_d(i) = \frac{p_d(i)}{r_d(i)}$$

for $i = 2, \ldots, k-1$. Then the flow rate-idle time equation (4.5) can be written

$$I_u(i) = \frac{1}{E(i)} + \frac{1}{e_i} - I_d(i-1) - 2, i = 2, \ldots k - 1 \qquad (4.24)$$

or

$$I_d(i) = \frac{1}{E(i+1)} + \frac{1}{e_{i+1}} - I_u(i+1) - 2, i = 1, \ldots k - 2. \qquad (4.25)$$

The algorithm consists of three parts: an Initialization, Step 1, and Step 2.

1. Initialization. Set

$$p_d(i) \quad = \quad p_{i+1}, i = 1, \ldots, k-1$$

$$r_d(i) \quad = \quad r_{i+1}, i = 1, \ldots, k-1$$

$$p_u(i) \quad = \quad p_i, i = 1, \ldots, k-1$$

$$r_u(i) \quad = \quad r_i, i = 1, \ldots, k-1$$

2. Perform Step 1 and Step 2 alternately until the Termination Condition is satisfied.

   (a) Step 1. For $i = 2, \ldots, k-1$ calculate $I_u(i)$ from (4.24), $r_u(i)$ from (4.6) and (4.16). $E(i)$ is replaced by $E(i-1)$ in both (4.16) and (4.24).

   (b) Step 2. For $i = k-2, \ldots, 1$ calculate $I_d(i)$ from (4.25), $r_d(i)$ from (4.7) and (4.22). $E(i-1)$ is replaced by $E(i)$ in (4.22) onlyq .

Termination Condition   Dallery, David, and Xie stop the algorithm when the changes in p_u, r_u, p_d, r_d from one iteration to the next are sufficiently small. Other stopping criteria are possible, such as (4.1) being satisfied sufficiently closely.

4.2.3 Numerical results

Figures 4.7[7] and 4.8[8] describe the production rate (E) and total in-process inventory ($I = \bar{n}_1 + \bar{n}_2$) of a three-machine, two-buffer transfer line. The fixed parameters are $r_1 = r_2 = r_3 = .2$, $N_1 = N_2 = 5$, $p_1 = .05$, and p_2 and p_3 are varied. (Actually, these results were not produced by the decomposition method described here, but by that of Gershwin and Schick, 1983). As p_2 and p_3 increase, E decreases; but I increases with p_3 and decreases with p_2. Evidently E does not approach 0 as p_3 goes to 1. This is because we assume that a part is always produced in the same time step when a repair is completed. Even if failure is certain, one part is produced for each failure.

Figure 4.9[9] represents a design problem: a firm has a production process that requires 9 machines. All the machines have the same reliability parameters $r = .019$ and $p = .001$, and they all require the same operation time. The firm is willing to allocate buffer space, but does not know how to divide it among the machines. Two plans are considered in Figure 4.9: divide it equally among all the machines (in eight equal parts), or divide it in two equal parts and put one part between the third and fourth machines, and the other between the sixth and seventh. The graph has the total space on the horizontal axis and the production rate on the vertical axis. Evidently, dividing it equally is better when there is a lot of storage space, and worse when there is only a little.

Figure 4.10[10] demonstrates the effect of increasing line length on production rate. The horizontal axis is k, the length of a transfer line, and the vertical axis is E. Two sets of lines are considered: in both, the machines have reliability parameters $r_i = .1$ and $p_i = .1$. In one, all the buffers have size 5 and in the other, the sizes are all 10. In both cases, the production rates decrease with k, apparently to non-zero limit.

Figure 4.11[11] describes both lines of Figure 4.10 with $k = 20$ in more detail. It shows how average inventory is distributed. The horizontal axis is buffer number, and the vertical axes is average buffer level. (Note that there are two scales: the solid bars are for $N = 5$, and the scale is on the left; the hollow bars are for $N = 10$, and the scale is on the right.) Note that the bars at the upstream side of the line are large and that those on the right are small. The greatest change in buffer levels occurs near the ends of the line. The middle buffers all contain about the same amount of material. The exact middle buffer (Buffer 10) is exactly half full, on the average. Figures 4.10 and 4.11 suggest the following conjecture on long lines.

---

[7]Reprinted with permission from *Operations Research*, Vol. 31, No. 2, 1983, copyright 1983, Operations Research Society of America. No further reproduction permitted without the consent of the copyright owner.

[8]Reprinted with permission from *Operations Research*, Vol. 31, No. 2, 1983, copyright 1983, Operations Research Society of America. No further reproduction permitted without the consent of the copyright owner.

[9]Reprinted with permission from *Operations Research*, Vol. 35, No. 2, 1987, copyright 1987, Operations Research Society of America. No further reproduction permitted without the consent of the copyright owner.

[10]Reprinted with permission from *Operations Research*, Vol. 35, No. 2, 1987, copyright 1987, Operations Research Society of America. No further reproduction permitted without the consent of the copyright owner.

[11]Reprinted with permission from *Operations Research*, Vol. 35, No. 2, 1987, copyright 1987, Operations Research Society of America. No further reproduction permitted without the consent of the copyright owner.

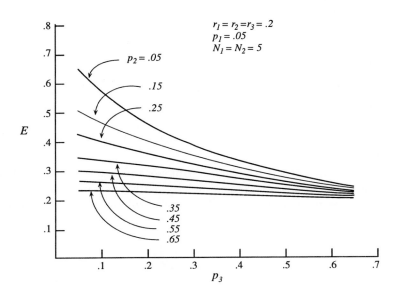

Figure 4.7: Production Rate *vs.* M_2 and M_3 Failure Probabilities for Three-Machine Deterministic Processing Time Line

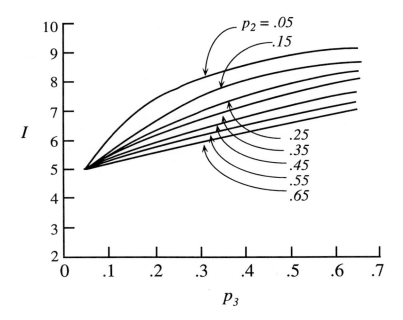

Figure 4.8: Total Average WIP *vs.* M_2 and M_3 Failure Probabilities for Three-Machine Deterministic Processing Time Line

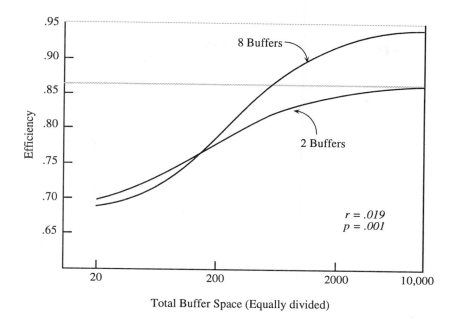

Figure 4.9: Efficiency *vs.* Total Buffer Space

Conjecture on infinitely long lines   Consider transfer lines with identical machines and buffers. We have seen that as the length of such a line with no buffers increases to infinity, the production rate decreases to zero. As the length of a line with infinite buffers goes to infinity, the production rate does not change; it remains equal to that of each machine. This raises a question: what is the limit of the production rate of a transfer line with finite buffers? Is it zero?

We are not able to give a definitive answer to that question. However, based on the decomposition equations of this section, we can offer a conjecture. If we *assume* that the production rate has a limit, and if the approximate equations of this section are good for infinitely long lines, then we derive an approximate formula here for the limiting production rate.

In an infinitely long transfer line with identical machines and buffers,

$r_i = r$, for each i, $-\infty < i < \infty$,

$p_i = p$, for each i, $-\infty < i < \infty$,

$N_i = N$, for each i, $-\infty < i < \infty$,

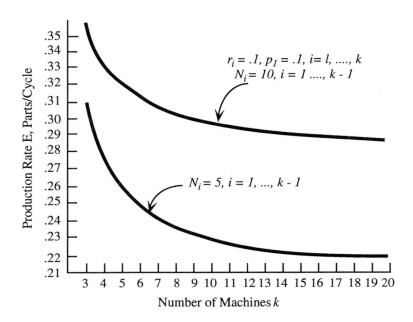

Figure 4.10: Very Long Lines: Efficiency *vs.* Number of Machines

the decomposed pseudo-machines are all identical and symmetric. That is, for each i,

$$r_u(i) = r_u(i-1) = r_d(i) = r_d(i-1)$$

$$p_u(i) = p_u(i-1) = p_d(i) = p_d(i-1).$$

Then from (4.6) and (4.7), $r_u(i) = r_d(i) = r$ for all i. From (4.5),

$$\frac{2p_u}{r} = \frac{1}{E} + \frac{1}{e} - 2. \qquad (4.26)$$

The pseudo-machines of each two-machine line have parameters r and p_u, and the buffer has size N. Equation (4.26) is one relationship between p_u and E. Another is the efficiency as a function of the parameters for a two-machine, deterministic processing time line. Together, they determine both E and p_u. Experiments show that this is a good approximation to the numerical solution of the decomposition equations for very long lines with identical machines and buffers.

For example, if $r = .09$, $p = .01$, and $N = 20$, then $p_u = 0.01950$ and $E = .7563$. In an 80-machine line, $p_u(40) = p_d(40) = .01944$ and $E = .7568$. Agreement with the approximation is best in the center of the line, far away from the boundaries.

See also the closely related work of de Kok (1990).

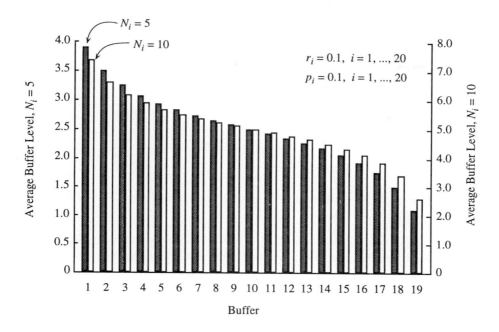

Figure 4.11: Very Long Lines: Distribution of WIP

4.3 Exponential Processing Time Model

In this section, we present a decomposition method to approximate the performance of a transfer line L with exponentially distributed up-, down-, and processing times. The method is similar to that of Section 4.1. Figures 4.12[12] and 4.13[13] illustrate the decomposition for this case.

The transfer line L is decomposed into a set of two-machine lines $L(i), i = 1, \ldots, k$. Their buffers have the same sizes as those of L. Pseudo-machine $M_u(i)$ models the part of the line upstream of B_i and $M_d(i)$ models the part of line downstream from B_i. We assume that the random behaviors governing flow into and out of B_i can be characterized by six exponentially distributed random variables with parameters $\mu_u(i), p_u(i), r_u(i), \mu_d(i), p_d(i)$, and $r_d(i)$. The key to the decomposition method is to find these parameters so that the material flow into and out of the buffers of the two-machine lines closely matches the flow into and out of the corresponding buffers of the long line L. Six equations per buffer, or $6(k-1)$ conditions, are required to determine the parameters.

For every Buffer B_i, the states of the line upstream of B_i are aggregated into two groups,

---

[12]Reprinted from *IIE Transactions*, Vol. 19, No. 2. Copyright 1987, Institute of Industrial Engineers, Norcross, GA 30092

[13]Reprinted from *IIE Transactions*, Vol. 19, No. 2. Copyright 1987, Institute of Industrial Engineers, Norcross, GA 30092

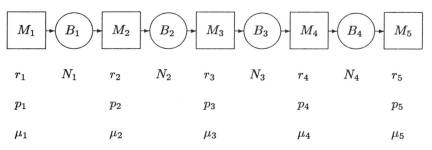

Figure 4.12: Five-Machine Exponential Processing Time Flow Line

represented by the up and down states of $M_u(i)$. A similar aggregation applies to the states of the line downstream of B_i. The decomposition method is based on the assumption that the behavior of $M_u(i)$ can be characterized by three exponential processes with the parameters $\mu_u(i)$, $r_u(i)$, and $p_u(i)$, and that the behavior of $M_d(i)$ can be characterized by exponential processes with parameters $\mu_d(i)$, $r_d(i)$, and $p_d(i)$. That is, the system consisting of $M_u(i)$, $B(i)$, and $M_d(i)$ is the kind of two-machine line studied in Sections 3.7 and 3.8. (Buffer $B(i)$ has the same size as the real Buffer B_i.) This aggregation is not exact. It is adopted here to characterize the most important features of the behavior of the transfer line in a simple approximate way.

In this section, we derive the equations for the unknown variables $\mu_u(i)$, $p_u(i)$, $r_u(i)$, $\mu_d(i)$, $p_d(i)$, and $r_d(i)$, $i = 1, \ldots, k$. They are based on the equation of conservation of flow, the flow rate-idle time relationship, the resumption of flow equations, and a new set, called the interruption of flow equations.

We first define the up and down states of the pseudo-machines $M_u(i)$ and $M_d(i)$.

4.3.1   Definitions: up and down

We say that $M_u(i)$ is down if material is not flowing into B_i because of a failure upstream. $M_u(i)$ is not down when some upstream machine is taking unusually long to do an operation. Therefore, $M_u(i)$ is said to be down when either M_i is down; or M_i is up, B_{i-1} is empty, and M_{i-1} is down; or some machine further upstream is down, with all buffers between it and B_i empty, and all intervening machines up. See Figure 4.14[14]. (Note that the intervening machines must be up, because otherwise the buffers would not be empty.) We use the terms *up* and *operational* synonymously. $M_u(i)$ is up if it is not down.

Formally, $M_u(i)$ is down if, for some $j \le i$:

1. *M_j is down;* and

---

[14]Reprinted from *IIE Transactions*, Vol. 19, No. 2. Copyright 1987, Institute of Industrial Engineers, Norcross, GA 30092

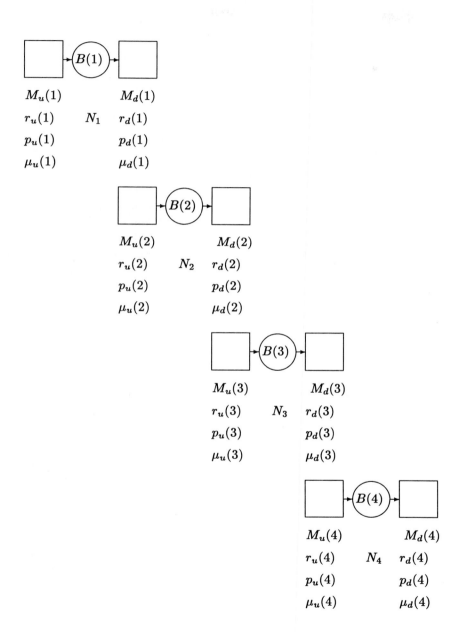

Figure 4.13: Exponential Processing Time Transfer Line Decomposition

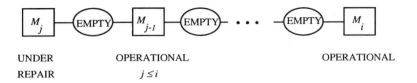

UNDER   OPERATIONAL   OPERATIONAL
REPAIR $j \leq i$

Figure 4.14: $M_u(i)$ Down

2. M_h *is up, all h: $j < h \leq i$; and*

3. $n_h = 0, j \leq h < i$.

Therefore the time when $M_u(i)$ is down is the time when the flow into B_i is interrupted due to an upstream machine failure. This is distinguished from the case in which the flow is interrupted due to an upstream machine taking a long time to perform an operation, and causing the intermediate buffers to empty. In that case, $M_u(i)$ is considered to be up.

An equivalent recursive definition is: $M_u(i)$ is down if

1. M_i *is down, or*

2. $n_{i-1} = 0$ *and* $M_u(i-1)$ *is down.*

$M_u(i)$ is up for all other states of the transfer line upstream of Buffer B_i. Therefore, $M_u(i)$ is up if

1. M_i *is operational and* $n_{i-1} > 0$, *or*

2. M_i *is operational,* $n_{i-1} = 0$ *and* $M_u(i-1)$ *is up.*

Including $n_{i-1} = 0$ in the second alternative is not necessary since it does not change the set of states in which $M_u(i)$ is up. It is convenient to include it, however, because doing so makes the two alternatives mutually exclusive. We do the same below for $M_d(i)$ up.

Similarly, $M_d(i)$ is down if

1. M_{i+1} *is under repair, or*

2. $n_{i+1} = N_{i+1}$ *and* $M_d(i+1)$ *is down.*

$M_d(i)$ is up if

1. M_{i+1} *is operational and* $n_{i+1} < N_{i+1}$, *or*

2. M_{i+1} *is operational ,* $n_{i+1} = N_{i+1}$ *and* $M_d(i+1)$ *is up.*

We identify $M_u(1)$ with M_1 and $M_d(k-1)$ with M_k. Thus $M_u(1)$ is up if M_1 is up and down if M_1 is down; and the same for $M_d(k-1)$. With this classification of the up and down states of the pseudo-machines and the assumption of exponentially distributed transition times between states, the parameters $\mu_u(i), r_u(i), p_u(i), \mu_d(i), r_d(i)$, and $p_d(i)$ are the rates of the exponential distributions. They have the meanings:

$r_u(i)\delta t = $ probability that $M_u(i)$ goes from <u>down</u> to <u>up</u> in $(t, t+\delta t)$, for small δt;

$p_u(i)\delta t = $ probability that $M_u(i)$ goes from <u>up</u> to <u>down</u> in $(t, t+\delta t)$ if it is not blocked, for small δt;

$\mu_u(i)\delta t = $ probability that a piece flows into B_i in $(t, t+\delta t)$ when $M_u(i)$ is up and not blocked, for small δt;

$r_d(i)\delta t = $ probability that $M_d(i)$ goes from <u>down</u> to <u>up</u> in $(t, t+\delta t)$, for small δt;

$p_d(i)\delta t = $ probability that $M_d(i)$ goes from <u>up</u> to <u>down</u> in $(t, t+\delta t)$ if it is not starved, for small δt;

$\mu_d(i)\delta t = $ probability that a piece flows out of B_i in $(t, t+\delta t)$ when $M_d(i)$ is up and not starved, for small δt.

4.3.2 Derivation of equations

Now we are ready to derive the $6(k-1)$ equations needed to approximate the transfer line.

Interruption of Flow The first two sets of equations describe the interruptions of flow caused by machine failures. By definition,

$$p_u(i)\delta t = \text{prob}\left[\alpha_u(i;t+\delta t) = 0 \,\Big|\, \alpha_u(i;t) = 1 \text{ and } n_i(t) < N_i\right],$$

or,

$$p_u(i)\delta t = \text{prob}\left[M_u(i) \text{ down at } t+\delta t \,\Big|\, M_u(i) \text{ up and } n_i < N_i \text{ at } t\right]. \tag{4.27}$$

Substituting the recursive definition of $M_u(i)$ down, we have

$$p_u(i)\delta t = \text{prob } [\{M_i \text{ down at } t+\delta t\} \text{ or}$$

$$\{n_{i-1}=0 \text{ and } M_u(i-1) \text{ down at } t+\delta t\} \Big|$$

$$M_u(i) \text{ up and } n_i < N_i \text{ at } t]. \tag{4.28}$$

Since $\{M_i \text{ down}\}$ and $\{n_{i-1}=0 \text{ and } M_u(i-1) \text{ down}\}$ are mutually exclusive events, Equation (4.28) can be written as

$$p_u(i)\delta t = \text{prob } \left[M_i \text{ down at } t+\delta t \Big| M_u(i) \text{ up and } n_i < N_i \text{ at } t\right]$$

$$+\text{prob } \left[n_{i-1}=0 \text{ and } M_u(i-1) \text{ down at } t+\delta t \Big|\right.$$

$$\left. M_u(i) \text{ up and } n_i < N_i \text{ at } t\right]. \tag{4.29}$$

The first term is the probability that M_i fails in $(t, t+\delta t)$ while processing a workpiece; that is, $p_i\delta t$. The second term in (4.29) is

$$\text{prob } \left[n_{i-1}=0 \text{ and } M_u(i-1) \text{ down at } t+\delta t \Big| M_u(i) \text{ up and } n_i < N_i \text{ at } t\right]$$

$$= \text{ prob } \left[n_{i-1}=0 \text{ and } M_u(i-1) \text{ down and } M_d(i-1) \text{ up at } t+\delta t\right.$$

$$\left. \Big| M_u(i) \text{ up and } n_i < N_i \text{ at } t\right]$$

$$+ \text{ prob } \left[n_{i-1}=0 \text{ and } M_u(i-1) \text{ down and } M_d(i-1) \text{ down at } t+\delta t\right.$$

$$\left. \Big| M_u(i) \text{ up and } n_i < N_i \text{ at } t\right].$$

Since it is not possible for n_{i-1} to be 0 and $M_d(i-1)$ to be down at the same time, this is

$$\text{prob } \left[n_{i-1}=0 \text{ and } M_u(i-1) \text{ down at } t+\delta t \Big| M_u(i) \text{ up and } n_i < N_i \text{ at } t\right]$$

$$= \text{ prob } \left[n_{i-1}=0 \text{ and } M_u(i-1) \text{ down and } M_d(i-1) \text{ up at } t+\delta t\right.$$

$$\left. \Big| M_u(i) \text{ up and } n_i < N_i \text{ at } t\right].$$

If $n_{i-1} = 0$ and $M_u(i-1)$ is down and $M_d(i-1)$ is up at $t + \delta t$, then,

1. $n_{i-1} = 1$ and $M_u(i-1)$ is down and $M_d(i-1)$ is up at time t, and $M_d(i-1)$ performs an operation in $(t, t + \delta t)$, with probability $\mu_d(i-1)\delta t$, *or*

2. $n_{i-1} = 0$ and $M_u(i-1)$ is up and $M_d(i-1)$ is up at time t, and $M_u(i-1)$ fails in $(t, t + \delta t)$, with probability $p_u(i-1)\delta t$, *or*

3. $n_{i-1} = 0$ and $M_u(i-1)$ is down and $M_d(i-1)$ is up at time t, and nothing happens in $(t, t + \delta t)$, with probability $1 - r_u(i-1)\delta t$.

$M_d(i-1)$ could not have been down at time t because $n_{i-1} = 0$. Consequently, the second term in (4.29) is

$$
\text{prob} \left[n_{i-1} = 1 \text{ and } M_u(i-1) \text{ down and } M_d(i-1) \text{ up at } t \right.
$$

$$
\left. \left| M_u(i) \text{ up and } n_i < N_i \text{ at } t \right] \mu_d(i-1)\delta t \right.
$$

$$
+ \quad \text{prob} \left[n_{i-1} = 0 \text{ and } M_u(i-1) \text{ up and } M_d(i-1) \text{ up at } t \right.
$$

(4.30)

$$
\left. \left| M_u(i) \text{ up and } n_i < N_i \text{ at } t \right] p_u(i-1)\delta t \right.
$$

$$
+ \quad \text{prob} \left[n_{i-1} = 0 \text{ and } M_u(i-1) \text{ down and } M_d(i-1) \text{ up at } t \right.
$$

$$
\left. \left| M_u(i) \text{ up and } n_i < N_i \text{ at } t \right] (1 - r_u(i-1)\delta t). \right.
$$

The last term is 0 because, according to the recursive definition of $M_u(i)$ up, either $n_{i-1} > 0$ or $M_u(i-1)$ must be up at time t.

The first term of (4.30) is

$$
\frac{\text{prob} \left\{ \begin{array}{c} n_{i-1} = 1 \text{ and } M_u(i-1) \text{ down and} \\ M_d(i-1) \text{ up and } M_u(i) \text{ up and } n_i < N_i \end{array} \right\}}{\text{prob} \left[M_u(i) \text{ up and } n_i < N_i \right]} \mu_d(i-1)\delta t
$$

which is the same as

$$
\frac{\text{prob} \left[n_{i-1} = 1 \text{ and } M_u(i-1) \text{ down and } M_d(i-1) \text{ up} \right]}{E_u(i)} \mu_d(i-1)\delta t
$$

according to the definitions of $E_u(i)$ and $M_u(i)$ up and $M_d(i-1)$ up. Therefore, the first term of (4.30) can be written

$$\frac{\mathbf{p}(i-1;101)}{E_u(i)}\mu_d(i-1)\delta t$$

in which $\mathbf{p}(i-1;101)$ is the steady state probability of Line $L(i-1)$ being in state $(1,0,1)$. The second term of (4.30) is

$$\frac{\text{prob}\left\{\begin{array}{c}n_{i-1}=0 \text{ and } M_u(i-1) \text{ up and} \\ M_d(i-1) \text{ up and } M_u(i) \text{ up and } n_i < N_i\end{array}\right\}}{M_u(i) \text{ up and } n_i < N_i}p_u(i-1)\delta t$$

which is, by similar reasoning,

$$\frac{\mathbf{p}(i-1;011)}{E_u(i)}p_u(i-1)\delta t$$

The sum of these two probabilities, the second term of (4.29), is

$$\frac{\mathbf{p}(i-1;001)}{E_u(i)}r_u(i-1)\delta t,$$

according to Equation (3.104) of Section 3.8.1. Therefore, the parameter $p_u(i)$ is given by

$$p_u(i) = p_i + \frac{r_u(i-1)\mathbf{p}(i-1;001)}{E_u(i)}. \tag{4.31}$$

In a similar manner, we obtain

$$p_d(i) = p_{i+1} + \frac{r_d(i+1)\mathbf{p}(i+1;N10)}{E_d(i)}. \tag{4.32}$$

Here, $\mathbf{p}(i+1;N10)$ is the steady state probability that line $L(i+1)$ is in state $(N,1,0)$.

Resumption of Flow   This second pair of equations describes the recovery from machine failures. The derivation is similar to that of Equations (4.6) and (4.7). By definition,

$$r_u(i)\delta t = \text{prob}\left[M_u(i) \text{ up at } t+\delta t \middle| M_u(i) \text{ down and } n_i < N_i \text{ at } t\right]. \tag{4.33}$$

Substituting the definition of $M_u(i)$ up,

$$r_u(i)\delta t = \text{prob}\left[\{M_i \text{ up and } \{n_{i-1} > 0 \text{ or}\right.$$

$$\{n_{i-1} = 0 \text{ and } M_u(i-1)\text{up}\} \text{ at } t+\delta t \middle| \tag{4.34}$$

$$\left.M_u(i) \text{ down and } n_i < N_i \text{ at } t\right].$$

Using the equivalent notation

$$\{n_{i-1} > 0 \text{ or } \{n_{i-1} = 0 \text{ and } M_u(i-1) \text{ up }\}\} = \text{ NOT } (n_{i-1} = 0$$

$$\text{and } M_u(i-1) \text{ down }),$$

(4.35)

and decomposing the conditioning event, Equation (4.34) can be written as

$$r_u(i) = A(i-1)X(i) + B(i)X'(i),$$

(4.36)

where we define

$$X(i) = \text{ prob } [\{n_{i-1} = 0 \text{ and } M_u(i-1) \text{ down}$$

$$\text{and } n_i < N_i\} \text{ at } t \Big| \{M_i \text{ down or } \{n_{i-1} = 0 \text{ and } M_u(i-1)\text{down}\}$$

$$\text{and } n_i < N_i\} \text{ at } t]$$

$$A(i-1) = \text{ prob } \Big[\{M_i \text{ up and NOT } (n_{i-1} = 0 \text{ and } M_u(i-1) \text{ down}) \text{ at } t + \delta t\}\Big|$$

$$\{n_{i-1} = 0 \text{ and } M_u(i-1) \text{ down and } n_i < N_i\} \text{ at } t\Big]$$

$$X'(i) \quad = \text{prob } [\text{ complement of the event of } X(i)]$$

$$= 1 - X(i)$$

$$B(i) = \text{ prob } \Big[\{M_i \text{ up and NOT } (n_{i-1} = 0 \text{ and } M_u(i-1) \text{ down}) \text{ at } t + \delta t\}\Big|$$

$$\{M_i \text{ down and } n_i < N_i \text{ at } t\}\Big].$$

This decomposition is possible because $\{n_{i-1} = 0\}$ and $\{M_i \text{ down}\}$ are disjoint events. M_i cannot fail when it is starved from processing and when it fails, it has to be processing one piece of material. We now evaluate all the four conditional probabilities in (4.36). From the definition of conditional probability,

$$X(i) = \frac{\left\{ \begin{array}{c} \text{prob } [\{n_{i-1} = 0 \text{ and } M_u(i-1) \text{ down }\} \text{ and} \\ (\{M_i \text{ down}\} \text{ or } \{n_{i-1} = 0 \text{ and } M_u(i-1) \text{ down}\}) \text{ and } \{n_i < N_i\} \text{ at } t] \end{array} \right\}}{\text{prob } [\{M_i \text{ down or } \{n_{i-1} = 0 \text{ and } M_u(i-1) \text{ down}\} \text{ and } n_i < N_i\} \text{ at } t]}$$

Since $\{M_i \text{ down}\}$ and $\{n_{i-1} = 0\}$ are disjoint, the numerator is the probability that line $L(i-1)$ is in state $(0, 0, 1)$. This probability is $\mathbf{p}(i-1; 001)$. The denominator is the probability of the conditional event of (4.33), that is, probability of $\{M_u(i)$ down and $n_i < N_i\}$. This probability can be calculated by using the relationship

$$r_u(i)\text{prob } [M_u(i) \text{ down and } n_i < N_i] = p_u(i)\text{prob } [M_u(i) \text{ up and } n_i < N_i],$$

as given by Equation (3.119) of Section 3.8.3. Thus, the denominator is

$$\text{prob } [M_u(i) \text{ down and } n_i < N_i] = \frac{p_u(i)E_u(i)}{r_u(i)},$$

and therefore

$$X(i) = \frac{\mathbf{p}(i-1;001)r_u(i)}{p_u(i)E_u(i)}.$$

$A(i-1)$ is the probability of $M_u(i-1)$ going from down to up in $(t, t + \delta t)$; that is, $r_u(i-1)\delta t$. $B(i)$ is approximately the probability of M_i been repaired in $(t, t + \delta t)$; that is, $r_i \delta t$. Therefore, Equation (4.36) can now be written as

$$r_u(i) = r_u(i-1)X(i) + r_i(1 - X(i)), \quad i = 2, \ldots, k-1. \tag{4.37}$$

Equation (4.37) shows that $r_u(i)$ is a convex combination of r_i and $r_u(i-1)$. A similar analysis yields

$$r_d(i) = r_d(i+1)Y(i) + r_{i+1}(1 - Y(i)), \quad i = 1, \ldots, k-2; \tag{4.38}$$

where

$$Y(i) = \frac{\mathbf{p}(i+1;N10)r_d(i)}{p_d(i)E_d(i)}.$$

Compare $X(i)$ and $Y(i)$ with (4.16) and (4.22).

Conservation of Flow   Conservation of Flow states that the production rates of all the decomposed two-machine lines $L(i)$ are the same. Thus

$$P_i = P_k = P(i) = P_u(i) = P_d(i), \quad i = 1, \ldots, k-1. \tag{4.39}$$

Flow Rate-Idle Time Relationship   The flow rate-idle time relationship is, according to (3.97) approximately,

$$P_i = e_i\mu_i \left(1 - \text{prob } [n_{i-1} = 0] - \text{prob } [n_i = N_i]\right). \tag{4.40}$$

This approximation may fail if, for some i, μ_i is larger than μ_{i-1} and μ_{i+1}. Since the buffers in the decomposed two-machine lines behave similarly to the corresponding buffers in the transfer line, we have

$$\text{prob } [n_{i-1} = 0] = p_s(i-1) \tag{4.41}$$

and

$$\text{prob } [n_i = N_i] = p_b(i) \tag{4.42}$$

where $p_s(i-1)$ is the probability that the buffer in line $L(i-1)$ becomes empty and $p_b(i)$ is the probability that $M_u(i)$ is blocked. These probabilities are calculated from the two-machine line formulas in Section 3.8.1.

Section 3.8.1 shows that the flow rate-idle time relationship for a two-machine line is

$$e_d(i-1)(1 - p_s(i-1)) = \frac{P_d(i-1)}{\mu_d(i-1)} \tag{4.43}$$

and

$$e_u(i)(1 - p_b(i)) = \frac{P_u(i)}{\mu_u(i)}. \tag{4.44}$$

Using these relationships and the conservation of flow equation, (4.40) can be written as

$$\frac{1}{e_i \mu_i} + \frac{1}{P} = \frac{1}{e_d(i-1)\mu_d(i-1)} + \frac{1}{e_u(i)\mu_u(i)}; \quad i = 2, \ldots, k-1. \tag{4.45}$$

Boundary Conditions The remaining six equations are satisfied by the boundary conditions

$$
\begin{aligned}
r_u(1) &= r_1 \\
p_u(1) &= p_1 \\
\mu_u(1) &= \mu_1 \\
r_d(k-1) &= r_k \\
p_d(k-1) &= p_k \\
\mu_d(k-1) &= \mu_k
\end{aligned}
\tag{4.46}
$$

4.3.3 Dallery-David-Xie algorithm — exponential model

The exponential DDX algorithm also consists of three parts: an Initialization, Step 1, and Step 2.

1. Initialization. For each two-machine line $L(i)$, the initial guesses for its parameters are:

$$p_d(i) \;=\; p_{i+1}, i = 1, \ldots, k-1$$

$$r_d(i) \;=\; r_{i+1}, i = 1, \ldots, k-1$$

$$\mu_d(i) \;=\; \mu_{i+1}, i = 1, \ldots, k-1$$

$$p_u(i) \;=\; p_i, i = 1, \ldots, k-1$$

$$r_u(i) \;=\; r_i, i = 1, \ldots, k-1$$

$$\mu_u(i) \;=\; \mu_i, i = 1, \ldots, k-1$$

2. Perform Step 1 and Step 2 alternately until the Termination Condition is satisfied.

   (a) Step 1. Let i range over values from 2 to $i = k-1$. Evaluate two-machine line $L(i)$, using the most recent values of $r_u(i-1)$, $p_u(i-1)$, $\mu_u(i-1)$, $r_d(i-1)$, $p_d(i-1)$, $\mu_d(i-1)$, to calculate $P(i-1)$ and $\mathbf{p}(i-1, 001)$. Using the values of $r_u(i)$, $p_u(i)$, $\mu_u(i)$, $r_d(i)$, $p_d(i)$, $\mu_d(i)$ from the previous iteration, evaluate the following quantities in the indicated sequence.

$$p_u(i) = p_i + \frac{r_u(i-1)\mathbf{p}(i-1, 001)\mu_u(i)}{P(i)} \tag{4.47}$$

$$X(i) = \frac{\mu_u(i)\mathbf{p}(i-1, 001)r_u(i)}{P(i-1)p_u(i)} \tag{4.48}$$

$$r_u(i) = r_u(i-1)X(i) + r_i(1 - X(i)) \tag{4.49}$$

$$e_u(i) = \frac{r_u(i)}{r_u(i) + p_u(i)} \tag{4.50}$$

$$\mu_u(i) = \frac{1}{e_u(i)} \left\{ \frac{1}{\frac{1}{P(i-1)} + \frac{1}{e_i\mu_i} - \frac{1}{e_d(i-1)\mu_d(i-1)}} \right\} \tag{4.51}$$

   (b) Step 2. Let i range over values from $k-2$ to $i = 1$. Evaluate two-machine line $L(i+1)$, with the most recent values of $r_u(i+1)$, $p_u(i+1)$, $\mu_u(i+1)$, $r_d(i+1)$, $p_d(i+1)$, $\mu_d(i+1)$, to calculate $P(i+1)$ and $\mathbf{p}(i+1, N10)$. Using the values of $r_u(i)$, $p_u(i)$, $\mu_u(i)$, $r_d(i)$, $p_d(i)$, $\mu_d(i)$ from the previous iteration, evaluate the following quantities in the indicated sequence.

$$p_d(i) = p_{i+1} + \frac{r_d(i+1)\mathbf{p}(i+1, N10)\mu_d(i+1)}{P(i+1)} \tag{4.52}$$

$$Y(i) = \frac{\mu_d(i)\mathbf{p}(i+1, N10)r_d(i)}{P(i+1)p_d(i)} \tag{4.53}$$

$$r_d(i) = r_d(i+1)Y(i) + r_{i+1}(1 - Y(i)) \tag{4.54}$$

$$e_d(i) = \frac{r_d(i)}{r_d(i) + p_d(i)} \tag{4.55}$$

$$\mu_d(i) = \frac{1}{e_d(i)} \left\{ \frac{1}{\frac{1}{P(i+1)} + \frac{1}{e_{i+1}\mu_{i+1}} - \frac{1}{e_u(i+1)\mu_u(i+1)}} \right\} \tag{4.56}$$

Termination Condition Terminate the algorithm when the greatest value of

$$| P(i) - P(1) |$$

is less than some specified value, for $i = 2, \ldots, k - 1$. Evaluate $\bar{n}(i)$ for $i = 1, \ldots k - 1$ from the two-machine lines to estimate the average buffers of the original line.

Comments Equations (4.51) and (4.56) are equivalent to the flow rate-idle time relationship (4.45) except that P is replaced by $P(i - 1)$ and $P(i + 1)$. The other equations are identical to the upstream and downstream interruption and resumption of flow equations. The only equation that is not explicitly enforced is conservation of flow, (4.39). However, this is the essence of the termination condition. Thus, if the algorithm converges and the termination condition is satisfied with a sufficiently small error parameter, the resulting $r_u(i)$, $p_u(i)$, $\mu_u(i)$, $r_d(i)$, $p_d(i)$, $\mu_d(i)$ satisfy all the decomposition equations (with the small error in (4.39)).

A proof of convergence is not available. However, in numerous experiments, the algorithm almost always converged.

This algorithm differs from that of Dallery, David, and Xie (1988) in that machines in this system have three parameters rather than two. Dallery, David, and Xie use the Resumption of Flow equations to propagate r_u and r_d, and the Flow Rate-Idle Time Relationship to calculate p_u and p_d. (It was a particularly clever stroke to use one equation to calculate two quantities, one in each direction.) The present algorithm uses the Resumption of Flow equations to propagate r_u and r_d. It uses the Interruption of Flow equations to propagate p_u and p_d. It uses the Flow Rate-Idle Time Relationship in essentially the same way that Dallery, David, and Xie did to calculate μ_u and μ_d.

4.3.4 Numerical results

Figure 4.15[15] compares the decomposition results for a three-machine line with simulation results (Choong and Gershwin, 1987). The horizontal axis is ρ_2 and the vertical axis is P. Note that the results are very close for small ρ_2, but deviate for large ρ_2. This is because when the middle machine is fast, the probability that the first buffer is empty and the second is full is not small. This violates an assumption that the decomposition was based on.

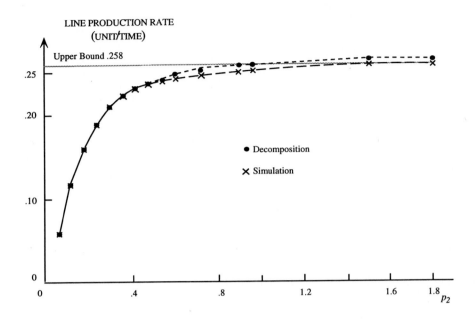

Figure 4.15: Simulation and Decomposition Results for Exponential Processing Time Line

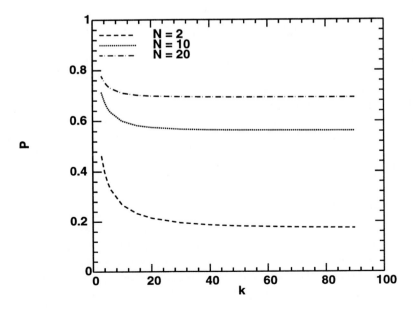

Figure 4.16: Production Rates for Long Exponential Processing Time Lines

i	Parameters			
	r_i	p_i	μ_i	N_i
1	.05	.03	.5	8
2	.06	.04	—	8
3	.05	.03	.5	

Table 4.1: Parameters for Exponential Processing Time Line

Figure 4.16 describes the behavior of a set of transfer lines with identical machines whose parameters are $r = .09$, $p = .01$, and $\mu = 1$. All buffers have the same size N. There are three sets of cases: $N = 2, 10$, and 20. Figure 4.16 shows production rates as a function of line length (k). The production rates are larger for larger buffers, and they decrease for greater length.

Conjecture on infinitely long lines   Just as in the case of the deterministic processing time line, a conjecture can be formulated on the limiting behavior of an infinitely long transfer line with identical machine (with parameters r, p, and μ) and buffers (with size N). If such a line does have a limiting behavior, and the decomposition is a good approximation, then

$$p_u(i) = p_d(i) = p_u \text{ for all } i$$

$$r_u(i) = r_d(i) = r \text{ for all } i$$

$$\mu_u(i) = \mu_d(i) = \mu_u \text{ for all } i$$

The interruption of flow equation becomes

$$p_u = p + \frac{r p_s \mu_u}{P} \tag{4.57}$$

in which p_s is $\mathbf{p}(0, 0, 1)$, the probability of starvation, in a two-machine transfer line both of whose machines have exponentially distributed repair, failure, and operation times with parameters r, p_u, and μ_u, and whose buffer has size N. P is the production rate of such a line.

The flow rate-idle time relationship becomes

$$\frac{1}{e\mu} + \frac{1}{P} = \frac{2}{e_u \mu_u}. \tag{4.58}$$

When (4.57) and (4.58) are solved simultaneously, the solution (p_u and μ_u) are close to the decomposition parameters of a long line, and the production rate P is close to that of the

---

[15] Reprinted from *IIE Transactions*, Vol. 19, No. 2. Copyright 1987, Institute of Industrial Engineers, Norcross, GA 30092

long line. For example, in a 20-machine line all of whose machines have parameters $r = .1$, $p = .1$, and $\mu = 1.$, and all of whose buffers have size 10, the production rate is .252 and the decomposition parameters of the middle buffer are $p_u(10) = .175$ and $\mu_u(10) = .929$. Solving (4.57) and (4.58) gives $P = .248$ and $p_u = .179$ and $\mu_u = .926$.

In a 90-machine line, all of whose machines have parameters $r = .09, p = .01$, and $\mu = 1$, and all of whose buffers have size 10, the production rate is .562 and the decomposition parameters of the middle buffer are $p_u(45) = .0263$ and $\mu_u(10) = .894$. Solving (4.57) and (4.58) gives $P = .561$ and $p_u = .0265$ and $\mu_u = .894$.

4.4   Research Problems

1. Perform extensive simulations to verify the claims that the arrival and departure processes into and out of buffers are similar to those generated by single machines. Determine experimentally when they are most and least similar.

2. Methods exist for evaluating long continuous material lines that work for homogeneous lines (those in which all μ_i are the same) or where a transformation is performed to homogenize a non-homogeneous line, or to otherwise convert a general continuous line into a form for which a solution method already exists. Such methods are restricted in that they only work on a limited class of systems, or because they add a layer of approximation onto techniques that are themselves approximate. A useful research goal would be to develop a decomposition method — similar to those in this chapter — for the continuous material line. Some of these methods, and some of the issues that make this task difficult, are described in Dallery and Gershwin (1992). A recent paper in this area is by Glassey and Hong (1993).

3. Find bounds on the accuracy and the speed of convergence of the decomposition method and the DDX algorithm.

4. Extend the research proposed in Section 3.11 to longer lines.

Other research problems are mentioned in Dallery and Gershwin (1992).

Exercises

1. What are $r_u(i)$ and $r_d(i)$ in lines in which all r_i are equal? Consider both the deterministic processing time and exponential lines.

2. Explain the shapes of Figures 4.7 and 4.8 intuitively.

3. Explain the large-storage behavior in Figure 4.9 intuitively. Can you predict the asymptotes? *Hint:* Use what you know about transfer lines with zero and infinite buffers.

4. What is the limiting average buffer level of the buffers of a long transfer line that are far from the ends of the line?

5. Is the limiting behavior of a long transfer line consistent with what we know for $N = 0$ and $N \rightarrow \infty$? That is, are the limiting production rates for $k \rightarrow \infty$ and for $N = 0$ and $N \rightarrow \infty$ consistent with the results of Section 3.3? *Hint:* write E in terms of r and p_u for $N = 0$ and $N \rightarrow \infty$.

6. Derive the Interruption of Flow equations for the deterministic processing time line.

7. Write a computer program (in any language you choose) to evaluate the deterministic processing time line using the DDX algorithm. Use the program of Chapter 3, Exercise 14 as a subprogram to evaluate the two-machine line quantities needed in the algorithm. Debug your program by comparing results with the graphs.

8. Numerical experiment. Make up parameters for two k-machine lines (either both deterministic processing time or both exponential processing time) that are the reverses of one another in the following sense:

$$r_i' \;=\; r_{k-i+1} \text{ for } i = 1, \ldots k,$$

$$p_i' \;=\; p_{k-i+1} \text{ for } i = 1, \ldots k,$$

$$\mu_i' \;=\; \mu_{k-i+1} \text{ for } i = 1, \ldots k, \text{ (for exponential processing time lines)}$$

$$N_i' \;=\; N_{k-i} \text{ for } i = 1, \ldots k - 1.$$

Can you observe any relationship between the production rates of the lines and between $\bar{n}_i'$ and $\bar{n}_{k-i+1}$? Try a few cases to be sure. Formulate a hypothesis about what is going on.

9. Numerical experiment. Make up parameters for a k-machine line (either deterministic processing time or exponential processing time) that are *symmetric* in the following sense:

$$r_i \;=\; r_{k-i+1} \text{ for } i = 1, \ldots k,$$

$$p_i \;=\; p_{k-i+1} \text{ for } i = 1, \ldots k,$$

$$\mu_i \;=\; \mu_{k-i+1} \text{ for } i = 1, \ldots k, \text{ (for an exponential processing time line)}$$

$$N_i \;=\; N_{k-i} \text{ for } i = 1, \ldots k - 1.$$

Can you observe any relationship between $\bar{n}_i$ and $\bar{n}_{k-i}$? In particular, if k is odd, look at $\bar{n}_j$, where $j = \left(\frac{k-1}{2}\right)$. Is there anything special about it? Try a few cases to be sure. Formulate a hypothesis about what is going on.

10. Using the simulation program you wrote for Exercise 15 of Chapter 3, and the DDX program you wrote for Exercise 7 above, compare simulation and approximate results for a set of lines. Does agreement (in production rates and average buffer levels) improve when you increase the length of the run? When you increase the length of the line? For what lines is agreement good, and for which is it poor? Is agreement in production rate better or worse than agreement in average buffer levels? Compare run time of simulation and approximation. Which would you rather use for line design?[16]

11. Transfer line design. The Tech Manufacturing Company is contemplating the acquisition of a transfer line to make digital adapters for its highly successful Tech-o-Tronic brand of multi-frequency desktop widgets.

The making of widget adapters is a multi-step process. It requires rough drilling, finished reaming, bolt insertion, and spot painting. Several different vendors have been invited to submit bids for the machines and buffers that will make up the line.

It is your job to pick the least expensive combination of machines and buffers that produces the required production rate of 500 parts per hour. Which of the following machines should the company purchase, and what size buffers should it have to minimize cost? Justify your answer. An answer within 1% of the optimum will be judged correct.

Assume that the value of parts in storage between the drilling and reaming stages is $10 per part, the value of parts between reaming and bolt insertion is $20 per part, and the value of parts between insertion and painting is $30.

The following is a summary of the information supplied by the vendors.

The ALPHA Machine Tool Company has a rough drilling machine that costs $25,000 that can do 11 operations per minute on the average and has a mean time to fail of 400 hours and a mean time to repair of 20 hours.

The ALPHA Machine Tool Company has a final reaming machine that costs $50,000 that can do 10.5 operations per minute on the average and has a mean time to fail of 500 hours and a mean time to repair of 20 hours.

The BETA Machine Tool Company has a rough drilling machine that costs $20,000 that can do an average of 10 operations per minute and has a mean time to fail of 150 hours and a mean time to repair of 30 hours.

The BETA Machine Tool Company has a final reaming machine that costs $45,000 that can do an average of 10 operations per minute and has a mean time to fail of 200,000 operations and a mean time to repair of 20 hours.

---

[16]Which answer do you think the author is looking for?

The GAMMA Machine Tool Company has a machine that can do both rough drilling and final reaming. It costs $80,000 and can process (perform both operations on) an average of 10 parts per minute and has a mean time to fail of 400 hours and a mean time to repair of 20 hours.

The INSERT-a-BOLT Model 25 can insert 2000 bolts per hour on the average with a mean time to fail of 1,000,000 operations and a mean time to repair of 10 hours. It costs $20,000.

The STUFF-a-BOLT Model 52 has an average production rate of 1000 bolts per hour with a mean time to fail of 500,000 operations and a mean time to repair of 10 hours. It costs $5,000.

The DROP-a-SPOT can paint 11 parts per minute, on the average, with a mean repair time of 10 hours and a mean time to fail of 400 hours. It costs $15,000.

Bibliography

[1] T. Altiok (1982), "Approximate Analysis of Exponential Tandem Queues with Blocking," *European Journal of Operations Research*, Vol. 11, 1982.

[2] J. A. Buzacott and J. G. Shanthikumar (1993), *Stochastic Models of Manufacturing Systems*, Prentice Hall, 1993.

[3] Y. F. Choong and S. B. Gershwin (1987), "A Decomposition Method for the Approximate Evaluation of Capacitated Transfer Lines with Unreliable Machines and Random Processing Times," *IIE Transactions*, Vol. 19, No. 2, pp. 150-159.

[4] Y. Dallery, R. David, and X.-L. Xie (1988), "An Efficient Algorithm for Analysis of Transfer Lines with Unreliable Machines and Finite Buffers," *IIE Transactions*, Vol. 20, No. 3, pp. 280-283, September, 1988.

[5] Y. Dallery, R. David, and X.-L. Xie (1989), "Approximate Analysis of Transfer Lines with Unreliable Machines and Finite Buffers," *IEEE Transactions on Automatic Control*, Vol. 34, pp. 943-953.

[6] Y. Dallery and S. B. Gershwin (1992), "Manufacturing Flow Line Systems: A Review of Models and Analytical Results," *Queueing Systems Theory and Applications, Special Issue on Queueing Models of Manufacturing Systems*, Volume 12, No. 1-2, December, 1992, pp. 3-94.

[7] A. G. de Kok (1990), "Computationally Efficient Approximations for Balanced Flowlines with Finite Intermediate Buffers," *International Journal of Production Research*, Volume 28, Number 2, pp. 410-419.

[8] S. B. Gershwin (1987), "An Efficient Decomposition Method for the Approximate Evaluation of Tandem Queues with Finite Storage Space and Blocking," *Operations Research*, pp. 291-305, March-April, 1987.

[9] S. B. Gershwin (1988), "An Efficient Decomposition Algorithm for Unreliable Tandem Queuing Systems with Finite Buffers," presented at the *First International Workshop on Queuing Networks with Blocking*, North Carolina State University, Raleigh, NC, May, 1988.

[10] S. B. Gershwin and I. C. Schick (1983), "Modeling and Analysis of Three-Stage Transfer Lines with Unreliable Machines and Finite Buffers," *Operations Research*, Vol. 31, No. 2, pp. 354-380, March-April, 1983.

[11] C. R. Glassey and Y. Hong (1993), "Analysis of Behaviour of an Unreliable n-Stage Transfer Line with $(n-1)$ Inter-Stage Storage Buffers," *International Journal of Production Research*, Vol. 31, No. 3, pp. 519-530, March, 1993.

[12] F. S. Hillier and R. Boling (1967), "Finite Queues in Series with Exponential or Erlang Service Times — A Numerical Approach," *Operations Research*, Vol. 4, pp. 286-303.

[13] R. O. Onvural (1988), "On the Exact Decomposition of Closed Queueing Networks with Finite Buffers," presented at the *First International Workshop on Queuing Networks with Blocking*, North Carolina State University, Raleigh, NC, May, 1988.

[14] B. A. Sevast'yanov (1962), "Influence of Storage Bin Capacity on the Average Standstill Time of a Production Line," *Theory of Probability and Its Applications*, Vol. 7, pp. 429-438.

[15] I. C. Schick (1978), "Analysis of a Multistage Transfer Line with Unreliable Components and Interstage Buffer Storages with Applications to Chemical Engineering Problems," MIT Chemical Engineering Department M.S. Thesis, 1978.

[16] I. C. Schick and S. B. Gershwin (1978), "Modeling and Analysis of Unreliable Transfer Lines with Finite Storage Buffers," MIT Electronic Systems Laboratory Report ESL-FR-834-6, September, 1978.

[17] Y. Takahashi, H. Miyahara, and T. Hasegawa (1980), "An Approximation Method for Open Restricted Queuing Networks," *Operations Research,* Vol. 28, No. 3, Part I, May-June 1980.

[18] B. Zimmern (1956), "Études de la Propagation des Arrets Aléatoires dans la Chaines de Production," *Revue Statist. Appl.*, Vol. 4, pp 85-104.

Chapter 5

Assembly/Disassembly Systems

5.1 Introduction

Assembly/Disassembly (A/D) systems (or networks) are queuing systems in which assembly and disassembly take place. An assembly operation is one in which two or more parts or subassemblies are brought together to form a single unit. A disassembly operation is one in which a single unit is separated into two or more parts or subassemblies. Almost anything that is manufactured is assembled, including cars, electronic equipment, windows and doors, and anything else that is composed of separate parts. Something similar occurs in computer systems, where Assembly/Disassembly networks are called *fork/join* queueing systems.

There are two kinds of assembly systems: (1) those that add relatively small components to a relatively large workpiece (such as printed circuit board assembly), and (2) those that put together subassemblies that have themselves already been assembled within the manufacturing system. The flow of materials in the first case is essentially the same as that in a transfer line and can be treated by the methods of Chapters 3 and 4. We treat systems of the second kind here as generalizations of transfer lines.

Assembly is more important in manufacturing, but we include disassembly operations because they add no difficulty, because they do appear occasionally, and because disassembly is useful in the analysis of equivalent systems, as discussed in Section 5.6. In addition, the removal of material can be thought of as a disassembly operation, and if any problem occurs in the waste handling system, production is affected.

In the systems studied in this chapter, parts arrive from outside and are processed at certain machines. There they may be disassembled into smaller parts or processed individually, and each component moves into a designated buffer. It then goes to another machine, at which it may be assembled with other parts, or further disassembled (or processed individually; or both assembled and disassembled). This continues until each part's processing is complete, and it leaves the system. Each buffer gets parts from a specific machine and sends parts to another specific machine. Each machine is connected to at least one buffer. A machine may have any number of upstream or downstream buffers, other than zero of both.

We assume that routing is entirely deterministic. That is, the path that each part follows in the system is known in advance, and the contents of each buffer are homogeneous. The only source of randomness is the variation of processing time in the machines. Just as in the case of transfer lines, no real-time decisions are considered in this chapter. An example of an Assembly/Disassembly (A/D) appears in Figure 5.1[1], in which squares represent machines and circles represent buffers.

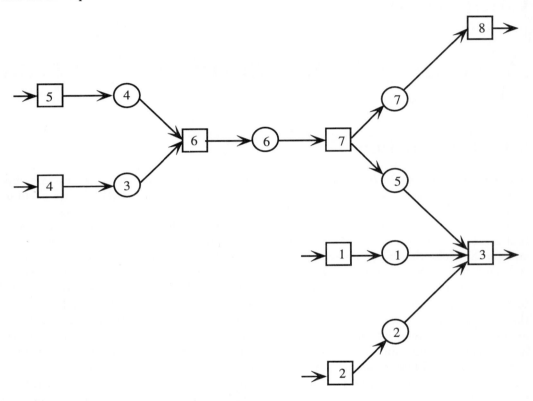

Figure 5.1: Assembly/Disassembly Network

A machine that has two or more upstream buffers performs assembly operations and is called an *assembly machine*. When it does an operation, it takes one part from each of them. A machine that has two or more downstream buffers is a *disassembly machine*. When it does an operation, it adds one part to each of them.

Machines are assumed to spend a random amount of time processing each item due, in

[1]Reprinted from *IIE Transactions*, Vol. 23, No. 4. Copyright 1991, Institute of Industrial Engineers, Norcross, GA 30092

part, to the failures and repairs of machines. When a machine is down, each of the immediate upstream buffers tends to accumulate material and each of the immediate downstream buffers tends to lose material. If this condition persists, one or more of the upstream buffers may become full or one or more of the downstream buffers may become empty. In that case, the machines upstream of the full buffers are blocked and prevented from working or the machines downstream of the empty buffers are starved and also prevented from working.

Idleness propagates through the network. In a transfer line, a failed machine tends to cause upstream machines to be blocked and downstream machines to be starved. In a more general A/D network, starvation propagates downstream, but it is also reflected by an assembly machine so that it propagates upstream as a blockage in a different branch of the network.

That is, if a machine fails, it may starve some of its downstream neighbors. Those machines may eventually starve their downstream neighbors, but they may also eventually block their upstream neighbors, other than the machine whose failure started the chain of events. Similarly, the machine that failed may block its upstream neighbors, and they may both block their upstream neighbors and starve their downstream neighbors, other than the machine whose failure started the chain of events.

For example, if Machine 7 of Figure 5.1 fails, it may starve Machine 3. Machine 3 may eventually block Machines 1 or 2. Or, Machine 7 might block Machine 6, which could block Machine 4 or Machine 5.

New issues arise in this more general class of networks which do not concern us in transfer lines. One is that the long term behavior of such systems may be strongly affected by their initial conditions. In technical terms, these systems may be *non-ergodic*. Specifically, in A/D networks with loops such as closed conveyor systems, the number of items in the loop remains constant for all time, and must be specified as a parameter in the same way that machine and buffer parameters are specified. As a consequence, performance measures (production rates and average buffer levels) are functions of the initial state. Tree-structured A/D networks (which are defined in Section 5.3 and which include transfer lines as a special case) do not have this difficulty.

Just as for transfer lines, the analysis of A/D systems is difficult because of the great size of the state space. In Section 5.2, we define a class of A/D networks which is a generalization of the deterministic transfer line models of Sections 3.5. Sections 5.3 and 5.4 present a method for the analysis (the calculation of throughput and average buffer levels) of the tree-structured subset of this class of systems. The method is an extension of the transfer line algorithms of Chapter 4. Numerical results which illustrate the behavior of these systems appear in Section 5.5.

Another issue is *equivalence*. We define it for another class of A/D networks in Section 5.6 and show that systems whose structures have certain features in common have behaviors that are closely related. This is a generalization of the notion of reversibility of transfer lines that appears in Exercise 8 of Chapter 4.

A third issue is the *instability* of some A/D networks. Using the algorithm of Sections 5.3 and 5.4 and the qualitative observations of Section 5.6, we show that tree-structured A/D networks with infinite buffers and at least one true assembly are inherently unstable, in the sense that the level of at least one buffer will grow without bound, regardless of the parameters of the line, or of which machine is faster than which. This is in contrast to transfer lines with infinite buffers (Section 3.3), in which instability only occurs when slow machines are further downstream than fast machines. This may explain why assembly has received so little attention in the queuing theory literature: most of that literature deals with the steady state behavior of systems with infinite buffers.

5.2 Model

The purpose of this section and Sections 5.3 and 5.4 is to describe an efficient method for calculating performance measures: the production rate and the average buffer levels. We follow the method of Section 4.2; first we describe how the real systems behave; then in Section 5.3 we describe an approximate decomposition; we describe an algorithm in Section 5.4 that follows the DDX algorithm (Section 4.2.2) very closely.

   The model described here is an extension of the deterministic processing time transfer line model of Sections 3.5 and 3.6. Here, we describe the assumptions, notation, and conventions that go beyond those of Section 3.5.1.

1. The network can be represented as a connected graph in which the machines are nodes and the buffers are arcs. $\mathcal{M}$ is the set of all machines in the network and $\mathcal{B}$ is the set of all buffers. The number of machines is k_M; there are k_B buffers. Each buffer is connected to exactly two machines, and is named b, or $b(j,i)$, or (j,i) if the machine upstream is j and the machine downstream is i. The machine upstream of Buffer b is called $u(b)$, and the machine immediately downstream of b is $d(b)$. (If $b = (j,i)$, then $j = u(b)$ and $i = d(u)$.)

2. The set of buffers upstream of Machine M_i is called $U(i)$ and the set of buffers downstream of i is $D(i)$. See Figure 5.2[2]. One of these sets may be empty. If $U(i)$ is empty and $D(i)$ is a single buffer, i is an *input port*. If $D(i)$ is empty and $U(i)$ is a single buffer, i is an *output port*. Input ports are never starved and output ports are never blocked.

3. Machine M_i is *blocked* if any one of the buffers in $D(i)$ is full. It is *starved* if any one of the buffers in $U(i)$ is empty. When a machine is blocked or starved, it cannot operate, even if it is operational, so it cannot fail.

4. As usual, α_i indicates the repair state of Machine M_i and n_b is the amount of material (the level) of Buffer b. The capacity of Buffer b is N_b, and $0 \le n_b \le N_b$. The state of the system is

$$s = (n_1, ..., n_{k_B}, \alpha_1, ..., \alpha_{k_M}).$$

---

[2]Reprinted from *IIE Transactions*, Vol. 23, No. 4. Copyright 1991, Institute of Industrial Engineers, Norcross, GA 30092

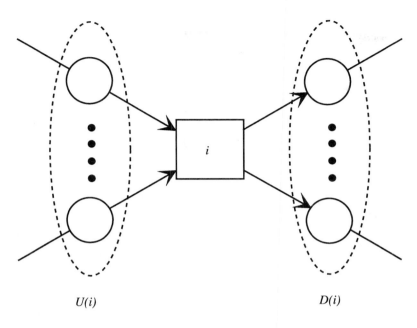

$U(i)$ $D(i)$

Figure 5.2: Assembly/Disassembly Network Notation

5. If Machine M_i is operational and neither starved nor blocked, it has probability p_i of failing. That is,

$$\text{prob} \left[\alpha_i(t+1) = 0\right|$$

$$\alpha_i(t) = 1, (n_b(t) > 0 \ \forall \ b \in U(i)), (n_b(t) < N_b \ \forall \ b \in D(i))\Big] = p_i. \qquad (5.1)$$

6. A Buffer b gains or loses at most one piece during a time unit. One piece is inserted into the buffer if the upstream machine $u(b)$ is operational and neither starved nor blocked. One piece is removed if the downstream machine $d(b)$ is operational and neither starved nor blocked. A buffer may fill up only after an operation is complete. Work on the next piece may not begin until the buffer is no longer full.

When machines $M_{u(b)}$ and $M_{d(b)}$ are neither starved nor blocked,

$$n_b(t+1) = n_b(t) + \alpha_{u(b)}(t+1) - \alpha_{d(b)}(t+1). \qquad (5.2)$$

More generally,

$$n_b(t+1) = n_b(t) + \mathcal{I}_b^u(t+1) - \mathcal{I}_b^d(t+1), \tag{5.3}$$

where $\mathcal{I}_b^u(t+1)$ is the indicator of whether flow arrives at Buffer b from upstream. That is,

$$\mathcal{I}_b^u(t+1) = \begin{cases} 1 & \text{if} & \alpha_{u(b)}(t+1) = 1 \\ & & \text{and } n_c(t) > 0 \; \forall \; c \in U(u(b)) \\ & & \text{and } n_c(t) < N_c \; \forall \; c \in D(u(b)) \\ \\ 0 & & \text{otherwise.} \end{cases} \tag{5.4}$$

The indicator $\mathcal{I}_b^d(t+1)$ of flow leaving Buffer b is defined similarly.

Steady-State Behavior   A steady-state distribution exists because the state space is finite. However, the steady state may be a function of the initial condition, so the system might be non-ergodic. An example is a system consisting of a single loop of machines and buffers (such as in Figure 5.8b) in which parts go from machine to buffer to machine without ever leaving the system, and where there is no opportunity for new parts to enter.[3] The number of parts in the system is constant. The steady-state distribution depends on the number of parts; therefore, the steady-state distribution depends on the initial state. Consequently, we can define

$$\mathbf{p}(s|s(0)) = \lim_{t \to \infty} \text{prob } \{ \text{ state of the system at time } t = s|$$

$$\text{state of the system at time } 0 = s(0)\}.$$

Performance Measures   The *production rate* of Machine M_i, in parts per time unit, is

$$E_i(s(0)) = \text{prob } \left[\alpha_i = 1 \text{ and } (n_b > 0 \; \forall \; b \in U(i)) \text{ and} \right.$$

$$\left. (n_b < N_b \; \forall \; b \in D(i)) \Big| s(0) \right]. \tag{5.5}$$

The *average level* of Buffer b is

$$\bar{n}_b(s(0)) = \sum_s n_b \text{ prob } (s|s(0)). \tag{5.6}$$

---

[3]The reader could reasonably ask what value there is in studying such a system. It can be quite useful when the parts are actually *pallets* or *fixtures* which move with parts. One machine is actually a load station, in which parts are assembled with the pallets. The machine immediately upstream is an unload station, in which parts are disassembled from the pallets. Or, a single machine does both operations.

Note that the steady-state performance measures depend on the initial state of the system. For example, for systems with loops, if the initial number of parts in a loops is 0, it will remain 0 forever, and the production rate and the average buffer levels will be 0. The goal of this section and Section 5.3 is to describe an efficient method for calculating E_i and $\bar{n}_b$ for tree-structured systems, in which the initial state does not influence the steady-state behavior.

Conservation of Flow   Because there is no mechanism for the creation or destruction of material, flow is conserved, or

$$E(s(0)) = E_1(s(0)) = E_2(s(0)) = \ldots = E_{k_M}(s(0)). \tag{5.7}$$

The Flow Rate-Idle Time Relationship   The isolated production rate of Machine M_i is

$$e_i = \frac{r_i}{r_i + p_i}. \tag{5.8}$$

The actual production rate E_i of M_i, which is less because of blocking or starvation, is

$$E_i(s(0)) = e_i \text{ prob } [n_b > 0 \ \forall \ b \in U(i) \text{ and } n_b < N_b \ \forall \ b \in D(i)|s(0)]. \tag{5.9}$$

This is a generalization of (3.17).

5.3   Decomposition Equations for Tree-Structured Networks

A *connected tree-structured A/D network* is one in which exactly one sequence of machines and buffers connects any two machines in the network. (The sequence need not follow the direction of material flow.) If there are $k = k_M$ machines, there are $k_B = k - 1$ buffers. This is a generalization of a transfer line.

Like transfer lines, A/D networks are difficult to analyze because of their large state spaces and their indecomposability. The decomposition described here generalizes that of Section 4.2; we approximate the steady-state behavior of a k-machine, $k - 1$-buffer system by that of $k - 1$ single-buffer systems. The parameters of the single-buffer systems are determined by relationships among the flows through the buffers of the original system. An algorithm is developed in Section 5.4 to calculate the parameters.

To emphasize the differences between the exact model and the approximate decomposition, we use subscripts to indicate machine or buffer index of parameters of System L, and parentheses to indicate the index of the two-machine decompositions $L(b)$. For example, $N(b) = N_b$, where N_b is the capacity of Buffer b of the system, and $N(b)$ is the capacity of the buffer of two-machine line $L(b)$. Since we are only dealing with tree-structured networks, in which the steady-state probability distribution is not a function of the initial state, we drop the argument $s(0)$ in the steady-state probabilities and steady-state performance measures.

Consider a system of two-machine lines $L(b)$. Their buffers b have the same capacities as those of the original A/D network. We seek the parameters (failure and repair probabilities $r_u(b), p_u(b), r_d(b), p_d(b)$) of the machines so that the behavior of the material flow in the buffers of the two-machine lines closely matches that of the flow in the buffers of A/D network L.

The rate of flow into and out of Buffer b in line $L(b)$ approximates that of Buffer b in L. The probability of the buffer of line $L(b)$ being empty or full is close to that of b in L being empty or full. The probability of resumption of flow into (and out of) the buffer in line $L(b)$ in a time unit after a period during which it was interrupted is close to the probability of the corresponding event in L. Finally, the average amount of material in the buffer of line $L(b)$ approximates the average material level in Buffer b in L. In order to find such parameter values, we use relationships among parameters and measures of a transfer line.

Pseudo-machine $M_u(b)$ models the part of the line upstream of b and $M_d(b)$ models the part of line downstream from b. There are four parameters per two-machine line (that is, per buffer in the A/D network): $r_u(b), p_u(b), r_d(b), p_d(b)$. Consequently, four equations per buffer, or $4(k-1)$ conditions, are required to determine them.

The decomposition method is based on the equation of conservation of flow (5.7), the flow rate-idle time relationship (5.11), and the resumption of flow equations developed below. The approach is to characterize the most important features of the A/D network in a simple approximate way, and to find a solution of the resulting set of equations.

For every Buffer b in L, define two-machine line $L(b)$, consisting of Buffer b, upstream machine $M_u(b)$ with parameters $r_u(b)$ and $p_u(b)$, and downstream machine $M_d(b)$ with parameters $r_d(b)$ and $p_d(b)$. The statistical properties of $M_u(b)$ are chosen to imitate those of the arrival process at Buffer b, and those of $M_d(b)$ represent the departure process. Let $E(b)$ be the efficiency or production rate of $L(b)$, let $p_s(b)$ be the probability of Buffer b being empty in $L(b)$, and let $p_b(b)$ be the probability of Buffer b being full in that two-machine line. $E(b), p_s(b)$, and $p_b(b)$ are functions of the four unknowns $r_u(b), p_u(b), r_d(b), p_d(b)$ through the two-machine line formulas of Section 3.6.4.

The objective of this section is to find a set of $4(k-1)$ equations for the $4(k-1)$ unknowns $r_u(b), p_u(b), r_d(b), p_d(b)$. The decomposition is represented in Figure 5.3[4].

Conservation of Flow   One set of conditions is related to conservation of flow:

$$E(b) = E(b_1), b \in \mathcal{B}, b \neq b_1. \tag{5.10}$$

where b_1 is any buffer in $\mathcal{B}$.

Flow Rate-Idle Time   It is useful to observe that in tree-structured systems, the probability of

---

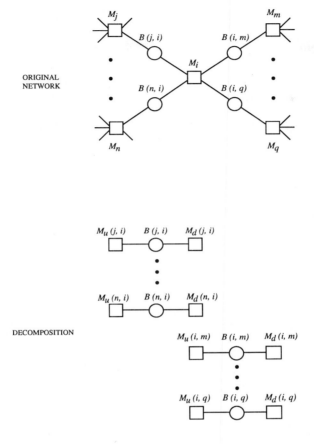

Figure 5.3: Assembly/Disassembly Decomposition

1. two or more buffers in $U(i)$ being empty at the same time, *or*

2. two or more buffers in $D(i)$ being full at the same time, *or*

3. one or more buffer in $U(i)$ being empty and one or more buffer in $D(i)$ being full at the same time

is small.

The probability of the last event is small because such states can only be reached from states in which $n_b = 1$ (for some $b \in U(i)$) and $n_c = N_c - 1$ (for some $c \in D(i)$) by means of a transition in which

1. Machine $M_{u(b)}$ is idle, *and*

2. $\alpha_i = 1$, *and*

3. Machine $M_{d(c)}$ is idle.

This event is rare because failures of M_i tend to fill buffers in $U(i)$ and empty buffers in $D(i)$. There is no single mechanism that does what is described here: empty buffers in $U(i)$ and fill buffers in $D(i)$. (The probability is not zero because there are possible sequences of failures and repairs of M_i and its neighbors that do this).

The other two events have small probabilities for the same reason. The production rate may therefore be approximated by

$$E_i \approx e_i \left[1 - \sum_{b \in U(i)} \text{prob } (n_b = 0) - \sum_{c \in D(i)} \text{prob } (n_c = N_c) \right] \tag{5.11}$$

which is an extension of (3.19).

The second set of conditions follows from (5.11):

$$E(i) = e_i \left\{ 1 - \sum_{b \in U(i)} p_s(b) - \sum_{c \in D(i)} p_b(c) \right\}, i \in \mathcal{M}. \tag{5.12}$$

Let u_i be the number of buffers in $U(i)$ and d_i be the number of buffers in $D(i)$. Then Equation (5.12), after some manipulation, can be written

$$\frac{p_i}{r_i} = (u_i + d_i - 1)(1 - \frac{1}{E}) + \sum_{b \in U(i)} \frac{p_d(b)}{r_d(b)} + \sum_{c \in D(i)} \frac{p_u(c)}{r_u(c)}, i \in \mathcal{M}. \tag{5.13}$$

This equation is an approximation since it follows from (5.11). It is an extension of Equation (4.2).

Resumption of Flow   In the following, we derive a set of equations of the form

$$r_u(i,m) = \sum_{(j,i) \in U(i)} r_u(j,i) X(j,i) + \sum_{(i,q) \in D(i), q \neq m} r_d(i,q) X'(i,q) +$$

$$r_i \left(1 - \sum_{(j,i) \in U(i)} X(j,i) - \sum_{(i,q) \in D(i), q \neq m} X'(i,q) \right), (i,m) \in \mathcal{B} \tag{5.14}$$

$$r_d(j,i) = \sum_{(\ell,i) \in U(i), \ell \neq j} r_u(\ell,i) Y(\ell,i) + \sum_{(i,q) \in D(i)} r_d(i,q) Y'(i,q) +$$

$$r_i \left(1 - \sum_{(\ell,i)\in U(i),\ell\neq j} Y(\ell,i) - \sum_{(i,q)\in D(i)} Y'(i,q) \right), (j,i) \in \mathcal{B} \quad (5.15)$$

which show the relationship between repair probabilities in neighboring two-machine lines and in the original line. Equation (5.14) says that the probability $r_u(i,m)$ of resumption of flow into a buffer (i,m), after a period of no flow, is a convex combination of the probabilities of resumption of flow into appropriate neighboring buffers. In fact, this is an equation of the form (2.2), where A is the event that flow from Machine M_i to Buffer (i,m) resumes after an interruption, where events $\mathcal{E}_j$ represent all the possible causes for the interruption, and where the conditional probabilities prob $(A|\mathcal{E}_j)$ are the coefficients $r_u(j,i)$, $r_d(i,q)$, and r_i. Similarly, Equation (5.15) says that the probability $r_d(j,i)$ of resumption of flow out of buffer (j,i), after a period of no flow, is a convex combination of the probabilities of resumption of flow into other appropriate neighboring buffers. Equations (5.14) and (5.15) are extensions of (4.6) and (4.7).

To derive (5.14) and (5.15) we must characterize the repair probabilities in the two-machine lines. To do that, we consider the meaning of failure and repair in those systems. Machine $M_u(i,m)$ in Line $L(i,m)$ represents, to Buffer $b(i,m)$, everything upstream of $b(i,m)$ in the A/D network. Thus, for every $i \in \mathcal{M}$, $(i,m) \in \mathcal{B}$,

$$\alpha_u[(i,m),t] = 1 \text{ iff} \qquad \{\alpha_i(t) = 1\} \text{ and}$$
$$\{n[(j,i),t-1] > 0 \; \forall \; (j,i) \in U(i)\} \text{ and}$$
$$\{n[(i,q),t-1] < N(i,q) \; \forall \; (i,q) \in D(i), q \neq m\}$$

$$(5.16)$$

$$\alpha_u[(i,m),t] = 0 \text{ iff} \qquad \{\alpha_i(t) = 0\} \text{ or}$$
$$\{n[(j,i),t-1] = 0 \text{ for some } (j,i) \in U(i)\} \text{ or}$$
$$\{n[(i,q),t-1] = N(i,q) \text{ for some } (i,q) \in D(i), q \neq m\}\}.$$

Compare the first part of (5.16) with definition of $\mathcal{I}_b^u(t)$. The second part of (5.16) is the logical negation of the first part. It says that a failure of $M_u(i,m)$ represents either a failure of Machine M_i or the emptying of at least one Buffer b in $U(i)$ (some buffer of the form $b(j,i)$) or the filling of at least one buffer c in $D(i)$ other than $b(i,m)$ itself. The emptying of b, in turn, is due to a failure of $M_{u(b)}$, and the filling of c is due to a failure of $M_{d(c)}$.

Because these conditions are mutually exclusive, the repair of $M_u(i,m)$ is the termination of whichever condition was in effect. Consequently, the probability of repair of $M_u(i,m)$ is r_i if the cause of the failure of $M_u(i,m)$ is the failure of M_i. If the cause of failure of $M_u(i,m)$ is the failure of $M_u(j,i)$, then the probability of repair is $r_u(j,i)$. If the cause of failure is the failure of $M_d(i,q)$, then the probability of repair is $r_d(i,q)$. This leads to Equation (5.14), in which $X(j,i)$ is the conditional probability that $M_u(j,i)$ is down given that $M_u(i,m)$ is down and $X'(i,q)$ is the conditional probability that $M_d(i,q)$ is down given that $M_u(i,m)$ is down.

If $r_u(i,m)$ is approximated as a constant, independent of the time t, the probability that a part enters Buffer $b(i,m)$ at time $t+1$ given that no part entered it (and it was not full) at time t is

$$r_u(i,m) = \text{prob} \left[\alpha_u[(i,m), t+1] = 1 \middle| \{\alpha_u[(i,m), t] = 0\} \text{ and} \right.$$

$$\left. \{n(i,m) < N(i,m) \text{ at } t-1\} \right] \qquad (5.17)$$

or,

$$r_u(i,m) \;=\; \text{prob} \left[\{\alpha_i(t+1) = 1\} \text{ and } \{n[(j,i), t] > 0 \; \forall \; (j,i) \in U(i)\} \text{ and} \right.$$

$$\{n[(i,q), t] < N(i,q) \; \forall \; (i,q) \in D(i), n \neq m\} \Big|$$

$$\Big\{ \{\alpha_i(t) = 0\} \text{ or}$$

$$\{n[(j,i), t-1] = 0 \text{ for some } (j,i) \in U(i)\} \text{ or}$$

$$\{n[(i,q), t-1] = N(i,q) \text{ for some } (i,q) \in D(i), n \neq m\} \Big\} \text{ and}$$

$$\{n[(i,m), t-1] < N(i,m)\} \Bigg] . \qquad (5.18)$$

Breaking down this expression by decomposing the conditioning event, we have

$$r_u(i,m) = \sum_{(j,i) \in U(i)} A(j,i)X(j,i) + \sum_{(i,q) \in D(i), q \neq m} A'(i,q)X'(i,q) +$$

$$B(i,m) \left(1 - \sum_{(j,i) \in U(i)} X(j,i) - \sum_{(i,q) \in D(i), q \neq m} X'(i,q) \right), i \in \mathcal{M} \qquad (5.19)$$

where we define

$$A(j,i) \;=\; \text{prob} \left[\alpha_u[(i,m), t+1] = 1 | \{n[(j,i), t-1] = 0\} \text{ and} \right.$$
$$\{n[(i,m), t-1] < N(i,m)\}] \qquad (5.20)$$

$$X(j,i) \;=\; \text{prob} \left[n[(j,i), t-1] = 0 \text{ and } \{n[(i,m), t-1] < N(i,m)\} | \right.$$
$$\{\alpha_u[(i,m), t] = 0\} \text{ and } \{n[(i,m), t-1] < N(i,m)\}] \qquad (5.21)$$

$$A'(i,q) \;=\; \text{prob} \left[\alpha_u[(i,m), t+1] = 1 | \{n[(i,q), t-1] = N(i,q)\} \text{ and} \right.$$
$$\{n[(i,m), t-1] < N(i,m)\}] \qquad (5.22)$$

$$X'(i,q) = \text{prob } [\{n[(i,q),t-1] = N(i,q)\} \text{ and } \{n(i,m),t-1] < N(i,m)\}|$$
$$\{\alpha_u[(i,m),t] = 0\} \text{ and } \{n[(i,m),t-1] < N(i,m)\}] \quad (5.23)$$

$$B(i,m) = \text{prob } [\alpha_u[(i,m),t+1] = 1|\{\alpha_i(t) = 0\} \text{ and }$$
$$\{n[(i,m),t-1] < N(i,m)\}] \quad (5.24)$$

This decomposition is exact because $\{n[(j,i),t-1] = 0\}$ and $\{n[(i,q),t-1] = N(i,q)\}$ and $\{\alpha_i(t) = 0\}$ are disjoint events. Machine M_i cannot fail if it is starved or blocked, and Machine M_i cannot become starved or blocked if it is down. We now evaluate the conditional probabilities.

The transition in (5.24) occurs when Machine M_i goes from down to up. Therefore

$$B(i,m) = r_i. \quad (5.25)$$

In (5.20), $A(j,i)$ is the probability of Buffer $b(j,i)$ making the transition from empty to non-empty. Buffer $b(j,i)$ being empty implies that machine M_j is down or starved by a buffer in $U(j)$ or blocked by a buffer in $D(i)$ other than $b(j,i)$. This is equivalent to saying that $M_u(j,i)$ is down.

The only way that $b(j,i)$ can become non-empty immediately after being empty is for $M_u(j,i)$ to recover. The probability of this event is, by definition, $r_u(j,i)$. Therefore,

$$A(j,i) = r_u(j,i). \quad (5.26)$$

Similarly,

$$A'(i,q) = r_d(i,q). \quad (5.27)$$

We now show that

$$X(j,i) = \frac{p_s(j,i)r_u(i,m)}{p_u(i,m)E(i)}. \quad (5.28)$$

Equation (5.21) can be written

$$X(j,i) = \frac{\text{prob } [n[(j,i),t-1] = 0 \text{ and } \{n(i,m) < N(i,m) \text{ at } t-1\}]}{\text{prob } [\{\alpha_u(i,m) = 0 \text{ at } t\} \text{ and } \{n(i,m) < N(i,m) \text{ at } t-1\}]} \quad (5.29)$$

because $\{\alpha_u(i,m) = 0 \text{ at time } t\}$ implies $\{n[(j,i),t-1] = 0\}$, and consequently the intersection of the events of the numerator and denominator of (5.29) (the events that appear in (5.21)) is the numerator event.

We have observed that the probability of a buffer in $U(i)$ being empty and a buffer in $D(i)$ being full at the same time is small. Therefore, the numerator of (5.29) is approximately the probability of $b(j,i)$ being empty. We assume $b(i,m)$ in $L(i)$ has the same probability of being empty as $b(i,m)$ in L, so the numerator is $p_s(j,i)$.

The denominator of (5.29) is calculated by making use of property (3.39) of a two-machine line:

$$
\begin{aligned}
r_u(i,m) \text{ prob } [\{\alpha_u(i,m) = 0\} \text{ and } \{n(i,m) < N(i,m)\}] &= \\
p_u(i,m) \text{ prob } [\{\alpha_u(i,m) = 1\} \text{ and } \{n(i,m) < N(i,m)\}] &= p_u(i,m)E(i). \quad (5.30)
\end{aligned}
$$

Thus, the denominator of (5.29) is

$$
\text{prob } [\{\alpha_u(i,m) = 0\} \text{ and } \{n(i,m) < N(i,m)\}] = \frac{p_u(i,m)E(i)}{r_u(i,m)} \quad (5.31)
$$

and (5.28) is established.

All quantities in (5.19) have now been evaluated, and the result is (5.14), in which $X(j,i)$ is given by (5.28). A similar analysis yields

$$
X'(i,q) = \frac{p_b(i,q)r_u(i,m)}{p_u(i,m)E(i)}, \quad (5.32)
$$

as well as Equation (5.15) for the second machine in line $L(j,i)$, where

$$
Y(\ell,i) = \frac{p_s(\ell,i)r_d(j,i)}{p_d(j,i)E(i)}, \quad (5.33)
$$

$$
Y'(i,q) = \frac{p_b(i,q)r_d(j,i)}{p_d(j,i)E(i)}. \quad (5.34)
$$

Finally, there are boundary conditions. Let $\mathcal{I}$ be the set of input ports and $\mathcal{O}$ be the set of output ports. For every $i \in \mathcal{I}$, let b be the buffer such that $i = u(b)$. Then

$$
\left.
\begin{aligned}
r_u(b) &= r_i \\
p_u(b) &= p_i
\end{aligned}
\right\} \quad (5.35)
$$

For every $j \in \mathcal{O}$, let b be the buffer such that $j = d(b)$. Then

$$
\left.
\begin{aligned}
r_d(b) &= r_j \\
p_d(b) &= p_j
\end{aligned}
\right\} \quad (5.36)
$$

There are a total of $4(k-1)$ equations among (5.10), (5.13)-(5.15), (5.28), (5.32)-(5.36) in $4(k-1)$ unknowns: $r_u(i,m), p_u(i,m), r_d(i,m), p_d(i,m), i,m \in \mathcal{M}, (i,m) \in \mathcal{B}$.

Interruption of Flow No additional equations are needed. However, further manipulation leads to another interesting result. Compare this with the Interruption of Flow equations of Section 4.3.2.

Equation (5.14) can be written

$$
r_u(i,m) = \sum_{(j,i)\in U(i)} r_u(j,i)\frac{p_s(j,i)r_u(i,m)}{p_u(i,m)E(i)} + \sum_{(i,q)\in D(i),q\neq m} r_d(i,q)\frac{p_b(i,q)r_u(i,m)}{p_u(i,m)E(i)} +
$$

$$
r_i\left(1 - \sum_{(j,i)\in U(i)} \frac{p_s(j,i)r_u(i,m)}{p_u(i,m)E(i)} - \sum_{(i,q)\in D(i),q\neq m} \frac{p_b(i,q)r_u(i,m)}{p_u(i,m)E(i)}\right), \quad (i,m)\in\mathcal{B}. \text{ (5.37)}
$$

This equation becomes, after multiplying by $p_u(i,m)$ and dividing by $r_u(i,m)$,

$$
p_u(i,m) = \sum_{(j,i)\in U(i)} \frac{p_s(j,i)r_u(j,i)}{E(i)} + \sum_{(i,q)\in D(i),q\neq m} \frac{r_d(i,q)p_b(i,q)}{E(i)} +
$$

$$
r_i\left(\frac{p_u(i,m)}{r_u(i,m)} - \sum_{(j,i)\in U(i)} \frac{p_s(j,i)}{E(i)} - \sum_{(i,q)\in D(i),q\neq m} \frac{p_b(i,q)}{E(i)}\right), \quad (i,m)\in\mathcal{B}. \quad \text{(5.38)}
$$

Equation (5.12) can be used to transform the last term into the following form:

$$
\frac{r_i}{E(i)}\left(\frac{E(i)p_u(i,m)}{r_u(i,m)} + p_b(i,m) + \frac{E(i)}{e_i} - 1\right), \quad (i,m)\in\mathcal{B}. \tag{5.39}
$$

Define

$$
e_u(i,m) = \frac{r_u(i,m)}{r_u(i,m) + p_u(i,m)} \tag{5.40}
$$

analogously to (5.8). Then, from the two-machine version of (5.9),

$$
E(i) = e_u(i,m)\left(1 - p_b(i,m)\right), \tag{5.41}
$$

and thus, the last term of (5.38) is simply p_i. Consequently, (5.38) can be written

$$
p_u(i,m) = p_i + \frac{1}{E(i)}\left(\sum_{(j,i)\in U(i)} p_s(j,i)r_u(j,i) + \sum_{(i,q)\in D(i),q\neq m} r_d(i,q)p_b(i,q)\right),
$$

$$
(i,m)\in\mathcal{B}. \text{ (5.42)}
$$

By a similar analysis,

$$p_d(j,i) = p_i + \frac{1}{E(i)} \left(\sum_{(\ell,i)\in U(i), \ell \neq j} p_s(\ell,i) r_u(\ell,i) + \sum_{(i,q)\in D(i)} r_d(i,q) p_b(i,q) \right),$$

$$(i,m) \in \mathcal{B}. \quad (5.43)$$

These equations describe how $p_u(i,m)$ and $p_d(j,i)$ propagate through the network. Note that while $r_u(i,m)$ and $r_d(j,i)$ are convex combinations of neighboring values and r_i, the failure probabilities are always greater than the probability of failure of the local machine, p_i.

5.4   Otero-DDX Algorithm

The algorithm described here, for solving the decomposition equations of Section 5.3 for a tree-structured A/D network, is based on the Dallery-David-Xie (DDX) algorithm of Section 4.2.2. We make no claims for convergence of the algorithm, uniqueness of the solution, or even whether a solution exists except to say that informal experience suggests that the algorithm converges whenever the machine parameters are on the same order of magnitude; and that it always seems to converge to the same quantities from different initial conditions. If it converges, it must converge to a solution of the decomposition equations. Experience also suggests that a numerical-coprocessor is helpful when the algorithm is run on a PC.

Evaluation Sequence   The DDX algorithm for a transfer line calculates r and p quantities in a natural order: that dictated by the shape of the line. In one phase, new values of $r_u(i)$ and $p_u(i)$ are chosen as functions of the just-calculated values of $r_u(i-1)$ and $p_u(i-1)$; in the other phase, new values of $r_d(i)$ and $p_d(i)$ are chosen as functions of the just-calculated values of $r_d(i+1)$ and $p_d(i+1)$. That is, the algorithm alternately proceeds down and up the line until the termination condition is satisfied.

There is no natural order in an A/D network. Therefore, we must create an *evaluation sequence* to traverse alternately in forward and reverse order. The evaluation sequence (1) determines the order in which the algorithm visits two-machine lines (that is, buffers) and (2) partitions the machines of the two-machine lines into two sets. It selects one machine of each line that it will visit during each phase of the algorithm. (For a transfer line, the DDX algorithm visits Lines $L(1)$, $L(2)$, ..., $L(k-1)$ and Machines $M_u(1)$, $M_u(2)$, ..., $M_u(k-1)$ in that order in the down phase; and Lines $L(k-1)$, $L(k-2)$, ..., $L(1)$ and Machines $M_d(k-1)$, $M_d(k-2)$, ..., $M_d(1)$ in that order in the up phase.) Evaluation sequences are not unique. In particular, the reverse of an evaluation sequence is an evaluation sequence. The partition is determined by the evaluation sequence.

The sequence is constrained by the following requirement. Each time the parameters of a machine are computed from a resumption of flow or flow rate-idle time equation, it is the only machine from its partition that appears in that equation whose parameters have not already been determined during the current phase. In the example below, the sequence starts at Buffer 7 of Figure 5.4[5]. The parameters of $M_d(7)$ are known by boundary conditions, but the parameters of $M_d(5)$ and $M_d(6)$ cannot yet be calculated. In the sequence chosen, $M_d(6)$ is deferred to the other phase, and $M_d(5)$ is obtained in the current phase after the branch connected to Machines 4 and 5 is analyzed. At that time, $r_d(5)$ can be obtained from (5.15) since $r_u(6)$ and $r_d(7)$ have already been determined in the current phase. Similarly, $p_d(5)$ can be obtained from the Flow Rate-Idle Time equation as modified below.

Notation Define the *evaluation sequence* $b(s), s = 1, ..., k - 1$ to be the order in which the algorithm visits each two-machine line during the Δ (for *down*) phase. During the Υ (for *up*) phase, it visits them in order $b(k - 1)$, $b(k - 2)$, ..., $b(1)$. Let $\mathcal{M}_\Delta$ be the set of machines that are visited in the Δ phase, and let $\mathcal{M}_\Upsilon$ be those that are visited in the Υ phase. Each of these sets contains exactly one machine from each two-machine line. The evaluation sequence is not unique. The partition is determined by the sequence.

Before constructing the sequence and partition, we first define

$$I_u(i, j) = \frac{p_u(i, j)}{r_u(i, j)}, \tag{5.44}$$

$$I_d(i, j) = \frac{p_d(i, j)}{r_d(i, j)}. \tag{5.45}$$

The Flow Rate-Idle Time equation (5.13) can be written

$$I_u(i, n) = \frac{p_i}{r_i} - u_i \left(1 - \frac{1}{E}\right) - \sum_{b \in U(i)} I_d(b) - (d_i - 1)\left(1 - \frac{1}{E}\right) - \sum_{c \in D(i), c \neq (i,n)} I_u(c)$$

or,

$$I_u(i, n) = \frac{p_i}{r_i} - \sum_{b \in U(i)} \left(1 - \frac{1}{E}\right) - \sum_{b \in U(i)} I_d(b) - \sum_{c \in D(i), c \neq (i,n)} \left(1 - \frac{1}{E}\right)$$
$$- \sum_{c \in D(i), c \neq (i,n)} I_u(c).$$

Because E is not known until the algorithm has terminated, we replace it by the most recent local values of $E(b)$. This equation is then replaced by

$$I_u(i, n) = \frac{p_i}{r_i} - \sum_{b \in U(i)} \left(1 - \frac{1}{E(b)}\right) - \sum_{b \in U(i)} I_d(b)$$
$$- \sum_{c \in D(i), c \neq (i,n)} \left(1 - \frac{1}{E(c)}\right) - \sum_{c \in D(i), c \neq (i,n)} I_u(c). \tag{5.46}$$

---

[5] Reprinted from *IIE Transactions*, Vol. 23, No. 4. Copyright 1991, Institute of Industrial Engineers, Norcross, GA 30092

Similarly, we can write

$$I_d(j,i) = \frac{p_i}{r_i} - \sum_{b \in U(i), b \neq (j,i)} \left(1 - \frac{1}{E(b)}\right) - \sum_{b \in U(i), b \neq (j,i)} I_d(b)$$

$$- \sum_{c \in D(i)} \left(1 - \frac{1}{E(c)}\right) - \sum_{c \in D(i)} I_u(c). \tag{5.47}$$

Construction of Evaluation Sequence   We now construct an evaluation sequence and corresponding partition $\mathcal{M}_\Delta$ for the Δ phase. The sequence for the Υ phase is the reverse sequence, and the partition $\mathcal{M}_\Upsilon$ is the set of machines not in $\mathcal{M}_\Delta$.

$s = 1$ Select any port. Then $b(1)$ is the buffer connected to that port. If it is an input port, $M_u(b(1)) \in \mathcal{M}_\Delta$ and $r_u(b(1))$ and $p_u(b(1))$ are determined by boundary conditions. If it is an output port, $M_d(b(1)) \in \mathcal{M}_\Delta$ and $r_d(b(1))$ and $p_d(b(1))$ are determined by boundary conditions. Increment s.

$s > 2$ Select any buffer $b(s)$ not among $b(1), ..., b(s-1)$ such that one of the following conditions is satisfied.

1. $M_u(b(s))$ is not already a member of $\mathcal{M}_\Delta$, but all the buffers that appear on the right side of (5.14) and (5.46) are among $b(1), ..., b(s-1)$. Then $r_u(b(s))$ is determined from (5.14), $I_u(b(s))$ is determined from (5.46), and $p_u(b(s))$ is determined from (5.44).

2. $M_d(b(s))$ is not already a member of $\mathcal{M}_\Delta$, but all the buffers that appear on the right side of (5.15) and (5.47) are among $b(1), ..., b(s-1)$. Then $r_d(b(s))$ is determined from (5.15), $I_d(b(s))$ is determined from (5.47), and $p_d(b(s))$ is determined from (5.45).

3. $b(s)$ is connected to a port. If it is an input port, $M_u(b(s)) \in \mathcal{M}_\Delta$ and $r_u(b(s))$ and $p_u(b(s))$ are determined by boundary conditions. If it is an output port, $M_d(b(s)) \in \mathcal{M}_\Delta$ and $r_d(b(s))$ and $p_d(b(s))$ are determined by boundary conditions.

If $s < k - 1$, increment s. If $s = k - 1$, stop.

As long as there are buffers not in $b(1), ..., b(s-1)$, there will always be a choice for at least one of these alternatives. There may be many choices. One possible approach to constructing a sequence is to start by picking a port arbitrarily, and then to proceed along its branch of the network until you reach a machine that is connected to more than two buffers. Then pick an available port closest to that machine. Proceed along the new branch until you again reach a machine that is connected to more than two buffers. There are two possibilities: (a) If it is the same machine you reached earlier, and you have reached it through all buffers connected to it except one, you can now work your way along the remaining branch connected to that machine, the one that you did not yet traverse. If there is more than one buffer connected to it not already visited, pick the next closest port and start again. (b) If it is not the same machine, pick a new port, preferably one closest to one of the machines that you are stuck at.

Evaluation Sequence Example   Consider the network of Figure 5.4. Table 5.1 indicates one possible evaluation sequence for this system.

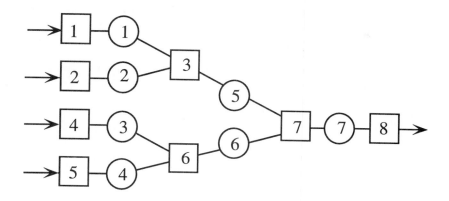

Figure 5.4: Eight-Machine Assembly/Disassembly Network

s	1	2	3	4	5	6	7
$b(s)$	7	4	3	6	5	2	1

$$\mathcal{M}_\Delta = \{M_d(7), M_u(4), M_u(3), M_u(6), M_d(5), M_u(2), M_u(1)\}$$
$$\mathcal{M}_\Upsilon = \{M_u(7), M_d(4), M_d(3), M_d(6), M_u(5), M_d(2), M_d(1)\}$$

Table 5.1: Evaluation Sequence for Figure 5.4

The procedure starts by selecting a port: in this case, Machine 8 and Buffer 7. Since the downstream machine of Buffer 7 is the port, $M_d(7)$ is in $\mathcal{M}_\Delta$ and $r_d(7)$ and $p_d(7)$ are determined by boundary conditions. Because the other machine that Buffer 7 is connected to is itself connected to two other machines, and because the sequence has not yet reached them, the next buffer must also be connected to a port. In this case, Buffer 4 is selected. This time, the upstream machine M_5 is the port, so $M_u(4) \in \mathcal{M}_\Delta$ and $r_u(4)$ and $p_u(4)$ are determined by boundary conditions. Again, Buffer 4 is connected to a machine that is connected to two other buffers, so the procedure again goes to a port. Buffer 3 is selected. Its upstream machine M_4 is again the port, so $r_u(3)$ and $p_u(3)$ are determined by boundary conditions and $M_u(3)$ is a member of $\mathcal{M}_\Delta$.

Buffer 3 is connected to a machine (M_6) that is connected to two other buffers, but only one of them (Buffer 6) has not yet been visited. Consequently Buffer 6 is the next member of the sequence and $M_u(6)$ is the next member of $\mathcal{M}_\Delta$. Similarly, Buffer 6 is connected to

Machine M_7 that is connected to two other buffers, only one of which (Buffer 5) has not already been visited. Therefore Buffer 5 is the next member of the sequence and $M_d(5)$ is the next member of $\mathcal{M}_\Delta$.

Now the procedure must again choose a port, and it picks Buffer 2. $r_u(2)$ and $p_u(2)$ are determined by boundary conditions. Finally, Buffer 1 is left. Its upstream parameters are determined by boundary conditions.

The Algorithm   As in Section 4.2.2, the algorithm consists of an Initialization, Step 1, and Step 2.

1. Initialization.

   (a) Select an evaluation sequence $b(s), s = 1, ..., k - 1$ and associated partition $\mathcal{M}_\Delta$ and $\mathcal{M}_\Upsilon$.

   (b) For every $M_d(b(s)) \in \mathcal{M}_\Upsilon$, and for every output port $M_d(b(s))$, set

   $$\begin{aligned} p_d(b(s)) &= p_{d(b(s))} \\ r_d(b(s)) &= r_{d(b(s))} \end{aligned}$$

   For every $M_u(b(s)) \in \mathcal{M}_\Upsilon$, and for every input port $M_u(b(s))$, set

   $$\begin{aligned} p_u(b(s)) &= p_{u(b(s))} \\ r_u(b(s)) &= r_{u(b(s))} \end{aligned}$$

2. Perform Step 1 and Step 2 alternately until the Termination Condition is satisfied.

   (a) Step 1. For $s = 2, \ldots, k - 1$ calculate the parameters of the machines in $\mathcal{M}_\Delta$. Calculate $I_u(b(s))$ from (5.46) and $r_u(b(s))$ from (5.14); or $I_d(b(s))$ from (5.47) and $r_d(b(s))$ from (5.15).

   (b) Step 2. For $s = k - 1, \ldots, 2$ calculate the parameters of the machines in $\mathcal{M}_\Upsilon$. Calculate $I_u(b(s))$ from (5.46) and $r_u(b(s))$ from (5.14); or $I_d(b(s))$ from (5.47) and $r_d(b(s))$ from (5.15).

Termination Condition   See discussion in Section 4.2.2.

Continuous Material System   Di Mascolo, David, and Dallery (1991) developed a similar method for the analysis of A/D networks with continuous material. For such systems, the approximation of Flow Rate-Idle Time equation that we use (5.13) is exact because the conditions in Section 5.3 concerning adjacent buffers simultaneously at their extremes are no longer merely very unlikely; they have probability 0.

Difficulties with Non-Tree Structured Networks   Networks that are not tree-structured have *loops* or *cycles*. That is, there is at least one machine such that it is possible to select a sequence of connected machines and buffers (without regard to the direction of material flow through them) that returns to that machine. The algorithm above cannot be used with such networks for two reasons:

1. The set of equations no longer makes sense. There are fewer boundary conditions (or even no boundary conditions, for an A/D network consisting of a single loop). This difficulty can be remedied by replacing the missing boundary conditions by a *specified-inventory* condition, when material flows in only one direction around a loop. That is, the total inventory — the sum of n_b around a loop — is constant over time. It must be specified for each such loop as a problem parameter, in the same way that r_i and p_i are specified. We can require that the sum of $\bar{n}_b$ have that value. (Other conditions can be constructed for loops in which material does not flow in only one direction. See Section 5.6.)

2. More importantly, the networks behave differently. One reason that the transfer line and tree-structured network decomposition algorithms work so well is that there is little or no correlation between buffer levels. If you are told the level of one buffer, you do not have much useful information about the level of another buffer. On the other hand, there can be a great deal of correlation in a loop network. If the total inventory around a loop is small enough to fit in one of the buffers, and you are told that it is all in that buffer, then you *know* that there is no inventory elsewhere. Furthermore, this is not a rare event: it can happen if the downstream machine is down long enough and the rest of the machines are up. To put it another way, the specified-inventory condition suggested above involves the *average* inventory, but a much stronger condition is true, involving the *actual* inventory. Consequently, the decomposition equations may not be appropriate for such networks.

5.5   Numerical Results

In this and later sections, the behavior of A/D networks and the algorithm is described in a set of examples.

8-Machine Network   We consider various cases of the eight-machine network of Figure 5.4. In Case 1, all the machines have $p_i = .1$ and $r_i = .1$; and all the buffers have $N_b = 10$. The solution, including $E, \bar{n}_b, r_u(b), p_u(b), r_d(b)$, and $p_d(b)$, appears in Table 5.2. Note the symmetry.

Case 2 is the same as Case 1 except that $p_7 = .2$. The results are presented in Table 5.3. The average levels of all the buffers upstream of Machine 7 have gone up, and the average levels of the buffer downstream of Machine 7 has gone down. The production rate has gone down. Symmetry is preserved.

Case 3 is the same as Case 1 except that $p_1 = .2$. The results are presented in Table 5.4. The average levels of Buffer 1, Buffer 5, and Buffer 7 have gone down, and those of all the

| Production Rate: .29354 | | | | | |
buffer	$\bar{n}$	r_u	p_u	r_d	p_d
1	7.3551	.1	.1	.1	.21462
2	7.3551	.1	.1	.1	.21462
3	7.3551	.1	.1	.1	.21462
4	7.3551	.1	.1	.1	.21462
5	5.6516	.1	.15210	.1	.18336
6	5.6516	.1	.15210	.1	.18336
7	2.6449	.1	.21462	.1	.1

Table 5.2: Results of Case 1.

| Production Rate: .25870 | | | | | |
buffer	$\bar{n}$	r_u	p_u	r_d	p_d
1	7.9444	.1	.1	.1	.26742
2	7.9444	.1	.1	.1	.26742
3	7.9444	.1	.1	.1	.26742
4	7.9444	.1	.1	.1	.26742
5	7.0529	.1	.13824	.1	.25283
6	7.0529	.1	.13824	.1	.25283
7	2.0555	.1	.26742	.1	.1

Table 5.3: Results of Case 2.

other buffers have gone up, in comparison to Case 1. This is because material enters Buffers 1, 5, and 7 at a lower rate than before, but leaves at the same rate. Material enters all the other buffers at the same rate as in Case 1, and leaves more slowly. The production rate has gone down. Symmetry is no longer preserved because the perturbation of the network is not symmetric.

Case 4 is the same as Case 1 except that $p_3 = .2$. The results are presented in Table 5.5. The average levels of Buffer 5 and Buffer 7 have gone down, and those of all the other buffers have gone up, in comparison to Case 1. This is because material enters Buffers 5 and 7 at a lower rate than before, but leaves at the same rate. Material enters all the other buffers at the same rate as in Case 1, and leaves more slowly. The production rate has gone down. Symmetry is not preserved because the perturbation of the network is not symmetric.

5.6 Equivalence

Introduction   Table 5.6 lists the results of the analysis of the network of Figure 5.1 with $p_i = .1$ and $r_i = .1$ for all the machines; and $N_i = 10$ for all the buffers.

Although Figures 5.1 and 5.4 are quite different, Tables 5.2 and 5.6 are identical except

buffer	Production Rate: .27328				
	$\bar{n}$	r_u	p_u	r_d	p_d
1	4.5640	.1	.2	.1	.17738
2	7.7077	.1	.1	.1	.24398
3	7.7077	.1	.1	.1	.24398
4	7.7077	.1	.1	.1	.24398
5	4.1089	.1	.21048	.1	.16416
6	6.5276	.1	.14388	.1	.22370
7	2.2923	.1	.24398	.1	.1

Table 5.4: Results of Case 3.

buffer	Production Rate: .26140				
	$\bar{n}$	r_u	p_u	r_d	p_d
1	7.9017	.1	.1	.1	.26292
2	7.9017	.1	.1	.1	.26292
3	7.9017	.1	.1	.1	.26292
4	7.9017	.1	.1	.1	.26292
5	3.4593	.1	.23927	.1	.15480
6	6.9609	.1	.13927	.1	.24739
7	2.0983	.1	.26292	.1	.1

Table 5.5: Results of Case 4.

for Buffer 5. A closer inspection reveals that the parameters of $M_u(5)$ and $M_d(5)$ are interchanged, and that $\bar{n}_5$ of Table 5.2 is $10 - \bar{n}_5$ of Table 5.6.

This is an example of *equivalence*. Two A/D systems are equivalent if they have the same number of machines and buffers, if there is a correspondence between the machines and buffers of the systems such that corresponding machines are connected to corresponding buffers (although the direction of flow through the buffers may be different), and corresponding machines and buffers have the same models and parameters. Systems that are equivalent have isomorphic Markov process models, and consequently have the same production rates, and identical or complementary average buffer levels.

The difference between Figures 5.1 and 5.4 is the direction of flow in Buffer 5 (as well as the changes in Machines 3 and 7 to make it possible). Note the equality of the production rates, the equality of all average buffer levels other than that of Buffer 5, and the complementarity of Buffer 5.

In this section, we study equivalence in Assembly/Disassembly systems in which the time to do each operation is an exponentially distributed random variable. The results are true for a much larger class of systems, including the deterministic processing time systems of Section 5.2, but they are easier to establish and illustrate in this simpler class of networks. It is important to note that we are *not* restricted to tree-structured networks so there are

| buffer | Production Rate: .29354 | | | | |
	$\bar{n}$	r_u	p_u	r_d	p_d
1	7.3551	.1	.1	.1	.21462
2	7.3551	.1	.1	.1	.21462
3	7.3551	.1	.1	.1	.21462
4	7.3551	.1	.1	.1	.21462
5	4.3484	.1	.18336	.1	.15210
6	5.6516	.1	.15210	.1	.18336
7	2.6449	.1	.21462	.1	.1

Table 5.6: Results of Figure 5.1

again k_M machines and k_B buffers, and k_M and k_B need not differ by 1.

System State and Markov Process Formulation   All notation and assumptions of Section 5.2 hold here, except that machines are reliable and the processing times are exponentially distributed. The rate that Machine M_i operates when it is neither starved nor blocked is μ_i.

The state of the system is then $n = (n_1, n_2, ..., n_{k_B})$. The system is a discrete state, continuous time Markov process (Section 2.3). The transition rate from state n to state m ($m \neq n$) is λ_{mn}, where $\lambda_{mn} = 0$, if m and n differ in more than one component, or if one component differs by more than 1. This is because two buffers will not change levels simultaneously, and because one buffer will not gain or lose more than one piece at a time. If $\lambda_{mn} \neq 0$, then $\lambda_{mn} = \mu_i$ where Machine M_i is the machine whose operation caused a buffer to gain or lose a piece. That is, if $m_c = n_c$ for $c \neq b$, and $m_b = n_b + 1$ then $i = u(b)$. If $m_c = n_c$ for $c \neq b$, and $m_b = n_b - 1$ then $i = d(b)$.

Steady-State Probability Distributions   The steady state probability distribution is given by the solution of (2.25) or (2.26) and normalization. Recall that even though a steady-state solution exists (because the state space is finite) it may depend on the initial state for non-tree-structured systems. Consequently, we can define

$$\mathbf{p}(n|n(0)) = \lim_{t \to \infty} \text{prob } \{ \text{ state of the system at time } t = n|$$

$$\text{state of the system at time } 0 = n(0)\}.$$

Then the steady state production rate of Machine M_i is

$$P_i(n(0)) = \mu_i \text{ prob } [(n_b > 0 \; \forall \; b \in U(i)) \text{ and } (n_b < N_b \; \forall \; b \in D(i)) \, |n(0)] \, .$$

Conservation of flow implies that we can define $P(n(0))$, where

$$P_i(n(0)) = P(n(0)) \; \forall \; i.$$

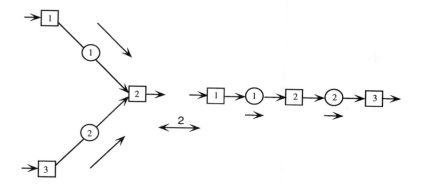

Figure 5.5: Equivalent Three-Machine Systems

The *average level* of Buffer b is

$$\bar{n}_b(n(0)) = \sum_n n_b \text{ prob } (n|n(0)).$$

Equivalence Theorem Let Z and Z' be two A/D exponential networks with the same number of machines and buffers. Assume that corresponding machines and buffers have the same parameters; that is, $\mu'_i = \mu_i, i = 1, ..., k_M$ and $N'_b = N_b, b = 1, ..., k_B$. Assume also that there is a subset of buffers Ω such that for $j \notin \Omega, u'(j) = u(j)$ and $d'(j) = d(j)$; and for $j \in \Omega, u'(j) = d(j)$ and $d'(j) = u(j)$. That is, there is a set of buffers such that the direction of flow is reversed in the two networks. Then

$$\lambda'_{m'n'} = \lambda_{mn}$$

in which $m'_j = m_j$ and $n'_j = n_j$ for $j \notin \Omega$, and in which $m'_j = N_j - m_j$ and $n'_j = N_j - n_j$ for $j \in \Omega$. That is, the transition equations for network Z' are the same as those of Z, except that the buffer levels in Ω are replaced by the amount of space in those buffers. In addition, the initial states are related in the same way: $n'_j(0) = n_j(0)$ for $j \notin \Omega$, and $n'_j(0) = N_j - n_j(0)$ for $j \in \Omega$.

As a consequence,

$$P'(n'(0)) = P(n(0))$$

$$\bar{n}'_b(n'(0)) = \bar{n}_b(n(0)), \text{ for } j \notin \Omega$$

$$\bar{n}'_b(n'(0)) = N_b - \bar{n}_b(n(0)), \text{ for } j \in \Omega$$

That is, the production rates of the two systems are the same, and the average levels of all the buffers in the systems whose direction of flow has not been changed are the same. The average levels of all the buffers in the systems whose direction of flow has been changed are complementary; the average number of parts in one is equal to the average amount of space in the other.

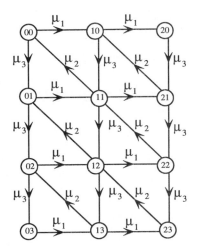

Figure 5.6: Graph of Three-Machine Assembly Network

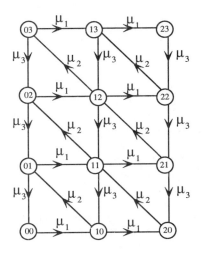

Figure 5.7: Graph of Three-Machine Transfer Line

Example: Three-Machine Systems   Figure 5.5 shows a three-machine assembly system and a three-machine transfer line. If we assume that the corresponding machines and buffers are the same in the two networks, then these systems satisfy the conditions above. Assume that in both networks, the machine service rates are μ_1, μ_2, and μ_3 respectively, and the buffer sizes are $N_1 = 2$ and $N_2 = 3$. Figures 5.6 and 5.7 show the graphs of the Markov processes of the two networks. The important feature to observe is that the graphs are identical except for the labeling of the nodes. Because the networks are tree-structured, the steady-state probability distributions are independent of initial conditions. The steady-state production rates of the two systems are the same; the average levels of Buffer 1 in the networks are the same; and the average levels of Buffer 2 in the networks sum to N_2.

Example: Transfer Line Reversibility   An important case of equivalence is the reversibility of transfer lines, which was observed in Exercise 8 of Chapter 4.

Example: Loop Networks   Figure 5.8 shows two networks which are equivalent if the corresponding parameters are equal. The number of parts in the loop network is constant because there is no way for parts to arrive or depart. This is not true in the other network; a different quantity remains constant. That quantity is the difference between the number of items in the upper branch and the number of items in the lower branch. The reason is that each time a disassembly occurs, one part is added to both branches. Each time an assembly occurs, one part is removed from both branches. The total in either branch does not change when any other event occurs.

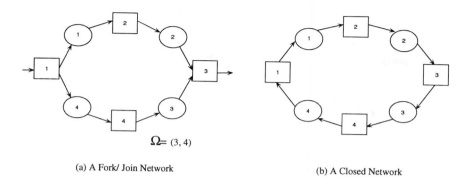

$\Omega = (3, 4)$

(a) A Fork/ Join Network

(b) A Closed Network

Figure 5.8: Two Networks with Loops

Example: Two-Machine Loop Networks Using the tools we now have, we can evaluate the production rate (P) and average distribution of material ($\bar{n}_1$ and $\bar{n}_2$) for a special case of a loop network. Assume that we have a two-machine, two-buffer loop system whose material flow and reliability behavior are the same as one of the types of two-machine transfer lines studied in Chapter 3. Let the buffer sizes be N_1 and N_2. We can transfer this into a two-machine, two-buffer A/D system with performance measures $P' = P$, $\bar{n}'_1 = \bar{n}_1$ and $\bar{n}'_2 = N_2 - \bar{n}_2$ as described above. Note that in the loop network, $n_1 + n_2 = n$, a constant that satisfies $0 \le n \le N_1 + N_2$; and that in the A/D system, $n'_1 - n'_2 = n_1 - (N_2 - n_2) = n_1 + n_2 - N_2 = n - N_2$, a constant which may be positive or negative.

We can now transform the new system into a two-machine, *one*-buffer transfer line. This is because the level in one buffer is determined when the level in the other is specified. To predict the behavior of Buffer 1, we need only observe the states of the machines and of Buffer 1, and not the level of Buffer 2. We can deduce everything we need to know about Buffer 2 from Buffer 1.

However, the range of values that n'_1 can take on is not simply $[0, N_1]$. This is because of the constraints imposed by the relationship between the buffer levels and by the buffer sizes. Since neither n'_1 nor n'_2 can be negative, we have

$$n'_1 \ge 0,$$

$$n'_1 \ge n - N_2.$$

Similarly $n'_1 \le N_1$, and, since $n'_2 \le N_2$, $n'_1 - (n - N_2) \le N_2$ or $n'_1 \le n$. To summarize,

$$\max(0, n - N_2) \le n'_1 \le \min(n, N_1).$$

Thus, the system consisting of Machine 1, Buffer 1, and Machine 2 has dynamics which are exactly like a two-machine transfer line, except that the minimal level of the buffer is $\max(0, n - N_2)$ and the maximal level of the buffer is $\min(n, N_1)$. This in turn has dynamics which are exactly the same as an ordinary two-machine transfer line with buffer size $\min(n, N_1) - \max(0, n - N_2)$. The performance measures of this line are P'' and $\bar{n}''$.

Then $P' = P''$ and $\bar{n}'_1 = \max(0, n - N_2) + \bar{n}''$. Consequently $\bar{n}'_2 = \bar{n}'_1 - n = \max(0, n - N_2) + \bar{n}'' + N_2 - n$. Finally, $P = P''$, $\bar{n}_1 = \max(0, n - N_2) + \bar{n}''$, and $\bar{n}_2 = n - \max(0, n - N_2) - \bar{n}''$. Compare with Exercise 16 of Chapter 3.

Other kinds of systems   Ammar (1980) showed equivalence for unreliable deterministic processing time systems; de Koster (1987) established equivalence for continuous material systems; Dallery, Liu, and Towsly (1990) showed that equivalence holds for general service time distributions; and many authors have studied reversibility for a wide variety of transfer line models.

5.7   Instability of Assembly/Disassembly Networks

There has been relatively little written on Assembly/Disassembly networks compared with the vast queueing theory literature. This may be due to one of the earliest results: Harrison (1973) found that assembly systems with infinite buffers are inherently unstable. That is, there is no steady state probability distribution, and that at least one buffer level increases without bounds. This result must have been discouraging to those who wished to study assembly systems by means of traditional queuing theory methods. This instability is not a concern in this chapter since we only consider systems with finite buffers.

Example   This instability can be illustrated with a simple system. Consider a three-machine deterministic processing time assembly system with machine parameters $r_1 = .81, p_1 = .19, r_2 = .85, p_2 = .15, r_3 = .80, p_3 = .20$. Let the sizes of its buffers be varied from very small to very large. The buffers are the same size ($N_1 = N_2 = N$). Machine 2 is the fastest machine, and Machine 3 is the slowest. Figure 5.9 demonstrates the variation of $\bar{n}_1$ and $\bar{n}_2$ with N. Figure 5.10 demonstrates the variation of E with N. These graphs have been obtained by using the algorithm of Section 5.4.

The limiting production rate is that of Machine 3: .8. This is because Machine 2 cannot perform assemblies any faster than material arrives in Buffer 1 and Buffer 2, and material arrives in Buffer 2 at a rate of .8 per time step. The average level $\bar{n}_1$ of Buffer 1 appears to increase without limit as $N \to \infty$, because material enters Buffer 1 faster than it can leave. The average level $\bar{n}_2$ of Buffer 2 appears to have an upper limit, because material can be removed from Buffer 2 faster than it can enter.

Equivalence and Instability   We can use equivalence concepts to demonstrate that all assembly systems are unstable when their buffers are infinite. Consider Figure 5.11. If we treat the input ports ($M_1, ..., M_k$) as representing arrival processes, this is a traditional queueing system, except for the assembly. If Machine M is the slowest machine, the system is clearly unstable, and all the buffer levels will grow without bound.

Therefore, we assume that some other machine is the slowest, say M_1. Now assume that all the buffers are finite, with sizes $N_1, ..., N_k$. We will let them grow, and deduce the limiting behavior of the buffer levels $\bar{n}_1, ..., \bar{n}_k$. Figure 5.12 is a system equivalent to Figure 5.11. Machine M has been transformed into a disassembly machine, the directions of flow through Buffers $B_2, ..., B_k$ and Machines $M_2, ..., M_k$ have been reversed. The steady-state average buffer levels are $\bar{n}'_1, ..., \bar{n}'_k$, and

$$
\begin{aligned}
\bar{n}_1 &= \bar{n}'_1 \\
\bar{n}_2 &= N_2 - \bar{n}'_2 \\
&\;\;\vdots \\
\bar{n}_k &= N_k - \bar{n}'_k
\end{aligned}
$$

Now let each of $N_1, ..., N_k \to \infty$. Each average buffer level $\bar{n}'_1, ..., \bar{n}'_k$ in Figure 5.12 approaches a *finite* limit because the slowest machine is M_1. Consequently, each of $\bar{n}_1, N_2 - \bar{n}_2, ..., N_k - \bar{n}_k$ remains finite as all the buffer sizes become infinite, and therefore each of $\bar{n}_2, ..., \bar{n}_k$ become infinite. Therefore, the system is unstable.

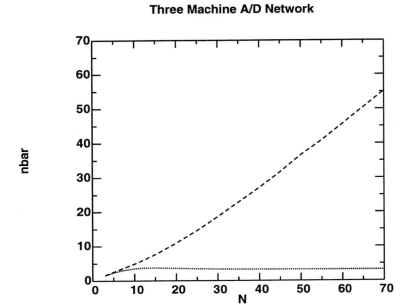

Figure 5.9: Average Buffer Levels of a Three-Machine Assembly/Disassembly Network

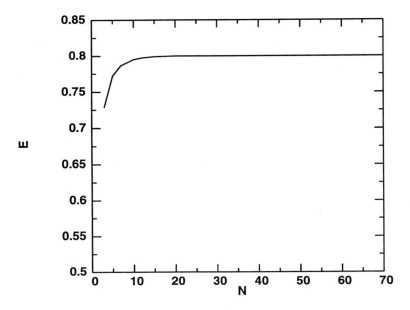

Figure 5.10: Production Rate of a Three-Machine Assembly/Disassembly Network

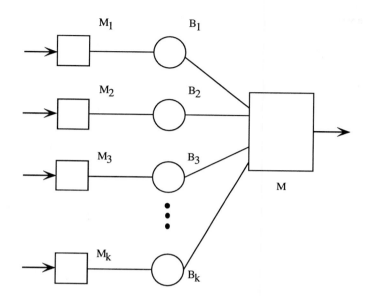

Figure 5.11: Assembly System

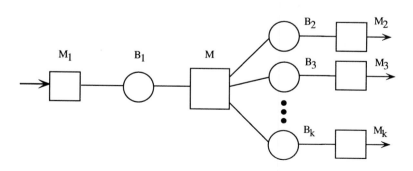

Figure 5.12: Equivalent System

Bibliography

[1] M. H. Ammar (1980), "Modeling and Analysis of Unreliable Manufacturing Assembly Networks with Finite Storages," MIT Laboratory for Information and Decision Systems Report LIDS-TH-1004; MIT EECS Master's Thesis.

[2] M. H. Ammar and S. B. Gershwin (1989), "Equivalence Relations in Queuing Models of Fork/Join Networks," *Performance Evaluation Journal*, Special Issue on *Queueing Networks with Finite Capacities*, Vol. 10, pp. 233-245, 1989.

[3] Y. Dallery, Z. Liu, and D. Towsley (1990), "Equivalence, Reversibility, and Symmetry Properties in Fork/Join Queueing Networks with Blocking," Technical Report MASI, No 90-32, Université Pierre et Marie Curie, Paris, June, 1990.

[4] M. B. M. de Koster (1987), "Approximation of Assembly-Disassembly Systems," Report BDK/ORS/87-02 of the Department of Industrial Engineering, Eindhoven University of Technology, Netherlands.

[5] M. Di Mascolo, R. David, and Y. Dallery (1991), "Modeling and Analysis of Assembly Systems with Unreliable Machines and Finite Buffers," *IIE Transactions*, Vol. 23, No. 4, December 1991, pp. 315-331.

[6] S. B. Gershwin (1991), "Assembly/Disassembly Systems: An Efficient Decomposition Algorithm for Tree-Structured Networks," *IIE Transactions*, Vol. 23, No. 4, December 1991, pp. 302-314.

[7] J. M. Harrison (1973), "Assembly-Like Queues," Journal of Applied Probability, Vol. 10, pp. 354-367, 1973.

[8] X. G. Liu (1990), "Toward Modeling Assembly Systems: Applications of Queueing Networks with Blocking," Ph. D. Thesis, University of Waterloo, Waterloo, Ontario, Canada.

[9] E. J. Muth (1979), "The Reversibility Property of Production Lines," Management Science, Vol. 25, No. 2.

[10] G. Y. Vives (1991), "Real-Time Scheduling of an Assembly Stage in a Production Stage," MIT Operations Research Center Master's Thesis, MIT Laboratory for Manufacturing and Productivity Report LMP-91-057.

Chapter 6

Jackson Network Models of Flexible Manufacturing Systems

6.1 Flexible Manufacturing Systems

A flexible manufacturing system (FMS) is a set of processing machines, a transportation system, a set of workpieces, a system for storing parts in processes, and a control system. Flexibility means that — unlike transfer lines or the Assembly/Disassembly networks studied in Chapter 5 — it is able to process more than one part type (*product flexibility*) or it is able to process the same part in more than one way (*process flexibility*).

As in the case of transfer lines, it is important to predict an FMSs most important performance characteristics, including its production rate and average in-process inventory. These are system design or planning issues. Because the system can make several part types, a new question arises that does not come up in transfer lines: which part should be loaded next? This is a real-time control issue.

In this chapter, we describe some work in calculating performance measures. Real-time control issues are treated in Chapter 9 and later chapters.

Comment This is an *extremely* brief overview of the field of queuing networks, and does not do it justice. Queuing networks, and their application to manufacturing systems is a large and growing area.

6.2   Queuing Network Models

Queueing networks are extensions of the $M/M/1$ queue of Chapter 2. The main strength of these, over less sophisticated models, is their ability to represent the delays that parts encounter in the system, and their ability to account for the less than full utilization of the bottleneck stations (Solberg, 1981). Because parts arrive at random and service times are random, a fully utilized station (one whose arrival rate equals its service rate) would exhibit instability and increasing delays.

The theory of networks of queues has developed gradually since the 1950s. It has had its main application and source of problems in computers and computer systems. There has been a great deal of interest in it among researchers in flexible manufacturing systems since the mid-1970s.

A network of queues, or queuing network, is a system in which customers arrive at a queue, wait until they are served, and then go to another queue or leave the system.[1] They spend a random amount of time in service, and therefore the time in each queue, and the total time in the system is random. The goal of the theory is to calculate such quantities as the steady-state probability distribution of the number of customers in the system, the throughput, the distribution of sojourn time (the length of time a customer spends in the system), etc.

The impetus behind the theory was (1) the analytic solution of a single $M/M/s$ queue, a single queue with Poisson process arrivals (exponentially distributed times between arrivals, exponentially distributed service times, s servers in parallel, and infinite waiting room); and (2) the observation that the output process from an $M/M/s$ queue in steady state is Poisson. Thus, if customers join a second queue with exponentially distributed service times, s' servers in parallel, and infinite waiting room, it can be analyzed as an $M/M/s'$ queue, and so can a third queue, and so forth. This is an elegant, surprising fact which can be used to analyze a tandem queuing system, a series of queues.

The same statement cannot be made about a general network of such queues. (In a general network, different customers can go to different queues when they depart from a server.) That is, the arrival processes and departure processes at queues may not be Poisson processes or independent. However, we can pretend that arrival and departure processes are Poisson, and that each queue is an $M/M/s$ queue, independent of all the others. Then we can derive formulas for the distribution of the number of customers, the throughput rate, and other quantities of interest. Such a derivation is incorrect, and not the procedure that Jackson followed. Amazingly, however, the formulas are correct. This is an even more elegant, surprising fact.

Limitations   Most of the literature on queuing networks makes a common set of assumptions. Buffers are almost always assumed to be infinite, so blocking never occurs. (One exception is Yao and Buzacott, 1986.) Consequently, they may only accurately predict the

---

[1]Queuing theory has its origins in telephone traffic and waiting lines in banks, and some of its jargon reflects this. In this chapter, we will freely switch among traditional queuing and manufacturing terminology. Thus parts are sometimes customers, machines are sometimes servers, and buffers are frequently queues.

performance of real systems in which blocking is an extremely rare event. In addition, they only work for a limited set of queue disciplines (the order in which customers in a queue are called to the server, such as first come, first served).

Queuing network models do not generally allow a system controller to observe the queue length or service duration at one station, and change the control policy of the whole system or of another station. This means that when failures occur (if they are modeled at all) or when a station takes an unusually long time to do an operation, the system is not allowed to take any kind of action in response. (The only feedback control that is allowed is that the service process at a station may be a function of the number of customers of each class at that station; or the total arrival rate from outside the system may be a function of the total number of customers in the system.)

All events are treated as random and deterministic processing times are not allowed, except by approximation. Scheduling of production events and any representation of non-production events (such as changes in setups or maintenance) are impossible or very awkward with these models.

In spite of all these limitations, queuing network models of FMSs are widely used and seem to work well. The field is a very active one in which much research is devoted to overcoming these limitations. In this chapter, we present a short summary of a small subset of these models and their application to FMSs.

6.2.1 The $M/M/s$ queue

Consider a single queue that is served by s identical machines. When one of the machines is idle and there is a customer waiting, the customer starts service at that machine. The arrival process to the queue is Poisson, and the service times are exponentially distributed. There is unlimited space for waiting customers. This is a generalization of the $M/M/1$ queue described in Chapter 2.

Let λ be the arrival rate of customers and μ be the service rate of each machine. Let

$$\rho = \frac{\lambda}{s\mu}$$

and let $f(n)$ be the steady-state probability that there are n customers in the system (waiting or in service). Then, if $\rho < 1$,

$$f(n) = \begin{cases} f(0)\frac{(s\rho)^n}{n!}, & n \leq s \\\\ f(0)\frac{s^s \rho^n}{s!}, & n \geq s \end{cases} \tag{6.1}$$

where $f(0)$ is the probability that there are no customers in the system. This quantity is such that distribution (6.1) satisfies

$$\sum_{n=0}^{\infty} f(n) = 1.$$

6.2.2   Jackson networks

Model   Consider a set of M queues. Queue i has s_i servers, each with exponentially distributed service time with rate μ_i. Queue i can get customers both from outside the system and from inside, and can send customers both outside and to other queues. Customers from outside arrive according to a Poisson process with rate γ_i. When customers complete service at Queue i, they flip a many-sided coin to decide where they go next; a customer leaving Queue i goes to Queue j with probability r_{ij} or leaves the system with probability

$$1 - \sum_{j=1}^{M} r_{ij}.$$

Open Network Solution   An *open network* is one in which $\gamma_i > 0$ for some i, and where

$$1 - \sum_{j=1}^{M} r_{ij} > 0$$

for some i (not necessarily the same i). That is, customers arrive from outside and depart from the system.

Let λ_i be the total rate at which customers arrive at Queue i. Then

$$\lambda_i = \gamma_i + \sum_{j=1}^{M} \lambda_j r_{ji}$$

if

$$\lambda_i < s_i \mu_i.$$

Customers arrive directly to Queue i from outside, and this contributes the γ_i term. Other customers come from other queues. The summation represents the fact that a fraction r_{ji} of the customers from Queue j go to Queue i, and we add it up for all j.

The total arrival process at a station is not Poisson and the queue lengths at the stations are not independent. But the following formula is correct anyway. Let $p(n_1, n_2, \ldots, n_M)$ be the steady-state probability distribution: the probability that there are n_1 customers at Queue 1, ..., n_M customers at Queue M. Let $f_i(n_i)$ satisfy (6.1), with s_i, λ_i, and μ_i in place of s, λ, and μ. Then

$$p(n_1, n_2, \ldots, n_M) = \prod_{i=1}^{M} f_i(n_i). \tag{6.2}$$

Closed Network Solution   A *closed network* is one in which $\gamma_i = 0$ for all i, and where

$$1 - \sum_{j=1}^{M} r_{ij} = 0 \text{ for all } i.$$

That is, no customers arrive from outside or depart. Now the set of n_is can no longer take on all possible combinations of values; instead, they must satisfy

$$\sum_{j=1}^{M} n_j = N, \tag{6.3}$$

where N is the fixed total number of customers in the system.

Let e_i be any set of numbers that satisfy

$$e_i = \sum_{j=1}^{M} e_j r_{ji}. \tag{6.4}$$

(e_i need not be the total rate at which customers arrive at Queue i. The e_is are sometimes called the *relative arrival rates*.)

Let $f_i(n_i)$ satisfy (6.1), with $s_i, e_i,$ and μ_i in place of $s, \lambda,$ and μ. Then, for all $n_1, \ldots, n_M$ that satisfy (6.3),

$$p(n_1, n_2, \ldots, n_M) = \frac{1}{G(M, N)} \prod_{i=1}^{M} f_i(n_i) \tag{6.5}$$

in which $G(M, N)$ is a normalization constant. That is, since

$$\sum_{\substack{n_i = 0, 1, \ldots \\ \sum_{j=1}^{M} n_j = N}} p(n_1, n_2, \ldots, n_M) = 1,$$

if we add (6.5) for all states, we must have

$$G(M, N) = \sum_{\substack{n_i = 0, 1, \ldots \\ \sum_{j=1}^{M} n_j = N}} \prod_{i=1}^{M} f_i(n_i).$$

The summations in the last two equations are over all possible values that $(n_1, n_2, \ldots, n_M)$ can take on.

Efficient algorithms (Buzen, 1973) exist for the computation of $G(M, N)$ for systems of practical size, although numerical difficulties arise as N grows. Approximation methods such as *mean value analysis* (Viswanadham and Y. Narahari, 1992; Buzacott and Shanthikumar, 1993) are also widely used.

Comments   This product form ((6.2) or (6.5)) is a very important property. It greatly simplifies the calculation of the steady-state probability distribution and of the performance measures. Many of the restrictive assumptions have been relaxed in the development of the theory of these networks, and the product form still applies.

One of the basic papers in this area is by Jackson (1963). A major extension appears in the paper by Baskett *et al.* (1975) (often referred to as BCMP). This paper allows many classes of customers; that is, the customers are labeled, and preserve their labels as they move from queue to queue. (In more recent work, customers can change their labels in a specified way.) There are different μ, γ, r, and N parameters for different classes. A variety of combinations of service time distributions and queue disciplines can be treated. The product form — an extension of (6.5) — still applies.

6.2.3   Application to FMSs

Solberg (1977, 1981) applies this theory to the prediction of performance of an FMS, and he contrasts it with the more simplistic "bottleneck model" (essentially the constraints of the linear programming formulation of Chapter 7). He says that the bottleneck model is too optimistic, and fails to take into account the effects of congestion and limited availability of parts.

In his model (represented in Figure 6.1)[2] there are $M - 1$ production stations and one transporter, which he regards as Station M. If we simplify his formulation, we define t_i as the average time a part spends at Station i in any one visit (for all stations, including the transporter), and v_i as the average number of times a part visits a station. (Note that v_M is then the average number of times a part visits the transporter, and therefore the average number of operations experienced by a part.) The *workload* w_i of a station is $t_i v_i$. The number of parts in the system is fixed at N, either as an operational policy or due to a limited number of fixtures.

A very simple routing scheme is considered:

$$r_{iM} \;=\; 1 \text{ if } i \neq M$$

$$r_{Mj} \;=\; q_j = \tfrac{v_j}{v_M} \text{ if } j \neq M$$

$$r_{ij} \;=\; 0 \text{ otherwise}$$

That is, parts go to the transporter with certainty whenever they complete an operation; after the transporter, parts go to Station j with probability $q_j = v_j/v_M$; and parts may not go from one workstation to another without passing through the transporter.

A solution of (6.4) is

$$e_j = \frac{v_j}{v_M}.$$

---

[2]With permission from Taylor and Francis, Ltd.

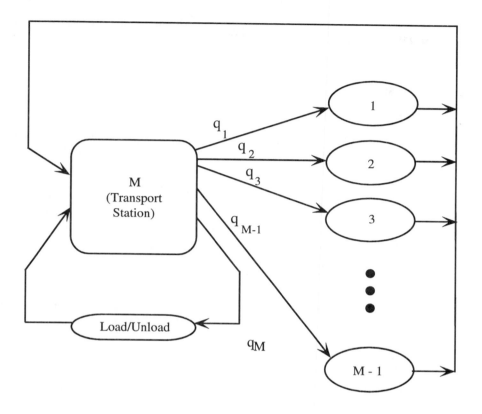

Figure 6.1: Solberg's FMS Queuing Network

Solberg shows that, for this system, the production rate P is given by

$$P = \frac{G(M, N-1)}{G(M, N)} \frac{1}{t_M},$$

and, since $G(M, N)$ is easy to calculate for this model, this is a simple way of calculating production rate for a flexible manufacturing system. Solberg gives a simple formula for the mean number of busy servers at a station, and, since (6.5) is an explicit representation of the probability distribution of the number of parts at each station, it is not hard to calculate such quantities as the mean number of parts at each queue or in the system, the probability of starvation of each station, etc.

Computational issues It is sometimes important to distinguish among different classes of parts, such as when different parts require different pallets, and there a limited number of each. It may be important to calculate the production rate of each part type. A product form solution is still valid, but the calculation of $e_{i\ell}$ (where i is the station and ℓ is the job class) and G, the normalization factor, becomes more complex. When the number of part classes becomes large, approximations are necessary to calculate the measures of performance.

6.3 Unreliable FMSs

Hildebrant (1980a, 1980b) considered FMSs with many part types whose machines failed and were repaired at random times, and where there was a specified amount of each type to be made. The problem he studied was to determine how to run the system while it was in each failure condition (each possible set of machines up or down) and to calculate the same performance measures discussed here. An approximation solution was obtained that determined a partial feedback rule. The idea was to think of the history of the production as divided into a set of failure conditions, and to determine the optimal set of requirements for each part type during each failure condition. Under each failure condition, the system can be thought of as a queuing network, and Hildebrant assumed it reached steady state.

If the operating parameters (such as the r_{ij} matrix for each part type) for each failure condition were known, and if the system persisted in each failure state long enough so that it reached steady state, the production rate of each part type for each failure condition would be known. If the fraction of time the system is in each failure condition were known, the overall production rate of each part type would be known.

The problem formulation is based on the following strategy: the fraction of time the system is in each failure condition can be estimated from MTTF and MTTR data for each machine. The set of production rates of each part type for each failure condition is treated as the unknowns in a nonlinear programming problem in which the objective is to minimize the expected time required until the production requirements are satisfied.

This approach is an important extension over the earlier work because it allows a response to machine failures. However, it is computationally complex and allows routing and dispatch strategies to be based only on the failure condition, and not on other important information, such as the amount of each part type that has been produced. This issue is treated in Chapter 9 and later chapters.

Exercises

1. Derive distribution (6.1). Draw a state transition diagram. Observe that the rate at which the number of customers (n) increases (goes from n to $n + 1$) is λ, independent of n, but that the rate of decrease (of going from $n + 1$ to n) is $n\mu$ if $n \leq s$ and $s\mu$ if $n \geq s$. What happens if $\rho \geq 1$?

Bibliography

[1] S.C. Agrawal (1975), *A Study of Approximations in Queuing Models*, Research Reports and Notes, Computer Systems Series, MIT Press, 1975.

[2] I.F. Akyildiz (1987), "Exact Product Form Solutions for Queuing Networks with Blocking," *IEEE Transactions on Computers*, Vol. C-37, pp. 121-126.

[3] I.F. Akyldiz (1988a), "On the Exact and Approximate Throughput Analysis of Closed Queuing Networks with Blocking," *IEEE Transactions on Software Engineering*, Vol. SE-14, pp. 62-71.

[4] I.F. Akyildiz (1988b), "Central Server Models with Multiple Job Classes, State Dependent Routing, and Rejection Blocking," *IEEE Transactions on Software Engineering*, Vol. 15, No. 10, pp. 1305-1312.

[5] F. Baskett, K. M. Chandy, R. R. Muntz, F. G. Palacios (1975), "Open, Closed, and Mixed Networks of Queues with Different Classes of Customers," *Journal for the Association of Computing Machinery*, Vol. 22, No. 2, April, 1975, pp. 248-260.

[6] G. R. Bitran and S. Dasu (1992), "A Review of Open Queueing Network Models of Manufacturing Systems," *Queueing Systems Theory and Applications, Special Issue on Queueing Models of Manufacturing Systems*, Volume 12, No. 1-2, December, 1992, pp. 95-133.

[7] O. Boxma and A. Konheim (1981), "Approximate Analysis of Exponential Queuing Systems with Blocking," *Acta Informatica*, Vol. 15, pp. 19-66.

[8] P.J. Burke (1956), "The Output of Queuing Systems," *Operations Research*, Vol. 4, pp. 699-704.

[9] P.J. Burke (1968), "The Output Process of a Stationary $M/M/s$ Queuing System," *The Annals of Mathematical Statistics*, Vol. 39, No. 4, pp. 1144-1152.

[10] J.A. Buzacott (1985), "Modeling Manufacturing Systems," *Robotics and Computer Integrated Manufacturing*, Vol. 2, No. 1, pp. 25-32.

[11] J.A. Buzacott and J.G. Shantikumar (1985), "On Approximate Queuing Models of Dynamic Jobshops," *Management Science*, Vol. 31, pp. 870-887.

[12] J. A. Buzacott and J. G. Shanthikumar (1992), "Design of Manufacturing Systems Using Queuing Models," *Queueing Systems Theory and Applications, Special Issue on Queueing Models of Manufacturing Systems*, Volume 12, No. 1-2, December, 1992, pp. 135-213.

[13] J. A. Buzacott and J. G. Shanthikumar (1993), *Stochastic Models of Manufacturing Systems*, Prentice Hall, 1993.

[14] J. Buzacott and D. Yao (1986a), "On Queueing Network Models of Flexible Manufacturing Systems," *Queueing Systems*, Vol. 1, pp. 5-27.

[15] J. Buzacott and D. Yao (1986b), "Flexible Manufacturing Systems: A Review of Analytical Models," *Management Science*, Vol. 32, No. 7, pp. 890-905.

[16] J. P. Buzen (1973), "Computational Algorithms for Closed Queuing Networks with Exponential Servers," *Communications of the ACM*, September, 1973, Vol. 16, No. 9, pp. 527-531.

[17] K. M. Chandy, J.H. Howard and D. F. Towsley (1975), "Approximate Analysis of General Queuing Networks," *IBM Journal of Research and Development*, Vol. 19, No. 1, January, 1975, pp. 36-42.

[18] W. M. Chow, E. A. MacNair and C. H. Sauer (1978), "Analysis of Manufacturing Systems by the Research Queuing Package," *Proceedings of Cambridge Philosophical Society*.

[19] A. E. Conway and N. D. Georganas (1989), "Queuing Networks — Exact Computational Algorithms," MIT Press, 1989.

[20] R. L. Disney (1975), "Random Flow in Queueing Networks: A Review and Critique," *AIIE Transactions*, Vol. 7, No. 3, pp. 268-288, September, 1975.

[21] W. J. Gordon and G. F. Newell (1967), "Closed Queuing Systems with Exponential Servers," *Operations Research*, Vol. 15, pp. 254-265.

[22] R. R. Hildebrant (1980a), "Scheduling Flexible Machining Systems when Machines are Prone to Failure," Ph. D. Thesis, MIT Department of Aeronautics and Astronautics, 1980.

[23] R. R. Hildebrant (1980b), "Scheduling Flexible Machining Systems Using Mean Value Analysis," *Proceedings of the 19th IEEE Conference on Decision and Control*, Albuquerque, New Mexico, December 10-12, 1980, pp. 701-706.

[24] J.R. Jackson (1957), "Networks of Waiting Lines," *Operations Research*, Vol. 5, pp. 518-521.

[25] J. R. Jackson (1963), "Jobshop-like Queuing Systems," *Management Science*, Vol. 10, No. 1, pp 131-142, October, 1963.

[26] F. P. Kelly (1979), "Reversibility and Stochastic Networks," Wiley, 1979.

[27] L. Kleinrock, *Queuing Systems; Volume I: Theory*, Wiley, 1975.

[28] A. J. Lemoine, "Networks of Queues: A Survey of Equilibrium Analysis," *Management Science*, Vol. 24, No. 4, pp. 464-481, December, 1977.

[29] Zhuang Li and K.S. Hindi (1990), "Mean Value Analysis for Multiclass CQN Models of FMSs with Limited Buffers," *European Journal of Operations Research*, Vol. 46, pp. 366-379.

[30] Zhuang Li and K.S. Hindi (1991a), "Approximate MVA for Closed Queuing Network Models for FMS with Block-and-Wait Mechanism," *Computers and Industrial Engineering*, Vol. 20, No. 1, pp. 35-44.

[31] Zhuang Li and K.S. Hindi (1991b), "Convolution Algorithm for Closed Queuing Network Models of Flexible Manufacturing Systems with Limited Buffers," *Information and Decision Technologies*, Vol. 17, pp. 83-90.

[32] R. O. Onvural, "Survey of Closed Queuing Networks with Blocking," *ACM Computing Surveys*, Vol. 22, No. 2, pp. 83-121, June, 1990.

[33] K. G. Ramakrishnan and D. Mitra (1989), "PANACEA: An Integrated Set of Tools for Performance Analysis," in *Modeling Techniques and Tools for Performance Analysis*, Elsevier North-Holland, Amsterdam, pp. 25-40.

[34] M. Reiser and S.S. Lavenberg (1980), "Mean Value Analysis of Closed Multichain Queuing Networks," *Journal of ACM*, Vol. 27, pp. 313-322.

[35] C.H. Sauer, M. Reiser and E.A. MacNair (1977), "RESQ - A Package for Solution of Generalized Queuing Networks," *Proceedings of 1977 National Computer Conference*, pp. 977-986.

[36] A. Seidmann, P.J. Schweitzer and S. Shalev-Oren (1987), "Computerized Closed Queuing Network Models of Flexible Manufacturing Systems: A Comparative Evaluation," *Large Scale Systems*, Vol. 12, pp.91-107.

[37] J. J. Solberg (1977a), "CAN-Q User's Guide, Report No. 9 (Revised)," School of Industrial Engineering, Purdue University, W. Lafayette, IN.

[38] J. J. Solberg (1977b), "A Mathematical Model of Computerized Manufacturing Systems," *Proceedings of the 4th International Conference on Production Research*, Tokyo, August, 1977. Published by Taylor and Francis, 1977.

[39] J. J. Solberg (1981), "Capacity Planning with a Stochastic Workflow Model," *AIIE Transactions*, Vol. 13, No. 2, June, 1981.

[40] B. N. Srikar and B. Vinod, "Performance Analysis and Capacity Planning of a Landing Gear Shop," *Interfaces*, Vol. 19, No. 4, July-August, 1989, pp. 52-60.

[41] N. Viswanadham and Y. Narahari (1992), *Performance Modeling of Automated Manufacturing Systems*, Prentice Hall, 1992.

[42] D. D. Yao and J. A. Buzacott (1986), "Models of Flexible Manufacturing Systems with Limited Local Buffers," *International Journal of Production Research*, Vol. 24, No. 1, pp. 107-118.

[43] W. Whitt (1983), "The Queuing Network Analyzer," *Bell Systems Technical Journal*, Vol. 62, pp. 2779-2815.

Chapter 7

Linear Programming

A linear program is a certain kind of mathematical problem which arises in a great variety of contexts (especially in resource allocation) and which is well understood. Because of its importance, there are many excellent texts on the subject. We do not discuss these problems exhaustively or in general; rather, we focus on issues that are needed in later chapters for the scheduling and planning of manufacturing systems.

7.1 Example

Two machines are available 24 hours per day. They are both required to make each of two part types. No time is lost for changeover. The times (in hours) required are:

Part	Machine 1	2
1	1	2
2	3	4

What is the maximum number of Type 1's we can make in 1000 hours given that the parts are produced in a ratio of 2:1? (That is, two Type 1's are made, on the average, for every Type 2, and we require up to 1000 hours of time on Machine 1 and up to 1000 hours on Machine 2.)

Formulation Let U_1 be the number of Type 1's produced and let U_2 be the number of Type 2's. Then the number of hours required of Machine 1 is

$$U_1 + 3U_2$$

and the number of hours required of Machine 2 is

$$2U_1 + 4U_2$$

and both of these quantities must be less than 1000. We must also satisfy the ratio constraint:

$$U_1 = 2U_2.$$

This leads to the following problem:

$$\max U_1$$

subject to

$$
\begin{array}{rcll}
U_1 + 3U_2 & \leq & 1000 & \quad(7.1)\\
2U_1 + 4U_2 & \leq & 1000 & \quad(7.2)\\
2U_1 & = & U_2 & \quad(7.3)\\
U_1 & \geq & 0 &\\
U_2 & \geq & 0 &
\end{array}
$$

The constraints are illustrated in Figure 7.1. Inequality (7.1), which is due to Machine 1, is not *effective*. That is, the solution does not satisfy it with equality. If it were changed by a little bit, the solution would not change. Because the constraint which is associated with Machine 2 is effective, Machine 2 is the *bottleneck*. Machine 2 is busy all the time; Machine 1 is not. The *constraint set*, the set of all possible solutions of the constraints of the problem, is the set of points on line segment AB, the set of points that satisfy (7.3), that lie between the origin (point A) and point B, the intersection of (7.2) (written with an equals sign, rather than an inequality) and (7.3). The solution is at that intersection.

7.2   General Formulation of Linear Programming Problems

Linear programming is a special case of nonlinear programming or optimization in which all the functions involved (the cost and the constraints) are linear. Assume $x \in \mathbf{R}^n, A \in \mathbf{R}^{m \times n}, b \in \mathbf{R}^m, c \in \mathbf{R}^n$. That is, x and c are n-dimensional vectors, b is an m-dimensional vector, and A is an $m \times n$ matrix. Then a linear programming problem is an optimization problem of the form

$$\min_x \sum_{j=1}^{n} c_j x_j$$

subject to

$$\sum_{j=1}^{n} a_{ij} x_j = b_i, i = 1, \ldots, m$$

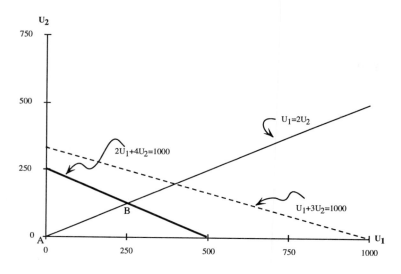

Figure 7.1: Constraint Set

$$x_j \geq 0, j = 1, \ldots, n$$

or, in vector form,

$$\min_{x} c^T x$$

subject to

$$Ax = b$$

$$x \geq 0$$

Slack Variables   Other, equivalent formulations are possible, particularly when *slack variables* are introduced. These are variables that are added to inequality constraints to put them in equation form, and do not enter the cost function.

Consider the problem

$$\min_{x'} \sum_{j=1}^{n'} c_j x_j'$$

subject to

$$\sum_{j=1}^{n'} a_{ij} x_j' = b_i, i = 1, \ldots, m'$$

$$\sum_{j=1}^{n'} a_{ij} x_j' \le b_i, i = m' + 1, \ldots, m$$

$$x_i' \ge 0, i = 1, \ldots, n'$$

Here, the first m' constraints must be satisfied with equality, while the rest are inequalities. We introduce a positive $(m - m')$-vector s, and reformulate the problem as

$$\min_{x', s} \sum_{j=1}^{n'} c_j x_j'$$

subject to

$$\sum_{j=1}^{n'} a_{ij} x_j' = b_i, i = 1, \ldots, m'$$

$$\sum_{j=1}^{n'} a_{ij} x_j' + s_{i-m'} = b_i, i = m' + 1, \ldots, m$$

$$x_i' \ge 0, i = 1, \ldots, n'$$

$$s_i \ge 0, i = 1, \ldots, m - m'$$

Now, if we let

$$x = \left(\begin{array}{c} x' \\ s \end{array} \right)$$

then x satisfies the form of the problem without inequality constraints and $n = n' + m - m'$.

For example, the problem of Section 7.1 is equivalent to

$$\min(-1)U_1$$

subject to

$$U_1 + 3U_2 + U_3 = 1000$$

$$2U_1 + 4U_2 + U_4 = 1000$$

$$U_1 = 2U_2$$

$$U_1 \geq 0$$

$$U_2 \geq 0$$

$$U_3 \geq 0$$

$$U_4 \geq 0$$

in which U_3 and U_4 are slack variables. Here, they represent the idle times of Machine 1 and Machine 2.

The constraint set of a linear program is always bounded by corners, straight lines, flat planes, and, in general, hyperplanes of various dimensions: a linear polyhedron. It need not be bounded. A *feasible solution* is a value of x that satisfies the constraints. It is in the interior or on the surface of the constraint polyhedron. It may or may not be optimal (that is, it may not minimize the cost). An *optimal solution* is a feasible solution that minimizes $c^T x$. There may be no optimal solutions, or there may be one, or there may be many. Because of the linearity of the problem, an optimal solution, if one exists, can always be found at a corner of the polyhedron. However, in some cases (which we will be very concerned about later in this chapter, and in Chapter 9), an optimal solution can also be found on an edge or on a face or in the interior.

7.3 Basic Solutions

Assume that there are more variables than equality constraints (that $n > m$) and that matrix A has rank m. That is, there are exactly m linearly independent columns in A. Then A can be partitioned into two parts, possibly after renumbering the x vector (and making corresponding changes to A and c):

$$A = (A_B, A_N)$$

in which A_B is the *basic part* of A. It is square $(m \times m)$ and invertible. The *non-basic part,*
A_N, is the rest of A. Correspondingly, we partition x:

$$x = \begin{pmatrix} x_B \\ x_N \end{pmatrix}$$

We choose

$$x_N = 0$$

so that

$$A_B x_B = b.$$

If

$$x = \begin{pmatrix} x_B \\ 0 \end{pmatrix}$$

is feasible, it is called a *basic feasible solution.*

The cost coefficient vector c can be partitioned similarly, and the cost is

$$c^T x = c_B^T x_B.$$

A basic feasible solution is a corner of the constraint polyhedron. To see this, recall that
x can also be partitioned as

$$x = \begin{pmatrix} x' \\ s \end{pmatrix}$$

where s is the vector of slack variables. Now n is the total number of variables, slack
and otherwise. Assume first that all constraints started out (before the addition of the
slack variables) as inequality constraints, that is, $m' = 0$. Assume also that the number of
inequalities was *greater* than the number of non-slack variables. (If not, the set of possible
x' is unbounded.) If n of the variables are 0, there are three possibilities: only x' variables
are 0; both x' and s variables are 0; and only s variables are 0. If only x' variables are 0,
the x' portion of the basic feasible solution is the origin of the x' space, and this is certainly
a corner of the polyhedron because none of the x variables may be negative. If both x' and
s variables are 0, the basic feasible solution is on a coordinate plane and also on one of the
planes of the form

$$\sum_{j=1}^{n} a_{ij} x'_j = b_i, i = 1, \ldots, m.$$

Such points are also corners because none of the x variables may be negative and it is not possible to have

$$\sum_{j=1}^{n} a_{ij} x'_j > b_i$$

for any i. Finally, if only s variables are 0, the basic feasible solution is the intersection of n' of the original inequality constraints. This determines a point in the positive orthant of n'-space, which is also a corner. Thus the picture of the constraint set is an object with one corner at the origin. Some of its faces meet at the origin and lie along coordinate planes. It is convex, and the rest of its faces lie in the positive orthant of the space.

If there are also some equality constraints, the constraint set is a slice of such an object.

7.4 The Fundamental Theorem

If there is a feasible solution, there is a basic feasible solution.

That is, if there is some point that satisfies the constraints, there is a corner point that satisfies the constraints.

If there is an optimal feasible solution, there is an optimal basic feasible solution.

If there is some point that satisfies the constraints and minimizes the cost, there is a corner point that satisfies the constraints and also minimizes the cost. If there is a point x that satisfies the constraints and minimizes the cost and is not a corner, then the corner point(s) that also minimizes the cost has the same cost as x.

7.5 The Simplex Method

The idea is to start at a corner (a basic feasible solution) and find another basic feasible solution whose cost is less. It is done by *pivoting*, or choosing a new set of linearly independent columns of A to form A_B. It consists of renumbering the x vector by switching one component out of x_B and replacing it with one component of x_N. The components that are chosen are those whose exchange would lower the cost the most. Geometrically, the method moves x along an edge from one corner of the polyhedron to an adjacent one, each time either lowering the cost or keeping it constant. It is guaranteed to converge to an optimal value of the cost if an optimum exists since the cost never increases and there are a finite number of corners.

This method is widely used because it generally converges in an acceptable amount of computer time. However, exceptions exist; there are problems that require excessive computer time. In addition, pivoting can introduce numerical errors. Some recently discovered methods overcome these difficulties (Karmarkar, 1984).

7.6   Parametric Linear Programming

7.6.1   Reduced cost

The purpose of *parametric linear programming* is to determine how the solution changes as we change some of the parameters (some components of A, b, or c). Recall that the solution is almost always on a corner. Therefore, as a parameter changes continuously, the solution at first does not change at all, and then jumps discontinuously to another corner. When the parameter takes on the value that caused the jump, all points in the region between the old and new corner are optimal.

To investigate the effects of changing a parameter, assume that we have found a solution of the problem for a nominal set of A, b, and c. Assume also that we have partitioned everything as described above. If we do not acknowledge that x_N is 0, we write:

$$\min c_B^T x_B + c_N^T x_N$$

subject to

$$A_B^T x_B + A_N^T x_N = b$$

$$x_B \geq 0$$

$$x_N \geq 0$$

However, we can use the equality constraint to eliminate x_B:

$$x_B = A_B^{-1} b - A_B^{-1} A_N x_N \tag{7.4}$$

so that the problem becomes:

$$\min \left(c_N^T - c_B^T A_B^{-1} A_N \right) x_N$$

subject to

$$A_B^{-1} A_N x_N \leq A_B^{-1} b \tag{7.5}$$

$$x_N \geq 0$$

Assume that each component of x_B is strictly positive. Then inequality constraint (7.5) is satisfied strictly (not with equality).

The only way for this problem to have $x_N = 0$ as a solution is for the coefficient of x_N in the cost function to be a vector with all components non-negative. (If some component of the cost vector were negative, we could reduce the cost by making the corresponding component of x_N positive. This would violate the assumption of the partitioning.)

Therefore, if we define the *reduced cost vector*:

$$c_R^T = c_N^T - c_B^T A_B^{-1} A_N$$

we know that

$$c_R^T \geq 0.$$

If this condition is satisfied strictly in all components, the solution is unique. If some components are zero, then the values of the corresponding components of x_N do not matter, as long as they are positive and (7.5) is satisfied. In this case, the solution is not unique. It may have any value along an edge, or on a face, or . . ., or in the interior, depending on how many components of c_R are 0.

7.6.2 Parameter changes

Suppose that a solution

$$x = \begin{pmatrix} x_B \\ x_N \end{pmatrix},$$

is found for an LP, and

$$c_R^T > 0$$

$$x_N = 0$$

$$x_B = A_B^{-1} b$$

Suppose the parameters of the problem are changed:

$$A' = A + \delta A$$

$$b' = b + \delta b$$

$$c' = c + \delta c$$

We investigate the effects of the changes on x. If the changes are small and the new problem is feasible, three things can happen.

(1) The old partition between basic and non-basic remains valid. The solution remains at the same corner as before, although the location of the corner may change. For this to happen, we must have

$$c'^T_R > 0$$

$$0 \leq A'^{-1}_B b'$$

Then the old partition is still valid and x'_N remains 0. However, x'_B is now

$$x'_B = {A'}_B^{-1} b'$$

Note that for some parameter changes, x_B does not change at all. In particular, if the cost c is modified but A and b are not, then x_B does not change. Geometrically, the polyhedron is unchanged, and the solution remains at the same corner.

(2) If, after the change, some component of the reduced cost c'_R is negative, the old partitioning is not valid. The solution must be recalculated. If the parameter change is small, the old solution is a good starting point for the simplex procedure.

(3) If, after the change, some component of the reduced cost c'_R is 0, the old partitioning remains valid. The solution need not be recalculated. However, other solutions are also valid, and all convex combinations of the old solution and the new solutions are valid.

We use these observations in scheduling manufacturing systems. In the formulation of Chapter 9, c changes while A and b stay constant.

7.6.3   Continuous parameter changes

Consider the situation where c changes continuously. That is, $c = c(s)$, a continuous function of a real number s. Since A and b are constant, the polyhedron does not change. Assume that when $s = 0$, the reduced cost $c_R(0)$ is strictly positive in all components. As s increases, some components of the reduced cost $c_R(s)$ increase and some decrease. (If none ever decrease, the solution $x(s)$ does not change and there is nothing further to discuss.)

Nothing interesting happens until s reaches a value such that one of the components of the reduced cost becomes equal to 0. At that point, the old solution is still optimal, but other points become optimal as well. This is because the corresponding components of $x_N(s)$ can become positive without increasing the cost. The new set of optimal solutions is an edge, or face, or higher dimensional object (depending on the number of components of c_R that are 0) that includes the old corner solution.

As s keeps changing, some components of $c_R(s)$ become negative. Now the old partition is no longer valid. The solution jumps abruptly to a new corner. This corner will be a member of the set of solutions that we found when those components of c_R were 0.

7.7   Example

$$\max_{x_1, x_2} x_1 + s x_2$$

subject to

$$3x_1 + 4x_2 \quad \leq \quad 1000$$

$$x_1 \quad \geq \quad 0$$

$$x_2 \quad \geq \quad 0$$

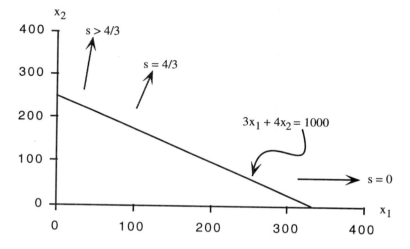

Figure 7.2: Constraint Set and Cost Vectors

The constraint set, and the objective coefficient vector, for three values of s, are illustrated in Figure 7.2. We must introduce a slack variable, x_3, and change the max to a min to put the problem in standard form:

$$\min_{x_1, x_2, x_3} \quad -x_1 - sx_2$$

subject to

$$3x_1 + 4x_2 + x_3 \quad = \quad 1000$$

$$x_1 \quad \geq \quad 0$$

$$x_2 \quad \geq \quad 0$$

$$x_3 \quad \geq \quad 0$$

Since there is one equality constraint, the basic part of the problem is 1-dimensional, and the non-basic part is 2-dimensional. At $s = 0$, the solution is

$$x_1 = \frac{1000}{3}, x_2 = 0, x_3 = 0.$$

This means that the basic part is x_1 and (x_2, x_3) form the non-basic part. Thus:

$$c_B = -1; c_N = \begin{pmatrix} -s \\ 0 \end{pmatrix}$$

$$A_B = 3; A_N = (4, 1)$$

so

$$c_R^T = (-s, 0) - (-1)\frac{1}{3}(4, 1) = \left(\frac{4}{3} - s, \frac{1}{3}\right)$$

which implies that the jump occurs at $s = \frac{4}{3}$. Note that at that value, the problem is essentially

$$\max 3x_1 + 4x_2$$

subject to

$$3x_1 + 4x_2 \leq 1000, x_1 \geq 0, x_2 \geq 0.$$

Thus, we are indifferent to the values of x_1 and x_2 as long as $3x_1 + 4x_2 = 1000$.
When $s \geq \frac{4}{3}$, the solution is

$$x_1 = 0, x_2 = 250, x_3 = 0.$$

To summarize: For $0 \leq s < \frac{4}{3}$,

$$x_1 = \frac{1000}{3}, x_2 = 0, x_3 = 0;$$

for $s = \frac{4}{3}$,

$$3x_1 + 4x_2 = 1000, x_1 \geq 0, x_2 \geq 0, x_3 = 0;$$

for $s > \frac{4}{3}$,

$$x_1 = 0, x_2 = 250, x_3 = 0.$$

Exercises

1. Consider the following optimization problem:

$$\max 12x_1 + x_2 + 7x_3$$

subject to

$$
\begin{array}{rcl}
3x_1 + 4x_2 - 19x_3 & \leq & 100 \\
5x_1 + 2x_2 & \leq & 0 \\
x_1 - 86 & \geq & 0 \\
x_2 & \leq & 13
\end{array}
$$

Find a change of variables to rewrite this into the standard form of Section 7.2.

2. Briefly describe the effect of changing some components of the b vector, in a way similar to the discussion of the effect of changing c in Section 7.6.3. Does x change discontinuously? Under what conditions does x change smoothly with b, and when does it vary in a non-smooth manner?

3. Describe the behavior of the solution of the problem in Section 7.7 for $s < 0$.

4. Describe the behavior of the solution to the following linear program as a function of s:

$$\max x_1 + sx_2$$

subject to

$$3x_1 + 4x_2 \leq 1000$$

$$5x_1 + 2x_2 \leq 1000$$

$$x_1 \geq 0$$

$$x_2 \geq 0$$

Draw the constraint set, and label the solution points for each value of s.

Bibliography

[1] M. S. Bazaraa and J. J. Jarvis, *Linear Programming and Network Flows*, Wiley, 1977.

[2] S. P. Bradley, A. C. Hax, and T. L. Magnanti, *Applied Mathematical Programming*, Addison-Wesley, 1977.

[3] G. B. Dantzig, *Linear Programming and Extensions*, Princeton University Press, 1963.

[4] G. Hadley, *Linear Programming*, Addison-Wesley, 1962.

[5] N. Karmarkar (1984), "A New Polynomial Time Algorithm for Linear Programming," *Combinatorica*, Volume 4, pp. 373-395, 1984.

[6] D. G. Luenberger, *Introduction to Linear and Nonlinear Programming*, Addison-Wesley, 1973.

[7] H. A. Taha, *Operations Research*, Macmillan, 1982.

Chapter 8

Dynamic Programming

Dynamic programming problems deal with the making of decisions over time. Chapter 2 provides four ways to classify a dynamic system:

- the nature of the time index;

- the nature of the state;

- whether the system is stochastic or deterministic; and

- whether or not there are decision variables that must be chosen as part of the evolution of the system.

There are no decision variables in the systems of Chapter 2. We introduce decision variables here. In later chapters, we use the results in determining real-time operating policies for manufacturing systems.

Dynamic programming problems are generalizations of calculus of variations and control theory problems. They are most important when they lead to feedback control policies: decisions that are made in response to events. We do not survey the entire field here; instead we focus on specific issues that we make use of in later chapters.

While dynamic programming problems are stated in terms of optimality, feedback is useful even when it results in merely acceptable behavior. This is a good thing, because, as we see in this and later chapters, the optimal solution is very often hard to obtain. On the other hand, some information on the structure of the solution is often easy to obtain, and approximations can be based on it.

8.1   Example — Discrete Time, Discrete State, Deterministic

Consider the network in Figure 8.1. Think of it as a transportation network, where the nodes are intermediate points and the links represent roads or other means of traveling from node to node. It could also represent a communications network.

The links are directed. That is, travel may proceed only in the indicated direction. The costs associated with traversing each link are also indicated. At several nodes (such as A and K) there are more than one possible outgoing links. There are no loops in the system. That is, once you leave a node, you cannot return to that node because there are no paths that lead back to it.

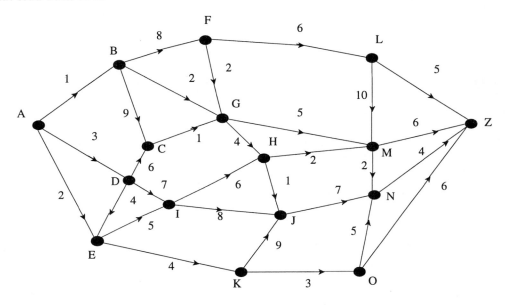

Figure 8.1: Link Costs from A to Z

Problem   Find the path (the sequence of nodes and links) from A to Z that minimizes the total cost.

Solution   Let $g(i,j)$ be the indicated cost of traversing the link from Node i to Node j, if a link exists. If the tth node to be reached on a path from A to Z is $i(t)$, then the path cost is

$$\sum_{t=1}^{T} g(i(t-1), i(t))$$

where T is the number of nodes on the path, $i(0) = A$, and $i(T) = Z$. Note that T is not specified; it is part of the solution. For every node i, let $J(i)$ be the optimal cost to go from Node i to Node Z (that is, the cost of the optimal path from i to Z). Then $J(i)$ satisfies

$$J(Z) = 0$$

and, if the optimal path from i to Z traverses link (i, j),

$$J(i) = g(i, j) + J(j).$$

Suppose that several links go out of Node i. Suppose that for each node j for which a link exists from i to j, the optimal cost $J(j)$ from j to Z is known. Then the optimal path from i to Z is the one that minimizes the sum of the costs from i to j and from j to Z. That is,

$$J(i) = \min_{j} [g(i, j) + J(j)] \tag{8.1}$$

where the minimization is performed over all j such that a link from i to j exists.

This suggests an algorithm to find the optimal path. For each node i, the cost $J(i)$ is calculated at the same time that the path from i to Z is determined.

1. Set $J(Z) = 0$. At this point, this is the only node whose cost has been calculated.

2. Look at all the nodes i whose costs $J(i)$ have not already been determined, and which are connected through a single link to nodes whose costs are already known. That is, consider only those nodes i such that

   - $J(i)$ has not yet been found, and
   - for each node j in which link (i, j) exists, $J(j)$ is already calculated.

   Now assign $J(i)$ according to (8.1).

   For example, assume that we are ready to calculate $J(K)$. We must already have found that $J(O) = 6$ and $J(J) = 11$. Then

   $$J(K) = \min \left\{ \begin{array}{c} g(K, O) + J(O) \\ \\ g(K, J) + J(J) \end{array} \right\}$$

   $$= \min \left\{ \begin{array}{c} 3 + 6 \\ \\ 9 + 11 \end{array} \right\} = 9.$$

   At each node i, note the cost $J(i)$ and the decision of which node j to visit next.

3. Repeat Step (2) until all nodes, including A, have costs calculated.

The optimal path starts at A and visits the nodes in the sequence determined by the decisions of Step (2). The cost of that path is $J(A)$. $J(i)$ and the optimal decisions are indicated in Figure 8.2.

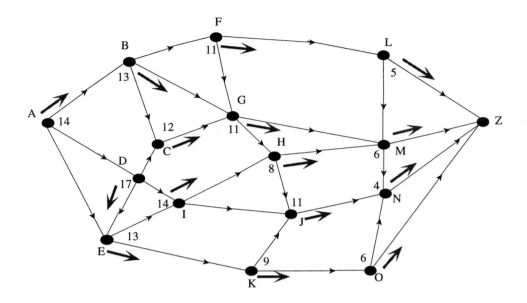

Figure 8.2: Minimal Costs to Z

Discussion   In spite of the simplicity of this problem, it is of great significance. Besides its practical use in the calculation of minimal cost paths in networks, it has features that appear in many dynamic programming problems. The important features are

- *the cost-to-go function $J(i)$;*

- *the one-step recursion equation (8.1) that determines $J(i)$;*

- *that the solution is determined for every i,* not just A and not just nodes on the optimal path;

- *that $J(i)$ depends on the nodes to be visited after i,* not those that were visited between A and i. The only thing that matters is the present state and the future. How the system got to its present state is not important. In this respect, it resembles Markov chains and processes.

Equation (8.1) is a fundamental equation. Some form of it is found in all the dynamic programming problems of this and subsequent chapters. This problem is one with discrete state (the current node) and discrete time (the number of links already traversed). Problems with continuous state and time have continuous versions of (8.1).

8.2 Example—Continuous Time, Mixed State, Stochastic

This example is a preview of Chapter 9. A machine can make two part types. It requires τ_1 time units to make Type 1 parts and τ_2 time units to make Type 2 parts. The machine is perfectly flexible in the sense that it can perform a Type 2 operation immediately after a Type 1 operation with no time lost or cost incurred for changeover (and vice versa). That is, the time for making a Type 1 and a Type 2 is $\tau_1 + \tau_2$, regardless of the order or other considerations. Assume that raw parts of both types are always available.

The machine sometimes fails. The time between the occurrence of the failure and the completion of the repair is exponentially distributed with mean $1/r$. The time between the completion of a repair and the occurrence of the next failure is exponentially distributed with mean $1/p$.

Whenever the machine is operational and not occupied in an operation, we are free to choose to initiate a Type 1 operation, to initiate a Type 2 operation, or to let the machine be idle. The problem is to decide which to do at all times.

We are required to make the two part types at rates d_1 and d_2. These two quantities can be considered to be constants for the time period of this problem. In fact, for every time t (after the start of the production run) the number of Type 1 parts produced must be as close as possible to $d_1 t$, and the number of Type 2 parts produced must be as close as possible to $d_2 t$. We are penalized for surplus because it leads to unnecessary inventory and we are penalized for backlog because it leads to downstream starvation.

For the problem to make sense, the demand should be feasible. That is, it should be possible to produce parts at those rates in the long run (assuming that we are not spectacularly unlucky). A necessary condition for this is that we have not required the machine to be busy more than 100% of the time. The fraction of time it is devoted to making Type j parts is

$$\tau_j d_j$$

for $j = 1$ and 2. To understand why this is true, see the example of Section 7.1. In that example, U_j parts are needed in 1000 hours, and each Type j part required τ_{ij} hours on Machine i (which are specified in the table). The amount of time Machine i is utilized in that 1000 hours is

$$\tau_{ij} U_j.$$

Therefore, the fraction of time that Machine i is busy making Type j parts is

$$\frac{\tau_{ij} U_j}{1000} = \tau_{ij} \frac{U_j}{1000} = \tau_{ij} d_j.$$

The fraction of time the machine is down is

$$\frac{p}{r + p}.$$

Thus, a condition on the problem data is

$$\tau_1 d_1 + \tau_2 d_2 + \frac{p}{r+p} \leq 1.$$

In other words, if your boss hands you the assignment of producing parts at rate d_1 and d_2 on this machine and this inequality is violated, protest because the assignment cannot be done.

Formulation Instead of dealing directly with the time instants at which we will load the two part types, we will instead deal with the production rates of the part types. We will allow these rates to vary with time, with the repair state of the machine, and anything else we choose. Once we find those rates, we have the further problem of actually loading parts at those rates, but we will assume that problem away for now.

Let u_j be the rate at which we produce Type j parts.[1] Let x_j be the surplus (if it is positive) or backlog (if it is negative). Then

$$x_j(t) = x_j(0) + \int_0^t u_j(s)ds - \int_0^t d_j ds,$$

$$= x_j(0) + \int_0^t u_j(s)ds - d_j t$$

since the integral of the production rate is the total amount produced and the integral of the demand rate is the total amount demanded.

This can also be written

$$\frac{dx_j(t)}{dt} = u_j(t) - d_j, \qquad x_j(0) \text{ specified.}$$

Then the cost criterion can be written

$$\min E \int_0^T g(x_1(t), x_2(t))dt$$

in which g is the cost for surplus or backlog, and the expectation E is taken over random failures and repairs.

If the machine is down at time t, we must have

$$u_j(t) = 0, j = 1, 2.$$

If the machine is operational at time t, the production rates must satisfy the instantaneous capacity constraints

$$\tau_1 u_1(t) + \tau_2 u_2(t) \leq 1,$$

---

[1]To actually schedule production, it is not enough to calculate rates. The rates must be achieved in the loading of discrete parts at discrete times. This issue is discussed in Section 9.4.4 where the *staircase strategy* is introduced.

$u_j(t) \geq 0.$

We can combine these statements by defining $\alpha(t)$ to be the repair state of the machine at time t. If the machine is up, $\alpha(t) = 1$; if it is down, $\alpha(t) = 0$. Then

$\tau_1 u_1(t) + \tau_2 u_2(t) \leq \alpha(t),$

$u_j(t) \geq 0.$

To summarize, the dynamic programming problem can be stated as

$$\min E \int_0^T g(x_1(t), x_2(t))dt \qquad \textbf{objective function}$$

subject to

$$\left. \begin{aligned} &\frac{dx_j(t)}{dt} = u_j(t) - d_j, \\[2mm] &\text{Markov dynamics for } \alpha \end{aligned} \right\} \quad \textbf{dynamics}$$

$$\left. \begin{aligned} &\tau_1 u_1(t) + \tau_2 u_2(t) \leq \alpha(t), \\[2mm] &u_j(t) \geq 0 \end{aligned} \right\} \quad \textbf{constraints}$$

$$x(0), \alpha(0) \text{ specified} \qquad \textbf{initial conditions}$$

The elements of a dynamic programming problem are the:

state all the information that is available to determine the future evolution of the system. In this problem, the state is x and α. In the previous problem, it was the current node. Even when the state is known, the future cannot be predicted. In the first example, it could not be known until the routing decisions were made; in this example, the future states of the machine will change randomly. The state of a dynamic programming problem is much like the state of a Markov process.

control the actions taken by the decision-maker. (It is also known as the *decision vari-able.*) In the first example, it is the next link chosen at nodes where there is a choice; here it is the instantaneous production rate vector u. As discussed below, u is often sought as a function of the state. In that case, the goal is a *control policy*. Here, the production rate u is sought as a function of whether the machine is up or down (since if it is down, no production will take place) and the surpluses x_1 and x_2. If x_1 is large and x_2 is small, the decision-maker will tend to produce Type 2 parts, and little or no Type 1 parts.

objective function the quantity that must be minimized; the measure of how good a proposed solution is. It is also called the *cost function* or *criterion.*

dynamics the evolution of the state as a function of the control variables and random events.

constraints the limitations on the set of allowable controls.

initial conditions the values of the state variables at the start of the time interval over which the problem is described. There are also sometimes **terminal conditions** such as in the network example. A function of the state x is specified at the terminal time T.

The problem described in this section is a dynamic programming problem because the cost is evaluated over time, and because present choices of action (u) influence the future. If we choose to make u large early in the interval $[0, T]$, we may cause x to be large and positive, and therefore incur large costs $g(x)$. If we make u small in the beginning, then later failures may make x large and negative, and also incur large costs $g(x)$. It is a stochastic problem because α is random. The state has a continuous component (x) and a discrete component (α). The time is continuous.

There are two important elements in the **solution** of a dynamic programming problem: the **control policy** and the **value function**. We have already described the control policy; the value function is the value of the cost function when the optimal control policy is applied. It is important to determine the value function for problems just like the given problem except with different initial conditions and times, so the value function has, as arguments, the initial conditions on the state and the initial time.

8.3   Types

There are many different kinds of dynamic programming problems. First, there is the same discrete/continuous time–discrete/continuous/mixed state classification as in Markov processes. Second, the problems may be stochastic as in Chapter 2 or deterministic. In Chapter 2 it would not be meaningful to consider deterministic systems; Markov processes are inherently stochastic.[2] However, deterministic dynamic programming problems are certainly meaningful.

There are further attributes. There are stochastic dynamic programming problems in which the full state may not be measured directly (usually for technological reasons). Instead, only part of the state is measured and the rest is inferred from the dynamic behavior of the system. An example is an airplane in which velocity is hard to measure directly, but acceleration is not. We will not deal with such problems in this book: we assume the states of our systems, which include surpluses, machine repair states, and machine setup states, are not hard to determine directly.

---

[2]Of course, deterministic dynamic systems are important: they include differential and difference equations.

Deterministic problems with continuous time and state variables are called *calculus of variations* problems and are very old. Problems with continuous state and

- discrete time, or

- inequality constraints, or

- stochastic elements

are called *optimal control* problems.

The difference between dynamic programming and calculus of variations is in point of view. Calculus of variations — being deterministic — takes the view that we are seeking a function of time, $u(t)$. This is sometimes called an *open loop control*. Dynamic programming takes the view that we are seeking a control which is a function of the state, $u(x)$, a *closed loop control*. If the system was deterministic (for example, if the machine never failed or if its availability were predictable) an open loop calculus of variations solution $u_i(t)$ would be satisfactory. The dynamic programming solution would find $u_i(x(t), t)$. The resulting functions of time are the same (for a deterministic system), but the solution techniques are different. Furthermore, only the latter is appropriate when the problem is stochastic.

Feedback can sometimes be appropriate when the real system is stochastic but can be modeled with a deterministic formulation. That is, the randomness is small enough so that the behavior can be predicted with a deterministic model with some accuracy. On the other hand, it is large enough to create some drift away from the deterministic prediction. Feedback can correct such drift. In such cases, it may not be important to model the randomness very precisely; the feedback calculated from the deterministic model may be enough to ensure good behavior. For further discussion, see Section 11.4.1.

Because of the diversity of problem types, there is no general formulation that includes all dynamic programming problems as special cases (the way there is for linear and nonlinear programming). However, an important class of deterministic problems has continuous time and continuous state:

$$\min_{\substack{u(t), \\ 0 \leq t \leq T}} \int_0^T g(x(t), u(t))dt + F(x(T))$$

such that

$$\frac{dx(t)}{dt} = f(x(t), u(t), t) \tag{8.2}$$

$x(0)$ specified

$$h(x(t), u(t)) \leq 0$$

in which $x \in \mathbf{R}^n, u \in \mathbf{R}^m, f \in \mathbf{R}^n, h \in \mathbf{R}^k$, and g and F are scalars. F is called the *terminal cost*. The specified problem data are $T, x(0)$, and the functions f, g, h, and F. The objective is to find the functions u and x.

The discrete-time, continuous-state counterpart is often written:

$$\min_{\substack{u(i), \\ 0 \le i \le T-1}} \sum_{i=0}^{T-1} g(x(i), u(i)) + F(x(T))$$

such that

$$x(i+1) = f(x(i), u(i), i) \tag{8.3}$$

$$x(0) \text{ specified}$$

$$h(x(i), u(i)) \le 0.$$

The comments after (8.2) apply here as well. Note that problem (8.3) is nothing more than a nonlinear programming problem. If f, g, h, and F are linear, this is a linear programming problem. If it is solved by NLP or LP methods, we get $x(i)$ and $u(i)$. We do not get $u(x(i), i)$.

8.4 Cost-to-go

Suppose we solve a dynamic programming problem like one of the last two. We can evaluate the cost function and call it J. Now we solve an identical problem, but with a different initial value $x(0)$. The cost function will change. Similarly, it would change if we started the problem at a time different from 0.

Define $J(x(s), s)$ to be the value of the cost function if we start the problem at $x(s)$ at time s. This is called the *cost-to-go* or *value function*. (The symbol V is often used.)

8.5 Discrete Time, Continuous State, Deterministic

Suppose we solve a dynamic programming problem. Then we pose a new problem which is identical to the first, except that its initial state and initial time are different. They are not completely arbitrary; they are on the optimal trajectory of the first problem. That is, the initial state and time of the new problem are not $x(0)$ and 0, but rather $x(t_1)$ and t_1, where the solution of the first problem is such that the value of the state at time t_1 is $x(t_1)$.

Then the *principle of optimality* says that the solution of the new problem is the same as the part of the trajectory of the old problem that starts at t_1. Put another way, if you are told that the solution to an optimal control problem passes through $x(t_1)$ at time t_1, then you can calculate its behavior after t_1 by solving the same problem with initial condition $x(t_1)$ at time t_1. You do not need to know what happened before this time.

This is not different from the advice that you should never look back. To get where you are going, forget where you have been. Think only about where you are and where you are heading. (This is great advice if you keep one thing in mind: it depends on a *full* description of the state. Knowing what to include in the state is not a mathematical problem. Rather, it is a problem of modeling, of really knowing what the problem is.)

This has the following consequence: if you are told that $(x(t_1), t_1)$ is on the optimal trajectory, and you are told the solution of the problem that starts at $(x(t_1), t_1)$, you only need to calculate the part of the trajectory from 0 to t_1.

On the other hand, suppose you were given $J(x, t_1)$ for some $t_1, 0 < t_1 < T$. This is a list of cost-to-go's from each possible initial state x for problems that start at time t_1. To determine the trajectory from 0 to t_1, you could solve the following problem:

$$\min_{\substack{u(i), \\ 0 \le i \le t_1 - 1}} \sum_{i=0}^{t_1-1} g(x(i), u(i)) + J(x(t_1), t_1)$$

such that

$$x(i+1) = f(x(i), u(i), i)$$

$$x(0) \text{ specified}$$

$$h(x(i), u(i)) \le 0.$$

Note that this problem is of the same form as (8.3) but with t_1 instead of T and $J(x(t_1), t_1)$ instead of $F(x(T))$. The principle of optimality implies that the value of $x(t_1)$ that this problem selects is the same as the value of $x(t_1)$ for the original problem. The value of $J(x(0), 0)$ that this problem selects is the same as the value of $J(x(0), 0)$ for the original problem. A very compact way of writing the last point is

$$J(x(0), 0) = \min_{\substack{u(i), \\ 0 \le i \le t_1 - 1}} \left\{ \sum_{i=0}^{t_1-1} g(x(i), u(i)) + J(x(t_1), t_1) \right\}.$$

Consider the one-step version of this equation. Instead of starting the problem at 0, we start it at $t_1 - 1$:

$$J(x(t_1 - 1), t_1 - 1) = \min_{u(t_1-1)} \{ g(x(t_1 - 1), u(t_1 - 1)) + J(x(t_1), t_1) \}. \qquad (8.4)$$

This says that if we knew the function $J(x(t_1), t_1)$, we could generate the function $J(x(t_1 - 1), t_1 - 1)$. But we can define

$$J(x(T), T) = F(x(T))$$

so, in principle, we can work backwards recursively from the final time T to generate the entire J function, and thus the optimal control. This is impractical because of the large number of values of the state space that would have to be treated — the "curse of dimensionality."

8.6   Continuous Time, Continuous State, Deterministic

Suppose we have a problem of the form (8.2). Then we can define

$$J(x(0),0) = \min \int_0^T g(x(t),u(t))dt + F(x(T))$$

where the minimization operation is subject to the constraints of (8.2). More generally, if $J(x,t)$ is the cost-to-go function,

$$J(x,t) = \min \int_t^T g(x(s),u(s))ds + F(x(T))$$

subject to the constraints of (8.2) except that the initial time of the problem is t, and the value of the state at time t is x.

Suppose $0 < t_1 < T$. Suppose we are given the function $J(x,t_1)$: the minimum value of the cost function integrated between t_1 and T, for all possible initial states x. That is, at some time t_1, we know the best possible trajectory during $[t_1, T]$ for each possible initial state x. (One of those x's is $x(t_1)$, the value of the state at time t_1 that is actually on the trajectory.) However, we know nothing about the problem during $[0, t_1]$. Then

$$J(x(0),0) = \min_{\substack{u(t), \\ 0 \le t \le T}} \left\{ \int_0^{t_1} g(x(t),u(t))dt + \int_{t_1}^T g(x(t),u(t))dt + F(x(T)) \right\}.$$

We can break up the minimization as follows:

$$J(x(0),0) = \min_{\substack{u(t), \\ 0 \le t \le t_1}} \left\{ \int_0^{t_1} g(x(t),u(t))dt + \right.$$

$$\left. \min_{\substack{u(t), \\ t_1 \le t \le T}} \left[\int_{t_1}^T g(x(t),u(t))dt + F(x(T)) \right] \right\}.$$

But

$$J(x(t_1), t_1) = \min_{\substack{u(t), \\ t_1 \le t \le T}} \left[\int_{t_1}^{T} g(x(t), u(t))dt + F(x(T)) \right]$$

so

$$J(x(0), 0) = \min_{\substack{u(t), \\ 0 \le t \le t_1}} \int_{0}^{t_1} g(x(t), u(t))dt + J(x(t_1), t_1)$$

subject to

$$\frac{dx(t)}{dt} = f(x(t), u(t), t)$$

$x(0)$ specified

$$h(x(t), u(t)) \le 0$$

This problem is of the same form as (8.2) but with t_1 instead of T and $J(x(t_1), t_1)$ instead of $F(x(T))$.

8.7 Bellman's Equation

If we perturb t_1, we get the one-step counterpart of (8.4):

$$J(x(t_1), t_1) = \min_{\substack{u(t) \\ t_1 \le t \le t_1 + \delta t}} \left\{ \int_{t_1}^{t_1 + \delta t} g(x(t), u(t))dt + J(x(t_1 + \delta t), t_1 + \delta t) \right\}$$

which can be approximated by

$$J(x(t_1), t_1) = \min_{u(t_1)} \left\{ g(x(t_1), u(t_1))\delta t + J(x(t_1 + \delta t), t_1 + \delta t) \right\} + o(\delta t).$$

In this approximation, $u(t)$ is treated as constant in the interval $t_1 \le t \le t_1 + \delta t$.

If J is differentiable,

$$J(x(t_1 + \delta t), t_1 + \delta t) = J(x(t_1), t_1) + \frac{\partial J}{\partial x}\delta x(t_1) + \frac{\partial J}{\partial t}\delta t + o(\delta t),$$

so

$$J(x(t_1), t_1) = \min_{u(t_1)} \left\{ g(x(t_1), u(t_1))\delta t + J(x(t_1), t_1) + \frac{\partial J}{\partial x}\delta x(t_1) + \frac{\partial J}{\partial t}\delta t \right\} + o(\delta t).$$

This can be further simplified:

$$-\frac{\partial J}{\partial t}\delta t = \min_{u(t_1)}\ \left\{g(x(t_1), u(t_1))\delta t + \frac{\partial J}{\partial x}\delta x(t_1)\right\} + o(\delta t)$$

since neither $J(x(t_1), t_1)$ nor $\partial J(x(t_1), t_1)/\partial t$ are functions of $u(t)$, for $t_1 \leq t \leq t_1 + \delta t$. Finally, we divide both sides by δt and let δt approach 0:

$$-\frac{\partial J}{\partial t} = \min_{u(t)}\left\{g(x(t), u(t)) + \frac{\partial J}{\partial x}\frac{dx(t)}{dt}\right\}$$

where we have dropped the subscript. This can also be written

$$-\frac{\partial J}{\partial t}(x, t) = \min_{u}\left\{g(x, u) + \frac{\partial J}{\partial x}(x, t)f(x, u, t)\right\}. \tag{8.5}$$

This is a nonlinear partial differential equation called *Bellman's equation*.[3] With an initial condition at the terminal time,

$$J(x, T) = F(x)$$

(8.5) determines $J(x, t)$. The Bellman equation is typically impossible to solve either analytically or numerically, although there are important exceptions.

How do we interpret this strange looking equation (8.5)? If we had a guess of $J(x, t)$ (for all x and t) we could confirm it by performing the minimization. If minimizing the right side produced a value which is equal to the left, the guess is correct.

Alternatively, we can think of the minimizing value of u in (8.5) as a nonlinear function of $x, \partial J/\partial x$, and t:

$$u = U\left(x, \frac{\partial J}{\partial x}, t\right).$$

If $\partial J/\partial x$ were a known function of x and t, U would be a feedback law. (Remember, however, that we are on somewhat shaky ground when we talk of a feedback law in a deterministic system.) From the definition of J, and because (8.5) is integrated backwards (since its initial condition is at T), J and $\partial J/\partial x$ summarize all we need to know about the future to make a good decision (u) at time t. Then

$$\frac{\partial J}{\partial t} = g\left[x(t), U\left(x, \frac{\partial J}{\partial x}, t\right)\right] + \frac{\partial J}{\partial x}f\left[x, U\left(x, \frac{\partial J}{\partial x}, t\right), t\right].$$

Even if we knew the function U, this would be a nonlinear partial differential equation and almost always impossible to solve, either analytically or numerically.

Both the Bellman equation and the one-step discrete version are important because they convert a minimization problem defined over an extended time interval into a minimization problem at a single time instant. In both, if we knew $J(x, t)$ for all x at some time t, we could find $u(x, t)$ for all x at the same t. This would allow us to calculate $J(x, s)$ for all x at some $s < t$, and we could work back to $t = 0$.

---

[3]It is also called the Hamilton-Jacobi-Bellman equation. In science, mathematics, and engineering, the more names something has, the more important it is. This is especially true when its names are people's names.

Example: Bang-Bang Control   Consider the following dynamic programming problem. The state x and the control u are scalars:

$$\min \int_0^\infty \mid x \mid dt$$

subject to

$$\frac{dx}{dt} = u$$

$x(0)$ specified

$$-1 \le u \le 1$$

Solution   Before solving the problem, we observe that it is possible to drive x to 0 in such a way that the objective will be finite. Then $x \to 0$ is part of the solution, because if x approaches some other value, the objective would be infinite.

In this problem, $f = u$ and $g = |x|$. Then (8.5) becomes

$$-\frac{\partial J}{\partial t}(x,t) = \min_{\substack{u, \\ -1 \le u \le 1}} \left\{ |x| + \frac{\partial J}{\partial x}(x,t)u \right\}. \tag{8.6}$$

To solve (8.6) we observe that $J(x,t)$ must have the form

$$J(x,t) = J(x).$$

This is because the problem is autonomous, or independent of t in the sense that none of the functions f, g, h, that define the problem are functions of t explicitly. In addition, because the time horizon is infinite, there is enough time to drive x to 0 or to the neighborhood of 0, regardless of the initial condition $x(0)$. Therefore, (8.6) becomes

$$0 = \min_{\substack{u, \\ -1 \le u \le 1}} \left\{ |x| + \frac{dJ}{dx}(x)u \right\}. \tag{8.7}$$

Also

$$J(0) = 0.$$

Note that the minimization problem in (8.7) is a (very simple) linear programming problem. Its solution is

$$
u = \begin{cases}
-1 & \text{if} \quad \dfrac{dJ}{dx}(x) > 0 \\[2ex]
1 & \text{if} \quad \dfrac{dJ}{dx}(x) < 0 \\[2ex]
\text{undetermined} & \text{if} \quad \dfrac{dJ}{dx}(x) = 0
\end{cases}
$$

In this case, $dJ/dx(x)$ is called the *switching function*. Consider the region (the set of x) in which $dJ/dx(x) < 0$, and thus where $u = 1$. In that region, (8.7) becomes

$$
0 = |x| + \frac{dJ}{dx}(x)
$$

or

$$
\frac{dJ}{dx}(x) = -|x|. \tag{8.8}
$$

Consider also the region where $dJ/dx(x) > 0$, and thus where $u = -1$. In that region, (8.7) becomes

$$
0 = |x| - \frac{dJ}{dx}(x)
$$

or

$$
\frac{dJ}{dx}(x) = |x|. \tag{8.9}
$$

To complete the solution, we must determine where the boundaries of the regions are. To do that, we observe that dJ/dx can only be 0 at $x = 0$. Therefore, u can only be 1 or -1, except at $x = 0$. In that case, it is clear that for all $x > 0, u = -1$, since $u = 1$ moves the state in the wrong direction. Similarly, for all $x < 0, u = 1$. Finally, for $x = 0$, the solution is $u = 0$. This is because any other value of u would move x from 0 and therefore raise the cost function.

Equations (8.8) and (8.9) become

$$
\frac{dJ}{dx}(x) = x
$$

so

$$
J = \frac{1}{2}x^2.
$$

To summarize, the solution is

$$
u = \begin{cases} 1 & \text{if} \quad x < 0 \\ 0 & \text{if} \quad x = 0 \\ -1 & \text{if} \quad x > 0 \end{cases}
$$

This example illustrates some of the characteristics of dynamic programming. It is relatively easy to determine the structure of the control policy. It is often less easy to determine exactly where boundaries are. In this case, we relied on intuition rather than only dynamic programming. When we find a solution, we can verify our intuition by plugging J and u into (8.6).

The term "bang-bang" is an old control engineering term that refers to the control banging back and forth between extremes. It would be more correct to call this a "bang-singular-bang" problem, since $x = 0$ is a *singular arc*, a region in which the value of the control is not determined by the minimization in the Bellman equation.

8.8 Continuous Time, Mixed State, Stochastic

Consider the following stochastic dynamic programming problem:

$$
J(x(0), \alpha(0), 0) = \min_u E \left\{ \int_0^T g(x(t), u(t)) dt + F(x(T)) \right\}
$$

such that

$$
\frac{dx(t)}{dt} = f(x, \alpha, u, t) \tag{8.10}
$$

$$
\text{prob } [\alpha(t + \delta t) = i \mid \alpha(t) = j] = \lambda_{ij} \delta t \text{ for all } i, j, i \neq j \tag{8.11}
$$

$$
x(0), \alpha(0) \text{ specified}
$$

$$
h(x(t), \alpha(t), u(t)) \leq 0
$$

The example in Section 8.2 is a special case of this formulation. In this problem, the state space is mixed: it has both discrete and continuous parts. Only the continuous part can be controlled. The derivation of the Bellman equation for this problem must take into account the randomness of α. This formulation includes an important assumption: that the source of randomness is Markovian. This means that, if at time t we are making a prediction about the state of the system at time $t + \delta t$, we need not look any further in the past than t. We use the methods of Section 2.3 to describe the behavior of α.

Let $\tilde{E}$ represent a conditional expectation operation. For any function $G(x, \alpha)$, $\tilde{E}G(x(t + \delta t), \alpha(t + \delta t))$ is defined as the conditional expected value of $G(x(t + \delta t), \alpha(t + \delta t))$ given the values of $x(t)$ and $\alpha(t)$. That is, we define

$$\tilde{E}G(x(t + \delta t), \alpha(t + \delta t)) = E\left\{ G(x(t + \delta t), \alpha(t + \delta t)) \Big| x(t), \alpha(t) \right\}.$$

Also, as usual,

$$\lambda_{ii} = -\sum_{j \neq i} \lambda_{ji}.$$

Let $H(\alpha)$ be some function of α. Then $H(\alpha(t + \delta t))$ is its value a short time in the future, and

$$\tilde{E}H(\alpha(t + \delta t)) = E\left\{ H(\alpha(t + \delta t)) \mid \alpha(t) \right\}$$

$$= \sum_j H(j)\text{prob}\left\{ \alpha(t + \delta t) = j \mid \alpha(t) \right\} \qquad \text{by definition of } \tilde{E}$$

$$= \sum_{j \neq \alpha(t)} H(j)\lambda_{j\alpha(t)}\delta t + H(\alpha(t))\left(1 - \sum_{j \neq \alpha(t)} \lambda_{j\alpha(t)}\delta t \right) + o(\delta t) \qquad \text{by definition of } \lambda$$

$$= \sum_{j \neq \alpha(t)} H(j)\lambda_{j\alpha(t)}\delta t + H(\alpha(t))\left(1 + \lambda_{\alpha(t)\alpha(t)}\delta t \right) + o(\delta t) \qquad \text{by definition of } \lambda_{ii}$$

$$= H(\alpha(t)) + \sum_j H(j)\lambda_{j\alpha(t)}\delta t + o(\delta t) \qquad \text{simplifying}$$

Then, to develop a Bellman's equation,

$$J(x(t), \alpha(t), t) = \min_{\substack{u(s), \\ t \leq s < T}} E\left\{ \int_t^T g(x(t), u(t))dt + F(x(T)) \right\}$$

$$= \min_{\substack{u(s), \\ t \leq s \leq t + \delta t}} \tilde{E}\left\{ \int_t^{t + \delta t} g(x(s), u(s))ds + J(x(t + \delta t), \alpha(t + \delta t), t + \delta t) \right\}$$

or,

$$J(x(t), \alpha(t), t) = \min_{u(t)} \tilde{E}\left\{ g(x(t), u(t))\delta t + J(x(t + \delta t), \alpha(t + \delta t), t + \delta t) \right\} + o(\delta t).$$

Assume J is differentiable. Expanding to first order,

$$J(x(t + \delta t), \alpha(t + \delta t), t + \delta t) =$$

$$J(x(t), \alpha(t + \delta t), t) + \frac{\partial J}{\partial x}(x(t), \alpha(t + \delta t), t)\delta x(t) + \frac{\partial J}{\partial t}(x(t), \alpha(t + \delta t), t)\delta t + o(\delta t),$$

so that

$$J(x(t), \alpha(t), t) =$$

$$\min_{u(t)} \tilde{E} \left\{ g(x(t), u(t))\delta t + J(x(t), \alpha(t + \delta t), t) + \right.$$

$$\left. \frac{\partial J}{\partial x}(x(t), \alpha(t + \delta t), t)\delta x(t) + \frac{\partial J}{\partial t}(x(t), \alpha(t + \delta t), t)\delta t \right\} + o(\delta t).$$

Now we must expand the expectation operation. Using the expansion of $\tilde{E}H(\alpha(t + \delta t))$ above,

$$J(x(t), \alpha(t), t) =$$

$$\min_{u(t)} \left\{ g(x(t), u(t))\delta t + J(x(t), \alpha(t), t) + \sum_j J(x(t), j, t)\lambda_{j\alpha(t)}\delta t \right.$$

$$\left. + \frac{\partial J}{\partial x}(x(t), \alpha(t), t)\delta x(t) + \frac{\partial J}{\partial t}(x(t), \alpha(t), t)\delta t \right\} + o(\delta t)$$

in which we have expanded J to first order and the derivatives to zero'th order. (Expanding the derivatives to first order would generate second order terms.) We have eliminated the expectation symbol. We can now move $J + (\partial J/\partial t)\delta t$ to the left, divide by δt, and get

$$-\frac{\partial J}{\partial t}(x(t), \alpha(t), t) =$$

$$\min_{u(t)} \left\{ g(x(t), u(t)) + \sum_j J(x(t), j, t)\lambda_{j\alpha(t)} + \frac{\partial J}{\partial x}(x(t), \alpha(t), t)\frac{dx(t)}{dt} \right\}.$$

Finally, we have

$$-\frac{\partial J}{\partial t}(x, \alpha, t) = \min_u \left\{ g(x, u) + \sum_j J(x, j, t)\lambda_{j\alpha} + \frac{\partial J}{\partial x}(x, \alpha, t)f(x, u, \alpha, t) \right\}. \qquad (8.12)$$

This is Bellman's equation for a continuous time, mixed (continuous and discrete) state, stochastic dynamic programming problem. It is exactly the same as the deterministic Bellman's equation except for the summation term. This was done in a very informal manner. We have freely interchanged minimizations, expectations, and limits. A proper derivation would consider all that very carefully.

Again, we can define the u that minimizes (8.12) as

$$u = U\left(x, \alpha, \frac{\partial J}{\partial x}, t\right)$$

but even if we knew U, J would satisfy a nonlinear partial differential equation which would almost always be impossible to solve, either analytically or numerically.

If $\partial J/\partial x$ were a known function of x and t, U would be a feedback law. U is a real feedback law because the problem is stochastic. The future is not known, even if the state at time t and the feedback law are known. Again, J and $\partial J/\partial x$ summarize all we need to know — or can guess — about the future to make a good decision (u) at time t.

In Chapter 9 we use Equation (8.12) to develop a control policy for a simple model of a flexible manufacturing system. The control u is the short term production rate. The state is (x, α), where x is the production surplus and α describes the repair states of the machines. This formulation is extended in later chapters to more complex manufacturing systems.

8.9   A Useful Approximation

Assume that the system dynamics (8.10) and (8.11) are such that

- f is independent of t;

- a steady state distribution exists for α;

- it is possible to find a control policy that keeps x bounded, or causes x to return to the same value over and over again for all time (such that the time between the returns has a bounded mean).

As a consequence, x and α can have steady state probability distributions. Assume also that T is very large. That is, many events (changes of α) occur before the end of the time interval.

Consider the time interval $[t_1, t_2]$, a subset of $[0,T]$. The time t_1 is sufficiently large that (x, α) reaches steady state; $T - t_2$ is sufficiently large that the approaching end of the interval does not affect decision-making in $[t_1, t_2]$. During this interval, the control law $u(x, \alpha, t)$ is approximately independent of t, so the probability distribution of u is approximately constant in t. (Then, from (8.12), $\partial J/\partial x$ must be approximately independent of t.) Consequently, $Eg(x(t), u(t)$ is approximately independent of t, for t in $[t_1, t_2]$.

Under these conditions, we can make a useful approximation. Let

$$J^* \approx Eg(x(t), u(t)), \text{ for all } t \in [t_1, t_2]$$

when the optimal control policy is used. Then J is approximately given by[4]

$$J(x(0), \alpha(0), 0) \approx J^*T + W(x(0), \alpha(0)). \qquad (8.13)$$

J^*, the average value of $g(x(s), u(s))$ during $[0, T]$, is the average rate of increase of

$$\int_0^t g(x(s), u(s)) ds$$

and $W(x, \alpha)$ is the cost of a deviation of x and α from their typical values. Since "typical values" is a rather imprecise concept, $W(x, \alpha)$ is defined only relatively. That is, we can pick one base value of (x, α), called (x^b, α^b), and set $W(x^b, \alpha^b) = 0$. W is often called the *differential cost*.

A more general version of (8.13) is

$$J(x, \alpha, t) \approx J^*(T - t) + W(x, \alpha).$$

Note that

$$\frac{\partial J}{\partial t} \approx -J^*; \qquad \frac{\partial J}{\partial x} \approx \frac{\partial W}{\partial x}.$$

Exercises

1. List the state, the control, the objective function, the dynamics, the constraints, and the initial conditions of the network problem of Section 8.1. (We are not looking for equations here: just catalog the parts of the problem.)

2. Formulate the dynamics of a system like that of Section 8.2 but where there are two machines, both flexible. Now the problem is not only to determine how much of each type to load into the system at each time t, but how to split it among the machines when both are operational.

    Hint: Define u_{ij} to be the rate of flow of Type j parts to Machine i.

3. A very important, practical class of problems are the *linear-quadratic* problems. Let Q and R be symmetric, R positive definite, and

    $$f(x, u, t) = Ax + Bu$$

    $$g(x, u, t) = \frac{1}{2} \left(x^T Q x + u^T R u \right)$$

    This can be written componentwise as

    $$f_i(x, u, t) = \sum_{j=1}^n A_{ij} x_j + \sum_{j=1}^m B_{ij} u_j, \, i = 1, \ldots, n$$

---

[4]See Kumar and Varaiya (1986), page 157 for this result for a similar problem.

$$g(x, u, t) = \frac{1}{2} \left(\sum_{i=1}^{n} \sum_{j=1}^{n} Q_{ij} x_i x_j + \sum_{i=1}^{m} \sum_{j=1}^{m} R_{ij} u_i u_j \right)$$

Write and solve the Bellman equation (8.5). *Hint:* Assume

$$J = \frac{1}{2} x^T S(t) x = \frac{1}{2} \sum_{i=1}^{n} \sum_{j=1}^{n} S_{ij}(t) x_i x_j.$$

Plug it into the Bellman equation and solve for u. Plug the resulting u back into the Bellman equation and find a differential equation for $S(t)$. This is enough; do not attempt to solve the differential equation.

4. Write the Bellman equation for the examples of Section 8.2 and of Exercise 2. Describe the feedback laws as well as possible without actually solving the problem.

Bibliography

[1] M. Athans and P. L. Falb (1966), *Optimal Control, An Introduction to its Theory and Its Applications*, McGraw-Hill, 1966.

[2] R. Bellman and R. Kalaba (1965), *Dynamic Programming and Modern Control Theory*, Academic Press, 1965.

[3] D. Bertsekas (1976), *Dynamic Programming and Stochastic Control*, Academic Press, 1976.

[4] D. Bertsekas (1987), *Dynamic Programming: Deterministic and Stochastic Models*, Prentice-Hall, 1987.

[5] S. P. Bradley, A. C. Hax, and T. L. Magnanti (1977), *Applied Mathematical Programming*, Addison-Wesley, 1977.

[6] A. E. Bryson and Y. C. Ho (1969), *Applied Optimal Control*, Blaisdell, 1969.

[7] F. H. Clarke (1989), *Optimization and Nonsmooth Analysis*, Les Publications CRM, Universite de Montreal, 1989.

[8] P. R. Kumar and P. Varaiya (1986), *Stochastic Systems: Estimation, Identification, and Adaptive Control*, Prentice-Hall, 1986.

[9] D. G. Luenberger (1979), *Introduction to Dynamic Systems — Theory, Models, and Applications*, Wiley, 1979.

[10] H. A. Taha (1982), *Operations Research*, Macmillan, 1982.

Chapter 9

Operating Flexible Manufacturing Systems—Responding to Machine Failures

9.1 Introduction

An example in Chapter 2 is concerned with a simple manufacturing system which is disturbed by machine failures, and in which some control is exercised. Chapters 3, 4, and 5 describe more complex manufacturing systems that are disturbed by machine failures and by the emptying and filling of buffers, but in which no control appears. All the systems studied in Chapters 2-5 involved only a single part type. In Chapter 6, a model of manufacturing systems with many part types is studied, but real-time control is not an issue.

In this chapter, we study systems involving many part types that are disturbed by machine failures. They are generalizations of the single-part type control problem of Section 2.6.2 and of the two-part type example of Section 8.2. As in Section 8.2, at every time instant that a machine is available, a system manager (human or computer) must decide which part to load, or if the machine is allowed to be idle. We use the mathematics developed in Chapters 2, 7, and 8. In later chapters, we study systems with disturbances other than failures, and in which there are other decisions than the initiation of operations.

The basic idea behind the policies developed here is to keep track of the capacity of the system, as it varies over time as machines fail and are repaired. Material is loaded at a time-varying production rate which is always within capacity. There may be a short-term bottleneck, which changes over time as different machines go up and down, and as the short-term production rate varies. A limited, measured amount of inventory (actually surplus) is allowed to compensate for future failures.

9.1.1   FMS phenomena and issues

FMS characteristics   For the purposes of this chapter, we define a *flexible manufacturing system* (FMS) as one whose machines are able to perform operations on a random sequence of parts with little or no time or other expenditure for changeover from one part to the next. That is, there is no greater cost for processing a Type 2 part at a flexible machine immediately after processing a Type 1 than there is for processing a Type 2 part at a flexible machine immediately after processing a Type 2. In some cases there is a choice of one or more stations for each operation. This allows production to continue even when a work station is out of service because of failure or maintenance.

In practice, the term FMS is most often applied to systems in which the operations at the work stations and the material handling system are entirely under computer control. Decisions such as which parts should be loaded into the system and what work stations each workpiece should visit next are made by the FMS control computer. Human intervention is necessary, but only when unusual or unanticipated events take place. It is important, therefore, to develop models and algorithms which allow the FMS controller to generate production schedules which satisfy demand requirements and to exercise control over the system so that the output conforms to the schedule.

In metal-cutting applications, the changeover time for parts in the same family is negligible when the machines are numerically controlled with a large number of tools available in a magazine or when operations are performed by robots. The FMS concept is not limited to metal cutting: printed circuit boards can be assembled, integrated circuits can be fabricated, and automobile parts can be made by means of FMSs.

The ability of an FMS to produce a family of parts simultaneously can result in reduced inventories and faster responses to changes in demand requirements, when compared to traditional production methods. However, production scheduling can become more complex because, at each time, there are more choices to be made. In addition, the use of a computer for loading and scheduling decisions requires that the scheduling algorithm must be determined in advance and stated explicitly. (When people do the scheduling, they sometimes do it in ways that they cannot explain. They sometimes make up methods as they go along. This can be acceptable if the resulting performance is satisfactory.) The high capital cost of an FMS means that efficient use of system resources is very important.

The assumption of flexibility allows us to assume, in this chapter, that we need to consider only two kinds of events: operations and failures. More realistic models are described in later chapters.

Example   Consider a flexible manufacturing system that makes large metal parts, such as engine blocks or gearboxes for large vehicles. The transport system of such an FMS is likely to be a set of AGVs (Automated Guided Vehicles), a cable car system, or a large conveyer. In any case, the transport system is likely to be able to hold only a small number of parts, and there is not likely to be much buffer storage space inside the system. In fact, any temporary storage is likely to be in the transport system, and an AGV or cable car is likely to be tied up with the part.

As a consequence, it is essential not to waste the limited storage that exists. Queuing should be held to an absolute minimum. It is much better to allow queuing to take place outside — in an upstream buffer — the system, since such storage does not use the transport system unproductively. In fact, using the transport system as a storage area can be even worse if the parts that are waiting for busy or failed machines are blocking other parts that can go to other, idle machines. Such a practice can lower the effective capacity of the system to something much less than the estimate described below.

Failures and Feedback The task of the controller is complicated by random failures of the work stations. A good production policy should anticipate failures and demand changes if it is to satisfy all of the objectives stated above. It is important that this policy employ feedback so as to respond to failures and to allow human operators (who can deal with a wider range of situations than envisioned by system planners) to override control decisions on rare occasions.

Operating policies for manufacturing systems must respond to machine failures and other important events that occur during production such as setups, demand changes, expedited batches, etc. Each of these events takes up time at a resource. Some events are controllable, such as production operations, in the sense that a manager may choose when they occur. Others are not controllable but are predictable, such as holidays.[1] Still other events are neither controllable nor predictable, such as machine failures. Controllability and other related concepts are defined for manufacturing systems in Chapter 10.

Feedback policies must be based on realistic models, and they must be computationally tractable. Computational tractability is an important concern because of the complexity of many manufacturing systems. Even for a very small, deterministic, idealization of a production system, the computational effort for combinatorial optimization renders it impractical for real-time control. Any control scheme must be based on a simplified representation of the system and a heuristic solution of the scheduling problem. In this and the next sections, we develop hierarchical scheduling and planning algorithms. The levels of the hierarchy correspond to classes of events that have distinct frequencies of occurrence.

In this section, only two kinds of events are considered:

- production operations on parts, and

- failures and repairs of machines.

Operations occur much more often than failures, and this allows the use of a continuous representation of material flow. A dynamic programming formulation based on this representation leads to a feedback control policy. In this formulation, the state of the system has two parts:

- a vector of real numbers $(x(t))$ that represents the surplus, the cumulative difference between production and requirements.

- a vector of integers $(\alpha(t))$ that represents the set of machines that are operational.

---

[1] The extent of controllability and predictability may depend on *who* is doing the controlling and predicting.

The object is to choose the production rate vector $(u(t))$ as a function of the state $(x(t))$ and $(\alpha(t))$ to keep the surplus $(x(t))$ near 0. The production rate (the continuous control variable) is restricted by linear inequality constraints that depend on the repair state. These constraints represent the instantaneous capacity of the system, and they express the idea that no machine, while it is operational, may be busy more than 100% of the time; and no machine, while it is not operational, may be used at all. The remaining chapters describe the extension of this work to the widest possible variety of phenomena and decisions in a manufacturing environment.

9.1.2   What is a schedule?

In normal usage, a schedule is a sequence of times when specified events will take place. This meaning is useful if these times can be specified precisely, and if the events will probably take place as scheduled. However, this meaning is too restrictive in a production environment for two reasons:

1. The environment is stochastic. Disruptive events occur frequently and prevent the planned events from taking place, or make the times that had been calculated less desirable than they were before the disruptions.

2. There are too many events. While computers can easily *record* the times at which events have taken place or will take place, even the fastest supercomputer with enormous memory cannot *calculate* optimal, or even satisfactory, times if there are too many events. In addition, human managers can usefully comprehend a schedule only of limited size.

Consequently, we change the meaning of "schedule." The following definition is intended to deal with the first issue.

Let $X(t)$ be the state of a system at time t. A *scheduling rule* is a set of functions $\{t_1(X(t),t),\ t_2(X(t),t),\ \ldots,\ t_n(X(t),t)\}$, $t_i(X(t),t) \geq t$ for all i, for the times at which future controllable events $\mathcal{E}_1, \mathcal{E}_2, \ldots, \mathcal{E}_n$ are planned to take place at time t. This is a feedback law; as $X(t)$ changes, the planned times $t_1, t_2, \ldots, t_n$ may change. For each t and $X(t)$, $\{t_1(X(t),t),\ \ldots\ t_2(X(t),t),\ t_n(X(t),t)\}$ is the *tentative schedule*. Controllable events are those whose times can be chosen. In this chapter, production operations are controllable events and machine failures are not. Event $\mathcal{E}_1$, for example, may be the loading of a Type 2 part on Machine 3. Event $\mathcal{E}_2$ may be the loading of a Type 1 part on Machine 5. At time 0, we may decide that $t_1 = 1$ and $t_2 = 4$. However, if Machine 5 goes down at time $t = 2$, we will have to choose a new value for t_2.

The network of queues models presented in Chapter 6 are not always adequate to either analyze or synthesize such policies. This is because analytic solutions of network of queues models do not allow controllable parameters (r_{ij} or μ_i, for example) to depend on states of the system other than local states.

As for the second issue, we deal with it in the rest of the book. Events in the near future must be specified precisely, even if tentatively; events further in the future need not be specified quite so precisely. We determine tentative future *rates* of controllable events, especially production rates.

9.1.3 Literature review

In this section, we review some of the literature of control theoretic models of flexible manufacturing systems.[2] The purpose of this literature has been to develop rules for deciding what action to take and when to take it in response to random events — especially failures and repairs — that occur during the production process. We emphasize the papers that have most influenced the work presented here.

Before describing manufacturing system control models, it is worthwhile to mention the control theory paper by Rishel (1975). This paper describes an abstract dynamic programming problem whose state has both a continuous and a discrete component. The control is a continuous vector (that is, a member of a real finite-dimensional vector space) that directly influences the continuous part of the state only. Rishel shows that the solution of the optimization problem divides the continuous part of the state space into regions. Associated with each region is a different feedback law. This problem is not quite a generalization of the production control problems described in this chapter because in Rishel's paper, the discrete part of the state influences the continuous dynamics directly. In the production control papers, the discrete part of the state determines the control constraint set. In spite of this difference, Rishel's paper has proved to be an important source of insight for these problems.

Deuermeyer and Pierskalla (1978) used a discrete time dynamic programming model to schedule production in a manufacturing system in which two kinds of raw material were used for two products. One of the raw materials yields both of the products in a fixed ratio; processing the other yields only one. Although the randomness in this system comes from stochastic demands rather than unreliable machines, the results have much in common with those presented below: dynamic programming methods, and a feedback control law in which the optimal decision is determined by dividing the state space into regions, and finding the region that the state is currently in.

Olsder and Suri (1980) proposed a dynamic programming model to describe the disruptive nature of machine failures. This model represented production with a vector of continuous variables. It represented machine repair states with a set of discrete variables. While this model illuminated many of the important issues that are relevant to production scheduling in systems with failure-prone machines, it could not be used for analytical solutions. However, Olsder and Suri were able to show that the state space is divided into regions, and that the optimal decision is determined by the region that the state is currently located in.

An alternative approach to the problem of failures is that of Hildebrant, in his Ph.D. thesis (1980), and Hildebrant and Suri (1980). These authors studied machine failures

---

[2]Much of this material has been taken from Maimon and Gershwin (1988). Reprinted with permission from *Operations Research*, Vol. 36, No. 2, 1988, copyright 1988, Operations Research Society of America. No further reproduction permitted without the consent of the copyright owner.

by extending existing network-of-queues models of FMSs. They represented the effects of failures as causing the FMS to change to other FMSs at random times. To get around the difficulty of solving a stochastic optimization problem, they assumed that the FMS could be described as a queueing network in steady state between these events. The introduction of failures and repairs was a major advance, and the technique showed reasonable improvement over existing heuristics for automated manufacturing (Hildebrant, 1980). See the discussion in Section 6.3.

Buzacott (1982) used dynamic programming methods to study a variety of issues in the operation of a two-stage transfer line subject to failure. The repair states of the machines and the level of material in the buffers constituted the system state. The controls included whether or not to operate machines, and where to dispatch a repair person. Related questions about FMS operations were also discussed in this paper.

Kimemia (1982) and Kimemia and Gershwin (1983) derived a closed loop solution to the problem of dispatching parts to machines in a failure-prone FMS. It is on this work, and on the papers that followed from it, that the present chapter is based. Their approach, like others', was to separate the relatively long term issues (the response to machine failures and to production backlogs and surpluses) from the short-term problem of part dispatching. Their main contribution was to find suboptimal strategies that are easy to calculate and that provide satisfactory performance.

The portion of the formulation which accounts for the behavior of the FMS between failures and repairs is modeled as a continuous-time, mixed state (having both discrete and continuous elements) dynamic programming problem. The discrete constituent of the state (α) is the vector of machine states. The other portion of the state, which satisfies a differential equation, is the vector of surpluses (x), the cumulative differences between production and demand. The objective is to minimize these differences. The production rate vector (u), the control, is constrained to be within a capacity set ($\Omega(\alpha)$) that is determined by the set of operational machines. A feedback control law, which determines the current production rate as a function of current machine state and current production surplus ($u(x, \alpha)$), is sought.

Since this is a dynamic program, the solution has two components. One is the calculation of the cost-to-go or value function $J(x, \alpha)$ (defined in Section 9.2.4). Since the calculation of J is performed once, it is the longest-term component of the scheduling rule. The other is the calculation of the control law, which requires J. This is the medium-term component. The short-term portion of the scheduling rule is the loading of parts in a way that agrees with the current production rates (determined from the medium-term control law).

Thus the solution now has three components: the long-term calculation of J (called C by Deuermeyer and Pierskalla and V by Olsder and Suri), which is equivalent to determining the regions in state space; the medium-term calculation of the current production rate, which is performed by determining which region the state is currently in; and the short-term dispatch of parts.

Kimemia and Gershwin (1983) described a four-level hierarchy, in which a route-splitting calculation appeared between the medium-term production rate calculation and the short-term part dispatch. Maimon and Gershwin (1988) found that it should not be separated from the production rate calculation. Consequently the hierarchy has three levels.

At the top, long-term level, Kimemia and Gershwin proposed a formulation which had, as an objective, the minimization of the surplus. They suggested an approximation in which they separated the solution of the Bellman equation into a number of subproblems (by replacing the capacity constraints with a set of approximating hypercubes). They then approximated the value function (J) for each subproblem by a quadratic.

The middle level of the hierarchy, which gives rise to a sub-optimal production rate vector u, is the maximum principle of an optimal control problem. Kimemia and Gershwin showed that this maximum principle is a linear programming problem for the scheduling problem. For the lower level, they developed an algorithm to choose part dispatch times to achieve flow rate u. Simulation experiments indicated that these procedures produced good performance for many problems.

More recent work by Gershwin, Akella, and Choong (1985) and Akella, Gershwin, and Choong (1984) led to improvements at all three levels. At the top level, because simulation results indicated that the behavior of a manufacturing system is highly insensitive to errors in the cost-to-go function, the Bellman equation was replaced by a far simpler procedure to generate the quadratic approximation for J.

Kimemia and Gershwin observed that one limitation to the performance of their scheduler was the tendency of the middle level to *chatter*, to jump rapidly between two adjacent corners of the capacity set. Gershwin, Akella, and Choong found a way to make use of the quadratic approximation of J to eliminate this phenomenon.

For the lowest (part dispatch) level, Gershwin, Akella, and Choong replaced Kimemia and Gershwin's algorithm with one that was simpler and more effective. Neither it nor its predecessor, however, was designed for complex precedence constraints or other restrictions. Developing heuristics to incorporate such constraints should not be difficult since the objective of the lower level problem is to meet a feasible rate rather than to optimize. The capacity constraints at the upper levels may have to be modified to reflect the complex precedence constraints.

Akella, Choong, and Gershwin described simulation experience with the improved form of the hierarchical scheduler. They reported that it worked well, even when the exact J function is replaced by a quadratic, and even when the coefficients of the quadratic are chosen crudely. They compared the hierarchical scheduler with other heuristic policies and observed that its performance was superior. They concluded that the exact J function is not important; as long as the loading policy restricts the loading of material to within the current capacity of the system and is reasonably sensible, it will do reasonably well.

Akella and Kumar (1986), Bielecki and Kumar (1988), and Sharifnia (1988) obtained analytic solutions for special cases of Kimemia and Gershwin's formulation. All three papers analyzed unreliable manufacturing systems that produce only one part type. Akella and Kumar's was the first to appear and it provided an exact solution to a system consisting of one unreliable machine. Bielecki and Kumar reformulated the problem and produced a much simplified solution technique. This version of the problem shows great promise of being extensible to a wide variety of cases.

An extension appears in Sharifnia's paper. There, the machine or set of machines has more than two operating states: the capacity of the system is the state of a continuous time Markov process. This is useful, for example, when there are many machines in a complex series-parallel arrangement. Each machine may fail independently of the others, and the capacity depends on which is operational at any given time. Another use may be in the hypercube approximation of Kimemia and Gershwin. Each of the decomposed subsystems is precisely the kind of single-part-type, multiple-machine-state system that Sharifnia studies.

A major limitation to this body of work is the limited set of phenomena that are treated: operations and failures. Real manufacturing systems exhibit a much richer catalog of events, including setups, preventative maintenance, absences of raw materials, engineering changes, training sessions for new personnel, expedited batches, and many others. Some of these events can be scheduled and others must be endured, but they all have the potential for disruption. A framework for treating a wide variety of events is described in Chapter 10. Setups are treated in detail in Chapter 11.

A second limitation is that buffer behavior is not treated. This literature deals only with cells: FMSs consisting only of a handful of machines. It is assumed that parts spend only a small amount of time in the system, and that the in-process inventory is small. When any machine fails, all parts that are destined for it are prevented from entering the system until it is repaired. This assumption clearly does not apply in all cases: for example, wafers may spend months in a semiconductor clean room. Consider a machine that wafers only reach fairly late in the process; after they have been in the facility for weeks, typically. It is not sensible to stop the flow of wafers into the clean room when that machine fails if its mean repair time is a matter of hours.

Recent work in this area by Van Ryzin (1987) and Van Ryzin, Lou, and Gershwin (1991) suggest two possible ways of dealing with this. Delays due to long operating times were approximated by replacing them with extra states. The resulting approximate system could be analyzed in much the same manner as the papers reviewed here. When the number of states was allowed to grow, the limiting middle level control law had a simple interpretation involving the amount of material recently loaded into the system.

Delays due to buffers were studied by performing numerical experiments on some simple systems (Van Ryzin, 1987; and Van Ryzin, Lou, and Gershwin, 1993). The tentative conclusion is that each subsystem — which is separated from the rest of the system by buffers — can be operated according to rules which are not very different from those described in this chapter: a surplus strategy (as in all the papers since Kimemia and Gershwin's); a buffer strategy (in which the controller tries to keep the buffer at a certain level); and a rule for switching between them. This was extended substantially by Bai (1991). It is discussed in Chapters 12 and 13.

9.2 Failure Hierarchy

9.2.1 Objective

Assume that we are seeking the control of a flexible manufacturing system that represents only an intermediate stage in a production process. It gets raw material from some upstream stage, and sends it to a downstream stage. It is desirable for it to receive material in as predictable a manner as possible, and to dispatch its output also in a predictable way.

To accomplish this, we will assume that a higher level, a central controller or manager specifies production plans to each stage in the factory. These plans are such that if each stage comes close to its plan, there will be small in-process inventory accumulation between stages and little or no danger of starvation.

Consider a single production stage, which is an FMS, and a single part type (j). In Figure 9.1[3], the horizontal axis represents time and the vertical axis represents the total amount of material of that type that has been produced at that stage, or that is required, up to time t. The solid line represents the requirements for that part type, and the dashed line represents the actual production. (The slope of the requirements curve is d_j and the slope of the production curve is $u_j(x(t), \alpha(t))$.) The difference between the two curves, the *surplus*, is $x_j(t)$. There is one such graph for each part type, and the set of all x_j is the vector x. The objective is to keep $x(t)$ close to zero, or, more precisely, to minimize

$$E \int_{t_0}^{T} g(x(s))ds$$

in which the expectation operation (E) is taken over all samples of $\alpha(t)$, the history of failures and repairs of machines.

9.2.2 Reason for hierarchy

One natural formulation of this problem is as a stochastic linear programming problem. We can define $t_{ij}(n)$ as the time that the nth copy of a Type j part arrives at Machine i. A set of constraints can be developed that say that a part cannot arrive at a station until the station has completed its previous operation. Alternatively, the problem can be formulated as a stochastic integer programming problem. Binary variables $\xi_{ij}(t)$ are introduced such that $\xi_{ij}(t)$ is 1 if a Type j part is at Machine i at time t, and 0 otherwise. Again, an appropriate set of constraints can be developed.

The first difficulty with both of these formulations is the very large number of variables. During a typical run, hundreds or thousands of copies of a part may be made. As a consequence, there may be thousands of t_{ij} or ξ_{ij} variables. Large integer programming problems are difficult and their solution methods are time-consuming. Finally, there are no standard methods for the solution of *stochastic* linear or integer programming problems.

Therefore, we describe a formulation in Section 9.2.4 which is not burdened by a large number of variables, and for which solution methods exist or can be developed that account for the randomness in the problem. It is based on a natural time scale decomposition of the problem.

---

[3]Reprinted from Srivatsan, Bai, and Gershwin (1993), with permission from Academic Press

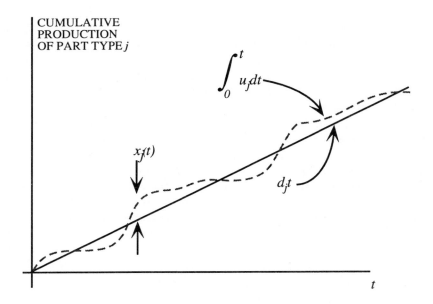

Figure 9.1: Cumulative Production and Demand

9.2.3   Hierarchy structure

In Section 9.2.4, we develop a model and a scheduling policy for an FMS whose machines fail at random times. We assume that failures occur much less often than operations. Each time a machine goes down, and each time a failed machine is repaired, the number of resources available for production is changed, and thus the short-term schedule should be changed. (If failures occur at roughly the same frequency as operations, they can be treated as random perturbations of operation times.) We do not consider multiple routes here. That is, each part type is assumed to have a fixed route through the system. Systems with multiple routes are considered in Section 9.6.1.

A three-level control hierarchy designed to compensate for work station failures and changes in part requirements is proposed. The hierarchy is illustrated in Figure 9.2. The objective of the FMS controller is to satisfy a known, possibly time-varying demand for a family of items that is dictated by the Master Production Plan, subject to constraints imposed by the resources available.

Assumptions on Lengths of Time Periods   The scheduling policy described here is based on a set of assumptions on the time scales of various classes of events that occur in the operation of a flexible manufacturing system:

- **The shortest time period is that of setup changes**: the switching among the operations to be performed on a family of parts. It is assumed that these times are

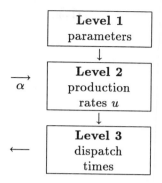

Figure 9.2: Three-Level Hierarchy

so short compared to the operation and failure times that they may be ignored for scheduling purposes. Systems in which setup times and costs are not negligible are discussed in Chapter 11.

- **The next time period is the typical duration of an operation.** Operation times are assumed to be orders of magnitude larger than setup times.

- **The next time period is the time between machine failures or repairs.** Mean times to failure and mean times to repair (MTTF and MTTR) are much longer than operation times.

- **The longest time period is the planning horizon.** It is assumed that demand can be specified for a time period much larger than the typical MTTF or MTTR.

- **The internal buffers are very small.** The amount of material that can be held in the system is so small that the time required for the buffers either to empty or to fill immediately after a machine goes up or down is small compared to the MTTFs and MTTRs. On the other hand, it is large enough to hold parts between the completion of one operation at one machine and the start of another at another machine. The dispatch policy is such that little material is in the system at any time.

- **The amount of time that parts spend in the system is very small** compared to the MTTRs and MTTFs.

Structure of Hierarchy   These assumptions on the relative values of times between events allow the following hierarchical structure.

Level 1: Parameter Calculation   At the highest level of the control scheme is the off-line calculation of the parameters of the control policy to be used in the flow level. If all problem data is known, this is required only once: when a scheduling policy is established. In practice, it may be prudent to include a long-term feedback loop to compile data on failure and repair rates and to update the control policy parameters.

Level 2: Flow Control — Production Rate Calculation   The flow control level determines the short-term production rates (u_j) of each member (j) of the part family. The rates are determined jointly because the parts share the time available at the work stations. The mix of parts being produced is adjusted continuously to take into account the random failure states (α_i) of the work stations. If, for example, a part cannot be made because a station has failed, the lost production of that part type must be made up when that station is repaired; and the time that is available at other machines is allocated to parts that can be made.

Using the control parameters determined in Level 1, the production rates are chosen in a way that anticipates station downtime. Adequate but not excessive surpluses (x) are maintained to track demand. The production rate vector u is a function of α and x, and is such that x tends to a value Z called the *hedging point*.

Level 3: Dispatch Time Calculation   At the lowest level is the dispatch of parts into the system. Times are selected at which parts are dispatched. These times are consistent with the production rates calculated at Level 2.

9.2.4   Hedging point problem

In this section, we describe the hedging point problem, whose solution leads to the calculations at Levels 1 and 2. It is based on a model of an FMS in which failures and repairs of machines are represented explicitly, but operations are not. Instead the frequencies of operations — the production rates — are calculated. The model is constructed so that we can take advantage of the methods of Sections 2.3, 2.6, and 8.8.

Level 2 Model of an FMS   The flow control level — Level 2 — of the FMS controller determines the production rates for all the part types in the family. The horizon is set by the FMS management and is on the order of one period of the master production plan. The dispatch level ensures that the actual output of the system is the same as that set by the flow controller. For the lower level of the hierarchy to be able to track the rates set by the flow controller, the rates must be feasible for the current system configuration at all times. It is important therefore for the flow controller to have complete and timely information on the operational status of all work stations.

The FMS consists of M work stations. Work station i $(i = 1, 2, \ldots, M)$ has L_i identical machines. The concept of work station is logical, not physical: the machines in a work station need not be located closer to one another than other machines.

A family of N part types is produced. The material flow is modeled as a continuous process. This kind of model ignores details which are treated at the lower level. Its precision is adequate for the time scale at this level, which is long compared to the time needed to produce individual parts.

Material flow   Let $u \in \mathbf{R}^N$ be the production rate vector for the part family. The demand rate is $d \in \mathbf{R}^N$ and is known in the interval (t_0, T). Define the surplus vector $x \in \mathbf{R}^N$ by

$$\frac{dx}{dt} = u - d. \tag{9.1}$$

The vector $x(t)$ measures the cumulative difference between production and demand for the parts. A negative value for a component of $x(t)$ gives the backlogged demand for the corresponding part. A positive value is the excess production. Ideally, parts in an FMS are produced as they are required, keeping the surplus close to zero.

In reality, many manufacturers do not allow the surplus to become negative. If the surplus is moving in that direction, some action is found to keep x positive, such as subcontracting to an alternative supplier, acquiring a new machine, or renegotiating delivery times with the customer. The model (and solution) described here is adequate for such systems, because its effect is to limit the amount of time that x is negative. In this case, it limits the frequency with which such expensive actions must be taken.

Repair states   In earlier chapters, each work station consisted of a single machine, which could be up or down. Here, we generalize this. Each work station consists of one or more identical machines. The entire manufacturing system consists of one or more non-identical work stations. The state of each work station is the number of its machines that are currently operational.

As in earlier chapters, we assume that a machine is either up or down. In reality, there may be partial failures in some kinds of systems. That is, a degraded machine may be able to do a subset of its normal set of operations, or it may be able to do all its operations but more slowly than normal, or it may only be allowed to do low-precision operations. The models described here can be extended to include these effects. In addition, we assume time-dependent failures in order to make the mathematics easier. That is, the probability of a failure is independent of production rate. In Chapters 3-5, we assume operation-dependent failures.

The state of the work stations is called the *machine state* and is denoted by an M-vector of integer variables $\alpha(t)$ with component α_i equal to the number of operational machines at Station i. Given that a machine at Station i is operational, the probability of a failure in an interval of length δt is $p_i \delta t$. The probability that a failed machine is repaired during such a time interval is $r_i \delta t$. The parameters p_i and r_i are the failure and repair rates for the machines at Station i. The dynamics of the machine state are therefore governed by

$$\text{prob } [\alpha_i(t + \delta t) = \ell + 1 \mid \alpha_i(t) = \ell] = \begin{cases} (L_i - \ell)r_i \delta t, & \text{for } 0 \leq \ell \leq L_i - 1 \\ 0, & \text{otherwise} \end{cases} \tag{9.2}$$

$$\text{prob } [\alpha_i(t + \delta t) = \ell - 1 \mid \alpha_i(t) = \ell] = \begin{cases} \ell p_i \delta t, \text{ for } 1 \leq \ell \leq L_i \\ \\ 0, \text{ otherwise} \end{cases} \tag{9.3}$$

Note that

$$\text{prob } [\alpha_i(t + \delta t) = m \mid \alpha_i(t) = n] = 0 \text{ if } \mid m - n \mid > 1. \tag{9.4}$$

That is, no more than one machine becomes operational or goes down at any instant. As in Section 2.3, it is convenient to define

$$\lambda_{mn} \delta t = \text{prob } [\alpha(t + \delta t) = m \mid \alpha(t) = n] + o(\delta t) \text{ for } m \neq n \tag{9.5}$$

and

$$\lambda_{mm} = - \sum_{n \neq m} \lambda_{nm}. \tag{9.6}$$

The times to failure and to repair are thus modeled by exponentially distributed random variables with rates p_i and r_i, respectively. The machine state therefore is modeled by an irreducible continuous time Markov process with a finite number of discrete states. Each state communicates with M neighbors, and transitions are due to the failure or repair of a single machine.

Other distributions must be used to model systems whose failure rates depend on the time since the last repair. However, in a practical implementation, the estimation of failure and repair time distributions is difficult. Even with the exponential assumption, however, it is not possible to solve the problem formulated here analytically or numerically. Since approximations seem to work well, it is not certain that much improvement would be gained for a real system if more accurate distributions were used.

Capacity   The production rate at each instant is limited by the capacity of the currently operational machines. At time t, the production rate must lie in a set $\Omega(\alpha(t))$ which depends on the machine state $\alpha(t)$ and is thus subject to sudden changes. The capacity set is a generalization of the inequality constraints on u in Section 2.6 and Section 8.2.

To define Ω, assume that U_j Type j parts are processed by the FMS in an interval $[t, t_1]$. Assume that each Type j part requires τ_{ij} time units at a machine at Work Station i before it leaves the system. (For this model, it is not important whether the part requires that time in a single interval, or it returns to the station more than once.)

Then the total amount of time that machines are occupied in Work Station i is

$$\sum_j \tau_{ij} U_j$$

time units. Assume that during the entire interval $[t, t_1]$, the number of Station i machines that are operational is constant, $\alpha_i(t)$. In that case, the total number of time units that are available at Station i is

$$\alpha_i(t)(t_1 - t).$$

Therefore, we must have

$$\sum_j \tau_{ij} U_j \leq \alpha_i(t)(t_1 - t).$$

The production rate of Type j parts is

$$u_j(t) = \frac{U_j}{t_1 - t}.$$

Thus

$$\sum_j \tau_{ij} u_j(t) \leq \alpha_i(t). \tag{9.7}$$

If we let $t_1 \to t$, then the number of machines that are operational during the whole interval does remain constant. Consequently, the production rate vector must satisfy (9.7) for every t. In addition, each component u_j must be positive or 0.

Thus, we can define the *capacity set* $\Omega(\alpha(t))$ as the set of u vectors which are positive and satisfy (9.7). This set is determined by linear inequalities and is therefore convex and polyhedral.

It would not be precise to denote capacity by a single number (the total number of parts flowing through the system per time) or even a vector (a rate for each part type). A set is required because of the sharing of resources among part types. The rate at which it is possible to manufacture one part is reduced by the production of other parts.

In fact, we have shown that capacity is not a single constant set, but rather a time-varying stochastic set. This is because of the random availability of the machines. For this chapter, this is all we need to consider. However, if one is doing long-range planning, the rapidly changing capacity sets described here are not helpful. We need still another capacity set: the average of all the $\Omega(\alpha(t))$ sets. As we show in later chapters, there are different capacity sets at each time scale, and thus at each level of the management and control hierarchy.

To summarize, the only u vectors that need be considered at time t are those that are in the set $\Omega(\alpha(t))$, which is given by

$$\Omega(\alpha(t)) = \left\{ \begin{array}{l} \text{the set of all } N\text{-vectors } u \in \mathbf{R}^N \text{ such that,} \\ \text{for all } 1 \leq i \leq M, 1 \leq j \leq N, \\[2mm] \displaystyle\sum_j \tau_{ij} u_j \leq \alpha_i(t), \\[4mm] u_j \geq 0 \end{array} \right\} \tag{9.8}$$

Problem statement   The Level 2 flow control problem can now be stated. Given an FMS, an initial surplus state $x(t_0)$ and machine state $\alpha(t_0)$, we wish to find a production plan for the time interval $[t_0, T]$ that minimizes the performance index

$$J(x(t_0), \alpha(t_0), t_0) = E\left\{ \int_{t_0}^{T} g(x(s))ds \mid x(t_0), \alpha(t_0) \right\} \tag{9.9}$$

subject to

$$\frac{dx}{dt} = u - d; \qquad\qquad\qquad x(t_0) \text{ specified} \tag{9.10}$$

$$\text{prob } [\alpha(t + \delta t) = m \mid \alpha(t) = n] = \lambda_{mn}\delta t \text{ for } m \neq n; \qquad \alpha(t_0) \text{ specified} \tag{9.11}$$

$$u(t) \in \Omega(\alpha(t)). \tag{9.12}$$

The minimization is over all functions $u(s)$, $t_0 \leq s \leq T$, such that $x(s), \alpha(s)$, and $u(s)$ satisfy constraints (9.10)-(9.12). The function $g(x(t))$ penalizes the controller for failing to meet demand and for getting too far ahead of demand. The performance index is thus the expected total penalty incurred by the controller in the interval $[t_0, T]$. The function is given by

$$g(x) = \sum_j g_j(x_j)$$

where each $g_j(s)$ is a scalar convex function satisfying

$$\lim_{|s| \to \infty} g_j(s) = \infty$$

$$\min_s g_j(s) = 0$$

$$g_j(0) = 0$$

The cost function $g(x)$ serves to enforce desired behavior on the controller. The ideal production policy would minimize the performance index by producing parts at exactly the demand rate, thereby keeping the buffer state at zero. Such a policy is impossible because of the failures of the machines.

Bellman equation   The solution $u(x, \alpha, t)$ of (9.9)-(9.12) is the optimal feedback control we are seeking. We now develop the Bellman equation for this problem which helps to characterize this function. While we cannot solve the Bellman equation for any but the simplest of problems, we can use its properties to help derive practical policies for realistic problems.

Define the optimal cost-to-go or value function J as

$$J(x(t), \alpha(t), t) = \min_u E \left\{ \int_t^T g(x(s)) ds \mid x(t), \alpha(t) \right\} \qquad (9.13)$$

where the minimization is over all functions $u(s), t \leq s \leq T$, such that $u(s) \in \Omega(\alpha(s))$ (9.12) and such that $x(s)$ and $\alpha(s)$ satisfy (9.10) and (9.11). Note that

$$J(x(T), \alpha(T), T) = 0.$$

The cost-to-go is thus the expected total penalty incurred by the controller for the remaining time, given that the buffer and machine states are x and α at time t. To derive the Bellman equation for this problem, we follow the development of Section 8.8.

For any δt,

$$J(x(t), \alpha(t), t) =$$
$$\min_u E \left\{ \int_t^{t+\delta t} g(x(s)) ds + J(x(t+\delta t), \alpha(t+\delta t), t+\delta t) \, \middle| \, x(t), \alpha(t) \right\} \qquad (9.14)$$

where now the minimization is over all functions $u(s), t \leq s \leq t + \delta t$, such that $u(s) \in \Omega(\alpha(s))$. This is because we do not have to worry about the behavior of $u(s)$ for $s > t + \delta t$; it is taken care of in $J(x(t+\delta t), \alpha(t+\delta t), t+\delta t)$.

For small δt, (9.14) becomes, approximately

$$J(x(t), \alpha(t), t) = \min_{u(t)} \left\{ g(x(t))\delta t + J(x(t), \alpha(t), t) + \sum_j J(x(t), j, t) \lambda_{j\alpha(t)} \delta t + \right.$$
$$\left. \frac{\partial J}{\partial x}(x(t), \alpha(t), t)\delta x(t) + \frac{\partial J}{\partial t}(x(t), \alpha(t), t)\delta t \right\} + o(\delta t) \qquad (9.15)$$

where *now* the minimization is over all $u(t)$ such that $u(t) \in \Omega(\alpha(t))$. If we replace $\delta x(t)$ by

$$\delta x(t) = \frac{dx}{dt}(t)\delta t = (u(t) - d)\delta t$$

and do the other manipulations of Section 8.8, we get

$$-\frac{\partial J}{\partial t}(x, \alpha, t) = \min_{u \in \Omega(\alpha)} \left\{ g(x) + \sum_j J(x, j, t)\lambda_{j\alpha} + \frac{\partial J}{\partial x}(x, \alpha, t)(u - d) \right\} \qquad (9.16)$$

for every x, α, and t.

This is the fundamental equation on which all subsequent work in this chapter is based. It is important to see that if J is known, (9.16) is a linear programming problem in u. This is because u appears linearly in the quantity to be minimized, and the constraints on u are linear inequalities.

9.3   Single-Machine, Single-Part-Type Example

Bielecki and Kumar (1988) examined a system with a single machine and a single part type. Such a system is not flexible in the sense defined above, but it illustrates some of the issues we study. In particular, they demonstrated, by means of the methods presented here, that it is not optimal to run the system at its full capacity whenever possible, because that would make the surplus grow excessively. Instead, when the surplus has reached a satisfactory level (the *hedging point*), production is slowed so that the rate of growth of surplus is set to zero. That is, once the surplus reaches the hedging point, the production rate is chosen to keep it there as long as possible. This system is exactly that of Section 2.6. Here, we derive the control law postulated there, and we calculate an optimal Z, a Z that minimizes a cost function.

In Bielecki and Kumar's problem, $M = N = 1$,

$$g(x) = g_+ x^+ + g_- x^-$$

where

$$x^+ = \left\{ \begin{array}{l} x, \text{ if } x \geq 0 \\ 0, \text{ otherwise} \end{array} \right. \qquad x^- = \left\{ \begin{array}{l} -x, \text{ if } -x \geq 0 \\ 0, \text{ otherwise} \end{array} \right.$$

and g_+ and g_- are positive penalties for producing too much (positive surplus) or too little (backlog). Note that

$$x^+ \geq 0, x^- \geq 0,$$

$$x = x^+ - x^-.$$

There is only one machine and it has only two repair states: up ($\alpha = 1$) and down ($\alpha = 0$). Therefore, $L_1 = 1$, and

$$\lambda_{01} = p; \lambda_{11} = -p;$$

$$\lambda_{10} = r; \lambda_{00} = -r.$$

The constraint set (9.8) is given by

$$\Omega(0) = \{0\},$$

$$\Omega(1) = \{u \mid 0 \leq u \leq \mu\}.$$

where $\mu = 1/\tau$ is the maximum production rate of the machine. We assume that the demand rate d is less than μ.

Bielecki and Kumar assume that T is very large. If we also assume that d is feasible, that

$$d < \frac{\mu r}{r + p}$$

then we can assume (8.13). This is because the conditions of Section 8.9 are satisfied: α has a finite set of possible values, and x can be made to return to the origin whenever the machine is up long enough.

This approximation is not valid if the demand is not feasible. In that case, x drifts systematically in the negative direction; roughly,

$$x(t) \approx x(t_0) + \left(\frac{\mu r}{r + p} - d \right) (t - t_0)$$

and J^* is not meaningful.

When the demand is feasible, this approximation is used here and extensively in later sections. Equation (8.13) is substituted into (9.16), which becomes, for $\alpha = 0$ and 1,

$$J^* = \min_{u \in \Omega(\alpha(t))} \left\{ g_+ x^+ + g_- x^- + \sum_j [(T - t)J^* + W(x, j)] \lambda_{j\alpha} + \frac{dW}{dx}(x, \alpha)(u - d) \right\}$$

where W is the differential cost. Since J^* is constant and

$$\sum_j \lambda_{j\alpha} = 0,$$

we have

$$J^* = \min_{u \in \Omega(\alpha)} \left\{ g_+ x^+ + g_- x^- + \sum_j W(x, j) \lambda_{j\alpha} + \frac{dW}{dx}(x, \alpha)(u - d) \right\}.$$

This can be further simplified:

$$\left. \begin{aligned} & J^* = g_+ x^+ + g_- x^- + W(x, 1)r - W(x, 0)r - \frac{dW}{dx}(x, 0)d, \text{ for } \alpha = 0, \\[2em] & J^* = \min_{0 \le u \le \mu} \left\{ g_+ x^+ + g_- x^- + W(x, 0)p - W(x, 1)p + \frac{dW}{dx}(x, 1)(u - d) \right\}, \\ & \qquad\qquad\qquad\qquad\qquad\qquad \text{for } \alpha = 1. \end{aligned} \right\} \quad (9.17)$$

The minimization does not appear in the $\alpha = 0$ case since there is no opportunity to select u; we must have $u = 0$. Since there is only one continuous state variable, the Bellman's equation reduces to the determination of two functions of a single variable ($W(x, 0)$ and $W(x, 1)$) and an unknown scalar J^*.

If $dW(x,1)/dx$ were known, the minimization in (9.17) would reduce to:

$$
\left.\begin{array}{l}
u = 0 \text{ if } \dfrac{dW}{dx}(x,1) > 0 \\[3mm]
u = \mu \text{ if } \dfrac{dW}{dx}(x,1) < 0
\end{array}\right\}
\tag{9.18}
$$

and u is not determined if $dW(x,1)/dx = 0$. Kimemia (1982) established that W for the optimal policy is convex. Therefore, its derivative is increasing in x, and there are three possibilities: $W(x,1)$ is increasing for all x, with a minimum at $-\infty$, $W(x,1)$ is decreasing for all x, with a minimum at $+\infty$, or there is a finite Z such that $dW(x,1)/dx < 0$ for $x < Z$ and $dW(x,1)/dx > 0$ for $x > Z$. In the first case, u is always 0, which is not reasonable. In the second case, u is always μ. The only reason for the machine to *always* be operated at full throttle is that there is not sufficient capacity. There is not much more to say in that case; in the following, we will assume that there is some excess long-term capacity.

Consequently, the optimal production rate is

$$
\left.\begin{array}{l}
u = 0 \text{ if } x > Z \\[2mm]
u = d \text{ if } x = Z \\[2mm]
u = \mu \text{ if } x < Z
\end{array}\right\}
\tag{9.19}
$$

for some Z which must be determined.[4] The middle condition is added to prevent *chattering*. Since dx/dt is negative when $x > Z$, and positive when $x < Z$, x would rapidly oscillate about Z if dx/dt were not 0 at $x = Z$. Thus the Bellman equation (9.17) and the convexity of W implies the form of the control law (9.19). This control law was assumed in Section 2.6.

To completely specify the control law, we must determine Z. In the following, we solve (9.17) for Z, J^*, and the functions $W(x,0)$ and $W(x,1)$. Feedback law (9.19) tends to move x to Z. When the machine goes down, x decreases since $dx/dt = -d$. When the repair occurs and $x < Z, x$ increases until $x = Z$, and then remains there. The surplus level Z is the *hedging point*. It is positive or zero ($Z \geq 0$) because x can only leave Z by decreasing. (If Z were negative, the cost incurred would be $-g_-x$, and would be increasing. If Z is positive, the cost incurred is first g_+x, which decreases until x reaches 0. Then it is $-g_-x$, and increases. There is a chance that the repair will occur before this cost gets too large.)

Equation (9.17) has a different behavior on each of three intervals in x. The intervals are:

$$I_1: \quad x > Z$$

$$I_2: \quad 0 < x < Z$$

$$I_3: \quad x < 0$$

---

[4]There might appear to be another possibility: if $W(x,1)$ is convex *but not strictly convex*. In that case, there might be an interval, rather than a single point, in which $u = d$. If that were true, however, $dW(x,1)/dx$ would be 0 over that entire interval. This is not possible, because it does not satisfy the Bellman equation.

Continuity properties $W(x, \alpha)$ is continuous in x because it is the solution of a set of differential equations.[5] However, the continuity properties of its derivatives are not as clear. Along with the differential equations, conditions on continuity or discontinuity are needed to determine W, but we must be careful to specify only independent, non-redundant, conditions. The solutions of the differential equations include a set of unknown constants of integration; the continuity conditions can be used to determine those constants if the conditions are independent. There are two places where the continuity of the derivatives of W is an issue: at $x = 0$ and at $x = Z$.

Consider the $\alpha = 0$ equation of (9.17) at $x = 0$. Since everything in this equation except $dW(x, 0)/dx$ is known to be continuous at $x = 0$, then $dW(x, 0)/dx$ must be continuous at $x = 0$ also. For the same reason, $dW(x, 0)/dx$ is continuous at $x = Z$, and if $Z \neq 0$, $dW(x, 1)/dx$ is continuous at $x = 0$.

At $x = Z$, u is not continuous. However, $\{dW(x, 1)/dx\}(u - d)$ must be continuous because everything else in the $\alpha = 1$ equation of (9.17) is continuous at $x = Z$. The discontinuity in $dW(x, 1)/dx$ at $x = Z$ must compensate just enough for the discontinuity in u to keep $\{dW(x, 1)/dx\}(u - d)$ continuous. Again, the magnitude of the discontinuity of dW/dx at $x = Z$ is not independent of the continuity of W at $x = Z$, and therefore cannot be used to further determine W.

If we specify that $W(x, 0)$ and $W(x, 1)$ are continuous at $x = 0$ and $x = Z$, then the continuity properties of the derivatives would be redundant, since they follow from the continuity of $W(x, \alpha)$. That is, we cannot use both the continuity of W at $x = 0$ and $x = Z$ and the continuity properties of dW/dx at $x = 0$ and $x = Z$ to determine the unknown constants of integration, since these conditions can be derived from one another.

Consider the behavior of the value function in the neighborhood of the hedging point. If the system is at $(Z, 1)$ at time t, there are two possibilities: it can still be at $(Z, 1)$ at time $t + \delta t$ if the machine does not fail during $[t, t + \delta t]$, or it can be at $(Z - d\delta t, 0)$ at time $t + \delta t$ if it does. Therefore, to first order,

$$
\begin{aligned}
J(Z, 1, t) = {} & (g(Z)\delta t + J(Z, 1, t + \delta t))(1 - p\delta t) \\
& + (g(Z)\delta t + J(Z - d\delta t, 0, t + \delta t))p\delta t + o(\delta t)
\end{aligned}
$$

or, using (8.13) in the form

$$
J(x(t), \alpha(t), t) \approx J^*(T - t) + W(x(t), \alpha(t)),
$$

we have

$$
\begin{aligned}
J^*(T - t) + W(Z, 1) = {} & (g(Z)\delta t + J^*(T - t - \delta t) + W(Z, 1))(1 - p\delta t) \\
& + (g(Z)\delta t + J^*(T - t - \delta t) + W(Z, 0))p\delta t + o(\delta t).
\end{aligned}
$$

---

[5] N. Srivatsan is responsible for many of the ideas on continuity and discontinuity presented here, especially (9.20).

By combining terms of the same order in δt and letting $\delta t \to 0$ (and observing that $g(Z) = g_+ Z$ since $Z > 0$), we obtain[6]

$$J^* = g_+ Z + (W(Z, 0) - W(Z, 1))p. \tag{9.20}$$

Solution of equations   In I_1, (9.17) becomes

$$\left. \begin{array}{l} J^* = g_+ x + W(x, 1)r - W(x, 0)r - \dfrac{dW}{dx}(x, 0)d, \text{ for } \alpha = 0, \\[3mm] J^* = g_+ x + W(x, 0)p - W(x, 1)p - \dfrac{dW}{dx}(x, 1)d, \text{ for } \alpha = 1. \end{array} \right\} \tag{9.21}$$

If we compare (9.20) with the $\alpha = 1$ equation of (9.21), we conclude that

$$\lim_{\substack{x \to Z \\ x > Z}} \frac{dW}{dx}(x, 1) = 0. \tag{9.22}$$

Since this limit follows from (9.20), (9.21), and the continuity of W, we cannot use it to determine the constants of integration. On the other hand, it and (9.22) establish that $W(x, 1)$ has a continuous derivative at its minimum, $x = Z$.

The analysis of Interval I_1 is a little simpler than that of the other intervals. Define $\mathcal{E}(x)$ as

$$\mathcal{E}(x) = \frac{p}{r + p} W(x, 0) + \frac{r}{r + p} W(x, 1).$$

We can think of $\mathcal{E}(x)$ as the expected value of $W(x, \alpha)$, for a given value of x, where α is treated as a random variable in steady state. By multiplying the equations of (9.21) by $p/(r + p)$ and $r/(r + p)$, respectively, and adding, we find

$$J^* = g_+ x - d \frac{d\mathcal{E}(x)}{dx}$$

so

$$J^* x = \frac{1}{2} g_+ x^2 - d\mathcal{E}(x) + dD$$

where dD is a constant of integration, or

$$\mathcal{E}(x) = \frac{1}{2d} g_+ x^2 - \frac{J^* x}{d} + D. \tag{9.23}$$

Similarly, we can define

$$\Delta(x) = W(x, 1) - W(x, 0).$$

---

[6]due to Srivatsan

Then, if we subtract the equations of (9.21), we can see that Δ satisfies

$$0 = \Delta(r+p) + d\frac{d\Delta}{dx} \tag{9.24}$$

so

$$\Delta(x) = Ce^{-ax}$$

where C is an unknown constant and

$$a = \frac{r+p}{d}.$$

Then, since

$$W(x,1) = \mathcal{E}(x) + \frac{p}{r+p}\Delta$$

$$W(x,0) = \mathcal{E}(x) - \frac{r}{r+p}\Delta$$

the solution of (9.21) is

$$\left. \begin{array}{l} W(x,0) = \dfrac{g_+ x^2}{2d} - \dfrac{J^* x}{d} - \dfrac{Cre^{-ax}}{r+p} + D \\[3mm] W(x,1) = \dfrac{g_+ x^2}{2d} - \dfrac{J^* x}{d} + \dfrac{Cpe^{-ax}}{r+p} + D \end{array} \right\} \tag{9.25}$$

Equation (9.25) could also be obtained by solving the pair of ordinary differential equations (9.17) directly in interval I_1 (by guessing a form for $W(x,0)$ and $W(x,1)$, plugging it into (9.17), forming an eigenvalue equation, etc.).

Similarly, in I_2, (9.17) becomes

$$\left. \begin{array}{l} J^* = g_+ x^+ + W(x,1)r - W(x,0)r - \dfrac{dW}{dx}(x,0)d, \text{ for } \alpha = 0, \\[4mm] J^* = g_+ x^+ + W(x,0)p - W(x,1)p + \dfrac{dW}{dx}(x,1)(\mu - d), \text{ for } \alpha = 1 \end{array} \right\} \tag{9.26}$$

and the solution is

$$\left. \begin{array}{l} W(x,0) = Ee^{-bx} - \dfrac{g_+(r+p)}{2bd(\mu-d)}x^2 + \left[\dfrac{(r+p)J^* + \frac{g_+r\mu}{bd}}{r(\mu-d)-pd}\right]x + F \\[5mm] W(x,1) = \dfrac{pd}{r(\mu-d)}Ee^{-bx} - \dfrac{g_+(r+p)}{2bd(\mu-d)}x^2 \\[4mm] \qquad + \left[\dfrac{(r+p)J^* + \frac{g_+r\mu}{bd}}{r(\mu-d)-pd} - \dfrac{g_+\mu}{bd(\mu-d)}\right]x + F \\[5mm] \qquad + \dfrac{1}{r}\left[J^* + \dfrac{d(r+p)J^* + \frac{g_+r\mu}{b}}{r(\mu-d)-pd}\right] \end{array} \right\} \tag{9.27}$$

where

$$b = \frac{r}{d} - \frac{p}{\mu - d} = \frac{r\mu - rd - pd}{d(\mu - d)}$$

and E and F are unknown constants.

The average capacity of the system is

$$\frac{r\mu}{r + p}.$$

That is the expected maximum production rate that the system can sustain. Therefore, for the problem to make sense,

$$\frac{r\mu}{r + p} - d > 0,$$

which implies that

$$b > 0.$$

Recall that $\{dW(x, 1)/dx\}(u - d)$ is continuous at $x = Z$. Since $u = \mu$ for $x < Z$, we must also have, by comparing (9.20) with the $\alpha = 1$ equation of (9.26),

$$\lim_{\substack{x \to Z \\ x < Z}} \frac{dW}{dx}(x, 1) = 0. \tag{9.28}$$

In I_3, (9.17) becomes

$$J^* = g_- x^- + W(x, 1)r - W(x, 0)r - \frac{dW}{dx}(x, 0)d, \text{ for } \alpha = 0,$$

$$J^* = g_- x^- + W(x, 0)p - W(x, 1)p + \frac{dW}{dx}(x, 1)(\mu - d), \text{ for } \alpha = 1.$$

The solution is

$$\left. \begin{aligned} W(x, 0) &= Ge^{-bx} + \frac{g_-(r + p)}{2bd(\mu - d)}x^2 + \left[\frac{(r + p)J^* - \frac{g_- r\mu}{bd}}{r(\mu - d) - pd} \right] x + H \\[2em] W(x, 1) &= \frac{pd}{r(\mu - d)}Ge^{-bx} + \frac{g_-(r + p)}{2bd(\mu - d)}x^2 \\ &\quad + \left[\frac{(r + p)J^* - \frac{g_- r\mu}{bd}}{r(\mu - d) - pd} + \frac{g_- \mu}{bd(\mu - d)} \right] x + H \\[1em] &\quad + \frac{1}{r}\left[J^* + \frac{d(r + p)J^* - \frac{g_- r\mu}{b}}{r(\mu - d) - pd} \right] \end{aligned} \right\} \tag{9.29}$$

where G and H are unknown constants.

Determination of constants So far, there are five independent conditions ((9.20) and continuity of $W(x,0)$ and $W(x,1)$ at $x = 0$ and $x = Z$) to determine eight unknowns $(J^*, Z, C, D, E, F, G,$ and $H)$. These conditions can be written as follows.

Equation (9.20):

$$W(Z,0) - W(Z,1) = \frac{J^* - g_+ Z}{p} = -Ce^{-aZ}.$$

(9.30)

Continuity of $W(x,0)$ at $x = 0$:

$$\lim_{\substack{x > 0 \\ x \to 0}} W(x,0) = \lim_{\substack{x < 0 \\ x \to 0}} W(x,0)$$

or, by comparing the expressions for $W(0,0)$ in I_2 and I_3,

$$W(0,0) = G + H = E + F$$

(9.31)

Continuity of $W(x,1)$ at $x = 0$:

$$\lim_{\substack{x > 0 \\ x \to 0}} W(x,1) = \lim_{\substack{x < 0 \\ x \to 0}} W(x,1)$$

or,

$$
\begin{aligned}
W(0,1) &= \frac{pd}{r(\mu - d)} G + H + \frac{1}{r}\left[J^* + \frac{d(r+p)J^* - \frac{g-r\mu}{b}}{r(\mu - d) - pd} \right] \\
&= \frac{pd}{r(\mu - d)} E + F + \frac{1}{r}\left[J^* + \frac{d(r+p)J^* + \frac{g+r\mu}{b}}{r(\mu - d) - pd} \right]
\end{aligned}
$$

(9.32)

Continuity of $W(x,0)$ at $x = Z$:

$$\lim_{\substack{x > Z \\ x \to Z}} W(x,0) = \lim_{\substack{x < Z \\ x \to Z}} W(x,0)$$

or,

$$
\begin{aligned}
W(Z,0) &= \frac{g_+ Z^2}{2d} - \frac{J^* Z}{d} - \frac{Cre^{-aZ}}{r+p} + D \\
&= Ee^{-bZ} - \frac{g_+(r+p)}{2bd(\mu - d)} Z^2 + \left[\frac{(r+p)J^* + \frac{g+r\mu}{bd}}{r(\mu - d) - pd} \right] Z + F
\end{aligned}
$$

(9.33)

Continuity of $W(x,1)$ at $x = Z$:

$$\lim_{\substack{x > Z \\ x \to Z}} W(x,1) = \lim_{\substack{x < Z \\ x \to Z}} W(x,1)$$

or,

$$
\begin{aligned}
W(Z,1) &= \frac{g_+ Z^2}{2d} - \frac{J^* Z}{d} + \frac{Cpe^{-aZ}}{r+p} + D \\
&= \frac{pd}{r(\mu - d)} E e^{-bZ} - \frac{g_+(r+p)}{2bd(\mu - d)} Z^2 \\
&\quad + \left[\frac{(r+p)J^* + \frac{g_+ r\mu}{bd}}{r(\mu - d) - pd} - \frac{g_+ \mu}{bd(\mu - d)} \right] Z + F \\
&\quad + \frac{1}{r}\left[J^* + \frac{d(r+p)J^* + \frac{g_+ r\mu}{b}}{r(\mu - d) - pd} \right]
\end{aligned}
\tag{9.34}
$$

Note that (9.30)-(9.34) is a nonlinear set of equations, but it is linear in all variables other than Z once Z is specified.

Determination of Z and J^*   If we assume the form of the feedback law (9.19), this system is exactly the same as that of the example of Section 2.6. Therefore, an alternative representation of the constant part of the cost function is simply

$$J^* = Eg(x) = g(Z)P(Z,1) + \int_{-\infty}^{Z} g(x)\left[f(x,0) + f(x,1)\right] dx \tag{9.35}$$

in which P and f form the steady-state probability distribution of x (Equations (2.56)-(2.60)). We must choose Z to minimize J^*.

If $Z \le 0$, then (9.35) becomes

$$J^* = -g_- Z P(Z,1) - \int_{-\infty}^{Z} g_- x\left[f(x,0) + f(x,1)\right] dx.$$

If $Z > 0$, it becomes

$$J^* = g_+ Z P(Z,1) - \int_{-\infty}^{0} g_- x\left[f(x,0) + f(x,1)\right] dx + \int_{0}^{Z} g_+ x\left[f(x,0) + f(x,1)\right] dx.$$

Evaluating and minimizing these expressions with respect to Z,

if $g_+ - b(g_+ + g_-) < 0$

$$Z = \frac{\ln\left(Kb(1 + \frac{g_-}{g_+})\right)}{b}$$

$$J^* = g_+(Z - K) + K(g_+ + g_-)e^{-bZ}$$

if $g_+ - b(g_+ + g_-) \geq 0$

$$Z = 0$$
$$J^* = Kg_-$$

where

$$K = \frac{\mu p}{b(\mu b d - d^2 b + \mu p)} = \frac{\mu p}{b(r + p)(\mu - d)}$$

Note that b is the same as in Section 2.6 and that Z is never negative.

Determination of G   It is possible to show, by using these equations, that $G = 0$. This is not a new condition since it comes from conditions already derived.

Summary   Now there are seven equations in eight unknowns. This is not a problem because $W(x, \alpha)$ cannot be completely specified from the differential equations and boundary conditions. If $W^0(x, 0)$ and $W^0(x, 1)$ form a solution of (9.17), then for any constant L, $W^0(x, 0) + L$ and $W^0(x, 1) + L$ also form a solution of (9.17). Recall from Section 8.9 that it must be possible to pick a state (x^b, α^b), and set $W(x^b, \alpha^b) = 0$. A convenient state for that purpose would be

$$(x^b, \alpha^b) = (Z, 1)$$

so that

$$W(Z, 1) = 0.$$

Adding L to $W(x, \alpha)$ is adding the same constant L to D, F, and H. In fact, equations (9.30)-(9.34) can be written so that D, F, and H appear only in $H - F$ and $F - D$.

Reality check — $G = 0$ We stated that the equations for the constants imply that $G = 0$. Here is an intuitive reason for this.

Suppose x is very negative. Since the problem is feasible, eventually x will return to 0. The time that it will take is approximately

$$T = \frac{-x}{\frac{\mu r}{r+p} - d}.$$

The cost incurred during this period is approximately

$$-\int_0^T g_- \bar{x}(s) ds$$

where

$$\bar{x}(s) = x + \left(\frac{\mu r}{r + p} - d\right) s$$

is the average trajectory. The value of this integral is

$$\frac{g_- x^2}{2\left(\frac{\mu r}{r+p} - d\right)}$$

which is precisely the quadratic term in (9.29). However, the exponential terms are much larger than the quadratic term if $G \neq 0$, since the exponent is positive and very large if x is very large and negative. Consequently,

$$G = 0.$$

Examples   Figure 9.3 shows $W(x,0)$ and $W(x,1)$ for a system in which $r = .09, p = .01, \mu = 1, d = .5, g_+ = 1$, and $g_- = 1$. For this case, $Z = 0$ and $J^* = 12.5$, and $W(x,0)$ and $W(x,1)$ are close to quadratic. Figure 9.4 shows $W(x,0)$ and $W(x,1)$ for a system which is identical except that $g_- = 10$. For this case, $Z = 4.928$ and $J^* = 9.928$, and $W(x,0)$ and $W(x,1)$ seem to be far from quadratic. In Section 9.4, we use a quadratic approximation of the value function to simplify the calculation of the production rate $u(x, \alpha)$.

Note that in both graphs, $W(x,1) < W(x,0)$. This is because it is easier to get to state $(Z, 1)$ from $(x, 1)$ than from $(x, 0)$. If $x < Z$, the difference is linear in x, and represents the cost of the surplus first decreasing (due to the machine being down) and then increasing before returning to the same value with the machine up. If $x > Z$, the difference is small, and diminishes as x increases. It is due to the greater probability of arriving at $x = Z$ with the machine down, if the machine is down now, than if the machine is up now.

Comments   To put this back into the hierarchical framework, the calculation of Z is all that is required from Level 1. Level 2 calculates $u(x, \alpha)$ according to feedback law (9.19) when $\alpha = 1$ and is forced to choose $u = 0$ when $\alpha = 0$. Level 3 loads parts into the machine at a rate equal to $u(x, \alpha)$. We discuss a version of Level 3, called the staircase strategy, in Section 9.4.4.

In this problem, it is easy to determine the form of the feedback law but harder to determine Z, and harder still to determine the value function. For larger systems, it remains easy to get the form of the feedback law, but generally impossible to go any further (to get the probability distribution or J) if we insist on analytic or even numerical solutions. However, W or J are not really important in themselves, but only in how they determine the behavior of the feedback law. In the following cases, we use what we know about the qualitative properties of J to derive feedback policies that work very well, even if they are not optimal.

The most important features of the solution of the problem of this section are:

- A Bellman equation was developed, and it led to a linear program. This linear program determined the instantaneous production rate as a function of the current machine state (α) and the current surplus state (x).

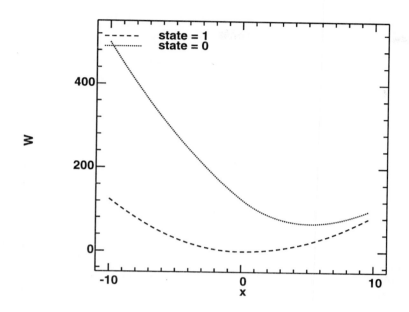

Figure 9.3: Solution of Bielecki-Kumar Problem when $Z = 0$

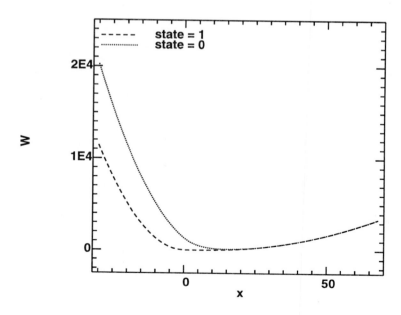

Figure 9.4: Solution of Bielecki-Kumar Problem when $Z > 0$

- The linear program *induces a partition* of the x space. That is, it divides the space into a set of regions (I_1, $I_2 \cup I_3$, and the boundary $x = Z$ between them) such that the optimal u is constant in each of these regions.

- All that is really important about the J function is that it is convex, and the location of its minimum. In at least some cases, a quadratic approximation of Z would not be far off.

- The minimum of J is called Z, the hedging point. It is the value of x that the system tries to bring x to, when it has sufficient short-term capacity.

- Letting $u = d$ when $x = Z$ prevents chattering. If there were no such rule, x would be moving frequently around Z.

- W is quadratic when x is negative.

We emphasize these points because we make use of them in the more complex systems that we study in the later sections of this chapter. Another point is that when the machine is sufficiently, but not perfectly reliable, the hedging point is 0. Thus, for some sufficiently reliable systems, the optimal policy can be obtained by ignoring the unreliability. While the policy found this way ($u(x, \alpha)$) is optimal, the cost-to-go (J^* and $W(x, \alpha)$) is not.

Figure 9.5 shows how Figure 9.1 looks when the system is operated according to the hedging point policy.

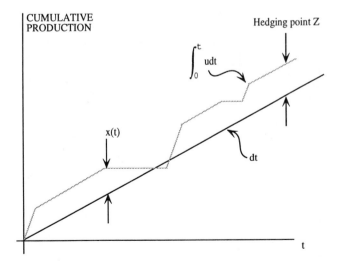

Figure 9.5: Cumulative Production and Demand Generated by the Hedging Point Policy

9.4 Larger Systems

9.4.1 Regions and boundaries

It is difficult to get an analytic solution even for the simple system described in Section 9.3, and the solution is complicated. We cannot expect that larger systems will be any easier to work with. Consequently, we use some of what we have learned about the simple case, and all of what we can find about more complex cases, to develop practical approximations. First we study the structure of Ω, then J, and finally the relationship between x and u.

Topology and geometry of Ω It is useful to discuss the features of the capacity set Ω in spaces of dimension $N > 1$. The minimization in (9.16) is a linear programming problem in which Ω is the constraint set. It is important to know that Ω is bounded, as well as the structure of the boundary of Ω. See Figure 9.6. Ω is a bounded polyhedron in u space. It is bounded because every part must go through at least one machine and take up some time on it. That is, for every n, there is some i such that $\tau_{ij} > 0$, and (9.7) implies that $u_j \leq L_i/\tau_{ij}$.

To use very general terms, the boundaries of polyhedra are unions of segments of hyperplanes. The lowest dimensional hyperplanes of Ω are the corners, which are of dimension 0. Edges and faces are affine subspaces of dimension 1 and 2. In general, the boundary of Ω is made up of hyperplanes h of dimension d_h. It is convenient to include the interior of Ω in this, which is of dimension N, so in general $0 \leq d_h \leq N$.

Because of the positivity constraints on $u_i (u_i \geq 0)$, Ω is located in the positive orthant of $\mathbf{R}^N$. Some $(N-1)$-dimensional faces of Ω pass through the origin and are orthogonal to the coordinate axes. They are the set of points in Ω in which, for some $i, u_i = 0$. Other $(N-1)$-dimensional faces are such that exactly one of the inequalities in (9.7) is satisfied with equality. Because all the coefficients of (9.7) are positive, the mth face formed that way intersects all the u_j axes such that τ_{ij} is positive, and is parallel to all those such that τ_{ij} is zero.

$(N-2)$-dimensional faces are formed when two of the inequalities in (9.8) are satisfied with equality, $(N-3)$-dimensional faces are formed when three of the inequalities are satisfied with equality, and so forth. Corners (0-dimensional faces) of Ω result when N of the inequalities are satisfied with equality.

Characteristics of optimal solution Equation (9.16) is the fundamental equation of manufacturing system control as developed here. The policies in this chapter and in much of the following are based on this equation or its variations. It determines the feedback law $u(x, \alpha, t)$ and the cost-to-go $J(x, \alpha, t)$ simultaneously. Its chief difficulty is that it is a nonlinear partial differential equation, generally of relatively high dimension (for a partial differential equation). It cannot be solved analytically (except for very special cases) or numerically. So what good is it? Why take up your time and energy with this?

Its value is that it allows us to determine some of the important features of the optimal u and J, and that information helps us to construct reasonably good suboptimal feedback

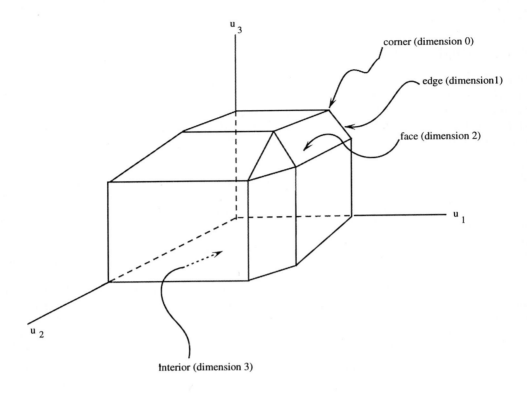

Figure 9.6: Polyhedron $\Omega(\alpha)$

laws. To justify a suboptimal feedback policy, it is important to remember that it is to be used in a factory environment. This means:

- Some of the parameters, especially p_i and r_i, are difficult to obtain precisely.

- The management is not likely to have a single, precise $g(x)$ function in mind, so some $g(x)$ probably would be constructed by the analyst (you). It would be constructed in a way that would assist computation (while still retaining important *qualitative* features). For example, if it were possible to find a $g(x)$ that would yield analytic solutions and have reasonable properties, it would certainly be used, even if it did not perfectly reflect all practical issues.

- Except in the 1-dimensional case, the exact optimal solution would be difficult to implement for reasons that are described below. Even if it could be calculated exactly, something a little different would actually be implemented.

- Simulation experience (described below) teaches that a good suboptimal feedback policy works well.

As a consequence, it is not necessary to get the exact optimal solution to this problem. We describe, in the following, the important features of the solution, and we construct a solution that has many of those features.

Note that u only appears explicitly in one place in (9.16). J is a function of the possible future values of u, but the minimization refers only to the value of u at time t. If J were known (or approximated), the optimal control would be determined by

$$\min_{u \in \Omega(\alpha(t))} \frac{\partial J}{\partial x}(x, \alpha, t)u. \tag{9.36}$$

The gradient $\partial J / \partial x$ can be regarded as a weighting on part production for an optimal control law defined by this expression. The calculation of the optimal value function J (the solution of (9.16)) takes into account the relative costs of backlogs and inventory storage determined by the functions $g_j(x_j)$. It also depends on the vulnerabilities of the part types; parts that need time at machines that are more likely to fail are more vulnerable than others. Thus a Part Type j that has a high g_j and is at the same time sensitive to machine failures would have correspondingly a large weighting $\partial J / \partial x_j$.

To develop practical strategies for calculating production rates u, we exploit whatever features of the Bellman equation (9.16) and of its solution that we can take advantage of. One feature was already used in the one-dimensional case of Section 9.3: the observation that if $T - t$ is large (compared with the mean time between changes in α),

$$J(x(t), \alpha(t), t) \approx (T - t)J^* + W(x(t), \alpha(t)), \tag{9.37}$$

where J^* is a constant, when the demand is feasible. As a result, the linear programming problem is actually

$$\min_{u \in \Omega(\alpha(t))} \frac{\partial W}{\partial x}(x, \alpha)u. \tag{9.38}$$

Features of LPs (9.36) and (9.38)

1. Equation (9.36) is a linear program in u. It is an optimization problem whose cost $(\partial J / \partial x)u$ and constraints $(u \in \Omega(\alpha(t)))$ are linear in u. (Remember that J is independent of u.) If we knew J, we could determine the optimal production rate vector u by solving this LP at every time instant t. The cost coefficients and the constraints vary with time t. They change abruptly as $\alpha(t)$ changes discretely. The cost coefficients also change continuously as x changes continuously.

2. The theory of dynamic programming tells us that J is differentiable in x and t and convex in x. J has a lower bound since it is an integral of g, and g is positive or 0.

3. Consider the change of J along an optimal trajectory. That is, calculate the change in J between t and $t + \delta t$ assuming that u is chosen according to (9.36). This *full* derivative is given by

$$\frac{dJ}{dt} = \frac{\partial J}{\partial t} + \frac{\partial J}{\partial x}\frac{dx}{dt}$$

or

$$\frac{dJ}{dt} = \frac{\partial J}{\partial t} + \frac{\partial J}{\partial x}(u - d).$$

But according to (9.36), u is chosen so that this quantity is as small as it can possibly be. Therefore u is chosen so as to achieve the greatest possible decrease in J.

From (9.38),

$$\frac{dW}{dt} = \frac{\partial W}{\partial x}(u - d)$$

is also minimal.

4. For a given α, the constraint set Ω is constant, but the cost coefficients of (9.38) are continuous functions of x. This, and the nature of linear programming, leads to important conclusions about the behavior of the controlled system.

If the cost coefficients of a linear program (of the form of (9.38)) are not all 0, the solution is at an extreme point (a boundary point) of the constraint set Ω. At an extreme point, at least one of the constraints of the linear program is satisfied with equality. Consequently, either one of the components of u — the production rate of one of the part types — is 0, or one of the machine inequalities (9.7) is satisfied as an equation. In the latter case, one of the workstations is fully utilized. The former condition occurs when there has been excessive production of some part type (that is, when the corresponding component of the surplus vector x is too large). The latter condition can be expected when one or more part types are behind (when components of x are negative or not positive enough).

In fact, for most values of the cost coefficients $\partial W/\partial x$ (and thus of x), the solution of the LP is at a corner u^c of capacity set Ω. For other values of x, there are edges or faces of various dimension such that any u on those edges or faces is optimal.

That is, *the linear program induces a partition of the x space* (Figure 9.7). We can label each corner, or edge, or face, or higher dimensional boundary hyperplane of $\Omega(\alpha)$, and then label each point in the x space with the name of the corner, or edge, or face, or higher dimensional boundary hyperplane of $\Omega(\alpha)$ that is optimal for that x. Most values of $\partial W/\partial x$ lead to corners of Ω. Only those gradients of W that are orthogonal to edges, faces, or higher dimensional boundary hyperplanes lead to those faces being optimal in (9.38). For each α, there is a different partition of x space.

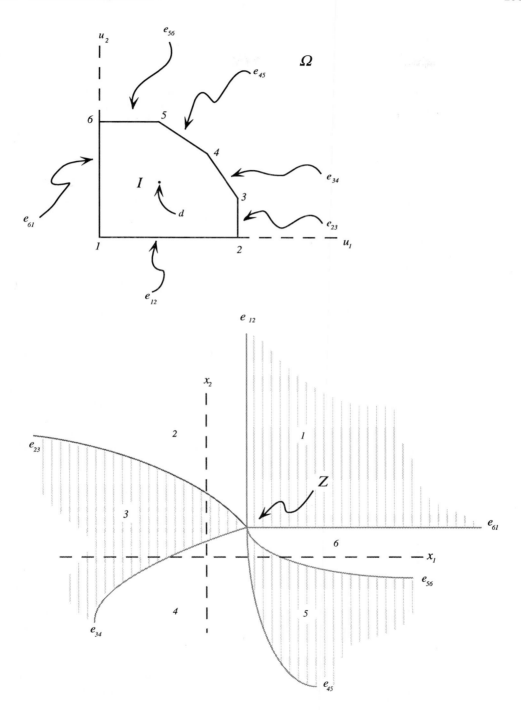

Figure 9.7: Ω and the Partition of x Space

Suppose the machine state α changes abruptly at some time t_0 due to the failure or repair of some machine. Immediately after the change, the state of the system is $(x(t_0), \alpha(t_0^+))$ (since $x(t)$ is continuous and $\alpha(t)$ is not). Most likely, $x(t_0)$ is in the interior of some region R^c corresponding to some corner u^c. Then, if the machine state does not change again too soon, the solution to (9.38) is $u(t) = u(x(t_0), \alpha(t_0^+)) = u(x(t), \alpha(t)) = u^c$ for $t_0 \leq t \leq t_1$ for some $t_1 > t_0$. That is, for some period of time, $x(t)$ remains in region R^c, so u remains constant. During this period, $x(t)$ is given by

$$x(t) = x(t_0) + (u^c - d)(t - t_0).$$

The production rate u remains constant until time t_1, when $x(t)$ reaches the boundary of R^c. At that point, u^c is no longer the unique solution of (9.38). It is a member of some hyperplane h, all points of which are equally optimal.

Simplifying Assertions and Assumptions   In the following, we make a set of simplifying statements. In some cases, they can be proved. For example, the behavior of u, as it jumps from corner to corner, to edge, to face, $\ldots$, to the interior of $\Omega(\alpha)$, and the corresponding behavior of x, is an example of the behavior of *singular* optimal control problems, and was studied by Rishel (1975). Other statements are true for an important set of special cases. Still others are helpful approximations.

1. There are two kinds of machine states $\alpha(t)$: those for which the demand rate d is feasible $(d \in \Omega(\alpha(t)))$; and those for which it is not. The former are called *feasible states*. These are the states in which the demand d could be satisfied if the state never changed. The behavior of the trajectory $x(t)$ depends crucially on whether $\alpha(t)$ is feasible or not. We study feasible states in detail here. If the state remained constant and feasible for a very long time, $u = d$ would be possible. This assumption allows Assumption 4, that the system is in steady state. The infeasible case is discussed briefly below.

2. For a given α, let R^c be the set of x for which the solution to (9.38) is unique, at a given corner u^c of $\Omega(\alpha(t))$. That is,

$$R^c = \left\{ x \in \mathbf{R}^N \,\middle|\, \frac{\partial W}{\partial x}(x, \alpha)u^c < \frac{\partial W}{\partial x}(x, \alpha)u, \text{ for all } u \in \Omega(\alpha), u \neq u^c \right\}.$$

Then we assume that for each corner u^c, R^c is a set of full dimension in $\mathbf{R}^N$. That is, some sphere is a subset of it.

Furthermore, for every 1-dimensional edge e in $\Omega(\alpha)$, there is an $N - 1$ dimensional surface R^e in $\mathbf{R}^N$ such that every point in e is an optimal u for every x in R^e. That is, for every $u \in e, u$ is a solution of (9.38). For every 2-dimensional face f in $\Omega(\alpha)$, there is an $N - 2$ dimensional surface R^f in $\mathbf{R}^N$ such that every point in f is an optimal u for every x in R^f. More generally, the set R^h of x for which every point u in

d_h-dimensional hyperplane segment h on the boundary of Ω is optimal, is a surface of dimension $N - d_h$, for every hyperplane segment h in Ω. This includes the interior of Ω. It is an N-dimensional subset of $\mathbf{R}^N$, every point of which is optimal for a special point (a 0-dimensional subset).

Consequently, almost every x is a member of some R^c, corresponding to a corner u^c of Ω. Further, we assume that if corner u^c is a member of hyperplane segment h, then set R^h forms part of the boundary of R^c. Thus, we have decomposed x space — $\mathbf{R}^N$ — in a way that is complementary to the decomposition of Ω.

3. For every α and t, $W(x, \alpha)$ is strictly convex in x. It is continuous in x and t, and piecewise smooth. The derivatives $\partial W / \partial x$ and $\partial J / \partial t$ exist and are continuous everywhere except possibly at the R^h sets. In some regions, W is close to quadratic.

4. T is sufficiently large that it makes sense to study the steady-state case: in which (9.37) is a good approximation. In that case, u is also a function only of x and α.

Hedging Point Assume that α is feasible and that α remains constant for a long time. Then W is decreasing. However, W has a lower bound, so W must approach a limit. Therefore x approaches a limit. We call that limit the *hedging point* and represent it by $Z(\alpha)$.

For x to approach this limit, dx/dt must approach 0. This implies that u approaches d, which is in the interior of $\Omega(\alpha)$. But we have assumed (Assumption 1 above) that whenever u is in the interior, x must be at some specific point corresponding to the interior (the hedging point $Z(\alpha)$). Since the entire interior of $\Omega(\alpha)$ corresponds to a single point in x space, and since the only way for x to remain at that point is for $u = d$, then u must not be in the interior if $x \neq Z(\alpha)$. Therefore, u jumps discontinuously from the boundary of Ω to d.

The hedging point, which is the minimum of $W(x, \alpha)$ with respect to x, is the optimal surplus (x) with which to hedge against future failures. When demand is close to the capacity of the system, recovery from a backlog is slow. The components of the hedging points are then at high surplus levels because otherwise failures quickly result in backlogs (negative x).

Boundaries and Chattering In the 1-dimensional problem, we need to add the condition $u = d$ when $\alpha = 1$ and $x = Z$. If we omit this condition, or allow u to have any other value at $x = Z$, then x would fluctuate rapidly around Z. This is because when $x > Z, \dot{x} = -d < 0$ and when $x < Z, \dot{x} = \mu - d > 0$.

A similar, but more complex condition is required in the multiple part type case. Here, when x crosses a boundary (for example when x leaves a region R^c for which a corner u^c is optimal), we must determine whether u in the new region is such that dx/dt points away from or toward the boundary just crossed. If it points away, there is no problem; x moves to the interior of the new region and away from the boundary. However, if it points toward the boundary, the possibility of chattering arises. Now x crosses back to the old region, for which u is such that x moves back to and crosses the boundary again. This repeats at high frequency.

Kimemia and Gershwin (1983) observed this behavior (Figure 9.8[7]). They implemented (9.38) in a simulation by solving it every time step (one minute). This worked well while x was in the interior of a region R^c. However, when x crossed certain boundaries between regions, this approach worked poorly. After $x(t)$ crossed such a boundary, which we call *attractive*, the value of u corresponding to the new region $R^{c'}$ was such that the derivative (9.1) pointed toward R^c. When $x(t)$ crossed the boundary back into R^c, the derivative pointed again to $R^{c'}$. Thus, $u(t)$ jumped between adjacent corners u^c and $u^{c'}$ of $\Omega(\alpha)$.

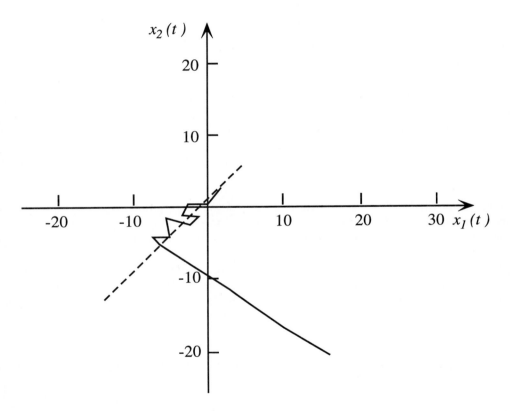

Figure 9.8: Chattering Trajectory

This kind of behavior is called *chattering* and is well known in the optimal control literature. Here, it causes the flow rate to change more frequently than parts are loaded

[7]Reprinted from *IIE Transactions*, Vol. 15, No. 4. Copyright 1983, Institute of Industrial Engineers, Norcross, GA 30092

into the system. As a result, if the demands on the system are near its capacity, it will fail to meet the demands. This was observed by Kimemia (1982).

This behavior is unsatisfactory and can be remedied by selecting a value of u in a way that is analogous to the simple case of Section 9.3. In Figure 9.9, let u^{c_1} and u^{c_2} be two adjacent corners of $\Omega(\alpha)$, and let R^{c_1} and R^{c_2} be the corresponding adjacent N-dimensional regions in x space. That is, for every x in R^{c_1}, u^{c_1} is the unique optimal solution of (9.16), and for every x in R^{c_2}, u^{c_2} is the unique optimal solution of (9.16).

Let e be the edge between u^{c_2} and u^{c_1} and let R^e be the corresponding N-1-dimensional region in x space. That is, for every x in R^e, every u in e is a non-unique optimal solution of (9.16). Furthermore, R^e forms the boundary between R^{c_1} and R^{c_2}.

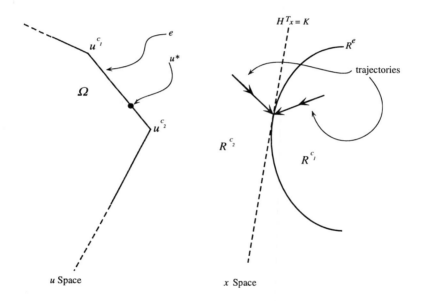

Figure 9.9: Prevention of Chattering

If x is in R^{c_1} and near the boundary R^e with R^{c_2}, there exists some vector H and scalar K such that $H^T x > K$. The same vector H satisfies $H^T x < K$ for x in R^{c_2} near the same boundary point and $H^T x = K$ for x in R^e in the same neighborhood. The plane $H^T x = K$ is the tangent to R^e at x. The values of H and K are determined below, in Equation (9.47).

Then, for small δt, there is some $u^e \in e$ such that $x(t+\delta t)$ is also on the boundary. Note that

$$x(t + \delta t) = x(t) + \frac{dx}{dt}\delta t + o(\delta t) = x(t) + (u^e - d)\delta t + o(\delta t).$$

This is because chattering occurs when u^{c_1} and u^{c_2} are such that x moves toward the common boundary from inside both regions. But this means that for x in R^{c_1} in that neighborhood,

$$\frac{d}{dt}(H^T x) < 0$$

and therefore

$$H^T \frac{dx}{dt} = H^T [u^{c_1} - d] < 0.$$

Similarly, for x in R^{c_2} in that neighborhood,

$$\frac{d}{dt}(H^T x) > 0$$

and therefore

$$H^T \frac{dx}{dt} = H^T [u^{c_2} - d] > 0.$$

If $u \in e$, there exists some $G, 0 \leq G \leq 1$ such that

$$u = G u^{c_1} + (1 - G) u^{c_2}.$$

Therefore, if $x \in R^e$ in the same neighborhood,

$$
\begin{aligned}
\tfrac{d}{dt}(H^T x) &= H^T (u - d) \\
&= H^T [G u^{c_1} + (1 - G) u^{c_2} - d] \\
&= G H^T [u^{c_1} - d] + (1 - G) H^T [u^{c_2} - d].
\end{aligned}
$$

Since the first term is negative and the second is positive, there is some G^* that makes the sum 0. Thus, we can avoid chattering by choosing

$$u^* = G^* u^{c_1} + (1 - G^*) u^{c_2} \in e$$

when x reaches R^e. The value of G^* is

$$G^* = \frac{H^T [u^{c_2} - d]}{H^T [u^{c_2} - d] - H^T [u^{c_1} - d]} = \frac{H^T [u^{c_2} - d]}{H^T [u^{c_2} - u^{c_1}]}.$$

However, this leads to another difficulty (in addition to the impossibility of computing W). It is not so severe, and is easily remedied once we find an appropriate approximate W. It is that the boundaries R^h in x space are curved. As a consequence, in order to choose u to keep x on the boundary, u must be a continuously varying function of t. This is not desirable. (Remember that u is the vector of production rates. Times for loading parts will be selected in such a way that these rates are realized. It would be much easier if the rates u were constant, or at least piecewise constant.)

In the following, we develop a method for choosing an approximate W and a piecewise constant $u(t)$. We choose a quadratic W, and this causes the boundaries to be straight.

Approximate solution — multiple part types In the following, we describe the implementation of all three levels of FMS control.

9.4.2 Top level: cost-to-go function

We present a quadratic approximation for the value function W. Not only does this reduce top level computation requirements, but it also simplifies the middle-level (maximum principle) computation. On the other hand, this is rather crude. More sophisticated estimates of W or the hedging point appear in Caramanis and Sharifnia (1991), Liberopolous (1993), Boukas (1991), Boukas and Haurie (1990), and Boukas, Haurie, and van Delft (1991).

The approximate cost-to-go function is

$$W(x, \alpha) = \frac{1}{2} x^T A(\alpha) x + b(\alpha)^T x + c(\alpha) \tag{9.39}$$

where $A(\alpha)$ is a positive definite diagonal matrix, $b(\alpha)$ is a vector, and $c(\alpha)$ is a scalar. In this section, we describe a method for choosing these coefficients for some values of α.

We have shown that the function $W(x(t), \alpha)$ is a decreasing function of t when α remains constant. The *hedging point* is the value of x that minimizes $W(x, \alpha)$ for fixed α. It is the value that x reaches if α stays constant for a long time and if α is feasible, that is, if $d \in \Omega(\alpha)$. The hedging point is important to the behavior and performance of the algorithm because it is the point that x spends most of its time either moving toward or resting at. It is the level to which one builds up surplus to compensate for future production losses due to machine failures.

Here, the hedging point is given by minimizing W in (9.39):

$$\left. \frac{\partial W(x, \alpha)}{\partial x} \right|_{x=Z} = 0 = AZ + b,$$

or,

$$Z_j(\alpha) = -\frac{b_j(\alpha)}{A_{jj}(\alpha)} \tag{9.40}$$

since A is diagonal.

In order to estimate the hedging point, there are two possible approaches. One (which may be superior) is to approximately decompose the problem into a set of one-dimensional problems of the form considered in Section 9.3. The values of x that minimize $W(x, 0)$ and $W(x, 1)$ are then used for the components of Z. (This is called the *hypercube approximation*.)

Another is illustrated in Figure 9.10[8] which demonstrates a typical trajectory of $x_j(t)$. Assume x_j has reached $Z_j(\alpha)$, the hedging point corresponding to the machine state before the failure. Then u_j is chosen to be d_j and x_j remains constant. This analysis produces a crude estimate for the hedging point, and is based on crude assumptions:

---

[8]Copyright 1985 by International Business Machines Corporation; reprinted with permission.

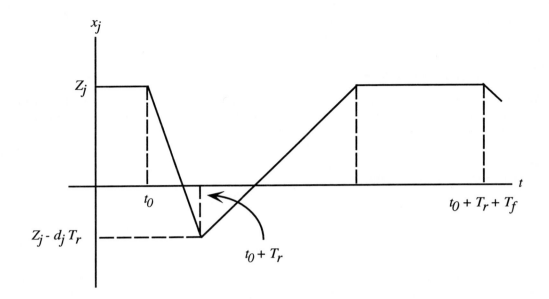

Figure 9.10: Simple Trajectory

1. There are only three possible production rates for each part type: a maximal rate, when all the machines required for a part are working, the demand rate d_j, and 0, when one of the required machines is down.

2. There is one hedging point for each part type, independent of the states of machines that the part does not require, and independent of the surpluses or production rates of the other part types.

A failure occurs at time t_0 that forces u_j to be 0. This causes x_j to decrease at rate $-d_j$. In fact, if the failure lasts for a length of time T_r, then the minimum value of x_j is

$$Z_j - d_j T_r. \tag{9.41}$$

Recall that T_r, the repair time, is a random variable. Just after the repair (at time $t_0 + T_r$), u_j is assigned the value μ_j. Assuming that this value is greater than demand d_j, x_j increases at rate $\mu_j - d_j$ until it reaches the hedging point Z_j. At that time, u_j resumes its old value of d_j and x_j stays constant until the next failure, at time $t_0 + T_r + T_f$. T_f is also a random variable.

To further simplify the analysis, we assume:

1. u_j is constant between the repair $(t_0 + T_r)$ and when x_j reaches Z_j.

2. T_r and T_f can be replaced by their expected values, the MTTR $(1/r)$ and MTTF $(1/p)$.

3. The cost function $g(\cdot)$ in (9.9) penalizes positive areas in Figure 9.10 with weight g_{j+} and negative areas with weight g_{j-}, where g_{j+} and g_{j-} are positive scalars.

The objective of this is to obtain an approximation for $W(\cdot, \cdot)$ and Z. We do this by choosing Z to minimize the total area under the positive and above the negative portions of the trajectory in Figure 9.10. We obtain

$$Z_j = \frac{\frac{1}{r}d_j(g_{j-}\mu_j + g_{j+}d_j) - \frac{1}{p}g_{j+}d_j(\mu_j - d_j)}{(g_{j+} + g_{j-})\mu_j} \tag{9.42}$$

This approach cannot be applied for machine states in which the demand is not feasible. Either there is no finite hedging point for such a state, or it is larger than (9.42).

$A_{jj}(\alpha)$ must be positive in order for W to be convex. Its value reflects the relative priority of Part Type j. Parts that have great value, or that would cause great difficulty if backlogged, or that pass through relatively unreliable machines should have large values of A_{jj}. For example, in some simulations we let A_{jj} be the number of machines that Part j passed through. This was because we treated all parts as equally valuable and because all machines had the same reliability parameters.

9.4.3 Middle level: maximum principle

In this section we describe an efficient method of computing the instantaneous production rates.

The optimal production rate vector $u(x, \alpha)$ satisfies linear programming problem (9.38) at every time instant t. This is a feedback law since the problem is specified only when x and α are determined. The numerical solution of (9.38) is implemented on-line at the middle level of the hierarchical algorithm. For every α, x space is divided into a set of N-dimensional regions R^c (open, connected sets) and the boundaries between them. Each region is associated with a corner u^c of $\Omega(\alpha)$. When x is in the interior of region R^c, the value of u that satisfies (9.38) is the corresponding corner u^c. We have already described how regions that correspond to corners are assumed N dimensional, and that regions corresponding to h-dimensional pieces of $\Omega(\alpha)$ are $N - h$ dimensional, and are boundaries of higher dimensional regions. In the following, we show how the assumption of a quadratic W simplifies the shapes of these regions and makes the production rates $u(x, \alpha)$ easier to calculate.

Cone-Shaped Regions   *When W is quadratic, the R^c regions are cones.* That is, if u^c is the production rate corresponding to x, then u^c is also the production rate corresponding to x', where

$$x' - Z = s(x - Z) \tag{9.43}$$

and s is a positive scalar.

Proof   The cost coefficient of u in (9.38) corresponding to x is $(Ax + b)^T$. Let x' satisfy (9.43). Then the cost coefficient of u corresponding to x' is $[Ax' + b]^T$, which can be written

$$[A(Z + s(x - Z)) + b]^T$$

or

$$[s(Ax + b) + (1 - s)(AZ + b)]^T .$$

Since Z satisfies (9.40), the second term vanishes. The factor s does not change the minimum of (9.38), so the same value of u is optimal for both x and x'.

In addition, the cones are convex.

Proof   A set S is convex if $x_1 \in S$ and $x_2 \in S$ implies that $x = cx_1 + (1 - c)x_2 \in S$ for $0 \leq c \leq 1$. In this case, x_1 and x_2 are in R^c if u^c minimizes both $(Ax_1 + b)u$ and $(Ax_2 + b)u$. In that case,

$$(Ax + b)u = (A(cx_1 + (1 - c)x_2) + b)u = c(Ax_1 + b)u + (1 - c)(Ax_2 + b)u.$$

Since u^c minimizes both terms, it minimizes $(Ax + b)u$. Therefore, x is in R^c, so R^c is convex.

Since all the regions are convex, they all have linear boundaries.

Linear Program   Here, we use the ideas in Chapter 7 to investigate the behavior of the solution u of linear program (9.38) when W is quadratic, α is constant, and x changes continuously. Linear program (9.38) can be written

$$\min C(x)^T u$$
subject to
$$Du = \alpha \qquad\qquad (9.44)$$
$$u \geq 0$$

in which u has been expanded with slack variables so that inequality constraint (9.7) can be written as an equality; D is a matrix whose elements are given by

$$D_{ij} = \begin{cases} \tau_{ij} \text{ if } j \text{ corresponds to Part Type } j \ (i.e., \text{ if } j \leq N) \\[2mm] 1 \text{ if } u_j \text{ is the slack variable for Machine } i \ (i.e., \text{ if } j > N \text{ and } i = j - N) \\[2mm] 0 \text{ otherwise} \end{cases}$$

and

$$C(x) = Ax + b = A(x - Z).$$

(Note that arguments α and t are suppressed.) The standard solution of (9.44) breaks u into basic (u_B) and non-basic (u_N) parts, with $C(x)$ and D broken up correspondingly. The basic part of D is a square, invertible matrix. By using the equality in (9.44), u_B can be eliminated, and the problem becomes

$$\left.\begin{array}{c} \min C_R(x)^T u_N \\[1em] u_N \geq 0 \\[1em] D_B^{-1} D_N u_N \leq D_B^{-1} \alpha \end{array}\right\} \qquad (9.45)$$

subject to

where

$$C_R(x)^T = C_N(x)^T - C_B(x)^T D_B^{-1} D_N \qquad (9.46)$$

is the reduced cost. If all components of C_R are positive, then the solution to (9.45) is $u_N = 0$. This and the corresponding u_B form an optimal solution to (9.44). Otherwise, $u_N = 0$ is not the optimal solution to (9.45), so the basic/non-basic split selected is not correct. (Note that there is always a feasible solution to (9.44), so there is always a feasible solution to (9.45). Since we are only concerned with whether $u_N = 0$ is optimal, the last inequality in (9.45) is not important.)

Since C is a function of x, the basic/non-basic breakup of this problem depends on x. That is, the set of components of u that are treated as basic varies as a function of x. At every x in region R^c, corner u^c is the optimal value of u for (9.44). In each region, then, there must be a basic/non-basic break-up of (9.44) which is valid throughout the region and not valid elsewhere. Consequently, $C_R(x)$ must be positive everywhere in its own region and it must have some negative components elsewhere. The boundaries of the regions are determined by some components of $C_R(x)$ being equal to zero.

Thus, we can define R^c as the set of all x such that all components of $C_R(x)$, defined by (9.46), are strictly positive. Similarly, the boundaries R^h of R^c are the set of all x such that the components of $C_R(x)$ are positive or zero, and at least one component is zero. $C(x)$, and therefore $C_N(x)^T$ and $C_B(x)^T$ are linear in x. Therefore $C_R(x)$ is also linear in x. Consequently, the boundaries R^h of the regions R^c are portions of hyperplanes.

Qualitative Behavior After a machine state change, $x(t)$ is almost always in the interior of a region. Since u is constant throughout a region, dx/dt is also constant. Thus, x travels along a straight line in the interior of each region. As indicated in Figure 9.9, such lines may intersect with one or more boundaries of the region. When x reaches a boundary, u and therefore dx/dt changes.

If the boundary is not attractive, $x(t)$ moves in the interior of the next region until it reaches the next boundary. The production rate vector u jumps to an adjacent corner. This behavior continues until $x(t)$ encounters an attractive boundary. At this time, the trajectory begins to move along the boundary and $u(t)$ jumps to a point on the edge of $\Omega(\alpha)$ between the corners corresponding to the regions on either side of the boundary.

This behavior continues: $x(t)$ moves to lower dimensional boundaries and $u(t)$ jumps to higher dimensional faces. It stops when either the machine state changes (that is, a repair or failure takes place) or $u(t)$ becomes constant. If the demand is feasible then the constant value for u is d. When that happens, x also becomes constant and its value is the hedging point. If the demand is not feasible, x does not become constant. Instead, some or all of its components decrease without limit.

Consequently, the entire future behavior of $x(t)$ would be determined from its current value if the machine state remained constant. This is because the change in machine states is the only source of randomness in this problem. We call this future behavior the *projected trajectory*.

It can be characterized by $(t_0, u_0, t_1, u_1, \ldots, t_k, u_k)$ in which t_0 is the time at which the machine state changed last, and u_0 is the solution to (9.38) for $x(t_0)$ and $\alpha(t_0)$. The time at which x reaches the first boundary is t_1, and u_1 is the value of u that satisfies (9.38) for $\alpha(t_0)$ and any $x(t_1)$ on the boundary and keeps $x(t)$ on the boundary. t_2 is the time that x reaches the next boundary when $u = u_1$, and u_2 is the value of u that satisfies (9.38) for $\alpha(t_0)$ and any $x(t_2)$ on the intersection of the two boundaries and keeps $x(t)$ on the intersection. The rest of the t's and u's are generated in this way until t_k, which is the last time that u changes, and u_k, which is the last value of u.

Remember that this is only the set of planned production rates. The only us that will actually be implemented (used as target rates for the bottom level of the hierarchy) are those that occur before the next change of α.

Calculation of the Projected Trajectory   Assume that the conditional future trajectory is to be calculated due to a machine state change at time t_0. As soon as the machine state change occurs (at t_0), linear program (9.44) is solved. Thus the basic/non-basic split is determined and the $C_R(x)$ function is known. In general, x appears in the interior of a region, and therefore all components of $C_R(x)$ are strictly positive. One or more components are zero on a boundary of a region.

The production rate vector at $t = t_0$ is denoted u_0. The production rate remains constant at this value until $t = t_1$, which is to be determined. In $[t_0, t_1]$, x is given by

$$x(t) = x(t_0) + (u_0 - d)(t - t_0)$$

where $x(t_1)$ is on a boundary. Then t_1 is the smallest value of t for which some component of $C_R(x(t))$ is zero. It is easy to calculate this quantity since C_R is linear in x and x is linear in t. Once t_1 is found, $x(t_1)$ is known. Define $h(x(t))$ to be the component of $C_R(x(t))$ that reaches zero at $t = t_1$. Because h is a linear scalar function of x, we can write

$$h(x) = H^T(x - x(t_1)), \tag{9.47}$$

where H is a vector of coefficients. In fact, this is the same H as in Figure 9.9, and $K = -H^T x(t_1)$.

For $t > t_1$, there are two possibilities. The trajectory may enter the neighboring region and travel in the interior until it reaches the next boundary. Alternatively, it may move along the boundary it has just reached. To determine whether or not the boundary is attractive, we must consider the behavior of $h(x(t))$ in its neighborhood.

We know that $h(x)$ is negative in the region across the boundary since this is how the regions are defined. We must determine whether h is increasing or decreasing on trajectories inside that region. If h is decreasing, x moves away from the boundary (where h is zero) into the interior. Also, if h is decreasing,

$$\frac{dh}{dt} = H^T(u_0 - d) < 0.$$

If h is increasing, trajectories move toward the boundary which must therefore be attractive.

One value of x which is just across the boundary is

$$\begin{aligned} \hat{x} &= x(t_0) + (u_0 - d)(t_1 + \epsilon - t_0) \\ &= x(t_1) + (u_0 - d)\epsilon. \end{aligned}$$

This is the value x would have if u were allowed to be u_0 until $t_1 + \epsilon$. Let $\hat{u}$ be the solution to (9.44) in the adjacent region. That is, (9.44) is solved with x given by $\hat{x}$. (This can be performed efficiently.) Let x^+ be the value of x at $t_1 + \epsilon$ if $\hat{u}$ were used after t_1. That is,

$$x^+ = x(t_1) + (\hat{u} - d)\epsilon.$$

Then

$$h(\hat{x}) = H^T(\hat{u} - d)\epsilon.$$

Therefore h is increasing and the boundary is attractive if and only if

$$H^T(\hat{u} - d) > 0.$$

If the boundary is not attractive, define $u_1 = \hat{u}$. Then the process is repeated to find t_2, $x(t_2)$, t_3, $x(t_3)$, and so forth until an attractive boundary is encountered. Recall that this is an on-line computation that is taking place at time t_0. The future trajectory is now being planned. If the boundary is attractive, a value of u must be determined which will keep the trajectory on it. Otherwise chattering will occur. For the trajectory to stay on the boundary,

$$h(x(t)) = 0$$

or, since $h(x(t_1)) = 0$,

$$\frac{d}{dt}h(x(t)) = H^T(u - d) = 0. \tag{9.48}$$

Although u is an optimal solution to (9.44), it is no longer determined by this linear program. In fact $u_0, \hat{u}$, and any convex combination of them are optimal. This is because one or more of the reduced costs is zero while x is on a boundary. Consequently, the new scalar condition (9.48) is required to determine the solution. The linear program is modified as follows:

$$\min C(x)^T u$$

subject to

$$Du = \alpha \qquad (9.49)$$
$$u \geq 0$$
$$H^T u = H^T d$$

Note that H is the coefficient of x in the component of the reduced cost vector that reached 0 (Equation (9.47)). The solution to (9.49) is the value of u that keeps the trajectory on the boundary. As before, this value is maintained until a new boundary is encountered.

New boundaries may still be attractive or unattractive. The same tests are performed: x is allowed to move slightly into the next region to determine the value of u. The time derivative of the component of the reduced cost that first reaches zero (h) is examined. If it is negative, the boundary is unattractive and the trajectory enters the new region. If it is positive, a new constraint is added to linear program (9.49).

Conjecture   Constraints, when added to (9.49), are not deleted. As the number of constraints increases, u is found on surfaces in $\Omega(\alpha)$ that increase in dimension and x is found in regions of decreasing dimension.

Since this is a finite dimensional system, this process must terminate. The vector $x(t)$ is eventually of the form

$$x(t) = x(t_j) + (u - d)t.$$

Assume d is feasible. Then when enough linearly independent constraints (9.48) have been added to (9.49), the only feasible solution is $u = d$ and x is constant. If d is not feasible, some or all of the components of $u - d$ are negative. The corresponding components of x decrease without limit until the next change of α.

Summary   If the state changes at time t_0, we do a series of linear programming calculations *at that time* that determines k and a table:

t_0	t_1	$\ldots$	t_k
u_0	u_1	$\ldots$	u_k

in which $t_1, t_2, \ldots, t_k$ are the times that x will reach boundaries, in the absence of future changes of α. The vectors $u_0, u_1, u_2, \ldots, u_k$ are the production rates to be used as targets in the lower level during time intervals $[t_0, t_1), [t_1, t_2), [t_2, t_3), \ldots, [t_k, \infty)$. If the demand is feasible, $u_k = d$. When α changes, the part of the table that has not been reached is simply discarded, and a new table is created.

9.4.4   Lower level: discrete part dispatch

Let

$$N_j(t) = \{\text{number of parts of Type } j \text{ loaded during } [0, t]\}.$$

Staircase strategy: Load a Type j part whenever

$$N_j(t) < \int_{t_0}^{t} u_j(s)ds \tag{9.50}$$

and whenever it is possible to load a part. It is often not possible because, for example, a machine is busy. In that case, wait until the machine is free. At that point, (9.50) will still be satisfied since the left side is constant and the right side is constant or growing.

The name comes from the shape of the graph of $N_j(t)$ (Figure 9.11). This strategy is easy to implement and is compatible with rule-based systems. It is easy to add other rules, if necessary. Additional rules may be required to resolve conflicts (such as what to do if two part types satisfy (9.50) at the same time); it may not matter what that rule is (as long as it is sensible) since conflicts will not arise very often. Conflicts do not arise very often because the set of rates $\{u_j\}$ is chosen to satisfy the capacity condition $u \in \Omega(\alpha)$.

With (9.50), we have fulfilled the promise of creating a scheduler: we have provided a method for selecting times for events. We have avoided complex combinatorial optimization and searches. The entire three-level hierarchy forms a scheduling rule, as defined in Section 9.1.2. The events $\mathcal{E}_i$ are the times at which parts are loaded into the system. The corresponding times t_i are the times in the future when (9.50) is satisfied. As long as the machine states (α) stay constant, those times can easily be calculated in advance. Whenever the machine state changes, the future of u is recalculated at Level 2, so the times that (9.50) is satisfied are recalculated at Level 1.

Infeasible States — Informal Discussion   When α is an infeasible state, we cannot assume (9.37). However, we can say something. Let us assume that g is of the form

$$g(x) = \sum_j g_j(x) = \sum_j \left[g_{j+} x_j^+ + g_{j-} x_j^- \right]$$

in which g_{j+} and g_{j-} are positive coefficients, and x_j^+ and x_j^- are as defined in Section 9.3. (In most cases, $g_{j-} > g_{j+}$ because backlog is worse than inventory.)

If α remains infeasible for a long time, at least some components of x will eventually become negative and stay negative. x will not approach a limit; at least some components will decrease without bound; and some components may approach a limit. Define $\tilde{x}(t)$ as the behavior of x for large t.

Define $\tilde{g}$ as the vector whose components are g_{j+} and g_{j-}, corresponding to the positive and negative components of x. Then

$$g(x) = \tilde{g}^T \tilde{x}.$$

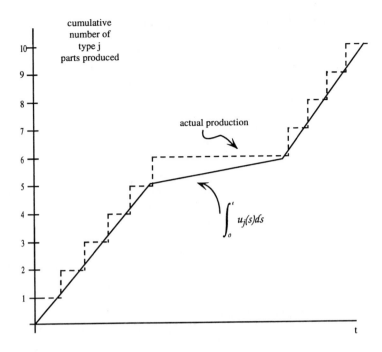

Figure 9.11: Staircase Strategy

(It seems fair to expect that *all* components of $\tilde{x}$ become very negative. If some component is positive and increasing, it means that it is desirable to collect unlimited inventory of some part type, even at the expense of increasing the rate of growth of the unlimited backlog of some other. If some component approaches a limit, there are others that are decreasing without bound. They could decrease at a lesser rate and therefore incur less cost if that component were allowed to decrease.)

Let us assume that u eventually becomes $\tilde{u}$, a constant (after α has been constant and infeasible for a long time). Then $\tilde{x}$ is given by

$$\tilde{x}(t) = x' + (\tilde{u} - d)t$$

for some x'. Thus

$$g(x(s)) = \tilde{g}^T(x' + (\tilde{u} - d)t).$$

Since u is chosen to minimize the integral of g, we can assume that the limiting value $\tilde{u}$ minimizes $\tilde{g}^T u$ subject to $u \in \Omega(\alpha)$. For this to be consistent, the components of u that are less than the corresponding components of d must also correspond to the components of $\tilde{x}$ that are negative.

The limiting behavior of J is given by

$$J(x,t) = \int_t^T g(x(s))ds = \int_t^T \tilde{g}^T(x' + (\tilde{u} - d)s)ds$$
$$= \tilde{g}^T x'(T - t) + \frac{1}{2}\tilde{g}^T(\tilde{u} - d)(T - t)^2.$$

This does not take into account in detail the behavior of x before it reaches its limiting behavior. Thus, we can extend (9.37) to infeasible states as follows:

$$J(x(t), \alpha(t), t) \approx (T - t)J^* + \frac{1}{2}\tilde{g}^T(\tilde{u} - d)(T - t)^2 + W(x(t), \alpha(t)),$$

where we can make the same assumption as earlier (9.39):

$$W(x, \alpha) = \frac{1}{2}x^T A(\alpha)x + b(\alpha)^T x + c(\alpha).$$

Therefore, the same analytic method as for feasible states applies for infeasible states *except* for the calculation of the $A(\alpha)$ and $b(\alpha)$ coefficients. In this case, the hedging point is less important (since the system can not rest at the hedging point as it does in the feasible state case), but the u that is the last solution to (9.49) is $\tilde{u}$, which must minimize $\tilde{g}^T u$ subject to $u \in \Omega(\alpha)$. This can help determine A and b.

9.5 Examples

9.5.1 Example 1: Two-part, two-machine system

To demonstrate the behavior of the hierarchical controller, consider the system of Figure 9.12[9]. Each station has two identical machines. Two parts are produced. The first part type requires two operations, one at each station; the second requires a single operation which can only be performed at the first station.

The operation times and reliability data for the system are given in Table 9.1. In this example, there are nine possible machine states. We discuss only two of them in detail: all machines operational $[\alpha = (2,2)]$ and one failed machine at Station A $[\alpha = (1,2)]$. The calculation of $W(x, \alpha)$ and $u(x, \alpha)$, however, must include all nine states.

The cost function is given by

$$g(x) = \mid x_1 \mid + \mid x_2 \mid,$$

or,

$$g_{1+} = g_{1-} = g_{2+} = g_{2-} = 1.$$

---

[9]Reprinted from *IIE Transactions*, Vol. 15, No. 4. Copyright 1983, Institute of Industrial Engineers, Norcross, GA 30092

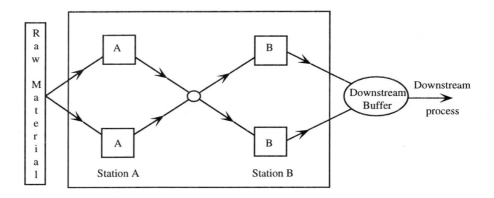

Figure 9.12: Four-Machine System

	Processing times		Reliability data	
	Part Type			
Station	1	2	MTTF	MTTR
A	0.33	0.67	300	30
B	0.33	–	300	30

Table 9.1: Example 1 Data (minutes)

The system is penalized equally for being ahead or behind demand requirements.

For this example, the top level computation — the calculation of W and $\partial W/\partial x$ — was a numerical solution of the Bellman equation. (This was possible because the state space was small, but it is not practical for the running of actual FMSs.) A quadratic function was fitted to the numerical W calculated in this way. The capacity sets for machine states (2,2) and (1,2) are shown in Figures 9.13[10] and 9.14[11] and 9.14 in u space. The effect of a Station A failure is evident. The demand rate $d(t)$ for the two part types are constant at 2.5 Type 1 and 1.25 Type 2 parts per minute. That is,

$$d = \begin{pmatrix} d_1 \\ d_2 \end{pmatrix} = \begin{pmatrix} 2.5 \\ 1.25 \end{pmatrix}$$

---

[10]Reprinted from *IIE Transactions*, Vol. 15, No. 4. Copyright 1983, Institute of Industrial Engineers, Norcross, GA 30092

[11]Reprinted from *IIE Transactions*, Vol. 15, No. 4. Copyright 1983, Institute of Industrial Engineers, Norcross, GA 30092

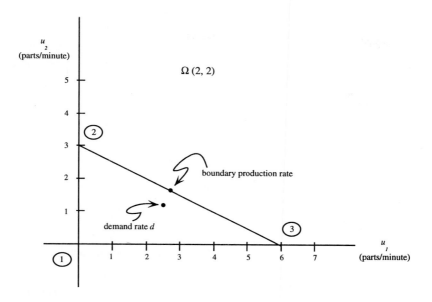

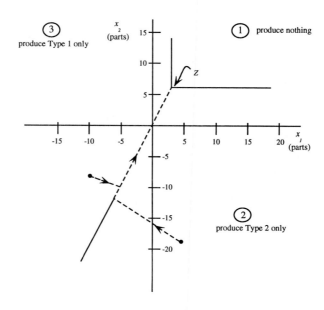

Figure 9.13: u Space and x Space for $\alpha = (2, 2)$

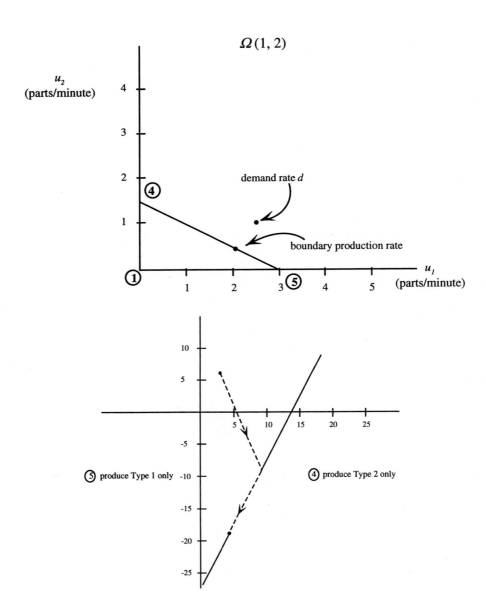

Figure 9.14: u Space and x Space for $\alpha = (1, 2)$

Production can exceed demand only in machine states (2,2) and (2,1). In all other machine states, the demand rate is beyond the capacity of the system. Of the two states we consider in detail here, (2,2) is feasible and (1,2) is not. Thus the control policy must find a way of producing in excess of requirements when $\alpha = (2,2)$ (although not too much in excess of requirements) because it will inevitably fall short when $\alpha = (1,2)$.

The control policy is characterized by the regions shown in Figures 9.13 and 9.14 in x space. In each region, the production rate vector is at an extreme point of a constraint set. It is indicated by the circled numbers. The approximate regions — those that are generated by the quadratic approximation of W — are shown.

Also shown in Figures 9.13 and 9.14 is a portion of the surplus trajectory for one run of the simulation. Initially, the system has all machines operating and the initial surplus $x(0)$ in Region 3. The whole production effort is devoted to making Type 1 parts, so x_1 increases and x_2 decreases, until x reaches the boundary between Region 3 and Region 2. The production rate vectors in these two regions both point toward the boundary. Consequently, the boundary is attractive. The trajectory moves on this boundary in the direction of increasing x_1 and x_2. This continues until the surplus reaches the hedging point, the intersection of all the boundaries. The production rate vector is changed to the demand rate vector and the surplus remains constant. That is, $u = d$, $\dot{x} = 0$, and $x = Z$. This situation persists until a machine fails.

When a Station A machine fails, the surplus x is found at a point in Region 5 of Figure 9.14. This point is the same as the hedging point of Figure 9.13, but the system is no longer at a hedging point. Initially only Type 1 parts are produced (since at Corner 5, $u = (3.0, 0)^T$). This results in an increase in the surplus of Type 1 parts and a decrease of the surplus of Type 2 parts (since $\dot{x} = (0.5, -1.25)^T$). Eventually, the surplus trajectory meets and stays on the boundary between Regions 4 and 5, and a mix of both parts is produced, keeping the trajectory on the boundary.

After approximately 25 minutes of this simulation, the failed machine is repaired and our attention must jump to a point in Region 2 of Figure 9.14. The production rate is then $u = (0, 3.0)$. Type 2 parts are produced at the maximum rate to clear the backlog caused by the failure. The surplus of Type 1 decreases and the surplus of Type 2 increases, leading to a trajectory that moves to the upper left. Production of Type 1 parts resumes when the surplus reaches the boundary between Regions 2 and 3, and the trajectory follows the boundary to the hedging point, where once again production is at the demand rate. A similar set of events can be constructed for any other sequence of failures and repairs.

Observations We have described a typical portion of a trajectory. In general, the production history consists of a set of such random cycles: starting from the hedging point and returning after some random length of time. Not every cycle is so simple. Sometimes a machine fails again before x returns to Z.

If the demand is small enough, the system spends most of its time at the hedging point. In this case, the location of the hedging point is the most important factor in determining the system's performance. The locations of the boundaries are not very important. According to (9.79), this is not unusual. If a machine's availability is 90%, and if $\mu = 1.5d$, then the

Station	Machine	Availability	Utilization
A	1	0.95	0.94
A	2	0.91	0.85
B	1	0.92	0.55
B	2	0.92	0.36

Table 9.2: Availability and Utilization

system is at the hedging point 70% of the time. (This is a highly simplified estimate.)

While one Station A machine was down, the surplus moved on a trajectory that caused both types of parts to fall behind. In effect, it shared the shortfall in capacity among the two part types.

Simulation Results   The system was simulated with an early form of the hierarchical scheduler, in which

1. the Level 3 controller was less effective than the one described above; and

2. chattering was not prevented.

Each station had an internal buffer with a capacity for five pieces and a last-in-first-out (LIFO) discipline. The simulation model was run for an equivalent of 14 hours. From the system parameters, all the machines should be available 90.9% of the time. The Station A machines should be utilized 91.7% of the time they are available and the Station B machines should be utilized 45.8% of the time they are available. The simulated availability and utilization of each machine are given in Table 9.2. Station A is the system bottleneck. The controller is able to attain utilizations of 94% and 85% at the two Station A machines. Station B on the other hand is lightly loaded with only 55% and 36% of the available time being used.

Simulation output data are shown in Table 9.3. On average, the production was 5.2 pieces behind demand for Type 1 parts and 4.2 for Type 2. The average in-process inventory in the system is 3.0 Type 1 pieces and 1.2 Type 2 pieces. At the end of the simulation, the system had produced the required number of Type 2 parts and was two Type 1 parts short of target. Thus the algorithm was able to track demand and at the same time keep the number of pieces inside the system small.

Although this example behaved well, more complex systems did not do so well with the rudimentary hierarchical scheduler (Kimemia, 1982). The Level 3 staircase policy, and the prevention of chattering have improved the performance of more complex systems.

Part	Average In-process Inventory	Average x	Demand	Production
1	3.0	-5.2	2083	2081
2	1.2	-4.2	1042	1042

Table 9.3: Production Data for the Simulation

9.5.2 Example 2: Two-part, three-machine example worked out in detail

Here, we work out a portion of a trajectory of a two-part, three-machine system in detail. This is only to illustrate the conclusions we have described. It is not necessary to do all this for an actual implementation. In particular, it is neither necessary nor practical to determine all the x space regions and boundaries.

For a fixed $\alpha = (1, 1, 1)$, the maximum principle (9.38) becomes

$$\min c_1(x)u_1 + c_2(x)u_2 \tag{9.51}$$

subject to

$$\tau_{11}u_1 + \tau_{12}u_2 + s_1 = 1 \quad [\text{Machine 1}] \tag{9.52}$$

$$\tau_{21}u_1 + \tau_{22}u_2 + s_2 = 1 \quad [\text{Machine 2}] \tag{9.53}$$

$$\tau_{31}u_1 + \tau_{32}u_2 + s_3 = 1 \quad [\text{Machine 3}] \tag{9.54}$$

$$u_1, u_2, s_1, s_2, s_3 \geq 0 \tag{9.55}$$

where

$$c_1(x) = A_{11}(x_1 - Z_1)$$

$$c_2(x) = A_{22}(x_2 - Z_2)$$

The slack variables are s_1, s_2, and s_3. They represent the fraction of time each machine is idle. If we write (9.51)-(9.55) in the form

$$\min c(x)^T u$$

subject to

$$Du = \alpha$$
$$u \geq 0$$

then

$$u = (u_1, u_2, s_1, s_2, s_3)^T$$

$c(x)^T = (x - Z)^T \bar{A}$, where

$$\bar{A} = [A_0] = \begin{bmatrix} A_{11} & 0 & 0 & 0 & 0 \\ 0 & A_{22} & 0 & 0 & 0 \end{bmatrix}$$

(Recall that A is chosen to be diagonal.) Since A must be positive definite, both A_{11} and A_{22} are positive.

$$D = \begin{bmatrix} \tau_{11} & \tau_{12} & 1 & 0 & 0 \\ \tau_{21} & \tau_{22} & 0 & 1 & 0 \\ \tau_{31} & \tau_{32} & 0 & 0 & 1 \end{bmatrix} \qquad \alpha = \begin{bmatrix} 1 \\ 1 \\ 1 \end{bmatrix}$$

Assume that

$$\left. \begin{array}{l} \tau_{ij} > 0 \\ \tau_{12} > \tau_{22} > \tau_{32} \\ \tau_{31} > \tau_{21} > \tau_{11} \end{array} \right\} \tag{9.56}$$

This assumption is used below to help determine the shape of Ω. The Ω set ((9.52) − (9.55)) is drawn in Figure 9.15 (in (u_1, u_2) space; not in $(u_1, u_2, s_1, s_2, s_3)$ space). The numbers on the edges indicate which machines correspond to which constraints. For example, Edge 1 is Equation (9.52), and represents the set of (u_1, u_2) such that Machine 1 is always busy (and that $s_1 = 0$).

The Shape of Ω   We have already established that Ω is bounded. Edges 1, 2, and 3 must slope downward because each $\tau_{ij} \geq 0$. Relationship (9.56) is part of what insures that Ω has the indicated shape: that there are five sides, that Edge 1 lies between the u_2 axis and Edge 2, that Edge 2 lies between Edge 1 and Edge 3, and that Edge 3 lies between Edge 2 and the u_1 axis. This is because the u_1 intercept of Edge i (if it were extended to the u_1 axis) is $u_1 = 1/\tau_{i1}$ and the u_2 intercept is $u_2 = 1/\tau_{i2}$. Consequently the smallest u_1 intercept is that of Edge 3, and the largest is that of Edge 1. The smallest u_2 intercept is that of Edge 1, and the largest is that of Edge 3.

Since we want to obtain the indicated shape (to keep the problem interesting and illustrative), we must also make sure that Edge 2 appears in the figure. That is, (9.56) does not guarantee that Machine 2 can be fully utilized. Specifically, we must impose conditions on the τ_{ij} so that the intersection of Edge 1 and Edge 3 is not feasible.

The intersection of Edges 1 and 3 is

$$u = \frac{1}{\tau_{31}\tau_{12} - \tau_{11}\tau_{32}} \begin{bmatrix} \tau_{12} - \tau_{32} \\ \tau_{31} - \tau_{11} \end{bmatrix}.$$

For this u to violate (9.53), the τ_{ij} must satisfy

$$\tau_{12} \left[\frac{\tau_{12} - \tau_{32}}{\tau_{31}\tau_{12} - \tau_{11}\tau_{32}} \right] + \tau_{22} \left[\frac{\tau_{31} - \tau_{11}}{\tau_{31}\tau_{12} - \tau_{11}\tau_{32}} \right] > 1. \tag{9.57}$$

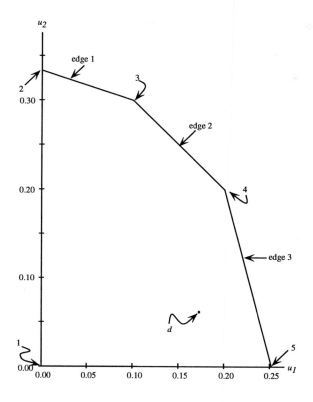

Figure 9.15: Capacity Set Ω in u Space

In drawing Figure 9.15, we have chosen

$$\tau_{11} = 1 \qquad \tau_{12} = 3$$
$$\tau_{21} = 2.5 \qquad \tau_{22} = 2.5$$
$$\tau_{31} = 4 \qquad \tau_{32} = 1$$

Locations of corners

Corner 1:

$$u_1 = u_2 = 0; s_1 = s_2 = s_3 = 1$$

Corner 2:

$$u_1 = s_1 = 0$$

$$u_2 = \frac{1}{\tau_{12}}$$

$$s_2 = 1 - \frac{\tau_{22}}{\tau_{12}}$$

$$s_3 = 1 - \frac{\tau_{32}}{\tau_{12}}$$

Corner 3:

$$s_1 = s_2 = 0$$

$$u_1 = \frac{\tau_{22} - \tau_{12}}{\tau_{11}\tau_{22} - \tau_{21}\tau_{12}}$$

$$u_2 = \frac{\tau_{11} - \tau_{21}}{\tau_{11}\tau_{22} - \tau_{21}\tau_{12}}$$

$$s_3 = 1 - \frac{\tau_{31}(\tau_{22} - \tau_{12}) - \tau_{32}(\tau_{11} - \tau_{21})}{\tau_{11}\tau_{22} - \tau_{21}\tau_{12}}$$

Corner 4:

$$s_2 = s_3 = 0$$

$$u_1 = \frac{\tau_{22} - \tau_{32}}{\tau_{31}\tau_{22} - \tau_{21}\tau_{32}}$$

$$u_2 = \frac{\tau_{31} - \tau_{21}}{\tau_{31}\tau_{22} - \tau_{21}\tau_{32}}$$

$$s_1 = 1 - \frac{\tau_{11}(\tau_{22} - \tau_{32}) - \tau_{12}(\tau_{31} - \tau_{21})}{\tau_{31}\tau_{22} - \tau_{21}\tau_{32}}$$

Corner 5:

$$u_2 = s_3 = 0$$

$$u_1 = \frac{1}{\tau_{31}}$$

$$s_1 = 1 - \frac{\tau_{11}}{\tau_{31}}$$

$$s_2 = 1 - \frac{\tau_{21}}{\tau_{31}}$$

Reduced costs To determine the regions in x space, we must determine the expressions for reduced costs for each corner. Recall that there is a different basic/non-basic split at each corner, and that

$$c_R(x)^T = c_N(x)^T - c_B(x)^T D_B^{-1} D_N.$$

The non-basic variables are those that are 0 at each corner.

Corner 1:

$$c_N = \begin{bmatrix} c_1(x) \\ c_2(x) \end{bmatrix} \quad c_B = \begin{bmatrix} 0 \\ 0 \\ 0 \end{bmatrix}$$

$$D_N = \begin{bmatrix} \tau_{11} & \tau_{12} \\ \tau_{21} & \tau_{22} \\ \tau_{31} & \tau_{32} \end{bmatrix} \quad D_B = \begin{bmatrix} 1 & 0 & 0 \\ 0 & 1 & 0 \\ 0 & 0 & 1 \end{bmatrix}$$

Then it is easy to determine that $c_R = c_N$. Therefore Region 1 is just

$$c_1(x) > 0,$$
$$c_2(x) > 0.$$

This can also be written

$$A_{11}(x_1 - Z_1) > 0$$

$$A_{22}(x_2 - Z_2) > 0$$

or, simply

$$x_1 > Z_1$$

$$x_2 > Z_2$$

This is intuitively reasonable: the set of points for which turning off the system is the correct strategy are those in which both components of the surplus are greater than the hedging point.

Corner 2:

$$c_N = \begin{bmatrix} c_1(x) \\ 0 \end{bmatrix} \quad c_B = \begin{bmatrix} c_2(x) \\ 0 \\ 0 \end{bmatrix}$$

$$D_N = \begin{bmatrix} \tau_{11} & 1 \\ \tau_{21} & 0 \\ \tau_{31} & 0 \end{bmatrix} \quad D_B = \begin{bmatrix} \tau_{12} & 0 & 0 \\ \tau_{22} & 1 & 0 \\ \tau_{32} & 0 & 1 \end{bmatrix}$$

and, after some effort,

$$c_R(x) = \begin{bmatrix} c_1(x) - \dfrac{\tau_{11}c_2(x)}{\tau_{12}} \\ \dfrac{-c_2(x)}{\tau_{12}} \end{bmatrix}.$$

Region 2 is determined by $c_R(x) > 0$ componentwise. Therefore, Region 2 is the set of (x_1, x_2) such that

$$\tau_{12}A_{11}x_1 - \tau_{11}A_{22}x_2 > \tau_{12}A_{11}Z_1 - \tau_{11}A_{22}Z_2$$

$$x_2 < Z_2$$

Corner 3:

$$c_N = \begin{bmatrix} 0 \\ 0 \end{bmatrix} \quad c_B = \begin{bmatrix} c_1(x) \\ c_2(x) \\ 0 \end{bmatrix}$$

$$D_N = \begin{bmatrix} 1 & 0 \\ 0 & 1 \\ 0 & 0 \end{bmatrix} \quad D_B = \begin{bmatrix} \tau_{11} & \tau_{12} & 0 \\ \tau_{21} & \tau_{22} & 0 \\ \tau_{31} & \tau_{32} & 1 \end{bmatrix}$$

and,

$$c_R(x) = \frac{1}{\tau_{11}\tau_{22} - \tau_{21}\tau_{12}} \begin{bmatrix} \tau_{21}c_1(x) - \tau_{22}c_2(x) \\ \tau_{12}c_1(x) - \tau_{11}c_2(x) \end{bmatrix}.$$

Region 3 is determined by $c_R(x) > 0$ componentwise. Note that

$$\tau_{11}\tau_{22} - \tau_{21}\tau_{12} < 0.$$

Therefore, Region 3 is the set of (x_1, x_2) such that

$$\tau_{21}c_2(x) - \tau_{22}c_1(x) < 0$$

$$\tau_{12}c_1(x) - \tau_{11}c_2(x) < 0$$

or

$$\tau_{21}A_{22}x_2 - \tau_{22}A_{11}x_1 < \tau_{21}A_{22}Z_2 - \tau_{22}A_{11}Z_1$$

$$\tau_{12}A_{11}x_1 - \tau_{11}A_{22}x_2 < \tau_{12}A_{11}Z_1 - \tau_{11}A_{22}Z_2$$

Corner 4:

$$c_N = \begin{bmatrix} 0 \\ 0 \end{bmatrix} \quad c_B = \begin{bmatrix} c_1(x) \\ c_2(x) \\ 0 \end{bmatrix}$$

$$D_N = \begin{bmatrix} 0 & 0 \\ 1 & 0 \\ 0 & 1 \end{bmatrix} \quad D_B = \begin{bmatrix} \tau_{11} & \tau_{12} & 1 \\ \tau_{21} & \tau_{22} & 0 \\ \tau_{31} & \tau_{32} & 0 \end{bmatrix}$$

and,

$$c_R(x) = -\frac{1}{\tau_{21}\tau_{32} - \tau_{31}\tau_{22}} \begin{bmatrix} \tau_{32}c_1(x) - \tau_{31}c_2(x) \\ \tau_{22}c_1(x) + \tau_{21}c_2(x) \end{bmatrix}$$

Region 4 is determined by $c_R(x) > 0$ componentwise. Since

$$\tau_{21}\tau_{32} - \tau_{31}\tau_{22} < 0,$$

Region 4 is the set of (x_1, x_2) such that

$$\tau_{32}c_1(x) - \tau_{31}c_2(x) > 0$$

$$\tau_{22}c_1(x) + \tau_{21}c_2(x) > 0$$

or

$$\tau_{31}A_{22}x_2 - \tau_{32}A_{11}x_1 > \tau_{31}A_{22}Z_2 - \tau_{32}A_{11}Z_1$$

$$\tau_{21}A_{22}x_2 - \tau_{22}A_{11}x_1 > \tau_{21}A_{22}Z_2 - \tau_{22}A_{11}Z_1$$

Corner 5:

$$c_N = \begin{bmatrix} c_2(x) \\ 0 \end{bmatrix} \quad c_B = \begin{bmatrix} c_1(x) \\ 0 \\ 0 \end{bmatrix}$$

$$D_N = \begin{bmatrix} \tau_{12} & 0 \\ \tau_{22} & 0 \\ \tau_{32} & 1 \end{bmatrix} \quad D_B = \begin{bmatrix} \tau_{11} & 1 & 0 \\ \tau_{21} & 0 & 1 \\ \tau_{31} & 0 & 0 \end{bmatrix}$$

and,

$$c_R(x) = \begin{bmatrix} c_2(x) - \dfrac{\tau_{32}c_1(x)}{\tau_{31}} \\ \dfrac{c_1(x)}{\tau_{31}} \end{bmatrix}$$

Region 5 is determined by $c_R(x) > 0$ componentwise. Therefore, Region 5 is the set of (x_1, x_2) such that

$$\tau_{31}A_{22}x_2 - \tau_{32}A_{11}x_1 > \tau_{31}A_{22}Z_2 - \tau_{32}A_{11}Z_1$$

$$x_1 < Z_1$$

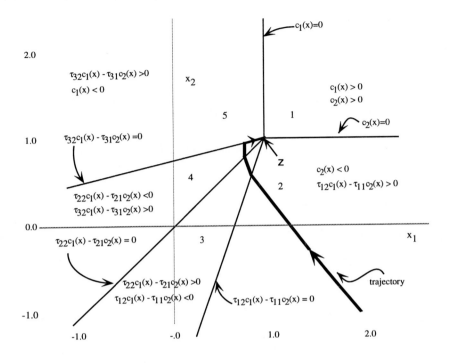

Figure 9.16: x Space Partitions and Trajectory

Figure 9.16 demonstrates the partitioning of x space. To draw this figure, we have assumed the τ_{ij} indicated above and

$$Z_1 = Z_2 = 1$$

$$A_{11} = 1; A_{22} = 1$$

The boundaries are

- Between R^1 and R^2: $x_2 = 1; x_1 > 1$

- Between R^2 and R^3: $3x_1 - x_2 = 2; x_1 < 1$

- Between R^3 and R^4: $x_1 = x_2; x_1 < 1$

- Between R^4 and R^5: $x_1 - 4x_2 = -3; x_1 < 1$

- Between R^5 and R^1: $x_1 = 1; x_2 > 1$

Observations

1. Once A and Z are known, and therefore $c(x)$ is known, the locations of the boundaries are independent of d. Recall, however, that A and Z depend on d as well as all other problem data parameters.

2. If Z is changed, all the boundaries change. However, the change is very special: the whole x space is translated by the change in Z. Thus, the shapes of the regions do not change. Again, recall that the optimal Z depends on all the problem data parameters.

A Trajectory   Assume that

$$d = \left[\begin{array}{c} .2 \\ .05 \end{array} \right]$$

and that at $t = t_0 = 0$,

$$x(0) = \left[\begin{array}{c} 2 \\ -1 \end{array} \right].$$

This initial condition is in Region 2.

Region 2

$$u(0) = \left[\begin{array}{c} 0 \\ .333 \end{array} \right] \quad \text{(Corner 2)}$$

Therefore

$$\dot{x} = \left[\begin{array}{c} -.2 \\ .283 \end{array} \right]$$

so

$$x(t) = \left[\begin{array}{c} 2 - .2t \\ -1 + .283t \end{array} \right].$$

The trajectory stays in Region 2 until it hits the boundary between Region 2 and Region 3:

$$3(2 - .2t_1) - (-1 + .283t_1) = 2$$

or,

$$t_1 = 5.66$$

and,

$$x(t_1) = \left[\begin{array}{c} -.87 \\ .60 \end{array} \right]$$

Region 3   In Region 3,

$$u = \begin{bmatrix} .1 \\ .3 \end{bmatrix}$$

so that

$$\dot{x} = \begin{bmatrix} -.1 \\ .25 \end{bmatrix}.$$

If we let

$$h = 3x_1 - x_2 - 2,$$

then $h > 0$ in Region 2, $h < 0$ in Region 3, and $h = 0$ on the boundary between them. In Region 3,

$$\frac{dh}{dt} = 3(-.1) - .25 < 0$$

so the boundary between Regions 2 and 3 is not attractive. In Region 3,

$$x(t) = \begin{bmatrix} .87 - .1(t - t_1) \\ .60 + .25(t - t_1) \end{bmatrix}.$$

The trajectory stays in Region 3 until t_2, the time it hits the boundary between Region 3 and Region 4:

$$.87 - .1(t_2 - t_1) = .60 + .25(t_2 - t_1)$$

or,

$$t_2 = 6.41$$

and,

$$x(t_2) = \begin{bmatrix} .79 \\ .79 \end{bmatrix}.$$

Region 4   In Region 4,

$$u = \begin{bmatrix} .2 \\ .2 \end{bmatrix}$$

so that

$$\dot{x} = \begin{bmatrix} 0 \\ .15 \end{bmatrix}.$$

If we let

$$h = x_1 - x_2,$$

then $h > 0$ in Region 3 and $h < 0$ in Region 4. In Region 4,

$$\dot{h} = -.15 < 0$$

so the boundary between Regions 3 and 4 is not attractive. In Region 4,

$$x(t) = \begin{bmatrix} .79 \\ .79 + .15(t - t_2) \end{bmatrix}.$$

The trajectory stays in Region 4 until t_3, when it hits the boundary between Region 4 and Region 5:

$$.79 - 4(.79 + .15(t_3 - t_2)) = -3$$

or,

$$t_3 = 12.30$$

and,

$$x(t_3) = \begin{bmatrix} .79 \\ .95 \end{bmatrix}$$

The boundary between R^4 and R^5   On this boundary, $h = x_1 - 4x_2 + 3 = 0$. This is an attractive boundary because in Region R^4,

$$\frac{dh}{dt} = 0 - 4(.15) < 0$$

and in R^5, where $u = \begin{bmatrix} .25 \\ 0 \end{bmatrix}$,

$$\frac{dh}{dt} = .05 - 4(-.05) > 0$$

Therefore, $h = 0$ and $\dfrac{dh}{dt} = 0$, so

$$\dot{x}_1 = 4\dot{x}_2$$

and,

$$u_1 - d_1 = 4(u_2 - d_2). \tag{9.58}$$

The best production rate vector to achieve this is a convex combination of Corners 4 and 5:

$$u = G \begin{bmatrix} .2 \\ .2 \end{bmatrix} + (1-G) \begin{bmatrix} .25 \\ 0 \end{bmatrix} = \begin{bmatrix} .25 - .05G \\ .2G \end{bmatrix}.$$

Then, to satisfy (9.58),

$$.2G - .05G - .2 = 4(.2G - .05)$$

or,

$$G = .29$$

and

$$u = \begin{bmatrix} .235 \\ .059 \end{bmatrix}$$

and the trajectory stays on this boundary until

$$x = \begin{bmatrix} .79 + .035(t_4 - t_3) \\ .95 + .009(t_4 - t_3) \end{bmatrix} = \begin{bmatrix} 1 \\ 1 \end{bmatrix}$$

or,

$$t_4 = 18.23.$$

The trajectory has now reached the hedging point. It stays there indefinitely. In an actual implementation, this scenario could be interrupted at any time with a repair or a failure of a machine.

Summary

- Between $t_0 = 0$ and $t_1 = 5.66$, $u = u(0) = \begin{bmatrix} 0 \\ .333 \end{bmatrix}$ (Corner 2),

- Between $t_1 = 5.66$ and $t_2 = 6.41$, $u = u(1) = \begin{bmatrix} .1 \\ .3 \end{bmatrix}$ (Corner 3) ,

- Between $t_2 = 6.41$ and $t_3 = 12.30$, $u = u(2) = \begin{bmatrix} .2 \\ .2 \end{bmatrix}$ (Corner 4),

- Between $t_3 = 12.30$ and $t_4 = 18.23$, $u = u(3) = \begin{bmatrix} .235 \\ .059 \end{bmatrix}$ (Edge 3),

- For $t > 18.23$, $u = d = \begin{bmatrix} .2 \\ .05 \end{bmatrix}$ (Hedging Point).

Table 9.4 represents these times and rates in the tabular form of Section 9.4.3.

These times and rates are all calculated at $t = t_0$, and the rates become the targets for the staircase strategy at the lowest level of the hierarchy: the portion of the hierarchy that determines precisely when to dispatch parts.

			m		
	0	1	2	3	4
t_m	0	5.66	6.41	12.30	18.23
u_m	$\begin{bmatrix} 0 \\ .333 \end{bmatrix}$	$\begin{bmatrix} .1 \\ .3 \end{bmatrix}$	$\begin{bmatrix} .2 \\ .23 \end{bmatrix}$	$\begin{bmatrix} .235 \\ .059 \end{bmatrix}$	$\begin{bmatrix} .2 \\ .05 \end{bmatrix}$

Table 9.4: Times and Rates

9.5.3   Example 3: N-part, one-machine system

This example shows how the hedging point strategy leads to a set of intuitively reasonable rules for operating a simple manufacturing system. Consider a system consisting of a single machine that performs operations on a set of parts. The operation times τ are all the same. The values of all the parts are the same, so we may choose $A_{jj} = 1$. The demand for Type j parts is d_j and the demand is feasible. The capacity set can be written

$$\sum_{j=1}^{N} \tau u_j \leq \alpha; \qquad u_j \geq 0, \qquad j = 1, ...N.$$

When $\alpha = 1$, this is an N-dimensional object with $N+1$ corners. One of the corners is the origin. Corner u^m $(m = 1, ...N)$ is of the form

$$u_m^m = \frac{1}{\tau}$$

$$u_j^m = 0; \qquad j \neq m$$

A three-dimensional version of this is represented in Figure 9.17. Since the demand is feasible, the demand vector is strictly in the interior of the capacity set when the machine is up. That is,

$$\sum_{j=1}^{N} d_j < \frac{1}{\tau}$$

Let the hedging point of Type j parts be Z_j. The real-time feedback control law is:

- When $\alpha = 0, u = 0$.

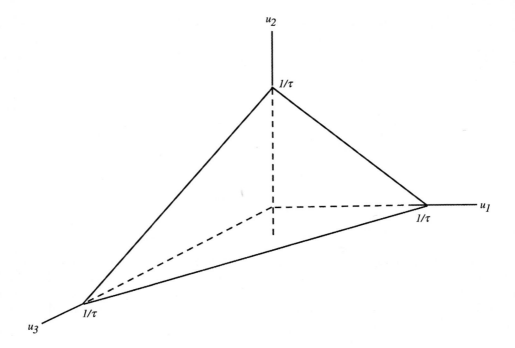

Figure 9.17: Capacity Set for Example 3

- When $\alpha = 1$, select production rate vector u to satisfy

$$\min \sum_{j=1}^{N} (x_j - z_j) u_j \tag{9.59}$$

such that

$$\sum_{j=1}^{N} u_j \leq \frac{1}{\tau}$$

$$u_j \geq 0, \quad j = 1, ... N.$$

As usual,

$$\frac{dx_j}{dt} = u_j - d_j.$$

When $\alpha = 0$, all components of the surplus decrease. The part types with higher demand lose surplus faster than those with low demand.

To analyze LP (9.59) when $\alpha = 1$, add a slack variable called u_{N+1}. In that case, the LP can be written

$$\min \sum_{j=1}^{N} (x_j - z_j) u_j \tag{9.60}$$

such that

$$\sum_{j=1}^{N+1} u_j = \frac{1}{\tau}$$

$$u_j \geq 0, \quad j = 1, ... N+1$$

Then (9.60) fits into the usual framework in which D is a $1 \times (N+1)$ matrix of 1's:

$$D = \{\overbrace{1, 1, ..., 1}^{N+1}\}$$

and $C(x)$ is the $N+1$ vector:

$$C(x)^T = \{x_1 - Z_1, x_2 - Z_2, ... x_N - Z_N, 0\}.$$

There are $N+1$ basic solutions, each corresponding to a corner of the capacity set. They are numbered so that the m'th basic solution corresponds to u^m above, for $m = 1, ..., N$, and the $N+1$st basic solution is the origin. For each basic solution,

$$D_B = \{1\}; \quad D_N = \{\overbrace{1, 1, ..., 1}^{N}\}.$$

That is, D_B is a 1×1 matrix, consisting of a single 1, and D_N is a $1 \times N$ matrix of 1's.

If $m \leq N$, then C_B is the 1-vector whose element is $x_m - Z_m$ and C_M is the N-vector formed by removing the m'th component of C. That is,

$$C_B = x_m - Z_m$$

$$C_N^T = \{x_1 - Z_1, x_2 - Z_2, ..., x_{m-1} - Z_{m-1}, x_{m+1} - Z_{m+1}, ..., x_N - Z_N, 0\}$$

If $m = N+1$, this basic solution corresponds to the corner at the origin. Then

$$C_B = 0$$

$$C_N^T = \{x_1 - Z_1, x_2 - Z_2, ..., x_N - Z_N\}$$

To determine the control action, we must find the reduced cost vectors. We use Equation (9.46). For $m \leq N$,

$$
\begin{aligned}
C_R^T &= \{x_1 - Z_1, x_2 - Z_2, ..., x_{m-1} - Z_{m-1}, x_{m+1} - Z_{m+1}, ..., x_N - Z_N, 0\} \\
&\quad -(x_m - Z_m)\{1, 1, ..., 1\} \\
\\
&= \{(x_1 - Z_1) - (x_m - Z_m), (x_2 - Z_2) - (x_m - Z_m), ..., \\
&\quad (x_{m-1} - Z_{m-1}) - (x_m - Z_m), (x_{m+1} - Z_{m+1}) - (x_m - Z_m), ..., \\
&\quad (x_N - Z_N) - (x_m - Z_m), -(x_m - Z_m)\}
\end{aligned}
$$

If $m = N + 1$, then

$$
C_R^T = C_N^T = \{x_1 - Z_1, x_2 - Z_2, ..., x_N - Z_N\}.
$$

Recall that for corner m of the capacity set to be optimal, all components of the corresponding reduced cost vector must be positive or 0. Therefore, the only way for m to be $N + 1$ (for the optimal u to be 0), is for $x_j \geq Z_j$ for all j. To put it in words, if all the surpluses are greater than their hedging points, stop producing. Turn the machine off.

For $m \leq N$

$$
\begin{aligned}
(x_j - Z_j) - (x_m - Z_m) &\geq 0; j \neq m \\
-(x_m - Z_m) &\geq 0
\end{aligned}
$$

That is, surplus m must be less than its hedging point, and it must be further below its hedging point than any other part type is below its hedging point. If the hedging points Z_j were all 0, Part Type m would have to be behind and further behind than anything else.

Suppose that this is the case strictly:

$$
\begin{aligned}
x_j - Z_j &> x_m - Z_m; \quad j \neq m \\
x_m &< Z_m
\end{aligned}
$$

In that case, we choose Corner m of the capacity set, and the surplus dynamics are

$$
\frac{dx_m}{dt} = \frac{1}{\tau} - d_m > 0
$$

$$
\frac{dx_j}{dt} = -d_j < 0; \quad j \neq m
$$

That is, Surplus m, which was the worst, is getting better, and all the other surpluses are getting worse. Eventually there will be a tie: at some time in the future, there will be some $k \neq m$ such that x satisfies

$$
\begin{aligned}
x_k - Z_k &= x_m - Z_m; \quad k \neq m \\
x_j - Z_j &> x_m - Z_m; \quad j \neq m, j \neq k \\
x_m &< Z_m
\end{aligned}
\tag{9.61}
$$

This represents a boundary between Region m and Region k. It is an attractive boundary because in Region k, x_k is increasing while x_m and all other surpluses are decreasing. Therefore, we must take care to avoid chattering. When the trajectory reaches this boundary we must add a constraint to LP (9.60) to keep the trajectory on the boundary.

We find the constraint by differentiating (9.61):

$$u_k - d_k = u_m - d_m$$

or,

$$u_k - u_m = d_k - d_m \tag{9.62}$$

The linear program that the new production rate vector satisfies is (9.60) with the additional constraint (9.62). We know that the surplus is on the boundary between Region m and Region k, and that surpluses m and k are equally below their hedging points, and further below their hedging points than all the others. Therefore u_m and u_k are as large as possible and all other u_j ($j \neq m$ and $j \neq k$) are 0. Consequently, u_m and u_k satisfy (9.62) and

$$u_m + u_k = \frac{1}{\tau}.$$

These are two equations in two unknowns. The solution is

$$u_k = \frac{1}{2}\left(\frac{1}{\tau} + d_k - d_m\right)$$
$$u_m = \frac{1}{2}\left(\frac{1}{\tau} + d_m - d_k\right)$$

Because the demand is feasible, these rates are both positive. In addition, they satisfy

$$u_k > d_k,$$
$$u_m > d_m.$$

Thus, we choose a production rate vector that keeps Type k and Type m equally far below their hedging points, and catching up, and allows the other part types, which are closer to their hedging points, to fall behind.

Again, there will eventually be a tie (unless, of course, the machine fails first). This time there will be a three-way tie when Types k and m improve enough and the worst of the others falls behind enough. The process repeats: the machine is divided in three ways so that the three part types furthest behind catch up as fast as possible and remain equally far behind, and the others get no attention so they fall behind. This continues until there is a four-way tie, and so forth.

Finally (unless the machine fails) there will be an N-way tie. All the parts types are equally far behind. That is,

$$x_j - Z_j = x_1 - Z_1, j = 2, ..., N.$$

Now the machine's resources are divided among all the part types in such a way that they all remain equally far behind their hedging points. They all reach their hedging points simultaneously, and they stay there until the inevitable eventual failure, when the entire process repeats.

Implementation There are two ways that this solution can be implemented. One way would be as a special case of the general approach described in this chapter: the production rates are chosen according to the linear program, with additional constraints as needed. The rates are then converted to loading times according to the staircase policy.

A second way would be to implement the rules that we have derived here, and to interpret them as directly pertaining to loading times rather than production rates. For example, the simplest form of such a rule is *Load the part that is furthest behind its hedging point.* This may be adequate in this case, but it can get more complicated when the operation times and relative values are not all the same. See Exercise 8, and, as a generalization to systems with non-negligible setup times, see the discussion of CLB policies in Section 11.4.4. See the example in Section 10.5 for a generalization of this policy to a system of three machines.

9.5.4   Example 4: Two-part, one-reliable-machine system

In this example, we present the exact solution of the two-part type, one-machine problem in which the machine does not fail, that is, in which $p = 0$. This is an artificial problem; since the machine does not fail, the hedging point Z is 0, and once x reaches 0, it stays there. However, there is a transient cost $W(x)$ of moving the surplus vector once from x to 0. The solution presented here is excerpted from Connolly (1992).

Why study this problem? It is reasonable to assume that if the machine is unreliable but p is small, the optimal boundaries are close to those of the reliable machine. Perhaps they are even *the same* as those of the reliable machine. This is the situation in Section 9.3: if the machine is sufficiently reliable, and the cost of positive surplus is great enough, the boundary (the location of the hedging point) is the same as if the machine were perfectly reliable.

Since the machine is reliable, and there is no other source of randomness in the problem, the controller can move the surplus state anywhere it chooses, and can keep it constant for as long as it wants. The optimal thing to do is to move the state to the origin, and to keep it there forever. Consequently, the origin is the hedging point. The only question remaining is to determine the best way of getting x to 0.

The surplus space is divided into three regions because Ω is a triangle. Corner 1 is $u = 0$; Corner 2 is $u_1 = 0, u_2 = 1/\tau_2 = \mu_2$; Corner 3 is $u_1 = 1/\tau_1 = \mu_1, u_2 = 0$.

Connolly shows that either

- Region 1 is the set of all x such that $x_1 \geq 0$ and $x_2 \geq 0$.

- Region 2 is the set of all x such that $x_1 \geq 0$ and $x_2 \leq 0$.

- Region 3 is the set of all x such that $x_1 \leq 0$.

or a similar set of boundaries are optimal. This set is optimal if

$$K = \frac{g_1 - \mu_1}{g_2 - \mu_2} > 1$$

If $K < 1$ Region 1 is the same, but Region 2 is the set of all x such that $x_2 < 0$ and Region 3 is the remainder of the space. If $K = 1$, it does not matter what u is when $x_1 < 0$ and $x_2 < 0$, as long as the machine is fully utilized.[12] In the following, we describe only the $K > 1$ case.

The Bellman equation becomes

$$0 = \min_{u \in \Omega} \left\{ g(x) + \frac{\partial W}{\partial x}(x)(u - d) \right\} \tag{9.63}$$

where Ω is the triangle given by $\{u | u_i \geq 0; \tau_1 u_1 + \tau_2 u_2 \leq 1\}$. *(Why is $J^* = 0$?)* The solution of this equation is piecewise quadratic.

In Region 1, $dx/dt = -d$, so all trajectories are straight lines pointing toward the southwest. They hit either the $x_1 = 0$ boundary or the $x_2 = 0$ boundary, depending where they start. In Region 2, $dx_1/dt = -d_1 < 0; dx_2/dt = \mu_2 - d_2 > 0$, so all trajectories are straight lines pointing toward the northwest. They hit either the $x_1 = 0$ boundary or the $x_2 = 0$ boundary, depending where they start. In Region 3, $dx_1/dt = \mu_1 - d_1 > 0; dx_2/dt = -d_2 < 0$, so all trajectories are straight lines pointing toward the southeast. They all hit the $x_2 = 0$ boundary. All three boundaries are attractive, since all trajectories move toward the boundaries, and none move away from them.

In Region 1, $W(x)$ must be such that

$$\frac{\partial W}{\partial x_1} > 0 \text{ and } \frac{\partial W}{\partial x_2} > 0 \tag{9.64}$$

since $u = 0$ minimizes

$$\frac{\partial W}{\partial x_1} u_1 + \frac{\partial W}{\partial x_2} u_2$$

subject to $u \in \Omega$.

Equation (9.63) becomes

$$0 = g_{1+} x_1 + g_{2+} x_2 - \frac{\partial W}{\partial x_1} d_1 - \frac{\partial W}{\partial x_2} d_2 \tag{9.65}$$

in Region 1.

Because the machine is reliable, we have boundary conditions that we would not have otherwise: the attractiveness of the boundaries means that if x starts on a boundary it stays on it; and the reliability means that failures also will not move it from the boundary.

---

[12] After reading the rest of the example, decide what the surplus trajectory must do after it reaches one of the axes.

Consequently, we can easily determine the cost W on either boundary: it is just the integral of g. That is,

$$\text{if } x_2 = 0, W = \frac{g_{1+}x_1^2}{2d_1}$$

$$\text{if } x_1 = 0, W = \frac{g_{2+}x_2^2}{2d_2}$$

These form boundary conditions for (9.65). The complete solution in Region 1 is

$$W = \frac{g_{1+}x_1^2}{2d_1} + \frac{g_{2+}x_2^2}{2d_2}$$

which can also be written

$$W(x) = \frac{1}{2}x^T A^1 x$$

where

$$A^1 = \begin{bmatrix} \frac{g_{1+}}{d_1} & 0 \\ 0 & \frac{g_{2+}}{d_2} \end{bmatrix}$$

This solution satisfies the differential equation and boundary conditions; and it also has another interpretation. For any point x in Region 1, the surplus follows a trajectory that starts at x and moves in the $-d$ direction to either the x_1 axis or the x_2 axis. It then moves along the axis until it reaches the origin. The expression for W is the integral of $g_{1+}x_1 + g_{2+}x_2$ along the trajectory. It is interesting to note that the expression is the same, no matter which axis the trajectory reaches first.

In Region 2, the derivatives of W must satisfy

$$\frac{\partial W}{\partial x_1} > 0 \text{ and } \mu_1 \frac{\partial W}{\partial x_1} - \mu_2 \frac{\partial W}{\partial x_2} > 0 \tag{9.66}$$

so that Corner 2 is the optimal solution of the linear program. In Region 3, where Corner 3 is the solution,

$$\frac{\partial W}{\partial x_2} > 0 \text{ and } \mu_1 \frac{\partial W}{\partial x_1} - \mu_2 \frac{\partial W}{\partial x_2} < 0 \tag{9.67}$$

Before we can complete the solution, the rest of the surplus space must be further subdivided. In Region 2, as in Region 1, some trajectories reach the x_1 axis first, and some reach the x_2 axis first. However, in Region 2, the expressions for W differ. This is because when x moves along the x_1 axis, $x_1 > 0$ so $u_1 = 0$ and $u_2 = d_2$. That is, x_1 is allowed to decrease and x_2 is kept constant. On the other hand, when x moves along the x_2 axis, $x_2 < 0$. Consequently, $u_1 = d_1$ and $u_2 = u_{2b} = (1 - \tau_1 d_1)/\tau_2 = \mu_2(1 - d_1/\mu_1)$. This is the production rate vector that keeps x_1 constant and allocates all remaining production capacity to Type 2. These two situations are not the symmetric opposites of one another, so the expressions will not, in general, be the same. Let us denote the portion of Region 2 in which trajectories eventually hit the x_1 axis as Region 2A, and the portion where they hit the x_2 axis as Region 2B. The boundary between them is the trajectory that hits the origin without first moving along either axis. This trajectory is given by $x_1/d_1 + x_2/(\mu_2 - d_2) = 0$.

That is, Region 2A is the subset of Region 2 such that $x_1/d_1 + x_2/(\mu_2 - d_2) > 0$ and Region 2B is the subset where $x_1/d_1 + x_2/(\mu_2 - d_2) < 0$.

A similar split occurs in Region 3, but there are three subregions. Region 3A is the set of x such that trajectories emanating from them hit the x_2 axis where $x_2 > 0$. All other trajectories hit the x_2 axis where $x_2 < 0$ (except for those on the boundary between the subregions, which hit the origin without first moving along an axis). The further split is along the x_1 axis; trajectories that start above the axis incur some cost due to positive x_2; that is, g_{2+} appears in the expression for W. This quantity does not appear in the expression for W when $x_1 < 0$ and $x_2 < 0$.

Therefore, Region 3A is the subset of Region 3 in which $x_1/(\mu_1 - d_1) + x_2/d_2 > 0$; Region 3B is the subset of Region 3 in which $x_1/(\mu_1 - d_1) + x_2/d_2 < 0$ and $x_2 > 0$; and Region 3C is where $x_1 < 0$ and $x_2 < 0$. The partitioning of the surplus space appears in Figure 9.18.

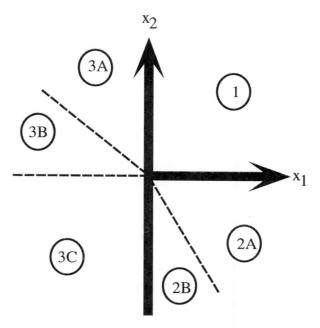

Figure 9.18: Regions and Subregions of the Surplus Space

In general, if x is in Region c (where $c = 1, 2A, 2B, 3A, 3B, 3C$),

$$W(x) = \frac{1}{2} x^T A^c x$$

where A^c is given in Table 9.5.

$$A^1 \quad = \quad \begin{bmatrix} \frac{g_{1+}}{d_1} & 0 \\ 0 & \frac{g_{2+}}{d_2} \end{bmatrix}$$

$$A^{2A} \quad = \quad \begin{bmatrix} \frac{g_{1+}}{d_1} & 0 \\ 0 & \frac{g_{2-}}{\mu_2 - d_2} \end{bmatrix}$$

$$A^{3A} \quad = \quad \begin{bmatrix} \frac{g_{1-}}{\mu_1 - d_1} & 0 \\ 0 & \frac{g_{2+}}{d_2} \end{bmatrix}$$

$$A^{2B} \quad = \quad \begin{bmatrix} \frac{g_{1+}}{d_1} + \frac{g_{2-} - \mu_2(\mu_2 - d_2)}{(u_{2b} - d_2)\mu_1 d_1} & \frac{g_{2-} - \mu_2}{(u_{2b} - d_2)\mu_1} \\ \frac{g_{2-} - \mu_2}{(u_{2b} - d_2)\mu_1} & \frac{g_{2-}}{u_{2b} - d_2} \end{bmatrix}$$

$$A^{3B} \quad = \quad \begin{bmatrix} \frac{g_{1-}}{\mu_1 - d_1} + \frac{g_{2-} - \mu_2 d_2}{(u_{2b} - d_2)\mu_1(\mu_1 - d_1)} & \frac{g_{2-} - \mu_2}{(u_{2b} - d_2)\mu_1} \\ \frac{g_{2-} - \mu_2}{(u_{2b} - d_2)\mu_1} & \frac{g_{2+}}{d_2} + \frac{g_{2-} - \mu_2(\mu_1 - d_1)}{(u_{2b} - d_2)\mu_1 d_2} \end{bmatrix}$$

$$A^{3C} \quad = \quad \begin{bmatrix} \frac{g_{1-}}{\mu_1 - d_1} + \frac{g_{2-} - \mu_2 d_2}{(u_{2b} - d_2)\mu_1(\mu_1 - d_1)} & \frac{g_{2-} - \mu_2}{(u_{2b} - d_2)\mu_1} \\ \frac{g_{2-} - \mu_2}{(u_{2b} - d_2)\mu_1} & \frac{g_{2-}}{u_{2b} - d_2} \end{bmatrix}$$

Table 9.5: Expressions for A^c

All of the expressions in Table 9.5 satisfy the differential equation. The expressions for adjacent regions also satisfy continuity. That is, for x on the boundary between Regions 1 and 2A, $W^1(x) = W^{2A}(x)$, for x on the boundary between Regions 1 and 3A, $W^1(x) = W^{3A}(x)$, and for x on the boundary between Regions 2B and 3C, $W^{2B}(x) = W^{3C}(x)$.

The expressions for adjacent subregions satisfy continuity of W and its first derivatives.

For example, for x on the boundary between Regions $2A$ and $2B$,

$$W^{2A}(x) = W^{2B}(x)$$

$$\frac{\partial W^{2A}(x)}{\partial x_1} = \frac{\partial W^{2B}(x)}{\partial x_1}$$

$$\frac{\partial W^{2A}(x)}{\partial x_2} = \frac{\partial W^{2B}(x)}{\partial x_2}$$

and the same kind of statements are true along the other boundaries between subregions.

Finally, these expressions also satisfy the conditions for optimality of the production rate vectors: inequalities (9.64), (9.66), and (9.67).

Interpretation and Implementation We can interpret this policy as determining which part type is better to devote effort to first. The product $g_{i-\mu_i}$ is the rate at which we can diminish the cost of a backlog if we devote all resources to Type i parts. If $K > 1$, $g_{1-\mu_1} > g_{2-\mu_2}$, and it is better to bring x_1 to 0 as fast as possible. Once $x_1 = 0$, we can devote all necessary resources to keep $x_1 = 0$, and use whatever is left to moving x_2 to 0.

Compare this policy with that of Example 3. These seem to be two quite different policies: either *load the part that is furthest behind its hedging point* or *rank order the parts in advance, and load the highest ranking part that is below its hedging point*. Note, however, that in Example 3 we assumed that all parts were equally valuable. This is similar to the case here in which $K = 1$.

Recall also that neither of these policies is exactly optimal for a case with failures (to say nothing of all the other real-world phenomena that plague a factory). Example 3 describes only the behavior of the hedging point policy with an assumed quadratic cost function and a guessed hedging point; the present example is the optimal solution for a system without failures.

9.5.5 Example 5: A Proposed IBM automated card assembly line

In 1984, at IBM's General Products Division at Tucson, an automated card assembly line was designed to be built in stages, through a series of "minilines." The portion of the system of interest to us is the stage consisting of insertion machines. (The system was designed, although never fully implemented. We use it as an example for the techniques described here.) See Figure 9.19[13] and Gershwin, Akella, and Choong (1985), and Akella, Choong, and Gershwin (1984). This example is a summary of the last reference.

Printed circuit cards from an upstream storage area arrive at the loading area of the insertion stage. Each card is placed in a workholder, and the card/workholder unit is introduced into the system. It goes to the machines where the required electronic components

---

[13]Copyright 1985 by International Business Machines Corporation; reprinted with permission.

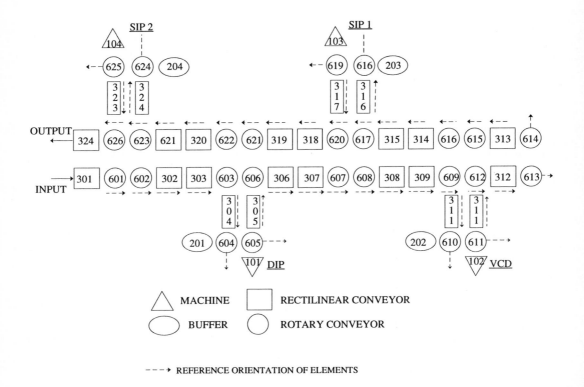

Figure 9.19: Insertion System

are inserted. It then exits the system and goes to the downstream stages: testing and soldering machines. There are several types of insertion machines, each of which inserts one mechanically distinct type of component. The common ones are SIPs (Single In-line Package Inserter), DIPs (Dual In-line Package Inserter), MODIs (Multiform Modular Inserter) and VCDs (Variable Center Distance Inserter). By loading different components, the line could have been used to assemble a variety of cards. In order to concentrate on the operational issues of the FMS, we assume that component loading has already been determined. The changeover time is small among the family of parts producible with a given component loading. We restrict our attention to a system that consists of a DIP, a VCD and two SIPs. Each of the machines also has an associated buffer, which can hold 30 parts.

Transportation System   The workholders are loaded at Input Station 301 and then move to each of the required machines. Movement is along straight or rotating elements. The

Machine i	Operation time τ_{ij} (seconds) Part Type j					
	1	2	3	4	5	6
1	40	40	0	0	20	60
2	0	0	60	30	40	40
3	0	100	0	0	70	0
4	0	0	0	80	0	80
Demand Rate d_j (parts/second)	.0080	.0070	.0060	.0070	.0025	.0040

Table 9.6: Operation Times and Demand Rates

straight elements are used to move parts in a single, fixed direction, and are represented by rectangles. The rotating elements are for 90 degree turns, and are represented by circles.

Movement of cards in the vicinity of a work station (insertion machine, associated buffer, and transport elements) follows a common pattern. Cards arrive at a rotating element like 603 and either turn toward the insertion machines, or move straight on. The cards going to machines (such as 101) either wait at input elements like 605, or go into buffers like 201. After all the required components have been inserted, a similar movement takes the card out of the insertion machine and onto output element 305. After element 606 is rotated toward the work station, the card is placed on it. Element 606 is rotated back to its original position and the card is then loaded onto the next transportation element (306). Finally, after going through the entire system, the cards exit from output element 324.

Machine Parameters and Part Data   There are random perturbations that affect the system other than machine failures. These include machine tool jams, which occur sometimes when a machine tries to insert a component. Rather than regarding them as failures, it is convenient to consider this small but regular disturbance (approximately once every 100 insertions) as part of the processing time. We limited our experiment to only six types to better examine the hierarchical policy. Typical demand rates are listed in Table 9.6. Also shown in Table 9.6 are the operation times required by each card type at each of the machines. They include the processing time and the time to move in and out of each machine.

The mean time to fail (MTTF), the mean time to repair (MTTR), and the efficiency e = (MTTF/(MTTF+MTTR)) of the machines are listed in Table 9.7.

Loading   Loading describes how heavily the machines in a system must be utilized to satisfy demand. Since each part has a fixed route, the average utilization is $(\sum_j \tau_{ij} d_j / e)$,

Machine	MTTF (minutes)	MTTF (minutes)	Efficiency (%)	Utilization (%)
1	600	60	90.91	97.68
2	600	60	90.91	91.10
3	600	60	90.91	96.03
4	600	60	90.91	96.58

Table 9.7: Machine Parameters

the ratio of the total machine time required to the expected machine time available. Table 9.7 displays the average utilizations for the machines in the configuration reported in the simulation experiment. This is not IBM data; it was created to impose a heavy loading on the simulated production system. The actual utilization in any sample simulation run depends on the time history of machine failures and repairs during that run. This time sequence determines the actual amount of time a machine is available.

Simulation Results   A detailed simulation was written to test the hierarchical scheduling policy and to compare it with other reasonable policies. The simulation indicated that the method behaves very well. The performance measures that were used were the total production during a day, average work-in-process, and production balance. The latter measured how well production adhered to the specified ratio of production requirements for different parts.

It was not vulnerable to parameter variations. A variety of different A and b coefficients were chosen for W in (9.39). This made almost no difference in the performance of the algorithm. See Table 9.8.

To define *balance*, let

$$P_i = \frac{\text{number of Type } i \text{ parts produced during the run}}{\text{number of Type } i \text{ parts required during the run}}.$$

Then balance is defined as

$$\frac{\min P_i}{\max P_i}.$$

It is important that balance be near 100% to ensure that only what is required is produced. In particular, if the cards will eventually be assembled into the same pieces of equipment, any deviation from 100% can result in incomplete production.

A variety of alternative policies was formulated to compare with the hierarchical policy. These policies shared the same structure but were increasingly sophisticated.

Run	Total Produced	Balance	WIP
Reference	98.1	90.4	11.81
Increased A	98.0	95.0	12.64
Increased Hedging points	98.3	92.2	11.58
Increased A and hedging points	97.8	96.0	12.62

Table 9.8: Hierarchical Policy Runs with Varying Control Parameters

1. Policy X. If more than N parts are in the system, do not load a part. If N or fewer parts are in the system, load the part that is furthest behind or least ahead of demand. Do not allow any part type to get more than K parts ahead of demand.

2. Policy Y. This is the same as Policy X, except that there are six thresholds, one for each part type. If there are N_i or fewer Type i parts in the system, and Type i is less than K parts ahead of demand, load a Type i part.

3. Policy Z. This is the same as Policy Y, except that threshold i is set to zero whenever any machine is down that part i must visit.

On all measures, the hierarchical method was superior: production was greater; work-in-process was less; and balance was closer to 100%, indicating that material was produced in nearly the specified ratio. It was more robust, in that it was less affected by disruptive events. The difference between its performance on good days and bad days was less than the difference for other strategies.

In particular, Table 9.9 illustrates the behavior of Policy X. Compare with Table 9.8. Policies Y and Z had better performance, but not as good as the hierarchical policy.

9.6 Extensions

9.6.1 Multiple routes (process flexibility)

So far, we have dealt only with product flexibility, in which each machine can do operations on more than one part type. In this section, we briefly discuss process flexibility, in which a part entering the FMS has more than one path through the system to complete its processing requirements. The proportion of parts that should follow each of the available paths is chosen

N	Total Production (%)	Balance (%)	WIP
11	82.2	74.8	11.00
16	87.1	82.9	15.98
20	89.5	87.3	19.96
22	91.1	88.4	21.95

Table 9.9: Policy X with Varying N

by the route control level of the controller. The objective is to meet the production rate dictated by the flow controller while minimizing congestion and delay within the system. The material in this section is a summary of Maimon and Gershwin (1988). Examples appear in that paper.

Let y_{nm}^k be the rate at which Type n parts arrive at Work Station m for Operation k. (Since only a few operations among all those that are possible are performed on each part type, most of these variables are 0.) We do not study how flow is divided among the machines in a workstation. The rate of arrival of parts for a given operation at a given station is the same as the rate for the same parts for any other operation at any other station, and the same as the rate of arrival of those parts at the system. This is a conservation of flow statement, and may be written

$$u_n = \sum_m y_{nm}^k \text{ for any } k \text{ and } n. \tag{9.68}$$

In this section, we formulate an optimization problem whose solution is the optimal set of y_{nm}^k variables as a function of time. A suboptimal solution is presented in Maimon and Gershwin (1988).

Capacity   The rate of flow of material into the system is limited by the rate at which machines can do operations. Each operation takes a finite amount of time, and no machine can be busy more that 100% of the time. A fundamental assumption is that there is no buffering inside the system. This reduces the total work in process, but increases the need for effective routing and scheduling.

Let $\tau_{nm}^k y_{nm}^k$ be the amount of time that a machine in Work Station m requires to do Operation k on a part of Type n. The rate at which machines of that station have to do such operations has already been defined as y_{nm}^k.

During a short interval of length ΔT, the expected number of operations performed by the machines is $y_{nm}^k \Delta T$. (It is assumed that the interval is short so that no repairs or failures take place during it.) The total amount of time that all of the machines of Station m are performing Operation k on Part Type n is $y_{nm}^k \tau_{nm}^k \Delta T$. The expected total amount of time that the machines of Station m are performing all operations on all part types is

$$\sum_n \sum_k y_{nm}^k \tau_{nm}^k \Delta T.$$

The total amount of time available on all the machines of Station m is $\alpha_m \Delta T$ if α_m machines are operational. Therefore,

$$\sum_n \sum_k y_{nm}^k \tau_{nm}^k \leq \alpha_m.$$

To summarize, the y flow rates must satisfy the following set of equations and inequalities:

$$y_{nm}^k \geq 0 \ \forall k, m, n \tag{9.69}$$

$$\sum_n \sum_k y_{nm}^k \tau_{nm}^k \leq \alpha_m \text{ for every Station } m. \tag{9.70}$$

$$\sum_m y_{nm}^k = \sum_m y_{nm}^{\kappa_n} \text{ for all } k \neq \kappa_n \text{ and all Part Types } n, \tag{9.71}$$

where κ_n is the name of the first operation performed on parts of Type n. Denote by $\Omega(\alpha)$ the set of all y flow rates that satisfy (9.69)-(9.71).

Dynamic Programming Formulation   The optimization problem can be written:

$$\min J(x_0, \alpha_0, 0)$$

subject to

$$\frac{dx}{dt} = u - d$$

Markov dynamics for α

$$y \in \Omega(\alpha)$$

where

$$J(x, \alpha, t) = \min_{y \in \Omega(\alpha)} E \left[\int_t^T g(x(s)) ds \,\middle|\, x(t) = x, \alpha(t) = \alpha \right]. \tag{9.72}$$

Solution   If we approximate

$$J(x(t), \alpha(t), t) \approx J^*(T - t) + W(x(t), \alpha(t))$$

for $t \ll T$ as usual, the Bellman equation takes the following form:

$$J^* = \min_{y \in \Omega(\alpha)} \left\{ g[x(t)] + \sum_n \frac{\partial W}{\partial x_n} \left(\sum_m y_{nm}^{\kappa_n} - d_n \right) + \sum_\beta \lambda_{\alpha\beta} W(x, \beta, t) \right\}. \tag{9.73}$$

If (9.73) has a solution, the optimal control y satisfies the following linear programming problem. Recall that the cost coefficients are time-varying.

$$\min \sum_n \frac{\partial W}{\partial x_n} \left(\sum_m y_{nm}^{\kappa_n} \right) \tag{9.74}$$

subject to

$$y \in \Omega(\alpha)$$

The solution y of (9.74) is a feedback control law since W and Ω are functions of x and α.

The cost-to-go J is positive since it is the expected value of the integral of g, a positive quantity. Recall the discussion in Section 8.9 that concludes that there is one degree of freedom in specifying W. Since J is positive for all x, α, and t, it is possible to pick W to be positive for all x and α.

Feedback law (9.74) minimizes

$$\frac{dW}{dt} = \sum_n \frac{\partial W}{\partial x_n} \left(\sum_m y_{nm}^{\kappa_n} - d_n \right) \tag{9.75}$$

while α is constant. This is because y appears in (9.73) only in the same term in which it appears in (9.75). If α remains constant long enough, and there is a $y \in \Omega(\alpha)$ such that (9.75) is negative, then J eventually reaches a minimum. As before, we call the value of x that produces this minimum the *hedging point* and write it $Z(\alpha)$. If possible, the production rate should remain at a value that keeps x at the hedging point. A positive hedging point serves as insurance for future disruptions.

After W reaches this minimum, W and x are both constant. Therefore, at the minimum,

$$\sum_m y_{nm}^{\kappa_n} - d_n = 0. \tag{9.76}$$

If there is no $y \in \Omega(\alpha)$ that satisfies (9.76), then W cannot reach a minimum for finite x. That is, the production lags behind the demand requirements and $x(t)$ decreases. This is because too many machines are down in state α to allow production to equal demand.

Quadratic W The simulation experience reported in this chapter for single-route systems suggests that the solution of linear programming problem (9.74) might provide a satisfactory scheduling and routing algorithm even if an approximate quadratic W function is used. In addition, it is likely that the repair and failure processes are not actually exponential, not actually independent of the machine utilizations, and do not have the exact λ parameters that would be used in (9.73) if an exact solution could be calculated. Also, the g function does not necessarily represent true costs, but rather is chosen to obtain a desired behavior. For these reasons, it would be a mistake to work very hard[14] to get an exact W.

Therefore, a reasonable strategy is to select a W function that has the correct qualitative properties and that is easy to calculate and work with. Such a function is positive and has a minimum at the hedging point (for every α such that the demand is feasible for that α). Just as in the single-route case described above, we suggest

$$W = \frac{1}{2}x^T A(\alpha)x + b(\alpha)^T x + c(\alpha).$$

9.6.2 Other extensions

Operation Dependent Failures We argue, in Chapter 3, that most failures are operation dependent, so it is unsatisfying to assume time dependent failures in this chapter. Problem (9.16) would still be a linear program if the model were generalized by letting $\lambda_{\alpha\beta}$ be a function of u (or y) of the form

$$\lambda = \lambda^0 + \lambda^1 u \tag{9.77}$$

in which λ^0 and λ are constants. This would allow operation-dependent, as well as time-dependent, failures because it would represent a failure rate that increases with increasing production rate. Linear program (9.38) becomes

$$\min_{u \in \Omega(\alpha(t))} \left(\lambda^1 + \frac{\partial W}{\partial x}(x, \alpha) \right) u. \tag{9.78}$$

which is a linear program. Equation (9.77) is a reasonable assumption, because λ^0 represents the rate of failure of a machine in an idle station, and $\lambda^1 u$ is the additional failure rate which is due to usage. This change does not appear to be important. It affects the optimal solution of the dynamic programming problem, but since experience indicates that the value of J in the feedback law is not critical, this change should not have a great affect on the performance of the policy. (Representing λ according to (9.77) would change the interpretation of the hedging point as the value of x that minimizes J.) See Choong (1988) and Hu, Vakili, and Yu (1991).

A related extension is one in which the cost function g is a function of u as well as x. This would represent costs that are functions of production rates. An example would be personnel costs.

---

[14]This refers, of course, only to factory managers and software developers. Graduate students, professors, and other researchers should always try to get analytical solutions. Interesting and even useful surprises sometimes occur.

More Events, Setups, Starvation, and Blockage   In Chapter 10 we propose a way of extending the hierarchy of this chapter to handle more kinds of events, particularly when there are more than two distinct frequency classes, as there are in this chapter. Chapter 10 is general; it is made more specific in Chapter 11, where we consider the event of changing the setup of a machine. This occurs when machines are not quite flexible as the ideal assumed here; when the time required, or the cost expended, to change a machine from operations on one part type to operations on another is not negligible. These are not random, like failures, but they are undesirable. They must occur if all the parts are to be produced.

Chapters 12 and 13 bring into the control hierarchy events that are studied in Chapters 3, 4, and 5: the emptying and filling of buffers. These are disruptions just as failures are, but they must be treated somewhat differently. We can influence when they will occur by the control policy.

9.7   Research Problems

Some research problems have already been mentioned. Others include:

1. Extend the analytic solutions described here (the one-machine, one-part-type problem of Section 9.3; the deterministic one-machine, two-part-type problem of Example 5) to larger systems.

2. Develop a more satisfactory approximation for the hedging point. In particular, if the part types can be approximately decoupled — for example, using the *hypercube approximation* proposed by Kimemia and Gershwin (1983) in which the polyhedral capacity set is replaced by a hypercube — then hedging points can be obtained for each one by means of the results of Section 9.3 or of Sharifnia (1988).

Exercises

1. Let $M = 3$ (3 classes of machines), $L_i = 2$ for $i = 1, 2, 3$ (2 identical machines in each class), and $N = 2$ (2 part types). Let τ_{ij} be given by

$$\tau_{11} = 1; \tau_{12} = 4$$

$$\tau_{21} = 2; \tau_{22} = 3$$

$$\tau_{31} = 3; \tau_{32} = 1$$

in hours. How many possible capacity sets Ω are there? Draw them all. Let the long range average requirements be

$$d = \begin{pmatrix} .3 \\ .3 \end{pmatrix} \text{ parts per hour.}$$

Indicate which repair states α are such that $d \in \Omega(\alpha)$. Supposed a feedback policy is proposed in which $u = d$ for all such states. Would this policy work well? If not, suggest simple ideas about how to improve it.

2. For the Bielecki-Kumar problem (Section 9.3), find Ex. What is the probability that $x > Z$ when Z is optimal? Does it matter whether Z is optimal?

3. Also for the Bielecki-Kumar problem, show that $\mathcal{E}(x)$ and $\Delta(x)$ can be usefully defined for Intervals I_2 and I_3. Let

$$\mathcal{E}(x) = -pdW(x,0) + r(\mu - d)W(x,1)$$
$$\Delta(x) = W(x,1) - W(x,0)$$

To get an equation for $\mathcal{E}$, multiply the $\alpha = 0$ Bellman equation by p and the $\alpha = 1$ equation by r and add them; to get an equation for Δ, multiply the $\alpha = 0$ equation by $(\mu - d)$ and the $\alpha = 1$ equation by d and add them. Suggest an interpretation for $\mathcal{E}$ and Δ.

4. Let $\mu = 1$ part per minute, $d = .5$ parts per minute, $x(0) = 0$ parts, and $\alpha(0) = 1$. Assume that failures occur at times 42 minutes, 80 minutes, and 136 minutes, and that the down times last 15 minutes, 10 minutes, and 12 minutes. Estimate reasonable values for r and p. If $g_+ = 1$ and $g_- = 10$, calculate Z. Using the strategy described in Section 9.3, calculate and graph $u(t)$ and $x(t)$ for $0 \le t \le 160$ minutes. Also graph the cumulative production and demand. (Draw the last two on the same axes.) Are cumulative production and demand close to one another? Calculate

$$\int_0^{170} (g_+ x^+ + g_- x^-)dt.$$

Complete the hierarchy: suggest times at which parts should be loaded into the system. Is the total number of parts loaded close to the cumulative production calculated above?

5. Confirm (9.42). What additional assumptions on the relative values of parameters were made in drawing Figure 9.10? In particular, what guarantees that the lowest point in that picture is negative; and what guarantees that x eventually reaches the hedging point under the assumptions made here?

6. Demonstrate that the fraction of time that a given part type spends away from its hedging point is approximately

$$\frac{p}{r + p} \frac{\mu_j}{\mu_j - d_j} \qquad (9.79)$$

7. An FMS has three sets of machines and makes two part types. The times required for each part type on each machine are given by the following table (in minutes):

τ_{ij} machine (i)	part (j) 1	2
1	5	0
2	10	5
3	0	10

The mean time between failures for each machine is 450 minutes. The mean time to repair is 50 minutes.

- Write the expressions that define the capacity set $\Omega(\alpha)$, in which α_i is the number of Type i machines available. Sketch the capacity set if $\alpha_1 = \alpha_2 = \alpha_3 = 1$. Sketch the capacity set if $\alpha_1 = \alpha_2 = 1; \alpha_3 = 0$.

- Sketch the average capacity set if there are a total of two machines of each type.

- Assume a demand rate $d = \begin{pmatrix} .08 \\ .15 \end{pmatrix}$. For which values of α is the demand feasible?

- Assume an approximate cost-to-go function

$$J(x,\alpha) = \frac{1}{2}\left((x_1 - Z_1(\alpha))^2 + (x_2 - Z_2(\alpha))^2\right)$$

in which the hedging points, $Z(\alpha)$, are given in Table 9.10. Are they reasonable hedging points? Why or why not? If you don't think they are reasonable, come up with a better set, and explain why they are better.
Draw the x space boundaries for $\alpha = (2, 1, 2)$ and $\alpha = (2, 2, 2)$.

α_1	0	0	0	0	0	0	0	0	0	1	1	1	1	1	1	1	1	1	2	2	2	2	2	2	2	2	2
α_2	0	0	0	1	1	1	2	2	2	0	0	0	1	1	1	2	2	2	0	0	0	1	1	1	2	2	2
α_3	0	1	2	0	1	2	0	1	2	0	1	2	0	1	2	0	1	2	0	1	2	0	1	2	0	1	2
Z_1	100	100	100	100	100	100	100	100	100	100	100	100	100	100	20	100	20	10	100	100	100	100	20	10	100	10	1
Z_2	100	100	100	100	100	100	100	100	100	100	100	100	100	100	20	100	20	10	100	100	100	100	20	10	100	10	1

Table 9.10: Hedging Points

- Describe, with words, equations, and sketches, the production rate and surplus history if the system starts at $t = 0$ with $x = 0$ and $\alpha = (2, 2, 2)$; and a Type 2 machine fails at $t = 200$, is repaired at $t = 1200$, and no other failures occur before the surplus returns to the hedging point. At what time does it return to the hedging point?

8. Do Example 3 of Section 9.5 but with the operation times τ_j all different.

Bibliography

[1] R. Akella, J. P. Bevans, and Y. Choong (1985), "Simulation of a Flexible Electronic Assembly System," Massachusetts Institute of Technology Laboratory for Information and Decision Systems Report, LIDS-R-1485, March, 1985.

[2] R. Akella, Y. Choong, and S. B. Gershwin (1984), "Performance of Hierarchical Production Scheduling Policy," *IEEE Transactions on Components, Hybrids, and Manufacturing Technology*, September, 1984.

[3] R. Akella and P. R. Kumar (1986), "Optimal Control of Production Rate in a Failure Prone Manufacturing System," *IEEE Transactions on Automatic Control*, Vol. AC-31, No. 2, pp. 116-126, February, 1986.

[4] R. Akella, O. Z. Maimon, and S. B. Gershwin (1990), "Value Function Approximation Via Linear Programming for FMS Scheduling," *International Journal of Production Research*, Volume 28, No. 8, August, 1990, pp. 1459-1470.

[5] S. X. Bai (1991), "Scheduling Manufacturing Systems with Work-In-Process Inventory Control," Ph. D. Thesis, MIT Operations Research Center, September, 1991.

[6] D. Bertsekas (1976), *Dynamic Programming and Stochastic Control*, Academic Press, 1976.

[7] T. Bielecki and P. R. Kumar (1988), "Optimality of Zero-Inventory Policies for Unreliable Manufacturing Systems," *Operations Research*, Volume 36, No. 4, July-August, 1988, pp. 532-541.

[8] E. K. Boukas (1991), "Techniques for Flow Control and Preventive Maintenance in Manufacturing Systems," *Control and Dynamic Systems*, Volume 48, Academic Press, 1991.

[9] E. K. Boukas and A. Haurie (1990), "Manufacturing Flow Control and Preventive Maintenance: A Stochastic Control Approach" *IEEE Transactions on Automatic Control*, Vol. 35, No. 9, pp. 1024-1031, September, 1990.

[10] E. K. Boukas, A. Haurie, and C. van Delft (1991), "A Turnpike Improvement Algorithm for Piecewise Deterministic Control," *Optimal Control Applications and Methods,* Volume 12, pp. 1-18, 1991.

[11] J. A. Buzacott (1982), " 'Optimal' Operating Rules for Automated Manufacturing Systems," *IEEE Transactions on Automatic Control,* Vol. AC-27, No. 1, February, 1982, pp 80-86.

[12] M. C. Caramanis and G. Liberopolous (1992), "Perturbation Analysis for the Design of Flexible Manufacturing System Flow Controllers," *Operations Research,* Volume 40, No. 6, November-December, 1992.

[13] M. C. Caramanis and A. Sharifinia (1991), "Near-Optimal Manufacturing Flow Controller Design," *International Journal of Flexible Manufacturing Systems,* Vol. 3, No. 4, pp.321-336, 1991.

[14] Y. F. Choong (1988) "Flow Control Approach for Batch Production Scheduling with Random Demand," Massachusetts Institute of Technology, Ph. D. Thesis, Department of Mechanical Engineering, May, 1988.

[15] S. Connolly (1992), "A Real-time Policy for Performing Setup Changes in a Manufacturing System," Master's Thesis, Operations Research Center, MIT, May 1992; MIT Laboratory for Manufacturing and Productivity Report LMP-92-005.

[16] B. L Deuermeyer and W. P. Pierskalla (1978), "A By-Product Production System with an Alternative," *Management Science,* Vol. 24, No. 13, September, 1978, pp. 1373-1383.

[17] S. B. Gershwin (1986), "Stochastic Scheduling and Setups in a Flexible Manufacturing System," in *Proceedings of the Second ORSA/TIMS Conference on Flexible Manufacturing Systems,* Ann Arbor, MI, August, 1986, pp. 431-442.

[18] S. B. Gershwin, R. Akella, and Y. F. Choong (1985), "Short-Term Production Scheduling of an Automated Manufacturing Facility," *IBM Journal of Research and Development,* Vol. 29, No. 4, pp 392-400, July, 1985.

[19] E. L. Hahne (1981), "Dynamic Routing in an Unreliable Manufacturing Network with Limited Storage," MIT Laboratory for Information and Decision Systems Report LIDS-TH-1063, February, 1981.

[20] R. R. Hildebrant (1980), "Scheduling Flexible Machining Systems when Machines are Prone to Failure," Ph. D. Thesis, MIT, 1980.

[21] R. R. Hildebrant and R. Suri (1980), "Methodology and Multi-Level Algorithm Structure for Scheduling and Real-Time Control of Flexible Manufacturing Systems," *Proc. 3rd International Symposium on Large Engineering Systems,* Memorial University of Newfoundland, July, 1980, pages 239-244.

[22] J.-Q. Hu, P. Vakili, and G.-X. Yu (1991), "Optimality of Hedging Point Policies in the Production Control of Failure Prone Manufacturing Systems," Boston University, Department of Manufacturing Engineering, September, 1991.

[23] J. G. Kimemia (1982), "Hierarchical Control of Production in Flexible Manufacturing Systems," MIT EECS Ph. D. Thesis; MIT LIDS Report No. LIDS-TH-1215 (1982).

[24] J. Kimemia and S. B. Gershwin (1983), "An Algorithm for the Computer Control of a Flexible Manufacturing System," *IIE Transactions* Vol. 15, No. 4, pp 353-362, December, 1983.

[25] P. R. Kumar and P. Varaiya (1986), *Stochastic Systems: Estimation, Identification, and Adaptive Control*, Prentice-Hall, 1986.

[26] G. Liberopolous (1993), "Flow Control of Failure Prone Manufacturing Systems: Controller Design Theory and Applications," Ph.D. Thesis, Boston University, 1993.

[27] X.-C. Lou, J. G. Van Ryzin, and S. B. Gershwin (1987), "Scheduling Job Shops with Delays," in *Proceedings of the 1987 IEEE International Conference on Robotics and Automation*, Raleigh, NC, March-April 1987.

[28] D. Luenberger (1973) *Introduction to Linear and Nonlinear Programming*, Addison-Wesley, 1973.

[29] O. Z. Maimon and Y. F. Choong (1985), "Dynamic Routing in Reentrant Flexible Manufacturing Systems," *Robotics and Computer-Aided Manufacturing*, Vol. 3, pp. 295-300.

[30] O. Z. Maimon and S. B. Gershwin (1988), "Dynamic Scheduling and Routing for Flexible Manufacturing Systems that have Unreliable Machines," *Operations Research*, Volume 36, No. 2, March-April, 1988, pp. 279-292.

[31] G. J. Olsder and R. Suri (1980), "Time-Optimal Control of Flexible Manufacturing Systems with Failure Prone Machines," *Procroceedings of the 19th IEEE Conference on Decision and Control*, December, 1980.

[32] R. Rishel (1975), "Dynamic Programming and Minimum Principles for Systems with Jump Markov Disturbances," *SIAM Journal on Control*, Vol.13, No.2, February, 1975.

[33] A. Seidmann and P. Schweitzer (1984), "Part Selection Policy for a Flexible Manufacturing Cell Feeding Several Production Lines," *IIE Transactions* Vol. 16, No. 4, pp 355-362, December, 1984.

[34] A. Sharifnia (1988), "Production Control of a Manufacturing System with Multiple Machine States," *IEEE Transactions on Automatic Control*, Vol. AC-33, No. 7, pp. 620-625, July, 1988.

[35] A. Sharifnia (1993), "Stability and Performance of Distributed Production Control Methods Based on Continuous Flow Models," *IEEE Transactions on Automatic Control*, to appear.

[36] N. Srivatsan (1993), "Synthesis of Optimal Policies for Stochastic Manufacturing Systems," Ph. D. Thesis, MIT Operations Research Center.

[37] N. Srivatsan, S. X. Bai, and S. B. Gershwin (1992), "Hierarchical Real-Time Integrated Scheduling of a Semiconductor Fabrication Facility," to appear in the *Control and Dynamic Systems* series, published by Academic Press, edited C. T. Leondes.

[38] R. Suri and R. R. Hildebrant (1984), "Modelling Flexible Manufacturing Systems Using Mean Value Analysis," *J. Mfg. Systems,* Vol. 3, No. 1, 27-38, 1984.

[39] J. N. Tsitsiklis (1987),"Convexity and Characterization of Optimal Policies in a Dynamic Routing Problem" *JOTA* Vol. 44, No. 1, pp 105-135, 1984.

[40] G. J. Van Ryzin (1987), "Control of Manufacturing Systems with Delay," MIT Laboratory for Information and Decision Systems Report LIDS-TH-1676, June, 1987.

[41] G. J. Van Ryzin, X.-C. Lou, and S. B. Gershwin (1991), "Scheduling Job Shops with Delays," *International Journal of Production Research,* Volume 29, Number 7, pp. 1407-1422, 1991.

[42] G. J. Van Ryzin, X.-C. Lou, and S. B. Gershwin (1993), "Production Control for a Tandem Two-Machine System," *IIE Transactions*, to appear.

Chapter 10

Hierarchical Scheduling and Planning of Manufacturing Systems

10.1 Introduction

Chapter 9 deals with a highly simplified manufacturing system, one in which only two kinds of phenomena take place: operations and machine failures. We reduce the computational effort required to schedule such a system by taking advantage of a common observation: failures, in most cases, occur less frequently than operations, and take up much more time each time they occur.

In this chapter,[1] we extend the method of Chapter 9 to a manufacturing system with more kinds of events. We use the computations of Chapter 9 as building blocks in a more elaborate hierarchy. We continue to make the assumption that frequencies and durations of different kinds of phenomena are very different, but we no longer assume that there are only two kinds.

Most manufacturing systems are large and complex. It is natural, therefore, to divide the control or management into a hierarchy consisting of a number of different levels. Each level is characterized by the length of the planning horizon and the kind of data required for the decision-making process. Higher levels of the hierarchy typically have long horizons and use highly aggregated data, while lower levels have shorter horizons and use more detailed information. The nature of uncertainties at each level of control also varies.

Typically, the managers of a manufacturing firm make production plans for finished products by considering forecasts of demand, sales, raw material availability, inventory levels,

---

[1] Portions reprinted, with permission, from S. B. Gershwin (1989), "Hierarchical Flow Control: A Framework for Scheduling and Planning Discrete Events in Manufacturing Systems," *Proceedings of the IEEE, Special Issue on Dynamics of Discrete Event Systems*, Vol. 77, No. 1, pp. 195-209, January, 1989. ©1989 IEEE.

and plant capacity. Frequently, they use *Materials Requirements Planning* or *MRP* (Orlicky, 1975). From the resulting high level plan, the requirements for the components that go into the final products can be determined. The various departments that are responsible for the manufacture of the components schedule their activities so as to meet the requirements dictated by the master production and the materials requirements plans (Halevi, 1980; Hitomi, 1979). Unfortunately, MRP does not account for the finite (and varying) capacity of a manufacturing system.

The goal of this chapter and of the following material is to put this process on a firmer, more systematic footing, and to extend it downwards to the real-time control of material movement. Operating policies for manufacturing systems must respond to important discrete events such as machine failures, setups, demand changes, expedited batches, etc. These feedback policies must be based on realistic models, and they must be computationally tractable. In this chapter, we develop a hierarchical framework for research and algorithm development in scheduling and planning. The structure of the hierarchy is systematically based on the characteristics of the specific kind of production that is being controlled. The levels of the hierarchy correspond to classes of events that have distinct frequencies of occurrence.

There have been many hierarchical scheduling and planning algorithms, some quite practical and successful. (For example, see the NBS conference proceedings edited by Jackson and Jones, 1986; Anthony, 1965; and many other works.) However, outside of the works of Sethi and his colleagues, there has been little systematic justification of this structure. The main goal of the approach described here and in Chapter 13 is a framework for studying and synthesizing such structures.

Figure 10.1 illustrates some of the issues that are considered here. It is a graph of the cumulative production and demand for one part type (j) among many that share one machine (i). This machine is *not* flexible in the sense described in Chapter 9. Some time is lost, and some cost is incurred, each time the machine is changed from being able to make one part type to making another. This may be because tools are changed and the new tools must be calibrated, or for many other reasons. This phenomenon is very common. It is worthwhile to try to reduce the amount of time or money that is spent in changing setups, but that is not the problem we treat here. Here, we assume that the costs are fixed, and we attempt to manage the system as well as possible given those costs. In drawing this graph, we have assumed that setup changes are infrequent events. Failures are assumed to occur much more often than setup changes, and much less often than operations. Assumptions like this — that important events occur at very different frequencies — form the basis of the hierarchy of this chapter.

A long term production rate (u_{ij}^1) is specified for Type j parts, and its integral is represented by the solid straight line. It is not possible to follow this line exactly because the machine is set up for Type j parts only during a set of time intervals. During such intervals, the medium term production rate u_{ij}^2 must be greater than u_{ij}^1, because during the other intervals — while it is set up for other part types, or while the setup is being changed — u_{ij}^2 is 0. The integral of u_{ij}^2 (the dashed line) is staircase-like (Figure 9.11), close to the integral of u_{ij}^1.

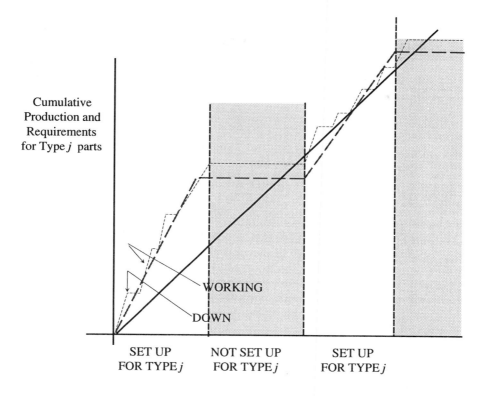

Figure 10.1: Cumulative Production and Demand in a Multiple-Time-Scale Environment

The dashed line cannot be realized either. The machine is unreliable, and while it is down, its production rate u_{ij}^3 is 0. Consequently, while it is up and configured for Type j, it must be operated at a short term rate u_{ij}^3 greater than that of the dashed line. The dotted line, which represents this phenomenon, is again staircase-like, and is close to the dashed line. Finally, the actual cumulative production graph (which requires too much resolution to be plotted) is a true staircase. It has vertical steps at the instants when parts are loaded, and it is flat otherwise. It is very close to the dotted line.

If the relative frequencies were different — if setups were much more frequent than failures — a graph like Figure 10.1 could be drawn. It would look similar, but the labels on the time axis and on the graph would be interchanged. In either case, control hierarchies could be constructed, but they would be different.

In this chapter, we formalize this hierarchy, and extend it to an arbitrary number of levels (and distinct classes of events) and several machines. We must introduce some new concepts to help us to deal with the great diversity of phenomena. They include

1. activities, a generalization of operations, failures, and set-up changes,

2. the distinction between controllable and uncontrollable activities and events,

3. the distinction between predictable and unpredictable activities and events,

4. the classification of events and activities by frequency, and the organization of a hierarchy according to this classification,

5. the Level k observer, who can observe and understand events that occur at roughly the frequency of the events of Level k of the hierarchy, but for whom more frequent events go by in a blur, and for whom less frequent events arrive like a *deus ex machina*. For this observer, they can be seen but not predicted in any sense or influenced.

6. setup changes, the change of tooling, for example, of a machine which allows it to operate on a new part or set of parts. Setup changes are controllable events which must be scheduled carefully because they take up machine and worker time (that is, capacity) and can cost money. They should not be too frequent, because of their costs, but they should also not be too infrequent. This is because infrequent setup changes can lead to large lots, large inventories, and long times for parts to spend in the factory. We describe a *framework* for dealing with setup changes in this chapter; we describe some specific problems and solutions in Chapter 11.

10.1.1 Literature survey

There is a large literature in scheduling (Graves, 1981). Many papers are based on combinatorial optimization/integer programming methods (Lageweg, Lenstra, and Rinnooy Kan, 1977 and 1978; Papadimitriou and Kannelakis, 1980) or mixed integer methods (Afentakis, Gavish, and Karmarkar, 1984; Newson, 1975a and 1975b; Wagner and Whitin, 1958). Because of the difficulty of the problem, authors are limited to analyzing computational complexity, or proposing and analyzing heuristics.

An important class of problem formulations is that of hierarchical structure (Bitran, Haas, and Hax, 1981; Dempster *et al.*, 1981; Graves, 1982; Hax and Meal, 1975; and others). The goal is to replace one large problem by a set of many small ones because the latter is invariably easier to treat. These methods are often used but there is no general, systematic way of synthesizing hierarchies for large classes of stochastic scheduling problems. A full critical survey of the hierarchical management and control literature appears in Libosvar (1988a, 1988b).

Multiple time scale problems have been studied in the control theory (Saksena, O'Reilly, and Kokotovic, 1984) and Markov chain literature (Delebecque, Quadrat, and Kokotovic, 1984). Caromicoli (1987) and Caromicoli, Willsky, and Gershwin (1987, 1988) treat a manufacturing system example with methods from the multiple-time-scale Markov literature. We use insights from these methods to develop a systematic justification for hierarchical analysis. A philosophical influence on this work is found in Koestler (1967, 1978).

This chapter is based on Gershwin (1987a, 1989). Xie (1988) treats a closely related problem — one with failures only, but two different failure modes, at two different levels —

with the methods of Gershwin (1989). Additional simulation experiments were performed by Darakananda (1989) and Violette (1993).

Some justification for the hierarchical structure is provided by Lehoczky *et al.* (1991). A great deal of significant work on real-time hierarchical scheduling control of manufacturing systems has been performed by Sethi and his colleagues. This seminal work is described in a large number of papers, and is summarized in Sethi and Zhang (1993) and presented at greater length in Sethi and Zhang (1994).

10.1.2 Chapter outline

Section 10.2 describes the manufacturing systems that we are considering. It establishes terminology and discusses the basic concepts for the present approach: capacity and frequency separation. Section 10.2.5 builds on the frequency separation to derive a small set of results that form the foundation of the hierarchy. Control in the hierarchy is described in detail in Section 10.4. A simple example appears in Section 10.5, and conclusions are drawn in Section 10.6.

10.2 Production Events and Capacity

In this section, we discuss some of the discrete events that occur during the production process. We define terminology to help describe these events. We categorize events in two ways: the frequency with which they occur; and the degree of control that decision-makers can exert over them. We define capacity, and show how capacity is affected by production events.

10.2.1 Definitions

A *resource* is any part of the production system that is not consumed or transformed during the production process. Machines — both material transformation and inspection machines, workers, pallets, and sometimes tools — if we ignore wear or breakage — can be modeled as resources. Workpieces and processing chemicals cannot.

For the purposes of this and succeeding chapters, we define *event* as a change in the discrete part of the state or a discontinuous change in a rate or a parameter. Discontinuous changes in rates occur in the exercise of the hedging point policy, as shown in Chapter 9. This is a special case of the definition of event that appears in Chapter 2.

An *activity* is a pair of events associated with a resource. The first event corresponds to the start of the activity, and the second is the end of the activity. Only one activity can appear at a resource at any time. For example, drilling 3/8" holes in Type 12 parts is an activity: an operation. Other examples include machine failures, preventative maintenance, routine calibration, inspection, and training sessions. A *disruption* is an undesirable activity.

The activities that a resource may be able to perform at a given time may be limited by its current *configuration* or *setup*. These terms refer to physical attributes of a resource —

such as the tooling of a machine — that can be changed. When to change the configuration (when to set up) is an important managerial decision.

Setting up is a special kind of activity. Configurations must be changed so that the full range of material that is demanded can be produced. If it is done too frequently, a resource's capacity for productive work is diminished, but if it is done too infrequently, excessive inventory and response time results. One of the goals of the work presented here is to create a framework for scheduling all activities, including setups.

Examples of production systems that involve setups are machine tools that can support a variety of different cutting edges at different locations, and ion implanters (in semiconductor fabrication) that can support different impurities. In the first case, changing tools involves removing and replacing cutters, and calibration of the new tools. In the second, the chamber must be cleaned. These activities are time-consuming, and must not be done too often.

Let i be a resource and j an activity. Define $\gamma_{ij}(t)$ to be the *activity state* of Resource i. This is a binary variable which is 1 if Resource i is occupied by Activity j at time t, and 0 otherwise. This notation is a generalization of α (except that now $\gamma_{ij}(t) = 1$ means that Activity j is taking place at Resource i, and if that activity is a failure, it means that Machine i is down. Earlier, $\alpha_i(t) = 1$ means that Machine i is up.).

For many resources and activities, only one activity may be present at the resource at any time. For example, at any given time, a machine may be doing an operation on a Type 1 part, or an operation on a Type 2 part, or it may be undergoing a setup change, or it may be under repair, or ..., but not more than one of these at any time. This may be expressed symbolically as

$$\sum_j \gamma_{ij}(t) \leq 1. \tag{10.1}$$

Define $\sigma_{ij}(t)$ to be the *configuration state* of Resource i. This is a binary variable which is 1 if Resource i is configured for Activity j at time t, and 0 otherwise. Assume Resource i is set up for Activity j at time t. Then if it is not performing j at time t, it will be able to perform j when its current activity ends without losing time or incurring other cost for the changeover. Configurations are not exclusive the way activities are. Some resources (like flexible machine tools) can be set up for many activities at the same time.

Activity state $\gamma_{ij}(t)$ can be 1 only if $\sigma_{ij}(t)$ is 1. As a consequence, (10.1) can be made more precise:

$$\sum_{j, \sigma_{ij}(t)=1} \gamma_{ij}(t) \leq 1. \tag{10.2}$$

Here, the summation is only over activities j for which Resource i is configured at time t, that is, over all activities that can be performed with no change of set up.

Every activity has a *frequency* and a *duration*. To define frequency, let $N_{ij}(T)$ be the total number of times that Resource i is occupied by Activity j in $(0, T)$. Then define the *Activity j frequency* (or *rate*) by

$$u_{ij} = \frac{1}{T} N_{ij}(T). \tag{10.3}$$

This is the frequency with which Type j activities occur at Resource i. It satisfies $u_{ij} \geq 0$. If Activity j is a production operation, then u_{ij} is a production rate. However, u_{ij} may also represent the frequency of doing maintenance, changing setups, experiencing failures, etc.

Let T_{ij}^{σ} be the total time that Resource i spends in configurations that allow Activity j. Then we can define the *conditional Activity j rate*,

$$u_{ij}^{\sigma} = \frac{1}{T_{ij}^{\sigma}} N_{ij}(T). \tag{10.4}$$

Let τ_{ij} be the average duration of Activity j at Resource i. It satisfies $\tau_{ij} \geq 0$. Durations may be random or deterministic, but we assume that they are not under the control of the decision-maker.

Observation If the system is ergodic and in steady state,

$$\tau_{ij} u_{ij} = E\gamma_{ij}. \tag{10.5}$$

Proof Consider a sample history of the system. The total time that Resource i is occupied by Activity j in $(0, T)$ is

$$\int_0^T \gamma_{ij}(t)dt. \tag{10.6}$$

The average duration satisfies

$$\tau_{ij} = \frac{\int_0^T \gamma_{ij}(t)dt}{N_{ij}(T)} = \frac{\frac{1}{T}\int_0^T \gamma_{ij}(t)dt}{u_{ij}}. \tag{10.7}$$

If the system is ergodic and in steady state, then the time average of a quantity is the same as its expected value, so the numerator is $E\gamma_{ij}$ and (10.5) is proven. The assumption that the system is in steady state is an important one. In later sections, the dynamics of the system is divided into subsets, each considered over different time scales. Each subset has a different time period which is required for it to reach steady state.

Since the system is in steady state,

$$\text{prob} \, (\sigma_{ij} = 1) = \frac{T_{ij}^{\sigma}}{T}. \tag{10.8}$$

Therefore,

$$u_{ij} = u_{ij}^{\sigma} \text{prob} \, (\sigma_{ij} = 1). \tag{10.9}$$

Note also that

$$E\gamma_{ij} = E(\gamma_{ij} \mid \sigma_{ij} = 1)\text{prob} \, (\sigma_{ij} = 1) \tag{10.10}$$

since $E(\gamma_{ij} \mid \sigma_{ij} = 0) = 0$, so that

$$u_{ij}^\sigma = \frac{E(\gamma_{ij} \mid \sigma_{ij} = 1)}{\tau_{ij}}. \tag{10.11}$$

Since only one activity may occur at a resource at one time, the fraction of Resource i's time that is spent on Activity j is $\tau_{ij}u_{ij}$. This is called the *occupation* of Resource i by Activity j. We can also define $\tau_{ij}u_{ij}^\sigma$ as the *conditional occupation* of i by j, given that it is set up for j. The conditional occupation can be less than 1 if Resource i is flexible and is used for other activities in addition to j.

Example Type 1 parts arrive at Machine 1 at a rate of 1 per hour (u_1). They undergo operations that take 20 minutes (τ_{11}). Therefore Machine 1 is occupied by making Type 1 parts for 1/3 of its time.

10.2.2   Capacity

From (10.1),

$$1 \geq E \sum_j \gamma_{ij}(t) = \sum_j \tau_{ij}u_{ij} \text{ for all resources } i. \tag{10.12}$$

This is the fundamental capacity limitation: no resource can be occupied more than 100% of the time.

Example In addition to the Type 1 parts, we wish to send Type 2 parts to Machine 1 for an operation that takes 25 minutes (τ_{12}). There is a demand of one Type 2 part every 35 minutes (u_2). This is not possible because it violates (10.12).

Equation (10.12) can be sharpened, since activities can only occur while the resource is configured for them. By taking the conditional expectation of (10.1),

$$1 \geq \sum_j E(\gamma_{ij}(t) \mid \sigma_{ij}(t) = 1) = \sum_{j,\sigma_{ij}(t)=1} \tau_{ij}u_{ij}^\sigma \text{ for all resources } i. \tag{10.13}$$

The set of all activity rate matrixes u that satisfies (10.13) is the *capacity set* Ω. It is important to observe that capacity is a set — a polyhedron — and not a scalar. Here we have defined capacity as a constant set. In later sections, capacity is described as a function of the state of the system. This means that *capacity is a stochastic set*.

10.2.3   Frequency separation

Dynamic models always have two parts: a constant part and a time-varying part. In all dynamic models, there is something that is treated as unchanging over time: some parameters, and, most often, the structure of the model. For example, the deterministic processing time transfer line model described in Chapter 3 is a conventional one in which there are static quantities (r_1, p_1, r_2, p_2, N), a static structure, and dynamic quantities (n, α_1, α_2).

Recently, the dichotomy between static and dynamic has been extended to systems with multiple time scales, modeled as differential equations or Markov chains. At one end of the scale, there are quantities that are treated as static. The other variables are divided into groups according to the speed of their dynamics. Because of this grouping, it is possible to simplify the computation of the behavior of these systems. Approximate but reasonably accurate techniques have been developed to calculate the effects of the slower and faster dynamics of adjacent groups on each group of variables.

The essential idea is: when dealing with any dynamic quantity, treat quantities that vary much more slowly as static; and model quantities that vary much faster in a way that ignores the details of their variations. This is the central assumption of the hierarchical decomposition presented here.

Assumption 1   The events and activities can be grouped into sets $\mathcal{L}_1, \mathcal{L}_2, \ldots$ such that for each set $\mathcal{L}_k$, there is a characteristic frequency f_k satisfying

$$0 = f_1 \ll f_2 \ll \ldots \ll f_k \ll f_{k+1} \ll \ldots \tag{10.14}$$

The rates satisfy

$$j \in \mathcal{L}_k \Rightarrow f_{k-1} \ll u_{ij} \ll f_{k+1} \tag{10.15}$$

where u_{ij} is the frequency of event or Activity j at Resource i. This statement means that the activities and events in class $\mathcal{L}_k$ have frequencies that are much closer to each other, and to f_k, than to the frequency of any other activity or event.

Figure 10.2 represents two kinds of production that satisfy this assumption. The horizontal axis represents frequency and the vertical axis represents occupation of some critical resource. Because of Assumption 1, all the event frequencies occur at distinct clusters. For example, note the careful enumeration of frequencies and time scales in Section 9.2.3. The time period over which a component of the system reaches steady state depends on the frequency classes of the activities that affect that component. It is on the order of $1/f_{k-1}$ if the lowest frequency activity is a member of $\mathcal{L}_k$.

A capacity set can be associated with each time scale k. Consequently, *capacity is a* <u>*set*</u> *of stochastic sets.*

We must make another assumption, which is also an extension of one of the assumptions made in Section 9.2.3: that parts spend a short time in the system. This differs from the model assumptions in Chapters 3-6. In Chapter 12 and 13, we bring some of the ideas of Chapters 3-6 together with those of Chapters 9-11, and relax this assumption. To state the assumption formally, let the lowest level of the hierarchy be called Level K, and assume that the activities treated at that level are production operations. Then the order of magnitude of the production rates is f_K. An operation time is roughly $1/f_K$ time units.

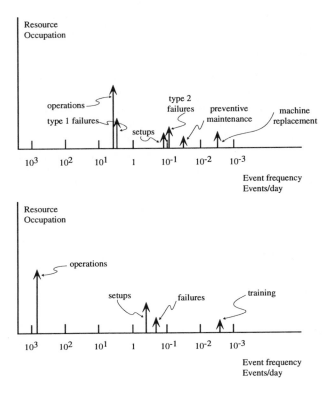

Figure 10.2: Spectrum of Events

Assumption 2   The average amount of time a part spends in the manufacturing system is much less than $1/f_{K-1}$ time units.

In Section 9.2.3, we assumed that the time that a part spent in the system was much less than the mean time between repairs or failures. Here, we generalize this to require that it is much less than whatever event is treated at the next-to-bottom level. The reason for this assumption is that if it is *not* true, there may be a resource that a part will not reach for a very long time compared with $1/f_{K-1}$. Whether or not the resource is available now, we cannot say whether it will be available when the part reaches it. This is because the machine is likely to change state long before it has to process the part. Therefore, there is no reason to develop a feedback law that depends on the state of that machine. We deal with these issues in Chapters 12 and 13.

10.2.4 Slowly varying, piecewise constant rates

In Sections 10.2.1 and 10.2.2, u_{ij} is treated as constant. However, it is convenient to allow u_{ij} to be slowly varying. That is, u_{ij} is not constant, but it changes slowly compared to the changes in γ_{ij}. An important special case is where u_{ij} is piecewise constant, and its changes occur much less often than those of γ_{ij}. This is the situation in Chapter 9. Equation (10.5) is now

$$\tau_{ij} u_{ij}(t) = E\gamma_{ij}(t). \tag{10.16}$$

This is established in the same manner as (10.5), but the bounds of the integral (10.6) are t_1 and t, where t_1 is the time of the most recent change in u_{ij}, and t is the current time. The quantity $u_{ij}(t)$ satisfies

$$N_{ij}(t) = \int_0^t u_{ij}(s)ds \text{ for } \tau_{ij} > 0,$$

or

$$N_{ij}(t) - N_{ij}(t_1) = \int_{t_1}^t u_{ij}(s)ds = (t - t_1)u_{ij}(t_1). \tag{10.17}$$

The assumption here is that many occupations of Resource i by Activity j occur in the interval (t_1, t): enough so that

$$E\gamma_{ij}(t) \approx \frac{1}{t - t_1} \int_{t_1}^t \gamma_{ij}(s)ds. \tag{10.18}$$

10.2.5 Degree of controllability and predictability

Events may or may not be under the control of the decision-maker. For the model constructed here, we say that an event is *controllable* if its time of occurrence may be chosen, whether or not there are constraints on that choice. An event is *uncontrollable* otherwise. An activity is controllable if its initial event is controllable, and it is uncontrollable otherwise. Operations are controllable, for example, and failures are not. Figures 10.3-10.5 represent a variety of activities with different degrees of control. Figure 10.3 shows the two repair states of a machine: operational and down. In this case, the times at which the transitions occur are beyond the control of the production personnel.

Figure 10.4 represents the operation states of a flexible machine. It can work on a family of four parts, and setup is not required. That is, after doing an operation on one part, the time required to do an operation on another part depends only on the new part, and not the identity of the part that preceded it. While the machine is in the idle state, it may be used to do an operation on any of the parts. When to make the transition, and what state to visit next, are entirely at the discretion of the manager. Once that decision has been made, however, the manager loses control. The time required to perform the operation may or may not be known, but it cannot be chosen, and the next state must be the idle state.

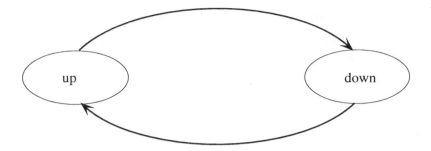

Figure 10.3: Failure and Repair States

Figure 10.5 displays the configuration states of a machine which can do operations on three families of parts. There is a substantial setup time to switch the machine from operations on one family to another. While the system is set up for any one family, it can remain that way indefinitely. The manager can choose when to switch out of the current family and which family to switch into next. However, the system then goes to the appropriate setup state. (While it is there, tools are changed, calibration is performed, test parts are made, etc.) It stays in that state for a length of time which is not under the control of the manager. (Again, it may or may not be known, but it cannot be chosen.) After that, the system goes to the new family state, and the series of events repeats.

We say that an event is *predictable* if it is uncontrollable but its time of occurrence is known in advance. It is *unpredictable* otherwise. We do not distinguish, in the notation developed here, between controllable, uncontrollable, predictable, and unpredictable events. However, the specific formulations of the dynamic programming problems (the hedging point problems) must take this into account.

In formulating our models, we concentrate on activities rather than events that are not activities. Such events include demand changes, for example. When the demand changes, there is certainly an important change in the problems to be solved, but it cannot be represented by an activity occupying a resource. This emphasis reflects the current state of research in this area, and not at all the relative importance of these phenomena.

In Table 10.1, we list a sample of the activities and non-activity events that can be seen in factories. (It is by far not an exhaustive list.) They are classified according to their controllability, their predictability, and whether they are events or activities. This is a rough classification; some of these events or activities may have different characteristics in different factories, and some may be controllable by some people but not by others. Having classified these phenomena this way does not mean that there is no longer any distinction among those that are classified together; they still may have different effects on the production processes.

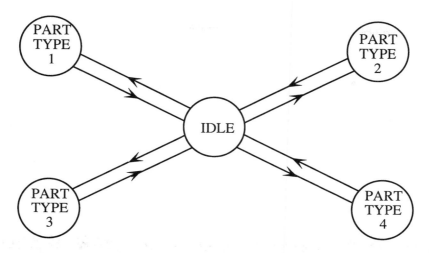

Figure 10.4: Production States

10.2.6 Effects of events

The goal of the factory is to make money by producing material that customers want. The only events that directly further this goal are the production events (operations), and only if they are chosen correctly. The direct effects of all the other events (failures, setups, maintenance, etc.) work against this goal since they take up time at resources and do not produce parts. Some of them are essential and others are inevitable.

When any activity occurs, it prevents all other activities from occurring at the same resource. Thus a low frequency, high occupation activity is a major disturbance to the system. During such an activity, the resource it occupies is unavailable for a very long time (as seen by the high frequency events). This may not simply shut down all production; instead, it may temporarily restrict only some kinds of production. Such disruptions greatly complicate the scheduling problem.

10.2.7 Purpose of the decomposition

It is possible to represent the scheduling problem as an integer program, particularly if time is discretized. (See Section 9.4.2.) However, this almost always leads to a problem which cannot practically be solved even in the absence of random events. Heuristics are often employed, and are sometimes useful for specific cases. The goal of the approach described below is to formulate the problem in a way that will provide a general methodology for developing approximate feedback solutions for stochastic scheduling problems in manufacturing systems.

The solution approach is based on a reformulation of the problem in which the large

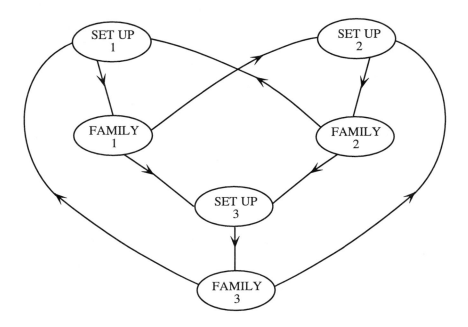

Figure 10.5: Setup States

set of binary variables that indicate the precise times of events is replaced by a small set of real (continuous) variables representing the rates at which events occur. This is a good approximation because of the large differences in frequencies among these events. Eventually, the binary variables are calculated, but by a much simplified procedure (for example, the staircase strategy).

10.2.8   Relationship with earlier chapters

The goals of this chapter are somewhat more general than those of the earlier chapters, and consequently the notation and terminology is a little more abstract.

Failure states   In particular, γ represents the state of any discrete quantity in the factory, and changes in γ represent a broad class of events. Special cases include operations and failures. When γ represents failures, however, its meaning is opposite that of α. That is, α_i is the failure state of Machine i: if $\alpha_i = 0$, Machine i is down, and if $\alpha_i = 1$, Machine i is up. This can also be expressed in γ notation: if j refers to the failure activity, then if $\gamma_{ij} = 1$, the failure activity is taking place at Machine i (that is, the machine is down); if $\gamma_{ij} = 0$, the failure activity is not taking place at Machine i (or, the machine is up). But

A. CONTROLLABLE	B. UNCONTROLLABLE
A.1 ACTIVITIES	**B.1 ACTIVITIES**
operations maintenance setup changes calibration	**B.1.1** *unpredictable* failures repair times worker absence vendor non-delivery starvation blockage **B.1.2** *predictable* holidays, lunch, and other breaks training sessions
A.2 NON-ACTIVITY EVENTS	**B.2 NON-ACTIVITY EVENTS**
acquisition of new equipment	demand changes engineering changes rejection rework

Table 10.1: Examples of Events and Activities

while the same idea is expressed, the notation has been reversed:[2]

$$\gamma_{ij} = 1 - \alpha_i.$$

Durations When j is an operation, τ_{ij} has exactly the same meaning as in Chapter 9. When j is a failure, τ_{ij} is simply the mean time to repair, or

$$\tau_{ij} = \frac{1}{r_i}.$$

Rates When j is an operation, u_{ij} has the same meaning as before: production rate. Consistency requires two subscripts here. It is not necessary to include the machine subscript

---

[2]Usually, the price for greater generality is more complex notation.

in Chapter 9 because — except for Section 9.6.1 — it is assumed that all parts of the same kind go to the same set of machines. (In that section, we have to introduce rate variables that do have complicated subscripts and superscripts.)

When j is a failure, $1/u_{ij}$ is the mean time between failures. If failures are time-dependent,

$$\frac{1}{u_{ij}} = \frac{1}{r_i} + \frac{1}{p_i}.$$

If failures are operation-dependent, it gets a little more complicated.

10.3   The Spectrum and the Hierarchy

In this section, we define the variables of the hierarchy and we describe the purposes of the calculations that take place at each of the levels. In the following sections, we propose problem formulations for those calculations. In Sections 10.3.1 and 10.3.4, we treat a restricted version of the hierarchy: one without configuration changes. Setups are introduced into the hierarchy in Sections 10.3.5 and 10.3.6.

10.3.1   Definitions

Levels, Frequencies, and the Level k Observer   The structure of the hierarchy is based on Assumption 1: that events tend to occur on a discrete spectrum. Classes of events have frequencies that cluster near discrete points on the spectrum. The control hierarchy is tied to the spectrum. Each level k in the hierarchy corresponds to a discrete point on the spectrum and thus to a set of activities. This point is the characteristic frequency f_k (and $1/f_k$ is the characteristic time scale) of those activities.

At each level of the hierarchy, events that correspond to higher levels (lower frequencies, and smaller values of k) can be treated as discrete and constant or slowly varying. Events that correspond to lower levels can be described by continuous (real) variables. These variables can be treated as though they are deterministic.

The approach is to define a set of rate or frequency variables for every activity. These quantities represent the behavior of the system in an aggregated way. At each level, we calculate optimal values for those aggregate variables. Optimal, here, means that they must be close, on the average, to the corresponding values chosen at the higher levels. However, they must respond to events that occur at their own level.

Define the *level* $L(j)$ of Activity j to be the value of k in Assumption 1 associated with this activity. That is,

$$L(j) = k \text{ if } j \in \mathcal{L}_k \tag{10.19}$$

in (10.15). We choose the convention that less frequent activities are higher level activities and have smaller values of k; lower levels have larger values of k.

We introduce the concept of a *Level k observer or manager*. Such an observer has a precise model only of events that occur with frequencies near f_k (in the sense of Assumption 1). In some cases, there is such a model because the observer/manager affects the events. The observer has greatly simplified models of events that occur at frequencies far from f_k.

Quantities that change with much lower frequencies (such as production goals that are selected by higher level managers) are treated as constant. Even after they change, the observer is not able to anticipate future changes. Events that occur with much higher frequencies — such as changes in γ or σ — cannot be distinguished in detail. This observer also cannot see activities whose duration is much less than $1/f_k$.

The Level k observer is able to see frequencies of lower level (higher frequency) events, and may even have a model of how the frequencies change. However, changes in the frequencies are themselves events. For a Level k observer to have a precise model of changes in higher frequencies, the changes must occur at frequencies near f_k. The hedging point problem is a method of selecting frequencies of high frequency events.

After the example, we formally define Level k quantities. These are values of system states as perceived by a Level k observer. The frequencies of high frequency events, as seen by this observer, depend on the current states of low frequency activities, and expectations must be conditioned on the current states of low frequency activities. First we present an example to make this concrete.

10.3.2 Example

Consider a system in which there are two machines that work in parallel performing operations on a single part type. Each machine is maintained four times per year (and is down a full week each time); failures happen roughly once per week (and occupy 8% of each machine's time while it is not undergoing maintenance); and operations take one hour. The system is run 24 hours per day.

A hierarchy can be constructed with long range planning at Level 1, maintenance at Level 2, failures at Level 3, and operations at Level 4. See Figure 10.6. The Level 1 manager chooses long range average maintenance frequencies and operation rates (the former in accordance with the instructions of the manufacturer of the machines or according to the company's own studies on the relationship between preventative maintenance and reliability; the latter to satisfy long range demand forecasts). This manufacturing system is capable of producing 1.754 parts per hour, in the long run (because one machine is available 8 weeks out of 52, and two machines are available 44 weeks out of 52, and each machine works 95% of the time it is available).

The activity states are γ_{ij}, where i = machine number = 1 or 2; and j = activity number. Maintenance is $j = 1; j = 2$ is failure; $j = 3$ is production operation.

Level 1 The Level 1 capacity set Ω^1 is the set of all Level 1 rates, the set of all u_{13}^1 and u_{23}^1 such that

$$0 \leq u_{13}^1 \leq .877; \qquad 0 \leq u_{23}^1 \leq .877$$

Assume that the long range demand rate is $u_{13}^1 + u_{23}^1 = 1.6$ parts per hour.

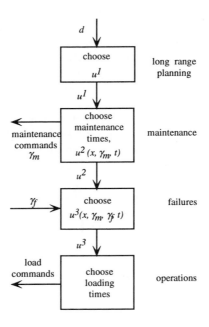

Figure 10.6: Hierarchy for Example System

Level 2 The Level 2 manager selects and announces the actual times to perform maintenance, and calculates the production rates $u_{i3}^2(\gamma_{11}, \gamma_{21})$ during the periods that the system is in each maintenance state. For example, the Level 2 manager selects u_{13}^2 (0,0), the Level 2 production rate of Machine 1 while neither machine is being maintained. Here, a Level 2 rate means that the effects of Level 3 events (failures and repairs) are averaged out. The capacity sets $\Omega^2(\gamma_{11}, \gamma_{21})$ are

$$0 \leq u_{13}^2(0,0) \leq .95 \qquad\qquad 0 \leq u_{23}^2(0,0) \leq .95$$
$$0 \leq u_{13}^2(0,1) \leq .95 \qquad\qquad 0 \leq u_{23}^2(1,0) \leq .95$$
$$0 = u_{13}^2(1,0) \qquad\qquad\qquad 0 = u_{23}^2(0,1)$$
$$0 = u_{13}^2(1,1) \qquad\qquad\qquad 0 = u_{23}^2(1,1)$$

A possible set of production rates is: the system will produce $u_{13}^2 = (0,1) = u_{23}^2(1,0) = .9$ parts per hour during periods while one machine is undergoing maintenance, and $u_{23}^2(0,0) = .864$ parts per hour ($i = 1, 2$) during periods while no machine is undergoing maintenance. The average production rates are $u_{13}^1 = u_{23}^1 = (0,0) = .8$, since both machines are available for 44/52 of the time, Machine 1 is available and Machine 2 is being maintained for 4/52 of the time, and Machine 2 is available and Machine 1 is being maintained for 4/52 of the time.

Note that this manager is only concerned with the average effects of failures, but is concerned with the actual maintenance states.

Level 3   The Level 3 manager must choose production rates $u_{i3}^3(\gamma_{11}, \gamma_{21}, \gamma_{12}, \gamma_{22})$ for each maintenance state and each failure state. The targets are $u_{i3}^2(\gamma_{11}, \gamma_{21})$. Now the capacity sets $\Omega^3(\gamma_{11}, \gamma_{21}, \gamma_{12}, \gamma_{22})$ are $(i = 1, 2)$:

$0 = u_{i3}^3(0, 1, 1, 0)$	(Machine 2 being maintained; Machine 1 under repair)
$0 = u_{i3}^3(1, 0, 0, 1)$	(Machine 1 being maintained; Machine 2 under repair)
$0 \le u_{13}^3(0, 1, 0, 0) \le 1$	(Machine 2 being maintained; neither machine under repair)
$0 = u_{23}^3(0, 1, 0, 0)$	(Machine 2 being maintained; neither machine under repair)
$0 = u_{13}^3(1, 0, 0, 0)$	(Machine 1 being maintained; neither machine under repair)
$0 \le u_{23}^3(1, 0, 0, 0) \le 1$	(Machine 1 being maintained; neither machine under repair)
$0 = u_{i3}^3(0, 0, 1, 1)$	(neither machine being maintained; both machines under repair)
$0 \le u_{13}^3(0, 0, 0, 1) \le 1$	(neither machine being maintained; Machine 2 under repair)
$0 = u_{23}^3(0, 0, 0, 1)$	(neither machine being maintained; Machine 2 under repair)
$0 = u_{13}^3(0, 0, 1, 0)$	(neither machine being maintained; Machine 1 under repair)
$0 \le u_{23}^3(0, 0, 1, 0) \le 1$	(neither machine being maintained; Machine 1 under repair)
$0 \le u_{i3}^3(0, 0, 0, 0) \le 1$	(neither machine being maintained or under repair)

A set of feasible rates is $(i = 1, 2)$:

$$
\begin{aligned}
&u_{i3}^3(0, 1, 1, 0) = 0 \qquad && u_{i3}^3(0, 0, 1, 1) = 0 \\
&u_{i3}^3(1, 0, 0, 1) = 0 \qquad && u_{13}^3(0, 0, 0, 1) = .909 \\
&u_{13}^3(0, 1, 0, 0) = .947 \qquad && u_{23}^3(0, 0, 0, 1) = 0 \\
&u_{23}^3(0, 1, 0, 0) = 0 \qquad && u_{13}^3(0, 0, 1, 0) = 0 \\
&u_{13}^3(1, 0, 0, 0) = 0 \qquad && u_{23}^3(0, 0, 1, 0) = .909 \\
&u_{23}^3(1, 0, 0, 0) = .947 \qquad && u_{i3}^3(0, 0, 0, 0) = .909
\end{aligned}
$$

The average of the Level 3 production rates of all the states in which $(\gamma_{13}, \gamma_{23}) = (0, 1)$ are $u_{13}^2(0, 1) = .9$ (since Machine 1 is down with probability .05 and up with probability .95), and $u_{23}^2(0, 1) = .0$. Similarly, the average production rates of the states in which $(\gamma_{13}, \gamma_{23}) = (1, 0)$ are $u_{23}^2(1, 0) = .9$ and $u_{13}^2(1, 0) = .0$. The other averages of Level 3 production rates are the corresponding Level 2 quantities.

The Level 3 quantities are chosen so that their expectations are the corresponding Level 2 quantities, and the Level 2 quantities are chosen so that their expectations are the corresponding Level 1 quantities. These are conditional expectation relationships, and they are generalized below. The hedging point policy is a more sophisticated choice of lower level rates that satisfy the upper level expectations, and is described in detail in Chapter 9. This policy allows the rates to depend on the amount of material produced, as well as the states of the machines.

Level 4   The task of the Level 4 manager (or worker, or material handling system) is to load parts onto the machines (that is, to choose γ_{i3}) to meet the last set of rates. The staircase policy, which is described in Section 9.4, is one possible way of doing this. Whenever the number of Type j parts loaded on Machine i is less than the time integral of u_{ij}^3, and there are no impediments (such as the machine being occupied), a new part is loaded. If there are impediments, wait until they are cleared.

10.3.3   Level k states and rates

In this section, we develop the capacity sets at each level of a hierarchy, and the relationships among rates at each level. In later sections, we will describe how to calculate $u^k(\gamma, \sigma)$ (the hedging point strategy) and how to determine times for discrete events (such as maintenance at Level 2 and loading of parts at Level 4).

Let $\gamma_{ij}^k(t)$ be the *Level k activity state of Resource i*. This is defined, only for activities j whose level is k or higher, as

$$\gamma_{ij}^k(t) = \gamma_{ij}(t) \text{ for } L(j) \le k. \tag{10.20}$$

Define γ^k as the matrix whose components are γ_{ij}^k. Its dimensionality depends on k. It is the low frequency part of γ, whose components change at frequencies much less than, or roughly equal to f_k. It is the only part of γ accessible to a Level k observer.

In the example,

$$\gamma^2 = \left[\begin{array}{c} \gamma_{11} \\ \gamma_{21} \end{array} \right]$$

$$\gamma^3 = \left[\begin{array}{cc} \gamma_{11} & \gamma_{12} \\ \gamma_{21} & \gamma_{22} \end{array} \right]$$

Let E_k be the *Level k expectation operator*. It is the conditional expectation, given that all Level m quantities $(\gamma_{ij}^m(t), m \le k)$ remain constant at their values at time t. That is, for any random variable z,

$$E_k z(t) = E(z \mid \gamma_{ij}^m = \gamma_{ij}^m(t), \text{ for all } i, j, \text{ such that } L(j) \le m \le k). \tag{10.21}$$

This is a Level k quantity because it is a function of γ^k. Its frequency of variation is roughly f_k.

Let u_{ij}^k be the *Level k rate of Activity j* at Resource i. It is defined only if the level of Activity j is lower than k, that is, $L(j) > k$. This is a representation of the high frequency part of γ that makes sense to the Level k observer. The Level k rate of Activity j is the frequency that a Level k observer would measure that Activity j occurs while all Level m events $(m \leq k)$ are held constant at their current values. This rate is defined as

$$u_{ij}^k(t) = \frac{E_k \gamma_{ij}(t)}{\tau_{ij}} \text{ for } L(j) > k. \tag{10.22}$$

Note that

$$u_{ij}^k(t) \geq 0. \tag{10.23}$$

It is important to note that u^k is a function of the current value of γ^k, the Level k activity state. Thus, u^k is a stochastic process. In the example, u^1 is a constant, u^2 is a function of γ^2, and u^3 is a function of γ^3.

The conditioning event of E_k is a subset of that of E_{k-1}. This is because the set of quantities held constant for E_{k-1} is a subset of that for E_k. Consequently,

$$E_{k-1}\left(E_k \gamma_{ij}\right) = E_{k-1}\gamma_{ij}. \tag{10.24}$$

Taking the Level $k-1$ expectation of (10.22),

$$E_{k-1}u_{ij}^k = E_{k-1}\frac{E_k \gamma_{ij}(t)}{\tau_{ij}}. \tag{10.25}$$

But this is equal to $\dfrac{E_{k-1}\gamma_{ij}(t)}{\tau_{ij}}$ according to (10.24). This implies that

$$E_{k-1}u_{ij}^k = u_{ij}^{k-1}. \tag{10.26}$$

That is, the Level $k-1$ rate of an activity is the Level $k-1$ expectation of the Level k rate of the activity. This is a very important observation, because it relates quantities at different levels of the hierarchy.

In the example, (10.26) is satisfied by all rates. In particular,

$$E_1 u_{13}^2 = \frac{4}{52}u_{13}^2(0,1) + \frac{4}{52}u_{13}^2(1,0) + \frac{44}{52}u_{13}^2(0,0) = .8 = u_{13}^1$$

$$E_2 u_{13}^3(t_1) = (.05)u_{13}^3(0,1,1,0) + (.95)u_{13}^3(0,1,0,0) = .9 = u_{13}^2(0,1)$$

where t_1 is any time that $\gamma_{11} = 0$ and $\gamma_{21} = 1$.

Recall that the rate matrix u_{ij}^k is defined only for $L(j) > k$. Therefore the dimensionality of u^k is generally smaller than that of u^{k-1}. Another way of writing (10.26) is

$$E_{k-1}u^k = \text{ proj } (u^{k-1}, k), \tag{10.27}$$

where proj (z, k) is the projection of vector z onto the space of u^k. The vector u^{k-1} has more components than u^k because it includes the rates of activities which are discrete at Level k. The proj operator removes them.

If $L(j) > k$, Level k of the hierarchy calculates u_{ij}^k. How that calculation is performed depends on the degree of control of Activity j. If Activity j can be initiated by the decision-maker rather than by nature, then u_{ij}^k is chosen to satisfy (10.26).

All activities j appear in three different guises in the hierarchy.

- At their own level ($k = L(j)$), they appear as pairs of discrete events (the start and the end of the activity). This is, of course, exactly what they are. No approximate representation is possible.

- At higher levels in the hierarchy ($k < L(j)$), however, their details are ignored, and they are represented by rates (u_{ij}^k).

- At lower levels ($k > L(j)$), they are treated as constant at their current values.

If $k = L(j) - 1$, then

$$u_{ij}^{L(j)-1} = \frac{E_{L(j)-1}\gamma_{ij}}{\tau_{ij}}. \tag{10.28}$$

This is the interface between discrete and continuous. For both control and data processing, this equation expresses the lowest level relationship between rates and discrete events.

Controllable activities are chosen from top down. That is, a rate u_{ij}^1 is chosen initially. Then ($k > 1$) is chosen to satisfy (10.26) and other conditions (according to the hedging point strategy of Chapter 9) for increasing values of k until $k = L(j)$. At that point, γ_{ij} is chosen to satisfy (10.28) according to the staircase strategy.

On the other hand, (10.28) and (10.26) have different interpretations when Activity j is not controllable (for example, machine failures). In that case, the expectations are statistical operations, in which data are collected and sample means are found. The rate $u_j^{L(j)-1}$ is calculated from (10.28) by observing the values of γ_{ij}. If $L(j) < k - 1$, (10.26) is repeated for decreasing values of k.

10.3.4   Capacity in the hierarchy

For each k, the sum in (10.1) can be broken into two parts:

$$\sum_{j,L(j)>k} \gamma_{ij} \leq 1 - \sum_{j,L(j)\leq k} \gamma_{ij}^k \tag{10.29}$$

in which (10.20) is applied to the high-level sum on the right side. If we take a Level k expectation of (10.29), the right side is not affected. From (10.22),

$$\sum_{j,L(j)>k} \tau_{ij} u_{ij}^k \leq 1 - \sum_{j,L(j)\leq k} \gamma_{ij}^k. \tag{10.30}$$

This equation is the basic statement of capacity in the hierarchy. It limits the rates at which lower level events can occur as a function of the current states of higher level events. If any high level activity is currently at Resource i, that resource is not available for any low level events. In that case, the right side of (10.30) is 0 and all u_{ij}^k that have a positive coefficient must be zero. If none of the higher level activities in (10.30) are currently taking place, this inequality becomes

$$\sum_{j, L(j) > k} \tau_{ij} u_{ij}^k \leq 1. \tag{10.31}$$

In the example, the feasible set of values for u^k was exhibited as a function of γ^k.

Capacity is thus a function of hierarchy level and, since it depends on the state of the system, a stochastic function of time. We define the *Level k capacity set* as

$$\Omega^k(\gamma^k) = \left\{ u^k \,\middle|\, \sum_{j, L(j) > k} \tau_{ij} u_{ij}^k \leq 1 - \sum_{j, L(j) \leq k} \gamma_{ij}^k \;\; \forall i; \;\; u_{ij}^k \geq 0 \;\; \forall j, L(j) > k \right\}, \tag{10.32}$$

the set of positive rates that satisfy (10.30).

This set is the constraint on the hedging point strategy (Chapter 9). It limits the choice of rates u^k as a function of the current state of the system. Note that the condition

$$u^k \in \Omega^k(\gamma^k) \tag{10.33}$$

is a necessary but not sufficient condition. That is, $\Omega^k(\gamma^k)$ was constructed so that every sequence of events must satisfy (10.33). However, we have not demonstrated that for every u^k that satisfies (10.33) there corresponds a feasible sequence of events. We assume sufficiency in the following, however. See Lasserre (1992).

The configuration state is added to the definition of the capacity set in Section 10.3.6.

10.3.5   Setups in the hierarchy

Setups, or configuration changes, are special activities. They are distinctive in that after a setup is performed, the set of activities that can occur is changed. Note also that σ can be changed only after some specific activity (a setup change) is performed. The purpose of this section is to establish how setups are viewed by observers at different levels, and to describe the effects of setup changes on different levels' capacity. The scheduling of setup changes is discussed in Chapter 11.

To incorporate setups in the hierarchy, we make the following observations:

1. Changes of setup are activities that share many characteristics with other activities, such as operations. Thus, while the setup of a machine is being changed, the machine cannot be occupied by any other activity (that is, it cannot be used to perform operations, it cannot undergo maintenance, and it is fair to assume that it cannot fail). Symbolically, changing Resource i from being able to perform Activity j_1 to being able to perform Activity j_2 is itself an Activity j_3; and j_1, j_2, and j_3 are among the values of j that appear in (10.1).

2. Since changes of setups are activities, they have frequencies. Therefore, setup changes appear at appropriate levels in the hierarchy. If there were only one kind of setup change, the system would look very different above the setup change level than below.

(a) Above this level, changes of setup could not be observed because they occur too frequently, and they take too little time to do. The observer would be aware that there is an activity called "changing setups," but it would only know its frequency and not the precise time when any setup change occurs. Since changes in setup occur at great speed, the system would appear *always* to be set up for *all* activities.

(b) Below the level of setup changes, the system would appear to be always, or never, set up for each activity.

3. More generally, there may be many different setup changes, and they may appear at different hierarchy levels. For example, there may be major and minor setups, in which changes among broad classes of parts are done infrequently, and changes within the classes occur frequently.

Assume $L(j) > k$. Let σ_{ij}^k be the *Level k configuration state*. It is given by

$$\sigma_{ij}^k(t) = \begin{cases} 1 \text{ if Activity } j \text{ can be performed at Resource } i \text{ before time } t + \delta \\ 0 \text{ otherwise} \end{cases} \quad (10.34)$$

where $\delta \ll \frac{1}{f_k}$.

Observation   If $\sigma_{ij}^k(t) = 1$, then $\sigma_{ij}^{k-1}(t) = 1$.

Proof   Since $\sigma_{ij}^k = 1$, Activity j can be initiated at Resource i before time $t + \delta$, where $\delta \ll 1/f_k$. But $1/f_k \ll 1/f_{k-1}$. Therefore, Activity j can be initiated at Resource i before time $t + \delta$, where $\delta \ll 1/f_{k-1}$, so $\sigma_{ij}^{k-1} = 1$.

Similarly, if $\sigma_{ij}(t) = 1$, then $\sigma_{ij}^k(t) = 1$. Recall that γ and σ without superscripts refer to the true activity and configuration states. More generally, if $\sigma_{ij}^k(t) = 1$, then $\sigma_{ij}^\ell(t) = 1$, for all $\ell < k$.

We must extend the definition of Level k expectation to include σ:

$$E_k z(t) = E(z \mid \gamma_{ij}^m = \gamma_{ij}^m(t), \sigma_{ij}^m = \sigma_{ij}^m(t), \text{ for all } i, j, \text{ such that } L(j) \le m \le k). \quad (10.35)$$

Using this definition of E_k, we still use (10.22) to define u^k. Thus, u^k is now a function of the current Level k setup (σ^k) as well as the current Level k activity state (γ^k).

Define the *Level k conditional activity rate*,

$$u_{ij}^{\sigma k} = \frac{E_k(\gamma_{ij} \mid \sigma_{ij}^k = 1)}{\tau_{ij}} \text{ if } L(j) > k. \quad (10.36)$$

This is the frequency at which Resource i performs Type j activities during the time that it is configured for that activity at Level k.

By the same reasoning that led to (10.9),

$$u_{ij}^k = u_{ij}^{\sigma k} \text{prob} \, (\sigma_{ij}^k = 1). \quad (10.37)$$

10.3.6 Capacity and setups in the hierarchy

If $L(j) > k$, then

$$\sigma_{ij}^k = 0 \Rightarrow \gamma_{ij}^k = 0 \text{ and } u_{ij}^k = 0.$$

If we take a Level k expectation of (10.29), we now find, according to (10.35),

$$\sum_{\substack{j,\sigma_{ij}^k=1 \\ L(j)>k}} \tau_{ij} u_{ij}^k \leq 1 - \sum_{j,L(j)\leq k} \gamma_{ij}^k \tag{10.38}$$

We now define the Level k capacity set as

$$\Omega^k(\gamma^k, \sigma^k) = \left\{ u^k \,\middle|\, \sum_{\substack{j,\sigma_{ij}^k=1, \\ L(j)>k}} \tau_{ij} u_{ij}^k \leq 1 - \sum_{j,L(j)\leq k} \gamma_{ij}^k \,\forall i; \right.$$

$$u_{ij}^k \geq 0; \tag{10.39}$$

$$\left. u_{ij}^k = 0 \text{ if } \sigma_{ij}^k = 0 \,\forall i,j, L(j) > k \right\}.$$

This is the set of all positive rates that satisfy (10.38), and for which all the machines are set up at Level k.

We can define the *Level k Flexibility* of the system as the number of part types for which the capacity set $\Omega^k(\gamma^k, \sigma^k)$ allows the production rates to be positive. It is the number of part types that can be produced with the current values of γ^k and σ^k. Flexibility, like capacity, varies with hierarchy level, and thus time scale.

10.4 Control in the Hierarchy

The goal of the hierarchical scheduler is to select a time for each controllable event. This is performed by solving one or two problems at each Level k. We emphasize control: scheduling and planning. Data-gathering and processing is also an important function of the hierarchy, but is not discussed here. The hierarchy is illustrated in Figure 10.7. The two problems are:

Problem 1 Find u_{ij}^k (for all $j, L(j) > k$) satisfying (10.26) and (10.38) (and possibly other conditions). One possible solution is the hedging point strategy.

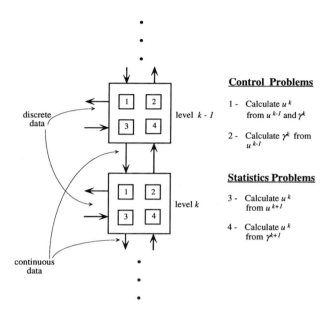

Figure 10.7: Architecture

Problem 2   Find γ_{ij}^k (for all j, $L(j) = k$) satisfying

$$E_{k-1}\gamma_{ij}^k = \tau_{ij}u_{ij}^{k-1} \tag{10.40}$$

(and possibly other conditions). One possible solution is the staircase strategy, although, as we discuss in Chapter 11, it is not appropriate for setups.

At the top level of the hierarchy ($k = 1$), required rates of some of the controllable activities are specified as input data, for example, production rates and maintenance frequencies. Other rates may not be specified, such as setup frequencies. We assume that rates of uncontrollable events are known. The frequency associated with the top level is 0. Consequently, there is no Problem 2 at that level, and Problem 1 reduces to a static optimization to determine the unspecified rates of controllable activities. The function of Problem 1 here is to choose all the rates that are not specified. The vector u^1 is the target rate vector for Level 2.

Recall that at each level of the hierarchy, there exists some activity that can be described as a time-varying set of discrete events. These activities may or may not be controllable. At Level $k > 1$, if there are any controllable activities, we solve Problem 2. (An example is the change in setup of a machine.) Controllable activities are thereby initiated in such a way that their rates of occurrence are close to the target rates that are determined at Level $k - 1$.

Then we solve Problem 1 to determine the Level k rates u_{ij}^k of occurrence of all activities j whose frequencies are much higher than f_k. These rates are refinements of u_{ij}^{k-1}, the target rates determined at Level $k-1$. They differ from the higher level rates in that they are affected by the Level k discrete events. These events, if they are controllable, were chosen by Problem 2 at this level. However, even if the Level k events are not controllable, the Level k rates differ from the higher level rates. These rates are then the targets for Level $k+1$.

For example, if at Level k we choose setup times, the production rates must be calculated so that they are appropriate for the current setup. If we are making Type 1 parts at the rate of 4 per day, but the necessary machine is only set up for that part on Tuesdays, then we must work at a rate of 20 per day on Tuesday and 0 Type 1 parts per day during the rest of the week.

Similarly, the activities associated with Level k may not be controllable, such as machine failures. It is still necessary to refine the production rates. If the overall requirements for Type 1 parts are 20 per day, and the machine is down 10% of the time, *and failures occur several times per day,* then the appropriate strategy is to operate the machine at a rate of 22.2 parts per day while it is up. Note that this only makes sense if failures are much more frequent than setups and much less frequent than operations. If not, related but different calculations must be performed in a different order. That is, a different hierarchy is appropriate.

An important feature of this hierarchy is that rates u_{ij}^k are always chosen to be within the current capacity of the system. When a Level m event occurs $(m \le k)$, the capacity set (10.39) changes. Problem 2 is then re-solved to keep the rates feasible. As mentioned earlier, this is necessary for feasibility. In many simulation experiments, it appeared to be sufficient as well.

10.5 Example

In this section, we describe an example of the hierarchical control of a manufacturing system in which the only important events are operations and failures. We describe the control of a system with operations, setup changes, and failures in Section 11.4.1, but the theory of control of such systems is far less complete.

This example demonstrates the behavior of a system operated according to a hierarchical hedging point policy. When one machine is down, the policy allocates the capacity of the remaining machines to the parts that can be made without it. That is, the policy is *opportunistic.* Also, the policy ignores lower level events while it is responding to higher level events.[3]

---

[3] This feature is not important here because the system is simple, but can have an important impact on the computational effort for complex systems.

10.5.1   System and policy

System   We analyze the system of Figure 10.8. Ten part types are made on three machines. All the parts are first processed on Machine M_1. Part Types 1-5 get second operations on Machine M_2, and Types 6-10 get their second operations on Machine M_3. The operation times for all the part types are .84 time units on Machine M_1, and 1 time unit on Machines M_2 and M_3. For M_1, the MTTF is 900 time units and the MTTR is 100; for M_2 and M_3, the MTTF is 800 and the MTTR is 200. There are homogeneous buffers (buffers that hold only a single part type at a single production stage) upstream of each of the machines. These buffers each have size 1. The demands for all the part types are different. The demand rate for Type j parts is $d_j = .0164j$ parts per time unit. The system is initialized with all machines operational and surpluses equal to 0.

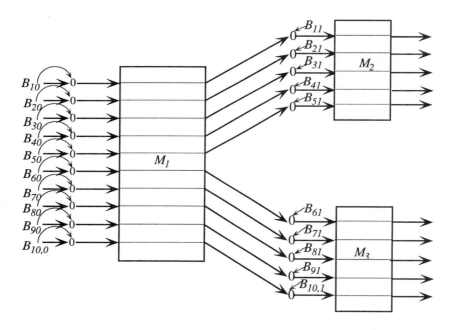

Figure 10.8: Example Manufacturing System

Policy   The policy is divided into three control levels and a top level (Level 1) which passes along the long term demands. The responses to the failures of Machine M_1 are treated by the Level 2 controller and the responses to the failures of Machines M_2 and M_3 are treated by the Level 3 controller. The loading of parts is scheduled by the Level 4 controllers.[4]

---

[4]In fact, since HIERCSIM 3.5 was written for the pyramid-shaped controller of Chapter 13, there are actually three Level 4 controllers, one for each machine. However, because the buffers are small, this

The Level 2 hedging points are all 10 and the Level 3 hedging points are all 5. The cost coefficient matrices (A^k) are all identity matrices.

When M_1 fails, the Level 2 controller adjusts the Level 2 target rates u_j^2 to within the current capacity, which is $u_j^2 = 0$. When M_1 recovers, Level 2 allocates production according to the hedging point policy, as seen at Level 2, as a function of the Level 2 surpluses, x_j^2. If M_1 stays up long enough, all Level 2 surpluses eventually reach their hedging points. Failures of M_2 and M_3 are ignored by this controller.

When M_1 fails, and therefore $u_j^2 = 0$, the Level 3 controller chooses $u_j^3 = 0$. When M_2 fails, the Level 3 controller adjusts the Level 3 target rates u_j^3 to within the current capacity. In particular, $u_j^3 = 0$ for $j = 1, \ldots, 5$. The rest of the target, u_j^3 for $j = 6, \ldots, 10$, is chosen according to the Level 3 surpluses, x_j^3 for $j = 6, \ldots, 10$. Similarly, when M_3 fails, $u_j^3 = 0$ for $j = 6, \ldots, 10$, and u_j^3 for $j = 1, \ldots, 5$, is chosen as a function of x_j^3 for $j = 1, \ldots, 5$.

10.5.2 Results

Overall performance   The system was simulated for 5000 time units using HIERCSIM 3.5 (Violette, 1993). Over this period, the production of each part type was equal to its demand plus its hedging points. For example, the total demand for Type 1 parts was $(5000)(.16)=80$ and the sum of the Level 2 and Level 3 hedging points was 15. The total production was 96. Figure 10.9 shows the Levels 1, 2, and 3 production targets of the Type 1 parts during $[0, 5000]$. The actual production, from Level 4, is indistinguishable from Level 3 at this resolution.

Because the buffers were small, the in-process inventory was small. Cycle times were short on the average, and only large when a part was caught in the system by a machine failure.

Short-term behavior

1. *Why some hedging points are not reached by time 600*   Figures 10.10-10.12 display the performance of the system in more detail, during the interval from 200 time units to 600 time units. By time 5000, the production of Part Type j, for each j, was almost exactly equal to $Z_j^2 + Z_j^3 + 5000d_j$, the sum of the Level 2 and Level 3 hedging points and the demand rate for that part times 5000. However, production had not reached $Z_j^2 + Z_j^3 + 600d_j$ by time 600. This was because M_1 was down for 68.4 time units between time 0 and time 600.

   For the system to reach its Level 2 and Level 3 hedging points by time 600, it would have had to produce a total of $600(d_1 + \ldots + d_{10})=641.2$ parts. Since operations on Machine M_1 require .84 time units, this much production would have required at least 538.6 time units at that machine. This time plus the failure time of M_1 adds up to more than 600 time units, and this is why the hedging point could not possibly have been reached by time 600 in this run of the simulation. In fact, the situation was

difference is not important to the simulation results.

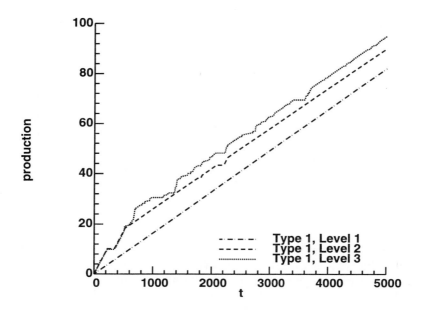

Figure 10.9: Type 1 Production Targets — [0, 5000]

probably worse than this. All 10 internal buffers were likely to be full most of the time that all three machines were operational. Consequently, M_1 was idle for a substantial amount of time when it was not down.

2. *Why hedging points for Types 1-5 are reached at time 600* This system is not well-balanced. Machine M_3 is much busier than M_2 because it must produce the high-volume parts, but it is not faster than M_2. As a consequence of the low demands that Part Types 1-5 place on M_1 and M_2, the system can reach the hedging points for those parts more quickly than those of the other part types.

3. *Level 2 behavior* Figure 10.10 shows the production targets and actual production (Level 4) for Type 1 parts during [200, 600]. During this run of the simulation, Machine M_1 failed at time 224.7. It was repaired at time 293.0, but Type 1 parts were not scheduled by the Level 2 controller until much later. (The reason for this is discussed in Item 5 below.) Type 1's Level 2 hedging point is reached after time 500, and the Level 2 target production line is parallel with the demand (Level 1) line.

4. *Level 3 behavior* Level 3 is more interesting. In Figure 10.10, when the Level 2 line is flat, the Level 3 line is flat also. However, Machine M_2 was down from 366.7 to 376.7, so no Type 1 production took place then. This was beneath the notice of the Level 2

controller, but Level 3 had to respond to it. Notice that the Level 3 controller decrees that production must be stepped up for a short time after the repair so as to meet the Level 2 target plus the Level 3 hedging point.

In this simulation run, the Level 3 production rate of Type 1 jumped at time 504.7, dropped to a very low value at time 518.0, and then returned to the same pace as before. Why should this happen?[5]

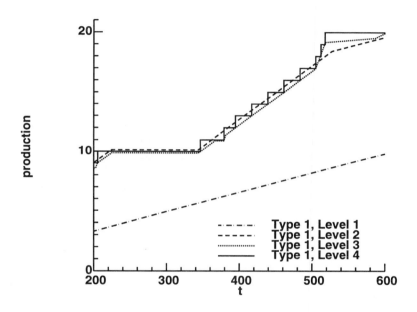

Figure 10.10: Type 1 Production and Targets — [200, 600]

5. *A simple explanation of Level 2 behavior* Figure 10.11 shows the Level 2 production targets for all ten part types. The Part 1 line is the lowest; Part 2 is next; and so forth up to Part 10. (The Part 6 line is dotted so it will be more easily distinguished from the Part 5 line.)

Recall that M_1 failed from time 224.7 to 293.0, and this attracted the attention of the Level 2 controller. This figure seems to show that production resumed immediately for Types 5 and 10 parts, and later for the other parts.

It is not hard to understand why the controller would want to produce Type 10s as soon as possible. Since the demand for Type 10 is the largest, the Type 10 surplus x_{10}^2 is likely to be most negative. But why does it produce Type 5s immediately, when the demand for Types 6-9 are all greater?

---

[5]See Item 6.

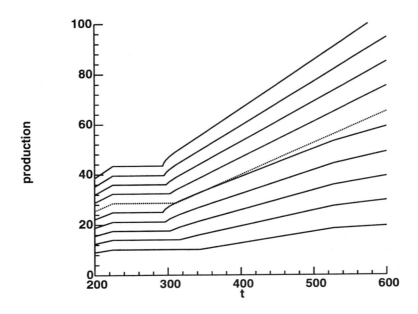

Figure 10.11: Level 2 Production Targets, all Part Types — [200, 600]

The reason is that Buffers B_{61}-$B_{10,1}$ are all full because M_1 can put parts in them faster than M_3 can take them out. These buffers were probably full before the failure. In addition, M_1 does not have to work full time to produce enough parts to keep M_3 fully occupied. The time that M_1 is not devoting to Types 6-10 is available for Types 1-5. Of those parts, the Type 5 surplus is most negative, so Type 5 parts get the capacity before Types 1-4.

Consequently, the Level 2 production policy appears to be an extension of the policy of Example 3 of Chapter 9. The policy is:

- Among Types 6-10, produce the part whose surplus is furthest behind its hedging point (usually Type 10 immediately after a failure).

- When two part types are tied for this distinction, produce them both in such a way as to keep their surpluses equally far behind.

- Continue until all surpluses are equally far behind their hedging points, and then bring them to the hedging points together and keep them there.

- This will keep M_3 fully loaded, but will leave M_1 with time available. During such time, produce Types 1-5, and follow the same strategy as above for them.

This explains why Types 5 and 10 are produced before the others, and why Type 1s are not produced until long after the repair.

6. *Level 3 response to failures*   During [200, 600], M_2 failed at time 366.7 and was repaired at time 376.7; and M_3 failed at time 504.7 and was repaired at time 518.0. Figure 10.12 indicates that Types 1-5 were not produced during [366.7, 376.7]. This is because these parts need M_2. Consequently, Machine M_1 did not have any of its time allocated to those parts during that period, and it was able to make more Type 6-10 parts than usual. This is why the Types 1-5 lines are flat and the Types 6-10 lines are steeper than usual during [366.7, 376.7]. However, this effect is small because the time period is short, and because not much M_1 capacity is freed up by not producing Types 1-5.

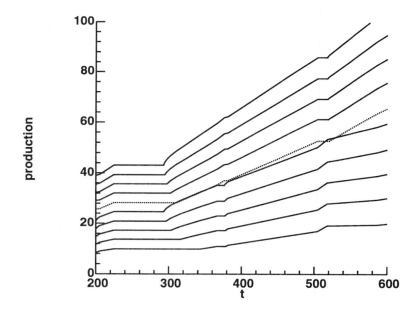

Figure 10.12: Level 3 Production Targets, all Part Types — [200, 600]

The opposite happened during [504.7, 518.0] when M_3 was down. Now Types 6-10 could not be produced, and M_1 was free to devote much more of its time to Types 1-5. The effect is much more pronounced because the time period is a little longer, and because a great deal of capacity was made available in this way. After the repair of M_3 was complete, the Level 3 controller slowed down the production of Types 1-5 to try to bring Types 6-10 to their hedging points as soon as possible. This shows the opportunistic nature of this scheduler.

For descriptions of other simulations of this hierarchical controller, see Violette (1993) and Violette and Gershwin (1991).

10.6   Summary and Conclusions

10.6.1   Overview of results

The purpose of this chapter has been to generalize the special theory that is presented in Chapter 9. The formulation in Chapter 9 is appropriate only for systems in which the only events and phenomena are operations and failures and repairs. There are no provisions for other events or activities like setups or maintenance, and material handling issues — such as buffers being empty or full, inventory costs, and delays — are assumed away.

In this chapter, we have taken a step to overcome one of these limitations. We have developed a framework to deal with other events and activities (in a system in which the material handling questions are still ignored). This framework is based on the observation that in many systems, different kinds of events tend to occur at widely different frequencies, and taking advantage of it leads to a hierarchical decomposition of scheduling computations. The building blocks of the hierarchy are generic (although they are not yet all available), but how they are put together is specific to each factory.

The simulation results indicate that the method works well for the small system of Section 10.5. The total amount of material produced was close to that which was required, and the maximum deviation from the nominal production trajectory was not large. Similar results have been demonstrated elsewhere (Darakananda, 1989; Xie, 1989; Violette, 1993).

Section 10.5 has shown that the structure of the hierarchy is dependent on the parameters of the system. The structure cannot be completely determined without first executing the top level. In more complex cases, the lower level structure can depend on higher level events. That is, the hierarchy structure may prove to be dynamic. This may be a problem if it requires excessively complex computer programs.

10.6.2   State of knowledge

Chapter 9 can be thought of as furnishing two of the modules of the hierarchy: the hedging point strategy for responding to failures, and the staircase structure for loading parts. In Chapter 11, we describe some recent work on the setup change module. Many more modules are needed, for example for maintenance, for yield failures, and for demand changes.

In Chapters 12 and 13, we take a step toward the further generalization of the hierarchy: to incorporate the inventory issue; that is, to relax Assumption 2 (Section 10.2.3) and allow parts to spend a long time in the system. This is a fact of life in most existing factories. It means that we must define a concept of space in a factory, and allow scheduling decisions to depend only on appropriately local events.

Bibliography

[1] P. Afentakis, B. Gavish, U. Karmarkar (1984), "Computationally Efficient Optimal Solutions to the Lot-Sizing Problem in Multi-stage Assembly Systems," Management Science, Vol. 30, No. 2, February, 1984, pp. 222-239.

[2] R. Akella, Y. F. Choong, and S. B. Gershwin (1984), "Performance of Hierarchical Production Scheduling Policy," *IEEE Transactions on Components, Hybrids, and Manufacturing Technology*, Vol. CHMT-7, No. 3, September, 1984.

[3] R. Akella and P. R. Kumar (1986), "Optimal Control of Production Rate in a Failure Prone Manufacturing System", *IEEE Transactions on Automatic Control*, Vol. AC-31, No. 2, pp. 116-126, February, 1986.

[4] R. N. Anthony (1965), *Planning and Control Systems: A Framework for Analysis*, Harvard University, 1965.

[5] G. R. Bitran, E. A. Haas, and A. C. Hax (1981), "Hierarchical Production Planning: A Single-Stage System," *Operations Research*, Vol. 29, No. 4, July-August, 1981, pp. 717-743.

[6] C. A. Caromicoli (1987), "Time Scale Analysis Techniques for Flexible Manufacturing Systems," MIT EECS Master of Science Thesis, MIT Laboratory for Information and Decision Systems Report LIDS-TH-1725, December, 1987.

[7] C. A. Caromicoli, A. S. Willsky, and S. B. Gershwin (1987), "Multiple Time Scale Analysis Techniques of Manufacturing Systems," MIT Laboratory for Information and Decision Systems Report LIDS-TH-1727, December, 1987.

[8] C. A. Caromicoli, A. S. Willsky, and S. B. Gershwin (1988), "Multiple Time Scale Analysis of Manufacturing Systems," Analysis and Optimization of Systems, Proceedings of the Eighth International Conference on Analysis and Optimization of Systems, Antibes, France, June, 1988, 12 pages.

[9] Y. F. Choong (1988), "Flow Control Approach for Batch Production Scheduling with Random Demand," MIT Ph.D. Thesis, MIT Laboratory for Manufacturing and Productivity Report LMP-88-010, May, 1988.

[10] B. Darakananda (1989), "Simulation of Manufacturing Process Under a Hierarchical Control Algorithm," MIT Master's Thesis, EECS, May, 1989.

[11] F. Delebecque, J. P. Quadrat, and P. V. Kokotovic (1984), "A Unified View of Aggregation and Coherency in Networks and Markov Chains," *International Journal of Control*, Vol. 40, No. 5, November, 1984.

[12] M. A. H. Dempster, M. L. Fisher, L. Jansen, B. J. Lageweg, J. K. Lenstra, and A. H. G. and Rinnooy Kan, (1981), "Analytical Evaluation of Hierarchical Planning Systems," *Operations Research*, Vol. 29, No. 4, July-August, 1981, pp. 707-716.

[13] S. B. Gershwin (1986), "Stochastic Scheduling and Setups in a Flexible Manufacturing System," in *Proceedings of the Second ORSA/TIMS Conference on Flexible Manufacturing Systems*, Ann Arbor, MI, August, 1986, pp. 431-442.

[14] S. B. Gershwin (1987a), "A Hierarchical Framework for Discrete Event Scheduling in Manufacturing Systems," in *Discrete Event Systems: Models and Applications*, IIASA Conference, Sopron, Hungary, August 3-7, 1987, Edited by P. Varaiya and A. B. Kurzhanski, Number 103 of the series *Lecture Notes in Control and Information Sciences*, Springer-Verlag.

[15] S. B. Gershwin (1987b), "A Hierarchical Framework for Manufacturing System Scheduling: A Two-Machine Example," *Proceedings of the 26th IEEE Conference on Decision and Control*, Los Angeles, CA, December, 1987.

[16] S. B. Gershwin (1989), "Hierarchical Flow Control: A Framework for Scheduling and Planning Discrete Events in Manufacturing Systems," *Proceedings of the IEEE, Special Issue on Dynamics of Discrete Event Systems*, Vol. 77, No. 1, pp. 195-209, January, 1989.

[17] S. B. Gershwin, M. Caramanis, and P. Murray (1988), "Simulation Experience with a Hierarchical Scheduling Policy for a Simple Manufacturing System," *Proceedings of the 27th IEEE Conference on Decision and Control*, Austin, TX, December, 1988.

[18] S. B. Gershwin, R. Akella, and Y. F. Choong (1985), "Short-Term Production Scheduling of an Automated Manufacturing Facility," *IBM Journal of Research and Development*, Vol. 29, No. 4, pp. 392-400, July, 1985.

[19] S. C. Graves (1981), "A Review of Production Scheduling," *Operations Research*, Vol. 29, No. 4, July-August, 1981, pp. 646-675.

[20] S. C. Graves (1982), "Using Lagrangean Relaxation Techniques to Solve Hierarchical Production Planning Problems," *Management Science*, Vol. 28, No. 3, March, 1982, pp. 260-275.

[21] G. Halevi (1980), *The Role of Computers in Manufacturing Processes*, Wiley, 1980.

[22] A. C. Hax and H. C. Meal (1975), "Hierarchical Integration of Production Planning and Scheduling," *Studies in Management Sciences*, Vol. 1, Logistics, North Holland/TIMS.

[23] K. Hitomi (1979), *Manufacturing Systems Engineering*, Taylor and Francis, 1979.

[24] R. H. F. Jackson and A. W. T. Jones (1986), editors, *Real-Time Optimization in Automated Manufacturing Facilities*, Proceedings of a Symposium Held at the National Bureau of Standards, Gaithersburg, MD, January 21-22, 1986, NBS Special Publication 724.

[25] J. Kimemia and S. B. Gershwin (1983), "An Algorithm for the Computer Control of a Flexible Manufacturing System," *IIE Transactions*, Vol. 15, No. 4, pp. 353-362, December, 1983.

[26] A. Koestler (1967), *The Ghost in the Machine*, Macmillan, 1967.

[27] A. Koestler (1978), *Janus, A Summing Up*, Random House, 1978.

[28] B. J. Lageweg, J. K. Lenstra, and A. H. G. and Rinnooy Kan (1977), "Job-Shop Scheduling by Implicit Enumeration," *Management Science*, Vol. 24, No. 4, December 1977, pp. 441-450.

[29] B. J. Lageweg, J. K. Lenstra, and A. H. G. and Rinnooy Kan (1978), "A General Bounding Scheme for the Permutation Flow-Shop Problem," *Operations Research*, Vol. 26, No. 1, January-February, 1978, pp. 53-67.

[30] J. B. Lasserre (1992), "New Capacity Sets for the Hedging Point Strategy," *International Journal of Production Research*, Vol. 30, No. 12, December, 1992, pp. 2941-2949.

[31] J. Lehoczky, S. Sethi, H. M. Soner, and M. Taksar (1991), "An Asymptotic Analysis of Hierarchical Control of Manufacturing Systems Under Uncertainty," *Mathematics of Operations Research*, Vol. 16, No. 3, August, 1991, pp. 596-608.

[32] C. M. Libosvar (1988a), "Hierarchies in Production Management and Control: A Survey," MIT Laboratory for Information and Decision Systems Report LIDS-P-1734, January, 1988.

[33] C. M. Libosvar (1988b), "Hierarchical Production Management The Flow-Control Layer," Thesis for the degree of Docteur de l'Universite de Metz, April, 1988.

[34] X.-C. Lou, J. G. Van Ryzin and S. B. Gershwin (1987), "Scheduling Job Shops with Delays," in *Proceedings of the 1987 IEEE International Conference on Robotics and Automation*, Raleigh, NC, March-April, 1987.

[35] O. Z. Maimon and S. B. Gershwin (1987), "Dynamic Scheduling and Routing For Flexible Manufacturing Systems that have Unreliable Machines," *Operations Research*, Vol. 36, No. 2, pp. 279-292, March-April, 1988.

[36] O. Z. Maimon and G. Tadmor (1986), "Efficient Low-Level Control of Flexible Manufacturing Systems," MIT Laboratory for Information and Decision Systems Report LIDS-P-1571, June, 1986.

[37] E. F. P. Newson (1975a), "Multi-Item Lot Size Scheduling by Heuristic, Part I: With Fixed Resources," *Management Science*, Vol. 21, No. 10, June, 1975, pp. 1186-1193.

[38] E. F. P. Newson (1975b), "Multi-Item Lot Size Scheduling by Heuristic, Part II: With Variable Resources," *Management Science*, Vol. 21, No. 10, June, 1975, pp. 1194-1203.

[39] J. Orlicky (1975), *Materials Requirements Planning*, McGraw-Hill, 1975.

[40] C. H. Papadimitriou and P. C. Kannelakis (1980), "Flowshop Scheduling with Limited Temporary Storage," *Journal of the ACM*, Vol. 27, No. 3, July, 1980.

[41] J. Perkins and P. R. Kumar (1988), "Stable, Distributed, Real-Time Scheduling of Flexible Manufacturing/Assembly/Disassembly Systems," *Proceedings of the 27th IEEE Conference on Decision and Control*, Austin, TX, December, 1988.

[42] P. J. Ramadge and W. M. Wonham (1985), "Supervisory Control of a Class of Discrete Event Processes," Systems Control Group Report No. 8515, University of Toronto.

[43] R. Rishel (1975), "Dynamic Programming and Minimum Principles for Systems with Jump Markov Disturbances," *SIAM Journal on Control*, Vol. 13, No. 2, February, 1975.

[44] V. R. Saksena, J. O'Reilly, and P. V. Kokotovic (1984), "Singular Perturbations and Time-Scale Methods in Control Theory: Survey 1976-1983," Automatica, Vol. 20, No. 3, May, 1984.

[45] S. P. Sethi and Q. Zhang (1993), "Asymptotic Optimality of Hierarchical Controls in Stochastic Manufacturing Systems: A Review," working paper in preparation, Faculty of Management, University of Toronto, 1993.

[46] S. P. Sethi and Q. Zhang (1994), *Hierarchical Decision Making in Stochastic Manufacturing Systems*, Birkhäuser, 1994.

[47] C. S. Schneeweiss and H. Schroder (1992), "Planning and Scheduling the Repair Shops of the Deutsche Lufthansa AG: A Hierarchical Approach," *Production and Operations Management*, Volume 1, Number 1, Winter, 1992, pp. 22-33.

[48] A. Sharifnia (1988), "Production Control of a Manufacturing System with Multiple Machine States," *IEEE Transactions on Automatic Control*, Vol. AC-33, No. 7, pp. 620-625, July, 1988.

[49] H. M. Soner, J. Lehoczky, S. Sethi, and M. Taksar (1988), "An Asymptotic Analysis of Hierarchical Control of Manufacturing Systems Under Uncertainty," *Proceedings of the 27th IEEE Conference on Decision and Control*, Austin, TX, December, 1988.

[50] J. G. Van Ryzin (1987), "Control of Manufacturing Systems with Delay," MIT EECS Master of Science Thesis, MIT Laboratory for Information and Decision Systems Report LIDS-TH-1676, June, 1987.

[51] J. Violette (1993), "Implementation of a Hierarchical Controller in a Factory Simulation," M.S. Thesis, MIT, Department of Aeronautics and Astronautics, June, 1993.

[52] H. M. Wagner and T. M. Whitin (1958), "Dynamic Version of the Economic Lot Size Model," *Management Science*, Vol. 5, No. 1, October, 1958, pp. 89-96.

[53] X.-L. Xie (1988), "Hierarchical Production Control of a Flexible Manufacturing System," SAGEP Project, INRIA-Lorraine, Vandoeuvre, France.

[54] X.-L. Xie (1989), "Controle Hierarchique d'un Systeme de Production Soumis a Perturbations," Doctoral Thesis, University of Nancy, Nancy, France.

Chapter 11

Setups

11.1 Introduction

Many manufacturing systems can process more than one kind of part. In most, a significant cost in time or money is incurred each time a production resource is set up for the processing of a new part type after it has been used for another type.[1] For example:

- In mechanical parts production, cutting tools often must be changed when part types are changed. If a machine is computer-controlled, the control program usually must be changed. Changing the tools can take a significant amount of time: the old tools are removed, the new tools are inserted, the new tools may have to be calibrated, and some parts may be initially produced that fail inspection.

- In printed circuit board assembly, the components are delivered to insertion or pick-and-place machines on tape on large reels or in long tubes. A set of boards can be made without changing setups from one board to the next if the boards are populated by parts on a set of component feeders that can be mounted together. Whether or not this is possible depends on how similar the boards are, and how many feeders the machine can hold.

- In semiconductor fabrication, certain processing steps, such as ion implantation, require the introduction of chemicals into a chamber. Before the chamber can be used for wafers[2] requiring a new set of chemicals, the previous chemicals must be cleaned

---

[1]This is a good example of the ambiguity of some manufacturing systems terms. Some authors call such systems *flexible* because they are able to work on more than a single part type; other authors call them *inflexible* because of the changeover cost. We offer a possible resolution of this issue in Section 10.3.6 with the concept of *Level k flexibility*. This formalizes the notion that whether a system is considered to be flexible or not depends on the perspective — the time scale — of the person doing the considering. Another approach would be to reserve these terms for a limited range of comparisons. If two systems are the same in all respects except that some of the setup times of one are shorter than those of the other, that system is *more flexible* than the other.

[2]the silicon disks on which integrated circuit chips are made. They are also called *slices*.

out. This can be a time-consuming, expensive operation. There may be several wafer types, and several different operations, that use the same chemicals.[3] Consequently, the scheduling problem involves grouping together as many part types as possible for such steps.

- When products such as cars are painted, it is advantageous to group together the items that will be painted the same color. This is because changing colors requires costly, time-consuming cleaning. Moreover, it may take less cleaning effort to change the painting station to a darker color than to a lighter one. Very similar considerations apply to the making of sheet steel or aluminum. When the metal is cut into sheets of various widths, the cutting blades must be repositioned whenever a new width must be produced. It is preferable to make progressively smaller widths because the rollers that move the metal are damaged by the edges of the sheet. If a large sheet follows a small one, it will be marked by the roller; if a small sheet follows a large sheet, there will be no damage. Whenever there is a changeover to a larger sheet, the roller must be repaired.

The setup scheduling problem is to decide (1) when to stop the resource from doing its current operation[4], and (2) which part type to start making next. If changes are performed too often, high changeover costs are incurred; and, if too much time is spent changing setups, there is not sufficient time to produce enough of the product to meet demand. On the other hand, if setups are not performed often enough, inventory levels and cycle times are large.

In this chapter, as elsewhere in this book, we consider systems in which many copies of each part are made. If only one copy of each part were produced, the setup time is just a part of the operation time. Similarly, we assume that parts have not already been grouped into *lots* or *batches* of specified size. If they were, then we may as well treat such lots as though they are parts, and the setup time is part of the operation time for such parts. We assume that we are not required to make all parts of each type in a single lot for the same reason. We assume that we can decide when to change setups; such decisions are what this chapter is all about.

The major goal of this chapter is to discuss methods for making these decisions in real time, as a function of the current state of the system, in the style of the previous two chapters. Other formulations are also described because this style is not appropriate for all problems. Only small, simplified systems are considered; efficient methods for managing more complex systems are not available. There has been an enormous literature on the subject of setups, lot sizes, and related issues. We do not survey very much of it; we mostly focus on the small portion that fits into our real-time control framework.

Some complex issues Before we focus on the very limited set of issues that we can deal with, it is worthwhile to indicate how vast the setup scheduling problem really is. Some

---

[3]This is one reason why *flexibility* is a complicated concept: there may be zero setup times among wafers that use the same chemicals, but large setup times among those that use different chemicals. Is the machine flexible?

[4]This is only an issue when the size of the order does not dictate the size of the run — for example, when orders are very large and must be delivered over time in small lots, rather than all at once.

issues that schedulers must consider include:[5]

- Setup time can be a function of the number of parts produced, the run time, the numbers of part types to be made, or the number of resources currently available. However, we assume that setup time is independent of anything under a scheduler's control. The duration of a setup change can be random, due to variable characteristics of raw material, irregular occurrences of engineering changes, or other causes. We treat setup time as constant for most of this chapter. (The exception is Section 11.5.)

- Setup times may also depend on whether the machine sees the parts on a first or second pass (that is, after rework).

- As indicated above, setups often involve tool changes. Tools can be changed individually or several can be changed together in a magazine. Setups might also involve inspection.

- The time when setups occur may be dictated by shift changes, or by the end of the week. This imposes constraints on scheduling.

- Many manufacturing operations include three activities: setup, process, and teardown. The teardown is *not* the next setup. Rather, it is the activity of bringing the machine to a clean, standard condition. Setup and teardown may require different resources. See Exercise 1.

- In some factories, there are setup specialists, who must be scheduled. Some setup activities do not require the full attention of the specialist, so the specialist can work on several machines at once. This can add to the complication of scheduling (as well as cost accounting).

- There are sometimes hierarchies of setups. That is, part types are organized into a set of nested groups of groups, where there are many lower level groups, which are subsets of a few higher level groups. The time required to change production among part types in a lower level group is small; the time required to change production among part types that are not in the same lower level group, but that are in the same middle level group, is larger; the time required to change production among part types in different lower level and different middle level groups is still larger. Such an organization influences the sequence of setup changes. This is described in more detail below.

- Setup costs may include material consumption, due to testing or to the time required for process stabilization.

---

[5]I am grateful to Kenneth McKay for these observations.

Setup time and cost reduction   Just as improvements can be achieved by reducing the frequency and duration of failures, savings can also be realized by reducing duration (and possibly also the frequency) of setup changes. One way to do this is to buy many machines. For each operation, devote one machine to each part type, or to each set of part types that require the same setup (for example, one ion implanter for boron and one for phosphorus). This is sometimes, but certainly not always, economically sensible. The study of techniques for economically grouping parts is called *group technology* (Smith, 1989; Kusiak, 1990). Another approach is to change setups during shifts when no production is taking place.

Reducing the duration of the setup change is beyond the scope of this book. However, we should mention that some useful actions are to keep materials, such as the tools for the new parts, near where they are needed for the change; to train workers specifically for changing setups; to do as much as possible off-line while the machine is still producing the previous part type; and to study the change in detail to eliminate unnecessary steps.

Computational effort   Once the system and objectives have been identified and modeled appropriately, the most critical issue in real-time scheduling and planning of manufacturing systems is the computational effort required to achieve good performance. We deal with both the computational effort and the randomness of a special class of manufacturing systems — FMSs — in Chapter 9. For this special class, it is possible to perform much of the scheduling computation on production rates (the hedging point problem), and then to convert the rates easily into loading times (the staircase strategy). This is better than working directly with loading times because (1) there are far fewer rate variables than loading time variables; and (2) we can use standard techniques, such as linear programming, for the rate variables.

Not all problems lend themselves so easily to such a simplification. In particular, the scheduling of setup forces us to confront the discrete nature of manufacturing. That is, there does not seem to be any easy way to deal with setup frequencies, or other aggregate quantities, and to then convert them into setup change times. Some small steps in this direction are described in this chapter.

Relationship with earlier chapters   One goal of this chapter is to provide results that are analogous to those of Chapter 9. We would like to provide real-time closed loop policies for deciding when to change setups, for systems in which the only activities are setup changes and operations. We would then embed these results in the hierarchical framework of Chapter 10. We would go further and use the spatial decomposition ideas of Chapter 12 for systems with setups, failures, and buffers, and then synthesize it all in Chapter 13 for systems with setups, failures, and buffers, and with events that occur at different frequencies.

However, this goal is not fully achieved. Real-time closed loop methods for dealing with setups are less developed than real-time closed loop methods for failures. This is an issue of both *science* and *mathematics* as the terms are used in Chapter 1. That is, we have only an incomplete empirical knowledge of the setup-related phenomena that affect scheduling; and the mathematical and computational tools require more work. Consequently, this chapter is not as deep as Chapter 9. This does *not* mean that systems with setup changes are less important; on the contrary, almost every multiple-product manufacturing system in existence at this writing requires setup changes, and very, very few conform to the flexibility and continuous demand assumptions of Chapter 9. They may not fit the assumptions of the models presented here precisely either, but many researchers are working to improve the models and results. In spite of the limitations on the theory of scheduling setups, there are good reasons to study it. It can help generate insights into the issues and problems. In some cases, if it is used creatively, it can provide estimates or upper or lower bounds on performance or other useful quantities.

Chapter overview Section 11.2 provides some definitions that pertain to the pattern of setup change costs and times. Some of the literature of non-real-time setup change planning is described in Section 11.3. Section 11.4 presents a model of a system in which setups are changed in real time on the basis of the system state. The model and feedback policy are developed in the hierarchical framework of Chapter 10. Section 11.4 also reviews some recent literature on real-time setup changing. Section 11.5 briefly sketches a different kind of factory and solution method. It is important that the reader be warned that the material in Sections 11.4 and 11.5 is found only in the research literature, and has not been implemented on the factory floor. Section 11.6 suggests some research problems.

11.2 Setup Structures

Define s_{ij} as the *setup time*, the time required to change a machine from being able to make Part Type i to being able to make Part Type j. Define A_{ij} as the *setup cost*, the dollar cost that must be expended (for labor, materials, etc.) each time such a setup change is performed. A setup change from i to i is not allowed, so s_{ii} and A_{ii} are not meaningful. Important computational advantages can be obtained if the sets of s_{ij} and A_{ij} have special structure.

For some purposes, only the setup time, or only the setup cost is relevant. In such cases, the following definitions are applied when the relevant quantities satisfy the conditions, and the irrelevant quantities are ignored.

If s_{ij} and A_{ij} depend only on j (that is, if $s_{ij} = s_j$ and $A_{ij} = A_j$ for all i and j), then the setups are said to be *non-sequence dependent*. Otherwise, they are *sequence-dependent*.

Sequence-dependent setups may be hierarchically organized. In many cases, the part types may be grouped into clusters such that the setup change time and cost to change from one part to another within a cluster is much less than the time and cost required to change from a part in one cluster to a part in another. This is because the parts within each cluster are more similar to each other than they are to parts in other clusters. The clusters themselves may be grouped into clusters; Burman (1993) describes a machine with four levels of setups: major setups, minor setups, major adjustments, and minor adjustments. (See Section 11.5.) Major setups take on the order of 240 time units, minor setups require about 90 time units, major adjustments take close to 45 time units, and minor adjustments are around 15 time units in duration. Operation times are very short: 0.0056 time units.

Another kind of system is where the part types can be ordered in a series, and the setup time and cost to change from i to j depend on the location of i and j in the series. The car-painting case in Section 11.1 is an example of a one-way series; Burman (1993) refers to a system with a two-way series in which the cost and time to go from i to j is the same as the cost and time to go from j to i.

Significance of structures In many problems, the only way to achieve a useful solution is to find a special structure that can be exploited. Setup scheduling for systems in which there is no such structure to s_{ij} and A_{ij} can be extremely difficult (in the sense that it can require a great deal of computer time and computer memory). For example, in the capacitated lot size problem (Section 11.3.2), setups are assumed to be sequence-independent. One of the sets of problem data is r_{ik}^δ, which represents the load imposed on the capacity of Resource k by one setup of Product i. If setups were allowed to be sequence-dependent, it would be necessary to include, instead, r_{ijk}^δ, to represent the load imposed on Resource k by one setup change from Product i to Product j. Another example is the hierarchical structure: as described in Section 11.5, this structure can be exploited to yield a simple algorithm to sequence setup changes.

11.3 Planning Setup Changes Without Feedback

This section reviews part of the literature that deals with the advanced planning of setup changes, *not* real-time decision-making. The models described here are historically or economically important, and form a good starting point for the real-time scheduling models in later sections. The *Economic Order Quantity* model of Section 11.3.1 deals with the ordering (rather than the production) of a single part type. The Wagner-Whitin formulation (also in Section 11.3.1) is an elegant extension that allows demand to vary with time. Its solution has a simple, interesting property which is described below.

The Wagner-Whitin formulation is extended in Section 11.3.2 to deal with multiple part types and capacity limitations. The *Economic Lot-Sizing Problem* of Section 11.3.3 includes a more detailed model of the resources to be set up. In general, these problems are difficult to solve, and their solutions are not characterized by simple properties. An extension of this model is used in the real-time scheduling methods that appear in Section 11.4.

11.3.1 Economic order quantity (EOQ)

The simplest model of lot sizing is the Economic Order Quantity or EOQ model. The EOQ model is not for a true setup situation because it deals with only a single part type, it treats the acquisition of raw materials rather than their production, and material is acquired at discrete times rather than continuously due to ordering costs and not setup costs. We discuss it because there is a similar trade-off between ordering and inventory costs as that between setup and inventory costs.

A simple version appears in Silver and Peterson (1985). (There are dozens of variants.) In this model, there is a single part type and there is a constant demand rate d for that item. Each time the firm obtains a lot of Q items, it must pay $A + vQ$ dollars for that lot. The unit cost is v, and the cost of ordering is A.

Assume that the firm orders Q items when its inventory level is exactly 0, and it receives them instantly. For the next Q/d time units, the inventory is depleted at a constant rate d until it is 0, at which point the firm obtains its next lot of Q items. A graph of inventory as a function of time is presented in Figure 11.1. The average inventory level is $Q/2$. If c is the dollar cost per time unit of holding an item in inventory, then $cQ/2$ is the average inventory holding cost per time unit.

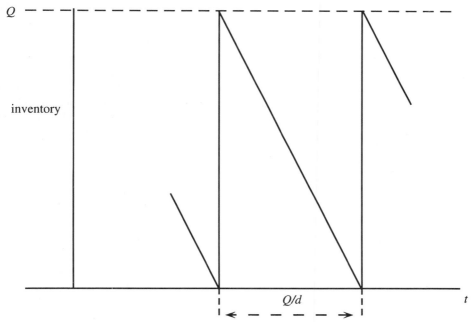

Figure 11.1: Inventory *versus* Time for EOQ Model

Now consider the total costs over a long time period of duration T. The total amount of material that must be acquired is Td, and it is obtained in lots of size Q. Therefore, the number of times that material is acquired is Td/Q, so the total cost of getting material is $(Td/Q)(A + vQ) = TdA/Q + Tdv$. Finally, the total cost, including both acquisition and inventory holding cost, is

$$\frac{TdA}{Q} + Tdv + \frac{TcQ}{2} = T\left\{ \frac{dA}{Q} + dv + \frac{cQ}{2} \right\}.$$

This cost is large when Q is small because materials are ordered frequently, and consequently ordering costs are incurred frequently. This is reflected in the first term. The cost is large when Q is large because inventories are large. This is expressed in the last term.

The economic order quantity is the value of Q that minimizes the total cost. The derivative of the cost with respect to Q is

$$T\left\{-\frac{dA}{Q^2}+\frac{c}{2}\right\}$$

which is 0 for the optimal Q. Therefore, the EOQ is given by

$$Q=\left(\frac{2dA}{c}\right)^{\frac{1}{2}}. \tag{11.1}$$

While this approach leaves out a great deal, it can be used to define a real-time scheduling policy. First, find all the quantities that appear on the right side of (11.1) and evaluate Q. Then, monitor the inventory level. Whenever it reaches 0, order Q. This is a feedback, or real-time control, policy because the action (ordering) is based on a measurement of the state of the system (the inventory). Although a simple model is used in its derivation, this policy, or an extension, can be implemented in a real environment. Figure 11.2 shows the effect of this policy when the demand is random.

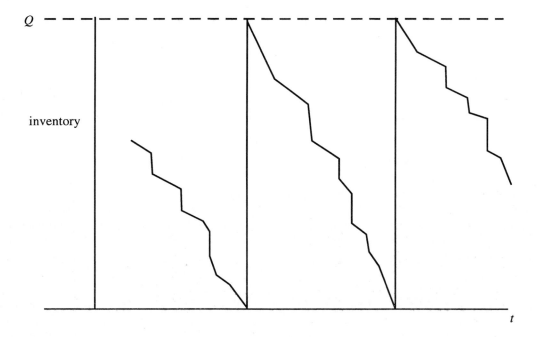

Figure 11.2: Inventory *versus* Time with Random Demand

Extensions Silver and Peterson (1985) adapt this approach for a known, time-varying demand. They (1) calculate the EOQ on the basis of average demand, (2) express the EOQ in terms of time (an *n*-month supply), (3) and then always acquire enough for that number of months, based on the projected demands.

Other phenomena that have been studied include random demand (for which *safety stock* is used to reduce the frequency of *stockouts*, or unfulfilled orders) and non-instantaneous deliveries of raw material. All these extensions involve the introduction of real-time decision-making.

Wagner-Whitin Wagner and Whitin (1958) study the scheduling of setups and production in a deterministic system with known, but time-varying demands. This formulation is appropriate for *production planning* rather than real-time scheduling.

The objective to be minimized is the cost of holding inventory. The Wagner-Whitin model is an extension of the EOQ model, and there is no real interaction among different part types. (This is because capacity does not play a role, and because a setup is assumed to take place if a part is manufactured during time period t regardless of whether the same kind of part was manufactured during time period $t-1$.) Consequently, this is a single-part type formulation; if the factory makes more than one kind of part, the problem is solved for each one independently.

Time is discretized into periods of fixed length and material is treated as a continuous quantity. The problem data include T, the number of periods; i_t, the interest charge per unit of inventory held from time t to time $t+1$; s_t, the setup cost in period t; and d_t, the demand in period t. The decision variables are x_t, the amount manufactured in period t.

The state variable is I_t, the inventory, which satisfies

$$I_t = I_0 + \sum_{j=1}^{t-1} x_j - \sum_{j=1}^{t-1} d_j \geq 0.$$

To discuss the setup, Wagner and Whitin introduce a binary function $\delta(x_t)$:

$$\delta(x_t) = \begin{cases} 0 & \text{if} \quad x_t = 0 \\ 1 & \text{if} \quad x_t > 0 \end{cases}$$

If a part is produced in period t, some resources will have to be set up. The function $\delta(x_t)$ is used to indicate that a setup cost is incurred when even a small amount of the product is made.

The problem is formulated as a dynamic programming problem with value function f_t. It satisfies

$$f_t(I) = \min_{\substack{x_t \geq 0 \\ I + x_t \geq d_t}} \{i_{t-1}I + \delta(x_t)s_t + f_{t+1}(I + x_t - d_t)\}, t = 1, ..., T,$$

$$f_{T+1}(I) = 0.$$

They derive an optimal algorithm for this problem. We will not describe it here, except to say that in the optimal solution, $x_t = 0$ for many t, and if x_t is nonzero, $I_t = 0$. Define t' to be the next time such that $x_{t'}$ is nonzero. Then

$$x_t = \sum_{j=t}^{t'-1} d_j.$$

That is, new production occurs only when the inventory goes to zero. At that time, the amount of material that is produced is exactly enough to meet the demand until the next time that production is planned to occur (which is the next time when inventory goes to zero). Such a procedure only makes sense because the system and the demand are assumed to be deterministic.

11.3.2   Mixed integer programming formulations of the lot-sizing problem

Integer programming problems are optimization problems all of whose unknown variables are integers. *Mixed integer programming problems* are optimization problems whose unknown variables include both integers and continuous numbers. Such problem formulations are often undesirable because (1) they are based on deterministic models, and (2) they are usually very difficult to solve (in the sense that they require very long computer times). If a problem can be formulated in some other way, it probably should be; but sometimes there is no alternative.

CLSP   Newson (1975a) extends the Wagner-Whitin formulation to include capacity limits. Multiple part types are represented explicitly. The objective to be minimized includes costs due to setups, production, and holding inventory. This problem is called the *Capacitated Lot Size Problem* or CLSP. Like the Wagner-Whitin model, this representation is appropriate for production planning rather than real-time scheduling.

Time is again discretized into periods of fixed length. Material is treated as a continuous quantity. The problem data include T, the number of periods; h_i, the inventory holding cost per unit of Type i parts per period ($i = 1, ..., N$); v_i, the production cost per unit of Type i parts; s_i, the setup cost for Type i parts; and d_{it}, the demand for Type i parts in period t. The setups are assumed to be sequence-independent.

Capacity limitations are expressed by $r_{ik}^{\delta}, r_{ik}^{x}$, and R_{kt}: r_{ik}^{δ} is the "capacity absorption for one setup of product i on resource k"; r_{ik}^{x} is the "per unit capacity absorption of product i on resource k"; and R_{kt} is "the level of resource k available in period t." That is, however R_{kt} is expressed (in whatever units), r_{ik}^{δ} is the amount of it consumed by a single setup, and r_{ik}^{x} is the amount of it consumed by a producing a single Type i part, when resource k is set up for it. Limits on the indexes are $t = 1, ..., T$, $k = 1, ..., K$ (the number of resources), and $i = 1, ..., N$ (the number of product types).

The decision variables include I_{it}, the amount of inventory of Product (or Part Type) i at the end of period t; and x_{it}, the amount of Product i produced in period t. If this were formulated as a dynamic programming problem, I_{it} would be the state variable and x_{it} would be the control variable.

There are only two kinds of constraints. The first is the inventory dynamics:

$$I_{i,t-1} + x_{it} - I_{it} = d_{it}; \quad i = 1, ..., N; t = 1, ..., T;$$

$$I_{i0} \geq 0 \text{ specified}; \quad i = 1, ..., N.$$

This equation is the same as (9.1) except that time is discrete and not continuous.

The capacity constraint is

$$\sum_{i=1}^{N} \left[r_{ik}^{\delta} \delta(x_{it}) + r_{ik}^{x} x_{it} \right] \leq R_{kt}; \quad k = 1, ..., K; t = 1, ..., T$$

in which $\delta(x_{it})$ has the same meaning as in the Wagner-Whitin formulation.

Additional constraints include

$$x_{it} \geq 0; \quad i = 1, ..., N; t = 1, ..., T;$$
$$I_{it} \geq 0; \quad i = 1, ..., N; t = 1, ..., T.$$

The cost to be minimized is

$$f = \sum_{i=1}^{N} \sum_{t=1}^{T} s_i \delta(x_{it}) + v_i x_{it} + h_i I_{it}.$$

This formulation is highly simplified and limited: setup change times are sequence-independent; periods are long compared with setup times; and there is no provision for saving a setup time if the same part type is produced in two successive time periods. (These simplifications are appropriate for a long time scale formulation.) Nonetheless, this is still not an easy problem to solve. There is no explicit or analytic solution (one that can be expressed in a formula) or other simple statement about the solution. Newson and others provide heuristics and numerical techniques. This is typical of these problems.

The Traveling Salesman Problem Consider a sequence-dependent set of setups, and consider the problem of selecting a cycle of setups to be repeated may times. Assume that each part will be produced exactly once during the cycle. The goal is to minimize the total time or total cost incurred during the cycle. This can be formulated as a *traveling salesman problem* in which a salesman must visit a set of cities (setups) and return home, where the cost to travel from city to city is known, and where the goal is to minimize the total cost.

The traveling salesman problem has been studied for many years, and has generated a long, interesting literature, but no simple efficient algorithm has been found to provide an exact solution. The problems described in this chapter are similar to traveling salesman problems — when setups are sequence-dependent — but they involve additional variables (such as production rates) and they allow setups to be visited more than once during a tour. Consequently, we will always be looking for good simplifying assumptions or approximate algorithms.

11.3.3   Economic lot scheduling problem (ELSP)

The goal of the *Economic Lot Scheduling Problem* (ELSP) is also the scheduling of several products on one or more identical machines. The demand rate for products is assumed constant, the time horizon is infinite, and no backlog is permitted. The system is in steady state, and the problem is that of finding lot sizes that minimize the average setup and inventory holding costs per unit time. A review of the ELSP literature appears in Elmaghraby (1978).

This section is based on Dobson's (1987) formulation. The goal is to select a sequence of setups to be repeated cyclically over a long period of time. The sequence is chosen to minimize the total cost, which is the sum of inventory holding cost and setup cost. Backlogs are not allowed. This formulation differs from that of Section 11.3.2 in that setup behavior is modeled more precisely. It is more restrictive in that the demand rate is required to be constant. It is appropriate for shorter time horizon.

The simplest example of a setup sequence is the *round-robin* sequence, $\{1\text{-}2\text{-}3\text{-}...\text{-}N\}$. Other sequences may be more desirable, however. For example, if the demand for Part Type 1 is much higher than the others and inventory costs are high, $\{1\text{-}2\text{-}1\text{-}3\text{-}1\text{-}4\text{-}...\text{-}N\}$ might be a better sequence. Complex sequences are possible, even when there are few part types. For example, $\{1\text{-}2\text{-}3\text{-}1\text{-}2\text{-}3\text{-}1\text{-}2\text{-}3\text{-}1\text{-}2\text{-}1\text{-}3\}$ is a a three-part-type sequence. The only rule for defining a sequence is that the same part type cannot appear twice in succession. The period between setup changes during which the system makes a single part type is a *production run*.

Problem data   Let $\mu_i = 1/\tau_i$ be a known production rate of Type i parts $(i = 1, ..., N)$, when the machine is set up for that type. Let d_i be the demand rate, h_i be the inventory holding cost, A_i be the setup cost, and s_i be the setup time for Type i. These quantities are assumed known, and are the problem data. Note that this is again assumed to be a sequence-independent set of setups.

Decision variables   Assume that there are n setup changes in the cycle, and F^j is the name of the part type that is produced after the jth setup change — the part type that is produced in the jth production run. The cycle is repeated many times; the part that is produced after the $n + 1$st setup is F^1. Each part must be set up and produced at least once in the cycle, so $n \geq N$. The total time for the cycle is T and the duration of the jth production run is t^j. The machine is idle for I^j time units during the jth production run. The decision variables, which must be determined, are T, n, F^j, t^j, and I^j, $j = 1, ..., n$.

Constraints   These quantities must satisfy a set of constraints. First, the total amount required of Part Type i over a cycle is $d_i T$. If Part Type i is produced after the jth setup, the amount produced is $\mu_i t^j$. Define $K_i = \{j | F^j = i\}$. This is the set of times in the cycle that Part Type i is produced. Then

$$\sum_{j \in K_i} \mu_i t^j = d_i T \tag{11.2}$$

where the sum is over all the setup changes in the cycle in which the machine is set up for Type i.

Second, Dobson assumes that the inventory level of Type i reaches zero just as production of Type i is about to begin, and that this is true each time in the cycle that Type i is produced.[6] Assume that $F^k = i$. That is, Type i is produced after the kth setup in the cycle. Assume that the next position in the cycle when Type i is produced is m. That is, for $j = k+1, \ldots, m-1$, $F^j \neq i$, and $F^m = i$. (Since the setup changes occur in a cycle, m may be less than k, and j and m must be interpreted modulo n.) In order for the inventory to just reach zero, the number of Type i parts produced during the kth interval must be exactly the same as are consumed during the kth, the $k+1$st, ..., and the $m-1$st. That is,

$$\sum_{j \in \mathcal{J}(k,m-1,n)} d_i(t^j + s^j + I^j) = \mu_i t^k$$

or,

$$\sum_{j \in \mathcal{J}(k,m-1,n)} (t^j + s^j + I^j) = \frac{\mu_i t^k}{d_i} \tag{11.3}$$

in which

$$\mathcal{J}(k, m-1, n) = \begin{cases} \{k, k+1, \ldots, m-2, m-1\} & \text{if } m-1 > k \\ \{1, 2, \ldots, m-2, m-1, k, k+1, \ldots, n-1, n\} & \text{if } m-1 < k. \end{cases}$$

Third, the total amount of production, setup, and idle time over a cycle must be the length of the cycle:

$$\sum_{j=1}^{n} (t^j + s^j + I^j) = T. \tag{11.4}$$

Costs   During production run k, the inventory level starts at 0 and increases while production of Type $i = F^k$ occurs. Since demand depletes inventory at rate d_i, the net rate of increase in inventory during production run k is $\mu_i - d_i$, and the maximum inventory level is $(\mu_i - d_i)t^k$. Inventory returns to 0 at time $\mu_i t^k / d_i$ after the start of production run k, according to Equation (11.3). See Figure 11.3. The average inventory level during this period is half the maximum. The inventory cost of Type i parts produced during production run k is h_i times the average inventory level times the length of the time interval in Equation (11.3). That is, the inventory cost of Type i parts produced during production run k is

$$h_i \left(\frac{1}{2}(\mu_i - d_i)t^k \right) \left(\sum_{j \in \mathcal{J}(k,m-1,n)} (t^j + s^j + I^j) \right) = \frac{1}{2} h_i(\mu_i - d_i)\frac{\mu_i}{d_i}(t^k)^2.$$

---

[6] Compare with the Wagner-Whitin solution.

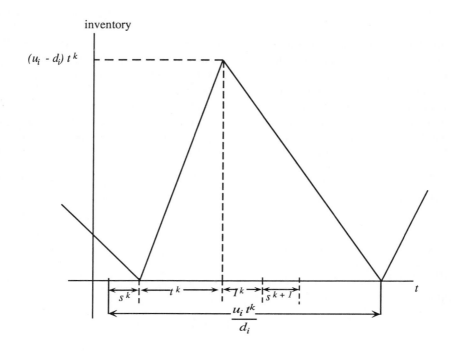

Figure 11.3: Details of Part Type i Inventory History

The objective is to minimize the total cost of setups and holding inventory over a long period. This is equivalent to minimizing the average cost over the cycle. The quantity to be minimized is

$$\frac{\sum_{j=1}^{n} \left(\frac{1}{2} h_{F^j} (\mu_{F^j} - d_{F^j}) \frac{\mu_{F^j}}{d_{F^j}} (t^j)^2 + A^j \right)}{T}. \tag{11.5}$$

Some of the decision variables are discrete (n and F^j) and some are continuous (T, t^j, and I^j). Conceptually, the optimization can be thought of as taking place in two stages: for every possible n and $F^1, ..., F^n$, minimize (11.5) with respect to T, t^j, and I^j, $j = 1, ..., n$, subject to (11.2)-(11.4). The solution is determined by the n and $F^1, ..., F^n$ such that the cost is minimized overall. This may not be a practical solution approach because of the large number of possible sets of n and $F^1, ..., F^n$.

Computation issues   There are two ways of dealing with the computational effort due to the integer variables. Both involve giving up on the idea of an exact solution, and settling for a satisfactory approximation. (1) Accept the fact that there must be integers, but limit

n. The number of different $\{F^1, ..., F^n\}$ is determined by n. Not only will this restrict the computational effort, but it will also bound the complexity of the cycle. However, there are still a *large* number of possibilities that must be considered. (2) Another approach would be to find a solution to this problem that bypasses the integer variables. To do this, we introduce *setup frequencies*.

Setup frequencies Recall that $K_i = \{j|F^j = i\}$. Then $n_i = \text{card}(K_i)$ (the *cardinality* of K_i, the number of members of set K_i) is the number of times that Part Type i is produced. Dobson calls n_i the *relative frequency* with which Type i parts are produced. We define

$$f_i = \frac{n_i}{T}$$

as the *setup frequency*, the frequency with which the machine is set up for Type i parts.

Rationality constraints If the optimization problem has a finite solution, then all the n_i are finite integers, and the frequencies are rational multiples of one another.

This can be expressed as

$$\frac{f_i}{f_j} = \frac{n_i}{n_j} \quad n_i, n_j \text{ positive integers, for all } i, j. \tag{11.6}$$

The values of integers n_i determine the length of the setup circuit (T). For example consider a machine with $f_1 = f_2 = f_3 = 1$ setup per day. We can choose the sequence of setups $\{1\text{-}2\text{-}3\}$ corresponding to these frequencies and $T = 1$ day. Now suppose f_3 were increased to 1.01 setups per day. Then a setup sequence that corresponds exactly to the new frequencies requires setting up 100 times for Type 1 parts, 100 times for Type 2 parts and 101 times for Type 3 parts in a time interval.[7] T is 100 days.

If the rationality constraints are imposed, the problem involves integers. Dobson (1987) provides an approximate solution that relies on relaxing constraint (11.3), and relaxing the requirement that the relative frequencies (n_i) be integers. But if the f_is are not rational multiples of each other, then $T = \infty$; there is no repeating finite cycle. To make T finite, one can slightly modify the target frequencies such that they are rational multiples of each other. However the circuit could still be very long. A larger modification of the frequencies might reduce the n_is further, but it might also be costlier. See the discussion of chaos in Section 11.4.5.

Calculating the f_is without calculating the sequence $\{F^1, ..., F^n\}$ is adequate if the purpose of the problem is to allocate resources between setups and production, as in the Level 2 problem below. If the purpose is actually to schedule setups and production, however, it is necessary to solve something like the ELSP. This is still a computational burden: even if the frequencies are known to be equal because $n = N$, there are $(N - 1)!$ possible sequences.[8]

---

[7]for example $\{1\text{-}2\text{-}3\text{-}1\text{-}2\text{-}3\text{-}1\text{-}2\text{-}3\text{-}1\text{-}2\text{-}3\text{-}...\text{-}1\text{-}3\text{-}2\text{-}3\}$

[8]On the other hand, consider the following *Conjecture: in this case, the cost is independent of the sequence.* But if $n \neq N$ or if the frequencies are not equal, the cost will not be independent of the sequence, and there will be many more sequences.

Interdependence constraints   Each setup frequency is bounded by the other setup frequencies. For example, if the machine produces only two part types, then whenever we change from one part type, we always produce the other part type. The two part types must have equal setup frequencies, or $f_1 = f_2$. If the machine produces three part types, valid setup sequences include {1-2-3} or {1-2-1-3}. In the first sequence, the setup frequencies are equal ($f_1 = f_2 = f_3$) while in the second, $f_1 = 2f_2 = 2f_3$.

However, there are some sets of frequencies which do not correspond to any sequence of setups, even if they satisfy the rationality constraint. For example, it is not possible to switch into Type 1 five times, Type 2 once and Type 3 once during an interval.[9] Consequently, it is not possible to have $f_1 = 5f_2 = 5f_3$.

In general, conditions that the frequencies must satisfy in order to correspond to a realistic sequence of setups are

$$f_j \leq \sum_{\substack{i = 1 \\ i \neq j}}^{N} f_i; \qquad j = 1, 2, ..., N. \tag{11.7}$$

We present a formulation of an optimization problem involving setup frequencies in Section 11.4.1, where we discuss the Level 2 problem.

Extensions   One possible extension would allow the production rate to take on more different values. In the above formulation it can be μ_i (which is specified) or 0 (the production rate during the idle periods). A reasonable extension would be three values: 0, d_i, and μ_i. The latter is the maximum possible production rate while the machine is set up for Type i; the other possibilities are letting the machine be idle and producing at the demand rate. These possibilities are the same as those for the one-part type hedging point problem (Section 9.3). Another extension would be to consider *sequence-dependent* setups.

11.4   Real-Time Setup Scheduling with Flow Models

The purpose of a real-time setup scheduler is to choose the times to change setups, and the new parts to be made, as a function of the current condition of the system. In this section, we develop models that are based on the assumption that machines are reliable. Failures and other events actually occur, but only at frequencies very different from that of setup changes.

11.4.1   Deterministic formulation

Justification for a deterministic model in a stochastic world   In principle, if a system is deterministic, then feedback is not necessary. Since the whole future is predictable, the optimal sequence of events can be chosen just once, and the resulting plan is carried

---

[9]Why not? Try to construct such a sequence.

out for the rest of time. In reality, no real system is deterministic. But there are three important reasons to study deterministic systems with feedback.

1. They are usually easier to study than stochastic systems. The analysis of a deterministic system often provides a starting point for the study of a related stochastic system.

2. In some cases, the optimal feedback controller for a deterministic system is a good controller for a stochastic system:

   (a) In the framework of Chapter 10, there are two classes of stochastic systems for which the feedback controller for a deterministic system would be a good approximation to an optimal feedback controller.

      i. In one, failures or other random events (such as random operation times) occur much *more* frequently than setup changes. In formulating the deterministic setup level feedback controller, only the average behavior of the random events is modeled. In such a system, the total production and the surplus are always slightly different from what is predicted by a deterministic setup level controller. Feedback allows the controller to adjust its decisions about when to change setups. If the disruptions caused by the lower level randomness are not too great, the deterministic model is a good approximation.

      ii. The other class is where failures occur much *less* often than setup changes. When the machine is up, the setup controller has enough time to bring the system to the neighborhood of a desirable state (such as a higher level hedging point), and to keep it there. However, when the machine fails, the surplus state may be forced to go far from such a state. The duration of the failure, and thus the value of the surplus after the repair, is not known in advance. It must be determined after the repair is completed, and the setup times chosen appropriately. If the frequency of the higher level randomness is small enough, a second failure rarely occurs before the surplus gets to the desirable state, so the deterministic model is a good approximation. This is the case that the hierarchy below is designed for, although the approach is appropriate for other cases as well.

   (b) The solution of the Bielecki-Kumar problem (Section 9.3) shows that for some sufficiently reliable unreliable systems, the optimal strategy is *the same as* (not merely close to) the optimal policy for a deterministic system.[10] In these systems, the hedging point Z is 0.

3. Even deterministic systems can behave in unpredictable ways. As we describe in Section 11.4.5, systems with setups can be *chaotic*. Chaos is a phenomenon that has recently gotten a great deal of attention. It is a complex behavior that is seen in deterministic, often surprisingly simple, systems. In practical terms, it means that

---

[10]The strategy is the same, but the value function (J or W) is not.

the precise future of the system cannot be predicted with a simple formula, and that even a detailed simulation cannot be accurate because small perturbations grow into major errors. While feedback seems to cause chaos in the class of systems with setups described in Section 11.4.5, it also keeps the systems bounded.

Context for Model The model described in the following is appropriate for cases in which other phenomena occur much more or much less frequently than setup changes. In particular, if material must be shipped at discrete points in time (*due dates*), then the setup changes are much *less* frequent than those points. (The opposite is true in the model of Section 11.5.) This is what allows us to represent the demand process by dt. Failures, maintenance, variations in processing times, are very frequent or very infrequent. Failures, setup changes, and operations are assumed to be the most important. These are treated explicitly in the hierarchy described below.

Consider the multistage manufacturing system illustrated in Figure 11.4 in which one stage is much less flexible than the others. This machine can work on the same set of parts as the others, but it is much more time-consuming for this machine to change part types than any other. Set up *costs* are not treated in this analysis. Only inventories and disruption propagation are considered. The system has five machines and it makes three part types. Eighteen buffers are shown, and they are assumed to be *homogeneous*. That is, each buffer holds only identical, interchangeable parts. All the parts in a buffer are of the same type, and are at the same production stage. There are three classes of buffers: very small, intermediate, and very large.

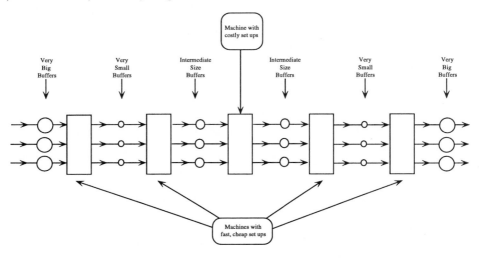

Figure 11.4: Multistage System

Failures occur infrequently, but when they do, the whole line is down for a long time. The whole line is down because some failures affect all the machines at the same time, such as power failures; and because other failures affect single machines directly — like tool breakage — but there are no buffers within the system large enough to prevent the propagation of the stoppage. The very large buffers most often stop the propagation of disruptions due to failures from this system to the outside world. They also prevent the propagation of similarly severe disruptions from outside to inside this system. After one of these major failures, the line must work hard to catch up to its hedging point, as described in Chapter 9.

The very small buffers hold only one or two parts. They do not prevent disruptions from propagating, but they hold a part or a space ready so a machine can work on a new part immediately after it finishes an operation on the previous part.

The intermediate buffers are included to prevent the propagation of the down time due to setting up the relatively inflexible machine. When the machine is being changed from doing operations on Type i parts to operations on Type j parts, it is not working on any parts. We would like the other machines to keep working while that machine is being changed over, but this is only possible if there are buffers of appropriate sizes near it. Assume that the two adjacent Type i buffers have space for roughly $s_i \mu_i$ parts (where μ_i is the rate that the least flexible machine makes Type i parts). This is the amount of material that could have been processed by the machine during the time it is being set up, if it were working instead. If that machine is the fastest machine in the line while it is producing, then upstream buffers will tend to have space, and downstream buffers will tend to have material, when setup changes are initiated. This allows the upstream and downstream portions of the line to keep operating while the setup change is taking place.

Demand is high, so capacity cannot be wasted. When the inflexible machine is set up for making Type i parts, all the other machines also make Type i parts. While it is being changed over to Type j, the other machines make either Type i or Type j parts or undergo faster i-to-j changeovers.

We focus on scheduling the relatively inflexible stage since it sets the pace for the rest of the line. The line produces a set of parts for which there are specified demand rates, and it is important to produce each kind of material as close as possible to those rates. (This could be because inventory is expensive or perishable, or because the parts are assembled or otherwise shipped together in a fixed ratio.)

As in many other cases of real time control, we will have to be satisfied with satisfactory, rather than optimal, behavior. In the following, we describe a four-level hierarchy with setup changes at Level 3. We describe optimization problems at Levels 2 and 3, but we do not offer exact solutions. We describe heuristic solutions for the Level 3 problem.

Model We deal with a single machine which requires τ_i time units to make a Type i part, $i = 1, ..., N$, and which requires s_j time units (the *setup time*) to change from operating on Type i parts to operating on Type j parts, $j = 1, ..., N, j \neq i$. The maximum rate at which the machine can produce Part Type i when it is set up for it is $\mu_i = 1/\tau_i$. The order of magnitude of all the s_j are the same. The demand for Type i parts is d_i per time unit, and d_i is constant. Failures (at rate p) and repairs (at rate r) are much less frequent than setup changes. That is (if we assume that the setup frequency is on the order of $1/s_j$),

$$p \ll \frac{1}{s_j}, r \ll \frac{1}{s_j}; j = 1, ..., N.$$

Hierarchical framework   To be more complete, we classify events by frequency according to the formalism of Section 10.2.3. Following Equations (10.14) and (10.15), we have $f_1 = 0$ and $\mathcal{L}_1$ is empty. Then

$$\begin{aligned}
f_2 &= p \sim r \\
f_3 &= \frac{1}{s_1} \sim \frac{1}{s_i}, i \neq 1 \\
f_4 &= d_1 \sim \frac{1}{\tau_1} \sim d_i \sim \frac{1}{\tau_i}, i \neq 1
\end{aligned}$$

where $\sim$ means *is on the same order of magnitude as*. $\mathcal{L}_2$ consists of failures, $\mathcal{L}_3$ is the set of setup changes, and $\mathcal{L}_4$ is the set of operations.

For the problem to be meaningful, the machine must have sufficient capacity to meet the demand. That is,

$$\sum_i \tau_i d_i < \frac{r}{r + p}. \tag{11.8}$$

The scheduling can be organized according to the four-level hierarchy of Figure 11.5. Setup changes characterize Level 3 of this hierarchy, and failures are treated at Level 2. Level 3 schedules setups to meet the targets dictated by Level 2.

Frequency separation assumption The frequency of failures and repairs (the Level 2 events) is small enough compared with those of setups and operations so that after a repair is completed, the system usually returns to its Level 3 steady state and remains there for some time before experiencing another disturbance. (Specifically, the system most often returns to the limit cycle described in Section 11.4.3 if a corridor policy is used.) During most such transient periods, there are no disturbances, so the Level 3 control policy can be calculated as if the system were reliable, but in a transient surplus state. That is, a deterministic model can be used to schedule setup changes for such a system.

Level 1   As usual, we include a top level to represent all the activities that are done only once during the whole horizon. That includes collecting all the data, establishing the hierarchy structure, and calculating the Level 2 control parameters.

Level 2   The goal at Level 2 is to select production and setup rates in response to changes in the repair state of the machine and the surplus. The Level 2 problem is a combination of the FMS scheduling problem of Chapter 9 (in particular, the single-machine, multi-part type problem of Exercise 8), the ELSP formulation of Section 11.3.3, and additional constraints

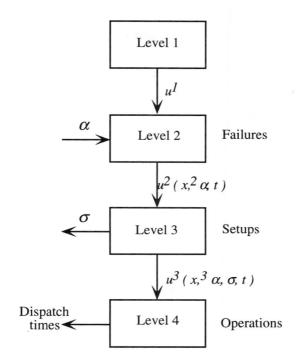

Figure 11.5: Four-level Hierarchy for a Manufacturing System with Setups

on setup frequencies. This problem determines both production rates and setup frequencies as a function of Level 2 surpluses. (Since there is only one machine, the production rates and setup frequencies are 0 when it is down.) The Level 2 rate vector w^2 consists of production rates and setup frequencies. In the notation of Section 11.3.3,

$$w^2 = \begin{pmatrix} u^2 \\ f^2 \end{pmatrix}.$$

When the machine is up, it is either recovering from a failure or it is at its hedging point. In the former case, w^2 changes as surpluses change. That is, both production rate and setup rates change over time.

Production rate u^2 is the production rate target for the Level 3 problem. Setup rate f^2 is *not* used as a target in Level 3. It appears in the Level 2 formulation to guarantee that the solution of the Level 2 problem is feasible, that some fraction of the machine's time is correctly allocated to setup changes.

Let $x_i^2(t)$ denote the Level 2 production surplus/backlog of activity i. Then if i denotes operations on Type i parts, $x_i^2(t)$ is the difference between the cumulative production and cumulative demand of activity i at time t. In principle, we could define the setup surplus as well: if j denotes setup changes for Type i parts, $x_j^2(t)$ is the difference between the cumulative number of setup changes already performed and the cumulative requirements for setup changes for Type i at time t. However, this is not needed for setup scheduling.[11] Consequently, we define production surplus only, and do not consider setup surplus. The dimensionality of x^2 is the number of part types.

The dynamics of the production surplus vector is given by

$$\frac{dx^2}{dt} = u^2 - d.$$

The dynamics of the machine state variable α are the Markov process dynamics of Chapter 9.

In Chapter 9, we formulate a stochastic dynamic program to determine production rates for a system without setup changes. From the Hamilton-Jacobi-Bellman equation, we know that, at each time instant, the optimal production rate is a solution of the following linear program:

$$\min_u \frac{\partial W}{\partial x}(x, \alpha)u \tag{11.9}$$

$$u \in \Omega(\alpha)$$

where $W(x, \alpha)$ is the differential cost (8.13), α is the repair state of the system, and $\Omega(\alpha)$ is the capacity set. The capacity set is convex, and an optimum solution can always be found at a vertex. The x space is divided into regions. Each vertex of the capacity set is optimal for the LP for all x in one of the regions. This policy moves the surplus vector along a straight line until it reaches a boundary between regions. At this point the solution u changes to an adjacent vertex of the capacity set. If the new u pushes the trajectory back to the same boundary, the boundary is attractive. In such cases, u is chosen at an extreme of the capacity set such that the x trajectory remains on the boundary. If additional variables and linear constraints were added to this problem, the form of the solution would not change very much.

In this system, setup changes occur much more frequently than failures. We therefore construct a hierarchy in which Level 2 has w^2 playing the role of u in the hedging point controller of Chapter 9. Let f_i^2 be the setup rate into Part Type i that is calculated at Level 2. We formulate a dynamic programming problem, similar to (11.9), which includes the f_i^2s as control variables. The capacity set is modified to account for the setup rate variables f_i^2 and additional constraints. The solution to the HJB equation determines activity rate

---

[11] Gershwin, Caramanis, and Murray (1988) found that keeping the cumulative number of setups near a target is *not* a good idea, even though keeping the cumulative number of parts produced near a target is. This is because parts have value in themselves, whereas setups do not. To put it another way, if a factory is all caught up in everything except one part type, it should work hard to bring that part type up to date, possibly even if it causes others to fall behind. However, if it is caught up in everything except that it hasn't done enough setups, it should *not* work hard to perform the missing setups. To make it even more concrete: if you usually take a shower every day, but you have gone a week without bathing, you don't have to take eight showers. One will suffice.

targets (production rates and setup rates) that are passed down to the next lower hierarchy level.

The objective function of the Level 2 optimization problem is

$$J^2 = \min \int_0^T g^2(x^2(t))dt, \tag{11.10}$$

the same as (9.9), where $g^2(x^2)$ is

$$g^2(x^2) = \sum_{i=1}^N g_i^2(x_i^2)$$

$$g_i^2(x_i^2) = \begin{cases} g_{i+}^2 x_i^2, & \text{if } x_i^2 \geq 0 \\ -g_{i-}^2 x_i^2, & \text{if } x_i^2 \leq 0 \end{cases} \quad g_{i+}^2, g_{i-}^2 \geq 0$$

The horizon T is assumed to be very long; it is long enough so that many failures take place in $[0, T]$.

The Level 2 optimization problem has several types of constraints. They are

- **Capacity constraints** The activities that share machine capacity include operations, setup changes, failures and repairs. The capacity constraint states that the total time used by all the activities cannot be greater than the total available time at the machine. This constraint is a special case of (10.39):

$$\sum_{i=1}^N \tau_i u_i^2 + \sum_{i=1}^N s_i f_i^2 \leq \alpha. \tag{11.11}$$

The two terms represent the fraction of the available time taken up by processing and setup changes, respectively. Compare (11.11) with (11.8). Equation (11.8) is a constraint on the parameters of the problem; (11.11) is a constraint on the decision variables.

This constraint shows that the more often setups occur, the less capacity is available for production. This is important if production falls far behind; to catch up quickly, setups should be done infrequently. On the other hand, if production is not far behind, there is enough capacity to do setups more often, and to keep inventory low.

- **Hierarchy constraints** If setups are performed too often or too infrequently, the assumptions of the hierarchy are violated. Therefore, we impose

$$\phi^3 \alpha \leq f_i^2 \leq \Phi^3$$

where ϕ^3 and Φ^3 are low and high frequencies that satisfy (10.15) for $k = 3$. (That is, $\phi^3 \sim \Phi^3 \sim 1/s_1$.) The lower bound includes α because if $\alpha = 0$, then $f_i^2 = 0$.

These constraints should not be satisfied with equality very often. If one of these constraints is often satisfied with equality, the assumptions on frequency separation may not be correct. That is, the system often wants to change setups at a frequency that threatens to violate the assumptions about relative frequencies. Consequently, they cannot be used to artificially impose a hierarchical structure.

- **Interdependence constraints** Each set of Level 2 setup rates must satisfy (11.7). That is,

$$f_j^2 \leq \sum_{\substack{i=1 \\ i \neq j}}^{N} f_i^2; \qquad j = 1, 2, ..., N.$$

- **Awkward constraints** The following three constraints are difficult to handle because they involve integers or logical conditions.

  - **Rationality**

    $$\frac{f_i^2}{f_j^2} = \frac{n_i}{n_j} \text{ for some positive integers } n_i, n_j; \text{ for all } i, j \qquad (11.12)$$

  - **No production implies no setups.**

    If $u_i^2 = 0$, then $f_i^2 = 0$. $\qquad (11.13)$

    That is, if Type i parts are not being made, there is no need to set up the machine for them.

  - **Production of only one part type implies no setups.**

    If $u_i^2 \neq 0$ and $u_j^2 = 0, j \neq i$, then $f_j^2 = 0$ for all j. $\qquad (11.14)$

    If only one part type is being made, there is no need to change setups.

Even if we ignore the rationality constraints, constraints (11.13) and (11.14) make the problem non-convex. Consequently, finding a satisfactory non-optimal solution will require problem simplification.

Simplification One simplification would be to ignore these awkward constraints. Ignoring the rationality constraints might lead to setup frequencies which are not integer multiples of one another, which would imply a complex, non-cyclic progression of setup changes. Ignoring the other constraints would cause the Level 2 dynamic program to allocate capacity for useless setups. We would then simply ignore those setups at Level 3.

An improvement would be to replace the resulting u^2 target in the Level 3 formulation by another vector of production rates. Component i of this vector is d_i if Part Type i is at its hedging point at Level 2; otherwise it is Ku_i^2, where K is a scale factor such that this vector uses all available capacity.

If we ignore these awkward constraints at Level 2, the problem is of the same form as in Chapter 9, with some additional linear constraints. For more discussion, see Section 11.6.

Level 3   The objective at this level is to choose setup times (no longer setup frequencies) and short term production rates. Here we study a system similar to that of Chapter 9, except that there are setup changes instead of failures. Minimizing inventory is not important at Level 3; the inventory required to decouple the effects of setup changes is far smaller than that which is required to decouple the effects of failures (as a result of the relative frequency assumptions made for this system). Consequently, optimization is not critical, as long as reasonable, stable behavior is assured.

The Level 3 production rate, u_i^3, is the quantity that is sought. Part of the state of the system is the *surplus vector*, whose component $x_i^3(t)$, is the difference between cumulative production and cumulative demand for Part Type i at time t. The surplus satisfies

$$x^3(t) = \int_{t_0}^{t} u^3(s)ds - u^2(t - t_0) + x^3(t_0) \tag{11.15}$$

where t_0 is the last time that u^2 was changed by the Level 2 controller. Equation (11.15) can also be written

$$\frac{dx^3}{dt} = u^3 - u^2, \qquad\qquad x^3(t_0) \text{ specified.} \tag{11.16}$$

The objective function,

$$J^3 = \min \int_{t_0}^{T} g^3(x^3(t))dt, \tag{11.17}$$

is of the same form as (9.9) and (11.10), where $g^3(x^3)$ is given by

$$g^3(x^3) = \sum_{i=1}^{N} g_i^3(x_i^3)$$

$$g_i^3(x_i^3) = \begin{cases} g_{i+}^3 x_i^3, & \text{if } x_i^3 \geq 0 \\ -g_{i-}^3 x_i^3, & \text{if } x_i^3 \leq 0 \end{cases} \qquad g_{i+}^3, g_{i-}^3 \geq 0$$

The horizon T is assumed to be very long; it is long enough so that many setup changes take place in $[t_0, T]$.

At Level 3, setups are treated individually. Therefore, there is no use for setup frequency variables; instead, we must define *setup states*. Let σ be the setup state of the system. It can be one of the following[12]

$$
\sigma = \begin{cases} i & \text{if the machine is producing Part Type } i \\ (i,j) & \text{if the machine is changing from producing Part Type } i \\ & \quad \text{to producing Part Type } j, \end{cases} \tag{11.18}
$$

$$
i = 1, ..., N; j = 1, ..., N; i \neq j
$$

and the only possible transitions of σ are

$$
\begin{array}{ccc} \sigma = i & \rightarrow & \sigma = (i,j) \\ \sigma = (i,j) & \rightarrow & \sigma = j \end{array} \qquad i = 1, ..., N; j = 1, ..., N; i \neq j \tag{11.19}
$$

The time at which a transition from $\sigma = i$ to $\sigma = (i,j)$ takes place can be chosen, so this is a controllable event. However, σ must remain in state (i,j) for exactly s_j time units (s_{ij} time units if the setups were sequence-dependent). For each setup state σ we have a different Level 3 capacity set. The decision to choose setup times, then, is one of choosing among the possible capacity sets. The machine capacity constraint at Level 3 dictates that the total amount of time that the machine is occupied within a setup state must not be more than 100%. Therefore, if $\sigma = i$, then $u_j^3 = 0$ (for all $j \neq i$) and u_i^3 can take on values over the interval $[0, \mu_i]$.

The object of real-time scheduling is to choose the setup state $\sigma(t)$, and the production rate vector $u^3(t)$ which is a function of $x^3(t)$, $\sigma(t)$, and t to minimize the cost integral (11.17).

To state the Level 3 dynamic programming problem, we must introduce a new state variable, t_σ, which is only defined when $\sigma = (i,j)$. It is the time since the setup change started. When $t_\sigma = s_j$, the setup change is completed, and $\sigma = j$. Note that σ is a very peculiar variable. It is a state variable, but when $\sigma = i$, it is also a control variable, in that the manager can change it to $\sigma = (i,j)$ whenever he or she chooses. Note also that α is not a state variable at this level; it is a constant parameter. It is a state variable at Level 2, and its dynamics are defined there.

The Level 3 dynamic programming problem is

$$
J^3 = \min_{\sigma(t), t_0 \leq t \leq T} \int_{t_0}^{T} \sum_{i=1}^{N} g_i^3(x_i^3(t)) dt \tag{11.20}
$$

subject to

---

[12]It is sometimes convenient to say *producing Part Type i* rather than *set up to produce Part Type i*. If a machine is set up to produce Part Type i, but is not currently producing it, we will say that it is producing Part Type i at rate 0.

- dynamics:

$$\frac{dx^3}{dt} = u^3(x^3, \sigma, t) - u^2.$$

  - If $\alpha = 1$, then
    * if $\sigma(t) = i$, then $\sigma(t^+) = i$ or $\sigma(t^+) = (i, j)$;
    * if $\sigma(t) = i$ and $\sigma(t^+) = (i, j)$, then $t_\sigma(t) = 0$;
    * if $\sigma(t) = (i, j)$, then $\dfrac{dt_\sigma}{dt} = 1$;
    * if $\sigma(t) = (i, j)$ and $t_\sigma < s_j$, then $\sigma(t^+) = (i, j)$.
    * if $\sigma(t) = (i, j)$ and $t_\sigma = s_j$, then $\sigma(t^+) = j$.

  - If $\alpha = 0$, then σ is constant.

  $x^3(t_0), \sigma(t_0), t_\sigma(t_0)$ specified.

- capacity constraints:

$$\tau_i u_i^3 \leq \alpha, \quad u_j^3 = 0 \qquad \text{if} \quad \sigma = i; \quad i, j = 1, ..., N; \quad j \neq i$$

$$u_i^3 = 0 \qquad \text{if} \quad \sigma = (j, m); \quad i, j, m = 1, ..., N; \quad j \neq m$$

$$u_i^3 \geq 0, \qquad i = 1, ..., N$$

No solution to this problem is known. Just as in Chapter 9, we seek control policies that provide satisfactory rather than optimal behavior.

Behavior The goal of this level is to choose setup change times consistent with the setup rates calculated at Level 2 and to set the production rate targets for Level 4. The Level 2 production rates are piecewise constant functions of the Level 2 surplus. If the Level 2 production rate vector has only a single non-zero component, the Level 3 production rate vector will have the same single non-zero component. The Level 2 surplus trajectory follows a straight line until it reaches a boundary between two regions. The Level 2 surplus trajectory then stays on the boundary if the boundary is attractive. When that happens, the corresponding Level 2 production rate vector will have more than one non-zero component. The Level 3 production rate vector cannot have more than one non-zero component, so it will alternate among different vectors, each with one non-zero component that is the same as one of the non-zero components of the Level 2 production rate vector. (It will also be 0 while the setup is being changed.) Based on the results of the single part-type problems in Chapter 9, it is reasonable to conjecture that the Level 3 production rate for the part type that the machine is set up for can have one of three values: 0, d_i, or μ_i.

Level 4 To complete the hierarchy, we must say something about the loading level. There is really not much of a scheduling problem here, since the Level 3 production rate vector has at most only one non-zero component. The machine is set up for the corresponding part type. If the Level 3 rate is μ_i, then the Level 4 strategy should be to load that part as fast as possible with no idle time. If it is d_i, then a staircase policy may be most effective.

11.4.2   Discussion of dynamic systems behavior

Before we introduce the heuristic policies that yield satisfactory behavior for Level 3, it is useful to discuss the possible behaviors of a dynamic system. A deterministic dynamic system can behave in one of three ways:

- It can be *unstable*. That is, over time its state moves further and further away (not necessarily monotonically) from a reference point. This kind of behavior is seen in both deterministic and stochastic systems. The buffer level of an $M/M/1$ queue (Section 2.3.6) is unstable when its arrival rate (λ) exceeds its service rate (μ). The surplus of a manufacturing system also demonstrates this behavior if the demand is greater than the capacity (which is essentially the same phenomenon) or if it is scheduled *very* badly (for example, if one part type is never made).

- The state of the system can approach a point or a limit cycle. The state moves closer and closer to a reference point, or its behavior becomes more and more nearly periodic over time. This is *stable*.

- The system can be *chaotic*. The state eventually moves to within a bounded region and never escapes after that. However, it does not approach a point or become periodic. A trajectory of such a system can look random, but it is not.[13] A similar behavior is exhibited by an ideal *pseudo-random number generator*, which looks random but always generates the same sequence of values when it has the same starting point (the *seed*), and which generates a very different sequence if the seed is changed by even a tiny amount.[14]

If a stable or chaotic (bounded) behavior is possible, it is preferable to an unstable behavior. Since no solution is known to the Level 3 optimization problem of Section 11.4.1, the remainder of Section 11.4 presents heuristics that produce stability or sometimes chaos, and a discussion of their characteristics.

11.4.3   Corridor policy for Level 3

In this section, we translate the Level 2 rate targets into Level 3 production rates and setup times. Whenever the Level 2 production rates are non-zero for only a single part type, the

---

[13]We are using the term chaotic in the specific, narrow, technical sense that has recently become popular in the scientific literature. The popular usage includes ideas of disorder and unpredictability — something is chaotic if it is a mess. Here, we want to separate randomness from chaos. Not every messy, hard to predict system is chaotic.

[14]Actual pseudo-random number generators are periodic. Good ones have very, very long periods.

Level 3 production rate vector is the same as the Level 2 vector, and there are no setups (or possibly one, at the time the vector changes). However, whenever two or more Level 2 rates are simultaneously non-zero, Level 3 must determine a sequence of production rate vectors that have only one non-zero element, and a sequence of appropriate setup change times.

The corridor policy does this by constructing a corridor around any Level 2 trajectory segment whose production rate vector has more than one non-zero rate. The corridor is made up of a set of planes (the walls, ceiling, floor of the corridor) that are each labeled with the name of a part type; when the trajectory hits a plane, the setup is changed so that the machine can make the associated part. To guarantee satisfactory behavior, there are certain restrictions on the planes. The corridor is a feedback control policy that chooses setup change times as a function of production surplus. If the corridor is chosen carefully, the trajectory converges to a cyclic sequence of production runs for the different part types, as shown in Figure 11.6 for $N = 2$.

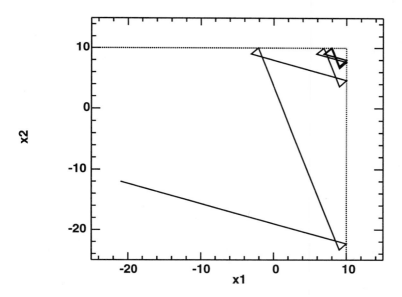

Corridor Policy -- Two Part Types

Figure 11.6: The Corridor Policy

The vertex of the corridor is near the Level 2 hedging point, and the corridor increases in width as each component of x^3 goes to $-\infty$. Consequently, when surplus is very negative, the trajectory has to travel a long distance from one plane to the next. When the surplus is near the Level 2 hedging point, setup changes are more frequent. Thus, more capacity is allocated to production when the system is far behind, and more is allocated to setup changes when the system is nearly caught up. Inventories are therefore larger during periods when the goal is to catch up as soon as possible; and they are smaller when the system can afford to change setups often enough to keep them small.

In the stability analysis described below, the machine is assumed always to be operated at its maximum production rate. As we indicated earlier, it might be better to allow it to be idle, or to operate at the demand rate for some of the time.

Equal setup frequencies   *Round-robin* policies are those for which there is a cycle of setup changes in which each part type appears exactly once, and where the cycle is repeated indefinitely. In the ELSP formulation (Section 11.3.3), $n_i = 1$ for all i. In this case, all the setup frequencies are equal[15], or $f_1 = f_2 = ... f_N$.

For round-robin policies, the corridor policy can be expressed as follows. Let $a_i, i = 1, ..., N$, and b be a set of vectors. Corridor plane i is defined as the set of all x^3 such that $a_i^T x^3 = b_i$. Assume that at time $t = t_0$, the initial setup is $\sigma(t_0)$ and the initial surplus is such that $a_k^T x^3(t_0) < b_k$ for some $k \neq \sigma(t_0)$. Then for $t > t_0$, let $\sigma(t) = j$. Whenever $a_i^T x^3(t) = b_i$ for some i, the setup state is changed from $\sigma = j$ to $\sigma = (j, i)$. For some vectors $a_i, i = 1, ..., N$ and b, the corridor policy leads to a desirable behavior. To state the conditions, we must define u_σ^3. It is the Level 3 production rate vector when the setup state is σ. Clearly $u_\sigma^3 = 0$ when $\sigma = (i, j)$; when $\sigma = i$, the ith component is μ_i, and all other components are 0. Then

A system operated according to a corridor policy converges to a periodic round-robin sequence of setups, if

> *For $i = 1, 2, ... N; j = 1, 2.... N; i \neq j$,*
>
> $a_j^T(u_i^3 - u^2) > 0$ if $j = i \pmod{N} + 1$;
>
> $a_j^T(u_i^3 - u^2) < 0$ otherwise
>
> *For all i,*
>
> $a_i^T u^2 > 0$.

The first condition insures that, if the machine is set up for Type i, the surplus is moving closer to Plane j, where j is the next part type in the cycle after i. (The mod operation means that if $j < N$, $i = j + 1$, and if $j = N$, $i = 1$.) This is because

$$\frac{d}{dt}(a_j^T x^3(t) - b_j) = a_j^T \frac{dx^3(t)}{dt} = a_j^T(u_i^3 - u^2),$$

and if it is positive, $a_j^T x^3(t) - b_j$ is getting closer to 0, so x^3 is getting closer to Plane j. If it is negative, $a_j^T x^3(t) - b_j$ is getting further from 0, so x^3 is getting further from Plane j. This condition requires that the surplus move toward Plane j *only* when $j = i \pmod{N} + 1$.

---

[15]On the other hand, equal setup frequencies does *not* imply a round-robin policy. For example, consider the cycle {1-2-3-1-3-2} for $N = 3$.

The last condition says that when the setup is being changed, the surplus vector x^3 moves away from all planes. This is because

$$\frac{d}{dt}(a_i^T x^3(t) - b_i) = a_i^T \frac{dx^3(t)}{dt} = a_j^T(-u^2) < 0.$$

Consequently, the only time that x^3 moves toward Plane j is if the machine is currently set up for Part i, and i precedes j in the setup cycle. When the machine is set up for something else, and when the setup is being changed, it moves away from Plane j. These conditions are very conservative. It is easy to find (by simulation experiment) sets of a_j and b vectors that do not satisfy these conditions, and yet lead to stable round-robin policies. It is just as easy to find sets of a_j and b vectors that do not satisfy these conditions, and lead to stable non-round-robin policies, or to apparent chaos.

Example Let $N = 3$. Let u^2 and $u_i^3, i = 1, 2, 3$ be given by

$$u^2 = \left\{ \begin{array}{c} 1 \\ 1 \\ 1 \end{array} \right\}; u_1^3 = \left\{ \begin{array}{c} 4 \\ 0 \\ 0 \end{array} \right\}; u_2^3 = \left\{ \begin{array}{c} 0 \\ 4 \\ 0 \end{array} \right\}; u_3^3 = \left\{ \begin{array}{c} 0 \\ 0 \\ 4 \end{array} \right\}$$

Then

$$b = \left\{ \begin{array}{c} 10 \\ 10 \\ 10 \end{array} \right\}; a_1 = \left\{ \begin{array}{c} 0 \\ 1 \\ 0 \end{array} \right\}; a_2 = \left\{ \begin{array}{c} 0 \\ 0 \\ 1 \end{array} \right\}; a_3 = \left\{ \begin{array}{c} 1 \\ 0 \\ 0 \end{array} \right\}$$

satisfy the above conditions. We switch the machine into Type 1 when x_2^3 reaches 10; we switch the machine into Type 2 when x_3^3 reaches 10; and we switch the machine into Type 3 when x_1^3 reaches 10.

Figure 11.7 shows $x_1(t)$ *versus* t for this policy and this system when $s^T = (1, 1, 1)$.

Example The same u^2, u_i^3 $(i = 1, 2, 3)$, b, and a_i $(i = 2, 3)$ but

$$a_1 = \left\{ \begin{array}{c} -0.3 \\ 1.0 \\ 0.5 \end{array} \right\}$$

do not satisfy the conditions. However, numerical experience indicates that the system converges to a stable round-robin setup change policy anyway. Here, we switch the machine into Type 1 when $-0.3x_1^3 + x_2^3 + 0.5x_3^3$ reaches 10; we switch the machine into Type 2 when x_3^3 reaches 10; and we switch the machine into Type 3 when x_1^3 reaches 10.

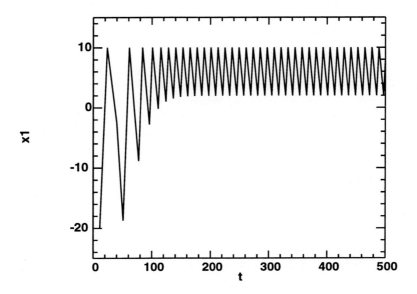

Figure 11.7: Corridor Policy with a Stable Limit Cycle

Example   The same u^2, u_i^3 $(i = 1, 2, 3)$, b, and a_i $(i = 2, 3)$ but

$$a_1 = \left\{ \begin{array}{c} -0.3 \\ 1.0 \\ 2.0 \end{array} \right\}$$

also do not satisfy the conditions. In this case, numerical experiment indicates that the system converges to a stable *non*-round-robin setup change policy. Here, we switch the machine into Type 1 when $-0.3x_1^3 + x_2^3 + 2x_3^3$ reaches 10; we switch the machine into Type 2 when x_3^3 reaches 10; and we switch the machine into Type 3 when x_1^3 reaches 10.

Unequal setup frequencies   Now consider a manufacturing system where the Level 2 target setup rates f_i^2 are unequal. The limit cycle contains more than one production run for some part types. The non-round-robin limit cycle can be obtained as an extension of the corridors that give a round-robin limit cycle in a related system with more part types.

Let the setup frequencies at Level 2 be such that Part Type i has n_i production runs in the optimal limit cycle. That is, in the ELSP notation of Section 11.3.3, $n_i = \text{card}(K_i)$, $f_i/f_j = n_i/n_j$, and $n = \sum_i n_i$. Consider another system with the following characteristics:

1. Corresponding to Part Type i in the original system, there are n_i part types in the

new system. A part type in the new system is denoted by π_{ij} if it corresponds to the jth production run of Part Type i in the original system; $j = 1, ..., n_i$.

2. The target rate u_{ij}^2 for Part Type π_{ij} satisfies

$$\sum_{j=1}^{n_i} u_{ij}^2 = u_i^2; \qquad u_{ij}^2 > 0$$

For example

$$u_{ij}^2 = \frac{1}{n_i} u_i^2.$$

The maximum production rate for Part Type π_{ij} is $1/\mu_i$.

3. The initial value of surplus for Part Type π_{ij} is $x_{ij}^3(t_0) = x_i^3(t_0)/n_i$. The dynamics of $x_{ij}^3(t)$ can be written

$$\frac{dx_{ij}^3}{dt} = u_{ij}^3 - u_{ij}^2$$

in which u_{ij}^3 is the current value of the production rate of Part Type π_{ij}.

4. Setup changes from Part Type π_{ij} to Part Type π_{ik} do not occur.[16]

Vectors a_{ij} and b are chosen for the new system to create corridors in the higher dimension surplus space. These vectors satisfy the stability conditions listed above as well as the last rule. There is a plane for Part Type π_{ij}, for each i and j. Whenever the surplus hits the π_{ij} plane, we change the setup to Part Type π_{ij}; that is, we change the setup to Part Type i. Since only one u_{ij}^3 is positive at any time,

$$u_i^3 = \sum_{j=1}^{n_i} u_{ij}^3.$$

Consequently

$$\frac{dx_i^3}{dt} = \sum_{j=1}^{n_i} \frac{dx_{ij}^3}{dt} = \sum_{j=1}^{n_i} (u_{ij}^3 - u_{ij}^2) = u_i^3 - u_i^2$$

so x_i^3 has the same stability properties as x_{ij}^3.

Corridors are chosen (for the new system) such that they satisfy the stability conditions, as well as the last rule enumerated above. Setup changes to Part Type i are initiated when

---

[16]Why not?

the surplus trajectory in the new system hits the corridor plane corresponding to any Part
Type π_{ij}. The surplus trajectory in the new system converges to a round-robin sequence of
setups. This implies that the surplus in the original system converges to the optimal limit
cycle consistent with the setup rates calculated at Level 2.

This is a feedback policy because the setup change decision is made on the basis of x^3.
If the actual system is a little different from the model (because of higher level or lower level
randomness or other reasons) the actual trajectory may differ from that predicted by the
model. However, if the error is not too great, the system will still be stable.

11.4.4 Clear-a-fraction

A class of similar policies that can be used for Level 3 of the hierarchy are the *Clear-a-
fraction* policies of Perkins and Kumar (1989) and Kumar and Seidman (1990). These
real-time scheduling policies make setup change decisions based on buffer levels upstream of
a machine. The stability of these policies has been established and bounds for the work-in-
process inventory have been found. In this chapter, we describe clearing policies for single
machines. We defer the discussion of multiple-machine policies to Chapter 12.

Single machine Consider a system in which there is one machine doing operations on N
part types. Part Type i arrives at rate d_i at Buffer i upstream of the machine. The number
of Type i parts in Buffer i at time t is $b_i(t)$. Then buffer level vector $b(t)$ satisfies

$$\frac{db}{dt} = d - u$$

If x is the usual surplus, this means that

$$\frac{db}{dt} = -\frac{dx}{dt}$$

Therefore $x + b = c$, a constant.

There are a set of related policies:

CLB: *Clear the largest buffer* Keep the machine working on the part type it is currently
working on until its buffer is cleared (emptied). Then switch to the buffer with the
largest b_i.

CLW: *Clear the largest work* Keep the machine working on what it is currently working on
until that buffer is cleared; then switch to the highest value of $\tau_i b_i$.

CAF: *Clear-a-fraction* This is a class of policies. For some ϵ, keep the machine working on
what it is currently working on until that buffer is cleared; then switch to *any* buffer
i such that $b_i \geq \epsilon \sum_j b_j$. CLB and CLW are members of this class of policies.

Comparison with corridor policy The CLB policy can be stated as: if $\sigma = i$ and $b_i = 0$, then switch to the largest b_j. Since $x + b = c$, this is the same as: if $\sigma = i$ and $x_i = c_i$, then switch to the Type j such that $c_j - x_j$ is largest. Assume each vector a_i of the corridor policy is a column of the identity matrix as in the first example of the corridor policy. Then the corridor policy can be stated as: if $x_i = c_i$, then switch to a specific Type j.

Comparison with hedging point policy If c is the hedging point, the CLB policy says that the part selected next is the one whose surplus is furthest behind its hedging point. This is exactly the part type that is chosen in the single machine example in Chapter 9, in Example 3 and Exercise 8. The difference is that in that example, the *next part type* decision is made every time an operation is performed, whereas here the decision is made only when a buffer is cleared.

Setups and Failures Lou, Sethi, and Sorger (1992) prove that the CLW policy is stable for a system in which the machine is unreliable.

11.4.5 Chaos

Real-time setup change policies can lead to chaos. Consider the following example, which is a modification of the above examples of the corridor policy.

Example Let u^2, u_i^3 ($i = 1, 2, 3$), and b be the same as above, and let

$$a_1 = \left\{ \begin{array}{c} -1 \\ 1 \\ 2 \end{array} \right\}; a_2 = \left\{ \begin{array}{c} 0.4 \\ -0.2 \\ 1.0 \end{array} \right\}; a_3 = \left\{ \begin{array}{c} 1 \\ 0 \\ 0 \end{array} \right\}$$

This does not satisfy the stability conditions above, and simulation experience suggests it produces apparent chaos. In this example, we switch the machine into Type 1 when $-x_1^3 + x_2^3 + 2.0x_3^3$ reaches 10; we switch the machine into Type 2 when $0.4x_1^3 - 0.2x_2^3 + x_3^3$ reaches 10; and we switch the machine into Type 3 when x_1^3 reaches 10.

Figure 11.8 shows $x_1(t)$ *versus* t for this policy and this system when $s^T = (1, 1, 1)$.

Explanation One characteristic of a chaotic system is *sensitivity to initial conditions*. That is, if the initial state $x(0)$ is changed by a little bit, some future state $x(t)$ changes by a large amount. (This does not imply instability. The perturbed $x(t)$ need not go to ∞. Both the unperturbed $x(t)$ and the perturbed $x(t)$ can remain within a bounded region, but they differ by a much larger amount than the initial perturbation.)

The corridor policy exhibits chaos when the trajectory comes very close to the intersection of two corridor planes. At such a time t, the unperturbed trajectory can hit one plane, and the perturbed trajectory, which, in $[0, t]$, is very close to the unperturbed trajectory, can hit the other. The two trajectories then move off in very different directions after t. The

Corridor Policy -- Chaos

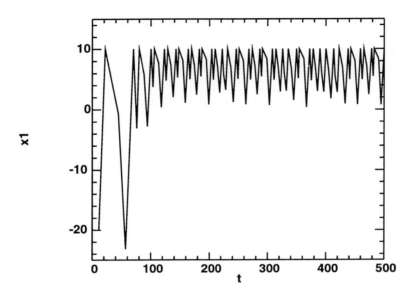

Figure 11.8: Corridor Policy with a Chaotic Trajectory

sequences of setups are identical in $[0, t)$; they are completely different after t. Conditions are not known on the system parameters that determine whether chaos will occur.

Is chaos bad?   Chaos certainly *sounds* bad in a factory. But chaos need not mean disorder; it only means that it is hard to predict the future. A future that is hard to predict is less desirable than one that is easy to predict. It makes it tougher for people to make plans. Life would be easier if the system followed a simple pattern (for example, paint white cars on Mondays and Thursdays, and blue cars on Tuesdays, Wednesdays, and Fridays). However, the factory may have to sacrifice performance — for example, it might be necessary to keep more inventory around — in order for managers to obtain such a simple behavior.

11.5   Random Setups and Due Dates

Burman (1993) describes a system that differs from the one in Section 11.4 in two major ways: the setup times are random, and demand cannot be represented by a continuous process. Demand cannot be represented by a continuous process because due dates are infrequent compared with setup frequencies.

Orders arrive each Monday that must be filled on Friday. The orders for the subsequent

Friday are known with high reliability, although not certainty. Orders for different customers are sometimes for the same part type, so there can be fewer setups required than orders.

The fixed arrival and delivery times, which are less frequent than the setup changes, make the methods of Section 11.4 inappropriate. There is nothing to be gained by setting up for a given part type more than once per week; and orders must be delivered, so if there is not enough material in inventory for all the orders for a given part type in a week, the machine *must* be set up.

The issue is that capacity is limited. If no material were kept in inventory, so that each order would have to be produced in the week that it arrives, it would not be possible to meet demand in most weeks. The problem is to decide how much inventory to produce each week. If some of this week's orders were produced last week, demand can probably be met. If this leaves some time available on the machine, we can use it to produce some of next week's orders.

The reason that this leads to a savings of time is that setups can be reduced by this strategy. The orders from next week that we produce this week are those for some of the same part types that we are making this week for this week's orders. As a consequence, the machine does not have to be set up for the same part type once this week and once next week; one setup suffices for both weeks if we do all the work this week for this week's and next week's orders for the same part types.

Burman approaches this problem by breaking it into two parts: a setup sequencing problem, and real-time lot sizing problem. The sequencing problem determines a minimum-time sequence of setups for the parts that are required in the current week. Such a sequence maximizes the time left for other activities. The real-time lot-sizing problem uses this time by scheduling production of some of the orders of the following week.

Setup sequencing problem   A set of parts must be produced during the current week. The setup sequencing problem — a traveling salesman problem — is that of finding the sequence that minimizes the expected setup time. When the setups have a hierarchical structure (Section 11.2), a greedy algorithm[17] creates a nearly optimal setup sequence. The greedy algorithm described by Burman chooses one of the parts in the current lowest-level cluster to set up next. If all those parts have already been selected, the algorithm chooses one in the nearest higher level cluster, and so forth. (Another way of saying this is that it chooses one of the parts that has not already been chosen, and whose setup time is minimal. Conway, Maxwell, and Miller (1967) call this a "closest unvisited city" algorithm.) This algorithm is run once each week.

Real-time lot sizing problem   The goal of the real-time lot sizing problem is to decide whether to add an order due next week to the current week's production. A dynamic programming problem was formulated, numerical results were obtained, and a set of simplified heuristics were developed based on those solutions. The heuristic that seemed most

---

[17]A *greedy* or *myopic* algorithm is one that selects its next move on the basis of immediate, local optimality. It does not plan far ahead; it grabs whatever gives it short-term gains. This is usually a poor strategy, but there are special cases in which it leads to optimal or near-optimal results.

promising was the following: assume that the ith uncontrollable event occurs at time T^i. At that time, calculate T_{UP}^i, the *unplanned production time*. This is the amount of time left until the end of the week after time allocated to mandatory production and setups or to variability has been deducted. (The latter is a hedge against random setup times or other sources of randomness.) The time required for an order of the same part type for the next week is compared with T_{UP}^i. If T_{UP}^i is greater, the order is produced.

11.6   Research Problems

Because of the incomplete nature of the material of this chapter, the field is open for much new research. A small number of such problems are enumerated here.

1. Find a satisfactory solution to the Level 2 problem of Section 11.4. Determine bounds on the error if the awkward constraints are relaxed. Find a solution to the static version of the problem.

2. A possible decomposition of the Level 2 problem (again without the awkward constraints) is as follows. Define $S = \sum_{i=1}^{N} s_i f_i^2$. Then (11.11) becomes

$$\sum_{i=1}^{N} \tau_i u_i^2 \leq \alpha - S.$$

   A solution procedure would be to iterate as follows. If $\alpha = 1$,

   0. Guess $S, 0 \leq S \leq 1$.
   1. Solve the following:

$$L = \min_{u} \frac{\partial W^2}{\partial x^2}(x^2, 1)u^2$$

      subject to

$$\sum_{i=1}^{N} \tau_i u_i^2 \leq 1 - S$$

$$u^2 \geq 0$$

   2. Solve

$$\min L$$

      subject to

$$S = \sum_{i=1}^{N} s_i f_i^2$$

$$\phi^3 \le f_i^2 \le \Phi^3$$

$$f_j^2 \le \sum_{\substack{i=1 \\ i \ne j}}^{N} f_i^2; \qquad j = 1, 2, ..., N.$$

3. If the u^2 and f^2 parameters have not yet converged, go to Step 1.

Does this converge? How fast? Does it converge to the correct solution? Here, S can be interpreted as the fraction of time that the machine is undergoing setup changes. Step 2 might be accomplished by performing a sensitivity analysis on Step 1. If the system is at the Level 2 hedging point, S and therefore the f_is can be large. Otherwise, S should be small. Note that this may be difficult to implement in real-time because of the iteration process.

3. Choose planes for the corridor policy of Section 11.4.3 to give desired behavior, such as specified setup frequencies. Investigate other corridor shapes.

4. Find *necessary* conditions for the corridor policy to yield a stable, round-robin cycle. (The conditions above are *sufficient*.) Find conditions to guarantee a stable, non-round-robin cycle. Find conditions to guarantee chaos.

5. Develop a corridor policy for multiple machine systems.

Exercises

1. For a static optimization problem, such as the ELSP, the same computational advantages can be obtained as for sequence-dependent setups if s_{ij} and A_{ij} depend only on i ($s_{ij} = s_i$ and $A_{ij} = A_i$ for all i and j). This is because the performance is the same if time is reversed; in the original case, the time is lost and the cost is incurred each time the machine is changed *into* a setup; in this case, time is lost and the cost is incurred each time the machine is changed *out of* a setup.

   Show that the same advantages are obtained if $s_{ij} = s_i^{out} + s_j^{in}$ and $A_{ij} = A_i^{out} + A_j^{in}$ for all i and j.

2. Write a simple simulation to demonstrate the corridor and clear-a-fraction policies. Experiment with them, and exhibit a variety of different kinds of behavior.

3. Show that CLB is CAF with $\epsilon = 1/N$, where N is the number of part types. Show that CLW is CAF with

   $$\epsilon = \frac{1}{(N-1)\frac{\tau_1}{\tau^*} + 1}$$

where

$$\tau^* = \max_{j \geq 2} \tau_j.$$

Bibliography

[1] K. Baker (1974), *Introduction to Sequencing and Scheduling*, Wiley, 1974.

[2] G. R. Bitran, and H. Matsuo (1986),"Approximation Formulations for the Single Product Capacitated Lot Size Problem," *Operations Research*, Vol. 34, No. 1, January-February, 1986, pp. 63-74.

[3] M. H. Burman (1993), "A Real-Time Dispatch Policy for a System Subject to Sequence-Dependent, Random Setup Times," Master's Thesis, MIT Operations Research Center, 1993.

[4] M. H. Burman and S. B. Gershwin (1992), "An Algorithm for the Scheduling of Setups and Production to Meet Due Dates," *Proceedings of the 1992 IEEE International Conference on Robotics and Automation,* Nice, France, May, 1992.

[5] J. J. Carreno (1990), "Economic Lot Scheduling For Multiple Products on Parallel Identical Processors," *Management Science*, Vol 36, No. 3, March, 1990, pp. 348-358.

[6] C. Chase and P. J. Ramadge (1992), "On Real Time Scheduling Policies For Flexible Manufacturing Systems," *IEEE Transactions on Automatic Control*, Vol. 37, No. 4, pp. 491-496, April, 1992.

[7] C. Chase, J. Serrano, and P. J. Ramadge (1993), "Periodicity and Chaos from Switched Flow Systems: Contrasting Examples of Discretely Controlled Continuous Systems," *IEEE Transactions on Automatic Control*, Volume 38, Number 1, January, 1993, pp. 70-83.

[8] S. Connolly (1992), "A Real-time Policy for Performing Setup Changes in a Manufacturing System," Master's Thesis, MIT Operations Research Center, May, 1992; MIT Laboratory for Manufacturing and Productivity Report LMP-92-0005.

[9] S. Connolly, Y. Dallery, and S. B. Gershwin (1992), "A Real-Time Policy for Performing Setup Changes in a Manufacturing System," *Proceedings of the 31st IEEE Conference on Decision and Control*, Tucson, Arizona, December 16-18, 1992.

[10] R. W. Conway, W. L. Maxwell, and L. W. Miller, *Theory of Scheduling*, Addison-Wesley, 1967.

[11] R. L. Devaney, *An Introduction to Chaotic Dynamical Systems*, Addison-Wesley, 1989.

[12] G. Dobson, "The Economic Lot Scheduling Problem: Achieving Feasibility Using Time-Varying Lot Sizes," *Operations Research*, Vol. 35, No 5, 1987, pp. 764-771.

[13] S. E. Elmaghraby, "The Economic Lot Scheduling Problem (ELSP): Review and Extensions," *Management Science*, Vol. 24, No. 6, February, 1978, pp. 587-598.

[14] S. French, *Sequencing and Scheduling*, Wiley, 1982.

[15] S. B. Gershwin, M. Caramanis, and P. Murray (1988), "Simulation Experience with a Hierarchical Scheduling Policy for a Simple Manufacturing System," *Proceedings of the 27th IEEE Conference on Decision and Control*, Austin, TX, December, 1988, pp. 1841-1849.

[16] S. K. Goyal (1984), "Determination of Economic Production Quantities for a Two-Product Single Machine System," *International Journal of Production Research*, Vol. 22, No. 1, 1984, pp. 121-126.

[17] S. C. Graves (1981), "A Review of Production Scheduling," *Operations Research*, Vol. 29, No. 4, July-August, 1981, pp. 646-675.

[18] J. Hu and M. Caramanis (1992), "Near Optimal Set-up Scheduling for Flexible Manufacturing Systems," Technical Report, Department of Manufacturing Engineering, Boston University, Boston, MA, 1992; *Proceedings of the Third Rensselaer Polytechnic Institute International Conference on Computer Integrated Manufacturing*, Troy, New York, May 20-22, 1992.

[19] P. C. Jones and R. R. Inman (1989), "When Is The Economic Lot Scheduling Problem Easy?," *IIE Transactions*, Vol. 21, No. 1, March, 1989, pp. 11-20.

[20] U. Karmarkar (1987), "Lot Sizes, Lead Times, and In-Process Inventories," *Management Science*, Volume 33, Number 3, March, 1987, pp. 409-418.

[21] P. R. Kumar and T. I. Seidman (1990), "Dynamic Instabilities and Stabilization Methods in Distributed Real-time Scheduling of Manufacturing Systems," *IEEE Transactions on Automatic Control*, Vol. 35, No. 3, pp. 289-298, March, 1990.

[22] A. Kusiak (1990), *Intelligent Manufacturing Systems*, Prentice-Hall, 1990.

[23] T. W. E. Lau (1991), *Dynamic Capacity Allocation in Manufacturing Systems with Significant Setup Times*, M.S. thesis, Department of Manufacturing Engineering, Boston University, October, 1991.

[24] E. L. Lawler, J. K. Lenstra, A. H. G. Rinnooy Kan, and D. B. Shmoys (1985), *The Traveling Salesman Problem*, Wiley, 1985.

[25] S. Lou, S. Sethi, and G. Sorger (1991), "Analysis of a Class of Real-Time Multiproduct Lot Scheduling Policies," *IEEE Transactions on Automatic Control*, Vol. 36, No. 2, pp. 243-248, February, 1991.

[26] S. Lou, S. Sethi, and G. Sorger (1992), "Stability of Real-Time Lot Scheduling Policies for an Unreliable Machine," *IEEE Transactions on Automatic Control*, Volume 37, Number 12, December, 1992, pp. 1966-1970.

[27] W. L. Maxwell and J. A. Muckstadt (1985), "Establishing Consistent and Realistic Reorder Intervals in Production-Distribution Systems," *Operations Research*, Vol. 33, No. 6, November-December, 1985, pp. 1316-1341.

[28] E. F. P. Newson (1975a), "Multi-Item Lot Size Scheduling by Heuristic, Part I: With Fixed Resources," *Management Science*, Vol. 21, No. 10, June, 1975, pp. 1186-1193.

[29] E. F. P. Newson (1975b), "Multi-Item Lot Size Scheduling by Heuristic, Part II: With Variable Resources," *Management Science*, Vol. 21, No. 10, June, 1975, pp. 1194-1203.

[30] J. Perkins and P. R. Kumar (1989), "Stable, Distributed, Real-Time Scheduling of Flexible Manufacturing/Assembly/Disassembly Systems," *IEEE Transactions on Automatic Control*, Vol. 34, No. 2, pp. 139-148, February, 1989.

[31] A. Sharifnia, M. Caramanis, and S. B. Gershwin (1991), "Dynamic Set-up Scheduling and Flow Control in Manufacturing Systems," *Discrete Event Dynamic Systems: Theory and Applications,* Volume 1, pp. 149-175, 1991.

[32] E. A. Silver and R. Peterson (1985), *Decision Systems for Inventory Management and Production Planning*, Second Edition, Wiley, 1985.

[33] S. B. Smith (1989), *Computer-Based Production and Inventory Control*, Prentice-Hall, 1989.

[34] N. Srivatsan and S. B. Gershwin (1990), "Selection of Setup Times in a Hierarchically Controlled Manufacturing System," *Proceedings of the 29th IEEE Conference on Decision and Control*, Hawaii, December, 1990.

[35] H. M. Wagner and T. M. Whitin (1958), "Dynamic Version of the Economic Lot Size Model," *Management Science*, Vol. 5, No. 1, October, 1958, pp. 89-96.

[36] P. H. Zipkin (1991), "Computing Optimal Lot Sizes in the Economic Lot Scheduling Problem," *Operations Research*, Vol. 39, No. 1, January-February, 1991, pp. 56-63.

Chapter 12

Spatial Decomposition of Scheduling

Chapters 3, 4, and 5 treat systems with buffers that are controlled by a simple policy whose goal is to maximize the production rate. Chapters 9, 10, and 11 deal with systems without buffers, but with more complex objectives, and consequently more complex control policies. The goal of this chapter is to combine some features of the systems of Chapters 3 and 4 with some features of those of Chapter 9. A further synthesis takes place in Chapter 13, where the ideas of Chapter 10 are added.

What appears here and in the next chapter is, like the material in Chapter 11, a long way from the last word on the subject. Considerable research remains to be done, to bridge the gap between the first part and the last part of the book, to improve the policies, and to add to the set of phenomena that are treated by control methods.

12.1   Introduction

12.1.1   Motivation

The methods of Chapters 9 and 10 are based on the assumption that the manufacturing system is small, in the sense that parts spend a short time in it. More precisely, the length of time a part spends in the system of Chapter 9 is small compared with the mean time to fail or the mean time to repair of any machine. In Chapter 10, if the lowest level is that of operations, the length of time a part spends in the system is assumed to be smaller than the mean arrival time of activities or events at the level just above operations (Assumption 2, Section 10.2.3). Consequently, as soon as any machine in the system fails, the production rates for all parts throughout the system are recalculated.

These assumptions are very limiting. In some kinds of manufacturing, parts can spend months in the production system.[1] If a machine fails that a part is not going to reach for weeks, and the repair is likely to take hours or days, there is no reason to prevent the part from entering the system. In fact, if we do, we are treating the system like one with buffers of size 0, and wasting machine capacity by creating unnecessary idle time. In this chapter, we extend the methods of Chapter 9 to systems with non-zero buffers. We also calculate buffer sizes that allow the system to meet the production requirements without excessive in-process inventory.

12.1.2 Inventory control

In order for a productive event — an operation — to occur in a factory, at least two things must come together: a part and a workstation. Sometimes, more than two are required, including a person, more parts (if the operation is an assembly), consumable materials (such as coolant for machining operations or deionized water for semiconductor operations), a pallet or fixture, etc. It is very unlikely that they all will arrive at precisely the same instant. That is, a part will not very often arrive from its previous operation at close to the same moment that the machine completes its last activity. More often, the part arrives while the machine is still busy, or the part arrives to find the machine idle. This is because of unequal operation times, machine failures, setup changes, demand that fluctuates above and below capacity, and many other causes. As a consequence, something must wait for something else.

We have different names for the waiting of different things. When machines wait, it is called *low utilization*. When parts wait, it is called *inventory*. Both of these are undesirable. Both can be reduced by reducing setup times and the frequencies and duration of failures and other disruptions. But beyond that, there is a conflict: inventory can be reduced by having redundant equipment (such as backup machines, or machines that are very fast so that they can catch up quickly after a failure); and capital requirements can be reduced by allowing inventory to accumulate in anticipation of future disruptions. The focus of this chapter is the minimization of inventory for a given set of capital equipment. Inventory is treated as a dynamic quantity, and capital is treated as fixed.

For all the reasons in Section 1.3, it is desirable for inventory to be as small as possible. On the other hand, Chapters 3 and 4 show that if inventory is too small, performance goals (such as production rates) may not be achievable. The analysis of the simple policy of Chapters 3, 4, and 5 determines the minimal inventory required for a given production rate. However, there are disadvantages to this policy: in particular, the variability (discussed in Section 3.2) appears to be high. It seems reasonable that different policies could reduce variability, possibly at the expense of requiring more inventory. We investigate such policies here.

Just as in Chapter 11, we must point out that there is a very large literature on inventory control, and that the reader must search elsewhere to find a survey of it. The goal here is to extend the framework established in Chapter 9 to include inventory management. A

---

[1]This, of course, is undesirable. Just as in the case of failures and setups, something ought to be done about reducing it. Until that happens, however, we must account for it in real-time schedulers.

further extension, that encompasses the ideas of Chapter 10, appears in Chapter 13.

12.1.3 Practical approaches

Just-in-Time A widely discussed philosophy is that of *just-in-time*. This is not so much a policy as a goal: to keep inventory as small as possible by producing what is needed only at the time it is needed. There are two major difficulties with the implementation of just-in-time.

1. It is often implemented by edict *("Reduce inventories! NOW!")* without any systematic methods for doing so. If buffers are haphazardly reduced, production goals cannot be met, and workers under pressure will find ways of hiding inventory surreptitiously. Large covert buffers are much worse than large acknowledged buffers.

2. The real goal of just-in-time is much wider than those of this book. It is to improve manufacturing by changing many of the things that we have assumed constant: system parameters such as failure and repair rates, and even system structure. The basic mechanism is that when inventories are reduced, problems become much more visible. There is pressure to repair machines faster, and to redesign processes to reduce failure rates and increase repair rates. Workers' suggestions about their own procedures and about process and product design must be solicited and respected. This can work if there is an atmosphere of mutual confidence among workers and management. It will fail otherwise. The evaluation of such a policy is beyond the scope of this book.[2]

MRP *MRP* or *Material Requirements Planning* systems are comprehensive computer-based systems for regulating the acquisition of material and the scheduling of production. (See Orlicky, 1975.) Computers were introduced into factories to keep track of the large volumes of information that arise from complex and varying production. It became clear that data should be managed in a consistent manner, and that good information could be used to help to keep inventories small and deliveries on time. MRP systems were developed to do this, and the initial challenge in their development was the collection and orderly management of data. (The more recent challenge is to use this data in the most effective way.)

The basic concepts of MRP scheduling are the *master production schedule*, the *bill of materials*, and *lead time*. The master production schedule is a statement of due dates and quantities of end items (goods to be delivered). The bill of materials is a list of components of each assembled item, including subassemblies of end items. It leads to a tree-like assembly structure for each end item. The lead time is the typical time required between production operations.

---

[2]It is beyond the scope for *two* reasons: one is the difference between human behavior and that of the simple systems we are describing here; the other is the fact that you cannot say anything about how much things can be improved without knowing those things in great detail. In particular, you cannot predict how much a machine's failure rate can decrease without knowing the design of the machine, and how to redesign it.

For each end item, production operations are scheduled backwards according to the lead times and the bill of materials from the master schedule. If an item is due at time T, and its last operation has a lead time of Δ, then that operation is scheduled to start at time $T - \Delta$. This same reasoning applies to each stage of production. If an operation is an assembly, then it has one previous operation for each component of the assembly. From this timing logic, minimal inventory requirements can be calculated.

This simple logic has two kinds of limitations. First, it is not clear how to determine the lead times. There is no straightforward way of computing them. If historical lead times are used, they can institutionalize the effects of past practices. Second, this logic must be adapted in each implementation to deal with all the additional complicating phenomena of real production: random demand, unreliable machines, random processing times, setup changes, finite buffers, etc. Most importantly, it does not account for finite machine capacity. That is, it assumes that the lead time for an operation is constant regardless of the load on the machine performing it.

Kanban   A simple version of a *Kanban* policy is described by Mitra and Mitrani (1990). Production stage k of a manufacturing system has C_k cards, or Kanbans. When a part arrives for an operation, a card is associated with it until the part leaves that stage for the next operation. If all C_k Kanbans of Stage k are already attached to parts (regardless of whether the parts are waiting for an operation at Stage k, or undergoing the operation, or waiting for a Kanban for Stage $k + 1$), no new parts can be admitted. In effect, there is a storage area of size C_k associated with Stage k. The machine of Stage k, the C_k cards, and the parts that are currently associated with those cards together form a *Kanban cell*. When a demand for a product arrives, it is satisfied by a part from the final stage of the process and thereby frees a Kanban in that stage. When there is a free Stage 1 Kanban, a part is drawn from raw material.

Kanban control differs from transfer line control. In a transfer line, the machine is always at one end[3] of the storage area. In a Kanban system, the machine is inside the cell. To put it another way, a transfer line storage area contains parts that have already received service from the associated machine[4], whereas a Kanban cell has parts awaiting service from the associated machine, receiving service from that machine, and waiting to be admitted to the next area. When a buffer is full in a transfer line, the upstream machine is idle due to blockage; when all the cards in a Kanban cell are associated with parts, the machine keeps operating until all the waiting parts in that area have been processed.

The Kanban policy is often described as a *pull* policy because demands propagate from the downstream end of the line. The last stage relinquishes a finished part when a demand arrives; this frees a Kanban which becomes a demand for the previous stage, and so forth.[5]

---

[3]upstream in our notation, but it could be downstream with only notation changes and no change in behavior

[4]or, with notation changes, are awaiting service

[5]This is usually contrasted with so-called *push* policies, in which material is pushed into the upstream end whenever there is an opportunity, without regard to demand or downstream inventory. In reality, of course, people stop pushing sooner or later.

If there were always parts in the last stage, orders would be met immediately. In reality, the only way to guarantee this would be to have a very large inventory at the last stage. Alternatively, inventory can be distributed throughout the system, but still, the smaller the inventory, the longer the delay between receiving and meeting orders. There is no easy way of calculating the performance of a Kanban system, and no easy way of determining the best distribution of cards other than by experimentation.

If orders arrive in nearly equal intervals and operation times are nearly deterministic, then little inventory is needed. As usual, the more variability there is in a system, the more inventory is needed to compensate for it.

There are many variations of the Kanban policy. In one, several stages are regulated together by the same set of cards. Buzacott and Shanthikumar (1993) describe a general framework that includes MRP, Kanban, and other policies as special cases.

MRP, Kanban, and a synthesis The advantage of the MRP scheduling policy is that it is aware of a schedule of future requirements, and knows when material is due. It is simplistic, however, in not explicitly treating randomness, finite capacity, and many other issues, and must compensate by extending lead times and therefore increasing inventories. Kanban regulates production according to inventory, but has no way of accounting for future requirements. The goal of this chapter is to combine the concepts of inventory, finite machine capacity, unreliable machines, and finite buffers in an extension of the MRP and Kanban policies. This policy uses *two* kinds of information to regulate production: future requirements (here summarized in the demand rate vector d) and local inventory levels.

12.1.4   Related literature

Most of the material in this chapter is based on the real-time inventory and production control work of Bai (1991). This was in turn based on earlier work by Van Ryzin (Van Ryzin, 1987; Van Ryzin, Lou, and Gershwin, 1993) in which a numerical solution of a two-machine line (similar to that of Section 12.2) was obtained. Further analysis of this system appears in Lou, Sethi and Zhang (1993). Similar concepts for the approximation of two-machine and longer lines were studied by Eleftheriu (1989) and Eleftheriu and Desrochers (1991)

12.1.5   Chapter overview

Following Bai's approach, we analyze a two-machine, one-buffer, one-part-type system in Section 12.2. The main issue in that section is the extension of the dynamic programming methods of Chapter 9 to simple systems with buffers. We extend those results to k-machine, $(k-1)$-buffer, one-part-type tandem systems in Section 12.3. The critical issue is to deal efficiently with the propagation of disturbances from machine to machine through buffers. In Section 12.4, we treat k-machine, $m(k-1)$-buffer, m-part-type tandem systems. Here, we must treat the allocation of machine time among competing part types. General networks are treated in Section 12.5. The new complication in this section is the possible *reentrant* nature of the production process. This is important in semiconductor fabrication, where parts can visit the same machine many times.

The distinction between surplus and inventory   In Chapters 3, 4, and 5 we speak of buffer level or inventory, and never of surplus. In Chapters 9 and 10 we speak of surplus, and never of buffer level or inventory. In this chapter, we bring these concepts together.

When there is a single stage, or a single point at which surplus or inventory is measured, then surplus is the same as inventory when surplus is positive, and it is the same as backlog when it is negative. More generally, the surplus measured at the *final* stage is the same as finished goods inventory or backlog. In the rest of this chapter we have buffers — and buffer levels — similar to those of the first part of the book. We generalize the concept of surplus, however, by defining surplus at each stage of the process. Surplus is closely related to (but not the same as) buffer level, and, as a consequence, we must introduce bounds on surplus.

Implementation issues   In this chapter, we devise methods for calculating short term production rates in real time as a function of machine repair states, surpluses, and buffer levels. These short term rates must be converted into loading decisions. There are two ways in which this can be done. (1) The most general is the staircase strategy of Section 9.4.4, or some similar policy. (2) In some cases, the policy for determining production rates has a simple interpretation which can be implemented directly. Examples 3 *(Load the part which is furthest behind its hedging point.)* and 4 *(Load the most valuable part which is below its hedging point.)* of Chapter 9 are instances of this.

12.1.6   Relationship with transfer line chapters

When the demand d on the single-part-type systems of Sections 12.2 and 12.3 is very high, the systems cannot meet it. In that case, they act like the continuous material transfer line of Chapter 3. (One difference is that the models here are assumed to have time-dependent failures, whereas those of the transfer line chapters have operation-dependent failures.) In one of his simulation experiments, Bai (1991) ran a long line, single-part-type system with infeasible demand. He found that the actual production was close to that predicted by one of the long line decomposition techniques of Chapter 4. (A similar effect would occur if the hedging point were chosen to be so high that the surplus could never reach it during an entire simulation run.)

12.2   Two-Machine, One-Part-Type Systems

In this section, we study two-machine, one-buffer, single-part-type systems (Figure 12.1). The purpose is to create a building block for more complex systems; the relationship between this section and those that follow is similar to the relationship between the two-machine line models of Chapter 3 and the decomposition methods of Chapter 4. The style is similar to that of Chapter 9.

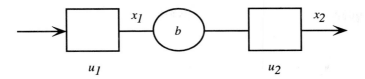

Figure 12.1: Two-Machine, One-Part-Type System

12.2.1 Dynamic programming formulation

The model is similar to the continuous material, two-machine transfer line of Section 3.10. However, instead of always operating both machines at their maximum possible rates (subject to starvation and blockage), we have the option of running the machines at lower rates.

Parameters The machines fail at random times and stay down for random durations. Just as in Chapter 9, we assume time-dependent failures. Both down times and up times are exponentially distributed with means $1/r_i$ and $1/p_i$, respectively, for $i = 1, 2$. The operation time at Machine i is τ_i and the demand rate for the part is d (a scalar, since there is only one part type). The processing times are assumed to be small compared with the time to fail and time to repair. It is convenient to define $\mu_i = 1/\tau_i$. We assume that

$$d < \frac{\mu_i r_i}{r_i + p_i}, \qquad i = 1, 2.$$

Consequently, $d < \mu_i$, for $i = 1, 2$.

A buffer of size B is located between the two machines. Machine 1 is never starved and Machine 2 is never blocked. A machine can be starved or blocked only when it is operational. B can be either a physical parameter, which specifies the amount of material that we are *able* to hold; or a control parameter which specifies the amount of material that we are *willing* to hold. In the former case, B is specified; in the latter, it must be determined.

States, dynamics, and constraints As usual, α_i represents the repair state of Machine i. We define x_i to be the *Stage i production surplus*. It satisfies

$$\frac{dx_i}{dt} = u_i - d, \qquad x_i(t_0) \text{ specified}, \qquad i = 1, 2 \tag{12.1}$$

where u_i is the production rate of the ith operation. The number of parts in the buffer, the *buffer level*, is represented by a continuous variable b which satisfies

$$\frac{db}{dt} = u_1 - u_2, \qquad b(t_0) \text{ specified}. \tag{12.2}$$

From (12.1) and (12.2), we have

$$b(t) = x_1(t) - x_2(t), \qquad t \geq t_0 \tag{12.3}$$

if $b(t_0)$ satisfies

$$b(t_0) = x_1(t_0) - x_2(t_0).$$

The buffer level must satisfy

$$0 \leq b \leq B. \tag{12.4}$$

This is called a *state variable inequality constraint* in the control theory literature.

Objective   The goal of scheduling the production system is to meet the demand with minimal costs due to deviation (in the sense of Figure 9.1), and due to inventory. We would like x_i and b to be as close as possible to 0. We summarize the costs due to x_i and b in a convex function $g(x, b)$ which has its minimum at $x_1 = x_2 = b = 0$ and which grows as $|x| \to \infty$. An example is

$$g(x, b) = \sum_{i=1}^{2} \left[g_{i+} x_i^+ + g_{i-} x_i^- \right] + g_b b \tag{12.5}$$

where x_i^+ and x_i^- are defined in Chapter 9 and g_b is the cost of in-process inventory. An important special case is where $g_{1+} = g_{1-} = 0$, where only inventory and final surplus enter into the cost directly.

We formulate a dynamic programming problem which involves the minimization of the integral of g over a long time. As in Chapter 9, we are not able to solve this problem exactly; the goal is to derive a solution structure, and then to use that structure to construct a simple controller. We find that the structure is again a partition of x space.

Given an initial surplus $x(t_0)$ and machine state $\alpha(t_0)$, the production control policy is determined by the dynamic programming problem

$$J(x(t_0), \alpha(t_0), t_0) = \min_u E \left\{ \int_{t_0}^{T} g(x(s), b(s)) ds \mid x(t_0), \alpha(t_0) \right\} \tag{12.6}$$

subject to (12.1), (12.2), (12.4), exponential unreliable machine dynamics for α, and

$$0 \leq u_i \leq \mu_i \alpha_i, \qquad i = 1, 2. \tag{12.7}$$

These constraints are very simple. When $\alpha_1 = \alpha_2 = 1$, they define a rectangle in u space whose four corners are $(u_1, u_2) = (0, 0), (0, \mu_2), (\mu_1, 0)$, and (μ_1, μ_2).

Maximum principle This is a continuous time, mixed state, stochastic problem of the kind considered in Section 8.8. Its solution is determined by the Bellman equation (8.12). If J is approximated by (8.13),

$$J(x, \alpha, t) \approx J^*(T - t) + W(x, \alpha).$$

The optimal production rate satisfies

$$\min_{u} \frac{\partial W}{\partial x_1} u_1 + \frac{\partial W}{\partial x_2} u_2 \qquad (12.8)$$

subject to (12.4) and (12.7). Unfortunately, (12.4) is expressed in terms of b and not u. This constraint can be treated in a similar way as boundaries are treated in Chapter 9. Here $b = 0$ and $b = B$ form boundaries that are like the attractive boundaries of Section 9.4.1. When b reaches 0 or B, it can either retreat from that value or stay constant, but it may not pass through 0 or B. Consequently, u_1 and u_2 must satisfy

$$\begin{aligned} &\text{if } b = 0, \text{ then } u_2 \leq u_1 \\ &\text{if } b = B, \text{ then } u_1 \leq u_2. \end{aligned} \qquad (12.9)$$

Equations (12.9) are called *conditional constraints*. They and (12.2) insure that when $b = 0$, $db/dt \geq 0$ and when $b = B$, $db/dt \leq 0$, so that (12.4) is not violated. Therefore, the feedback law is (12.8) subject to (12.7) and (12.9).

12.2.2 Optimal policy

In this section, we briefly characterize the optimal policy. Note that neither analytic nor computational solutions are available, and few rigorous theorems have been proved.

Linear programming problem (12.8) is similar to (9.38), and has the same consequences: the surplus space is partitioned into regions. In this case, it is also constrained by (12.4), or

$$0 \leq x_1 - x_2 \leq B. \qquad (12.10)$$

Because (12.7) forms a rectangle, x space is divided into four regions. In one, both u_1 and u_2 are 0; in one, they are both maximal; and in the other two, one is 0 and the other is maximal. The control u tends to drive x toward a boundary (a boundary between regions, or a boundary that satisfies (12.10) with equality), and then to keep it on it.

When both machines are operational ($\alpha_1 = 1$ and $\alpha_2 = 1$), Figure 12.2 illustrates the regions in x space. The two straight lines are the *zero-buffer* ($b = 0$) and *full-buffer* ($b = B$) boundaries. The feasible region of x space lies between them (12.10). The other curves are the sets of points in which one of the coefficients of the objective function in (12.8) is zero ($\partial W / \partial x_i = 0$). The x space is divided into four mutually exclusive regions which correspond to the four extreme points of the constraint set. In each region, the production rate u is constant. The four regions intersect at a point $Z = (Z_1, Z_2)$ called the *hedging point*. The feedback controller (12.8) always attempts to drive the system to the hedging point, and to keep it there.

A *feasible* hedging point Z is one that satisfies

$$0 \leq Z_1 - Z_2 \leq B. \tag{12.11}$$

It seems fair to assume that an optimal hedging point will be feasible. On the other hand, we construct heuristic policies based on non-optimal hedging points. While the hedging points from these policies are always feasible, other methods may not have such a guarantee unless (12.11) is imposed. If Z is not feasible, it is not obvious where the system drives the surplus.

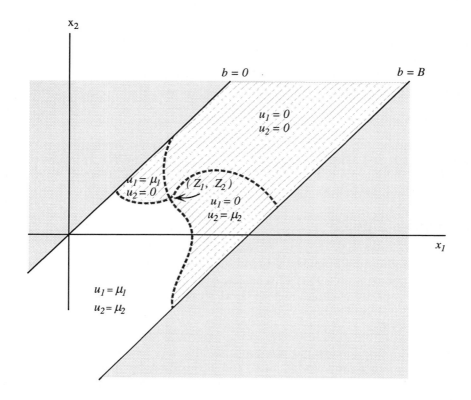

Figure 12.2: Optimal Partition of x Space

Since the production rates are constant in every region in x space, they do not have to be calculated at every time instant. They must be computed only when machine state α changes or when production surplus x reaches a boundary. In fact, once the boundaries are known, it is easy to calculate when x will reach a boundary (if a change in α does not occur first) and which region x will enter next. It is reasonable to assume that W is convex. Then if it has a finite minimum, it has a unique minimum (since $W = $ constant does not satisfy the Bellman equation. See Section 9.3.).

12.2.3 Heuristic policy

It is difficult to determine the optimal partition. Consequently, Bai (1991) develops a heuristic partition; he argues on intuitive grounds that the boundaries should be orthogonal to the axes, and then he locates them using a nonlinear program. The optimal value function W is also difficult to find, and only of interest in determining the shapes and positions of the optimal boundaries. In the spirit of the approximations in Chapter 9, we develop the boundaries directly and do not attempt to construct the W function. It should be noted that the boundaries that are constructed are straight lines, and they are consistent with a quadratic approximation of W in (12.8).[6]

We assume that the most desirable short term behavior is for Machines 1 and 2 to be as decoupled as possible. That is, if the buffer is neither empty nor full, the choice of u_1 should be independent of x_2 and α_2; and the choice of u_2 should be independent of x_1 and α_1. The only way for this to happen is for the boundaries to be vertical and horizontal, orthogonal to the axes. See Figure 12.3.

Since each region in Figure 12.3 must correspond to one corner of the capacity set (12.7), then the region in which $x_1 > Z_1$ and $x_2 > Z_2$ must be where $u_1 = u_2 = 0$. If production rate u_i were equal to μ_i, then $dx_i/dt > 0$, so x_i would increase without bound. For the same reason, the region in which $x_1 < Z_1$ and $x_2 < Z_2$ must be where $u_1 = \mu_1$ and $u_2 = \mu_2$.

Consequently, we can approximate the optimal policy for (12.6) by the optimal policy for the Bielecki-Kumar problem (Section 9.3) for each machine, when the buffer is neither empty nor full. That is, if $\alpha_i = 1$, and Machine i is neither starved nor blocked, then we choose

$$\left.\begin{array}{lll} u_i = 0 & \text{if} & x_i > Z_i \\ u_i = d & \text{if} & x_i = Z_i \\ u_i = \mu_i & \text{if} & x_i < Z_i \end{array}\right\}$$

which is the same as (9.19). More generally, since these production rate decisions are based on maximizing a quantity linear in the production rate,

$$\left.\begin{array}{lll} u_i = 0 & \text{if} & x_i > Z_i \\ u_i = d & \text{if} & x_i = Z_i \\ \text{maximize } u_i & \text{if} & x_i < Z_i \end{array}\right\}$$

if $\alpha_i = 1$, in which the maximization is subject to (12.7) and (12.9).

If Machine 2 is starved, then u_2 is reduced to the current value of u_1; if Machine 1 is blocked, then u_1 is reduced to u_2. This policy is the same as (12.8) subject to (12.7) and

---

[6]It is sometimes convenient to use a W function in describing the real-time scheduling policy. In that case, we derive a $\tilde{W}$ from the boundaries and the hedging point, rather than deriving the boundaries and the hedging point from W. See (12.12).

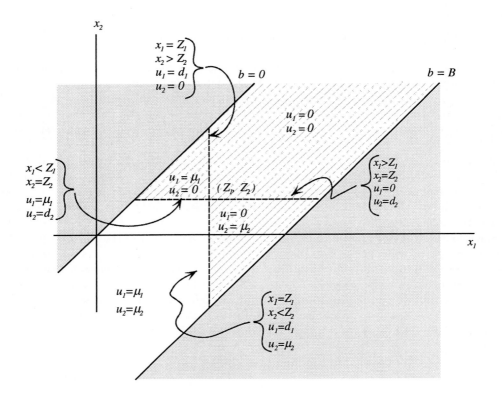

Figure 12.3: Heuristic Partition of x Space

(12.9), in which W is replaced by

$$\tilde{W} = \frac{1}{2}A_{11}(x_1 - Z_1)^2 + \frac{1}{2}A_{22}(x_2 - Z_2)^2.$$

(12.12)

The only issues remaining are the location of the hedging point Z, and the size of the buffer, B, if that is a control parameter. A nonlinear programming problem formulation to determine Z_1, Z_2, and B is developed by Bai (1991). The decomposition equations are derived in a spirit similar to that of Chapter 4, although the details are very different. It is summarized in Section 12.2.5.

12.2.4   System behavior under the heuristic policy

Behavior when both machines are up   Suppose that the system is not at the hedging point. If $x_1 > Z_1$, then $u_1 = 0$ and $dx_1/dt = -d_1 < 0$, so x_1 decreases. If $x_1 < Z_1$ and Machine 1 is up and not blocked, then $u_1 = \mu_1$ and $dx_1/dt = \mu_1 - d_1 > 0$, so x_1 increases.

Thus, as long as the machine is up and not blocked, x_1 moves toward the hedging point Z_1. Furthermore, if $x_1 < Z_1$, there is no way for x_1 to become greater than Z_1, since the maximum value that dx_1/dt can have when $x_1 = Z_1$ is 0. In other words, any state in which $x_1 > Z_1$ is transient.

Similarly, if $x_2 > Z_2$, then x_2 decreases. If $x_2 < Z_2$ and Machine 2 is up and not starved, then $u_2 = \mu_2$ and x_2 increases. As long as the machine is up and not starved, x_2 moves toward Z_2. Any state in which $x_2 > Z_2$ is transient.

If $x_1 < Z_1$ and $x_2 < Z_2$ and $0 < b = x_1 - x_2 < B$, then $u_1 = \mu_1$ and $u_2 = \mu_2$. Both x_1 and x_2 increase. Whether b is increasing, decreasing, or remaining constant depends on the speeds of the machines. From (12.2),

$$\frac{db}{dt} = \mu_1 - \mu_2$$

so the buffer level is increasing if the first machine is faster than the second, decreasing if it is slower, and staying constant if their speeds are equal.

Depending on the speeds of the machines and the starting point (the value of x when both machines are up immediately after a repair), one of the following will occur first[7]:

1. $b = 0; x_1 < Z_1; x_2 < Z_2$;

2. $0 < b < Z_1 - Z_2; x_1 < Z_1; x_2 = Z_2$;

3. $Z_1 - Z_2 < b < B; x_1 = Z_1; x_2 < Z_2$;

4. $b = B; x_1 < Z_1; x_2 < Z_2$.

The first event cannot occur if the first machine is faster than or has the same speed as the second, and the last event cannot occur if the first machine is slower than or has the same speed as the second. That is, Event 1 can only occur if $\mu_1 < \mu_2$, and Event 4 can only occur if $\mu_1 > \mu_2$.

Let us assume for a moment that neither machine fails before the surplus vector x reaches the hedging point. Then the possible sequences of events are the following:

- If Event 1 occurs, then we know that $\mu_1 < \mu_2$. Since Machine 1 is not blocked, $u_1 = \mu_1$. Since Machine 2 is starved, u_2 is maximized subject to (12.7) and (12.9), so $u_2 = \mu_1$ and b remains equal to 0. Since $b = 0$, $x_1 = x_2$, and they increase together.

  We have assumed that the hedging point is in the feasible region of x space, so $Z_1 - Z_2 \geq 0$. Consequently, as x moves along the zero-buffer boundary, x_2 reaches Z_2 while x_1 is still strictly less than Z_1. The policy says that when $x_2 = Z_2$, we must have $u_2 = d$ so x_2 remains constant. Production rate u_1 is still equal to μ_1, so x_1 increases, and therefore b increases. This continues until $x_1 = Z_1$, at which time u_1 is reduced to d, and x remains constant.

---

[7]It is possible, but not very likely, that the first event to occur will be $b = Z_1 - Z_2; x_1 = Z_1; x_2 = Z_2$.

- Similarly, if Event 4 occurs, then we must have $\mu_1 > \mu_2$,. We select $u_1 = u_2 = \mu_2$, so b remains equal to B, and x_1 and x_2 increase together. In fact, $x_1 - x_2 = B$. This time, x_1 reaches Z_1 before x_2 reaches Z_2 because $Z_1 - Z_2 \leq B$. At this time, u_1 is set equal to d, so x_1 remains constant while x_2 continues to increase. That is, x moves on a vertical line from the full buffer boundary to the hedging point. The buffer level b decreases until the hedging point is reached.

- If Event 2 is the first to happen, precisely the same sequence of events occurs as those after x_2 reaches Z_2 following Event 1. Similarly, if Event 3 occurs first, it is followed by the same sequence of events as those after x_1 reaches Z_1 following Event 4.

Behavior when one machine is down When a failure occurs, the behavior of the surplus trajectory depends on where x is at that time. Assuming that no repair occurs and that only one machine is down, the following describes the trajectory.

- If x is in the interior of the non-transient region (that is, if $x_1 < Z_1$ and $x_2 < Z_2$), and Machine i fails while Machine j stays up, then $u_i = 0$ and $u_j = \mu_j$. Therefore x_i decreases and x_j increases. This persists until b reaches 0 or B or x_j reaches Z_j.

- If b reaches 0, it must have been Machine 1 that failed. In that case, b remains at 0, $x_1 = x_2$ and $dx_i/dt = -d$. If the failure occurred when b was already 0, the same thing happens if Machine 1 was the one that failed. If Machine 2 failed, then x will move in the interior as described above until b reaches B or x_1 reaches Z_1.

- If b reaches B, Machine 2 was the cause of the failure. Then b remains at B, $x_1 - x_2 = B$ and $dx_i/dt = -d$. If the failure occurred when b was already at B, the same thing happens if Machine 2 was the one that failed. If Machine 1 failed, then x will move in the interior until b reaches 0 or x_2 reaches Z_2.

- The most important case is when a failure occurs while the system is at the hedging point. If Machine i fails, x_i decreases and x_j stays constant. That is, the surplus either moves down the vertical line (if Machine 2 fails) that passes through the hedging point or to the left on the horizontal line (if Machine 1 fails). If Machine 1 fails, the buffer eventually empties. If Machine 2 fails, the buffer fills up. In either case, x_1 and x_2 decrease together after the buffer boundary is reached.

Finally, when both machines are down, both x_1 and x_2 decrease at rate d, and the buffer level stays constant.

12.2.5 Estimating the hedging point and other parameters

Bai proposes an approximation for the purpose of determining Z_1, Z_2, and B. It is based on the assumption that the surplus usually reaches the hedging point after one failure and before the next failure. Therefore, the typical buffer level just before a failure is

$$Z^b = Z_1 - Z_2. \tag{12.13}$$

Bai defines f_i^b and f_i^s to be the fractions of time that Machine i is starved or blocked. A machine can be starved or blocked only when it is operational. Because the first machine is never starved and the last is never blocked, $f_1^s = f_2^b = 0$. To determine an estimate of f_2^s, observe that the average period during which Machine 1 is up and down is $1/p_1 + 1/r_1$. During such a period, the machine is down for time $1/r_1$. This period can be further divided into the time when both machines are down (whose total average duration is called β_1), the time when Machine 1 is down and Machine 2 is up and producing (β_2), and the time when Machine 1 is down and Machine 2 is up but starved (β_3).

Then, if we assume that Machines 1 and 2 fail independently, β_1 is given by

$$\beta_1 = \left(\frac{1}{r_1} + \frac{1}{p_1}\right)\left(\frac{p_1}{r_1 + p_1}\right)\left(\frac{p_2}{r_2 + p_2}\right) = \frac{1}{r_1}\left(\frac{p_2}{r_2 + p_2}\right).$$

This assumption is consistent with the assumption of time-dependent failures.

To determine β_2, Bai defines $\bar{u}_2$ to be the average production rate of Machine 2 while it is producing. (It would be μ_2 if the machine were not slowed down when the system reaches it hedging point. It must be between d and μ_2.) The amount of time that Machine 2 operates while Machine 1 is down is the time it takes to work off the material in the buffer, or $\beta_2 = Z^b/\bar{u}_2$. To determine $\bar{u}_2$, observe that

$$d = \frac{r_2}{r_2 + p_2}(1 - f_2^s)\bar{u}_2 \tag{12.14}$$

because Machine 2 must produce at rate d in the long run. It can only produce when it is up and not starving. Therefore,

$$\beta_2 = \frac{r_2(1 - f_2^s)Z^b}{(r_2 + p_2)d}.$$

Finally, β_3 is determined by

$$\beta_3 = \left(\frac{1}{r_1} + \frac{1}{p_1}\right)\left(\frac{r_2}{r_2 + p_2}\right)f_2^s.$$

These time durations satisfy

$$\beta_1 + \beta_2 + \beta_3 = \frac{1}{r_1}$$

which can be expressed as

$$\frac{1}{d}Z^b + \frac{r_1 + p_1}{r_1 p_1}f_2^s - \frac{1}{d}Z^b f_2^s = \frac{1}{r_1}. \tag{12.15}$$

Similarly, if $Z^s = B - Z^b$ is the amount of space in the buffer when the system is at its hedging point,

$$\frac{1}{d}Z^s + \frac{r_2 + p_2}{r_2 p_2}f_1^b - \frac{1}{d}Z^s f_1^b = \frac{1}{r_2}. \tag{12.16}$$

There is an upper bound on the fractions of time that the buffer can be empty or full, which is determined by the demand rate and the machine reliabilities. From $(12.14)^8$,

$$d \le \frac{r_2}{r_2 + p_2}(1 - f_2^s)\mu_2. \tag{12.17}$$

Similarly,

$$d \le \frac{r_1}{r_1 + p_1}(1 - f_1^b)\mu_1. \tag{12.18}$$

Determination of B   These equations form the constraints of a nonlinear programming problem for the determination of B. In the following problem, the decision variables are f_1^b, f_2^s, Z^b, and Z^s. Recall that $Z^b + Z^s = B$. The problem is

$$\min \ Z^b + Z^s$$

subject to (12.15), (12.16), (12.17), (12.18), and

$$f_1^b, f_2^s, Z^b, Z^s \ge 0.$$

Determination of Z_1 and Z_2   Since $Z^b = Z_1 - Z_2$, one more fact is needed to determine Z_1 and Z_2. Bai determines Z_2 by (1) estimating

$$\Delta_2 = Z_2 - \bar{x}_2 \tag{12.19}$$

the difference between Z_2 and the average value of x_2, and (2) choosing the average value of x_2.

Machine i failures are still assumed to occur when surplus x_i is at its hedging point Z_i. Therefore, x_i deviates from Z_i during the failure, and for some time after the repair. To simplify, assume that the duration of the failure is $1/r_i$. When the repair occurs, $x_i = Z_i - d/r_i$. After the repair, the Machine i production rate is μ_i, so the *catch-up time* t_{ci}, the time required to bring x_i back to Z_i, satisfies $(\mu_i - d)t_{ci} = d/r_i$. The average deviation of x_i from Z_i due to failures is therefore

$$\delta_i^r = \frac{1}{2}\frac{\frac{d}{r_i}\left(\frac{1}{r_i} + t_{ci}\right)}{\frac{1}{r_i} + \frac{1}{p_i}} = \frac{r_i p_i}{r_i + p_i}\frac{d}{2r_i}\left\{\frac{1}{r_i} + \frac{d}{r_i(\mu_i - d)}\right\}$$

or,

$$\delta_i^r = \frac{r_i p_i}{r_i + p_i}\frac{d}{2}\left(\frac{1}{r_i}\right)^2\frac{\mu_i}{\mu_i - d}. \tag{12.20}$$

Similarly, if δ_i^s and δ_i^b are the average deviations due to starvation and blockage,

$$\delta_i^s = \frac{r_i p_i}{r_i + p_i}\frac{d}{2}\left(\frac{f_i^s}{p_i}\right)^2\frac{\mu_i}{\mu_i - d}, \tag{12.21}$$

---

^{8}Compare this with (3.248) and all the other versions of the Flow Rate-Idle Time relationship.

$$\delta_i^b = \frac{r_i p_i}{r_i + p_i} \frac{d}{2} \left(\frac{f_i^b}{p_i} \right)^2 \frac{\mu_i}{\mu_i - d}, \tag{12.22}$$

and

$$\Delta_2 = \delta_i^r + \delta_i^s + \delta_i^b. \tag{12.23}$$

Finally, Z_2 is chosen so that $\bar{x}_2 = 0$. Therefore, $Z_2 = \Delta_2$ according to (12.19), and, from (12.13), $Z_1 = Z_2 + Z^b$. All control parameters have now been determined.

12.2.6 Simulation performance

This approximation cannot be expected to be very close to optimal; the g function of (12.6) does not appear in it at all. On the other hand, it is easy to use, and it is not obvious how to reflect the g cost in a simple approximation.

Bai reports considerable simulation experience for this and all the other models of this chapter. We will only summarize his observations here by saying that the hedging points and buffer sizes obtained this way yield satisfactory performance. That is, the systems meet demand (when demand is feasible) and the in-process inventories are not large.

12.3 Single-Part-Type Tandem Systems

The two-machine, one-part-type methods of the previous section extend readily to k-machine, one-part-type lines (Figure 12.4).[9] The dynamic programming problem still divides the space into regions; the state variable inequality constraints still restrict the state space, and still add boundaries that lead to conditional constraints. The approximate region boundaries are still orthogonal to the axes.

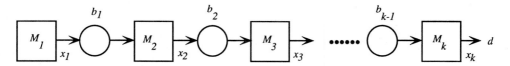

Figure 12.4: k-Machine, One-Part-Type System

12.3.1 Control Policy

Dynamic Programming Problem   The dynamic program is an extension of the problem for the two-machine, one-part-type system. Here, there is one production rate (u_i) and

---

[9]with permission of the Massachusetts Institute of Technology.

one surplus (x_i) for each machine $(i = 1, \ldots, k)$, and one buffer level (b_i) for each buffer $(i = 1, \ldots, k - 1)$.

The problem is to find

$$J(x(t_0), \alpha(t_0), t_0) = \min_u E \left\{ \int_{t_0}^{T} g(x(s), b(s)) ds \mid x(t_0), \alpha(t_0) \right\} \tag{12.24}$$

subject to

$$\frac{dx_i}{dt} = u_i - d, \qquad x_i(t_0) \text{ specified}, \qquad i = 1, \ldots, k$$

$$b_i(t) = x_i(t) - x_{i+1}(t), \qquad t \geq t_0, i = 1, \ldots, k - 1$$

$$0 \leq b_i \leq B_i, \qquad i = 1, \ldots, k - 1$$

$$0 \leq u_i \leq \mu_i \alpha_i, \qquad i = 1, \ldots, k.$$

and the dynamics of α_i are those of the exponentially unreliable machine used throughout this book.

Maximum Principle   The optimal control is the solution to the following linear program:

$$\min_u \sum_{i=1}^{k} \frac{\partial W}{\partial x_i} u_i$$

subject to

$$0 \leq u_i \leq \mu_i \alpha_i, \qquad i = 1, \ldots, k. \tag{12.25}$$

and

$$0 \leq b_i \leq B_i, \qquad i = 1, \ldots, k - 1$$

in which W comes from (8.13).

If buffer level b_i is neither 0 nor B_i, then Machines i and $i+1$ can be controlled independently of each other. If the buffer is empty or full, then they are linked as in the two-machine case. The last set of constraints is therefore replaced by the conditional constraints:

$$\begin{aligned} &\text{if } b_i = 0, \text{ then } u_{i+1} \leq u_i \\ &\text{if } b_i = B_i, \text{ then } u_i \leq u_{i+1} \qquad i = 1, \ldots, k - 1. \end{aligned} \tag{12.26}$$

Implementable Linear Program As usual, the true, optimal W seems impossible to determine. Therefore, we assume a set of region boundaries that are extensions of the earlier ones.

For each i, there is a hedging point Z_i. Let u_i^{max} be the maximal possible value of u_i. It is determined by the capacity (12.25) and conditional constraints (12.26). If $\alpha_i = 1$, the policy is

$$\left.\begin{aligned} u_i &= 0 & \text{if} \quad x_i > Z_i \\ u_i &= \min\{d, u_i^{max}\} & \text{if} \quad x_i = Z_i \\ u_i &= u_i^{max} & \text{if} \quad x_i < Z_i \end{aligned}\right\}$$

Again, this policy is the same as the maximum principle, but where the exact W is replaced by

$$\tilde{W} = \frac{1}{2}\sum_{i=1}^{k} A_{ii}(x_i - Z_i)^2.$$

12.3.2 Nonlinear programming problem for parameters

To implement this policy, we must obtain control parameters $B_1, \ldots, B_{k-1}, Z_1, \ldots, Z_k$. The only thing that is new is that the nonlinear programming problem for the buffer sizes must be generalized. Besides the more complex notation due to the larger system, there is one more difference: in the two-machine case, Machine 1 could be blocked but not starved, and Machine 2 could be starved but not blocked. Here, any machine other than the first and the last can be both starved and blocked.

Let $B_i = Z_i^b + Z_i^s$. Then the nonlinear programming problem becomes

$$\min \sum_{i=1}^{k-1} \left(Z_i^b + Z_i^s \right)$$

subject to

$$\frac{1}{d}Z_{i-1}^b - \frac{1}{p_{i-1}}f_{i-1}^s + \frac{r_{i-1} + p_{i-1}}{r_{i-1}p_{i-1}}f_i^s + \frac{1}{r_{i-1}}f_i^b - \frac{1}{d}Z_{i-1}^b f_i^s - \frac{1}{d}Z_{i-1}^b f_i^b + \frac{1}{p_{i-1}}f_{i-1}^s f_i^b$$

$$= \frac{1}{r_{i-1}}, \qquad i = 2, \ldots, k. \tag{12.27}$$

$$\frac{1}{d}Z_i^s + \frac{1}{r_{i+1}}f_i^s + \frac{r_{i+1} + p_{i+1}}{r_{i+1}p_{i+1}}f_i^b - \frac{1}{p_{i+1}}f_{i+1}^b - \frac{1}{d}Z_i^s f_i^s - \frac{1}{d}Z_i^s f_i^b + \frac{1}{p_{i+1}}f_i^s f_{i+1}^b$$

$$= \frac{1}{r_{i+1}}, \qquad i = 1, \ldots, k-1. \tag{12.28}$$

$$d \le \frac{r_i}{r_i + p_i}(1 - f_i^b - f_i^s)\mu_i, \qquad i = 1, \ldots, k. \tag{12.29}$$

$$f_i^b, f_i^s, Z_i^b, Z_i^s \ge 0, \qquad i = 1, \ldots, k.$$

$$f_1^s = f_k^b = 0.$$

The equations for the hedging points are the same as in Section 12.2.5. Again, in spite of the many approximations and simplifications, Bai reports satisfactory simulation performance. See the comments in Section 12.2.6.

12.3.3   Virtual machines

The conditional constraints (12.26) have effects which are similar to those of machines in series. Consider Figure 12.5. The top picture represents a portion of the line; the bottom picture shows an equivalent three-machine line with no buffers.

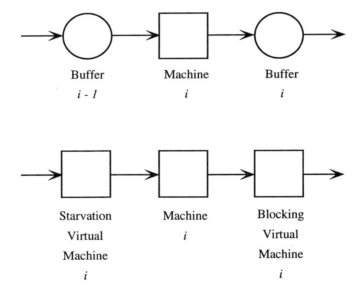

Figure 12.5: Virtual Machines for Single-Part-Type System

The flow of material from Buffer $i - 1$ to Machine i has rate μ_i when Machine i is operational and neither starved nor blocked, and $x_i < Z_i$; it has rate d when Machine i is operational and neither starved nor blocked, and $x_i = Z_i$; it has rate 0 if Machine i is down, or starved or blocked due to a machine elsewhere which has failed; and it has rate d or the rate of a slower neighboring machine if one of the buffers is empty or full due to the slow speed of that machine.

In the spirit of Chapter 4, suppose that the virtual machines of Figure 12.5 were chosen so that an observer in Machine i would see the same material flow behavior as if he or she were in Machine i of the real line. That is, *Starvation Virtual Machine i* has a very high speed whenever Buffer $i - 1$ is not empty; its production rate is 0 whenever Buffer $i - 1$ is empty due to an upstream failure; and otherwise, its production rate is the same as that of the limiting machine upstream. The high speed when Buffer $i - 1$ is not empty means that the production rate of this segment is determined by Machine i or Blockage Virtual Machine i. In addition, the transitions among those speeds has the same behavior as the corresponding transitions in the real line. *Blockage Virtual Machine i* operates similarly.

Unfortunately, it would be difficult to construct such machines, and harder yet to devise an optimal policy like that of Chapter 9. However, it is not hard to imagine what such a policy would look like. Define the state of the line with the virtual machines as $(\alpha_i^s, \alpha_i, \alpha_i^b)$, where α_i^s indicates whether the starvation virtual machine currently has a high speed, or one of the possible lower speeds (d or the speed of an upstream machine), or 0; and α_i^b is the state of the blockage virtual machine. Then, from the methods of Chapter 9 (suitably extended[10]), the production rate of this three-machine system would be a function of $(\alpha_i^s, \alpha_i, \alpha_i^b)$ and x_i. In fact, it is reasonable to guess that the optimal policy has the same structure that we have seen many times: the production rate of the three-machine system is set to its maximal possible value if x_i is less than a hedging point; it is 0 if x_i is greater than the current hedging point; and it is d when x_i is at the hedging point. Most likely, the hedging point would be a function of $(\alpha_i^s, \alpha_i, \alpha_i^b)$. An approximation for such a policy would be one with a single hedging point for all values of $(\alpha_i^s, \alpha_i, \alpha_i^b)$.

Benefit of virtual machines As a consequence, the control policy for this system can be approximated by the control policy of Chapter 9 for a single machine making a single part type. When the surplus is greater than the hedging point, turn the machine off. When it is less than the hedging point, run the machine at the maximum possible rate. That maximum may be determined elsewhere as a consequence of blockage or starvation. When it is equal to the hedging point, run it at the demand rate.

In more complex systems, particularly those of Section 12.6, we can use the virtual machine concept to add machine-like capacity constraints to the capacity set of the hedging point strategy. Consequently, the heuristic real-time controller uses the same machinery developed in Chapter 9 to select production rates as a function of surpluses and machine states.

Implementation issues When Buffer i becomes empty because Machine i is down or operating slowly, a new constraint is imposed on Machine $i + 1$. If that machine causes Buffer $i + 1$ to become empty, Machine $i + 2$'s controller gets an additional constraint. Such a chain of constraints must be recognized because when the original cause of the slowdown is removed, all of the machines are immediately affected. That is, when Machine i speeds

---

[10]Besides the fact that two of the machines have more than two states, the transitions among the states are not likely to be exponentially distributed.

up, we want to alter the constraints on Machines $i+1$ and $i+2$ instantly. The same is true for chains of blocked machines.

12.4   Multiple-Part-Type Tandem Systems

In this section we study k-machine, m-part-type tandem production lines. As shown in Figure 12.6,[11] the system consists of k machines and $(k-1)m$ buffers. Type j parts travel in a fixed sequence: Machine 1, Buffer $(1,j)$, Machine 2, ..., Buffer $(k-1,j)$, Machine k. Buffers are assumed *homogeneous*. That is, Buffer (i,j) holds only identical, interchangeable parts: Type j parts that have completed operations on Machine i and are waiting for an operation on Machine $i+1$. Machine 1 is never starved and Machine k is never blocked.

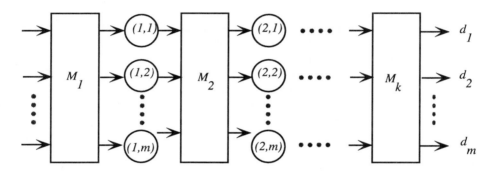

Figure 12.6: k-Machine, m-Part-Type System

In the previous systems, the real-time decision was whether to operate the machines at full speed or at a lower rate. Now, we must also decide in real time how much of each machine's time should be allocated among the parts.

Parameters   Each Type j part requires an operation with processing time τ_{ij} on Machine i. The demand for Type j parts is d_j. The failure rate of Machine i is p_i and its repair rate is r_i. The demand d_j must satisfy

$$\sum_{j=1}^{m} \tau_{ij} d_j \leq \frac{r_i}{r_i + p_i} \quad i = 1, \ldots, k.$$

Decision variables u_{ij} is the production rate of Type j parts at Machine i.

―――――――――――――

[11]with permission of the Massachusetts Institute of Technology.

State variables x_{ij} is the surplus of Type j parts at Machine i. b_{ij} is the level of Buffer (i, j). α_i is the repair state of Machine i.

Control parameters Buffer sizes B_{ij} can be specified, or they can be chosen as part of the control policy. We also seek hedging points Z_{ij}.

12.4.1 Dynamic optimization

The production control problem is formulated as a dynamic programming problem:

$$J(x(t_0), \alpha(t_0), t_0) = \min_u E\left\{ \int_{t_0}^{T} g(x, b)dt \mid x(t_0), \alpha(t_0) \right\} \tag{12.30}$$

subject to the capacity constraints

$$\left. \begin{array}{ll} \sum_{j=1}^{m} \tau_{ij} u_{ij} \leq \alpha_i & i = 1, \ldots, k \\ u_{ij} \geq 0, & i = 1, \ldots, k; j = 1, \ldots, m \end{array} \right\} \tag{12.31}$$

and the dynamics and the buffer constraints of the system are

$$\frac{dx_{ij}}{dt} = u_{ij} - d_j \qquad i = 1, \ldots, k; j = 1, \ldots, m$$

$$\frac{db_{ij}}{dt} = u_{ij} - u_{i+1j}, \qquad i = 1, \ldots, k-1; j = 1, \ldots, m$$

$$0 \leq b_{ij} \leq B_{ij}, \qquad i = 1, \ldots, k-1; j = 1, \ldots, m. \tag{12.32}$$

As earlier, the function $g(x, b)$ is a convex function which penalizes $x(t)$ and $b(t)$ for being too positive or too negative.

Conditional constraints Conditional constraints must be imposed on the feedback controller to insure that the surplus trajectory does not violate the buffer constraints (12.32).

$$\begin{array}{lllll} \text{if } b_{ij} = 0, & \text{then} & u_{i+1,j} \leq u_{ij}, & i = 1, \ldots, k-1; j = 1, \ldots, m \\ \text{if } b_{ij} = B_{ij}, & \text{then} & u_{ij} \leq u_{i+1,j}, & i = 1, \ldots, k-1; j = 1, \ldots, m. \end{array} \tag{12.33}$$

Optimal policy The solution of the optimization problem (12.30) satisfies the following linear program:

$$\min_u \sum_{i=1}^{k} \sum_{j=1}^{m} \frac{\partial W}{\partial x_{ij}} u_{ij} \tag{12.34}$$

subject to (12.31) and (12.33). W comes from (8.13).

12.4.2   Heuristic policy

As these problems get more complex, the prospect of an analytical or numerical solution for $W(x, \alpha)$ becomes more and more remote. Therefore, we look for a heuristic policy which is an extension of the earlier policies. In particular, we assume that each machine is treated independently of the others when its adjacent buffers are neither empty nor full. Such machines look very much like the one-machine, many-part-type systems of Example 3 and Exercise 8 of Chapter 9. The control parameters that we therefore must find are the hedging points Z_{ij} for each part type at each stage and the buffer sizes B_{ij}.

In order to estimate the control parameters, Bai cuts the machines in the original system into *partial machines* and separates them into m single-part-type approximate tandem systems (Figure 12.7).[12] Then he chooses the parameters and capacity for each partial machine such that the approximate tandem systems are as close as possible to the original system.

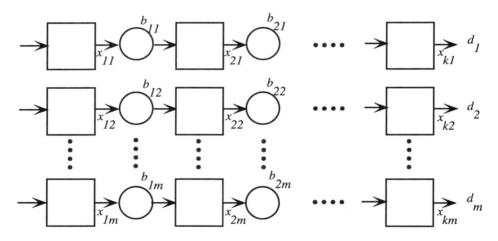

Figure 12.7: The Subsystems of the k-Machine, m-Part-Type System

Define M_{ij} to be the partial machine which performs the ith operation in approximate tandem system j, $i = 1, \ldots, k$; $j = 1, \ldots, m$. Each partial machine does only one operation. Approximate tandem system j is the kind of k-machine, single-part-type system studied in Section 12.3.

Buffer hedging level and buffer hedging space   Define Z_{ij}^b to be the *hedging level* of Buffer (i, j). It is the number of parts in the buffer when the system reaches the hedging point. It satisfies

$$Z_{ij}^b = Z_{ij} - Z_{ij+1}, \quad i = 1, \ldots, k-1; j = 1, \ldots, m. \tag{12.35}$$

---

[12]with permission of the Massachusetts Institute of Technology.

Define Z_{ij}^s to be the *hedging space* of Buffer (i, j). It is the room left for more parts in the buffer when the system reaches the hedging point. It is given by

$$Z_{ij}^s = B_{ij} - Z_{ij}^b, \quad i = 1, \ldots, k - 1; j = 1, \ldots, m. \tag{12.36}$$

Let f_{ij}^s and f_{ij}^b be the starvation and blockage fractions. The hedging buffer levels and spaces are determined by solving the nonlinear program of Section 12.3 for each j. In Equations (12.27) and (12.28), d is replaced by d_j. Equation (12.29) is replaced by

$$\sum_{q=1}^{m} \tau_{iq} d_q \leq \frac{r_i}{r_i + p_i} (1 - f_{ij}^b - f_{ij}^s) \quad i = 1, \ldots, k; j = 1, \ldots, m.$$

This inequality was derived by assuming that the maximum production rate that Machine i would produce Part Type j when it is up is

$$\phi_{ij} = \frac{d_j}{\displaystyle\sum_{q=1}^{m} \tau_{iq} d_q}.$$

That is, Partial Machine M_{ij} is a machine that has the same reliability parameters as Machine i, but it makes only Type j parts with capacity set given by

$$0 \leq u_{ij} \leq \phi_{ij} \alpha_i.$$

This simplification is only made for the purpose of calculating the control parameters. The real-time controller is not limited by this capacity set; it is limited by (12.31).

12.4.3 Buffer sizes and hedging points

The buffer sizes are given by

$$B_{ij} = Z_{ij}^b + Z_{ij}^s, \quad i = 1, \ldots, k - 1; j = 1, \ldots, m.$$

To determine the hedging points, we follow the same procedure as in Section 12.2.5. The average buffer levels are

$$\bar{b}_{ij} = Z_{ij}^b + (\Delta_{i+1,j} - \Delta_{ij}), \quad i = 1, \ldots, k - 1; j = 1, \ldots, m, \tag{12.37}$$

where Δ_{ij} is the *surplus loss*. $\Delta_{k+1,j}$ is defined to be 0; for $i = 1, \ldots, k$,

$$\Delta_{ij} = Z_{ij} - \bar{x}_{ij}$$

is approximately given by Equations (12.20)-(12.23), in which f_i^s is replaced by f_{ij}^s; f_i^b is replaced by f_{ij}^b; the factor $d/2$ is replaced by $d_j/2$; and the factor $\mu_i/(\mu_i - d)$ is replaced by

$$\frac{1}{1 - \displaystyle\sum_{q=1}^{m} \tau_{iq} d_q}.$$

As before, Z_{kj} is chosen so that $\bar{x}_{kj} = 0$, or

$$Z_{kj} = \Delta_{kj}$$

and, finally, the rest of the hedging points are found from

$$Z_{ij} = Z_{ij}^b + Z_{i+1,j}, \quad i = 1, \ldots, k-1; j = 1, \ldots, m.$$

12.4.4   Real-time scheduling

The heuristic real-time controller calculates the production rate vector by solving (12.34) with W replaced by

$$\tilde{W} = \sum_{j=1}^{m} \tilde{W}_j,$$

where

$$\tilde{W}_j = \frac{1}{2} \sum_{i=1}^{k} A_{iij} (x_{ij} - Z_{ij})^2.$$

To simplify, assume all $A_{iij} = 1$. As indicated earlier, when Machine i is neither starved nor blocked, it looks like the one-machine, many-part-type system of Exercise 8 of Chapter 9. Consequently, the same heuristic is equally applicable: devote all effort to the part type that is furthest behind its hedging point. It will start catching up, and all the others will lose ground. When two parts types are equally far behind their hedging points, split the machine between them so as to keep them equally far behind. They will both catch up, and all others will continue to fall further behind. Keep doing this until all parts have reached their hedging points, or until a failure or a starvation or a blockage occurs, if it occurs first.

When a starvation or a blockage occurs, the same policy is valid, but now the amount of effort that we can allocate to some part types may be limited by the conditional constraints. The rule is therefore to devote as much effort as possible to the part type that is furthest behind its hedging point. If that effort is limited by a conditional constraint, allocate as much as possible to the next part type, the one among all the remaining types that is furthest behind its hedging point. Continue allocating machine capacity in this way until either all capacity is allocated, or until you have reached the parts that are already at their hedging points. Share the remaining capacity in such a way as to keep them all at their hedging points, or let them fall behind together.

12.4.5   Virtual machines

Figure 12.8 is the extension of Figure 12.5 for tandem systems with multiple part types. The controller for this case can similarly be thought of as a hedging point controller of Chapter 9 of a flexible manufacturing system with $2m + 1$ machines and m part types. Each of the virtual machines — the machines that correspond to the buffers — processes only a single part type, and its production rate depends on whether its buffer is at an extreme.

When an upstream buffer is not empty or a downstream buffer is not full, the corresponding machine has a very high production rate. When the buffer becomes full or empty, its machine has its production rate reduced to that of the current production rate of its part type at the upstream or downstream machine.

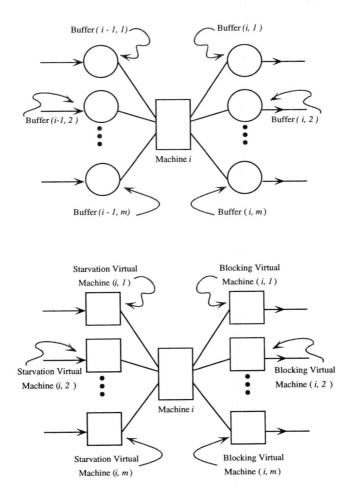

Figure 12.8: Virtual Machines for Multiple-Part-Type System

The comments in the previous section on keeping track of chains of empty or full buffers apply here as well.

12.5   Reentrant Systems

The next class of systems are those in which parts visit some of the same machines more than once. The most important class of such systems are semiconductor fabrication lines, in which wafers have multiple layers of wiring or microscopic electronic components. Each visit to the same machine does the same operation, but on a different layer. Printed circuit boards, in which parts are mounted on both sides, require two visits to the same machine.

We again assume that all buffers are homogeneous, that all the parts in each buffer are interchangeable. This means that only a single part type can be contained in each buffer. It also means that parts of the same type, but at different production stages, do *not* share the same buffer. Consequently, there are often more than $2m + 1$ buffers attached to a machine; the number may vary, and it depends on the number of times each part visits that machine.

It is convenient to define the *operation index* θ_{inj}, which may be 0 or 1. If $\theta_{inj} = 1$, then Type j parts receive their nth operation at Machine i; otherwise, they do not. The operation time, surplus, production rate, and buffer level vectors are defined accordingly: τ_{nj} is the operation time of the nth operation of Type j parts; x_{nj} is the surplus of Type j parts after they have obtained their nth operation; u_{nj} is the production rate of the nth stage of Type j parts; and b_{nj} is the number of Type j parts that have had their nth operation in the buffer that holds such parts. The number of operations for Type j parts — the upper limit of n — is L_j.

The procedure for developing a real-time scheduler in this case is similar to all the previous. The dynamic program can be stated but not solved exactly. We deduce a solution structure in which the surplus space is divided into regions. Based on this, we guess a heuristic: for each machine, create a small flexible manufacturing system consisting of the machine and all the virtual machines that correspond to its adjacent buffers. Then operate this flexible manufacturing system according to the hedging point policy of Chapter 9.

Parameters   The problem data are τ_{nj} as defined here, and r_i, p_i, and d_j as defined earlier.

Decision and state variables   The decision variables are u_{nj}. The state variables are x_{nj}, b_{nj}, and α_i.

Control parameters B_{nj} is the maximum allowable value of b_{nj}, and it can be specified or chosen. The hedging point Z_{nj} is the value that the policy drives x_{nj} toward.

12.5.1   Dynamic optimization

The following dynamic programming problem is formulated to determine the production control policy.

$$J(x(t_0), \alpha(t_0), t_0) = \min_u E\left\{ \int_{t_0}^{T} g(x, b)dt \mid x(t_0), \alpha(t_0) \right\} \tag{12.38}$$

subject to:

$$\sum_{\{j,n|\theta_{inj}=1\}} \tau_{nj}u_{nj} \leq \alpha_i, \quad i = 1, 2, \ldots, k;$$
$$u_{nj} \geq 0, \quad n = 1, \ldots, L_j; j = 1, \ldots, m \tag{12.39}$$

where the system dynamics and buffer constraints are

$$\frac{dx_{nj}}{dt} = u_{nj} - d_n, \qquad n = 1, \ldots, L_j; j = 1, \ldots, m \tag{12.40}$$

$$\frac{db_{nj}}{dt} = u_{nj} - u_{n+1,j}, \qquad n = 1, \ldots, L_j - 1; j = 1, \ldots, m \tag{12.41}$$

$$0 \leq b_{nj} \leq B_{nj}, \qquad n = 1, \ldots, L_j - 1; j = 1, \ldots, m, \tag{12.42}$$

and the dynamics of α_i are those of the exponentially unreliable machine.

Conditional constraints These constraints are the same as before, but the notation is different because we keep track of operation number rather than machine:

$$\begin{array}{llll} \text{if} \ \ b_{nj} = 0, & \text{then} & u_{n+1,j} \leq u_{nj}, & n = 1, \ldots, L_j - 1; j = 1, \ldots, m; \\ \text{if} \ \ b_{nj} = B_{nj}, & \text{then} & u_{nj} \leq u_{n+1,j}, & n = 1, \ldots, L_j - 1; j = 1, \ldots, m. \end{array} \tag{12.43}$$

Optimal policy The solution of the optimization problem (12.38) satisfies

$$\min_u \sum_{j=1}^{m} \sum_{n=1}^{L_j} \frac{\partial W}{\partial x_{nj}} u_{nj} \tag{12.44}$$

subject to (12.39) and (12.43). W comes from (8.13).

12.5.2 Heuristic policy

As in previous cases, we replace the exact W in the optimal policy by $\tilde{W}$ which provides reasonable boundaries. We choose

$$\tilde{W} = \frac{1}{2} \sum_{j=1}^{m} \sum_{n=1}^{L_j} (x_{nj} - Z_{nj})^2$$

and we must find good values for the hedging points Z_{nj} and buffer sizes B_{nj}.

As in the previous case, we first obtain buffer sizes, buffer hedging levels, and buffer hedging spaces by converting the actual system to a set of approximate single-part-type tandem systems, and obtaining those quantities for those systems using the method of Section 12.3. Because of the reentrant nature of this case, the lengths of the single-part-type systems differ; and the machine that performs operation n on Part Type j may be different than the machine that performs operation n on any other part type.

Buffer hedging level and space   As in the tandem multiple-part-type case, we replace the parameters of the nonlinear program of the single-part-type case with appropriate parameters from this system. They are also derived by creating fictitious partial machines; Partial Machine m_{nj} corresponds to Machine i if $\theta_{inj} = 1$.

Let f^s_{nj} and f^b_{nj} be the starvation and blockage fractions of Partial Machine m_{nj} in the imaginary Part Type j line. The hedging buffer levels and spaces are determined by solving the nonlinear program of Section 12.3 for each j. In Equations (12.27) and (12.28), d is replaced by d_j. Equation (12.29) is replaced by

$$\sum_{\{q,n|\theta_{inq}=1\}} \tau_{nq} d_q \leq \frac{r_i}{r_i + p_i}(1 - f^b_{nj} - f^s_{nj}) \quad n = 1, \ldots, L_j.$$

As in Section 12.4.2, this inequality was derived by assuming that the maximum production rate that Machine i would produce Part Type j when it is up is

$$\phi_{nj} = \frac{d_j}{\displaystyle\sum_{\{q,n|\theta_{inq}=1\}} \tau_{nq} d_q}.$$

That is, Partial Machine m_{nj} is a machine that has the same reliability parameters as Machine i (if $\theta_{inj} = 1$), but it makes only Type j parts with capacity set given by

$$0 \leq u_{nj} \leq \phi_{nj}\alpha_i.$$

This simplification is only made for the purpose of calculating the control parameters. The real-time controller is not limited by this capacity set; it is limited by (12.39).

12.5.3   Buffer sizes and hedging points

The buffer sizes are given by

$$B_{nj} = Z^b_{nj} + Z^s_{nj}, \quad n = 1, \ldots, L_j - 1; j = 1, \ldots, m.$$

To determine the hedging points, we follow the same procedure as in Section 12.2.5. The average buffer levels are

$$\bar{b}_{nj} = Z^b_{nj} + (\Delta_{n+1,j} - \Delta_{nj}), \qquad n = 1, \ldots, L_j - 1; j = 1, \ldots, m \tag{12.45}$$

where Δ_{nj} is the surplus loss. $\Delta_{L_j+1,j}$ is defined to be 0; for $n = 1, \ldots, L_j$,

$$\Delta_{nj} = Z_{nj} - \bar{x}_{nj}$$

is approximately given by Equations (12.20)-(12.23), in which f^s_i is replaced by f^s_{nj} (if $\theta_{inj} = 1$); f^b_i is replaced by f^b_{nj}; the factor $d/2$ is replaced by $d_j/2$; and the factor $\mu_i/(\mu_i - d)$ is replaced by

$$\frac{1}{1 - \sum_{\{q,n|\theta_{inq}=1\}} \tau_{nq} d_q}.$$

As before, $Z_{L_j j}$ is chosen so that $\bar{x}_{L_j j} = 0$, or

$$Z_{L_j j} = \Delta_{L_j j}.$$

and, finally, the rest of the hedging points are found from

$$Z_{nj} = Z_{nj}^b + Z_{n+1,j}, \quad n = 1, \ldots, L_j - 1; j = 1, \ldots, m.$$

12.5.4 Real-time scheduling

A heuristic real-time scheduling policy is similar to that of the other cases: production rate u_{nj} is chosen which satisfies

$$\min_u (x_{nj} - Z_{nj}) u_{nj} \tag{12.46}$$

subject to (12.39) and (12.43).

Virtual machines Again, the conditional constraints can be treated as virtual machines. However, a new phenomenon arises here, a kind of chattering, which was explored by Violette (1993).

Sometimes a sequence of buffers can all become empty because the first machine in the sequence is operating at a slow pace. Similarly, a sequence of buffers can all become full because the last machine in the sequence is operating slowly. Because conditional constraints must be imposed as soon as buffers become empty or full, and because they must be removed as the buffers become non-empty or non-full, a sequence of empty buffers (or a sequence of full buffers) that forms a loop can lead to chattering. In particular, if a critical buffer is empty but is about to become non-empty, then some production rates must be recalculated immediately. The chattering arises when one of those rates determines whether that buffer is going to become non-empty.

Consider a system in which parts travel in a loop. The first machine in the loop is also the last machine. That is, it does the first operation on the parts. After that, the parts go into the first buffer, the second machine, the second buffer, and so forth until they reach the last buffer. Then, they re-enter the first machine for their last operation, and finally they leave the loop.

Suppose the buffers become empty because the first machine in the loop is doing the first operation at a low rate. This might happen because some other part type is further from its hedging point, and there is limited capacity at that machine available for this operation on this part. As parts leave the first machine, they travel through the loop, and return to that same machine for the last operation. Suppose that the buffers are not empty at first, but that they become empty one by one, starting with the buffer immediately downstream from that machine. All the production rates around the loop had been higher than that of the first machine doing the first operation on that part type, but as the buffers become empty, each of the machines is slowed to the speed of the first machine doing the first operation in the loop.

Recall that all the machines except the first do a single operation on the part. The first machine does two operations: the first and the last. Suppose that before the last buffer became empty, the first machine was doing the last operation at a higher rate than it was doing the first operation. (Perhaps controller (12.46) made this decision because the surplus for the part at its early stage was at its hedging point, but the surplus for the later stage of the part was below its hedging point.)

When the last buffer becomes empty, a chain of conditional constraints is imposed, leading back to the rate at which the first machine is doing the first operation. This new conditional constraint limits the rate that (12.46) can choose for the first machine to do the last operation. Since the rate at which it does the last operation is slower than before, more capacity is available for that machine to do the first operation. Consequently, the first operation is now performed at a faster pace than before.

But since the rate of the first operation was limiting all the machines, all the machines in the loop can now work faster, including the first machine doing the last operation. That is, the conditional constraints, which limited all later production rates, is relaxed. Since (12.46) evidently prefers to see the first machine devoting more effort to the last operation, it then restricts the speed of the first operation, and the cycle repeats. All of this happens very rapidly, so it is fair to call it chattering.

In fact, it happens before any decisions are communicated to move material. This is taking place during the computations of rates, not in response to any events happening on the production floor. For that reason, this chattering is a little different from that of Chapter 9. There, the chattering was potentially real, in the sense that if we did not take action to avoid it, parts would be loaded according to chattering production rates. We would observe it in high frequency rate recalculations and erratic loading of parts. Here, the chattering manifests itself in an infinite loop in a computer program.

The solution is first to detect that this may be happening, and then impose a new constraint on that machine: that under these circumstances, the rate at which it does the first operation is equal to the rate that it does the last operation. All the intermediate operations are also done at the same speed, and the buffers stay empty.

12.6　Cells and Virtual Machines

Here, we briefly describe one last generalization. In either of the two multiple-part-type cases, suppose that instead of single machines between buffers, there are cells — groups of machines with no buffers among them. The systems studied in Chapter 9 are examples of cells. We propose that such a system be operated according to the procedure described here: that for each cell, a controller like (12.46) is used. Instead of a single-machine constraint like (12.39) being imposed on each cell, now there are as many real capacity constraints as there are machines in that cell. There are the same virtual machine constraints as for the other cases: two for each part type (except for raw material entering the system and finished goods leaving). See Figure 12.9.

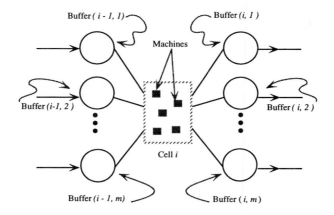

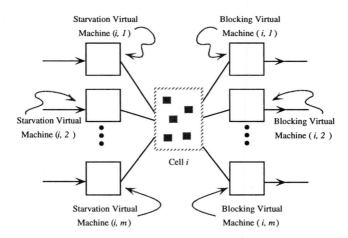

Figure 12.9: Virtual Machines for a Cell

12.7   Other Policies for Networks of Machines

Buffer priority, *due date*, and Clear-a-fraction (Section 11.4.4) policies have been developed for real-time distributed scheduling by Kumar and his colleagues. The goal of distributed scheduling is to allow most decisions to be made on a local basis, without extensive coordination, and for the system to demonstrate satisfactory performance. This work was done for the scheduling of complex production such as semiconductor fabrication, in which parts visit the same machines many times.

The buffer priority policies assume homogeneous buffers. When a machine completes an operation, the scheduler must decide which buffer to choose the next part from.[13] Due date policies make decisions based on when parts must be delivered. The policies that have been studied include the following.

- *First Buffer First Served* (Buffer Priority) A part is chosen from the first non-empty buffer that parts visit. For example, if a machine is visited for the third operation, the fifth operation, and the tenth operation of a process, parts waiting for the third operation are served when the machine becomes available. If there are no parts waiting for the third operation, the machine is used for parts waiting to get their fifth operation, and so forth.

- *Last Buffer First Served* (Buffer Priority) A part is chosen from the last non-empty buffer that parts visit. In the example above, a part waiting for the tenth operation has priority. If there are no such parts, one waiting for the fifth operation is chosen. If there are no tenth-operation or fifth-operation parts waiting, a third-operation part is chosen.

- *First Come First Served* The first part to arrive at the machine, of those that are currently waiting, is chosen. (This is actually neither a buffer priority nor a due date policy, but it was analyzed in a network using similar methods.)

- *Earliest Due Date* (Due Date) Among the parts that are waiting at a machine, the one that is due first is chosen.

- *Least Slack* (Due Date) For each buffer, there is a number which can be, but need not be, an estimate of the remaining delay in the system. The *slack* is the due date minus this number. The part with the least slack is chosen.

Kumar and his colleagues have found conditions for these policies to be stable (in the sense that delays and buffer levels do not increase without limit). They have also done extensive simulation testing, and have concluded that the Least Slack policy is almost always far superior to the others, in the sense that it produces small delays and small variances of delay. They have also studied the clearing policies (Section 11.4.4) in networks for systems with and without setup changes. They find conditions for stability and examples of instability when the conditions are not satisfied.

---

[13]If the parts are identical, it does not matter which part is chosen from a buffer, once the buffer is chosen. If the parts are not identical, they can be ordered according due date.

Sharifnia has studied NINE (non-idling-non-exceeding) policies for systems without se-tups, which can be viewed as generalizations of the staircase and Clear-a-fraction policies (when they are restricted to such systems). In a NINE policy, there is a hierarchical sched-uler with at least two levels. At the level above the lowest level, feasible production rates are chosen to meet some performance objective. At the lowest level, a part is loaded onto a machine when the machine is idle and (1) the part is present, waiting in a buffer for an operation on that machine, and (2) the total production to date for that part type does not exceed the integral of the production rate for that part type. Thus, the machine can only be idle if it is starved, or if, among all the parts that are present, the machine has gotten slightly ahead of the integral of the production rate. In fact, it cannot get more than one part ahead of this requirement. Sharifnia (1993) shows that even in a complex network where starvation is possible, these policies do not fall behind, and that buffer levels do not grow without limit.

12.8 Research Problems

1. Demand is not described very well by a constant rate. To some extent, we can account for demand variations by including an artificial last machine, whose failures and repairs represent the stochastic nature of demand. However, this is not completely satisfactory because the only information that is propagated upstream is the average demand and the blockage or repair state of the next machine. Consequently, we have gained little by this approach if demand variations are much greater than variations due to machine failures.

   A better approach can based on the hierarchy of Chapter 13. If demand variations are larger than reliability variations, they are treated at a higher level in the control hierarchy. When a major change in demand occurs, it is propagated as far upstream as necessary from the last stage. As d changes, the affected control parameters are changed appropriately. Investigate the effectiveness of this approach, and how to implement it.

2. Improve the approximate method for calculating hedging points by including the cost function g.

3. Following the style of Chapter 4, develop a method for calculating hedging points by decomposing the system into a set of one-machine systems. In these systems, failures represent starvations or blockages, as well as the actual failures, of the correspond-ing machine. Find the hedging point of each system using the method of Section 9.3. Reintroduce buffers and estimate frequencies and durations of starvations and blockages as a function of these hedging points. Iterate.

4. Estimate the variance of production. How much do these policies reduce variance? What is the tradeoff between inventory and variance?

5. Vives (1991) extended Bai's methods to production systems with a single assembly stage. He observed some symmetries which were reminiscent of the equivalence results of Section 5.6. Extend Vives' decomposition to more complex systems.

6. Extend Bai's methods to systems in which finite buffers are shared by different part types.

7. Extend these methods to systems with non-exponential failures. Consider a machine that exhibits a decreasing failure rate. It is more likely to fail during a time interval soon after an interruption than during a later interval of the same length. It may be wise to keep it idle after a repair or a starvation or a blockage until there is enough material upstream and space downstream so that it can work for a long time before it is in danger of another interruption due to starvation or blockage.[14] How can such a policy be developed as an extension of the policy studied in this chapter?

Exercises

1. Write the Bellman equations for all the dynamic programming problems in this chapter.

2. Show that the $g_b b$ term in (12.5) adds no generality. That is, show that for some set of $\tilde{g}_{i+}$ and $\tilde{g}_{i-}$, (12.5) is equivalent to

$$\tilde{g}(x) = \sum_{i=1}^{2} \left[\tilde{g}_{i+} x_i^+ + \tilde{g}_{i-} x_i^- \right].$$

Note that $\tilde{g}_{1-}$ and $\tilde{g}_{2+}$ could be negative. What does this mean? Does this lead to undesirable behavior, such as x_2 growing without bound, or $g \to -\infty$ as $x_2 \to +\infty$? *Hint:* consider (12.3) and (12.4).

---

[14]Observation reported by Gary Sullivan.

Bibliography

[1] S. X. Bai (1991), "Scheduling Manufacturing Systems with Work-In-Process Inventory Control," Ph. D. Thesis, MIT Operations Research Center, September, 1991.

[2] X. Bai and S. B. Gershwin (1990a), "Scheduling Manufacturing Systems with Work-In-Process Inventory Control: Single-Part-Type Systems," MIT Laboratory for Manufacturing and Productivity Report LMP 90-003; also MIT Microsystems Research Center, VLSI Memo No. 90-604; Operations Research Center Working Paper OR 218-90, June, 1990.

[3] X. Bai and S. B. Gershwin (1990b), "Scheduling Manufacturing Systems with Work-in-Process Inventory Control: Nonlinear Formulation of Single Part Type Systems," *Proceedings of the 29th IEEE Conference on Decision and Control,* Hawaii, December, 1990. MIT Laboratory for Manufacturing and Productivity, LMP 90-016.

[4] X. Bai and S. B. Gershwin (1990c), "Scheduling Manufacturing Systems with Work-In-Process Inventory Control: Reentrant Systems," MIT Operations Research Center Working Paper OR 242-91, March, 1991.

[5] X. Bai and S. B. Gershwin (1993), "Scheduling Manufacturing Systems with Work-In-Process Inventory Control: Multiple-Part-Type Systems," *International Journal of Production Research,* to appear.

[6] J. A. Buzacott and J. G. Shanthikumar (1992), "A General Approach for Coordinating Production in Multiple-Cell Manufacturing Systems," *Production and Operations Management*, Volume 1, Number 1, Winter, 1992, pp. 34-52.

[7] J. A. Buzacott and J. G. Shanthikumar (1993), *Stochastic Models of Manufacturing Systems*, Prentice Hall, 1993.

[8] M. N. Eleftheriu (1989) "On the Analysis of Hedging Point Policies of Multi-Stage Production Manufacturing Systems," Rensselaer Polytechnic Institute Ph. D. Thesis, CIRSSE Document 48, December, 1989.

[9] M. N. Eleftheriu and A. A. Desrochers (1991), "An Approximation Schema for the Estimation of Buffer Sizes for Manufacturing Facilities," *IEEE Transactions on Robotics and Automation*, Vol. 7, No. 4, pp. 551-562, August, 1991.

[10] C. R. Glassey and M. G. C. Resende, "Closed-Loop Job Release Control for VLSI Circuit Manufacturing," *IEEE Transactions on Semiconductor Manufacturing*, Vol. 1, No. 1, pp. 36-46, February, 1988.

[11] S. C. Graves (1986), "A Tactical Planning for a Job Shop," *Operations Research*, Vol. 34, No. 4, pp. 522-533, July-August, 1986.

[12] S. C. Graves, H. Meal, D. Stefek, and A. Zeghmi (1983), "Scheduling of Re-entrant Flow Shops," *Journal of Operations Management*, Volume 3, 1983, pp. 197-203.

[13] P. R. Kumar and T. I. Seidman (1990), "Dynamic Instabilities and Stabilization Methods in Distributed Real-time Scheduling of Manufacturing Systems, *IEEE Transactions on Automatic Control*, Vol. 35, pp. 289-298, March, 1990.

[14] S. Lou, S. P. Sethi, and Q. Zhang (1993), "Optimal Feedback Production Planning in a Stochastic Two-Machine Flowshop," *European Journal of Operational Research: Special Issue on Stochastic Control Theory and Operational Research*, to appear.

[15] C. Lozinski and C. R. Glassey, "Bottleneck Starvation Indicators for Shop Floor Control," *IEEE Transactions on Semiconductor Manufacturing*, Vol. 1, pp. 147-153, November, 1988.

[16] S. H. Lu and P. R. Kumar (1991), "Distributed Scheduling Based on Due Dates and Buffer Prioritization," *IEEE Transactions on Automatic Control*, Vol. 36, December, 1991.

[17] W. Maxwell, J. A. Muckstadt, L. J. Thomas, and J. VanderEecken, " A Modeling Framework for Planning and Control of Production in Discrete Parts Manufacturing and Assembly Systems," *Interfaces*, Vol. 13, No. 6, pp. 92-104, December, 1983.

[18] D. Mitra and I. Mitrani (1990), "Analysis of a Kanban Discipline for Cell Coordination in Production Lines. I," *Management Science,* Vol. 36, No. 12, pp. 1548-1566, December, 1990.

[19] J. Orlicky (1975), *Material Requirements Planning*, McGraw-Hill, 1975.

[20] J. Perkins and P. R. Kumar (1989), "Stable, Distributed, Real-Time Scheduling of Flexible Manufacturing/Assembly/Disassembly Systems," *IEEE Transactions on Automatic Control*, Vol. 34, No. 2, pp. 139-148, February, 1989.

[21] A. Sharifnia (1993), "Stability and Performance of Distributed Production Control Methods based on Continuous Flow Models," *IEEE Transactions on Automatic Control*, to appear.

[22] G. Van Ryzin (1987), "Control of Manufacturing Systems with Delays," MIT EECS M.S. Thesis, MIT Laboratory for Information and Decision Systems Report LIDS-TH-1676, June, 1987.

[23] G. J. Van Ryzin, X.-C. Lou, and S. B. Gershwin (1991), "Scheduling Job Shops with Delays," *International Journal of Production Research,* Volume 29, Number 7, pp. 1407-1422, 1991.

[24] G. J. Van Ryzin, X.-C. Lou, and S. B. Gershwin (1993), "Production Control for a Tandem Two-Machine System," *IIE Transactions,* to appear.

[25] J. Violette (1993), "Implementation of a Hierarchical Controller in a Factory Simulation," M.S. Thesis, MIT, Department of Aeronautics and Astronautics, June, 1993.

[26] G. Y. Vives (1991), "Real-Time Scheduling of an Assembly Stage in a Production Stage," MIT Operations Research Center Master's Thesis, MIT Laboratory for Manufacturing and Productivity Report LMP-91-057.

Chapter 13

Pyramid-Shaped Hierarchy and the General Framework

The methods of Chapter 12 are improvements over those of Chapter 9 because they account for the presence of buffers, and take advantage of their ability to reduce the propagation of disturbances among machines. In Chapter 9, if one machine fails, all machines in the system are immediately affected. In Chapter 12, the effect of a failure is deferred until an intervening buffer becomes full or empty; and if the repair is prompt enough, the effect is not propagated at all.

Suppose there are many classes of disruptions, with a wide range of frequencies and durations, as in Chapter 10. Suppose there are also buffers with a wide range of sizes. In that case, a brief failure will probably not propagate through a large buffer, but a major downtime will most likely pass through many small buffers, and disrupt many machines.

This suggests that the Chapter 10 hierarchy can be combined with the spatial decomposition of Chapter 12. High level controllers in the hierarchy deal with infrequent, major disruptions, and with the large portions of the factory that are found between large buffers. Low level controllers in the hierarchy respond to frequent, brief disruptions and manage the groups of machines between smaller buffers. There are few high level controllers and many low level controllers.

This leads to a pyramid-shaped extension to the hierarchical controller of Chapter 10. Its purpose is the same as the frequency and spatial decompositions of Chapters 10 and 12: to replace one big problem with many small ones. Not only is the set of small problems easier to solve, but the decomposition leads to decentralized control, which often has benefits in improved controller reliability.

Hierarchies are not new. They are so widespread — in businesses, armies, religions, governments, and universities — that there must be something useful about them. To construct a hierarchical organization for people, one must take into account their human nature, and

483

create a decent working environment. Such a consideration does not apply to organizations of machines, to which we restrict ourselves here. On the other hand, humans can sometimes deal effectively and creatively with vague instructions, or surprise their colleagues and themselves with bursts of energy in crises. Computers and other machines lack these capabilities. We therefore must construct hierarchical control systems for inanimate objects differently: such organizations must respond to disruptions in limited, but effective, ways; and they must allocate tasks to resources that have fixed capacities. Most importantly, the calculations required to make decisions must be performed quickly.

13.1 Characteristics of a Scheduler for a Complex System

A real-time control technique for complex, stochastic factories should be based on the following ideas:

- **Event Classification** Different kinds of events should be treated differently. Events should be classified according to controllability, frequency, and location. The control hierarchy should be determined by this classification:

  - **Controllability** Operations and setup changes are events that managers or workers can control, whereas machine failures are generally uncontrollable. The former are the objects of the scheduling algorithm, whereas the latter cause the algorithm to be invoked.

  - **Frequency (time scale)** Events that occur at very different frequencies need not be treated in detail together. A decomposition that allows a focus on one frequency class at a time reduces the real-time computational burden.

  - **Location** Similarly, events that occur at different locations need not be treated in detail together. Because of the low-pass filter effect of buffers, a decomposition that allows a controller to focus on one region of the factory also reduces computation. The extent of the region is determined by the sizes of buffers and the frequencies and durations of events to be managed.

- **Capacity** Capacity is a function of events. When machines go down, when set-up changes are performed, or when maintenance is taking place, the affected machines cannot do operations. This condition, however, is local and temporary. The scheduling of operations must respect these temporary capacity variations. The available capacity seen by a scheduler depends on the time scale over which the scheduling is performed. The detailed state of the system must be considered when short term schedules are calculated, but only an aggregate state is necessary for making longer term plans.

- **Scope** The scope of a controller — the portion of the factory floor for which a given controller is responsible — is a function of the frequency class of the events that it responds to. Controllers that treat infrequent, major (high level) events are responsible for the broad direction of large parts of the production system; controllers that deal with frequent, minor (low level) events are responsible for the detailed management of small parts of the system.

- **Scheduling by Tracking Feasible Targets** The scheduling objective is to keep production close to demand while keeping work-in-process inventory low. Each component of the scheduling hierarchy is given a feasible production target by its superior, and uses current data to translate that target into feasible short term targets for its subordinates. It also schedules controllable events that fall into its frequency and location domain. Feasible short term targets are those that satisfy the current, local capacity constraints.

- **Customized Structure** The structure of the hierarchy should depend on the nature of the factory and of its products. The number of levels, and the scope of the controllers should depend on the frequencies and locations of the events that occur. It should not be a fixed structure that is based *solely* on accounting conventions and reporting periods. It must accommodate such events, but it must also respond to the physical events of the factory itself. Every factory is unique, and the controller must adapt itself to the factory. The factory should not have to adapt to the controller.

13.2 Pyramid Hierarchy

13.2.1 Pyramid Structure

Consider a large, complex production system with many machines, many buffers, and in which many different kinds of events occur. These events have frequencies and durations that span many orders of magnitude. Such a system would be hard to control in a centralized way, so we want to decompose the real-time scheduler according to frequency, as in Chapter 10, and location, as in Chapter 12. A combination of the temporal and spatial decomposition leads to a pyramid shaped hierarchy (Violette and Gershwin, 1991; Violette, 1993). In the pyramid hierarchy, a few high level controllers treat low frequency events and control large portions of the factory. Many low level controllers react to high frequency events and control limited portions of the factory. The terminology and notation in this section is an extension of that of earlier chapters, particularly Chapter 10.

For example, consider the production system and four-level control hierarchy illustrated in Figure 13.1[1]. This tandem system makes only one part type. The numbers in the figure represent machines and the letters represent buffers. The relative buffer sizes are indicated by the sizes of the ovals. There is a wide range of events that take place at these machines, such as failures, worker absence, engineering changes, etc. These events are clustered into five frequency classes: $\mathcal{L}_2$, $\mathcal{L}_3$, $\mathcal{L}_4$, and $\mathcal{L}_5$. $\mathcal{L}_5$ is the set of operations, which are not explicitly represented in the figure.

---

[1]Reprinted from Srivatsan, Bai, and Gershwin (1993), with permission from Academic Press

Physical Machines and Buffers

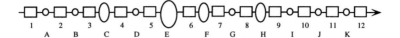

Pyramid-Shaped Hierarchy

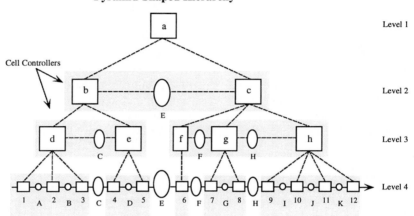

Figure 13.1: The Pyramid Hierarchy

Buffer E is a Level 2 buffer because it can always decouple Level 3 and lower level events, and sometimes it decouples Level 2 events. Buffers C, F, and H are Level 3 buffers and the other buffers are Level 4 buffers. The cell controllers at each level are also shown.

When a Level 4 event occurs at Machine 7, it sometimes causes Machine 8 to be starved, but it never[2] fills up Buffer F, and never causes Machine 6 to be blocked. When a Level 3 event occurs at Machine 7, it always causes Machine 8 to be starved. It sometimes empties Buffer H, which starves Machine 9; and it sometimes fills up Buffer F, blocking Machine 6. When a Level 2 event occurs at Machine 7, it always causes Machines 8-12 to be starved. It always blocks Machine 6. Sometimes it fills up Buffer E. When that happens, it always blocks Machines 1-5.

Cell **a** is the entire factory. The Cell **a** controller sets long term goals for the whole system. It has an estimate of the system's capacity, and it ensures that the production

---

[2]Well, hardly ever. It is tedious to write "almost never" and "almost always" over and over, but that is what is really intended in this discussion.

target is within it. Cell **b** consists of Machines 1-5 and Buffers A, B, C, and D. The Cell **b** controller selects the Level 2 hedging point and the Level 2 production rate targets for that part of the factory. That is, if the Level 2 production surplus for the part of the factory upstream of Buffer E is below its Level 2 hedging point, and there is currently no Level 2 disruption (a major failure in one of the Cell **b** machines, of Buffer E filling up) in effect, the Cell **b** controller demands that Cell **b** works at its maximum possible rate. (That maximum takes into account the average frequencies and durations of higher frequency events.) When the Cell **b** surplus reaches its hedging point, the Level 2 production target drops down to the target calculated by the Cell **a** controller, at Level 1.

If a major failure occurs in Cell **b**, the Level 2 production target is reduced to 0. If Buffer E becomes full, the Level 2 production target of Cell **b** is reduced to the current target of Cell **c** exactly as in the two-machine line of Section 12.2.

When Cell **b** determines its production rate target, it communicates it to Cell **d** and Cell **e**. The controllers of these cells must respond to higher frequency, shorter duration disruptions within their own boundaries. Cell **d** worries about short term disturbances in Machines 1, 2, or 3; Cell **e** worries about such events in Machines 4 and 5. Also, Cell **d** worries about Buffer C becoming full, and Cell **e** worries about the possibility that the same buffer might become empty. When any of these events happen, the affected cell finds itself with a reduced ability to work.

When Cell **d** is not impeded from working, it tries to exceed the Cell **b** production target by its hedging point. When it reaches that goal, it reduces its production rate to exactly equal to that goal. It does this by calculating shorter term production rate targets that it communicates to the controllers of Machines 1, 2, and 3. These machines respond to even shorter term disruptions according to the methods of Section 12.3.

Note that events must have been classified in advance. That is, when one kind of disruption occurs, it is known to be a Level 2 event, and when another kind of disruption occurs, it is known to be a Level 3 event. When these events occur, they are communicated to the controller that is programmed to deal with them.

Note also that Cell **b**, a Level 2 cell, is bounded by the entrance buffer to the factory (which is not shown in Figure 13.1) and Buffer E, a Level 2 buffer. The entrance and exit buffers are infinite — and therefore, Level 1 — buffers because they allow us to assume that the first machine is never starved and the last machine is never blocked. Cell **f**, a Level 3 cell, is bounded by Buffer E, a Level 2 buffer, and Buffer F, a Level 3 buffer. Cell **g**, another Level 3 cell, is bounded by Buffer F and Buffer H, both Level 3 buffers. In general, Level k cells are surrounded by Level k or higher level buffers (one upstream and one downstream for each part type).

13.2.2 Pyramid Decomposition

To construct a pyramid-structured controller, we first decompose the controller according to frequency. At each level k is a controller that responds to, or schedules, events whose frequencies are near f_k. Events whose frequencies are much less than f_k are treated at higher levels; and events that are much more frequent are represented only as rate variables in determining capacity sets, and in setting targets. This is an extension of Chapter 10 because among the Level k events are the emptying and filling of Level k buffers. A *Level k buffer* is one whose size is comparable to the number of parts produced during the duration of a typical Level k disruption. A Level k buffer is large enough to block the propagation of Level k disturbances, but too small to isolate Level $k-1$ disturbances.

Let us assume that buffers are homogeneous in the sense of Chapter 12, and that all the buffers that are adjacent to the same machine have the same level. Consider two sets of buffers. One set are Level k buffers, and the other are Level k or higher. Assume that when parts flow from one to the other, they do not pass through any other Level k or higher buffers between them. Then the set of machines and smaller (lower level) buffers between the two sets of Level k or higher buffers is a *Level k cell*.

Now construct a controller for Level k according to the methods of Chapter 12, particularly Section 12.6. The system is broken up according to Level k and higher level buffers. Smaller buffers are treated as though they are of size 0.

Level k Cell c is a set of machines and buffers that are treated together in the Level k spatial decomposition. The *Level k production rate* u_{cj}^k is chosen at this level. It is the production rate of Type j parts in this cell, as perceived by a Level k observer. The Level k surplus x_{cj}^k is estimated from differential equations like (12.40). *Level k hedging points* Z_{cj}^k are calculated for such cells. They are the values that the controller drives x_{cj}^k toward.

Let operations be numbered, and let the buffer that a part enters just after an operation have the same number. That is, if the last operation that Type j parts get in Cell c is Operation n, then the buffer after the last machine in Cell c for Type j parts is called Buffer β_{nj}. Its size is B_{nj}. Cell c' is the next cell that Type j parts visit after Buffer β_{nj}. The first operation that Type j parts get in Cell c' is Operation $n+1$.

The *Level k buffer level* b_{nj}^k is estimated from differential equations like (12.41). It differs from the buffer level as perceived by controllers at other levels, even though they are describing the same buffer. Consequently blockage and starvation are perceived differently at different levels, and a buffer may be seen as blocked at one level and not blocked at another. For this reason, virtual machines are assigned to levels, and the speed of a Level k virtual machine may differ from that of a virtual machine that represents the same event (blockage or starvation) due to the same buffer at a different level.

The scope of the controller — the factory floor space that the controller is responsible for — is a function of the frequency class k of the events that it responds to. Consider a Level m buffer ($m > k$), a buffer which is very small compared to the number of parts that can be processed during the duration of a typical Level k disruption. Such a buffer is transparent to these events. By contrast, buffers whose size is comparable to the duration of a typical Level k disruption, or larger, can limit the propagation of the effects of such events.

13.2.3   The Real-Time Level k Controller for Cell c

Let C be a Level $k-1$ cell, let c be a Level k cell, and assume that $c \subset C$. Each Level k cell c is separated from its neighbors by two sets of Level k or higher level buffers. (For each part type, there is an upstream and a downstream buffer, possibly the factory entrance or exit buffers.) The goal of the controller of Cell c at Level k is to ensure that the expected values of its production rates u_{cj}^k are equal to its Level $k-1$ target rates u_{Cj}^{k-1} over the time scale of Level $k-1$. The extension of Equation (10.26) for the cell at Level k is

$$E_{k-1} u_{cj}^k = u_{Cj}^{k-1}. \tag{13.1}$$

All the cells $c \subset C$ have the same target rates u_{Cj}^{k-1}. The hedging point controller for Cell c at Level k is constructed using the method suggested in Section 12.6 to choose rates that satisfy Equation (13.1).

For each part type j that is treated in Cell c, define the production surplus x_{cj}^k as:

$$x_{cj}^k(t) = \int_{t_0}^t u_{cj}^k dt - \int_{t_0}^t u_{Cj}^{k-1} dt$$

or,

$$\frac{dx_{cj}^k}{dt} = u_{cj}^k - u_{Cj}^{k-1}, \qquad x_{cj}^k(t_0) \text{ specified.}$$

Let Cell c' be the cell immediately downstream of Cell c for Type j parts. Then the Level k level of Buffer β_{nj} is given by

$$b_{nj}^k(t) = \int_{t_0}^t u_{cj}^k dt - \int_{t_0}^t u_{c'j}^{k-1} dt$$

or,

$$\frac{db_{nj}^k}{dt} = u_{cj}^k - u_{c'j}^{k-1},$$

$$b_{nj}^k(t_0) = x_{cj}^k(t_0) - x_{c'j}^k(t_0)$$

The buffer level must satisfy

$$0 \le b_{nj}^k(t) \le B_{nj}. \tag{13.2}$$

Virtual Machines Buffer β_{nj} is the buffer between operations n and $n+1$ for Process j. When Buffer β_{nj} is full or empty, Cell c's or Cell c''s capacity set is limited by the maximum flow rate through Buffer $u_{\beta_{nj}}^{max}$, which is determined by the neighboring cell. This is the conditional constraint

$$\begin{aligned} &\text{if } b_{nj} = 0, &&\text{then} &&u_{c'j} \le u_{cj}, \\ &\text{if } b_{nj} = B_{nj}, &&\text{then} &&u_{cj} \le u_{c'j} \end{aligned} \tag{13.3}$$

that is added to the capacity set in the form of a virtual machine. These constraints are generalizations of the many versions of the conditional constraints in Chapter 12 such as (12.43).

Real-time controller   To specify the linear program for a heuristic cell controller at Level k in a pyramid decomposition of a factory, we must define some symbols. The machines in Cell c are denoted by i. P_i and F_i are the sets of controllable and uncontrollable events that occur in Machine i. P_i includes operations on Type j parts, and F_i includes different failure modes. The real-time Level k production rate for Cell c is the set of u_{cj}^k that satisfy

$$\min \sum_{j \in P} A_{cj}^k (x_{cj}^k - Z_{cj}^k) u_{cj}^k$$

subject to

$$\sum_{j \in P} \tau_{ij} u_{cj}^k \leq \alpha_{ci}^k - \sum_{j \in F_i} \tau_{ij} u_{cj}^k \quad \forall i \in c$$

$$u_{cj}^k \geq 0 \tag{13.4}$$

and conditional constraints (13.3).

As usual, the lowest level of the hierarchy, the loading of parts, is managed by the staircase policy (Section 9.4.4) or some other technique for matching discrete events to target rates.

Conditions on Hedging Points   Hedging points must be chosen carefully to assure that the system exhibits desirable behavior. Here, we extend the concept of hedging point feasibility (Equation (12.11)) to the pyramid hierarchy.

Consider two segments of Process j in adjacent Level k cells c and c'. The last operation in Cell c on Process j is n and the first in Cell c' is $n + 1$. The process segments are separated by a Level k buffer of size B_{nj}. The hedging point of the upstream process is Z_{cj}^k and that of the downstream process is $Z_{c'j}^k$. When both process segment surpluses are at their respective hedging points, the amount of material b_{nj}^k in the buffer is equal to the difference in the hedging points

$$b_{nj}^k = Z_{cj}^k - Z_{c'j}^k. \tag{13.5}$$

The amount of material in the buffer is constrained as in (13.2). Therefore, the hedging points must satisfy

$$0 \leq Z_{cj}^k - Z_{c'j}^k \leq B_{nj}. \tag{13.6}$$

Consider the same two process segments at Level k, but this time the segments are separated by a buffer of Level $k - 1$, again of size B_{nj}. Major changes in the amount of material in the buffer are due to the Level $k - 1$ process segments. However, minor changes are possible at Level k. When the entire system is at its hedging point, the amount of material in the buffer is

$$b_{nj}^k = (Z_{cj}^{k-1} + Z_{cj}^k) - (Z_{c'j}^{k-1} + Z_{c'j}^k). \tag{13.7}$$

In general, feasible hedging points at Level k for a Level m buffer of size B_{nj}, where $m \leq k$, must satisfy

$$0 \leq \sum_{i=m}^k Z_{cj}^i - \sum_{i=m}^k Z_{c'j}^i \leq B_{nj}. \tag{13.8}$$

13.3 Designing and Scheduling Factories

13.3.1 Current Decision-Making Techniques

At present, production managers and workers make decisions — and academic researchers develop decision methods — in four major ways.

1. They improvise, based on common sense. Sometimes, this is adequate, but it cannot be effective when systems are large and complex, when there are many different decisions to be made, and when events happen frequently.

2. They use — or study — simple rules. Some rules are justified analytically or by simulation. However, exact analytical methods usually fail for complex systems. Often, there is no way of knowing if the rules are getting the best possible performance from the system.

3. They write simulations to analyze their proposed designs. This can become clumsy, as the comparisons between the line design exercises by simulation and by analytic modeling in Chapters 3 and 4 show.

4. They solve large scale optimization models of the production system. But because such calculations are time consuming, they cannot be run frequently, and the decisions are therefore not made in real time. Managers must improvise when random events occur between computations. Optimization models are usually based on crude models of the production system. These models are invariably deterministic, so they do not take randomness into account, and provide no explicit way of responding to a random event.

13.3.2 Suggested approach

You are an engineer who must develop a real-time scheduler for a factory, or a portion of a factory, that comes close to satisfying Assumption 1 of Section 10.2.3 (the assumption that events can be segregated according to frequency). Assume that it can be decomposed into portions that each satisfy Assumption 2 (the assumption that parts spend a short time in each of these portions of the factory) reasonably well. We assume also that solutions for all phenomena in the factory exist. (See Section 13.4.) Among other activities, you should

1. Collect data. Determine all the part types that are to be produced by the system to be controlled, and the demand rates for all of them. Determine all the resources. Determine all the events, activities, and other phenomena. Determine the timing for all phenomena: for example, average operation times, average down times and times between failures, average setup times, average times between maintenance, and so forth. If there are different classes of the same kind of event — such as minor and major setups — treat them as different events for the purpose of calculating averages and determining the structure of the hierarchy. Some data may not be available at this time; make educated guesses.

2. Determine if the demands are within capacity. If they are, proceed with Step 3. If not, discuss with senior management. Capacity must be expanded (by acquiring more capital or expanding working hours), or demand reduced (by turning away business or by subcontracting production[3]), or management must be made to understand the consequences on performance measures. (Some demands will not be satisfied, and delays will be large and growing.)

3. Formulate and solve the Level 1 problem to determine the frequencies of all controllable events, to determine route splits, etc. This will establish the structure of the hierarchy.

4. Develop all lower level controllers, including hedging point and staircase strategies, corridor strategies, etc.

5. Install a computer system that will collect real-time information, including notification each time an operation is completed, each time a machine goes up or down, each time a setup change is initiated and completed, etc. It must also convey commands, such as when to load parts, when to start setup changes, etc., to the production system. They must be conveyed directly to automated hardware such as robots or tool changers, or to computer terminals that instruct workers what to do next.

6. Implement the hierarchy on the computer system. Monitor its performance. Collect data; if the data of Step 1 is not correct, replace it. It may require that hedging points be recomputed; it may even require the hierarchy to be restructured.

13.4   Research Problems

The hierarchy described here is the subject of on-going research because there are many questions that must still be answered.

1. The set of phenomena to be treated should be expanded. At present, it only includes operations, failures, setup changes, and starvation and blockage. Other phenomena include scheduled maintenance, subcontracting, random demand, due dates, statistics/adaptive control, and many more.

2. Among the important outstanding research problems are proving that hierarchical decomposition is asymptotically optimal as times scales separate (see Sethi and Zhang, 1994); determining how to deal with systems in which time scales are not widely separated; formulating and solving the hedging point problem with non-Markov events (such as those generated by a corridor strategy); and developing sufficiency conditions for capacity (Lasserre, 1992).

3. To improve on the staircase policy, new formulations of deterministic scheduling problems are required in which the objective is to load material as close as possible to a

---

[3]Whether subcontracting is reducing demand or increasing capacity is a matter of taste and perspective.

given rate. (The staircase strategy is one possible solution to such a problem, but better solutions may exist.) Another research area of interest is in numerical solutions or better quadratic approximations for hedging point problems. In addition, bounds on the quality of quadratic approximations should be determined. See Sharifnia (1993).

4. We have not discussed at all the collection and processing of data in the hierarchy. Such problems are important because the rates of uncontrollable events are not known, as we have assumed here, but must be deduced from experience. This will require the solution of statistics problems.

   Essentially, Equations (10.22) and (10.26) are used in the opposite way from the way we have used them here. In the control hierarchy, the Level $k - 1$ rates of controllable activities are specified, and the corresponding Level k rates or activities are determined. In the statistical hierarchy, the Level k uncontrollable activities or rates are observed, and the corresponding Level $k - 1$ rates are calculated.

5. We have discussed two aggregation/decompositions. At least one more is important: the reduction of the number of product types at higher levels in the hierarchy. Many factories have an enormous number of products. Like events and resources, it should be possible to consider each product type in detail at the lower levels, and an aggregation of products at the higher levels.

Bibliography

[1] S. X. Bai, N. Srivatsan, and S. B. Gershwin (1990), "Hierarchical Real-Time Scheduling of a Semiconductor Fabrication Facility," *IEEE/CHMT IEMT (International Electronics Manufacturing Technology) Symposium*, Washington, DC, October 1-3, 1990. MIT Laboratory for Manufacturing and Productivity, LMP 90-011.

[2] J. Dayhoff and R. Atherton (1987), "A Model for Wafer Fabrication Dynamics in Integrated Circuit Manufacturing," *IEEE Transactions on Systems, Man, and Cybernetics*, Volume SMC-17, 1987, pp. 91-100.

[3] K. Fordyce, R. Dunki-Jacobs, B. Gerard, R. Sell, and G. Sullivan (1992), "Logistics Management System: An Advanced Decision Support System for the Fourth Decision Tier Dispatch or Short-Interval Scheduling," *Production and Operations Management*, Volume 1, Number 1, Winter, 1992, pp. 70-87.

[4] J. B. Lasserre (1992), "New Capacity Sets for the Hedging Point Strategy," *International Journal of Production Research*, Vol. 30, No. 12, December, 1992, pp. 2941-2949.

[5] K. N. McKay (1992), "Production Planning and Scheduling: A Model for Manufacturing Decisions Requiring Judgment," Ph. D. Thesis, University of Waterloo, Waterloo, Ontario, Canada.

[6] S. P. Sethi and Q. Zhang (1994), *Hierarchical Decision Making in Stochastic Manufacturing Systems*, Birkhäuser, 1994.

[7] A. Sharifnia (1993), "Stability and Performance of Distributed Production Control Methods based on Continuous Flow Models," *IEEE Transactions on Automatic Control*, to appear.

[8] N. Srivatsan, S. X. Bai, and S. B. Gershwin (1992), "Hierarchical Real-Time Integrated Scheduling of a Semiconductor Fabrication Facility," to appear in the *Control and Dynamic Systems* series, published by Academic Press, edited C. T. Leondes.

[9] G. Sullivan and K. Fordyce (1990), "IBM Burlington's Logistics Management System," *Interfaces*, Volume 20, Number 1, 1990, pp. 43-64.

[10] J. Violette (1993), "Implementation of a Hierarchical Controller in a Factory Simulation," M.S. Thesis, MIT, Department of Aeronautics and Astronautics, June, 1993.

[11] J. Violette and S. B. Gershwin (1991), "Decomposition of Control in a Hierarchical Framework for Manufacturing Systems," *Proceedings of the 1991 Automatic Control Conference*, Boston, June, 1991.

[12] L. Wein (1988), "Scheduling Semiconductor Wafer Fabrication," *IEEE Transactions on Semiconductor Manufacturing*, Volume 1, 1988, pp. 115-130.

Index